MODERN COOKERY

FOR TEACHING AND THE TRADE

VOLUME I

FIFTH EDITION

THANGAM E. PHILIP

Orient Longman

FOOD FUNDAMENTALS

FOREWORD TO THE FIRST EDITION

Minister for Food & Agriculture
Govt. of India

A desirable development in India, in recent years, has been the widespread application of science and technology to problems in the fields of food and nutrition. Better methods of processing and cooking can help to increase the effective availability of our food resources. A new kind of education in catering technology and applied nutrition has assumed importance in this context. Four full-fledged institutes of Catering Technology and Applied Nutrition have already been opened in the country. This is a welcome development.

Miss Thangam Philip, Principal of the Institute of Catering Technology and Applied Nutrition, Bombay, has written an exclusive book on cookery. It attempts to introduce new ideas in cookery and bakery and to change the pattern of our dietary. Miss Philip deals with scientific methods of cooking, planning of meals and improvement of the sense of taste and flavour.

I hope that this book will reach a wide and interested public. There is bound to be scope for suitable editions in various Indian languages also.

C. SUBRAMANIAN

New Delhi
5 May 1965

INTRODUCTION

In May 1965, the first edition of the book 'Modern Cookery for Teaching and the Trade' was published. The first volume was reprinted in 1974.

The two volumes have now been revised to update the theory and incorporate many more recipes (traditional and innovative) that the author has standardized to make the book a comprehensive reference book for the hospitality industry and a valuable text book for students training for the hotel and catering industry.

In the ensuing eleven years, the author has been continuously engaged in Food Education and Food Research and the revised volumes are the fruits of her efforts in these fields.

The popularity of the first edition, I am sure will ensure the success of the revised editions.

I wish the author every success in her revised edition of 'Modern Cookery for Teaching and the Trade', and hope she will continue with her work and publish further books in the field of Food.

C. BELFIELD-SMITH
Technical Expert,
Consultant to the United Nations

PREFACE

Modern Cookery for Teaching and the Trade, originally published in 1965, has been one of the most sought after and encyclopaedic books on Cookery published in India. An authentic selection of recipes from all parts of India and an easy-to-follow format have made the book an invaluable tool.

The book was published to meet the need for a standard book on Cooking and Baking for the rapidly expanding Institutes of Hotel Management and Catering Technology, the Food Craft Institutes and Institutes teaching Home Science. My long experience in food education, my love of cookery and my deep appreciation of foods, motivated me to accept this challenge.

The first print of this book soon sold out. The revised edition updated the food science section to incorporate new research findings and also included a comprehensive chapter on Food Commodities, their scientific or botanical names and their vernacular names.

A wide range of recipes—Indian, Western, Basic, Intermediate, Advanced and International as well as Bakery and Confectionery—have been covered. An intimate knowledge of the foods of different parts of India and abroad obtained by extensive travel and stay in the various regions of India and outside is the basis of selection. All the recipes in the book are the product of years of meticulous research and rigorous recipe-testing. The recipes are laid out in easy-to-follow steps and use easily obtainable ingredients. A special feature of presentation is that the ingredients as well as the methods of cooking have been itemized instead of being given in the usual narrative form. Fortification of popular recipes by addition of soya bean flour, multi-purpose foods, peanut flour, peanut butter, Balahar etc. is the theme of the chapter on ancillary foods. Such inputs not only improve the nutritive value of the food, but also increase palatability and sometimes keeping quality. This section has been very carefully selected after much experimental work to meet the needs of the changing times and as a means of providing low-cost, balanced meals.

In this fifth revised edition, the section on Indian Cuisine has been extended to cover several standardized traditional recipes from the rich heritage of our cuisine and several new, innovative recipes.

The increasing popularity of Chettinad food all over the country has prompted me to include a large, comprehensive section of Chettinad recipes in Volume II. Also included for this fifth edition is a section on Chocolate-making. This book, although primarily meant for students and the trade, will appeal to homemakers who wish to improve their repertoire and introduce variety into the daily food of the family. The section on equivalent weights and measures in Volume I allows the user to easily convert metric units like grams and kilograms into spoons and cups. For the sake of convenience, conversions from grams and kilograms to ounces and pounds have also been included.

The accelerated pace of globalization, the increase in tourism in our country and worldwide has brought cultures and nations closer, promoting interest in the cuisines of the different countries of the world. The two revised volumes provide a comprehensive selection of not only the foods from the different regions of India but also standardized recipes of gourmets' favourites found on the menus of great restaurants all around the world and will be an invaluable asset to all hotels interested in serving authentic and high class cuisine. The art of cuisine is, after all, an artistic science if not a scientific art and one in which the homemaker, the hotelier, the caterer and the student can all utilize their creative talents. It is hoped that this comprehensive book on cookery will be a stimulus for promoting this scientific art.

My sincere thanks are once again due to the staff of the Institute of Hotel Management, Catering Technology and Applied Nutrition, Bombay, for their unstinted assistance in the compilation and editing of the earlier editions of this book and for their generosity in making themselves available whenever I have needed their help for this revised edition.

THANGAM E. PHILIP

CONTENTS

Food Fundamentals

Names of Ingredients in Several Indian Languages

Indian Cookery

Western Cookery: Basic and Intermediate

Index

1 / DEFINITION OF "FOOD TECHNOLOGY"

Application of physical and chemical methods of processing foods from the time of harvest, slaughter or catch, during storage and till the time of consumption. The objectives of such processing are:

1. Improvement in aesthetic quality leading to better acceptability.
2. Enhancement of nutritive value.
3. Prevention of deteriorative changes.

Normal culinary practices are not included except those practised on a large scale or on a commercial basis.

2 / AIMS AND OBJECTIVES OF COOKING FOOD

1. Cooking partly sterilizes food. Above 40°C (104°F) the growth of bacteria falls off rapidly and in general it ceases above 45°C (113°F). Non-sporing bacteria are killed at temperatures above 60°C (140°F) for varying periods of time, e.g., to make milk safe, it is pasteurized at 63°C (145°F) for 30 minutes or at 72°C (161°F) for 15 seconds. Boiling kills living cells, with the exception of spores, in a few seconds. Spore-bearing bacteria take about 4 to 5 hours of boiling to be destroyed. To destroy them in a shorter period of time higher temperatures must be used.
2. Cooking helps to make food more digestible. Complex foods are often split into simpler substances during cooking. This helps the body to absorb and utilize the food more readily than if consumed in its raw form.
3. Cooking increases palatability.
4. Cooking makes food more attractive in appearance and, therefore, more appetizing.
5. Cooking introduces variety. Many different types of dishes can be prepared using the same ingredient.
6. Cooking helps to provide a balanced meal. Different ingredients combined together in one dish make it easier to provide a balanced meal.

3 / COOKING MATERIALS

Different raw materials are used in cooking to produce a complete dish. Each ingredient in a dish has a special part to play and a knowledge of what each food does is necessary to understand cooking thoroughly. Grouping the foods according to their use, makes it possible to remember the facts better. The materials are thus classified according to the part they play in making up a dish. Given below is a classification of raw materials.

1. Foundation ingredient. 2. Fats and oils. 3. Raising agents. 4. Eggs. 5. Salt. 6. Liquid. 7. Flavourings and seasonings. 8. Sweetening agents. 9. Thickening agents.

1. Foundation ingredient

Every dish has a foundation ingredient on which the other ingredients are based. The foundation ingredient can be a liquid or a solid. e.g., flour in bread, meat in roast, milk or stock in soups. When examining a recipe for proportions, all foods which serve the same purpose should be reckoned together. It is not only necessary to know the proportions of various ingredients but also the composition of the different ingredients and the action of heat on these. Heat may not affect the whole material but only certain constituents.

Food is composed of the following five constituents:

1. Carbohydrates. 2. Fats and oils. 3. Proteins. 4. Minerals. 5. Vitamins.

Action of heat on carbohydrates Generally starch swells up and becomes softer. Starch is enclosed within granules. These starch granules cannot be easily digested but heating makes them swell up and then burst and release the starch. Starch itself becomes gelatinized.

Sugar is changed into invert sugar (by a process where sucrose is broken down into glucose and fructose) when heated with fruit juices or other weak acids. In the presence of invert sugar, the solubility of sucrose is increased, and it tends to recrystallize more slowly. Inversion raises the boiling point and lowers the freezing point of a sugar solution. Invert sugar is slightly more easily digested and absorbed.

When sugar is boiled it passes through regular stages till it becomes caramelized at 163°C (325°F). The following are the stages thorough which it passes:

	°C	°F
Small thread	102°C	216°F
Large thread	103°C	218°F
Pearl	106°C	222°F
Soft ball	114°C	237°F
Hard ball	120°C	247°F
Soft crack	143°C	290°F
Hard crack	156°C	312°F
Caramel	163°C to 177°C	325°F to 350°F

Action of heat on protein Protein coagulates or sets when heated. The white of an egg is a good example. The coagulation process helps in keeping the nourishment within the food; it is sealed in by the formation of a coat on the outside. Hence, when boiling protein foods such as meat and fish, put them in hot water. When roasting meat, put it in an oven which is at a fairly high temperature, and then reduce the heat. Another action of heat on meat is the softening of the muscle fibres. Normal cooking methods cause the elastin in the connective tissue to shrink, and the collagen is converted into gelatin by heat in the presence of water, and as a result the muscle fibres separate and meat becomes tender. This is done more satisfactorily at a medium temperature than at a high temperature. Meat also shrinks during cooking. The higher the temperature the greater the shrinkage. Cooking at medium temperatures renders protein foods more digestible. The myoglobin in the muscle tissues and haemoglobin in the capillaries give meat its red colour. Both these decompose on heating causing the brown colour which is generally found in cooked meat. The change takes place at a temperature of 65ºC (149ºF). At high temperatures the protein itself gets denatured thus making it less nutritive.

Action of heat on fats Fat melts when it comes in contact with heat. At high temperatures fats decompose into fatty acids and acrolein. Darkening of fat is caused by cooking at high temperatures and also by the presence of carbonized breadcrumbs and small particles of cooked food. The temperature at which decomposition sets in, when an amount of fat is heated, is known as its smoke point. The specific temperature at which this takes place varies with different fats and is lowered by repeated heating. With repeated use, fat deteriorates, because of excessive temperature, moisture, air and the presence of carbonized crumbs and small pieces of food, to a point where it will just bubble in the pan, too weak to perform the function of frying. Abnormal absorption caused by frying for too long at too low a temperature also contributes to the breakdown. Fat also begins to thicken and become gummy. This condition is known as polymerization, and fat that has reached this stage is no longer fit for use.

Action of heat on minerals There is no appreciable loss of minerals due to cooking, excepting when cooking liquor is thrown out. Some minerals are made readily available by cooking.

Action of heat on vitamins Vitamin C is the only vitamin which becomes unstable when heated, although careful cooking helps to retain some of it. Vitamin A and D are not destroyed by ordinary methods of cooking. Vitamin B may be destroyed during cooking if cooked at high temperatures, e.g., baking of biscuits and manufacture of breakfast cereals, by the addition of baking soda, or when cooking liquor is thrown away.

Fats and oils

Fats are solid at normal temperatures and melt when heated. Those used in cooking are butter, margarine, lard, suet, dripping and hydrogenated fat.

Oils are liquid at normal temperatures but solidify at lower temperatures. The commonly used cooking oils are coconut oil, sesame oil, cotton-seed oil, olive oil, peanut oil, mustard oil, corn oil, and sunflower oil.

Hydrogenation of oils Whale oil, cotton-seed oil, soya bean oil, peanut oil, etc., are sold as shortenings of varying consistencies. The conversion of oil into fat is brought about by a process known as hydrogenation. This consists of treating oil under pressure and at a suitable temperature with hydrogen, in the presence of a catalyst, usually nickel. Under these conditions the unsaturated fatty acids present in the oil combine with the hydrogen. This chemical process brings about a physical change, the liquid oil becoming a solid fat. The unsaturated fatty acids are chiefly those of the oleic type but when hydrogenated, are converted into stearic acid which is solid. The varying consistencies are due to the process of hydrogenation being stopped at different stages. Fats are used in cooking either as shortening agents or as frying media.

Fats are used in confectionery to enrich the food and to impart to them shortening qualities. Collectively they are referred to as shortening agents. Their effect is to break down or destroy the toughness of gluten, so that instead of being hard and tough to eat, foods containing fat break off short and readily melt in the mouth.

The factors to look for in shortenings are:

(i) *Creaming value:* This affects the cake volume.
(ii) *Shortening value:* The shortness or shortening power it gives to the result. Shortness is necessary for the baking of biscuits, cookies, wafers and pastries.
(iii) *Stability:* Its keeping quality. If the stability is not good, the keeping quality of the product will be decreased.
(iv) *Consistency:* Hardness or softness depending on the purpose, e.g. hardness is needed for puff pastry, softness for cake-making.
(v) *Water absorption power:* Correlated to emulsification value of shortening.

As shortening agents, fats add to the nutritional and satiety values of flour mixtures and contribute to their characteristic flavour and texture. The type of fat and the way in which fat is incorporated affect the texture, as in shortcrust pastry, flaky pastry and puff pastry. As heat melts fat, cooking must be done at the correct temperatures so that the flour can absorb the fat as it melts. If the heat is insufficient, the fat runs out of the mixture and is wasted, besides leaving the food tough and dry. Fat which has been broken up into very fine particles, as in creaming, is more easily absorbed than fat left in large pieces, In general, the richer the pastry the hotter the oven, and the richer the cake the cooler the oven.

Fat as a frying medium functions in three ways. It serves to transfer heat to the articles to be fried, it adds to the nutritive value of the food and it contributes to the flavour of the food. Fat used as a frying medium should have a high smoke point, low congealing point, low moisture content, high stability and acceptable flavour.

Rendering of fat Rendering of fat is the process of melting to extract fat from fatty tissues. A good supply of dripping can be obtained by rendering down suet (fat surrounding the kidney of a cow or sheep) and pieces of fat from meat. This can be done in two ways:

1. Cut the fat into small pieces and place in a baking tin in a slow oven until the fat has melted and there are only crisp brown pieces of tissue left. Strain through a fine cloth into a clean basin pressing the tissues to squeeze out all fat.
2. Cut the pieces of fat as for above method. Place in a pan without a lid and with very little water. Boil until the water has evaporated and then heat very gently until the fat melts and leaves only crisp brown pieces of tissue. Strain as before.

In both cases the temperature should not be too high or else the fat will decompose.

Clarification This is a method of cleaning used fat. For this process, put fat in a pan with enough water to cover it. Bring to boil without covering. Strain and cool. Lift off the cake of fat floating on top, turn it upside down and scrape off any foreign particles sticking to the bottom. The fat is then heated gently till it stops bubbling, to remove all water particles.

Varieties of fats and oils

Fat/Oil	**Butter**
Source	Cream
Properties	Salted or unsalted. Difficult to handle when chilled, unique flavour and enriching qualities.
Uses	Not suitable for deep frying. For shallow frying, add 1 tbsp oil to raise smoking point.

Fat/Oil	**Margarine**
Source	Groundnuts; palm, coconut and fish oils, milk whey
Properties	Not easy to spread when chilled. Distinctive flavour not to everyone's taste.
Uses	As above but not used for its flavour. Economical for baking.
Fat/Oil	**Soft-blend margarine**
Source	As above
Properties	Will spread when chilled.
Uses	Excellent for all-in-one cake and pastry making.
Fat/Oil	**Low-fat spread**
Source	Blended vegetable oils
Properties	Half the calories of butter, less fattening than margarine.
Uses	Can be used for most baking, but not for pastry.
Fat/Oil	**Cholesterol-free spread**
Source	Vegetable oils
Properties	Spreads when chilled.
Uses	As above.
Fat/Oil	**Aerated white vegetable fat**
Source	Blended vegetable oils
Properties	More flavour than lard. Easy-to-mix, creamy texture.
Uses	Can be used for most purposes, but rather expensive for deep frying. Excellent for fork-mix pastry.
Fat/Oil	**Lard**
Source	Pork
Properties	White solid fat, very economical.
Uses	Good for shortcrust pastry when combined with margarine. Does not cream with sugar. Good for shallow frying.
Fat/Oil	**Suet**
Source	Lamb or beef
Properties	Hard white fat. Available shredded or solid.
Uses	Best used for suet pastry, pudding and stuffing.
Fat/Oil	**Spreading blend**
Source	Buttermilk, butter oil, vegetable oil
Properties	A mixture of butter and margarine. Low fat content. Just over half the calories of butter. Slight butter flavour. Spreads when chilled.
Uses	Suitable for all cooking, except frying. Baking results acceptable. Do not use for pastry.

Fat/Oil	**Corn oil**
Source	Corn
Uses	Suitable for all purposes, especially deep frying.
Fat/Oil	**Sunflower oil**
Source	Sunflower seeds
Uses	As above
Fat/Oil	**Sesame and almond oils**
Source	Sesame seeds, bitter almonds
Properties	Delicate flavour
Uses	All purposes.
Fat/Oil	**Olive oil**
Source	Olives
Properties	Distinctive flavour
Uses	Suitable for most purposes, but not for deep frying
Fat/Oil	**Soya bean oil**
Source	Soya beans
Properties	Distinctive flavour
Uses	Suitable for all purposes, but not ideal for dressings. Low shelf life.
Fat/Oil	**Coconut oil**
Source	Coconuts
Properties	Strong aroma and flavour
Uses	Used mainly in Kerala.
Fat/Oil	**Arachide oil**
Source	Groundnuts
Properties	Distinctive flavour
Uses	Suitable for all purposes.
Fat/Oil	**Blended oil**
Source	Vegetable and animal oils
Uses	Can be used for the same purposes as corn oil but needs straining after use if it is to be re-used for deep frying.
Fat/Oil	**Solid vegetable oil**
Source	Palms
Properties	Suitable for all purposes, except dressings because it solidifies when cold.

Raising agents

The function of a raising agent is to puff up the food so that it spreads and rises, thus making it light instead of close and heavy. The tiny air spaces caused by the raising agents are retained during the process of cooking. The leavening of the flour mixture is accomplished by the expansion of incorporated air and by the internal production and expansion of water vapour and carbon dioxide. When the product is heated, the air expands and part of the water vaporizes. The formation of carbon dioxide requires the presence of suitable micro-organisms or chemical agents. During the first part of heating, gas production is accelerated and the gas formed expands as the temperature rises. Gluten, a substance found in flour, develops when moisture is added, and helps to keep the raising agent within until the food sets, thus helping to make the food light. Gluten is a sticky, elastic substance which stretches as the air or gas expands and prevents these from escaping. The air or gas trapped in the mixture expands further when heated and makes the cooked food light. Too much raising agent raises the food too rapidly, breaks the surface and allows the gas produced to escape, and as a result the product sinks and becomes heavy.

Air as a raising agent Air is incorporated by sifting flour, by creaming shortening, by beating eggs or by beating the mixture itself.

Water vapour as a raising agent Water vapour is formed in quantities sufficient to raise the mixture when liquid and flour are in equal volumes.

Chemicals as raising agents Chemicals such as sodium bicarbonate, cream of tartar, baking powder, ammonium carbonate, etc., are added to mixtures to make food light. In each case the result is the production of carbon dioxide.

Baking powders are mixtures of sodium bicarbonate with some suitable acid such as cream of tartar, diluted with cornflour to give a product the desired strength. The cornflour also serves to separate the acid and the base, thereby increasing the stability of the mixture during shelf life. General proportions used are 1–2 tsp baking powder per 450 gm of foundation. The richer the mixture, the less the baking powder required. When the mixture is of an acidic nature, (as when sour milk, buttermilk, treacle, vinegar or jams made from acid fruits are used) the addition of cream of tartar or tartaric acid is not necessary, since the soda will act upon these other foods and cause the required gas to be given off. Four tsp baking powder is equal to approximately one tsp of soda in a carbon dioxide yield. In certain flour mixtures variations from neutrality are deliberately sought by including a reaction with either soda or cream of tartar, e.g., to get the dark, rich colour in chocolate cakes which many people prefer, sodium bicarbonate is used.

By the addition of yeast Carbon dioxide is produced either from sugar by yeast, or from a carbonate, usually sodium bicarbonate, by action of an acid.

Yeast consists of microscopic, unicellular plants which are capable of rapid multiplication when conditions are favourable and which obtain energy by breaking down sugars to carbon dioxide and alcohol. This process is known as fermentation, and is brought about by the enzyme zymase found in yeast. Yeast also produces enzymes which are able to split disaccharide sugars.

Dried yeast This is a mixture of yeast and cornflour or cornmeal pressed into cakes and dried. The yeast continues to live but in an inactive state. When furnished with warmth and moisture, it begins to develop and multiply, but this process is slow. Dried yeast has to be soaked in lukewarm water and mixed with very soft dough (sponge) for a preliminary period of development before all the other ingredients are added.

Activated dry yeast This develops more rapidly than dried yeast and is the type now available. It can be used in straight dough mixing. It is less perishable than compressed yeast. The shelf life of both dried yeast and activated dried yeast is longer at refrigerated temperatures than at room temperature.

Compressed yeast This is a moist mixture of yeast plants and starch. The yeast remains active and will grow and multiply rapidly when added to dough. It has to be kept at refrigerated temperatures and keeps well for only a few days. If held in the freezing compartment, it retains its activity for a longer period.

Eggs

Although hens' eggs are the most popular, eggs of turkeys, guinea fowls, ducks and geese are also used. Eggs are used in various forms in cooking:

1. As a leavening by foam formation to make the dish light, as in soufflés or meringues.
2. For binding, as in egg croquettes.
3. To improve flavour and colour, as in cakes.
4. To add to the nutritive value:
   (a) The protein of eggs is unexcelled in quality, and is used as a standard against which other food proteins are measured.
   (b) Eggs make a substantial contribution of vitamins A and D and also contain a small amount of B complex vitamins and minerals.
   (c) The essential fatty acids are more finely emulsified in eggs

than in any other food thus assuring easy, complete digestibility and ready utilisation.

5. To decorate and garnish dishes.
6. To enrich a mixture as in the case of rich cakes.
7. As a thickening, as in custards and cooked salad dressings.
8. For emulsification, as in mayonnaise sauce.
9. For coating, as in fried foods.
10. As the first semi-solid food taken by infants.
11. As a nourishing and easily digestible food for invalids.
12. As a quick-cooking and nourishing dish for breakfast or main meals.

The action of heat on proteins accounts for the principal changes that occurr when eggs are cooked. Both yolks and whites of eggs coagulate when heated. The temperature at which coagulation begins, the rate of coagulation and the firmness of the gel will depend on: (i) Intensity of heat, (ii) Length of heating period, (iii) The presence of added material such as water, milk, sugar and salt.

Acid and salt speed up the process of coagulation, e.g., to prevent disintegration of eggs when poaching, vinegar and salt are added.

Sugar increases the temperature at which coagulation takes place. When eggs are diluted by adding milk or water, the coagulation temperature is raised. If water is added instead of milk, coagulation results in a flocculent rather than a gelled structure.

An undiluted whole egg begins to coagulate at 57°–66°C (135°–150°F) and to gel at 70°–74°C (158°–165°F). The white of the egg alone starts coagulating at 58°–62°C (136°–144°F) and begins to gel at 62°–70°C (144°–158°F). In all cases, the higher the cooking temperature, the more rapid the coagulation and the firmer the gel. Changes associated with the cooking of eggs can however, be produced at temperatures much below boiling, by a longer heating period. The egg that is cooked for a longer period at a lower temperature is superior in nutritive value, as well as in flavour, to an egg cooked at a higher temperature for a shorter period.

The blue ring round the yolk of an egg, sometimes found in a hard-boiled egg, is due to the formation of ferrous sulphide. This is brought about by the union of iron released from the yolk of the egg and hydrogen sulphide from the white, which in turn is released from sulphur found in the white. The amount of such discoloration depends on time and temperature of cooking, and the age of the egg. Cooking for 30 minutes in water at 85°C (185°F) followed by rapid cooling, gives very little discoloration. Eggs which are six weeks or more old discolour rapidly. In any case, boiled eggs used for stuffing, garnishing etc., should be cooled quickly after boiling, after cracking or without cracking.

Characteristics of fresh eggs The shell of an egg may be either brown or white depending upon the breed of hen producing it. But, irrespective of colour, the shell of a fresh egg always has a delicate velvety appearance, called "bloom", that is due to the protective mucous coating which the shell has when the egg is laid. The inner air cell of a fresh egg is small. The contents when broken out from the shell show an upstanding, well-rounded yolk covered with a clinging layer of thick egg white, which, in turn is surrounded by a relatively smaller amount of thin egg white. The yolk may be either golden or light yellow, depending upon the amount of carotenoid pigments contained in it, and the white is practically colourless or possibly slightly opalescent. There is no odour other than that characteristic of eggs, and when cooked, the flavour will be excellent.

Deterioration of eggs As soon as the egg is laid, changes begin to take place which, if not checked by suitable storage conditions, result in undesirable deterioration. An account of these changes and their effects follows:

As shown in the shell With deterioration, the mucous protective covering of the shell soon disappears, leaving the shell shiny and more porous, so that moisture and carbon dioxide can pass more easily through it from the egg contents. This causes a loss in weight of the egg, a contraction of egg contents, and a resulting enlargement of the air space between the two membranous linings of the shell.

As shown in the egg white: Accompanying the loss of carbon dioxide through the shell, the reaction of the egg contents, especially of the egg white, changes from nearly neutral in the fresh white, to alkaline, becoming progressively more alkaline as the egg ages. It should be said, however, that factors other than the loss of carbon dioxide may be responsible for the increase in this alkalinity.

As egg deterioration progresses, the thick white gradually loses its firm, jelly-like consistency and decreases in volume, while the volume of thin egg white increases. These changes continue until the entire white portion becomes watery and drains away from the yolk when the egg is broken out of the shell. The cause of this change in thick egg white is not, at the present time, entirely clear, although various reasons have been advanced to account for it.

As shown in the egg yolk: Upon aging, the yolk of the egg also becomes more liquid and enlarges as water passes into it from the white through the enveloping vitellin membrane. As a result, the increasing volume of the yolk stretches the surrounding membrane and weakens it so that, in the broken-out egg, the yolk is no longer upstanding and well-rounded, but instead becomes wide and flat. Indeed, with continued aging, the membrane which encloses the yolk may become so weakened that it breaks when the egg is opened, and, as a consequence, the white and yolk cannot be separated from each other.

As shown by substances with off-odours: Finally, in aging eggs certain chemical reactions occur among the various egg components which yield compounds that impart characteristic and familiar off-odours and flavours; and if these reactions continue long enough, such eggs become inedible.

Among the compounds that are made from these reactions is the foul-smelling, gaseous substance, hydrogen sulphide. When eggs are heated for some time, as when hard-boiling them in the shell, this gas, formed chiefly in egg white, passes through the vitellin membrane and reacts with iron compounds in outer yolk areas to form ferrous sulphide which can be seen as a black, film-like deposit enveloping the yellow, hard-boiled yolk. Although this film can be encountered to a certain extent in a fresh egg, its formation can be largely avoided—if the aging of the egg has not been carried too far—by taking care not to prolong the cooking period unnecessarily, and by being careful to use the hard-boiled egg immediately.

Boiling eggs

Put enough water into a pan to cover the egg and bring it to the boil. Lower the egg into the water with a metal spoon.

Reduce the heat and cook gently for 3–4 minutes for a lightly cooked egg. For a moderately soft egg, allow 4–5 minutes. For a hard-boiled egg, allow 10 minutes.

Duck's eggs must be boiled for not less than 14 minutes.

Put the hard-boiled egg into cold water and leave to cool to prevent the formation of dark rings round the yolk.

Salt

Salt, although used in small quantities, is an essential ingredient for both sweet and savoury dishes. Salt helps to bring out the flavour of other ingredients. If too much is added, food becomes inedible, and too little makes food insipid. Gauging the right amount to be added is learned by experience. Salt adds to the nutritive value of food by providing an essential mineral, sodium chloride.

Salt has physical effects on the gluten of flour. In reasonable quantities it strengthens gluten and increases its resistance to the softening effects of fermentation. Too much salt on the other hand will remove the power of gluten to hold gas. Salt also acts as a preservative; it speeds up coagulation of eggs and lowers the freezing point of food.

Liquid

Liquid is necessary to bind dry ingredients together, to dilute food, to act as a cooking medium and to thin down a gravy or sauce. Milk, water, stock and fruit juices are the most commonly used liquids. Eggs may be used for binding.

When too little liquid is added, the food does not get cooked, or as in the case of cakes, it retards the action of raising agents, resulting in a hard, heavy cake. Gravies or soup containing insufficient liquid are 'stodgy'. Too much liquid results in a watery product, or, as in the case of cakes and puddings, makes them soggy.

Flavourings and seasonings

The taste and acceptability of food depends to a very great extent on the correct amounts of flavourings and seasonings. These are variable ingredients and the types and amounts necessary for different dishes must be carefully studied. To add just enough and no more should be the aim of every cook.

Those which combine taste and smell such as essences, cardamom, nutmeg, basil, thyme, etc., are called flavourings. Those which only enhance taste are seasonings, e.g., red chillies, mustard, pepper, etc.

Sweetening agents

These are not as necessary as salt. Their lack will not affect the texture of the food or the lightness of a dish. A bad cook generally adds too much sweetening to cover other faults.

The type of sweetenings used are:

(i) Sugar, (ii) Treacle, (iii) Jaggery or molasses, (iv) Syrups such as golden syrup, etc. (v) Jams, (vi) Honey, (vii) Fruit juices.

If too much sweetening is used, food becomes cloying and if too little is used, sweet dishes become tasteless.

Theory

Sugar

Type Granulated sugar (white)
Description Refined sugar medium-size
Uses All-purpose but for many tasks another type may be better or quicker.

Type Castor sugar
Description Refined white sugar with the smallest crystals
Uses Because it dissolves quickly it is especially good for cake-making, whisked sponges and sauces. Best for caramels and syrups.

Type	Icing sugar
Description	Made from sugar—relatively large crystals ground to a fine powder. Contains a small percentage of calcium phosphate to prevent clogging.
Uses	Finest and smoothest of all sugars. Best for icing for cake decorations, for meringues and for sprinkling and coating. Sometimes takes on a slight greyish tinge if sieved through a metal sieve or if a metal spoon is used.
Type	Preserving sugar
Description	Refined white sugar—relatively large crystals, makes it ideal for preserving.
Uses	Dissolves slowly and does not clog bottom of pan or form as much scum as granulated sugar when used for preserving. Can also be used (coloured) to decorate cakes and breads.

Thickening agents

Thin foods such as milk, soups, gravies, curries, etc., are often improved by the addition of a thickening agent. The thickening used also increases the nutritive value.

Starchy foods and eggs are commonly used as thickening but sugar will thicken a syrup, and gelatin will set a thin liquid if chilled. Ground onion, coconut and poppy-seeds are used for thickening curries in Indian cookery.

4 / WEIGHING AND MEASURING

This is a very important aspect of cookery, particularly for bulk food production. To obtain a standard product with a standard yield, as is essential for commercial foods, weighing and measuring must be done accurately.

A set of scales, measuring jugs, and standard measuring cups and spoons must be provided in every kitchen. The scales should denote both grams and ounces and the measuring jug both litres and pints. Weighing is more accurate than measuring but for expediency, measuring can be used. When measuring, it is better to use level measurements, as this is less subject to error. Spoons and cups vary greatly in size. Therefore test them carefully and always use the same utensils for measuring.

5 / PREPARATION OF INGREDIENTS

Solid foods which are to be mixed have to be reduced into sizes which will allow them to combine readily. A certain amount of preparation is thus necessary.

Washing This is done to remove superficial dirt. Wash vegetables, meat and fish in cold water before any preparation is done. If they are soaked for a long period or washed after cutting there is greater loss of water soluble minerals and vitamins.

Peeling and scraping Spoilt, soiled and inedible portions are removed. Skins of vegetables like potatoes, carrots, etc., or of fruits, are removed by either peeling or scraping. When peeling, remove as little of the fleshy part as possible.

Paring Remove surface layers by cutting as in paring an apple. A circular motion is used.

Cutting Reducing to small parts by means of a knife or scissors. When the reduction is done by a chopping knife or a food chopper it is known as chopping. Cutting into even-sized cubes is called dicing. Cutting into very fine pieces is mincing. Shredding is cutting into fine long pieces with a knife or shredder. Slicing is also cutting into thin long pieces, but these are not as fine as in shredding.

Grating Reducing to fine particles by rubbing over a rough, sharp surface.

Grinding Reducing to small fragments by crushing in a mill, a grinding stone or an osterizer.

Mashing This is a method of breaking up soft foods such as cooked potatoes or vegetables.

Sieving Passing through a mesh to remove impurities, to break down to even portions, or to enclose air.

Milling used for cereals, to remove husks, etc.

Steeping Extracting colouring and flavouring by allowing ingredients to stand in water generally at a temperature just below boiling point.

Centrifuging Promotion of separation through the application of a whirling force, e.g., separating cream from milk.

Emulsification Blending one liquid with another in which it is insoluble, e.g., oil and egg yolk in mayonnaise.

Evaporation Removal of excess moisture by heating.

Homogenization Subdivision of large drops into smaller ones by forcing them through a small opening under great pressure, e.g., fat in cream.

Methods of mixing foods

Beating This method can be used with thin mixtures or liquids. This should be done carefully with the aim of enclosing air. This term is used synonymously with whipping. e.g., beating of eggs.

Blending Mixing two or more ingredients thoroughly.

Cutting in Usually the incorporation of fat in flour and other sifted ingredients with a knife. This method produces a relatively coarse division of the fat and does not result in blending. e.g., cutting fat into pastry mixture.

Creaming Softening of fat by friction with a wooden spoon, generally followed by the gradual incorporation of sugar as in cake making.

Folding Mixing by a careful lifting and dropping motion. The edge of the spoon is used and the mixture is lifted, turned completely and gently replaced. All the movements in this method, though deft, should be so gentle that the different ingredients are almost coaxed together.

Kneading Manipulating by alternating pressure with folding and stretching. The food is pressed with the knuckles. The dough is brought from the outside of the bowl or basin to the centre and at the same time the bowl is moved so that a different section is kneaded each time. This ensures a thorough distribution of ingredients. eg., bread dough, chapati dough, etc.

Pressing This is done to shape foods like cutlets and sometimes as a method of subdivision to separate liquids from solids by weights or mechanical pressure, as for paneer.

Rubbing in Rubbing fat into flour using the tips of the fingers and thumb and lifting the hand out of the basin as in the case of shortcrust pastry. Rub until the mixture looks like breadcrumbs.

Rolling in Rolling butter or fat in a soft dough, e.g., puff pastry.

Stirring Mixing foods with a suitable tool such as a spoon by a circular motion in contact with the pan. Generally this is a gentle movement but is changed to suit different dishes, as when used to prevent sticking or burning in halwas and toffees. If used too vigorously, it tends to drive out air or other gas previously enclosed as raising agent.

6 / TEXTURE

Texture is the term used to describe the characteristics of a finished food product. The order in which the ingredients are added, the way of mixing and the method of cooking affect the resulting product.

A good cook should not only be able to distinguish between one texture and another but also be able to produce what he or she wants. Only by observation, experience and perseverance will a person be able to know what the correct texture of a particular product should be. A brief description of some commonly found textures and their correct occurrence is given below, but it must also be borne in mind that the difference between one texture and another is very fine.

Firm and close The air bubbles made by the raising agents are many but small, and the mixture is not in the least spongy. The fat included prevents the mixture from being too hard, e.g., in biscuits or plain short pastry.

Short and crumbly This is similar to firm and close, but more fat is added. e.g., in shortbread or nankhatais.

Spongy A soft and elastic texture showing inclusion of air, e.g., Swiss rolls, sponge cakes and idlis.

Light and even Holes are plentiful and of a fair size. The food is firm but not hard or tough. It is neither as short as pastry nor as spongy as sponge cakes, e.g., Madeira cake, Queen cake.

Flaky This is caused by the method of adding fat. Thin crisp layers are formed, separated by air pockets. The flakes themselves should not be tough, e.g. flaky and puff pastry, chiroti, etc.

There are some textures which are incorrect in any dish, e.g.:

Coarse Holes are large and uneven, and the food is sunken in the centre. This is brought about by the addition of too much raising agent or too little liquid.

Tough Coarse mixtures are also tough. Toughness is caused by too much liquid or through incorrect mixing. This will also result if too little fat is added.

Hard A bad fault brought about by the addition of too much liquid or too much pressure while mixing. Hard mixtures are usually heavy since the air enclosed is removed.

7 / METHODS OF COOKING FOODS

While the correct preparation of ingredients and correct mixing are necessary, greater skill is needed in the actual cooking of the food. The different methods of cooking are: 1. Roasting 2. Baking 3. Frying 4. Boiling 5. Poaching 6. Steaming 7. Stewing 8. Braising 9. Broiling 10. Grilling.

Roasting

Spit roasting The food to be cooked is brought into direct contact with the flame of a clear, bright fire. The food is basted with fat and also turned regularly to ensure even cooking and browning. This method, now known as spit roasting, is not often used as only good quality meats are suitable for it. Roast meats, however, have a very good flavour, and are still served in large hotels and in special restaurants and hotels, e.g., as barbecued meat.

Oven roasting This has now taken the place of spit roasting, because of its convenience, although only first class meat, poultry and vegetables are thus cooked. It is done in a closed oven with the aid of fat. The joint is raised out of the fat by means of bones or a trivet to prevent the meat from frying and becoming hard. Frequent basting, however, is essential. The food is put into a fairly hot oven for 5 to 10 minutes and the temperature is lowered to allow the joint to be cooked through. Cooking in a moderate oven for a longer time produces a better cooked joint than cooking at high temperature for a shorter period. There is also less shrinkage. Therefore, more portions can be obtained. Aluminium foil is now used in oven roasting. The joint is larded or browned in fat. A matignon [finely minced 2 medium carrots, 2 onions, 2 sticks of celery (heart), 1 tbsp ham, 1 sprig thyme, ½ a bay leaf crushed and stewed in butter] may or may not be used to cover the joint which is then wrapped tightly in aluminium foil and cooked in the oven till done. This method is an improvement on oven roasting as the meat retains its moisture and flavour.

Pot roasting This method is used to cook small joints and birds if no oven is available, but a thick heavy pan is essential. Enough fat is melted to cover the bottom of the pan. When the fat is hot the joint is browned. It is then lifted out and 2 or 3 skewers are put into the pan, on which the joint is placed. This is to prevent the joint from sticking to the pan. The joint should just touch the fat. The pan is then covered tightly with a well-fitting lid and cooked over a very slow fire. The joint could be basted if lean and turned occasionally to ensure even cooking. Prepared root vegetables and potatoes can also be cooked around the meat.

Baking

The food to be cooked is surrounded by hot air in a closed oven. The action of dry heat is modified by the steam which arises from the food whilst cooking. Bread, cakes, pastry, puddings, vegetables and potatoes may be cooked by this method.

Frying

This is a method of cooking whereby the food to be cooked is brought into contact with hot fat. Food cooked in this way is said to be indigestible, but if the method is correctly and carefully carried out, the food is quite suitable for normal people. The advantages of frying are: (i) Fried food is very appetizing. (ii) It is a quick method of cooking. (iii) The keeping quality of fried food is strengthened. It is however, an expensive method of cooking meat as only the best parts are suitable (chops, liver, etc.). For other foods and for reheating of food, frying is a good means of providing variety.

There are two types of frying: (i) shallow fat frying; (ii) deep fat frying.

Shallow fat frying Only a little fat is used and the food is turned over in order that both sides may be browned. Generally this method is applied to pre-cooked food unless the food takes very little time to cook (omelette, liver, etc.). Some foods contain sufficient fat in themselves (e.g., bacon, sausages, etc.) and additional fat is not necessary although some cooks prefer to use a little fat. Fat absorption is greater when food is shallow fried then deep fried.

Deep fat frying The food is completely immersed in hot fat and, therefore, a large quantity of fat is required. The quantity of fat requires some time to heat. Special care must be taken to prevent overheating of fat, as this spoils both the food and the fat. The fat decomposes at high temperatures.

If the fat is not hot enough the food breaks up and absorbs extra fat thus making the product unfit for consumption. Use a frying basket wherever possible to remove fried foods easily.

Almost all foods require coating before frying, since not only are the juices and flavour of the food to be kept in, but the fat must be kept out. Materials used are: (i) eggs and breadcrumbs; (ii) flour and milk (not suitable for deep fat frying); (iii) batter (flour, milk and eggs); (iv) thinly rolled pastry; (v) oatmeal or vermicelli; (vi) lamb or pig's caul; (vii) besan (gram flour or chick pea flour) batter.

Both sweets and savouries may be cooked by this method without the flavour affecting the fat or the food, provided correct principles are applied. Food cooked by deep fat frying has a much better appearance than that cooked by shallow fat frying as it is evenly browned.

General rules for frying

(i) Have the fire clear and hot.

(ii) Make the food into suitable sizes and shapes and see that it is free from cracks.

(iii) Apply coating evenly. The breadcrumbs used should not be coarse. Remove any excess and firmly press on loose crumbs.

(iv) When frying chicken dry off all moisture before dipping in flour.

(v) Use fat with a high smoke point. The fat must be quite still and at the right temperature required, before the food is put in.

(vi) Do not put in too many pieces of food at the same time as this will lower the temperature.

(vii) See that the temperature is not increased for increased output.

(viii) Follow a time and temperature chart.

(ix) Fry to a golden brown on both sides turning over the food if necessary.

(x) Drain well on absorbent paper and serve attractively.

(xi) Cover fats left in the fryer between frying periods and maintain at a temperature not higher than 200ºF.

(xii) Once fat has been used for frying, strain and store in cans in a refrigerator.

(xiii) Replenish the original volume with fresh fat after each frying period.

(xiv) Fat begins to thicken, getting to be what is known as gummy or syrupy, with continuous use. This condition is known as polymerization and such fats are more viscous than fresh fat. Since there are no known food additives for inhibiting this condition, fat that has reached this stage is no longer fit for use.

(xv) Fats that are used for frying should have high stability. Normally fats themselves do not get rancid during the frying process but rancidity in the finished product affects the keeping quality and acceptability of the product. For commercial purposes fat of over 100 hours stability is desired for continuous trouble-free frying.

(xvi) Darkening of the fat is caused by cooking at too high a temperature which carbonizes loose breadcrumbs and small particles of fried food. Such fat should be strained and replenished with fresh fat before being used again.

Boiling

Food is cooked by surrounding it with boiling or simmering liquid (stock or water). Only just sufficient liquid should be used to cover the food to be cooked. To retain nourishment and flavour in food, plunge into boiling liquid. Allow to reboil and then to simmer. The liquid thus obtained is known as 'Pot Liquor' and contains some nourishment and flavour. This should not be wasted. It can be used as a substitute for stock when stock is not available or cooled and used to prepare stock. If a well-flavoured stock is required, vegetables and meat should be put into cold water and allowed to cook gently. Salted or pickled meats should always be started in cold water.

Generally speaking, vegetables grown above the ground are cooked in boiling salted water and vegetables grown below the ground are started in cold salted water with the exception of new potatoes and new carrots. Dry vegetables are started in cold water. Salt is added only after the vegetables are tender.

Fish should be put into hot liquid and allowed to just simmer.

Poaching

Poaching is cooking slowly in a minimum amount of liquid which should never be allowed to boil but should be just off boil. Fish, fruits and eggs are poached. When poaching eggs, a little vinegar and salt are added to the liquid to help in quicker coagulation and thus prevent disintegration.

Steaming

The food to be cooked is surrounded by plenty of steam from fast boiling water directly or by having the food in a basin or other dish placed in steam or boiling water. This is a slow process of cooking and only easily cooked food can be prepared by this method.

Advantages of steaming

(i) Food cooked by this method is easily digested.
(ii) All nourishment and flavour are kept in the food.
(iii) Food cannot be easily overcooked.
(iv) Pudding basins and other containers need not be filled to the top, thus allowing room for food to rise and so making food light.

General rules for steaming

(i) Prepare the vessel and have the water boiling fast.
(ii) If a basin is to be used as a container inside the steamer, see that it is greased and covered with a well-fitting lid or with greaseproof paper. This is to prevent condensed moisture from falling on the food.
(iii) Keep a kettle of boiling water handy so that the water in the steamer can be replaced as it boils away. Frequent refilling however, should be avoided as this causes a draught on food.
(iv) Never allow the water in the steamer to go off the boil, except when preparing dishes with eggs as the main ingredients, such as custard. For this, water must be kept at the simmering point otherwise the custard will curdle.
(v) Dish food quickly and serve hot. An appropriate sauce must accompany steamed food to make it appetizing, as steamed food is generally bland.

Stewing

This is a very gentle method of cooking in a closed pan using only a small quantity of liquid. The food should never be more than half covered with the liquid and the food above this level is thus really cooked by steam. As the liquid is not allowed to boil during cooking the process is a slow one.

Advantages of stewing

(i) Cheap cuts of meat, old fowls and tough or under-ripe fruits may be prepared by this method as the slow, moist method of cooking softens fibres, rendering the food tender.

(ii) Meat and vegetables may be cooked and served together, making an appetizing dish, while saving fuel and labour.
(iii) Stewed food may be cooked in the oven after other food is cooked, or it may be cooked on the side of the fire or on a very small gas or oil flame, thus again saving fuel.
(iv) All nourishment and flavour are retained so the food is very appetizing.

General rules for stewing

(i) Have a pan with a well-fitting lid ready.
(ii) Prepare the food and cut into pieces convenient for serving.
(iii) Use tepid liquid, which is just sufficient to half cover the food.
(iv) Bring just to boiling point and then simmer very gently until the food is perfectly tender. Never allow a stew to boil for "a stew boiled is a stew spoilt".

Braising

This is a combined method of roasting and stewing in a pan with a tight-fitting lid. To be strictly correct this method requires a special pan but a casserole dish or stew pan makes a good substitute. The meat should be sealed by browning on all sides and then placed on a lightly fried bed of vegetables (generally root). Stock or gravy is added which should cover two- thirds of the meat. The flavourings and seasonings are then added. The lid is put on and the food is allowed to cook gently on the stove or in the oven. When nearly done the lid is removed and the joint is frequently basted to glaze it. This latter process is always done in the oven.

Broiling

Broiling is cooking by direct heat and is synonymous with grilling. In pan broiling, the food is cooked uncovered on hot metal such as a grill or a frying pan. The pan or grill is oiled slightly to prevent sticking. Excess fat accumulated while cooking should be poured off.

Grilling

Used synonymously with broiling. This is cooking by dry heat. The food is supported on a grid iron over the fire, or on a grid placed in a tin under a gas or electric grill, or between electrically heated grill bars.

Grilling over the heat This is cooking on greased grill bars with the help of fat over direct heat. Only first class cuts of meat, poultry and certain fish can be prepared this way. The grill bars are brushed with oil to prevent food from sticking, and can be heated by charcoal, coke, gas or electricity. The bars should char the food on both sides to give the distinctive flavour of grilling. The thickness of the food and the heat of the grill determine the cooking time. Grills are typical *a la carte* dishes and are ordered by the customer to the degree of cooking required, such as rare, medium rare, medium or well done.

Grilling under the heat-salamander Cooking on grill bars or on trays under direct heat. Steaks, chops, etc., are cooked on the bars but fish, tomato, bacon and mushrooms are usually cooked on trays. This method can also be used in the preparation of foods *au gratin* and when glazing is required.

Grilling between heat Food is cooked between electrically heated grill bars.

Infra-red grilling This is cooking by infra-red radiation. This method reduces cooking time considerably, e.g., a steak can be grilled in one minute.

8 / SOUPS

Aim of soup making

To prepare an appetizing, economical and easily digestible dish by extracting nourishment and flavour from the solid to the liquid.

Stock is the foundation of all good soups. Stock is made by putting solid food into cold water and by a long slow process of cooking extracting the nourishment into the liquid. The best stocks are made from meat and bones together, e.g., white consomme. Since this is expensive for household purposes as well as for institutional feeding, bones and leftovers are used. The following stocks are adequate as well as economical.

Bone stock Use any kind of bones, cooked or uncooked. Place in a pan. Cover with cold water, add a little salt and bring to the boil. Simmer gently to allow the scum to form on the surface then gently remove it. A little cold water could be added occasionally to accelerate the process. Skim well and for each 600 ml of liquid add one onion, one carrot and a bouquet garni. Put the lid on and simmer very slowly for at least 2 to 3 hours. Strain. Cool quickly and use.

Meat and bones not only contribute flavour but body. Body is largely made up of gelatine and other soluble products extracted from meat and bones.

Depending on the size of the bones and the way they are cut, stock from meat bones is simmered from 4 to 10 hours and poultry from 2 to 6 hours.

The best bones to use for stock are those from young animals. These contain more gelatine and the marrow contains more flavouring ingredients. Shin and knuckle bones are best with neck bones next. The bones are best cut into 4 lengths and split.

To make 5 litres of good stock use 2kg. of meat bones, 6 litres water, 12kg. of flavouring vegetables (mirepoix).

In a brown stock, the meat, bones and vegetables are first browned.

In a white stock, they are not browned. Also avoid using highly coloured vegetables such as carrots, beans etc.

Vegetable stock Use any mixture of vegetables, the outside leaves of cabbage, cauliflower stalks, celery stalks and leaves, shells of peas, etc. All these must be washed thoroughly to free them of grit, sand and worms. Shred vegetables and add to cold water. Cover and boil for 20 to 30 minutes. Strain and use.

Fish stock Cover the fish bones, skin, head and other trimmings with water or milk and water. Add 1 small onion, 2 cloves, ½ a bay leaf and a sprig of parsley. Bring to boil. Cover and simmer for 20 minutes. Strain and use.

Emergency stock Dissolve meat or yeast extract in boiling water or in pot liquor.

Pot liquor is the water in which meat, poultry, fish, vegetables, macaroni, etc., have been boiled for the table where the purpose is to retain as much nourishment and flavour in the solids as possible. This is done by putting the solids into hot water but still some nourishment and flavour escape into the liquid. This liquid (pot liquor) can be used as a substitute for stock.

No stock will keep for very long. Because stock is a good medium for bacterial growth, great care must be taken in its preparation and storage. In hot climates stock should be stored in a refrigerator and boiled to prevent spoilage. Cool quickly by emptying into shallow and clean bowls. Stock which contains starchy foods should not be used after 12 hours.

Consommé A clear soup prepared from beef, chicken or game stock, garnished with a variety of ingredients. This can be served hot or chilled. Consommé takes its name generally from the garnish, e.g. Consommé Julienne—consommé garnished with boiled matchstick-like strips of vegetables such as carrots, beans, turnips, etc. Consommé Royale—consommé garnished with savoury custard cubes.

Broth A good stock (beef, mutton or chicken) cooked with diced meat, vegetables and rice or barley and served with the solids. Some of the nourishment is retained in the solids by putting them into tepid liquid. Broths are also different from ordinary soups in having the thickening (rice, barley, macaroni, etc.) put in at the beginning and cooked with the other ingredients. Examples: scotch broth, minestrone, escudella-catalina, etc.

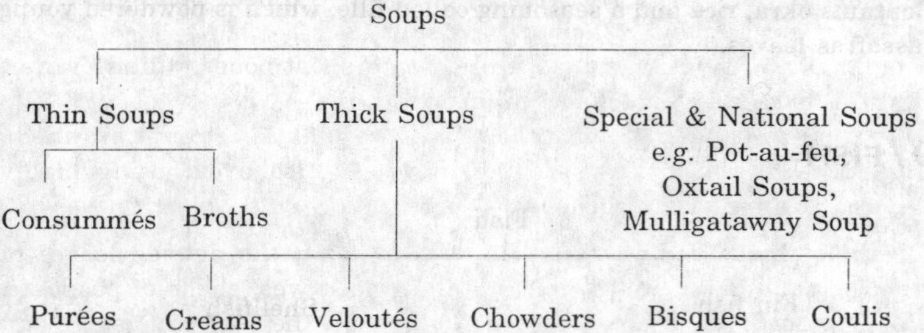

Potage or soupe These terms cover a wide variety of soups, e.g., potage bortsch, potage minestrone, potage mulligatawny, soupe au gumbo, soupe aux rognons, etc.

Purée A soup thickened by its main ingredient and passed through a sieve. Milk or a little flour blended with milk is added to prevent the purée from separating, but not as a thickening. The consistency of the soup should be like thick cream. Generally served with croûtons (fried cubes of bread). Examples: purée-de lentilles, purée de haricot blanc, purée Parmentier, purée de tomates, purée de pois frais.

Cream A soup of cream consistency which is generally made with vegetable purée mixed with béchamel or white sauce. It can be finished with cream if desired, e.g., créme de celeri, créme de tomato.

Velouté A thick soup made from white stock and roux, finished with a liason of yolks and cream.

Chowder An American soup resembling a stew made of meat, fish or vegetable with milk, salt pork and various seasonings. Crackers are generally added just before serving. Examples: prawn chowder, oyster chowder, pork chowder, vegetable chowder.

Bisques These are thickened fish soups generally made from shellfish and fish stock and thickened with cream. Diced fish is served in it. Example: bisque de homard.

The value of any soup will depend on the ingredients used. Clear soups are of value only to stimulate the appetite at the beginning of a meal while thick soups such as cream, velouté and purée, chowders, broths, etc., are nourishing as well as appetizing.

Coulis A term often used for thick soups made with a purée of shellfish, e.g. coulis d'écrevisses, coulis de crabes. Sometimes the term is also used for liquid purées such as chicken, game or vegetables.

Gumbo A regional dish that originated from the American South.

Contains okra, rice and a seasoning called fille, which is powdered young sassafras leaves.

9 / FISH

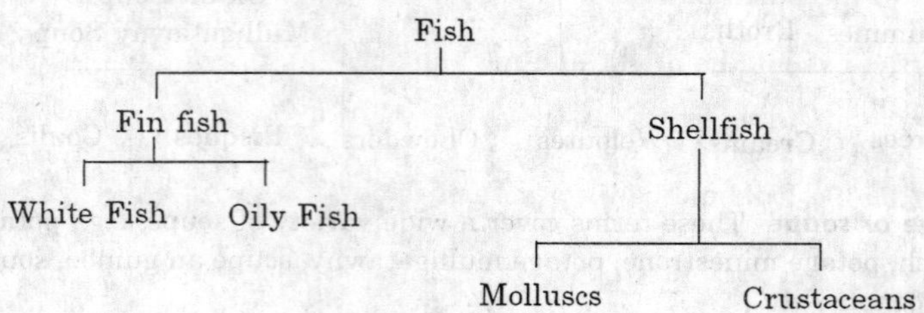

Fin fish are vertebrates and have skin and scales which cover the body. They move with the help of fins. They are subdivided into:

(1) *White fish* which are mainly flat fish, and contain oil only in the liver. Most of these are deep sea fish. Common local examples are pomfret, sole etc.

(2) *Oily fish* which are mainly round fish and contain fat all over the body. The amount of fat varies from 1.5% to 20% in different varieties. These fish are often pigmented and tend to be surface fish. Example: mackerels, sardines etc.

Shellfish, as the name denotes, have a shell covering the body. They are invertebrates. They are subdivided into:

(1) *Molluscs:* (a) Bivalves (e.g. oysters, scallops, mussels, clams and cockles) which have two distinctly separate shells joined by a hinge-like membrane. The movements of the shell are controlled by a strong muscle. When the muscle relaxes, the two halves of the shell fall open. The shell also opens when the organism dies, thus exposing the contents of the shell to contamination from outside, resulting in quick putrefaction.

(b) Univalves: (e.g. whelks and winkles). These are recognized by the characteristic spiral formation of their shells, which unlike those of bivalves are not divided into halves.

The shells of molluscs increase at the rate of one ring per year to allow for the growth of the organism. The age of the mollusc can thus be roughly estimated by the number of rings on the shell.

(2) *Crustaceans* have a segmented, crust-like shell (e.g. lobsters, crabs, prawns, shrimps). The shells of crustaceans do not grow with the

fish, unlike those of the molluscs, but are shed every year, with a new one forming to suit their new size.

How to select fish

The following points must be borne in mind when selecting fish:

(i) Eyes should be bright and not sunken.
(ii) Gills should be red.
(iii) The tail should be stiff.
(iv) The flesh should be firm and not flabby.
(v) The scales if any should be plentiful.
(vi) There should be no unpleasant odour.
(vii) To test a cut piece, press down with a finger, and if an impression is left then the fish is stale.
(viii) Any tendency for the raw flesh to come away from the bones is a dangerous sign.

Preparing fish for cooking

Scaling and cleaning

(i) To scale, use the blunt side of the knife. Holding the fish by the tail, scrape firmly from the tail towards the head. Wash well to remove any loose scales.
(ii) Remove fins and trim tail.
(iii) To clean fish such as herrings, mackerel, etc., slit the belly, using a pair of kitchen scissors, from the head to almost half way down. Remove the head if desired.
(iv) In the case of flat fish such as pomfret, etc., cut away the gills, and make a small opening in the belly. Remove the entrails and wash well. If the head is to be removed, do this with a semicircular cut at the base of the head.

To fillet the fish Slit the fish down the backbone with a sharp knife and separate the flesh from the backbone on each side with short sharp strokes. Then slit from the side and take out each fillet.

To bone herrings After slitting and cleaning, open gently. Turn over and place the inside on hard board. Press firmly along the backbone to loosen the bone. Turn over and starting at the head raise the backbone with the thumb and forefinger. Pull the bone steadily away from the fish. After pulling out the bone, rinse the fish well and drain.

Cleaning of fish

What not to do	*What to do*
Do not work without having a basin prepared to hold the fish bones, and another one for the offal.	Wash and dry fish with a clean swab. Cut off all the fins and trim the tail; remove the eyes if necessary.
Do not work directly on a table; use a chopping board.	Remove the scales, if any, by scraping them with a knife from tail to head, then remove the gills.
Do not throw the fish scales on to the table; remove them from the knife by wiping the knife against the side of the basin to collect them.	Remove all the entrails, roe, liver etc., from the gill-slits by pulling the gut out with a fork, or the hook of a small ladle handle. Make a small opening, 3½ to 5 cm. long, from the vent to the belly of fish such as herring, whiting, trout, and salmon, to remove the roe and clean the fish properly. For turbot, brill, etc. make the opening behind the head.
Do not mix different fish together; always begin with one kind and place them on one side to be washed with the others, when they have all been cleaned from inside.	
Do not have your table covered with scales or offal of fish. Keep your chopping-board and table clean by swabbing often.	After removing roe, such as herring roe, place them immediately in a basin of cold water.
Do not forget, when removing the entrails of a fish, to clear the bones of the blood vessels; and ensure that there is nothing left inside the fish by feeling with one finger.	If the head has to be removed, cut it from the gill in a V-shape.
Do not cut the ligament between the head and the body when removing the gills from small fish.	Wash the inside of the fish well under running cold water. With a clean swab or cloth dry the inside as well. Then inspect the interior of the fish carefully.
Do not burst open or cut off the belly of a small fish when cleaning the inside.	
Do not place a fish on a tray unless it has been well washed, dried and carefully examined.	

Cooking of fish

The flesh of fish is very delicate and, therefore, great care must be taken to prevent the flesh from breaking during cooking. When boiling or cooking fish, the liquid should be at simmering point before fish is added as the connective tissue in fish is softer and the quantity is less than in meat. When preparing fish stew or fish curry, fish is put into cold liquid to flavour the gravy as well. Whole fish may also be covered with a cold liquid and brought to boil. This is done to prevent shrinkage of the skin. Steaming is a better method of cooking fish as it is a gentle method. Fish cookery is not a special method of cooking. All methods of cooking can be applied bearing in mind that the delicacy of the flesh of the fish and the fat content of the fish determine the cooking method. The time taken is always much less than for cooking meat. An average timetable is as follows, but much depends on the size and shape of the fish.

Boiling and baking		10 minutes per 500 gm and 10 minutes over
Steaming		15 minutes per 500 gm and 15 minutes over.
Stewing		Half to three quarter of an hour from the time the stew begins to simmer.
Frying (for small fish or thin pieces)		about 5 minutes
Grilling		5 to 7 minutes
Lean fish	Steamed or Baked	Poached, deep-fried or baked in a sauce.
Oily fish		Baked, grilled or pan-fried.

Boiling of fish Fish is generally boiled in a court bouillon. This is made of salt, water, milk and lemon juice for sea fish with white flesh. For salmon, trout and shellfish and various types of river fish the following court bouillon is used.

Court Bouillon

Water	1 litre
Salt	15 gm
Vinegar	75 ml
Carrots(sliced)	60 gm
Onion (sliced)	60 gm
Bay leaf	1
Parsley stalks	2 to 3
Peppercorns	6
Thyme	1

Simmer all ingredients for 30 to 40 minutes.
Strain and use as required.

The stock after fish is boiled can be used as a base for different types of sauces. Fish is cooked when the flesh separates easily from the bone. Test at the thickest part nearer the bone. It there is no bone then the fish is considered done when a creamy substance begins to run from the fish.

Steaming of fish Place the fish in a steamer. Sprinkle with salt and pepper. The water in the steamer must be fast boiling all the time the fish is cooking, if large, the fish can be turned once. Test as for boiling.

Grilling of fish Heat the grill and grease the rack. Clean fish. Sprinkle over with salt, pepper and lime juice. Gashes should be made on the fish to allow heat to penetrate, otherwise the outside becomes dry before the inside is cooked. For large fish, baste frequently with melted fat. For oily fish such as herrings and sardines, no extra fat is required.

Frying of fish Fish can be fried whole, if small, or cut into steaks or fillets or pieces if large. For cut pieces, it is preferable to coat the fish with egg and breadcrumbs or seasoned flour and milk.

Baking of fish This method is most suitable for medium sized fish or the middle portion of a large fish. Scale and clean, but leave the head and tail on. Stuff the belly with a savoury forcemeat (11 gm fresh breadcrumbs, 60 gm fat, grated rind of half a lime, 2 tsp chopped parsley, ½ tsp mixed herbs, salt and pepper and egg or milk to bind). Sew up with a needle and coarse thread. Do not fill the fish too tightly. or it will burst, since the stuffing swells when it is cooked. Place the fish in a baking tray with a little fat, in a moderately hot oven, and cook till the flesh leaves the bones. To serve, remove the thread. Garnish with parsley and lemon. Serve with a sharp sauce.

Soused herring or mackerel Soused herrings and mackerel are served as an *hors d'oeuvre* or for breakfast. Scale and clean the fish. Cut off the head and tail. Remove entrails. Wash well. Put back roe if any. Place on a plate. Sprinkle over with a little salt and leave for a couple of hours. Drain the fish. Roll up and place in a casserole dish. To 500 gm of fish add 12 peppercorns, 1 bay leaf and a large onion thinly sliced. Pour over equal proportions of vinegar and water, the liquid being just sufficient to cover the fish. Bring quickly to boil and simmer for a few minutes before removing from the casserole. Serve garnished with parsley.

Shellfish

Choosing shellfish They should be bought in season as far as possible. They should be medium- sized and of good weight. It is best to buy them alive, particularly oysters, crabs, and lobsters. If they are dead, the following precautions must be taken: (a) The claws of crabs should be springy and not hanging down. (b) The eyes should be bright. (c) The tail of lobsters should spring back when stretched out. (d) Shrimps and prawns must be crisp. (e) Oyster shells should be tightly closed.

Preparing and serving shellfish Shellfish can be served in a variety of ways. Lobsters and crabs are boiled alive. The meat is removed after cooking, flaked and replaced in their own shells with sauces or served in salads or other cold dishes. The meat is mixed with sauce and served in patties, or in scallop shells or on toast and canapés. Smaller shellfish such as prawns and shrimps must be shelled first, the intestines (the black thread- like substance found at the back) removed, then washed and cooked. They are served whole, boiled or steamed, stewed or in curries, fried with masala or in batter, devilled and in soups. Shrimps and oysters can be covered with sauces. Lemon and vinegar are served with shellfish to aid in digestion.

What to serve with fish

When fish is served as a main dish, it is usually served with potatoes, a salad or a cooked vegetable and a sauce. Here are some suggestions.

FISH	POTATOES	VEGETABLES	ACCOMPANIMENTS
Fried or grilled	Fried, boiled or sautéed	Green salad, cole slaw, green peas or beans, carrots, tomatoes parsnips, cauliflower, onions.	Hollandaise, tartare, caper, tomato, mustard or cucumber sauces, lemon, parsley, butter, chutney, pickled beetroot or red cabbage.
Boiled or steamed	Boiled in jacket or mashed	Green peas or beans, carrots, tomatoes, spinach, celery, green salad, cucumber salad, parsnips, hot beetroot, sprouts, cauliflower, onions.	Hollandaise, cheese, horseradish, chutney, parsley, egg, fennel, anchovy or lemon sauces.
Baked	Baked, boiled or sautéed	Green peas or beans, carrots, green salad, tomatoes, cucumber salad, spinach, celery, parsnips, hot beetroot, sprouts, cauliflower, onions.	Hollandaise, mustard, anchovy, cucumber, tomato, tartare, caper or brown sauces, lemon, parsley, butter.

10 / MEAT

The term meat is generally applied only to butcher's meat—beef, mutton, lamb, pork and kid.

The tenderness of the meat depends on the age and feeding of the animal, on the hanging and preparation after killing. Muscle structures have an effect on the tenderness and the texture of the meat. The skeletal muscles are made up of fibres which are composed of proteins, salts and nitrogenous extractives. The fibres are grouped parallel to each other in bundles held together by connective tissue and surrounded by a sheath of heavier connective tissue. The size of the bundles varies with different muscles and determines to some extent the texture of the meat. There are two kinds of connective tissue, collagenous or white connective tissue and elastic or yellow connective tissue.

The flavour of meat is determined by various factors such as feeding, age, sex and maturity. The older the flesh the greater the flavour in most cases; young flesh is not so highly flavoured but is sweeter and more tender. Flesh of male animals is stronger in flavour than that of females unless the animal has been castrated. Well developed muscles are usually more strongly flavoured, e.g., chicken leg as compared with breast. The longer the meat is hung the stronger the flavour, owing to certain chemical changes. Meat should not be eaten immediately after killing. It has to be hung till tender. Shortly after death rigor mortis sets in and the muscles stiffen. Meat must be hung at 1° to 3°C (about 34° to 38°F) at least, till this passes off and until the acids which then develop have had a chance to soften the connective tissue. The enzyme present in the tissues also helps to make the meat render and more juicy. In cold countries this process takes at least 3 days but it is much quicker in warmer temperatures, varying between 12 to 24 hours. If so desired meat can be hung for a longer period. Not all meats should be hung like this and veal and pork particularly should be eaten fresh. They should also be thoroughly cooked before use.

Generally speaking, old meat and meat with considerable muscular development will be darker in colour and stronger in flavour. The flavour of the meat varies depending on the saltiness and sweetness of the blood, the species, the age and sex of the animal and the degree of maturity when eaten. Another factor is fat. Pork and mutton for example, have individual flavours depending on the fat. The third factor is the amount of sugar in the meat which on cooking tends to caramelize. Wherever possible select meat which is marbled. This is meat where the fat is interspersed between the muscle fibres and connective tissue. This shows good feeding. Marbling helps to keep the meat moist when cooked by dry methods. Marbled meat is also more nutritous.

There are no special methods of cooking meat and the fundamental methods of cooking can be deftly adapted to suit the particular joint. The amount of connective tissue present in the meat determines to a great extent the method of cooking. When connective tissue is present in large amounts, the meat, being tough, is cooked by moist methods. For those cuts which have only a small amount of connective tissue, dry heat cooking may be used. Long-fibred cuts of meat require longer cooking than short-fibred ones. They should be stewed or braised to make them tender. Shorter-fibred meat is cooked by dry heat. The most developed muscle fibres are usually the longest and these coarser fibres are found in the legs, neck and tail. The shorter fibres are found in the fillet, rump and loin.

Dry heat cooking (roasting, frying and grilling or broiling) develops the characteristic meat flavour, coagulates the proteins, thus making fibres firm, hardens the connective tissue, and changes the colour. This change in colour is caused by a change in the composition of haemoglobin. Shrinkage is observed in meat cooked by the dry heat method. Moist cooking (braising, boiling, stewing, etc.) besides developing flavour and coagulating the meat, softens the collagenous tissue, thus rendering meat tender. Elastic connective tissue is softened only slightly by moist heat. There is no shrinking in meat cooked by moist methods.

When cooking meat it is desirable to retain the juices in the fibres. Steaks, roasts, etc., are cooked either at a constant temperature of 149°C (about 300°F) for beef, veal and lamb and 177°C (about 350°F) for pork, or by the searing method, where the meat is cooked at a high temperature for the first 10 minutes and then cooked at a lowered temperature. This method was supposed to help in retention of juices but this has been disproved although the aroma, flavour and colour that accompany searing are preferred by some. Steaks are usually grilled at 204.5°C (about 400°F). Studies have illustrated that a lower oven temperature 171°–177°C (about 300°–350°F) as compared to a higher temperature 218.3°–232.2°C (about 425°–450°F) results in less drip loss, less shrinkage, increased juiciness and more uniform colour throughout a cut. Overcooking or extended cooking at high temperature denatures the protein of meat, eggs, fish and birds or they toughen or become stringy or all three.

If a roast is cooked at a high temperature, the time of cooking is decreased, but dripping and evaporation losses are higher, and the meat is not so evenly cooked. The degree of 'doneness' also affects this loss, the steak done 'rare' or 'underdone' showing less than that done 'medium' or 'well done'. A meat thermometer helps in determining the degree of 'doneness'. The thermometer should be inserted so that the bulb is at the centre of the cut but not in contact with the bone. For thin cuts the thermometer is not very satisfactory.

Meat meant for boiling should be dipped into salted boiling water and then allowed to simmer till tender. A pressure saucepan may be used to save time when cooking less tender cuts of meat. Care should be taken to prevent cooking of meat in a pressure cooker or at a high temperature longer than necessary, otherwise it becomes hard, dry and flavourless.

Frozen meat may be prepared by the same methods as fresh meat. It need not be thawed before cooking. If it is not thawed, however, the cooking time is considerably increased, to as much as two to three times the time required for cooking thawed or fresh meat. Thawing can be done in the refrigerator or at room temperature. When meat is not thawed, it does not retain a coating such as egg and breadcrumbs.

Tenderisers such as papain (taken from raw papaya) may be used to soften the fibres before cooking. These must be applied to the meat, which should then be allowed to stand for one hour for a cut of 2.5 cm.(1") thickness. The acidity of vinegar, lemon juice, curd, cider and wine which can be added before or during cooking also helps to tenderise meat.

Sign of quality Mutton and lamb (lamb is meat from a lamb under one year old):

(i) A good quality animal should be compact and evenly fleshed.
(ii) The lean flesh should be firm, of a pleasing dull red colour and of a fine texture or grain.
(iii) There should be an even distribution of surface fat, which should be hard, brittle and flaky in structure, and of a clear white colour.
(iv) In a young animal the bone is pink and porous, so that when it is cut, a small amount of blood can be seen. With progressive aging the bones become hard, dense, white and inclined to splinter when chopped.

Order of dissection

(i) Remove the shoulders.
(ii) Remove the breasts.
(iii) Remove the middle neck and scrag end.
(iv) Remove the legs.
(v) Divide the saddle from the best end.

Approximate weight of the carcass of an Indian animal:

Lamb: 10 kg. (22 lb.)
Mutton: 16.8 kg. (37 lb.)

Whereas the approximate weight of an English animal is:

Lamb: 14 kg. (32 lb.)
Mutton: 23 kg. (50 lb.)

Mutton and Lamb

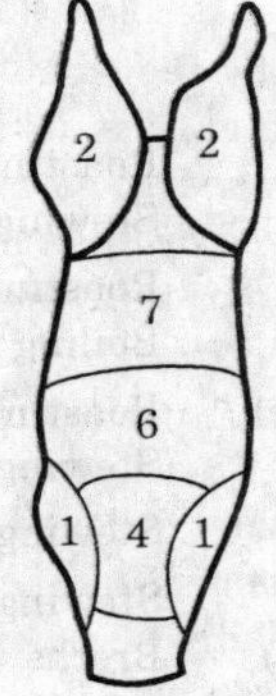

1. Shoulders (two)
2. Legs (two)
3. Breasts (two)
4. Middle neck
5. Scrag end
6. Best end
7. Saddle

Kidneys
Liver
Sweetbread
Tongue

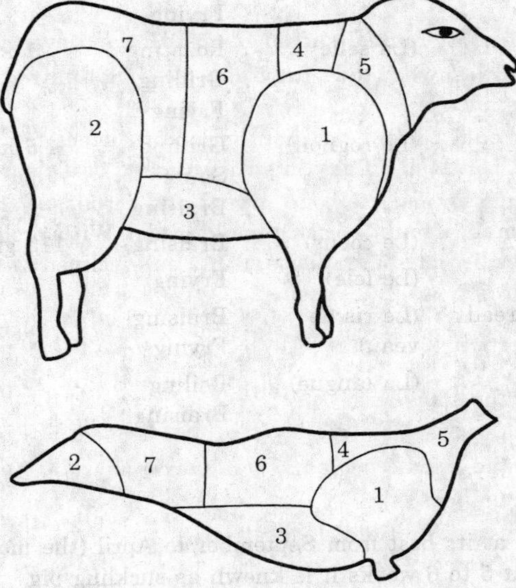

Joints and their uses

JOINTS	French	USES	APPROX. WEIGHT (Lamb)	(Mutton)
(i) Shoulder	(L'épaule)	Roasting Stewing	2.00 kg.	3.5 kg.
(ii) Leg	(Le gigot)	Roasting Boiling	2.75 kg.	3.75 kg.
(iii) Breast	(La poitrine)	Roasting Stewing	0.9 kg	1.75 kg.
(iv) Middle neck	(Le collet)	Stewing	1.15 kg.	1.7 kg.
(v) Scrag end	(Le côte décourverte)	Stewing Broths	450 gm.	0.9 kg.
(vi) Best end	(Le carré)	Roasting Grilling Frying	575 gm.	1.20 kg.
(vii) Saddle	(La selle)	Roasting Grilling Frying	1 kg.	3.5 kg.
(viii) Kidney	(Le rognon)	Grilling Sauté Braising	1.5 kg.	2.25 kg.
(ix) Heart	(Le coeur)	Braising	115 gm	60 gm.
(x) Liver	(Le foie)	Frying		350 gm.
(xi) Sweetbread	(Le ris de veau)	Braising Frying		
(xii) Tongue	(La langue)	Boiling Braising		

Pork

Fresh pork is at its best from September to April (the months with an 'r' in them). At 5 to 6 weeks it is known as suckling pig.

Sign of quality

(i) Lean flesh should be pale pink, firm and of a fine texture.
(ii) The fat should be white, firm, smooth and not excessive.
(iii) Bones should be small, fine and pinkish.
(iv) The skin or rind should be smooth.

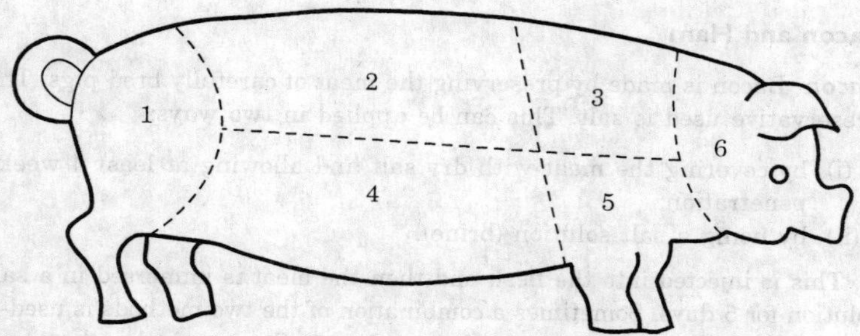

1. Leg
2. Loin
3. Spare-rib
4. Belly
5. Shoulder
6. Head (whole)
   Trotters
   Kidneys
   Liver

Order of dissection:

(i) Remove the head.
(ii) Remove the trotters.
(iii) Remove the leg.
(iv) Remove the shoulder.
(v) Remove spare ribs.
(vi) Divide loin from the belly.

Joints and their uses

JOINTS	French	USES	APPROX. WEIGHT
(i) Thigh	(La cuisse)	Roasting Boiling	4.55 kg.
(ii) Loin	(La longe)	Roasting Frying Grilling	5.45 kg.
(iii) Spare rib	(Le côte découverte de porc)	Roasting Pies	1.35 kg.
(iv) Belly (Breast)	(La poitrine)	Pickling Boiling	1.8 kg.
(v) Shoulder	(L'épaule)	Roasting Sausages Pies	2.7 kg.
(vi) Head (whole)	(La tête)	Brawn	3.6
(vii) Trotters	(Le pied)	Grilling Boiling	
(viii) Kidney	(Le rognon)	Sauté Grilling	
(ix) Liver	(Le foie)	Pâté	

Bacon and Ham

Bacon Bacon is made by preserving the meat of carefully bred pigs. The preservative used is salt. This can be applied in two ways:

(i) by covering the meat with dry salt and allowing at least 4 weeks penetration;
(ii) by using a salt solution (brine).

This is injected into the flesh and then the meat is immersed in a salt solution for 5 days. Sometimes a combination of the two methods is used—brine is injected into the meat and the sides are then stacked and covered with dry salt for 2 to 3 weeks. It is then matured for about 3 weeks under controlled temperature. Desirable bacteria acting on the meat juices and salt produce the characteristics associated with well matured bacon.

This bacon is now ready for sale as 'green' or 'pale' bacon. In certain parts of the world the bacon is preferred smoked. So it is then hung over smouldering wood dust for 2 days. This extracts excessive moisture and gives the bacon a distinctive flavour. Smoking also improves the preservation as it acts as an antiseptic. This is particularly suitable in hot climates.

Good quality, well cured bacon should have a pleasant smell; the rind should be thin and smooth, the fat firm and free from any yellow marks, the lean part a good deep pink colour and the flavour mild and mellow.

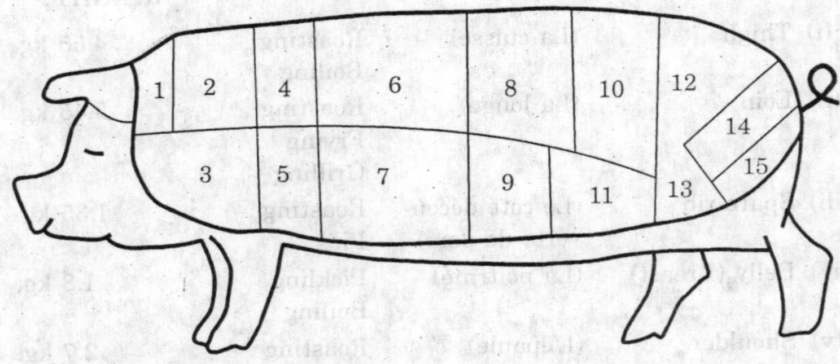

1. End Collar
2. Prime Collar
3. Fore Hock
4. Top Back
5. Top Streaky
6. Back and Ribs
7. Prime Streaky
8. Short Back
9. Thin Streaky
10. Long Back
11. Flank
12. Corner Gammon
13. Slipper
14. Middle Gammon
15. Gammon Flock

Ham and gammon Ham and gammon come from the hind leg of a pig. Gammon is cut off the side of a cured porker. Ham, on the other hand, is cut off at the fresh pork stage and includes a substantial part of the loin. It is cured after cutting, usually by the long process of dry salting.

Cuts and their uses

	CUT	USE
(i)	End collar	Boiling; Braising
(ii)	Fore hock can be bought boned and rolled	Boiling
(iii)	Prime collar	Boiling (either whole or cut into smaller pieces) Rashers can be fried or grilled.
(iv)	Top streaky	Thinly sliced rashers can be used for frying and grilling. Can be boned and boiled.
(v)	Top back (good lean cut)	Boiled or braised whole or cut into thin rashers and grilled.
(vi)	Back and ribs	Cut into rashers and grilled.
(vii)	Prime streaky (the best cut of streaky bacon).	Boiled in one piece or cut into rashers.
(viii)	Short back (one of the best cuts for breakfast frying)	Frying
(ix)	Thin streaky	Grilling Frying (Crisp and well cooked)
(x)	Long back	Sliced thinly and fried gently or grilled quickly.
(xi)	Flank (good cut to be served with liver or other meats and in a minced bacon recipe)	Boiling Frying
(xii)	Corner gammon (lean and well flavoured)	Boiling whole (serve hot or cold) or cut into rashers for grilling.
(xiii)	Slipper (gammon lean small cut)	Boiled whole or cut into rashers.
(xiv)	Middle gammon	Boiled whole (serve hot or cold) or lean rashers for frying.
(xv)	Gammon hock	Should be partly boiled and then baked (serve hot or cold.)

Beef

Signs of good quality

(i) The lean meat should be bright red with small flecks of white fat.

(ii) The fat should be firm, brittle in texture, creamy white in colour and odourless. Older animals and dairy breeds have fat which is usually deeper yellow in colour.

(iii) Beef in good condition should have streaks of fat running through the lean section and the flesh should rise again quickly after being pressed with the fingers. Any cut surface should present a slightly moist appearance to the touch.

Order of dissection A whole side is divided into the forequarter and hindquarter, the division being between the wing ribs and fore ribs.

Hindquarter

(i) Remove the rump, suet and kidney.
(ii) Remove the thin flank.
(iii) Divide the loin and rump from the leg. (The leg will consist of topside, silverside, thick flank and shin)
(iv) Remove the fillet.
(v) Divide the rump from the sirloin.
(vi) Remove the wing ribs.
(vii) Remove the shin.
(viii) Bone out the aitchbone.
(ix) Divide the leg into topside, silverside and thick flank.

Forequarter

(i) Remove the shank.
(ii) Divide in half down the centres.
(iii) Take off the fore ribs.
(iv) Divide into joints.

Joints and their uses

JOINTS	French	USES	APPROX WEIGHT
(i) Shin	Jambe de derrière (Jambe de devant)	Consommé, beef tea, stewing	4.00 kg.
(ii) Topside	Culotte de boeuf	Braising, stewing, second-class roasting	7.5 kg.
(iii) Silverside	Gîte à la noix, semelle	Salt beef	10.00 kg.

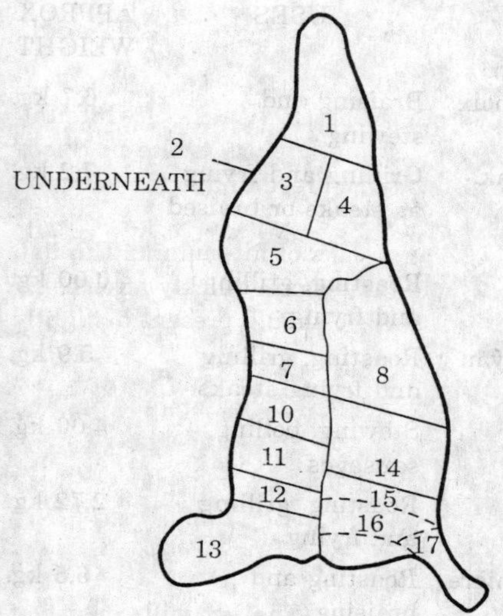

1. Shin
2. Topside
3. Sliverside
4. Thick flank
5. Rump
6. Sirloin
7. Wing ribs
8. Thin flank
9. Fillet
10. Fore rib
11. Middle rib
12. Chuck rib
13. Sticking piece
14. Brisket
15. Plate
16. Leg of mutton cut
17. Shank

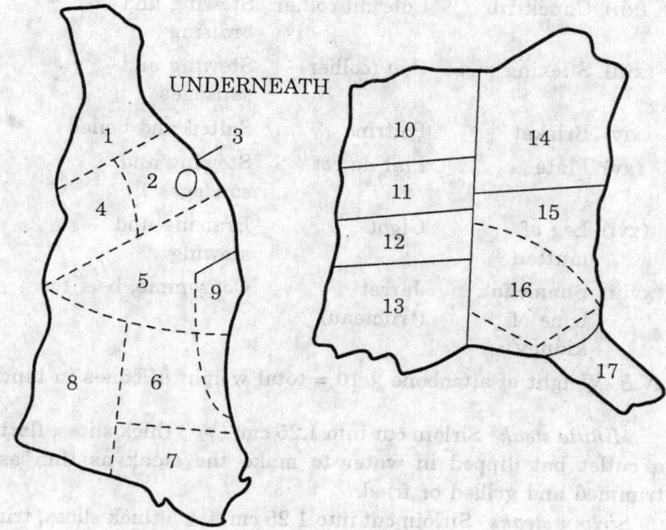

JOINTS	French	USES	APPROX WEIGHT
(iv) Thick flank	Gîte à la noix	Braising and stewing	6.7 kg.
(v) Rump	Rump steak, colutte de boeuf	Grilling and frying as steaks or braised	7.2 kg.
(vi) Sirloin	Aloyau	Roasting, grilling and frying	10.00 kg.
(vii) Wing ribs	Côte d'aloyau	Roasting, grilling and frying steaks	5.9 kg.
(viii) Thin flank	Bavette	Stewing, boiling, sausages	4.00 kg.
(ix) Fillet	Filet	Roasting, grilling and frying	2.72 kg.
(x) Fore rib	Côte première	Roasting and braising	6.5 kg.
(xi) Middle rib.	Côte découverte	Roasting and braising	8.00 kg.
(xii) Chuck rib	Côte du collier	Stewing and braising	4.08 kg.
(xiii) Sticking piece	Cou (collier)	Stewing and sausages	10.00 kg.
(xiv) Brisket	Poitrine	Salted and boiled	6.8 kg.
(xv) Plate	Plat de cot	Stewing and sausages	5.9 kg.
(xvi) Leg of mutton	Gigot	Braising and stewing	10.5 kg.
(xviii) Shank fat, bone of kidney	Jarret (trumeau)	Consommé, beef tea	4.08 kg. 7.2 kg.

N.B. Weight of aitchbone × 10 = total weight of bones in hind quarter.

Minute steak Sirloin cut into 1.25 cm. (½″) thick slices, flattened with a cutlet bat dipped in water to make the steak as thin as possible, trimmed and grilled or fried.

Sirloin steaks Sirloin cut into 1.25 cm. (½″) thick slices, trimmed and fried or grilled.

Double sirloin steaks Sirloin cut into 2.5 cm. (1″) slices, trimmed and fried or grilled.

Porterhouse and T-bone steak Complete slices of sirloin including the bone and fillet.

Châteaubriand This is a double fillet steak taken from the head of a fillet of beef, 3.5 to 10 cm. (1½"–4") thick, with an average weight of 340 gm. to 1 kg. It is generally served grilled at a temperature of 204.5ºC (about 400ºF), done to the taste of the customer.

Fillet steak These are approximately 115 gm. to 170 gm. in weight cut into 2.5 cm. (1") thick slices trimmed and grilled or fried.

Tournedos Taken from the middle portion of the fillet. Remove all fat.

Fillet mignon Taken from the tail end of the fillet. All fat and sinews are removed and it is minced or sliced as required.

Entrecôte steak A slice of steak cut between two bones of a rib of beef, or cut from the contrefilet (bone sirloin or undercut), and weighing about 650 gm.; sufficient for four persons.

Entrecôte minute Cut as above from the sirloin or contrefilet as thinly as possible, about 1 cm. (⅖") in thickness, well flattened, and served grilled or sauteéd.

11 / POULTRY

Choosing poultry

Only young birds are suitable for roasting; older birds may be boiled , steamed, braised or stewed. A roasting chicken should be about nine months to a year old; geese and other birds for roasting should not also be older than one year.

Signs of a young bird

(i) The feathers, especially the quills on the wings, should be easy to pull out.
(ii) There should be down all over the body, but especially under the wings.
(iii) No long hair on the body.
(iv) The skin should be white or clear and smooth.
(v) The feet should be supple, with smooth, even, over-lapping scales.
(vi) The comb and wattle should be small and not well developed.

Signs which show that a bird is fresh

(i) Feathers – light and fluffy.
(ii) Eyes – prominent and clear.
(iii) No marked or unpleasant smell.
(iv) Feet – moist and not stiff and dry
(v) Skin – clear with no dark or greenish tinge.

Points which denote good condition in ducks The breast should be plump. The bill and feet are yellow in young birds, but they darken with age. The webbing of the feet should be smooth, tender and easily broken, and the underbill soft and pliable.

Preparation

Storing poultry Fowls and ducks are best used fresh and should not be stored longer than 1 or 2 days before cooking. Protect them from flies and hang by the feet in a dry airy place.

Plucking If poultry is plucked while still warm the feathers are easier to remove.

(i) When plucking, do not sit in a draught or the feathers will blow about.
(ii) Put the bird on a large sheet of strong paper.
(iii) Take care not to tear the skin, especially when plucking game birds.
(iv) Hold the bird firmly with the left hand and pluck with the right.
(v) Pluck out small handfuls at a time, starting from under one wing then continue plucking until one side is completely clear.
(vi) Remove all the pin feathers with a knife.

Singeing A bird can be singed in either of the two following ways. Care should be taken not to scorch or blacken the skin.

(i) Hold the bird by its head and feet, and quickly and carefully singe off the hairs over a small gas jet.
(ii) Hold the bird in the left hand and singe with a lighted taper or paper spill.

The giblets These can be used for making stock for gravy to serve with the roast bird, for enriching the stock when the bird is boiled, or for making giblet pie or giblet stew. The liver and kidneys are not boiled with the fowl, as they tend to darken the meat. They may be half-cooked, chopped and used as part of the stuffing or cooked in other ways. Instructions for cleaning giblets are given below.

Liver: Carefully cut away the gall bladder, taking great care not to break it.

Stomach: Remove any fat and reserve it. Scrape the gizzard lining well.

Heart: Cut free of tubes, cut open, and scrape away all congealed blood.

Kidney: With a large bird, such as a turkey or goose, these are large enough to be used. Cut them open and cut out the core.

Neck: Scrape away all congealed blood.

Wash the liver, gizzard, heart, kidney and neck in salt water and rinse well.

Drawing the tendons If a bird is not young and tender, it is advisable to draw the tendons from the legs before roasting.

(i) Carefully cut through the skin of the leg at the knee joint, taking care not to cut the tendons at the same time.
(ii) Break the joint and swing the leg free to expose the tendons.
(iii) Pull out the tendons one at a time with a strong metal skewer. There will be 7 of them in each leg.

Stuffing Birds can be roasted, stuffed or unstuffed, but they are usually stuffed. Stuffing can be put inside the bird only, or both inside and at the crop, covered by the skin of the neck.

Veal forcemeat may be used for the inside and sausage meat for the crop or vice versa. Pack the veal forcemeat, or any similar stuffing, fairly loosely to allow for swelling.

Trussing

Method (A)

A trussing needle and some thin, clean string will be necessary. A trussing needle is a strong steel needle about 23 cm. (9") long with a large eye.

(i) Fold the skin of the neck over the back of the bird, and cross the tips of the wings over, to keep it securely in position.
(ii) Turn the bird breast upwards and put the tail through the vent.
(iii) Thread the trussing needle and pass it just under the top joint of the right wing through the bird and out through the same joint in the left wing. Run the needle back through the bird so that it enters and comes out just above the bottom joint of the wings.
(iv) Tie the ends of the string securely in a bow, taking care not to drag the flesh.
(v) Re-thread the needle, press the legs well into the sides towards the wings, plumping out the breast, and run the needle through the back of the bird, just under the thigh joint, and return through a point near the ends of the legs. Tie both ends of the string firmly together.

Method (B)

(i) Fold the skin of the neck over the stuffing and secure firmly with a small skewer.
(ii) Turn the bird breast upwards and put the tail through the vent.

(iii) Pass a large skewer through the wing pinions to hold them securely in position.

(iv) Tuck the legs well into the sides of the bird to plump out the breast, then tie the legs firmly together with a string; pass the string underneath the bird, cross it, then bring it up again and twist it round the wing. Skewer and tie firmly.

Trussing a fowl for boiling

(i) Cut the skin of the legs all round at the knee joint, crack the joints and pull the shanks off with as many of the sinews as possible.

(ii) Thread the trussing needle and secure the wings in the same way as for the roasting bird, or fix them securely with a skewer.

(iii) Carefully loosen the skin round the legs, and slip them into the body of the bird. Secure in position with the trussing needle and string or with a skewer.

WHAT TO SERVE WITH MEAT, POULTRY AND GAME

The following tables give some suggestions for vegetables, sauces and accompaniments for meat, game and poultry.

MEAT	POTATOES	OTHER VEGETABLES	SAUCES AND ACCOMPANIMENTS
		BEEF	
Roast	Roast or boiled	Any green vegetables, carrots, peas, green beans, parsnips, marrow or pumpkin.	Brown gravy, horseradish sauce, Yorkshire pudding.
Grilled steak	Fried or boiled	Fried onions or mushrooms, beetroot, water-cress, lettuce, grilled tomatoes.	Parsley, butter, tart jelly (currant, cranberry, etc.), grated horseradish.
Boiled	Boiled	Onions, tomatoes, turnips, carrots, beetroot.	Dumplings, tomato, parlsey, or horseradish sauce.
Stewed	Boiled	Any root vegetables.	Dumplings.
Braised	Mashed, boiled or baked	Peas, green beans, carrots, turnips, celery and any green vegetable.	Horseradish sauce, tart jelly, gravy.
Minced or hamburger	Boiled, mashed or fried	Carrots, tomatoes, peas, green vegetables.	Tart jelly, pickles, tomato sauce, gravy.
Cold	Boiled or potato salad	Beetroot, green salad.	Tart jelly, pickles, including cabbage or cucumber.
		LAMB OR MUTTON	
Roast mutton	Roasted or boiled	Peas, turnips, any green vegetable.	Savoury stuffing, currant jelly brown gravy, onion sauce.
Roast lamb	Roasted or boiled	Peas, turnips, any green vegetable.	Mint sauce.
Grilled or fried chops	Mashed or fried	Spinach, peas, green beans, tomatoes, mushrooms.	Mint sauce, mint or currant jelly, tomato or mushroom sauce, parsley butter.
Boiled leg	Boiled or jacket	Carrots, turnips, and any green vegetable.	Caper sauce, red currant jelly, pickled red cabbage, dumplings.
Stewed	Boiled or jacket	Carrots, celery, peas, green beans, turnips.	Pickled red cabbage dumplings.

(*contd.*)

MEAT	POTATOES	OTHER VEGETABLES	SAUCES AND ACCOMPANIMENTS
Braised	Boiled, mashed or baked in jacket	Turnips, onions, carrots, any green vegetable.	Mint sauce, tart jelly, pickled cucumber.
		PORK	
Roast	Boiled, roasted or mashed	Cauliflower, onions, cabbage, celery, tomatoes, spinach, sprouts.	Sage and onion stuffing, brown gravy, baked or fried apples or apple sauce, tart jelly, cranberry sauce.
Grilled or fried chops	Mashed or fried	Onions, carrots, celery, tomatoes, turnips.	Fried apple rings, tart jelly.
Boiled salt port	Boiled	Cabbage.	Pease pudding, tomato sauce, dumplings.
Grilled or fried gammon	Mashed or fried	Spinach, peas, tomatoes, or any green vegetable.	Apple sauce or fried apple.
Boiled bacon	Boiled	Cabbage, carrots, beetroot, turnips, beans.	Pease pudding, parsley sauce.
Sausages	Mashed	Any green vegetable, tomatoes.	Fried apple rings or apple sauce, fried bacon gravy, fried onions.
		VEAL	
Roast and braised	Boiled, roasted or mashed	Spinach, tomatoes, onions, beetroot.	Savoury stuffing, brown gravy, boiled bacon or salt pork.
Grilled or fried chops and cutlets	Mashed or fried	Tomatoes, carrots, celery, string beans.	Tomato sauce, apple sauce or fried apples, celery sauce, lemon.
Calf's head	Boiled	Green salad to follow.	Vinaigrette sauce with brains.
Liver	Fried, baked in jacket, boiled or mashed.	Spinach, tomatoes, green salad.	Bacon, brown gravy, savoury forcemeat.
		POULTRY AND GAME	
Roast chicken	Mashed, fried or roasted	Onions, cauliflower, peas, green beans, celery, watercress, green salad.	Savoury stuffing, currant jelly, bread sauce, brown gravy, bacon rolls.

(*contd.*)

MEAT	POTATOES	OTHER VEGETABLES	SAUCES AND ACCOMPANIMENTS
Boiled rabbit	Boiled or jacket	Onion, carrots, turnips and any green vegetable.	Boiled salt pork or bacon, dumplings, parsley sauce, mint sauce.
Roast duck	Boiled or roasted	Peas, carrots, turnips and any green vegetable, orange salad.	Apple sauce, sage and onion stuffing, tart jelly.
Roast turkey	Boiled, fried or roasted	Onions, peas, pumpkin, sprouts.	Sausages, cranberry sauce, brown gravy, chestnut stuffing, bacon rolls, bread sauce, celery sauce.
Roast goose	Roasted or boiled	Onions, carrots and any green vegetable.	Sage and onion stuffing, apple and prune stuffing, apple sauce, brown gravy, savoury stuffing, currant jelly, cranberry sauce.
Roast pheasant	Game chips, roasted, mashed or boiled	Onions, cauliflower, peas, green beans, celery, watercress.	Brown gravy, bread sauce, bacon rolls, fried beadcrumbs.
Roast venison	Roasted or boiled	Any green vegetable, carrots, onions.	Brown gravy, red currant jelly or red currant jelly melted in port wine.
Stewed or jugged hare	Boiled, jacket or mashed	Any green vegetable.	Red currant jelly, forcemeat balls.
Roast rabbit or hare	Roasted, backed, jacket or boiled	Any green vegetable, onions, carrots.	Red currant jelly, brown gravy, savoury stuffing.
Boiled chicken	Boiled	Any green or root vegetables.	Onion sauce, bread sauce, egg sauce, parsley sauce.
Snipe, quail, etc.	Game chips	Green salad, orange salad.	Serve on rounds of toast or fried bread, red currant jelly.

12 / VEGETABLES AND SALADS

Test for freshness

All vegetables, particularly green ones, are best when taken straight from the garden. But this is not always possible so it is essential that one should know how to judge a well-grown vegetable. A well-grown vegetable is usually tender and free from pests.

Vegetables are classified into three divisions:

(i) Root vegetables.
(ii) Leafy vegetables.
(iii) Other vegetables grown above the soil.

Root vegetables These should be firm and heavy for their size. They should be free from earth and grubs. Carrots should be heavy, smooth skinned and orange in colour.

Leafy vegetables These should be crisp and give a crunchy sound when squeezed. Break the vein of a leaf; it should give a sharp snap. It the leaves are limp, then the vegetable is not fresh.

Other vegetables Cabbage and cauliflower should be free from greenfly. The cabbage should have a firm heart and the outer leaves should stand the same test for freshness as green leafy vegetables. Cauliflower should have a close, white flower. Tomatoes should be of a rusty red colour and should not be soft. Runner beams and French beans should not be stringy. Peas should be full in the pod, and green. Ladies fingers should snap if the ends are broken. Brinjals should have a smooth skin and should not be heavy for their size.

Importance of vegetables in our diet

Vegetables play an important role in the human diet. Properly chosen and eaten, cooked or raw, they make an invaluable contribution toward the supply of vitamins and minerals. Root vegetables are good sources of carbohydrates, and pulses (peas, beans, lentils, etc.) of vegetable proteins. A good balance of ingredients essential for growth and maintenance in human beings is more easily attained by a diet made up of both plant and animal life. Vegetables also provide variety in a meal, help to make a meal attractive by introducing colour, and furnish roughage.

Mushrooms have been found to contain one or more antibiotics, one of which is effective against tuberculosis and germs which cause boils. Mushrooms which have always been a food favourite are rich in vitamins and low in calories. Seven average sized mushrooms have only 12 calories.

Whenever possible at least two vegetables should be served in addition to potatoes. Salads should be made popular and should be served at both meals.

SALADS are dishes made up of meat, poultry, game, fish, shellfish, eggs, vegetables, fruits and milk products—normally served cold but can be served hot or frozen. They can be made out of a single ingredient or a combination of ingredients. Salads are normally served as an accompaniment to the main course, a meal by itself or a sweet course (dessert). There should be special stress on hygiene as most of the ingredients are served raw. The ingredients used and the colour, flavour, texture and presentation may be varied according to the purpose.

There are four basic parts in a salad:

The Underliner These are generally greens either shredded or in large pieces. Tear the greens instead of cutting with a knife. The greens must be crisp and chilled. To keep the greens crisp, it is necessary to store them in a manner that retains the maximum amount of water in the cells. This could be achieved by storing them at refrigeration temperature in the hydrator drawer wrapped in a moist cloth or in a covered container. The loss of water in cells can be reversed. To do this reduce the temperature to 2–3°C (about 34°F), and moisten the greens. When the cells are once again filled with water the greens will be crisp.

The body or heart of the salad This will form the major component and can be made of one ingredient or a combination of ingredients. Ingredients should look sparkling fresh with each individual piece intact. Fruits are particularly fragile and should be handled as little as possible.

Dressings These make the salad more appetising although diet conscious people today eat their salads without a dressing. Dressings must be carefully selected. Depending upon the salad, the dressing could be either basic French or an emulsion. Pleasing flavours can be added to and variations made in the dressings by adding ingredients like cayenne pepper, tabasco sauce, diced hard boiled eggs, assorted herbs, a variety of cheeses, chutney, etc. Dressings should enhance the salad and not obscure it.

Garnish The garnish should be the focal point and should be carefully selected for its simplicity and to enhance eye appeal and flavour. Edible garnish is more appropriate than inedible ones. Sometimes the dressing is also used as a garnish by piping it in a decorative form on the salad.

Special stress should be given to the quality of ingredients, eye appeal, simplicity, neatness and contrast or harmony in colour and in texture. All ingredients should be edible, clean, fresh and free from defects, such as bruises, rotten spots, insects, dirt, sand and insecticide. Raw fruits and vegetables should be at their optimum stage of maturity. All inedible portions should be removed. Remove any excess moisture from ingredients as it thins the dressing, making it less effective.

The aesthetic qualities are determined by the form and shape of the food as well as by the colour. Skilfulness and artistic cutting and arranging of salad ingredients can create an appealing effect.

Try for an uncluttered appearance.

Always prepare salads as close to time of serving as possible.

Preparation of vegetables

They should be washed before peeling. A knife or a peeler may be used. The purpose of cutting is to ensure uniformity of size and even cooking. The types of cutting used for vegetables are dicing, chopping, grating, slicing, shredding, cutting into rings, mincing, etc. The object of preparation is to remove spoilt, soiled and indigestible parts.

Cooking vegetables

Fruits and vegetables are cooked for many reasons:

(i) To preserve them.
(ii) To soften the product.
(iii) To improve the flavour.
(iv) To increase the digestibility.

Whatever the methods of cooking applied, the objective is to lose as little as possible of the natural flavours, colour and nutrients.

Cooking affects the palatability of the vegetables, i.e., their texture, flavour and colour. While palatability may not affect the nutritive value of vegetables, it affects their desirability.

All the different methods of cooking can be effectively employed in the preparation of vegetables.

The effect of cooking on starch, protein and cellulose brings about the change in texture observed in vegetables when they are cooked. The predominant cause for change in texture will depend upon the composition of the vegetable. For example, with leafy vegetables which contain a high percentage of fibre, the change in texture is primarily due to the effect of cooking on the hemicellulose, whereas in potatoes the gelatinization of starch is the chief factor. While this is true, it has also been noted that the change in any one ingredient is not the only cause that makes vegetables tender. For example, gelatinization of the starch in a potato is completed before the potato is considered done.

As the amount of protein in vegetables is small, the effect of coagulation during cooking is not of great significance.

Alkalies such as baking soda aid in softening of vegetables as they speed up the solution of pectic substances and dissolve the hemicellulose. Acids, on the contrary, harden the vegetables, as acid precipitates pectin.

The texture of the cooked vegetables can be controlled to a great extent by the length of the cooking time. The longer the cooking period, the softer the product.

The flavour of vegetables depends upon many substances—sugar, acids, tannins and a variety of volatile substances. There is a predominance of sweetness in beetroot, peas, corn and carrots, but each vegetable has other ingredients which contribute to its characteristic flavour and aroma. The pronounced bitterness or astringency of certain vegetables is due to the presence of tannin. The characteristic odour of the onion family—chives, shallots, onions, garlic and leek—is due to a readily volatile substance—allyl propyl disuphide. As this substance is soluble in water the longer the vegetables are cooked in water, the milder is the flavour.

The colour of the cooked product will depend on the kind and amount of colour pigment, the method of cooking and the acidity of the cooking medium. The colour pigments of fruits and vegetables are cholorophyll, carotenoids, flavones and anthocyanins. Tannins, though not colour pigments, undergo chemical changes during cooking and thus affect the colour of many cooked vegetables.

Chlorophyll is made up of two compounds, chlorophyll 'a' and chlorophyll 'b'. Both are organic esters and both contain magnesium. The reactions taking place during cooking affect these radicals. Chlorophyll is slightly soluble in water but dissolves easily in many organic solvents. Like other esters it is subject to hydrolysis, the reaction taking place in the presence of alkali, forming chlorophyllins—salts of chlorophyll which are intensely green in colour.

In the presence of acids, chlorophyll undergoes another type of decomposition with the loss of magnesium from the molecule. The resulting compounds are called phaeophytins. They are yellow to brown in colour. Both reactions, with acids and with alkalis, are irreversible in the sense that chlorophyll cannot be formed again by treating the decomposed products with a neutralizing agent.

Any cooking process which involves the use of acids or alkalies will affect the colour of green vegetables. During the life of the plant the chlorophyll is held in the cytoplasm of the plant cells in such a way that it is protected from the regions of changing acidity. When cell life is destroyed, the constituents of the cells intermingle and the green colour fades, becoming yellow and brown.

When a green vegetable is cooked the cell structure gets slowly destroyed and the acid of the cells gradually comes in contact with the chlorophyll. Hence green vegetables cooked for long periods lose their greenness. If the cooking pan is kept open during cooking, some of the acids of the vegetables may evaporate, preserving some of the green colour. When soda is added to the water in which green vegetables are cooked there is no loss in colour. The alkali neutralizes the acidity of the vegetable and also speeds up the cooking process. Loss of colour also depends on the temperature of cooking. At high temperatures there is greater hydrolysis and, therefore, greater loss of colour.

Carotenoids include two types of colour pigments—the hydrocarbons, e.g. carotene as in carrots, and the oxygenated hydrocarbons, e.g. lutein, the colouring matter in egg yolk.

These pigments like all other hydrocarbons do not dissolve readily in water. They are also not affected by acids or alkalies. The oxygenated carotenoids are also chemically resistant to acids and alkalies as well as insoluble in water. Other carotenoids are xanthophyll, associated with carotene, lycopene (the red pigment in tomatoes and watermelon), zeaxanthin (the yellow pigment in egg yolks and corn), capsanthin (in red pepper) and fucoxanthin (in brown seaweed).

Anthocyanins are colour pigments which are found more in fruits and flowers than in vegetables. The colour varies from red to blue. Red or purple cabbage, purple broccoli, beets and skins of aubergine and radish contain large amounts of anthocyanins. There are 28 known anthocyanins. They differ in their degree of solubility and sensitiveness to conditions which produce colour changes. They are inclined to be red in acidic and blue in basic solutions. The colour changes of anthocyanins, unlike those of chlorophyll, are reversible.

While cooking vegetables containing anthocyanins, the loss of colour as well as change of colour must be considered. Beets lose their colour or 'bleed' during the preparation. This is due to the great solubility of anthocyanins. High temperatures bleach this pigment, the colour returning partly when it is cooled.

Natural acids in fruits increase the redness of the cooked fruit. The colour of cooked red cabbage depends on the acidity of the cooking water. Tap water gives it a purple colour. Red cabbage is produced by adding acid to the water. The addition of cooking soda gives a bluish product.

Flavones occur in all plants, but particularly in white onions, white cabbage, cauliflower, etc. In an acid medium, they are colourless, while in a basic medium they are yellow. The reaction like that of anthocyanin, is reversible. Vegetables such as cauliflower can be made to change colour from white to yellow and back by holding them in fumes of acid or ammonia. Flavones are readily soluble in water as can be observed from the colour of the alkaline vegetable water, which is yellow. During cooking it is important to see that white vegetables do not turn yellow. The addition of acids such as lime juice or vinegar will keep them white.

Boiling vegetables

Vegetables are usually put into boiling liquid. This is to prevent the nourishment escaping into the liquid and also to curtail the action of plant enzymes which have harmful effects on vitamins. The exceptions to this are dried vegetables and root vegetables which should be started in cold water. Salt is generally added to the water, except when cooking dry vegetables, which do not cook well if salt is added at the commencement. The lid is kept on generally, except when cooking green vegetables, where the volatile acids present in chlorophyll must be allowed to escape or else they will discolour the vegetables. Lime juice brings out the whiteness of cabbage and cauliflower if added before cooking.

Potatoes Scrub and scrape new potatoes, peel and eye old ones. Keep under water to avoid discolouration. To boil, put in salted water and cook till tender, drain and use as required.

Roast potatoes Parboil, drain and cook in dripping around the meat for at least 45 minutes.

Sauté potatoes Slice cold boiled potatoes and fry in very little fat till brown.

Potato chips Two methods are used:

(i) Peel and cut them in to finger lengths. Parboil, drain and put into hot fat. Remove when half done. Put into smoking fat or boiling fat and brown just before serving.

(ii) Cut the peeled potatoes into finger lengths. Dry on a towel. Deep fry in a pan till a faint blue smoke rises. Fry chips until golden brown. Drain on absorbent paper, add salt.

Spinach Remove the stalk and damaged leaves. Wash very thoroughly in several batches of water to remove grit and mud. Put into a pan. Add salt. Place over gentle heat. when the juice begins to run over spinach, raise temperature and boil for 15 minutes. Drain and chop or sieve as required. Add pepper and a small knob of butter to taste.

Before cooking spinach and other leafy vegetables, soak them for some time in water to which a little sugar has been added. This improves the flavour.

Green peas Shell peas and place in boiling water with ½ teaspoon of sugar, salt and a sprig of mint. Boil till tender. Drain. Take out the mint and add a little butter.

French beans String the beans. Slice them diagonally and cook in boiling salted water till tender (approx. 20 minutes). Cook with the lid off. Drain well and add a knob of butter.

Brussels sprouts Found in a temperate climate. Cooked the same way as cabbage but kept whole. Slit stalk end into four before cooking.

Cabbage Wash well, remove coarse leaves but use dark outer leaves. Cut in half. Remove the hard centre stalk, shred. Cook in a little boiling and salted water till tender (10 to 15 minutes approx.). Drain well. A few bacon rinds can be added to the water. Serve plain or tossed in melted butter.

Cauliflower Wash thoroughly, remove outermost leaves if necessary but leave some on. Turn over and cut across the stalk. Put the cauliflower into boiling salted water and cook for 20 to 30 minutes.

Broccoli Three types—white, green and purple.

Purple and green: To prepare, remove coarse stalks and wash the leaves and sprigs. Boil. Serve same way as cabbage or cauliflower. Particularly good with white sauce.

White: Prepare and cook as for cauliflower.

Turnips Peel rather thickly. Cook in boiling salted water till tender; this takes 20 minutes to one hour. Drain, add white pepper and salt and butter. The cooked turnips can also be mashed up.

Vegetable marrow Very young vegetable marrow may be boiled whole and unpeeled. Cook in salted water for 15 minutes. Drain and serve with melted butter. Large marrows must be peeled and the seeds removed. Drain well and serve sprinkled with brown breadcrumbs or with cheese sauce. Marrow may also be baked whole, (peeled or not) and stuffed with any savoury filling. Bake in a moderate oven at 177°C (350°F) for one hour. Cover the marrow with greased grease-proof paper.

Onion Remove the root and the outer skin. Apart from being used as a flavouring agent, onions can be boiled and served as a vegetable or used stuffed.

Tomatoes Grilled, fried, stewed, baked or raw.

Carrots Scrub and scrape lightly. Peel old ones. Cut into strips or into roundels. Add just enough water, salt and a little butter. Cook till the carrots are tender and the water has evaporated. Serve sprinkled with chopped parsley. Young carrots can be boiled whole.

Corn on the cob Remove the sheath and silk threads. Cook in salted, boiling water till tender. Serve with melted butter.

Sweet pepper Capsicum, red or green. This can be served cooked or raw. To prepare the pepper, wash, cut out the stalks and remove the seeds. Red and green peppers may be cooked together to make a colourful vegetable dish. Slice and cook in a little salted water. Add a knob of butter. They may also be served stuffed, baked, boiled or stewed.

Celery Wash celery thoroughly, using a brush to remove all soil. Separate the stalks. Tie into bundles. Cook in boiling salted water till tender. Drain and serve with white sauce.

Beetroot Cut out the stalks about 2.5 cm. (1") from the root, taking care not to damage the skin. Wash and boil in salted water till tender (about 2 hours). Peel off the skin. Cut into cubes or slices and either serve hot, coated with white sauce, or cold in vinegar.

Leeks Remove the coarse outer leaves. Cut out the roots and green top. Split the leaf end so that it can be washed thoroughly. Tie in bundles and boil in salted water. Drain. They are usually served with white or cheese sauce.

Broad beans Shell the beans. Cook them in boiling salted water and drain. Serve with parsley sauce. Skin older beans before serving.

Parsnips Peel thinly, using a potato peeler. Cut as required. Boil or bake.

Asparagus Cut the woody portion, scrape the white part lightly. Remove any coarse spine. Tie in bundles. Place upright in a pan of salted water and boil for 10 minutes. Then lay the asparagus flat and cook till tender. Drain well, remove the string and serve with melted butter.

Artichokes Only the lower parts of the leaves and lower sections are edible. Wash well. Cut off the stems and trim lower leaves if necessary. Place head downwards in boiling salted water and boil gently until tender, for about 30 minutes with the lid off. When cooked, the leaves should be easy to pull off. They may also be dipped in a thin batter and fried. Serve hot with melted butter or margarine or hollandaise sauce. Do not pour the sauce over the artichokes. The lower sections without the leaves may also be used, either raw or cooked, in salads.

Artichokes (Jerusalem) Scrub well, peel, and to keep them white until ready to be cooked, place in a bowl of water to which a little vinegar has been added. Boil or bake. Serve plain boiled in the same way as potatoes or with white sauce. A very good *au gratin* can be made with these artichokes. Can be served in soups, separately or with another vegetable such as celery.

Colour Reaction of Vegetable Pigments

Pigment	Vegetable	Colour in acid	Colour in alkali	Colour reaction to metals
Flavone	Cauliflower	Colourless (white)	yellow	Al-yellow Iron-brown
Anthocyanins	Red cabbage Beetroot	red	blue to green	Iron-blue Tin-purple
Carotenoids	Carrots	orange	orange	
Chlorophyll	French beans Spinach	olive green	bright green	Copper-bright Iron-green

13 / PULSE COOKERY

Nutritive function

Pulses are a good source of vegetable proteins and vitamin B complex. Being substances with very little taste, they should be combined with spicy and strong foods, e.g. bacon, ham, etc.

In Western preparations pulses are combined with onion, tomatoes, leeks, celery and bacon rind.

In Indian preparations pulses are combined with spices, coconut milk, tomatoes, leafy vegetables and herbs.

Cooking

(i) If with skin, soak overnight in boiling water to soften skin, e.g. haricot beans, thick peas, etc.

(ii) Wash first before soaking so that the pulses can be cooked in the same liquid in which they are soaked. Those with no skins like lentils can be soaked in cold water. Bring to boil and cook with lid on.

(iii) Add salt after cooking, as salt inhibits the normal cooking process of lentils and pulses. Those with skins can be made into a purée, as it is the skin that causes indigestion.

In Western preparations these foods are rarely served plain boiled. They are generally mixed with other foods and browned by baking or frying. Use liquids for soups and gravies.

14 / CHEESE

Cheese, one of the oldest known food products, is universally popular. The chemistry involved in changing semifluid milk into semisolid cheese is complex and many factors enter into the final curing of cheese to produce the different varieties but they all begin with the action of rennet or lactic acid which performs the same basic function, that of coagulating the milk proteins. Simply defined, cheese is the solid or casein portion of milk separated from the whey. The curdling of the casein is brought about by the action of rennet or lactic acid. The many different cheeses are the result of variation in the making and curing of each variety after initial curdling has taken place.

Many experiments and inventions in many countries of the world have produced cheeses ranging in texture from very soft to very hard and in flavour from extremely mild to very sharp. These cheeses are known by thousands of names, generally with names taken from the localities where they were first made.

Cheeses are classified into large general groups according to whether they are started by the rennet or lactic acid method. They may also be classified as unripened, mould ripened and bacteria ripened or as soft cheese, hard pressed cheese or blue veined cheese.

Cheese is one of the most highly concentrated of all protein foods. It is also readily digested. Experiments have shown that from 90 to 99% of all cheese is digested. It is also a complete protein. Since approximately 10 litres of fluid milk are required to make 1 kg. of cheese, cheese contains many of the nutrients of milk in highly concentrated form—milk proteins, fat, fat-soluble vitamins and minerals.

Wholemilk cheese contains the same properties as milk. Certain cheeses such as blue veined are made out of skimmed milk and, therefore, are less nutritious.

Normally cow's milk is used to make cheese, but certain well known cheeses are made from goat's milk. The texture of the cheese from goat's milk differs slightly from that of cow's milk. It is more crumbly. Sheep's milk can also be used. The quality of the cheese depends to a great extent on the breed and the condition of the animal and the fodder given to it. Cheshire cheese is said to owe its fine flavour to the wild radish on which the cows feed, and its special nature is due to the mineral in the soil. Cheshire cheese, therefore, cannot be made in any other place as cheddar cheese can.

Certain cheeses develop a blue vein in maturing. This is sometimes a purely natural development, often sporadic and unpredictable. Sometimes fresh cheese is innoculated with pieces of blue cheese to catch the mould by contact. In some cases special bacilli are introduced. The mould is sometimes strengthened by brushing the cheese clean while the skin is soft, dipping it in whey and then rubbing it slightly with butter. This is done once a day for 10 to 20 days. Sometimes cheese is pierced with a copper wire. The main classes of cheese are:

(i) Unripened soft cheese, e.g. Cottage cheese, Cream cheese, Neufchâtel.
(ii) Ripened in moulds by bacteria, e.g. Brie and Camembert.
(iii) Ripened by bacteria, e.g. Limbourger.
(iv) Semi-hard, ripened by bacteria in moulds, e.g. Gorgonzola, Roquefort and Stilton.
(v) Semi-hard, ripened by bacteria, e.g. Brick cheese, Munster.
(vi) Very hard cheese without gas holes, e.g. Cheddar, Edam, Gouda and Cheshire.
(vii) Very hard cheese with gas holes, e.g. Gruyère, Swiss Cheese, Parmesan.

Glossary of cheese terms

Acid, acidity a description of a pleasant tang; it can be a defect if too pronounced.

Ammoniated a term describing cheeses that smell or taste of ammonia, a condition that affects the rinds of overripe cheese, primarily those with bloomy rinds such as Brie and Camembert. A hint of ammonia is not necessarily objectionable.

Annatto a yellow-orange dye extracted from the seeds of a South American plant and used to colour such cheeses as Cheddar, Momolette, Double Gloucester, Edam and many others.

Bloomy rind the white fleecy rind that develops on certain surface-ripened cheeses like Brie, Camembert, Double or Triple Creams and some Chèvres. It is formed by spraying the surface of the cheese with spores of penicillium candidum while it is curing.

Chèvres the French term for goat cheeses.

Gummy a negative term used to describe an overly plastic texture, as well as overripe rinds that have become sticky or gooey. Gumminess is undesirable in any context.

Salty most cheeses have some degree of saltiness; those lacking in salt are said to be dull or flat. Pronounced saltiness is characteristic of some cheeses, but oversaltiness is a defect.

Springy a descriptive term for cheese with a resilient texture that springs back when gently pressed. Ripe or nearly ripe soft-ripened varieties should be springy.

CHARACTERISTICS, MODE OF SERVING AND PLACE OF ORIGIN OF THE COMMONLY USED CHEESES

	CHEESE	CHARACTERISTICS	MODE OF SERVING	PLACE OF ORIGIN
(i)	Cottage	Simplest of all cheese varieties. Uncured cheese made of cow's milk. Now made commercially from pasteurised skimmed milk to which lactic acid culture is added. Cream may be added if desired.	Salads, sandwiches, appetizers, cheesecakes and as paneer in Indian curries.	Uncertain.
(ii)	Cream Cheese	A soft uncured cheese made of cow's milk with cream added. The special richness and smoothness comes from the whole milk with added cream. One of the few world cheeses made by the lactic acid rather than the rennet method of coagulating the curd. It is extremely mild in flavour.	Salads, sandwiches and appetizers.	Uncertain.
(iii)	Neufchâtel	A soft rennet cheese made of cow's milk. Prepared in the same way as Cream Cheese with a slightly higher moisture content and lower fat content than Cream Cheese. Sometimes flavoured with pimento and other condiments.	Same as above.	France.
(iv)	Brie	Soft ripened cheese in small discs, made from cow's milk. One of the most famous and a great favourite in Europe.	Served after a meal and as a buffet cheese.	France.
(v)	Camembert	Soft ripened rennet cheese, made from cow's milk. Strong flavour like that of ammonia. It is a world favourite.	Served at the end of a meal with crackers, fruit, etc.	France.

(*contd.*)

	CHEESE	CHARACTERISTICS	MODE OF SERVING	PLACE OF ORIGIN
(vi)	Limburger	Soft, highly flavoured cheese made from cow's milk. One of the most delicate and difficult cheeses to make.	Served at the end of a meal.	Luttich, Belgium.
(vii)	Gorgonzola	Hard blue-veined cheese made of cow's milk.	Served after meals, also used for salads and buffets.	Gorgonzola, near Milan, Italy.
(viii)	Roquefort	Blue-veined, semi-hard. Has a sweet, piquant flavour. Only world-famous variety made from sheep's milk.	To be served at the end of a meal. Also used for salads and buffet services.	France.
(ix)	Stilton	Semi-hard, blue-veined cheese. Made of cow's milk (whole with added cream)—spicy flavour. Surface rind is crinkled and brown with the interior creamy white and marbled by blue veins.	Served at the end of a meal and with salads.	England.
(x)	Brick	Distinctly American cheese developed in the mid-nineteenth century. Texture ranges from very firm to fairly soft and elastic. Flavours vary from extremely mild to sharp, depending on degree of curing.	Sandwiches and buffets.	America.
(xi)	Munster	Semi-hard, whole milk cheese. European Munster is highly flavoured and sharp. American Munster is mild in flavour, the curing time being shorter.	Sandwiches and buffets.	Munster (originally in Germany, now in France).

(contd.)

	CHEESE	CHARACTERISTICS	MODE OF SERVING	PLACE OF ORIGIN
(xii)	Cheddar	One of the most popular and well-known cheeses of the world; made from cow's milk (whole or partly defatted). Hard and smooth. The English Cheddar is one of the oldest and best known of English cheeses. It is white in colour, close in texture and clean and mellow in flavour. American Cheddar, known as American Cheese, varies in colour from white to yellow. It is factory-produced, using lactic acid as a starter, with rennet added later.	Served after meals. Used in sandwiches and in preparation of foods.	Cheddar, England.
(xiii)	Edam	Round, cannonball-shaped, bright red cheese. Produced by dipping ripened cheese in red-coloured paraffin. It is hard and rubbery in texture. In flavour it is like Cheddar, but milder and sweeter. It is made out of partly defatted cow's milk.	Served after meals or for buffets.	Northern Holland.
(xiv)	Gouda	Semi-hard. It has the same flavour as Edam and is also dipped in red paraffin after ripening. It varies in size from Edam, weighing between 5–25 kg. (10–45 lbs.). Baby Goudas weighing about 500 gm. (1 lb) are now available. Goudas are made from partly defatted cow's milk.	Served after meals.	Southern Holland.
(xv)	Cheshire	One of the oldest of English cheeses made of cow's milk. A hard cheese characterized by its loose, flaky crumbly texture and sold in rich yellow colour or in its natural white colour.	Served after meals, or in such dishes as Welsh rarebit, fondues, etc.	Cheshire County, England.

(*contd.*)

	CHEESE	CHARACTERISTICS	MODE OF SERVING	PLACE OF ORIGIN
(xvi)	Gruyère	Hard, with gas holes, and a nut-like, salty flavour. Made of cow's milk, which is usually partly defatted.	Served after meals.	Gruyère, Switzerland.
(xvii)	Swiss cheese (known as Emmenthal in Switzerland)	One of the world's most famous cheeses. It is hard, with gas holes, and a nut-like, sweet flavour. Made from partly defatted cow's milk.	Served after meals, in sandwiches and with salads.	Emme Valley, Switzerland.
(xviii)	Parmesan	Hard, granular texture, sharp flavour. Made of partly defatted cow's milk.	Served after meals and for flavouring foods.	Parma and Lodi, Italy.
(xix)	Port-Salut	Semi-hard with rubbery texture and a flavour between Limbourger and Cheddar. It is made of whole slightly acid cow's milk. Oka cheese made in Canada belongs to the same family.	Served after meals.	Trappist Monasteries, France.
Some well known English cheeses:				
(i)	Derby	Close buttery texture with a pale honey colour. It is mild when young but develops a fuller flavour as it matures.	Served after meals and for flavouring foods.	England.
(ii)	Lancashire	Crumbly texture. Has a mild flavour when young but develops a full and rather pungent flavour as it matures.	Ideal for crumbling over soups, hot-pots, etc. Also well known for toasting quality.	England.
(iii)	Wensleydale	Flaky texture with subtle flavour. Clean, mild and slightly salty. It has an after taste of honey and is pale parchment in colour.	Used in preparation of foods.	Yorkshire, England.
(iv)	Double Gloucester	Velvet texture like butter, resembles Cheddar in flavour and has a pale straw colour.	Served after meals or with fresh fruit salad and cream.	England.

Processed Cheese

Pasteurized processed cheese is the food prepared by mixing together, with the aid of heat and the addition of a small amount of emulsifying agent (not exceeding 3% of the total weight of the finished product), one or more cheeses of the same variety or two or more varieties. The emulsifying agents commonly used are sodium phosphate and sodium citrate.

Many cheeses are available in pasteurized processed form. Among the most common ones are American Cheddar, Swiss, Brick, Limburger, etc. Processed cheeses are widely served after meals. For cooking they have several advantages. They melt smoothly and quickly without separation or stringiness. They are also uniform in flavour and texture.

Cooking of Cheese

Cheese cookery is an old art. Classic favourites like fondues, Welsh rarebit, macaroni and cheese, cheese pies and cheesecakes are well known. There are countless other dishes incorporating cheese which are of more recent origin. Cheese blends happily with many other food flavours and hence is a popular ingredient.

Cheese is a protein food and like all other proteins it is toughened by high heat. All cheese dishes should be cooked at low temperatures whatever the dish is. Whenever possible cheese should be melted in a double boiler or chafing dish rather than over direct heat.

Grate or chop cheese finely and dilute with some kind of starchy food such as flour, breadcrumbs, macaroni, etc.

Add a small pinch of bicarbonate of soda ½ tsp to a kg. (¼ tsp to a lb). This softens the cheese, prevents stringiness and makes it more digestible.

Cook by moist heat whenever possible, or at least see that there is some moisture included in the dish. If and when possible, add the cheese only at the last moment after the rest of the food has been cooked. This is to prevent long cooking of cheese.

Care of Cheese

The keeping quality of cheese varies greatly. Some of the hard varieties such as Swiss and Parmesan have a high keeping quality. Soft cheeses such as Camembert, Cream Cheese, etc. are highly perishable.

All cheeses require special care in handling once they are cut, for once cheese is cut it tends to dry rapidly. Mould may also form on any natural bulk cheese. This is in no way harmful, and can be cut off before being served without detriment to the quality of the remaining cheese.

Pasteurized processed cheese keeps well when left-over portions are rewrapped in the original paper and placed in the refrigerator. Bulk cheese or any hard cheese variety may be wrapped in wax paper, aluminium foil or plastic material. Tightly covered refrigerator dishes of plastic or glass are excellent for keeping cheese of all varieties.

All cheeses should normally be kept under refrigeration but before serving, they should be left out for a few hours. No cheese should be served chilled. The flavours of all cheeses are best when the cheese is neither cold nor over-warm.

15 / ACCOMPANIMENTS AND GARNISHES

A good cook not only takes pride in preparing a dish correctly but also in presenting it properly to appeal to the different senses. This is done by suitable decoration and the way it is placed on the serving dish. One of the chief points that must be borne in mind when both dishing and garnishing is neatness. Decoration that is done without restraint or badly carried out is worse than no decoration at all. Decoration done on hot dishes must be done quickly to prevent cooling of a dish which should be served hot. The colours of the garnish and the flavour should blend with the main dish. Proper garnishing has a three-fold role in food service. It helps "dress" the plate, "style" the product and adds colour, flavour and eye appeal of its own.

Accompaniments are dishes such as sauces, salads or vegetables which are used to make a dish complete. They provide variety and improve the nutritive value of the meal. What accompaniments should go with what, is usually determined by custom, based on a desire to enhance the flavour, to increase the digestibility and to improve a dish, e.g. roast beef with Yorkshire pudding, roast pork with apple sauce, roast duck with sage and onion stuffing and orange sauce, fried fish and chips with tartare sauce or tomato sauce, roast chicken with roast potatoes, buttered peas and bread sauce.

Forcemeat or stuffing are used to add flavour and piquancy to meat. They also help to increase bulk.

SAGE AND ONION STUFFING

Ingredients	*Quantity*
Onions	225 gm
Fresh breadcrumbs	50 gm
Salt and Pepper	to taste
Butter	30 gm
Powdered sage or Fresh sage (chopped)	1 tsp

Method

1. Boil chopped onions till tender, in just enough water. 2. Add butter and stir till melted. 3. Add remaining ingredients, mix well and use as required.

FORCEMEAT STUFFING

Ingredients	*Quantity*
Fresh breadcrumbs	115 gm
Suet, mutton dripping or Butter	50 gm
Grated lemon	½ lime
Chopped parsley	2 tsp
Mixed herbs	½ tsp
Salt and Pepper	to taste
Egg or milk to bind	

Method

1. Mix dry ingredients. 2. Add binding. 3. Mixture should be crumbly, should not be pressed heavily and not mixed too wet.

BREAD SAUCE

Ingredients	*Quantity*
Milk	300 ml
Onion	10 gm
Margarine	30 gm
Fresh breadcrumbs	50 gm
Cloves	2
Mace	a pinch
Lemon rind or a strip of lemon	
Seasoning	

Method

1. Boil the milk. Infuse the hot milk with onion, cloves, mace and lemon rind for 30 minutes. 2. Strain over fresh breadcrumbs, add seasoning and margarine; stir well to a smooth consistency. 3. Stand in a warm place to thicken. Reheat and beat well; add one tablespoon cream if desired.

Sauces

Sauce is a liquid adjunct to a dish such as meat, poultry and vegetables, used to moisten the food, to enhance the flavour, to provide contrast in taste or colour and sometimes to improve the digestibility (e.g. Roast pork with apple sauce); generally thickened by means of a liaison such as roux, egg, blood, etc.

"A correct sauce is that wonderful production of the culinary art which forms a pleasant and exquisite accompaniment to all kinds of fish, meat, poultry, game and vegetables." The skill and knowledge of a cook is shown in no other part of culinary art so clearly and prominently as in the way the sauces are prepared. To make a perfect sauce is the height of the art of cooking.

The most simple dishes can be made appetizing by the addition of a good plain sauce while the most *recherché* dishes can be improved and made still more palatable by a well-made sauce. Sauces in cookery are the essence of elegance. Every sauce, whether plain or rich, must possess a decidedly distinct flavour and character. Plain sauces should be simple and pure so that they taste of the materials employed, from which they take their name. Richer sauces always require a longer and slower process for their preparation.

Sauces were hardly made use of in English cookery till the beginning of the nineteenth century. Today there are at least 650 different types of sauces and gravies. A clever cook can devise as many varieties as he needs in sauces as an artist can paint pictures.

The art of sauce-making consists in preparing liquids from various materials by cleverly extracting and combining certain flavours into the liquid. Besides this, a good palate as well as the experience and skill of the most accomplished cooks and a thorough knowledge of the taste of those for whom the dish is being prepared, are necessary.

All sauces should be smooth, glossy in appearance, definite in taste, and light in texture.

Gravy is not a sauce. It is generally the juice of meat or vegetables seasoned but not thickened like a sauce. According to textbooks on cooking, a gravy may be called a sauce but a sauce cannot be called a gravy. Many of the more elaborate sauces have gravies as their foundation ingredient. It is easier to call a thinner liquid a gravy and a thicker one a sauce.

Liaison

The various processes of thickening sauces as well as soups are called 'Liaison'. There are six distinct methods known for thickening sauces:

(i) Liaison with roux.
(ii) Liaison with egg.
(iii) Liaison with butter and cream.
(iv) Liaison with kneaded butter and flour (manied).
(v) Liaison with blood.
(vi) Liaison with farinaceous products.

Roux The most popular and the most widely used thickening is roux. Roux is a mixture of flour and butter cooked to a definite degree – white, fawn or brown colour. Flour and butter are generally used in the same proportion. Roux can be prepared beforehand and stored, but it should be kept in airtight containers.

Approximately 60 gm of roux is required for 60 ml of liquid. If the roux is used cold, the stock used can be hot or cold. If mixed hot, the liquid, which should also be hot, must be gradually added to the roux away from the fire. This is then stirred over the fire till it boils. Roux should be allowed to cool slightly before the liquid is added to prevent the formation of lumps. All roux must be stirred constantly during the process of cooking.

White roux or 'Roux Blanc': This is a mixture of flour and butter cooked in a pan over a moderate fire without allowing it to get discoloured.

Blond roux or 'Roux Blonde': This is prepared by melting a certain quantity of butter and stirring in the same quantity or a little less of flour and by cooking it over a slow fire or in the oven till it gets a fawn colour.

Brown roux or 'Roux Brun': This is generally known as stock roux and can be prepared in bulk and stored. It is prepared more or less in the same way as 'Roux Blonde' but is cooked for a longer period to get a deeper brown colour. It is better to finish a brown roux in a slow oven so as to make it more brown without burning. This will also improve the aroma.

With brown and blond roux, a mirepoix is added to give the necessary flavouring to the sauce. Mirepoix is an essence or extract of meat and vegetables. The following ingredients are used: 225 gm bacon, 1 carrot, 1 bay leaf, 1 sprig thyme, 2 small onions, and 2 cloves garlic. Chop all ingredients and fry without browning.

Egg liaison This is a thickening composed of egg yolks beaten up and diluted with a small quantity of cream, milk or cold white stock. Cream is used more often than stock. When the soup or sauce is boiling it is removed to the side of the fire and a spoonful of the boiling liquid is added to the egg mixture gradually and then the whole is poured slowly into the sauce and stirred over the fire without allowing it to boil. It is passed through a tammy before it is served. This liaison is used largely for blanquettes, white ragoûts (usually of vegetables) and white fricassées.

Butter and cream liaison Butter and cream are incorporated in sauces and soups just before they are served. After the liaison has been added the sauce or soup is stirred vigorously without reheating. The flavour of the sauce alters if butter and cream are added too soon or if the sauce is allowed to boil after the addition of the liaison. The same applies to a plain butter liaison as well. Butter is added in small amounts the moment the sauce is taken off the fire. It is then stirred with a whisk and served without being reheated.

Kneaded butter and flour liaison Knead as much flour into the butter as it will absorb, to form a soft paste. Mix in small portions into a hot thin sauce. Stir constantly till the butter melts.

Blood liaison This is mostly used with hare or other game. It is made by preserving the blood of hare or game to which is added a little vinegar to prevent clotting. It is then strained through a fine sieve and generally added to the sauces.

Farinaceous liaison Arrowroot, cornflour, potato flour, rice flour or other farinaceous products are commonly used for thickening sauces. Dilute with a little cold milk, cold stock or water. Pour through a strainer into boiling liquid. Stir continuously until it boils. Simmer gently for 10 minutes.

16 / SPICES USED IN WESTERN AND INDIAN COOKERY

Down through the ages India has been known as the land of spices. Sweet or pungent, aromatic and seductive spices have played a special part in the life, legend and ritual of the country. With the march of time, although there have been several changes in the use of spices, their qualities for enhancing food still reign supreme.

The primary function of spices in Indian food is to improve the flavour of the dish. Many spices such as cloves, coriander, cumin seeds, cinnamon, etc., because of their volatile oil contents, impart various flavours to the food. These appeal to the sense of smell and render the food more palatable. The primary quality the common man looks for in a food product is its organoleptic quality (or the sense of taste), rather than its nutritive value. As a result even highly nutritious food is not accepted unless it is adequately spiced. It is only where pleasure to the eye and palate meet that food becomes fully acceptable. The best chefs of the world consider flavourings and seasonings absolute necessities for achieving this objective. The success of cooking depends largely on their aid. However, spices must be used with skill and, above all, sparingly. All palates do not crave highly spiced foods, yet most people demand that food should be adequately spiced, for the flavour of insipid food can be improved very much by the use of some suitable spice. Even the people of the West, particularly the English and Americans who have a tradition of bland food, are now introducing a variety of spices into their dishes and appreciating the added piquancy of the food. Western palates, however, are sensitive, and therefore can appreciate the subtle flavours more readily than we do, as unfortunately, owing to the continuous consumption of overspiced foods, we have lost this power. Whenever possible, only such spices should be used as bring out the natural flavours of the main ingredient, rather than imparting a new one. Intelligence, carefulness, thorough, sound judgement, a steady hand and a keenly perceptive palate are qualifications every cook must possess in order to prepare food that is appetizing and pleasant to the taste.

Besides enhancing the flavour and aroma of food, spices have a physiological action beneficial to our system. They act as a stimulus to the digestive system and help digestion in many ways.

Every spice used in the making of a curry is a preservative. All have some antiseptic value and many are carminatives, i.e. they tend to reduce flatulence as in the case of omum (ajwain) water given to babies. The traditional combination of spices used for certain dishes must have been made with this factor in mind, e.g. the use of ginger or mint with peas. Peas are flatulence-forming and ginger or mint counteracts this effect. Asafoetida, commonly used with pulses (dals) of various types functions in a similar manner.

Some spices are used to give colour to food, to improve eye appeal, e.g. turmeric in yellow rice, red chillies in vindaloo, rattanjog in roganjosh, etc. Spices also serve as a thickening agent in the preparation of curries, e.g. onion and poppy seeds.

The therapeutic value of spices is well known. Spices and herbs play a very important role in some of the simple but effective home remedies. Almost every spice has medicinal properties. Investigations are being conducted scientifically to elucidate the therapeutic properties of the various spices. Many have already been accepted and are being used today, e.g. aniseed (saunf) which has been used from prehistoric times as a flavouring for cough mixtures and as a herb tea to soothe the nervous system and induce sleep. Scientists have recently probed the effect of cloves on the digestion. Studies of clove oil have shown that it stimulates the flow of gastric juices and is non- injurious to the lining of the stomach. Garlic has been accepted in both India and China as one of the treasured spices and medicinal agents. It has been indicated in the treatment of numerous diseases such as haemorrhoids, rheumatism, dermatitis, abdominal pains, coughs, loss of appetite, etc. Although garlic is claimed to be useful in the treatment of such a variety of diseases, it is not popular because of its strong smell and pungency. Research has now made it possible to administer the active principle of garlic in a fairly concentrated form. Ginger tea is used commonly to ease an ailing stomach. Nutmeg is used medicinally to cure biliousness, diarrhoea and headaches. The ancients prized the seeds of fenugreek because of its stimulating effect on the digestive system.

To enhance the flavour and aroma of foods, spices may be used whole or in pieces, as in pulaos and biryanis, or in powdered or ground form. Indian cooks are artists in the use of spices. Money may limit the variety of spices used by some, but others are limited only by their own creative imagination. While freshly ground masalas (mixed curry spices) are preferred to powdered masalas, owing to the shortage of domestic labour there is a definite trend today towards using spices mainly in powdered form. Many combinations of spices to suit different tastes are marketed today as various forms of curry powders. When using spices in powdered form it is essential that the powders be extremely fine. Coarse powders do not blend well with the rest of the ingredients; this causes a separation thus allowing the spices to float. The fine powders should be mixed into a paste with vinegar or water and then fried well before meat or vegetables are added. Besides curry powders, practically all the dry spices such as coriander, turmeric, cumin, fenugreek, cloves, cinnamon, mustard, etc., can be cleaned, dried and powdered.

As a result of modern techniques, moist spices such as onion, garlic and ginger are now obtainable in powdered form. This process, while retaining the original flavours, improves the keeping quality of spices, and makes transportation more economical and easy. Onion powder is used commercially in the manufacture of processed meats and sausages, and for flavouring vegetables and meat. Garlic powder has many commercial uses and is also now being used by the housewife who wants a clean and convenient method of using this popular flavour. All powdered spices, however, must be kept in airtight containers to prevent spoilage and deterioration in aroma and flavour, caused by the evaporation of volatile oils. Ground masalas are also available in the market today. They are packed in plastic bags and sold, but the keeping quality of these is poor as they are susceptible to spoilage.

The liquid spices now available in the market as straight liquid spices, such as liquid red chillies, green chillies, ginger, coriander, cumin, garlic, nutmeg, cinnamon, cloves, cardamom, asafoetida, saffron, curry leaves, etc., or as ready-to-use compounds such as liquid masala for curries, pulao, mutton, fish, etc., have revolutionized the use of spices. These liquid spices are extracts of indigenous natural spices and are the result of years of research. By the separation of the active principles from the residual matter, concentrations are prepared. These are easy to use and are being used widely in the commercial manufacture of sauces, fruit juices, ketchups, salad dressings, tinned pulaos, curries, etc. They have a better keeping quality than curry powders, and mix readily with the rest of the ingredients, thus bringing a uniformity of colour and flavour to the food. They are clean, compact, suitable for transportation and storage and are available in glass bottles with droppers, ranging from 15 ml (½ oz) to 500 ml (1 lb). They impart original flavours and colours. Thickening agents such as ground onion, poppy seeds, coconut and coconut milk should still be added to maintain the desired texture of the food. For those spices where flavour is the primary function as in cardamom, cloves, cinnamon, nutmeg, etc., the liquid form can be used most effectively. It also makes it possible to be able to use out-of-season flavours. For example, when ginger or green chillies are not available, as in the summer months, the same flavours can be readily obtained by using liquid spices. Provided they are used carefully, liquid spices do not in any way increase costs, while at the same time they save labour and time.

Allspice

This is the berry of 'Eugenia Pimenta', a small tree grown in the West Indies. The berries are gathered when green and unripe and dried in the sun. Then they turn black. Large quantities of these are used for the manufacture of sauces and pickles sold commercially. The berries combine the flavour of cloves, cinnamon and nutmeg. This spice is also known as 'Jamaica Pepper'.

Cloves

A very old and important spice, the clove was known before the time of the early Egyptians. The word is taken from the Latin 'Clavus' and the French 'Clou' both meaning nail, which describes its shape. The clove tree (of the order of the myrtle) grows to a height of 9 metres. The unopened flower buds are carefully harvested. Upon browning, they lose half their weight. Cloves are used in both Western and Indian dishes, both savoury and sweet, e.g. pulaos, cooked ham, sauces such as béchamel sauce and bread sauce, meat dishes, fruit salads, baked apple, etc. The oil of cloves is used in dentistry to soothe toothaches, and its antiseptic properties are well known. It is grown on the islands of Zanzibar, Pemba and the East Indies, West India and other tropical regions.

Nutmeg and Mace

These are the only known cases of two different spices from the same fruit. Nutmeg is grown in the Dutch East Indies and Grenada in the British West Indies. The tree begins bearing fruit at the age of 8 years and continues to yield for half a century or more. In its wild state the tree grows to a height of about 22 m. or 70 ft. The nutmeg fruit resembles an apricot in size and shape. What we call the nutmeg is the seed. It is protected by a thin shell; the shell has a coat of orangy flesh which dries into mace. Although the aroma of mace is similar to that of nutmeg, separate uses exist for each. Nutmeg is used in Western and Indian dishes in puddings, sweetmeats, for flavouring egg and milk and in some curries. Mace is also used to flavour sauces, stocks, sweet dishes such as halwas as well as in betel nut mixtures. Nutmeg is used grated fine and mace coarsely crushed. When buying nutmegs choose those which are round, compact, of oily appearance and heavy for their size.

Mustard

A product of great antiquity and grown in most parts of the world, mustard is used in both Western and Indian preparations. It is used in the West in powdered form, as a table condiment and for flavouring sauces, etc. The pungency is more fully brought out when mustard is moistened with water (prepared mustard). In India it is used whole for tempering dishes, and in pickles. It is also an important ingredient in certain masala powders, e.g. vindaloo.

Cinnamon

This is taken from the bark of an evergreen tree belonging to the 'laurel' family and is chiefly cultivated in Ceylon and the East Indies. First the outer bark is stripped of the three-year-old branches, and then the inner bark is loosened and dried. The best cinnamon should not be too dark in colour and should be as thin as paper. It has a fragrant odour and its taste is pleasant and aromatic. It is used in both Western and Indian cookery, in cakes, buns, ketchup, pickles, in pulaos with cardamom and cloves, etc. It is used in the preparation of garam masala for curries.

Cardamom

This is the fruit of a reed-like plant, native of the mountains of the Malabar Coast, but cultivated in Jamaica as well. The fruit is a small pod and the seeds within the pods have a strong, sweetish flavour. The pods vary from 0.5–2 cm. (¼–1") and more in length. The small-sized ones are considered the best. Rich curries like khorma include cardamom. Powdered cardamom is a big favourite in cakes, puddings, halwas, etc. Pulaos and biryanis also depend on this spice for their popular flavour. Tincture of cardamom is used in stomach medicines.

Pepper

This is obtained from the seeds or berries of the plant 'piper nigrum' which grows in Malabar and other parts of India. Black pepper is made from dried whole berries, and white pepper from the same berries with the husk dried and removed. Pepper is one of the most universally popular spices, and is used in every type of savoury dish to improve flavour and to add to its piquancy. It is also one of the table condiments.

Mignonette pepper This is ordinary white pepper coarsely crushed.

Long pepper It is a spice similar in taste to ordinary pepper but not so pungent.

Cayenne pepper Dried fruits of the capsicum plant grown in the Cayenne Islands. This is red in colour, resembling the red chillies of India without being as pungent. This is used in Western cookery where pungency is required. e.g. for devilled prawns.

Krona pepper Bright red pepper from the Hungarian paprika. It is much milder than cayenne pepper and forms a palatable seasoning for Western savoury dishes.

Red chillies

Chillies are grown in large quantities in India and are used extensively in Indian savoury preparations. They also form an important ingredient of curry powders. Apart from being used as a condiment, they are also used in several medicinal preparations for the treatment of lumbago, neuralgia, rheumatism, etc. Although there are several varieties they fall under two main groups: Capsicum Anum and Capsicum Frutescens. The variety acuminatum (Capsicum Anum) is the principle source of commercially used red chillies.

Coriander

The fruit of a plant called 'Corianderum Sativum' of the parsley family. It is extensively used in the preparation of Indian savoury dishes and forms an essential ingredient of curry powders. It is used in the preparation of frankfurters (sausages) and by confectioners and distillers. The leaves are used for flavouring curries, in salads and chutney and as a garnish.

Turmeric

This is the aromatic root or rhizome of a plant grown in India and the West Indies. It is sold in root form and as powder. The hard resinous flesh of the dried root varies from a dark orange to deep reddish brown, but in the powdered form it exhibits a characteristic yellow colour. Turmeric is a member of the ginger family but has a different flavour. It is used in curry powder not only for imparting colour and flavour to curries but also because of its preservative qualities. Game and meats that are dried are soaked in liberal quantities of turmeric and salt. Turmeric is used freely in Indian medicines too. Plasters of it are applied in cases of bruises; as a dry dressing on open wounds; paste of turmeric and neem leaves is used to heal smallpox marks, and so on. Turmeric has sometimes been used to replace the more expensive saffron as a colouring agent.

Ginger

This is the tuberous root of a plant 61 cm. (2ft.) or more in height and is one of the few spices that grow underground. Ginger is mainly produced in Jamaica and to a less extent in Sierra Leone, China, Japan and India. Because of its stimulating and digestive properties it is employed medicinally for dyspepsia and colic. It is also frequently used to disguise nauseous tastes in medicines. The most common use of ginger is in making masalas, soft drinks, pickles and preserves, and in confectionery such as ginger biscuits, gingerbread, snaps, etc. Crystallized ginger is made from the young roots and is a delicacy. The best grades selected are called 'stem ginger'.

You can make instant pickle by chopping fresh ginger and green chillies and adding lemon juice together with salt. It is delicious specially one day after preparation.

Cumin seed

This is a herb of the caraway type, producing seeds of a pleasant smell and flavour which are very popular. It is most widely grown in several European countries, India and Mexico. The cumin plant is less than 30 cm high. The seeds come from the fruit and their slightly bitter taste is said to stimulate the appetite and digestive system. Cumin is added to curry powders and used whole in savouries, biscuits and fried rice. It is also used in the manufacture of liquors, pickles and sausages.

Fenugreek

These are the dried ripe fruits of an annual plant grown in many European countries and India. The fresh leaves and tender stalks are used widely as a vegetable. Because of their stimulating effect on the digestion they are administered medicinally even to horses and cattle. The seeds are used in making curry powders and fried whole for seasoning pickles and vegetables. When ground with water, fenugreek becomes a slimy paste and so is used to give batters smoothness.

Aniseed

The seed is small, oval in shape, somewhat similar to caraway and it grows in China, Mexico, Peru, Argentina, Spain, Malta, Syria, Lebanon, India, Pakistan, Hongkong and Egypt.

The seed is small, oval in shape, somewhat similar to caraway and is usually a greenish brown in colour. It is used in Western preparations and in Indian dishes. It is identified with the licorice flavour. It is used in making licorice confections, in baking, in the cordial anisette and other liquors. Its digestive properties are well known and it can be eaten plain after a meal.

Fennel seed

The dried fruit of a perennial herb of the parsley family, fennel is grown in Europe, India, Lebanon and Argentina. The seed has a licorice-like flavour resembling anise. Fennel is used both whole and ground. Bakers use it whole in Italy to stud breads and rolls. It is also used in sweet pickles, in the seasoning of soups, fish dishes, sauces, and in South Indian meat curries. It is also attributed with medicinal properties.

Caraway seed

Fruit of a perennial plant of the parsley family. It has a pleasant, slightly sharp flavour with a sweet undertone. It is a native of Europe. Caraway seed is mostly used whole and is the principal flavouring in rye bread, and is widely used in rolls, biscuit and cakes. It is also used in cheeses, sauerkraut, pickles, soups, meats and stews. It is the chief ingredient of 'Kummel Cordial'.

Aromatic herbs and plants

The ones commonly used are parsley, bay leaves, thyme, marjoram, sage, tarragon, chervil, chives, onions, shallots, garlic etc. The bouquet garni which is the mainstay of French cookery consists of sprigs of chervil, chives, thyme, bay leaves, tarragon and parsley.

Parsley It possesses a wonderful quality of masking the taste of a stronger flavour; so do not use too much of it when flavouring a dish. It plays an important part in cookery. It not only gives a finishing touch to stews and soups and sauces, but it is also used a great deal for garnishing purposes. Powdered parsley is an excellent herb which imparts a delicate flavour. To make powdered parsley, infuse some parsley leaves in boiling water for a few seconds. Drain and put into a hot oven to dry. Put through a sieve and use as required.

Tarragon and chervil The leaves of chervil possess a flavour which is appreciated by many people. Tarragon belongs to the same family as wormwood and the botanical name is 'Artemisia Dracunculus'. Of all the pot-herbs, tarragon and chervil give the strongest smell. They are used a great deal in French cookery for entrées, sauces, soups, salads, chaud-froids, etc. Tarragon leaves are also used for flavouring vinegar.

Thyme It belongs to the same family as mint. The leaves are used fresh or dry for stuffings, soups, etc.

It possesses a highly aromatic flavour and should, therefore, be used sparingly. Lemon thyme is a smaller variety and has a strong perfume like the rind of lemon. Leaves of ajwain (omum) can be used as a substitute for thyme.

Burnet This is not used much in cookery now except for salads. When bruised it smells like cucumber.

Capsicum There are several kinds of capsicum cultivated in the East and West Indies and in America. The capsicum fruit is both pungent and stimulating. In Mexico the pods are called chili and they are used to make hot-pickle and chili-vinegar. It is the powder of the dried seeds and pods that goes to make cayenne pepper (as a substitute use Kashmiri chilli powder). Capsicums are considered to be very wholesome.

Savory There are two varieties of this herb; one is called the "summer variety". It is taken from a flowery herb. Both varieties are used extensively in Western cookery.

Marjoram There are four kinds of marjoram. The sweet or knotted marjoram, originally a native of Portugal, is the one which is commonly used. It is used for soups, sauces, stews, etc., and used either fresh or dry.

Mint This belongs to a family of plants called 'Labiatae'. The spearmint or the 'Mentha Viridis' commonly cultivated in gardens has a better flavour and is the one used popularly in cooking. It has the property of removing flatulence.

Bay leaves The leaves of the common laurel are used in cookery to give a kernel-like flavour to stocks, mirepoix sauces, custards, puddings, blancmanges, and to the milk which is used for mixing cakes. They are generally dried and used.

Basil A favourite herb in French cookery. It has a flavour similar to that of cloves. It is used for making such things as mock turtle soup and clear soups made out of shellfish. It is also used for flavouring vinegar.

Onions The name onion is given to all plants of the onion tribe, e.g., leeks, garlic and shallots. The onion is, next to salt, the most valuable of all flavouring substances used in cookery. When onions, shallots or garlic are used in cookery they should be well blended with other flavours. Whenever onion is used as a condiment or seasoning and the article properly treated, the strong smell is removed.

Garlic This consists of groups of several bulbs called cloves, all enclosed in one membranous skin. When used carefully and sparingly, garlic is an excellent condiment. It is considered to be very wholesome and is a stimulant.

Shallots This bulbous root resembles garlic. It is a native of Palestine and was introduced to England by the Crusaders.

Carrots and turnips

Next to onions, these are considered to be the most important flavouring vegetables for soups and sauces. Besides being used for flavouring, carrots and turnips are largely used for garnishing certain dishes such as ragôuts, boiled meat, etc. They are also used as a vegetable and as a purée for soup.

Lemon

It plays an important part in sauces. The rind, juice and the essential oils contain valuable properties. The rind or peel is used for flavouring a variety of dishes. Generally the rind is grated, but the best way is to peel the rind with a very sharp knife as thinly as possible without touching the white part. Lemon rind is preserved in sugar.

When sour limes are in season buy them in large quantities. Extract the juice and mix one cup of salt to every four cups of juice. Shake well and keep in an airtight bottle—under refrigeration it keeps for months. Use whenever fresh lime is required.

Vanilla

This was first discovered by the Spaniards. It is the fruit of an orchid. The best variety is grown in Mexico. It has a delicious flavour and is largely used for flavouring puddings, custards, liquor chocolate, etc. For flavouring purposes it is better to use the vanilla pod or vanilla sugar rather than the essence of vanilla, since the odour of the essence escapes rapidly.

Curry powders

For some basic curry powders, see the recipes at the beginning of the Indian Cookery Section of this book.

17 / BEVERAGES

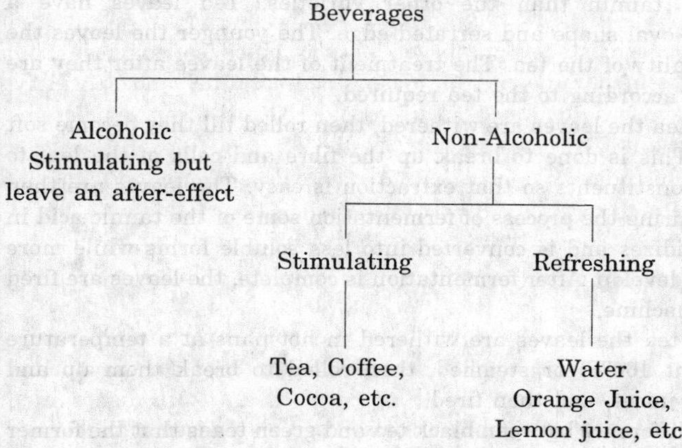

Function of Beverages

To prevent water depletion Water being one of the essential constituents of beverages it is very useful in making good the loss of water content in the blood stream, specially after heavy physical exertion.

Adequate supply of water is essential for the healthy functioning of all the tissues in the body. For an adult doing no manual work and when the weather is pleasant enough not to cause any excessive perspiration, three litres of water daily are necessary for good health. Two litres are obtained from food so one litre must be taken in the form of water and other beverages.

Refreshing and restorative Cold drinks in summer and hot drinks in winter have a greatly refreshing and restorative effect on the body particularly when fatigued.

Supplies vitamins Certain beverages like lime juice, Ovaltine, etc., are a source of vitamin supply.

Stimulating Alcoholic beverages are stimulating and have a definite value in case of illness, but if taken regularly even in moderate quantities, lessen the power of resistance to disease, and if taken in excess are very harmful.

Beverages such as tea, coffee and cocoa besides being refreshing are also stimulating but they do not have any after-effects.

Tea

The most popular non-alcoholic beverage, tea consists of the dried leaves of the tea plant grown in India, Ceylon, China and Japan. Chinese tea contains less tannin than the other varieties. Tea leaves have a characteristic oval shape and serrated edge. The younger the leaves the better the quality of the tea. The treatment of the leaves after they are picked varies according to the tea required.

For black tea the leaves are withered, then rolled till they become soft and mushy. This is done to break up the fibre and cells of the leaf to liberate the constituents so that extraction is easy. The leaves are then fermented. During the process of fermentation some of the tannic acid in the leaves oxidizes and is converted into less soluble forms while more essential oils develop. After fermentation is complete, the leaves are fired in a drying machine.

For green tea the leaves are withered in hot pans at a temperature of 71°C (about 160°F) or steamed, then rolled to break them up and liberate their juices, and then fired.

The chief difference between black tea and green tea is that the former is fermented while the latter is not. Since the purpose of fermentation is to make the tannin less soluble, an infusion of green tea has more tannin in it.

The best tea generally produces a pale-coloured infusion and the depth of colour is not necessarily a sign of strength. Freshly infused tea is harmless to normal digestion; continued infusion extracts the tannin, a bitter substance with a decidedly harmful effect upon the digestive organs.

Storage of dry tea Tea very quickly absorbs odours and moisture. So it should be kept in airtight containers, whether in the store or on the counter.

If the tea is in chests, they should be kept off the ground and at least 16 cm. or 6 inches away from the walls. This allows a current of air to circulate round the tea chest and averts dampness. Once a chest is opened it is advisable to put a close- fitting lid over it. When issuing tea from it, be sure that it is sent out in a tin fitted with a lid that can be firmly replaced after use, so that the natural aroma of the tea is retained.

Next in importance to the tea leaf is water, which is used for the preparation of tea. Water varies in different parts of the country. In some places water is hard and at other places it is soft. Tea which gives good results in soft water may not necessarily do so in hard water. For this reason samples of water drawn from different areas of the country are used for blending teas.

Water should not be too hard or too soft for making good tea. Artificially softened water is unsuitable for making tea and should be avoided.

Water should be freshly drawn before it is put on to boil.

Water which has been lying in the kettle for several hours or which has been boiled previously makes tea flat and insipid, as also, water which is allowed to continue boiling for some time before it is used. When the water used is off the boil, approximately half the leaves float and remain floating throughout the infusion. The rest remain at the bottom from the time the water is added. The movement of the leaves is very slight and tends to be from the bottom upwards. The flavour of the tea is poor.

With freshly boiled water approximately two-thirds of the leaves float from the start. There is a marked circulation of the leaves from the bottom to the top and from the top to the bottom. The liquor has good body and good flavour.

When water is overboiled all the leaves remain clotted at the bottom from the start of the infusion to the end. The liquor is thin and lacks flavour and character.

Rules for preparation of tea (in bulk or in small quantity)

(i) Use good tea and remember the recipe - one teaspoonful per person and one for the pot. The ideal is 60 gm of good tea to 4 litres of boiling water. There should be no guesswork; weigh or measure tea for each brew.

(ii) Use freshly drawn, freshly boiling water. Take water from a cold water tap, use it when it bubbles fiercely. An automatic boiler provides this, but if bulk boilers are used, two small ones are better and more economical than one large. Measured water may be boiled in metal pots (degchis) and transferred to another pot (already heated and containing tea leaves), or tea leaves can be put directly into the pot in which water has reached boiling temperature. Remove the pot from the fire and allow the tea to infuse for 5 minutes.

(iii) Heat the pot. Tea pots or urns in which tea is to be prepared should be heated before making tea. Unless this is done the water will go off the boil rapidly, thus preventing correct infusion of the tea leaves.

(iv) Take the teapot to the boiling water. The water must be at boiling point to enable the leaves to infuse properly, so the teapot should be brought near the boiling water outlet to ensure the shortest length of pour possible. To a measured quantity of water add a measured quantity of tea leaves and remove the pot immediately from the fire. Allow it to infuse for 5 minutes and strain. If electric or other boilers are used for boiling water, their outlet taps should be such that the maximum water can flow through them in the minimum of time.

(v) Brew for 5 minutes. Never more, never less. Tea should be made of good average strength to allow being watered down if necessary, as nothing can be done about strengthening tea which is too weak to start with. Removable infusers enable the leaves to be withdrawn easily and prevent stewing. Stir well before pouring.

Approximately 190 to 200 cups of tea can be obtained from 500 gm of tea leaves.

Adding of milk first or last does not make any significant difference in the taste of tea—but let people have their choice—some like to add milk first and some afterwards. Sugar must be added last. Tea is also taken hot with sugar and slices of lemon. This is known as Russian Tea.

Iced Tea Prepare strong tea. Pour over crushed ice on which is placed a sprig of mint. Top with lemon slices.

Tea contains the stimulating principle caffeine, tannin and some volatile oils.

Coffee

Coffee is the berry of a plant grown in Kenya, Ceylon, Brazil, West Indies, India and other places.

Coffee has become one of the important beverages in India. There has been a steady increase in the consumption of coffee in recent years. It is also one of the major plantation crops of India, particularly South India.

The two main varieties of coffee grown in India are, Coffee Arabica and Coffee Robusta. Coffee Arabica originated in Yemen in Arabia and was brought to India in the seventeenth century by a Muslim called Bababudan Sahib on his return from his visit to the Holy Land, Mecca. Coffee Robusta was brought to India from Java in 1910.

After the fully ripe berries are harvested, they are processed in two ways, by the 'wet' method or by the 'dry' method.

The 'wet' process is very elaborate. Ripe berries called cherries are first passed through pulpers where their outer skin is removed. The pulped beans are then allowed to ferment for about 12 to 36 hours. They are then washed in running water. This leaves the beans encased in a soft parchment covering. They are then dried in the drying yard. Great care is taken at this stage to see that only a little moisture remains and the parchment covering becomes brittle. This produces what is known as Plantation or Parchment Coffee.

The 'dry' method is a simpler process. Immediately after harvesting, the coffee berries are dried in the sun until the three layers—the outer skin, the sticky layer and the inner parchment covering—dry into a husk, leaving the beans loose inside. The beans are separated from the husk by being pounded in a mortar or passed through a huller. This is then graded and is called Native Coffee or Cherry Coffee.

In the days of sailing ships when a voyage to Europe took about six months or so, Native (Cherry) Coffee stowed away in damp holds lost its colour and became white. Later, when steamships went speedily through the Suez Canal, coffee drinkers in Europe complained that the coffee had lost its flavour. To overcome this, a new process known as 'monsooning coffee' was evolved. This is done in Mangalore and Tellicherry on the west coast of India.

When the monsoons break in early May or June, Native (Cherry) Coffee is evenly spread in layers from four to six inches thick, in airy godowns which are open on all sides. Every four or five days the beans are raked. They are then packed in gunny bags and stacked in piles so that the monsoon breeze can blow continuously on each bag. Once a week the beans are repacked or poured from one bag to another, so that they do not develop moulds and also to ensure uniform monsooning. After six weeks of this treatment the coffee becomes silvery white in colour and is considered fully matured and ready for export.

After the beans have been treated to make either 'parchment' or 'cherry' types, they are sent to the curing houses for the final process required to prepare the coffee for the market. It is here that the parchment is peeled off Parchment Coffee.

The stimulating principle in coffee is caffeine. It also contains tannin and some volatile and aromatic oils. As long as coffee is in good condition the distinctive aroma remains. It should always be stored in airtight containers. Refrigerated storage is best for keeping coffee.

Roasting and grinding The aroma and flavour associated with coffee is brought about by roasting. Roasting must be done evenly without any scorching. It should be done on a slow fire and the beans should be uniformly roasted. When the beans stop swelling and obtain a golden-brown colour, the roasting is complete. If roasting goes beyond this point the essential oils exude and the beans turn shiny. When it reaches this stage the coffee has no value. Roasting can be done in a charcoal roaster or in an electric roaster. A medium roast and grind is considered to give the best results.

Roasted beans keep fresh much longer than powder and so grinding must be done just before use. Too finely ground powder clogs up the filter if used, and deteriorates rapidly when stored. The coarser the powder, the less the extraction. As a standard for brewing coffee, 450 gms. (16 oz.) gives 53 cups [187.5 ml (6 fl.oz.) coffee, 62.5 ml (2 fl.oz.) milk per cup].

Coffee can be prepared by many methods. The pot method, the filter method, the urn brewing method and the vacuum brewing method are commonly used.

Just one cup of coffee does some amazing things to the body. The temperature of the stomach jumps up by 10–15%. Salivary glands double their flow; the heart beats 15% faster; the lungs work 13% harder; blood vessels dilate in the brain and near the heart; the metabolism rate goes up 25%; and the work-load of the kidney doubles.

General rules for making coffee

(i) Fresh coffee is the best; so buy quantities to last not more than a week.
(ii) Use the quantity required for making coffee.
(iii) Use freshly drawn water.
(iv) The coffee-maker must be rinsed with hot water before use and thoroughly washed and dried before being put away. Never brew less than three-fourths of the coffee-maker's capacity; use a smaller one instead.

Pot method

(i) Warm an earthenware pot or jug. Put in 3 level teaspoons of fresh coffee powder (coarse grind) for each 250 ml (8 oz.) cup.

(ii) Pour water which has started to boil over the powder and stir. Cover the pot and let it stand near the fire for 5 to 7 minutes.

(iii) Pour the coffee through a fine meshed sieve or cloth. Add milk and sugar to taste.

Filter method

Several types of filters are available. Stainless steel or brass filters are the best but the latter should be properly tinned, or else the coffee will be spoilt. Glass or china containers are good but are fragile. Copper should not be used.

(i) Put in 3 level teaspoons of coffee powder (fine or medium grind) to each 250 ml or 8 oz. cup. Press the plunger down lightly over the powder.

(ii) Pour water which has just come to boil over the plunger in a circular motion. Let it stand for 5 to 7 minutes.

(iii) Coffee can be poured out straight from the lower vessel and milk and sugar added as required.

Percolator method

(i) Place the ground beans in the centre section of a clean warm percolator on a fine strainer fitted inside and resting on a paper filter (a pinch of salt is mixed with the coffee).

(ii) Pour fresh boiling water slowly through the top section.

(iii) The water passes through the coffee, is strained and collects in the bottom section of the apparatus.

Cona coffee machine (a patent percolator) consists of two flameproof glass bowls joined by a glass drainer tube which also acts as a filter. A measured amount of ground coffee is placed in the top receptacle and water in the lower one. Heat is applied, causing the water to rise, meet and mix with the coffee. The whole operation is automatic, and the beverage returns to the lower bowl and is served immediately or placed on a warming unit to be held at 85°–88°C (about 185°–190°F) (never allow coffee to boil).

Coffee is made in large quantities in the urns using the filter or percolator method. It is then held at 85°–88°C (about 185°–190°F) temperature and should be served within the hour.

All equipment used for the preparation of coffee should be kept scrupulously clean. When using a Cona or other mechanical percolator be sure to:

(i) Scrub upper tube regularly with a stiff brush.

(ii) Remove rubber collars and wash all parts thoroughly.
(iii) Replace rubber collars when they become heat softened.

If *a coffee urn* is used

(i) Clean inside of urn after each batch.
(ii) Clean faucets at close of each day.
(iii) Leave plenty of water in urn when not in use.
(iv) Clean gauge glasses twice a week.
(v) Give urn a thorough cleaning twice a week.

Turkish coffee

Turkish coffee is rich and syrupy and has a peculiar aroma of its own, caused by the preliminary method of drying coffee: the 'wet' method. The ground coffee is first mixed with sugar in a small china or copper pot fitted with a long handle. Water is added, heat applied and the coffee is flavoured with rose water. It is served piping hot.

Cocoa

Cocoa, besides being a stimulant, is also a food. It is prepared from the seeds of a tree grown in South and Central America, the West and East Indies and along the Gold Coast and adjacent areas in Africa.

The pods are gathered in heaps and cut open with sharp rounded knives. The cocoa beans which are covered with a moist glistening white pulp are scooped out. Oxidation begins almost at once causing the beans to become brown. Therefore, as soon as possible, they must be placed on fermenting heaps or spread in the sun to remove the moisture so that they are not spoilt. However, fermentation is necessary to get the finest possible flavour. This is accompanied by a rise in temperature and the transformation of natural sugars to acetic and other acids. After several days, this operation is complete and the beans are allowed to dry. They are then ready to be packed and shipped.

In the manufacture of cocoa and chocolate the first step is thorough cleaning to remove any foreign substance which may be present. The beans are then roasted in revolving cylinders by currents of air heated to a temperature above 204.4°C (about 400°F). At exactly the right moment they pass from the roaster and are quickly cooled to prevent further change.

The beans are then conveyed into chambers where they are broken into fragments called nibs. At the same time the shells are lifted away from the nibs by air currents and removed from the chambers. The nibs are quite dry. They are then milled to reduce their size. In this process they pass between three sets of steel-encased grinding stones. Here the cocoa butter, the natural fat of the cocoa bean averaging about 55 per cent, is released from the cells in the form of a free-flowing liquor of rich, dark colour and heavy, distinctive aroma. This product is the basic ingredient of all forms of chocolate and milk chocolate.

Cocoa is the second derivative of chocolate liquor. After undergoing heat treatment for flavour development, the liquor is pumped into powerful hydraulic presses which expel the free-flowing cocoa butter until the original 55 per cent is reduced to less than half that quantity. The solid cakes of cocoa remaining in the presses are then ejected and reduced to a fine dry powder in crushers and pulverizers. The powder is then cooled and wind-sifted to get the pleasing brown colour and extreme fitness essential for high quality.

Cocoa contains theobromine and caffeine as well as starch, fats, nitrogenous bodies and salts, so it is both a stimulating drink, and a food.

Cocoa can be prepared in milk only, or in milk and water, mixed to suit the taste of the individual. The powder is mixed with sugar to avoid lumping. A little cold milk is added and a thick, even paste made. Either hot milk or hot milk and water are poured over. The preparation is then allowed to boil for a few minutes which improves the flavour. A pinch of salt added at the beginning enhances the flavour.

18 / REHEATING OF FOOD—RECHAUFFE COOKING

Although freshly cooked food is better than reheated food, in the interests of economy and food management, reheating of food forms an important part of cooking. A clever cook should take pride in seeing that the second appearance is appetizing and that the maximum amount of nourishment is retained. Great care must be taken in reheating food, particularly meat. Since it is already cooked, further cooking will toughen the fibres and harden the proteins, thus making the food indigestible. Therefore, the first rule is never recook, only reheat.

Food may be warmed in a moderate oven if carefully covered. If the vessel containing food can be placed in a tin containing water, overdrying is prevented. Steaming is one of the best methods of reheating as the heat is gentle and does not dry the food. A covering is necessary to prevent the condensed steam from falling on the food. Frequently it may be necessary to do more than just reheat and, therefore, an ingenious cook must find ways and means of using up cooked food to make new dishes, e.g., cutlets, minced coilops, shepherd's pie, hash, and curry can be made without having to recook.

Rules for reheating food

(i) Never recook, only reheat.

(ii) Make use of all scraps of food, e.g., vegetables, sauces, grayy, etc., but be sure that they are absolutely fresh.

(iii) Remove gristle, bone and skin but not fat unless in excess because fat helps to keep the food moist.

(iv) Divide finely so that flavourings and seasonings can penetrate quickly and the food can be reheated quickly to avoid recooking.

(v) Cook any ingredient such as vegetables before adding it to the food that has to be reheated, e.g., if a cutlet has to be made from roast, the potatoes should be boiled first and then mixed for binding. The short, quick reheating does not allow time for the cooking of raw ingredients.

(vi) Additional moisture is always necessary in the form of sauce or gravy as most of the original moisture will have been removed.

(vii) A binding is essential for croquettes, rissoles, etc., but see that the binding is properly cooked before being added, e.g., as with Panada.

(viii) Cooked meat and fish become insipid when cold. So they must be carefully seasoned and flavoured in reheating. Meat is improved by the addition of ham, tongue, salted meat, onions, tomatoes, mushrooms, curry paste and fresh vegetables, while fish is improved by the addition of lemon juice, parsley and other mixed herbs.

(ix) It is often necessary to coat food to protect it from direct heat and, therefore, merely reheat: e.g.

(a) Covering with potato as in shepherd's pie.
(b) Coating with egg and breadcrumbs.
(c) Enclosing in pastry as in mutton patties.
(d) Enclosing in batter as in pan rolls.

(x) Dish daintily and garnish neatly.

(xi) Serve with a good gravy or a sharp sauce as an accompaniment.

(xii) Serve hot. Half-warmed, reheated food is far from appetizing.

19 / BASIC PRINCIPLES OF COOKERY FOR INVALIDS

This is not a special method of cookery but we have to use our knowledge of baking, boiling, steaming, etc., and in addition follow some rules which apply specially to food prepared for the sick. An invalid usually has a weak appetite and needs tempting because strength can only be regained through taking suitable food. Wrong food may kill a patient, while badly prepared food will retard recovery. Good food, well cooked and served will do much towards saving the patient's life.

Convalescents vary in appetite according to the nature of their complaint. But whether they have good appetites or not, their food should be easily digestible as they cannot take as much exercise as a normal person.

Important points in catering for invalids

(i) Consult the doctor about the patient's diet and obey his instructions.
(ii) Choose food that will supply necessary nourishment and be suitable to the illness.
(iii) Serve food which can be easily digested because in sickness the digestive system is often impaired.
(iv) Serve well-balanced meats, but pay special attention to the constituents according to the nature of the illness. In some cases meat, starches and sugar may have to be taken sparingly or even eliminated.
(v) In a serious illness, food is usually given in liquid form and should be as varied as possible.
(vi) In convalescence see that the solid food is light, easily digestible and served in small quantities.
(vii) As convalescence proceeds, increase the food in amount and variety.
(viii) Serve the best quality possible. Food should be absolutely fresh.
(ix) Vary the food and the method of cooking as much as possible. This stimulates appetite.

Suitable dishes

Liquid Fresh fruit juice, barley water, beef tea, eggflip, lemonade or orangeade.

Soft food Made with milk, e.g., junket or milk jelly, custard puddings (baked or steamed), blancmange, broths, light soups, rice conjee, etc.

Solid food White fish, fowl, rabbit, sweetbread or pancreas, liver dishes (on the advice of a doctor), khitchdi, etc.

20 / PRINCIPLES OF FOOD STORAGE

The fundamental principle in the storage of food is to keep it clean, cool and covered. Periodical inspection is a must, and there should be a regular turnover of goods. Daily cleaning, weekly cleaning and spring-cleaning are necessary to keep food free from dust and dirt.

Access to food stores must be restricted. No food should be kept in the kitchen or larder, apart from what is required during the day. The storage room should be dry, well-lit, ventilated, vermin-proof and clean.

Cupboards and shelves should be of simple design without dust-collecting ornamentation, unnecessary ledges or panels. Doors should be so designed as to enable the whole shelf to be clearly visible and accessible when doors are opened. Shelves must be constructed for specific purposes. They should be so fixed that they could be easily taken down and re-erected to facilitate regular and thorough cleaning. They should be narrow enough to enable all the goods to be easily accessible. Wide wooden shelves should not be made of planks which are joined, tongued or grooved but of 5 cm. × 1.25 cm. (2" × ½") slats laid with a clearance of 3.75 cm. to 5 cm. (1½" to 2") between each slat. The one nearest to the wall should have a return board to form a lip. The back of the lip should be at least 5 cm. (2") from the wall, to leave room for the cleaning of the wall. Corners must be rounded, particularly where shelves on two walls meet at a corner, to avoid an uncleanable dust trap.

As far as possible avoid having shelves above windows. Special shelving covered with marble, hard stone or tiles should be set aside for such materials as fat. One part of the shelf should be set aside for glass receptacles. No foodstuff, even when in bins, boxes or cartons, should be stored directly on the floor. The bottom shelving should be at least 75 cm. (26") above the floor. Containers for food should be provided, the nature of the foodstuff determining the nature of the receptacle required. These should be smooth, impervious, easily cleanable, resistant to wear, denting, buckling, pitting, chipping, cracking and should withstand penetration by vermin, and the corrosive action of foods and cleaning compounds. Stainless steel, monel metal, vitrified china, glass or plastic should be used for moist unpackaged food or beverages, and galvanized steel for dry packaged and unpackaged foods. Solder must be nontoxic, and welded areas must be as resistant to corrosion as the parent metal. Food containers should stand clear of walls, should be kept scrupulously clean and unless the articles they contain are naturally wet, should be completely dry, both inside and outside.

Segregate food to be used promptly from the food that is to be held for some time. Use food in the order of priority—first in, first out.

Stocks should be inspected once a week. A stock list should be made to tick off inspection dates and to indicate conditions.

Keeping food clean not only means keeping it free from visible dirt, but also keeping it in such a way as to prevent the multiplication of germs. High temperature kills them, and freezing preserves bacteria in suspended animation. Hence food should be kept cool and dry. Perishables should be kept under refrigeration or, when no refrigeration is available, in the larder in closed containers or adequately protected with muslin or wire covers. Windows and doors should have fly-proof meshing.

Guide to storage of certain Fruits and Vegetables (R.H. 85 to 90%)

Commodity	*Temperature*		*Approximate Storage life*	*Approximate post-storage life*
	°C	°F	*(weeks)*	*(days)**
Apples	2°–3°	35°–38°	18	9
Apricots	–1°–0°	31°–32°	1–2	–
Bananas	11°–13°	52°–55°	3	1
Beans	0°–2°	32°–35°	2–3	–
Beetroot	0°–2°	32°–35°	6–8	–
Brinjal	8°–10°	47°–50°	3–4	–
Cashew apples	0°–2°	32°–35°	5	–
Cherries	–1°–0°	30°–32°	2–3	–
Carrots	0°–2°	32°–35°	13–17	–
Cabbage	0°–2°	32°–35°	9–13	–
Cauliflower	1°–2°	34°–35°	4–6	–
Guavas	8°–10°	47°–50°	4	–
Grapes	0°–2°	32° –35°	8	–
Grapefruit	5.5°–7°	42°–45°	8	3
Gooseberry (Indian)	0°–2°	32°–35°	8	3
Jackfruit	11°–13°	52°–55°	6	–
Lemons	5.5°–7°	42°–45°	6	3
Limes	8°–10°	47°–50°	8	–
Litchi	0°–2°	32°–35°	11	–
Mangoes:				
Alphonso	8°–10°	47°–50°	4	–
Badshapasand, Dashari, Dilpasand, Khuddus, Neelum, Raspuri, Safeda, Bangalore	5.5°–7°	42°–45°	4–6	3–4
Mangosteen	4°–5.5°	39°–42°	7	–
Oranges	5.5°–7°	42°–44°	18	–
Onions (R.H.70 to 75%)	0°–2°	32°–35°	17–26	–
Papaya	4°–5.5°	39°–42°	5	3
Passion fruit (purple)	5.5°–7°	42°–45°	3	–
Pears	–1°–0°	30°–32°	12	–

(contd.)

Commodity	*Temperature* °C	°F	*Approximate Storage life* *(weeks)*	*Approximate post-storage life* *(days)*[*]
Persimmons	0°–2°	32°–35°	7	–
Peaches	–1°–0°	30°–32°	4–6	–
Peas	0°–2°	32°–35°	2–3	–
Pineapples	8°–10°	47°–50°	6	–
Plums	–1°–0°	30°–32°	2–4	–
Pomegranates	0°–2°	32°–35°	7–11	1
Pommelos	5.5°–7°	42°–45°	23	–
Potatoes	3°	37°–38°	26–35	–
Radishes	0°–2°	32°–35°	6–8	–
Sapota (Chikkoo)	0°–2°	32°–35°	10	5
Tomatoes				
(a) ripe	4.5°–7°	40°–45°	1–1½	–
(b) mature (turning to yellow)	13°–15.5°	55°–60°	3–4	–
Turnips	0°–2°	32°–35°	2–3	–

[*]at a temperature of 21°–34°C (70°–93°F)

Poultry Dressed and ready to cook poultry deteriorates rapidly unless carefully handled and stored under properly controlled conditions. Freshly killed poultry, after dressing, should be drawn quickly, and wrapped loosely in waxed paper or aluminium foil and refrigerated. Such poultry can be kept for 2 to 3 days in a refrigerator at 3°C (about 38°F) or less.

Frozen poultry should be stored at –18°C (about 0°F) or less, and cooked soon after it has been defrosted. Generally speaking, frozen poultry should be used within 6 months after it has been processed to obtain satisfactory results.

Eggs Eggs are highly perishable products and care must be taken in handling and storage. Eggs should always be stored in a refrigerator. They may lose as much of their fresh quality in 3 days at room temperature as in 2 weeks in the refrigerator. Store with the large end up. At a range of temperatures and relative humidity varying from –2°C (about 28°F) and 85 per cent R.H. and 2°C (about 35° F) and 75 per cent R.H., eggs may be stored for as long as 9 to 10 months. Frozen eggs should be stored at –18° C (about 0° to 20°F).

Treating with oil or wax before refrigeration also extends shelf life for several months. A pure, colourless, odourless, tasteless mineral oil is used and the processing done under controlled conditions.

Milk Bottled pasteurized milk can be safely kept for at least 3 to 4 days at refrigerated temperatures preferably between –1º and 4.4º C (about 34º and 40º F).

Refrigerator-freezer-pantry shelf

Knowing how to store food properly, and for how long you can keep it, is very important: the food will be safe to eat; it will retain its flavour and texture; a high level of nutrients will be maintained; and you will not waste money on spoiled items.

Safety First The three types of bacteria responsible for most cases of food poisoning (Salmonella, Staphylococcus and Streptococcus) are present around us all the time. Normally, they are not trouble some, but if given the right (actually wrong) conditions, bacteria can multiply in a matter of hours to dangerous levels. The contributing factors to bacterial growth: temperatures between 10º–52ºC (about 50º–125ºF) and time. To thwart growth, do not be casual about handling food; always work with well-scrubbed utensils, cutting boards—and hands; cook or serve food as soon as possible after removing it from storage; refrigerate food immediately after the meal is over; always take precautionary care. It is often not possible to tell by taste or smell if food is contaminated.

Foods that need special care Give special attention to preparing and storing poultry, fish and sea food, meat, creamed mixtures, mayonnaise, puddings and stuffings. Bacteria find these foods a good media to grow in. In particular: do not stuff poultry the night before; the cold stuffing may not heat up to a safe temperature when you cook the bird. Never refrigerate cooked poultry with the stuffing in—store it separately. If you have bought cracked eggs, use them only where they will be thoroughly cooked (baked or hard-boiled); Salmonella, which may be present on shells, could contaminate cracked eggs.

Know-how about frozen foods It is safe to refreeze virtually all partially thawed foods if they still have ice crystals in them and are still firm in the centre. However, many foods (ice cream and uncooked baked goods, for example) will not maintain top quality. Meat, fish and poultry purposely thawed in the refrigerator and kept no more than one day may be refrozen. However, do not refreeze combination dishes—pies, stews, etc., that have been thawed. With the exception of fruit and juice concentrates, foods thawed accidentally in the freezer over a period of days (because of a power failure, etc.) should not be refrozen, unless, of course, they still have ice crystals. If food is completely thawed (on purpose or by accident), warmed to room temperature and left for more than two hours, throw it out. The exceptions: fruit and juice concentrates, which ferment when spoiled. Throw away fruit if flavour is "off".

Pantry-shelf storage Temperature: Store food in well ventilated cabinets—not over a cooking range or near refrigerator's exhaust. Use cool areas for storing large amounts of potatoes, onions, etc., and for long-term storage of canned foods.

Time: Though most staples and canned foods will keep indefinitely, buy no more than you expect to use in the recommended storage times given later. While foods will be safe beyond the recommended storage times, flavours will fade and textures will wilt. Date foods. Then check cabinets every six months and use up the oldest items.

Buying: Purchase the freshest-looking packages—messy or shop worn labels indicate old stock. Don't buy cans with swollen ends—the food has gone bad. Dented cans may be purchased, provided they are not punctured.

Home Canning: Use first-quality foods and the best techniques.

Temperature: From 1° to 4.5°C (about 34° to 40°F) is best. Above 4.5°C (40°F), food spoils rapidly. Check temperature with a refrigerator thermometer or an outdoor thermometer.

Time: Use foods quickly—do not depend on maximum storage time.

Wraps: Use foil, plastic wrap or bags, airtight containers. When meat, poultry or fish is bought in a plastic wrapped package, loosen ends of package to dry surface moisture—bacteria grow faster on moist surfaces.

General Care: Clean refrigerator regularly to cut down food odours. Remove spoiled foods immediately so that decay will not be passed on to other food.

Food	*Storage Time*	*Special Handling*
	STAPLES	
Baking powder	18 months	Keep covered and dry.
Bouillon cubes	1 year	Keep covered and dry.
Breadcrumbs, dried	6 months	Keep covered and dry.
Cereals	4 months	Keep covered and dry.
Chocolate, premelted	1 year	Keep cool.
semisweet	2 years	Keep cool.
unsweetened	18 month	Keep cool.
Coffee, cans (unopened)	1 month	Refrigerate after opening.
Coffee, instant (opened)	2 months	Keep lid tightly closed.
(unopened)	6 months	
Condensed and evaporated milk	1 year	Refrigerate after opening.

(*contd.*)

Food	Storage Time	Special Handling
Flour (all types)	1 year	Put in airtight container.
Gelatine (all types)	18 months	Keep in original packets.
Honey, jams, syrups	1 year	Keep tightly covered.
Nonfat dry milk	6 months	Put in airtight container.
Pasta	2 years	Keep tightly closed.
Pudding mixes	1 year	Keep in original packets.
Rice, white	2 years +	Keep tightly closed.
Salad dressing (all types)	3 months	Refrigerate after opening.
Salad oil	1–3 months	
Shortening, solid	8 months	Refrigeration not needed.
Sugar, brown	4 months	Put in airtight container.
confectioners	4 months	Put in airtight container.
granulated, molasses	2 years +	Keep tightly covered.
Tea	2 years	Put in airtight container.
CANNED AND DRIED FOODS		
Fruits, canned	1 year	Keep in cool spot.
dried	6 months	Put in airtight container.
Gravies, canned	1 year	
Meat, fish, poultry, canned	1 year	
Pickles, olives	1 year	Refrigerate after opening.
Soups, canned, dried	1 year	Keep cool.
Vegetables, canned, dried	1 year	Keep cool.
HERBS, SPICES AND CONDIMENTS		
Ketchup (opened)	1 month	
Herbs and spices		Transfer from cartons to airtight containers, keep away from sunlight.
whole spices	1 year	
ground spices	6 months	
herbs	6 months	Check aroma; when it fades replace.
Tabasco, Worcestershire	2 years +	
DAIRY PRODUCTS AT REFRIGERATED TEMPERATURES		
Butter, margarine	1–2 weeks	Keep tightly wrapped or covered. Hold only 2 day supply in butter keeper.
Buttermilk, sour cream or yogurt	5 days to 2 weeks	Keep tightly covered. Turn unopened yogurt and sour cream containers upside down to prevent surface from drying. Once opened, store right-side up.

(contd.)

Food	*Storage Time*	*Special Handling*
Cheese		Keep all cheese tightly packaged in moisture-resistant wrap. If outside of hard cheese gets mouldy, just cut away mould—it would not affect flavour. For longer storage, see freezer storage.
cottage	5 days	
cream	2 weeks	
hard and wax-coated cheeses-Cheddar, Edam,, Gouda, Swiss etc.		
large pieces		
(unopened)	3–6 months	
(opened)	3–4 weeks	
(sliced)	2 weeks	
Parmesan (grated)		See pantry-chart. Does not need refrigeration.
Processed (opened)	3–4 weeks	Unopened processed cheese need not be refrigerated.
Cream-light, heavy, half-and-half	3 days	Keep tightly covered. Do not return unused cream to original containers. This would spread any bacteria present in leftover cream.
Dips-sour cream, etc.		
commercial	2 weeks	Keep tightly covered.
homemade	2 days	Keep tightly covered.
Eggs	2 days	Keep small end of egg down, to centre yolks.
in shells	3 weeks	
whites	3 days	Store in covered container.
yolks	3 days	Cover yolks with water; cover container.
Milk		
evaporated (opened)		
pasteurized	4–5 days	Keep containers tightly closed.
nonfat dry, skimmed	3–4 days	Do not return unused milk to original container.
sweetened condensed	4–5 days	Remove entire lid of can to make pouring easier. Keep covered.
FRUITS AND VEGETABLES—FRESH		
Fruits		Sort fruit; discard bruised or decayed fruit. Do not wash before storing—moisture encourages spoilage. Store in crisper or moisture resistant bags or wrap. Keep fruit juices tightly covered.
apples	1 week	
berries, cherries	1–2 days	
citrus fruits	1 week	
citrus juices		
bottled, reconstituted		
frozen, canned	6 days	

(contd.)

Food	Storage Time	Special Handling
melons	1 week	
other fruit	3–5 days	It is not necessary to remove canned fruit from can. Wrap uncut cantaloupe, honeydew, etc., to prevent odour spreading to other refrigerated food.
Vegetables		
beets, carrots, radishes	2 weeks	Remove leafy tops, keep in crisper.
mushrooms	1–2 days	Do not wash before storing.
onions, potatoes, sweet potatoes		Refrigeration not needed. See pantry-shelf chart.
shredded salad greens, cabbage	1–2 days	Keep in moisture-resistant wrap or bags.
unshelled peas, corn on husks, etc.	3–5 days	Keep in crisper or moisture-resistant wrap or bags.
other vegetables	3–5 days	Keep in crisper or moisture-resistant wrap or bags.
MEAT, FISH AND POULTRY—FRESH UNCOOKED		
Meats		
beef, lamb, pork andveal chops	3–4 days	Store fresh meats loosely wrapped. Partial drying of surface increases keeping quality. If meat comes packaged in plastic wrap, loosen ends. Store in coldest part of refrigerator or in meat keeper.
ground meat	1–2 days	
roasts	5–6 days	
steaks	3–5 days	
stew meat	1–2 days	
variety meats (liver, heart, etc)	1–2 days	
Fish and shellfish		
fresh cleaned fish including steaks and fillets	1 day	Store loosely wrapped. Keep in coldest part of refrigerator or in meat keeper.
Clams, crab, lobster in shell	2 days	Cook only live shellfish.
seafood including shucked clams, oysters, scallops, shrimps	1 day	
Poultry ready-to-cook chicken, duck or turkey	2 days	Store loosely wrapped. Keep fresh poultry in coldest part of refrigerator or in meat keeper.

(*contd.*)

Food	*Storage Time*	*Special Handling*
	CURED AND SMOKED MEATS	
Bacon	5–7 days	Keep wrapped. Store in coldest part of refrigerator or in meat keeper. Times given are for opened packages of sliced meats. Unopened vacuum packs keep about 2 weeks.
Bologna	4–6 days	
Corned beef	5–7 days	
Dried beef	10–12 days	
Dry and semi-dry sausages (salami, etc.)	2–3 weeks	
Frankfurters	4–5 days	
Hams (Whole, halves)	1 week	
Hams, canned (unopened)	6 months	
Liver sausages	4–5 days	
Luncheon meat	3 days	
Sausages, fresh	2–3 days	
Sausages, smoked	2–3 days	
	CANNED FOOD AFTER OPENING	
Baby food	2–3 days	Store baby food covered. Don't feed baby from jar; saliva may liquefy food. Store all canned foods tightly covered. It is not necessary to remove food from can.
Fish and seafood	1 day	
Fruit	1 week	
Gravy, broths	2 days	
Meats	2 days	
Pickles, olives	1 month	
Poultry	1 day	
Sauce, tomato based	5 days	
Vegetables	3 days	
	OTHER FOODS	
Coffee	2 weeks	Keep tightly covered after opening
Honey, jams, jellies	2 weeks	Refrigeration not needed but storage life is lengthened if refrigerated.
Nuts	9 months	Refrigerate nuts after opening cans or packages. For longer storage, freeze.
Onions, potatoes sweet potatoes	2 weeks at room temperature	For longer storage, keep below 10°C (about 50°F), but not refrigerated. Keep dry, out of sun. Plan short storage in spring when sprouting is a serious problem.
Parmesan cheese	2 months	Keep lid tightly closed.

(*contd.*)

Food	Storage Time	Special Handling
Peanut butter		
unopened	9 months	Refrigeration not needed, but
after opening	2 months	it keeps longer if refrigerated.
Refrigerated biscuits, rolls pastries, refrigerated cookie dough	Expiry date on label	Products keep better if stored at the back of the refrigerator. where it is colder.
Soft drinks	3–6 months	
Syrups		Same as honey
Whipped topping mix	1 year	
Wines, table	2–3 days	Keep tightly closed.
cooking	2–3 months	Keep tightly closed.

Freezer storage

Temperature –18ºC (about 0ºF) or below is best. The maximum temperature should be –15ºC (about 5º F). Check temperature with freezer thermometer or outdoor thermometer, or use this rule of thumb: if the freezer does not keep ice cream brick solid, temperature is above the recommended level. If this is the case, do not plan to store food for more than a week or two.

Time Date foods with an "expiry date" according to maximum storage time recommended below. Longer storage is not dangerous, but flavours and textures begin to deteriorate.

Wraps Use foil, plastic bags and wraps, freezer wrap or freezer containers.

Commercially Frozen Foods Do not buy them if they are battered, a sign that they may have been partially thawed. If foods have been partially thawed, then refrozen, use them within a few days.

Home-Frozen Foods Use good-quality foods and proper techniques. Freeze foods quickly in coldest part of freezer, then store in another freezer area.

Food	Storage Time	Special Handling
MEAT, FISH AND POULTRY		
Meat—home frozen and purchased frozen		
bacon	1 month	If meat is purchased fresh on
corned beef	2 weeks	trays and in plastic wrap,
frankfurters	1 month	check for holes. If none,
minced beef, lamb and veal	4 months	freeze in this wrap for up to 1 month. For longer storage,
minced pork	3 months	wrap over with foil, plastic
ham slices	1 month	wrap or freezer wrap.

(*contd.*)

Food	*Storage Time*	*Special Handling*
ham whole	2 months	Other meats should be wrapped as above. Make package as airtight as possible. Keep frankfurters, bacon, etc., in vacuum packages to freeze. Put two layers of waxed paper between individual hamburger patties, chops, etc. Keep meat purchased frozen in original package. Thaw and cook according to label instructions.
luncheon meats	1 month	
Roasts		
beef	1 year	
lamb	9 months	
pork	6 months	
veal	9 months	
sausages, dry, smoked	1 month	
sausages, fresh	2 months	
Steaks		
beef	1 year	
lamb, veal	9 months	
pork	6 months	
Fish—home frozen and purchased frozen		
fillets and steaks from "lean" fish—cod, flounder, haddock, sole	6 months	To home-freeze fish, wrap in foil, plastic wrap or freezer wrap. Make package as airtight as possible. Freeze in coldest part of freezer. For best results, prepare fish as directed in authoritative freezing guide.
"fatty" fish—bluefish, mackerel, perch, salmon	3 months	
breaded fish	3 months	
clams	3 months	
cooked fish or seafood	3 months	
king crab	10 months	Keep fish purchased frozen in original wrapping. Thaw and cook according to label directions.
lobster tails	3 months	
oysters	4 months	
scallops	3 months	
shrimp, unbreaded	1 year	
shrimp, breaded	4 months	
Poultry—home frozen or purchased frozen		
chicken, whole or cut-up parts	1 year	For home freezing, prepare as directed for fish and seafood (above). Thaw commercially frozen poultry according to label directions. Cook all thawed poultry within 1 day.
chicken livers	3 months	
cooked poultry	3 months	
duck, turkey	6 months	
FRUITS AND VEGETABLES		
Fruit–home frozen or purchased frozen		
berries, cherries, peaches, pears, pineapple, etc.	1 year	

(*contd.*)

Food	Storage Time	Special Handling
citrus fruit and juice		
—frozen at home	6 months	
fruit juice concentrate	1 year	
Vegetables—home frozen or purchased frozen		
home frozen	10 months	Cabbage, celery, salad greens,
purchased frozen-cartons,		tomatoes do not freeze
plastic bags or boil-in-bag	8 months	successfully.
COMMERCIAL FROZEN FOODS		
Also see: meat, fish, poultry; fruits, vegetables; dairy products		
Baked goods		
breads, baked	3 months	Pick up frozen foods
breads, unbaked	2 months	immediately before going to
cakes		check-out counter. Place in
cheesecake	3 months	home freezer as soon as
chocolate	4 months	possible. Purchase only foods
fruit cake	1 year	frozen solid. Cook or thaw
sponge cake	2 months	according to label instructions.
yellow or pound	6 months	
pies		
cream, custard	8 months	
fruit	8 months	
Main dishes		
meat, fish and poultry pies	3 months	
meat, fish and poultry casseroles	3 months	
TV dinners	6 months	
HOME FROZEN FOODS		
Also see: meat, fish, poultry; fruits, vegetables; dairy products		
Breads	3 months	Package foods tightly in foil,
Cakes	3 months	plastic wrap, freezer wrap or
Casserole dishes:		watertight freezer containers.
meat, fish, poultry	3 months	For casseroles, allow head
Cookies, dough, baked	3 months	room for expansion.
Nuts	3 months	Freeze in coldest part of
Pies, unbaked	8 months	freezer.
DAIRY PRODUCTS		
Butter, margarine	9 months	Store in airtight freezer container or wrapped in freezer wrap.
Buttermilk		
sour cream or yogurt		Do not freeze.

(*contd.*)

Food	*Storage Time*	*Special Handling*
Cheese		
Camembert	3 months	Thaw in refrigerator.
Cottage, farmers' cheese (dry curd only)	3 months	Thaw in refrigerator. Do not freeze creamed cottage cheese—it gets mushy.
Cream cheese, Neufchâtel	1 month	Thaw in refrigerator.
Hard cheeses—Cheddar, Edam, Gouda, Swiss, Brick, etc.	3 months	Cut and wrap cheese in small pieces for freezer storage. When frozen, may show mottled colour due to surface moisture. Thaw in refrigerator.
Processed	3 months	
Roquefort, Blue	3 months	Becomes crumbly after thawing Still fine for salads and melting.
Cream—light, heavy. half-and-half	2 months	Heavy cream may not whip after thawing. Use cream for cooking. Thaw in refrigerator.
Cream, whipped	1 month	Make dollops of whipped cream; freeze firm. Place in plastic bag or carton; seal; store in freezer. Place on top of dessert to thaw.
Eggs		
in shells		Do not freeze.
whites	1 year	Store in covered container. Freeze in amounts for favourite recipes.
yolks	1 year	For sweet dishes: Mix one cup yolks with 1 tablespoon corn syrup or sugar. For other cooking: substitute ½ teaspoon salt for sugar.
Ice cream, ice milk, sherbet	1 month	Cover surface with plastic wrap or foil after each use to keep from drying out.
Milk	3 months	Freezing affects flavour and appearance. Use in cooking and baking. Allow room for expansion in freezer container. Thaw in refrigerator.

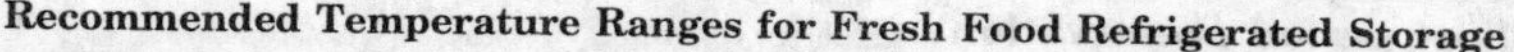

Recommended Temperature Ranges for Fresh Food Refrigerated Storage

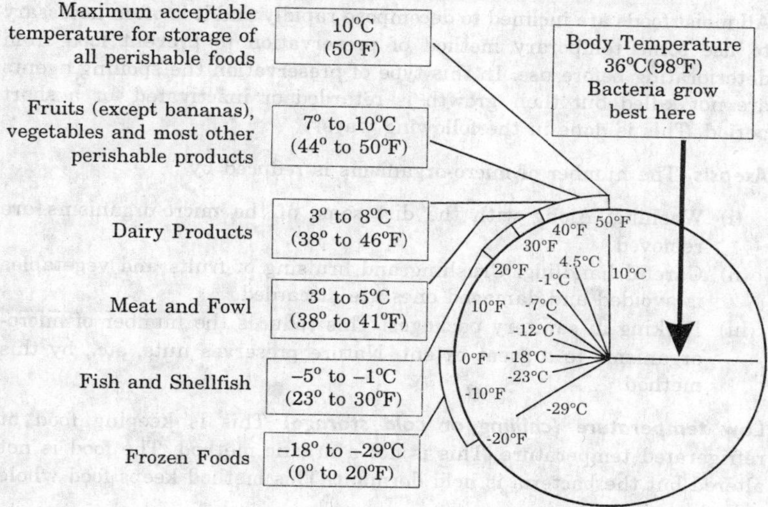

XXI. PRESERVATION OF FOOD

It is often convenient to preserve foods such as fish, eggs, fruits and vegetables while they are cheap and plentiful, for use when they are not. Careful preservation of food eliminates waste which may happen otherwise during a time of glut. It also helps to prevent undue fluctuation of prices.

Although preservation in one form or another has been practised throughout the world, it developed scientifically into a technology only after the First World War when it was found convenient to use preserved food for the armed forces. The technology has continued to progress, and preserved food is used by rich and poor in everyday life in the West. Easy transportation, variety in food and convenience in use have all added on to the popularity of preserved foods. The development of this technology has now made it possible to have preserved food of practically the same nutritive value and palatability standards as fresh foods.

The object of food preservation is to destroy or inactivate spoilage by micro-organisms, toxins produced by them and the chemicals present which are responsible for the deterioration of food. This has to be done without affecting the palatability of the food to be preserved, its colour, flavour and nutritive value.

Preservation can be divided into short or long period preservation.

Short period preservation

All moist foods are inclined to decompose rapidly and it is often necessary to use some temporary method of preservation to prevent food from deteriorating before use. In this type of preservation the spoiling agents are not killed but their growth is retarded or inactivated for a short period. This is done in the following ways:

Asepsis The number of micro-organisms is reduced by

(i) Washing: Along with the dirt some of the micro-organisms are removed.
(ii) Careful handling: Crushing and bruising of fruits and vegetables is avoided and damaged ones are discarded.
(iii) Packing in sanitary packages: This reduces the number of micro-organisms to a great extent. Nature preserves nuts, etc., by this method.

Low temperature (chilling or cold storage) This is keeping food at refrigerated temperature. This is not a drastic method. The food is not altered but the bacteria is held dormant. This method keeps food whole only for short periods.

Some fruits such as bananas however, spoil under refrigeration so they must be kept at 12°C (about 54°F).

Apples and hard fruits will keep for a long time in cold storage as long as they are wrapped in greaseproof paper.

Cold storage has been practised for thousands of years. In old temples and caves (e.g. Kanheri Caves, Bombay) one can see niches surrounded by running water to keep them cool. In Pompeii in Roman times each house had a food storage compartment cut out of rock with running water playing on it.

By heating Cooking of food and boiling of milk helps to preserve these longer than if left fresh.

By mild antiseptics Sugar and salt can be sprinkled over fruits and vegetables respectively that are to be used for the next day.

By removal of air If butter is spread over potted meat or egg is dipped in a wax emulsion it can be kept for a longer period than if untreated as the air that is necessary for growth of micro-organisms is not available.

Waxing fruits by means of sugarcane wax is another old method which is now being revived in India and is being developed on a commercial scale in Nagpur. The purpose is to exclude air by covering fruits and vegetables with wax emulsion. The results have been very encouraging.

Long period preservation

The storage life of foods is increased for a longer period by these methods:

Sun drying This is perhaps the oldest method of food preservation and has been used by hunters and travellers for generations. The method of preservation is the removal of moisture to render germs inactive. It has been extensively used in India and fish, meat, vegetables and fruits have been preserved by this method; e.g., dried fish, such as Bombay Duck, dried game meat, lentils, peas, chillies, etc., and dried fruits and nuts such as apricots, dates, raisins, cashewnuts, etc.

Dehydration Whilst sun-drying is a method of dehydration, by using mechanical devices this process has been speeded up considerably. Dehydration is the removal of moisture to the extent that mould growth does not flourish under carefully controlled conditions of air flow, temperature, and humidity, in a special piece of apparatus known as a dehydrator. By using dehydrators a more standard product is also obtained. Milk and eggs, for example, are roller-dried or spray-dried. The products can be successfully reconstituted. Dehydrated vegetables such as potatoes, peas, carrots, cabbage, etc., are extensively used. All vegetables must be blanched before being dehydrated (except onion, garlic, etc). Dehydrated food can be easily transported and does not need refrigerated storage. The storage space required is also reduced.

Salting This very often accompanies dehydration. When foods are just salted, this must be done at as low a temperature as possible. In tropical countries it must be done under refrigeration. Use salt that is as pure as possible, or else the impurities cause a bitterness in the fish or meat being salted.

Two methods are used:

(i) Rubbing the salt on the flesh of fish or meat.
(ii) Soaking in a brine tub. This method is used particularly for tongue, beef, pig's trotters and pig's head. Sometimes the brine solution is injected into the meat. Microbes cannot grow in a strong salt medium.

Smoking This is also a very old method of preservation. Fish or meat is exposed to the smoke of a slowly burning wood fire thus imparting a smoked flavour and assisting in the preservation of the food stuff.

Bacterial growth is stopped by the drying of the food surface and by the antiseptic action of certain constituents of the smoke, such as creosote, formaldehyde and acetic acid.

The wood must not contain any substance that will impart a foreign flavour to the food, nor must the temperature be too high, or else the food will become too dry, and the smoke will not be able to penetrate the food thoroughly.

Deep freeze This does not kill germs, but prevents them from being active. This method is being used more and more in recent years, with the advancement in refrigeration machinery.

Freezing is a relatively simple method of preserving food and is generally accepted as one of the most satisfactory ways of storing perishable foods. Research done in this field has shown that freezing food is the simplest and safest method of preservation provided one follows the five cardinal points: careful selection, proper packaging, freezing at –18°C (0°F) or lower, storage at –18°C (0°F) or lower with the minimum of fluctuation, and avoiding long storage.

Meat, poultry, poultry products, game, fruits and vegetables and prepared and cooked foods can be preserved by this method.

(i) Careful Selection. Careful selection is the first step in successful preservation as freezing does not improve the natural product, except in the case of beef. If quality products are to be taken from the freezer, only quality products should be frozen. Slime or bruises must be trimmed carefully from meat before it is frozen.

(ii) Proper Packaging. Experience has demonstrated that special packaging materials are necessary. Inferior or low grade materials should be avoided. A good packaging material should be:

(a) Clean and sanitary.
(b) Odourless, flavourless, and impervious to odours.
(c) Mechanically practical.
(d) Attractive and easily labelled.
(e) Protective against desiccation (freezer burn).
(f) Resistant to oxidation.
(g) Tough and not brittle at low temperature.
(h) Greaseproof and stain-proof.

Numerous papers, foils, plastic films, and waxes meet most of these requirements. Only materials that adequately protect the product should be used. There is quite a range in the prices of these materials. More expensive materials increase packaging costs, but the increased protection usually justifies the extra cost.

Even the best available wrapping material must be applied properly. The following suggestions are offered for best results in packaging meat:

(a) Use only approved wrapping paper or containers.
(b) Cut meat to suit needs. Avoid packages weighing more than 4.5 kgs. 2.5 kg. roasts are convenient.
(c) Be sure all sharp edges of bones are removed.
(d) Avoid rolling or folding steaks. Keep all packages as flat and square as possible.
(e) Interleave all pieces of meat with tissue paper.

(f) Maintain as complete contact between the meat and the paper as possible.

(g) Eliminate air from the packages, wrap tightly and seal.

(h) Mark each package clearly with name, locker number, cut of meat, weight, and the date frozen.

(iii) Freezing at –18ºC (about 0ºF) or lower: Foods should be frozen at –18ºC (about 0ºF) or lower, and packages should be loosely arranged while freezing, but when completely frozen they may be tightly stacked in the home unit or locker. "Sharp freezing" often refers to freezing at temperatures between –18ºC (about 0ºF) and –28ºC (about 20ºF), while "quick freezing" applies to still lower temperatures.

(iv) Storage at –18ºC (about 0ºF): The palatability and nutritive value of food are best preserved at –18ºC (about 0ºF) or lower. The storage temperature should not fluctuate above this, but experiments indicate that fluctuation below that temperature is not serious. Fluctuation of the storage temperature above –18ºC fosters dehydration even with the best of wrapping material. Ice or snow on the inside of the package usually indicates fluctuation above this temperature.

(v) Avoid long storage: Many people think that because freezing retards bacterial and enzymatic activity a frozen product will keep indefinitely. This is true only to a degree, as there is progressive deterioration in a frozen state. The rate is slow, but nevertheless specific; therefore time in storage should be limited. It is best to plan on a normal seasonal turnover. When meat is carefully handled, properly wrapped, sharp frozen, and stored at –18ºC (about 0ºF), it can be stored for a reasonable period of time. but deviation from the ideal in any one of the above factors may cause rapid deterioration.

It is recommended that beef be consumed within twelve months, fresh pork within six months and ground meat, especially pork sausages, within four to six months. Pork and pork products tend to develop rancidity early and cured pork products even earlier; therefore, it is a good practice to stock only a six months supply of pork at one time.

These are the five cardinal points for successful storage. They are not over-exacting and not beyond reach. It is believed that home freezer owners will be far wiser to have all their bulk processing done at the nearest commercial freezer plant and use the home unit only as a home reservoir. This will leave all processing to the professional at the plant, where adequate facilities and equipment are available, and thus relieve the householder. Where small quantities of food are to be handled, as a day's supply of peas, beans or strawberries from the garden, they may be handled safely and without materially influencing the storage temperature; but large quantities should be done in units intended for volume. The home unit is essentially a storage unit and not a processing unit.

Hermetically sealed containers The absence of air from any container is a principle of food storage. This method is used for biscuits, cereals and preserved food in bottles.

Canning and bottling In this method preservation of food is done in hermetically sealed containers sterilized by heat.

The word 'canning' is of American origin but is now used internationally in connection with preserving foods in tin containers. In its broader sense it also includes preservation by application of heat in glass containers as well. Tins are standardized. A1 T A2½ and A10 are the commonly used sizes in India. A10 has a capacity of about 3 litres and is used for the trade as it is an economical size.

The canning of vegetables, fruits, meat, fish, dairy products and most edible products cooked and uncooked, has reached a very high degree of efficiency. Each food item uses a special technique. Colouring agents if added in canned and bottled products are strictly controlled by the Food and Drugs Act. In India colouring agents are specially used for canning cherries and green vegetables.

By sugar Food products containing 60% sugar do not ordinarily spoil. Jam, jelly, marmalade, preserves, candy fruits, fruit syrups and confectionery are preserved by this method.

Gas storage Oxygen (air) is replaced by inert gases e.g. aerated water.

Acid Acids preserve foods by virtue of their hydrogen ion concentration, which produces a toxic effect on microbial protoplasm. e.g., pickles in vinegar.

By spices Essential oils of spices produce a toxic effect on micro organisms, e.g., as in pickles.

By vacuum packing Coffee powder, milk powder, etc.

By fermentation Alcoholic beverages, etc.

By chemical preservatives Sodium benzoate and potassium metabisulphite are the two preservatives permitted by the Food and Drugs Act.

Irradiation Preservation by irradiation is a new technique which is being explored at present. This is done by radiation of various frequencies ranging from the low frequency electric current to the high frequency gamma rays. In 1957 it was reported that 100 food items have been cleared for human testing. The obvious advantage of food preserved by this method is that food can be stored without refrigeration. Bacon, beans, and peaches have been kept for one year at 22ºC (about 72ºF) storage temperature without spoilage after irradiation treatment.

Ionized radiation produces some destruction of nutritive value, but not sufficient to be nutritionally significant. Experiments on irradiated powdered milk showed no loss of vitamins. This may be due to a lack of moisture.

Colour changes were noticed in strawberry and milk powder amongst the foods studied. There was some flavour change in the foods, the most noticeable being in ground beef. It is believed, however, that acceptability of the strangeness in odour will be only a matter of time.

Work done hitherto does prove, however, that irradiation as a form of food preservation although still in its infancy, has great possibilities.

Preservation by Antibiotics This is another method of preservation now under study. Much work has been done on Penicillin, Streptomycin, Aureomycin, Terramycin, Chloromycetin, Subtlin, Tetracyclin, Oxytetracyclin, Chlortetracyclin, etc.

Eviscerated chicken dipped in Aureomycin and stored at 4.4ºC (about 40ºF) was found fresh 7 to 14 days longer than untreated chicken.

Chlortetracyclin (aureomycin) is recognized as one of the most effective of the broad range of antibiotics.

This method is still in the experimental stage. Although food bacteriologists realize the advantage of the preservation of raw foods by means of a non-toxic antibiotic or the use of one in combination with reduced amounts of heat in the processing of canned foods, they are aware of certain problems that could arise with the use of antibiotics as preservatives.

(i) The effect of an antibiotic on a micro-organism is known to vary with the species or even with the strains of the organism. Hence the antibiotic may be effective against some spoilage organisms but not others, or against part of the population in a culture but not all.

(ii) Organisms are known to be able to adapt themselves to increasing concentrations of antibiotics, so that new resistant strains may develop. There is also the possibility that other organisms not yet significant in food spoilage but resistant to the antibiotic might assume new importance in food spoilage.

(iii) Effects of the antibiotic on the consumer, sensitization to it, changes in his intestinal flora and the development of strains of pathogen in the body resistant to that antibiotic, are all possibilities. It is, therefore, recommended that the antibiotics used for food preservation be other than those used for therapeutic reasons.

22 / PLANNING OF MEALS

It is the manager's responsibility to have a pattern and a plan for all operations so that it is possible to proceed with the least expenditure of time, effort, material and money, to supervise each area and at the same time direct the overall organization. One of the most important aspects of organization and planning in the food industry is 'Menu Planning'. The best results are obtained if the person in charge of the food production plans the menus in consultation with the chef.

Menu is a French word meaning minute details as applied to the kitchen bill, bill of fare, table card or programme of a meal. Its object is to present a list of dishes and courses, eatables and beverages.

In olden days the menu was not given. The banquet or dinner consisted of two courses. 10 to 40 dishes were set upon the table before the diners entered (hence the word *Entrée*) which when consumed were "Relieved" or 'Removed' by 10 to 40 other dishes; hence the words *Relevés* and *Removes*.

History of menus

Menus were first heard of as being adopted for table use in 1541, when at a banquet given by Duke Henry of Brunswick, His Grace had a sheet of paper by his side to which he occasionally referred. When questioned by one of his guests about what he was looking at, he answered that it was a programme of what they were eating and that it helped him to reserve his appetite for those dishes he liked. The idea was admired so much that it became generally known and adopted.

Another story is that at a dinner given in the year 1498 Count Hugo de Monfort was noticed to have a piece of written parchment near his plate, which he frequently consulted and when asked what it was explained that he had ordered the head cook to write on it the various dishes that were being sent from the kitchen.

The old fashioned bills of fare were usually written on large cards, gaudily ornamented.

Menu planning is the term used to denote the planning in advance of a dietary pattern for a given period of time.

By planning a menu, we can come to know what food-stuffs we are going to consume, and in what form, at scheduled meal times such as breakfast, lunch, tea, or dinner.

Menu planning is an art and menus are compiled rather than written and they present not only the picture of a truly balanced appetizing meal but also the complete operation of changing raw materials into cooked and served delicacies.

There are two classes of menus: *Table d'hôte* and *à la Carte*.

Table d'hôte will be a set menu, often with a choice in each course, at a set price that is charged whether or not the full menu is consumed. The food is usually cooked in advance.

À la Carte menus are those where each dish is priced separately. The customer can choose from the card as many dishes as he wants. The dish will be cooked to order and it is recognized that the customer will wait while the dish is cooked.

Factors that influence menu planning are:

1. Money to be spent (a) customer.
   (b) food services.
2. Type of customer.
3. Type of food service.
4. Availability of foods.
5. Seasonability of foods.
6. Balance.
7. Equipment.
8. Labour.
9. Leftovers in hand.
10. Appearance of the final product.
    (a) palatability (shape, flavour.
    (b) variety colour, texture.)
11. Menu-planning pattern.
12. Recipes to be used.
13. Food habits of the customer.
14. Policy of the establishment.

Nutritional requirement The nutritional needs of the people being catered for are an important consideration especially when planning set meals.

Nutritional needs differ for persons of various ages, sex and activity groups.

It is not necessary that we should have a balanced meal every time we eat. The day's meals together must be considered to see that the right quantity and quality are provided.

The number of meals per day may vary from 3 to 5.

The primary consideration should be quality and not quantity. As a rule our appetites will give us a rough idea regarding quantity but when calculating quantities for institutional or large-scale catering, it is safer to calculate the total quantity, allowing 2400C (calories) per day per adult man, and using this unit to determine the amount required for women and children. The occupation of the people you are catering for must also be considered. 300 calories more per hour for very hard physical work, 150 to 300 calories for medium work and 75 calories for ordinary physical work should be added to the original amount. Allow about 150 calories per person per day for wastage. No extra food is necessary for people with sedentary occupations.

Mere variety is not enough. A knowledge of the different constituents of food and their functions in the body and the sources from which these foods are obtained should be studied.

The different constituents of foods are carbohydrates, proteins, fats, minerals and vitamins. These are divided into:

(i) Body warmers and workers: These elements form the bulk of the food and are obtained from carbohydrates and fats. Although proteins can also be used for this purpose, it is wasteful to use a more expensive and less available food.

(ii) Body builders: These are proteins and some minerals; meat, fish, milk and milk products, eggs and soyabean are sources of complete or first-class proteins and therefore, are considered to be superior. Peas, beans, lentils and nuts are sources of second-class or partially complete proteins. A judicious mixture of these provides the best nutrition. Special stress must be laid on ensuring that when planning meals for vegetarians, a third of the proteins is obtained from the first category. When there is a shortage of first-class proteins it is a wise policy to distribute them though the three meals as proteins cannot be stored in the body. Minerals can be obtained from vegetables and fruits.

(iii) Body protectors: These are vitamins, minerals and proteins. It is very easy to overlook the body protectors, particularly vitamins, as they are found in food in small quantities. So special attention must be paid to them. Cooking and processing destroy some of the vitamins, particularly Vitamin C. This vitamin is highly unstable and will be destroyed by oxidation, leaching, heat or ageing. Vitamin B is lost in the cooking liquor, if the liquor is thrown out, and destroyed when soda is used for cooking. Therefore it is essential that raw fruit, fresh vegetables, salads and some nuts or pulses be included in the daily diet. In addition to these, beverages and roughage must be provided.

Another way of dividing food is as follows:

(i) For bones and teeth: Calcium is necessary and it cannot be utilized without Vitamin D. Foods rich in calcium are milk and cheese; vegetables contain smaller quantities. Vitamin D is found in animal fat.

(ii) For flesh and muscles: These need proteins which are obtained from milk and milk products, meat, fish, poultry, eggs, soyabean and a second-class variety from peas, beans, lentils, and nuts.

(iii) For blood: This needs iron which besides giving red colour to the blood helps to transport oxygen to the various parts of the body.

(iv) Food for protection: Such as minerals and vitamins. Vitamin A for growth, respiratory organs, skin and eyes. Vitamin B for healthy digestive system, nervous system and good appetite and for metabolism of carbohydrates. Vitamin C for cells of the body, clear skin, bright eyes and general good health. Vitamin D for fixing calcium and phosphorus in bones and teeth.

(v) Food for energy and warmth: Fat and carbohydrates. It is a good plan when planning meals to put in body-building and protective food first and then add other foods to satisfy hunger.

When planning meals for children, besides a knowledge of their nutritional needs, the fact must be borne in mind that partaking of food is a significant social and educational experience. Food should be plain, well-cooked, easily chewed, free from strong flavours and odours. There should be interesting variety in colour, flavour and texture. Meals should be served well and meal-time should be pleasant, free from undue stress and resentment.

Old people should have less calories (not more than 1500). Food should be easily chewed. Protective food such as vitamins and mineral should form the chief part. There should be less carbohydrates and fats.

Foods served in commercial restaurants, cafeterias, industrial canteens and hotel dining rooms may constitute only a part of the daily consumption of foods. They should be planned to meet a third of the calorie requirement. Such institutions should so plan their meals that patrons will be able to readily select foods necessary for their bodily needs. This is facilitated by the arrangement of foods for a given meal into menus classed as light, medium and heavy. The inclusion of leafy vegetables and salad plates is a nutritionally sound principle.

Budget The following points must be considered:

(i) Money available for food.

(ii) Cost of raw material.

(iii) Proper ratio between high and low-cost dishes.

Type of service Menus should be planned in relation to type of service e.g. cafeteria or seated service, etc., and the distance over which food must be transported for service. When meals are served in decentralized units from a central kitchen, a master menu with modifications should be used.

Availability and seasonability Seasonal foods are, besides being economical, also better in quality. These must be studied and included. It is also important to consider availability of food when planning menus.

Balance The following points must be considered:

(i) Light to heavy and back to light.
(ii) Vary the sequence of preparation, e.g. cold or hot.
(iii) Change seasoning, flavouring and presentation.
(iv) Ensure that garnishes are in harmony with their main dishes.

Equipment and work space Menu should conform to limitation of equipment and physical facilities.

Labour

(i) Skill and number of employees must be considered.
(ii) Avoid too many last-minute processes.
(iii) Avoid too many long jobs especially for one cook.
(iv) Avoid overly complicated processes or emphasis on wrong kinds of food. Plan meals that the staff can do well.
(v) Have records of time and yield.
(vi) Allow time for portioning and garnishing.

Leftovers in hand For wise and economic management, leftovers should be considered and the menu altered or the necessary adjustment made.

Appearance of the final product Food should be palatable to be acceptable and hence recipes should be tried out and standardized before a dish is put on the menu. The tastes of the people catered to should be studied. New foods should be introduced gradually.

To make food attractive and to break monotony, variety in colour, texture and flavour must be introduced, e.g. Cream of tomato soup, Fish colbert with French fried potatoes, Chicken fricassée with fresh peas and fruit salad or Puri and chole, Moghlai biryani, Palaksag, Tomato cucumber, Onion raita and Phirnee. As eye-appeal stimulates the appetite, relate the colours of the garnish with the basic ingredient. Natural colours should be used for food. Do not over-garnish.

Food habits of the customer This is important when catering in industrial canteens, schools, institutions, hospitals, etc. For example Jains and most Brahmins are strict vegetarians. Sikhs may eat only 'Jhatka meat'. Orthodox Jews may need Kosher meat. Bengali Brahmins may eat fish but not meat.

Policy of the establishment Certain establishments may not serve certain foods because of their policy, e.g. beef, or ham, bacon and pork.

In order to have well-planned menus it is necessary to have a well worked-out menu pattern which is suitable to the clientele, and workable as it relates to staff and equipment.

Well planned menu-making techniques

(i) Plan regular uninterrupted time for making your menus when you are not too fatigued. Choose a quiet place.

(ii) Have available all records, charts and books which will be helpful.

(iii) Have a well organized, classified and usable menu chart. This will be a guide to menu making and will, if kept up to date, suggest ideas and help to prevent monotony and repetition in menu making. Ideas for menu charts can be collected from books, magazines, visits to restaurants and many other sources.

(iv) Formulate a workable menu-pattern. This means that the menu-pattern should be planned to meet the needs of the various groups of individuals served, and should be based on definite information.

(v) Make menus one week in advance. Use menu charts and other sources to get interest, variety and nutritional adequacy, and to avoid repetition. Re-check menus daily to use up leftovers and to meet other problems.

The arrangement of an elaborate dinner is an art in itself and consists of selecting the various courses so that the dishes harmonize with each other. The following points are helpful:

(i) Each dish should be different in composition and mode of cooking.

(ii) The choice of individual dishes must be excellent, each dish should be well cooked, tastefully dressed and yet distinct in character.

(iii) The harmonizing effect is obtained by so arranging the dishes that each one is distinct from the other, bearing no relation in appearance to the preceding or following dish.

(iv) A judicious selection of the raw materials with special regard to the season of the year must be made in all cases.

(v) The various meats and materials forming one course must not be repeated in the same menu from one course to another.

(vi) The various kinds of sauces used in the preparation and as the accompaniment must each be distinctly different in colour, taste and flavour.

(vii) If there are two soups, one ought to be clear and the other cream. If the cream soup is made of vegetables the clear soup must not contain any vegetables.

(viii) When two or more types of fish are to be served the first should be boiled—generally a large fish—and the second fried, grilled or broiled.

(ix) The entrée should always be classified so that light dishes such as rissoles, bouchées, croquettes, quenelles, kromeskies, etc., are served first.

(x) If there are two relevés, poultry is served before butcher's meat. The most important point is to have dressed relevés before plain roasts. This is followed by the sweet (entremet), savoury, dessert and cheese. Sometimes the savoury is served before the sweet.

Having compiled the menu, it must be written down. Use correct words and phrases. Choose the language easily understood by the type of client being served.

First-class establishments use the French language. Ordinary establishments use English with a few common and easily understood foreign terms. Canteens use descriptive, easily understood English.

Do not mix languages. Always call an Irish stew by that name, or by the name used in the country of origin. Well known terms like *hors d'oeuvre*, etc., may be used when writing menus in English.

Some cooks give new names to old dishes, or give dishes names which have no bearing on the preparation. This causes confusion and disappointment so this practice must be avoided.

When writing the menu it is very important to see that words are properly spelt. Call dishes by their proper names. Do not mask or disguise. Use the following formula:

(i) Name the article—pomfret, lamb, duckling.
(ii) Add the place of origin—Bombay Pomfret, Punjab Lamb, Kerala Duckling.
(iii) Name the part used—Fillet of Bombay Pomfret, Saddle of Punjab Lamb, Breast of Kerala Duck.
(iv) Name the method of cooking—poached, roasted, braised.
(v) Add the garnish—in white wine, boulangre, and green peas.
(vi) Then having finished up with rather a long list of words, streamline the name leaving out the least important.
(vii) Finally add the sauce where necessary, Apple Sauce for the duck, Redcurrant Jelly for the saddle, etc.

How to avoid errors

(i) Never write the word "gravy" on the menu.
(ii) Add after the main name any sauce which is served separately.
(iii) Add after the main name any accompaniment which is served separately viz: Yorkshire pudding, Cheese straws, etc.
(iv) Parsley is not put on the menu except where it is part of a dish, e.g. Parsley Potatoes.
(v) Watercress may be added either after the main word or by adding it with the word *and.*
(vi) Sauces and garnishes go directly after the dish to which they belong. Add the vegetable after the main dish and its garnish or

sauce; and add the potatoes after the vegetable; add the salad after the roast or the cold dish.

(vii) Do not translate literally, e.g. Chasseur means hunter, Bonne Femme means good woman—in these cases either keep the original word or describe the dish as "with mushroom sauce" etc.

(viii) When something is grilled it cannot also be "à la meunière". "A la" is only used to denote "in the fashion of", "after or in the style of". This means that it may be used when in the style of a certain town, country, place, etc., such as "a l'anglaise", "à la française", "à la portugaise", etc. It might also mean "in the" as in "à la crème". But where a dish is named after somebody it will not have the words "à la" but go straight on to the name, e.g. Peach Melba. In the case of Vichy carrots the word "vichy" belongs to the water there and the correct term is, therefore, "Carrottes Vichy".

(ix) Do not translate words which are very well known like Mayonnaise, Hollandaise, Consommé, Yorkshire pudding, etc.

(x) Do not add fancy names not properly understood, like Grilled Plaice à la meuniére.

(xi) Do not write 'soup and a roll': this looks clumsy.

(xii) Do not write Smoked Salmon Hollandaise. Salmon Hollandaise is hollandaise sauce mixed with poached fresh salmon.

(xiii) Do not repeat the garnish as a vegetable. The word 'Bruxelloise' means with brussels sprouts. Vichy means with carrots, Clamart means with peas, Boulangre means with baked potatoes, and so on.

(xiv) Avoid over-descriptive words.

Correct sequence of courses Make sure that the sequence of courses is correct. Take as a sample those given later under respective headings.

A few alterations are allowed sometimes; a savoury may be served before the sweet. The vegetable course is sometimes put before the roast. Cheese is sometimes served before the sweet.

Make sure that alternative dishes follow the same order of appearance as in a full menu, e.g. if it is fish or meat, then write the fish course first.

Correct sequence of garnishes and accompaniments First comes the main name of the dish, followed by the garnish which is to be served separately or the sauce which is served separately. Then the vegetables and then the potatoes.

Menu Card as a tool for merchandising the food

(i) Use good quality paper or papier maché or parchment or silk.

(ii) The print should be good and clear, in indelible ink, clean and elegant looking. Words should be correctly spelt. The prices should be up-to-date. A card with old prices crossed out looks untidy.

(iii) A medium-sized menu card is preferable to a too large or small one.

(iv) A menu card should have an attractive layout; one of topical interest is a good choice.

(v) There should be variety and contrast without confusing the customer.

SUGGESTED DISHES

Breakfast Menu			*Notes*
1st	Course: *Fruit*	a. Fresh grapefruit, melon, juices. b. Stewed compoté of figs, prunes, apples, mixed fruit. Baked apple.	
2nd	Course: *Cereals*	Cornflakes, grapenuts, shredded wheat, etc., and always—porridge. Sometimes add the words—Hot or cold milk or cream.	
3rd	Course: *Eggs*	Scrambled, fried, boiled, poached, omelettes; with bacon (streaky or back), tomatoes, mushrooms.	Where this is the main course, it will follow the fish.
4th	Course: *Fish*	Grilled mackerel, kippers, herrings, bloaters, fish cakes, haddock, kedgeree. Fried plaice, sole, whiting, meunière. Usually plain, sometimes with tartare sauce.	There are usually just single names.
5th	Course: *Meats, Hot*	Grilled bacon (back and streaky), ham, gammon, sausage, lamb's kidney, calves' liver, with sautéed or fried potatoes or potato fritters. Bubble and squeak, mushrooms, tomatoes.	
6th	Course: *Meats, cold*	Ham, tongue, pressed beef, rarely, poultry or butcher's meat; with plain or sautéed potatoes where not included above.	Salad may be served but not put on the menu.
7th	Course: *Preserves*	Marmalade, jam, honey.	

8th Course:	*Fresh Fruit*	Apples, pears, peaches, grapes, bananas, oranges, etc.
9th Course:	*Beverages*	Coffee, tea, drinking chocolate.
10th Course:	*Breads*	Rolls, crescents, toast, brioche, etc.

Generally speaking, a breakfast will consist of three courses:

Fruit or cereal.

Eggs, fish or meat with or without potatoes.

Preserves and toast, rolls, coffee.

Luncheon menus These do not follow as strict a pattern as those for dinners—they are generally smaller, with less courses, but more choice within each course. Whereas in dinners there are many dishes considered beneath a dinner standard, most dinner dishes can be served at lunch.

The emphasis at luncheon is placed on stews, grilled meats, cold buffet and steamed puddings, all of which are seldom or never used at a dinner.

1st Course:
- (a) *Cocktails:* Fruit or shellfish.
- (b) *Fruit:* Grapefruit, melon, fresh figs, and fruit juices.
- (c) *Shellfish*, etc.: Caviar, oysters, seagulls' eggs, snails, potted shrimps.
- (d) *Smoked Foods:* Salmon, trout, ham, salami and sausages.
- (e) *Hors d'oeuvre.*

2nd Course: *Soup:* clear, petite marmite, consommé base, veloute, creams, purées, bisques.

3rd Course: *Farinaceous:* macaroni, spaghetti, ravioli, gnocchis, etc.

4th Course: *Eggs:* All kinds excluding boiled eggs, but including omelettes.

5th Course: *Fish:* Steamed, poached deep or shallow but without complicated garnishes, grilled, meunière, fried, prime herrings, skate, etc., shellfish, hot mussels and scallops, cold lobster.

6th Course: *Entrées:* Stews (brown), blanquette, navarm fricassée, hot pot, pies, puddings, oxtail, goulash, boiled meats, braised meats, salt meats, veal scallops, veal cutlets, lamb cutlets and noisettes, pork cutlets, liver, calves' head, pig's feet, tripe, vienna steak, Hamburg steak, sausages (braised), minces, réchauffé dishes, braised game, hare, salamis of game, pilaws. All served with vegetables and potatoes.

OR

7th Course: *Roast:* Mostly butcher's meat, rarely poultry or game. With vegetables and potatoes.

OR

8th Course: *Grills:* All the grilled meats including chicken with garnishes. With a vegetable or grilled vegetables and fried potatoes.

OR

9th Course: *Cold buffet:* All the cold joints, poultry, game, pies, terrines, cold fish—salmon, lobster, trout, crab, etc., in aspic or with a salad and sometimes a boiled or mashed potato.

AND/OR

10th Course: A *vegetable dish:* hot or cold asparagus, globe artichokes, seakale.

OR

11th Course: *Soufflé:* Cheese, spinach, mushroom, etc.

12th Course: *Sweet:* Steamed pudding, pancakes (not as often as at dinner), milk puddings, fruit—stewed, baked, salad, flans, apple dumplings, pies, tart, fritters, trifle, jelly, egg custards, bavaroise, gâteaux savarin, babas,, charlottes, profiteroles. Various ices and coupes (not featured as much as at dinner), French pastries.

13th Course: *Cheeses:* All varieties with celery, radishes, biscuits and butter.

14th Course: *Dessert:* All fresh fruits.

15th Course: *Coffee.*

Tea menus In hotels, cooked meals are seldom provided at teatime, other than boiled or poached eggs, but in commercial (public) restaurants the emphasis is on "high teas"—and like canteens. they serve lighter snacks more on the lines of a snack bar.

Suggested tea dishes (high teas)

Sandwiches Very small, dainty, white and brown bread, well buttered. Eggs and cress; tomato, lettuce, cucumber; chutney, savoury paste filling, sometimes chicken; foie gras (not often), smoked salmon (not often).

Hotplate foods and buns Buttered buns, scones, teacakes, sally lunns, scotch pancakes.

Doughnuts, waffles, samosas, sausage rolls, pakoras, mutton patties.

Bread and butter White, wholemeal, currant, fancy and proprietary brands.

Preserves Jams, lemon curd, honey, etc. (not marmalade).

Toasted items Toast, teacakes, scones, crumpets, buns, etc. Cheese toast, farinaceous and savoury toasted items as in a snack bar.

Eggs Boiled, fried and omelette.
Pastries All varieties, afternoon tea pastries (small), gâteaux, etc.
Ices Plain ices: all varieties of sundaes.
Tea Indian, Ceylon, China, Russian and iced.

Dinner menus Here we come to the real art of menu compilation, with a choice of the most esteemed, rarest and exotic dishes. Balance must be perfect throughout the long complicated number of courses, and here too the language is of the highest classical order.

1st Course:
(a) *Cocktails:* Fruit, shellfish, but rarely juices.
(b) *Fruit:* Melon (cantaloupe), fresh figs, rarely grapefruit halves.
(c) *Shellfish*, etc.: Caviar, oysters, seagulls' eggs, prawns, snails, frogs, tunny fish, sardines, potted shrimps.
(d) *Smoked food:* Salmon, eel, cod roe, ham, sprats, trout, salami, breast of goose, foie gras, sausages.
(e) *Hors d'oeuvre:* Usually served hot (chauds)—often in a special way called 'zakouski'.

2nd Course: *Soup:* Consommé and consommé base, veloutés creams, bisques, bortsch.

3rd Course: *Fish:* Deep poached salmon, blue trout. Shallow poached with all the garnishes. Prime fish. Hot shellfish, lobster, crab, crayfish, Dublin Bay prawns, scallops (never mussels).
Meunière with garnishes: Sole, trout, salmon. Fried: sole sometimes, or whitebait. No other fish.
Grilled (seldom): lobster, sole, salmon.
Cold fish: Salmon, trout, pomfret, sole, almost always in aspic.

4th Course: *Entrées:* These are lighter dishes—generally small and garnished. Vegetables are not served when a relevé follows the entrée. Examples: the sautés, tournedos noisette, cutlet of veal (not viennoise), vol au vent, sauté of chicken, fried chicken, hot mousse.

5th Course: *Relevés with Vegetable and Potatoes:* These are usually larger than entrées, larger joints which have to be carved, butcher's meat which never appears as roast on a dinner menu is here poled and usually accompanied with a sauce. Examples: Chicken pole, casserole en cocotte, poled saddle, whole fillet of beef, boned sirloin, braised ham, tongue, duck.

6th Course: *Sorbet:* Here in a long menu the diners stop, as it were, to get their second wind, and to refresh their appetite. Serve a sorbet, which is a light sherbet ice, flavoured with champagne or a liqueur.
Sometimes cigarettes are handed round and the first speech is made; they then pass on to the next part of the dinner.

7th Course: *Roast:* Roast game and poultry but never butcher's meat, served with salad—generally a compound salad, or when plain, something exotic like Belgian endives, rose petals, etc. It is served in a bowl.

8th Course: *Cold dish:* Foie gras, cold mousses, timbales, terrines and the like.

9th Course: *Vegetable dish:* Asparagus, globe artichokes, seakale, truffles, vegetable marrow, sometimes a soufflé, very delicate, like asparagus.

10th Course: *Sweet, hot and cold:* Soufflés, pancakes, fritters. Iced soufflés, baked ice cream, bombes, biscuits, coupe (melbas and the like) always accompanied by petit fours.

11th Course: *Savouries:* All types (these may sometimes be served before the sweet, as in Europe). Savoury soufflés.

12th Course: *Cheeses:* All types with celery, radishes, biscuits, and butter.

13th Course: *Dessert:* All the fresh fruits and nuts.

14th Course: *Coffee.*

Supper menus Have less variations than for either Lunch or Dinner, fewer in number and the dishes are lighter, except at Supper Balls.

1st Course: (a) *Cocktails:* Shellfish, caviar, lapwings' eggs, prawns, snails.

(b) *Smoked Foods:* Smoked salmon, trout, ham.

(c) *Soup:* Consommé and consommé base soups and particularly soups a l'oignon and green turtle soup.

2nd Course: (a) *Fish:* Fried, grilled, (seldom poached), haddock, kippers, Cold fish—Salmon, trout, lobster.

(b) *Entrées:* The sautés, tournedos noisette, cutlets, veal sweetbreads, vol au vent, liver and sometimes small birds braised and poêled.

(c) *Roasts:* Very seldom.

(d) *Grills:* Particularly the grills for supper.

with vegetables: Most kinds can be served, but as most of the supper dishes are fish, well garnished entrées or grills, vegetables will not often be necessary.

and potatoes: Most varieties are served with emphasis on the fried ones which fit in with the grills and most entrées.

or cold dishes: Cold meats, poultry, foie gras, mousse, timbales, terrines, etc. with salad: most varieties.

3rd Course: (a) *Sweets:* Hot soufflés, pancakes, fritters, etc. Cold iced soufflé bombes, biscuits, glacé coupes, accompanied by petit fours.
(b) *Savoury:* Most kinds are served.
(c) *Cheese:* Most varieties.
(d) *Dessert:* All the fresh fruits and nuts.
(e) *Coffee:* Always.

Banquet menus: (lunch) The usual lunch dishes are used (bearing in mind the suitability of service and keeping the dishes hot). It is not usual to include farinaceous dishes or eggs. Stews are avoided and savouries rarely served, but much may be made of cheese and biscuits. The menu again is shorter than its dinner equivalent and the service as a rule is fast and takes the following form.

1st Course: (a) *Cocktails:* Fruit, shellfish, smoked fish.
(b) *Hors d'oeuvre*, or
(c) *Soups.*

2nd Course: *Fish:* (see list under lunch menus).

3rd Course: *Entrée:* (excluding stews and rechauffé dishes) but including dinner entrées, roast joints, grills or cold meats. With vegetables and potatoes or salads and potatoes.

4th Course: *Vegetable dish:* Asparagus if in season.

5th Course: (a) *Sweets:* With emphasis on the hot variety including bombes, biscuit glacé as at dinner.
(b) *Cheeses:* Most varieties with biscuits and celery or radishes.
(c) *Dessert:* Rarely.
(d) *Coffee:* Always.

Banquet menus (dinner) Here is the chance to excel in the choice of the menu and the full menu as set forth for normal Dinner may be followed.

Light buffets Light buffets may be required for all kinds of catering—to augment a long function (dance) some hours after the main meal, for tea dances, supper dances and the like. The light buffet can be of two sorts, an inclusive "help yourself" running buffet—where the food is displayed for everyone to choose—or an à la carte buffet which is served by waiters and not usually displayed. The à la carte will follow the same lines as a displayed buffet but may include less of the smaller items and more of those prepared to order in the kitchen. The general arrangements will be a boxed-in line of tables, where guests can walk around with enough space inside for the servers. The à la carte buffet will include a menu card (priced) and waiter service. The menu should consist of items easily eaten with the fingers, though forks and serviettes will be provided. In connection with this kind of work one often hears of a "Fork Luncheon" or "Fork Buffet" and the idea behind this means that guests will probably be standing (that is, tables will not be provided nor chairs) and food will be any items easily eaten with a single implement (fork or spoon) while the guest is standing with the plate in one hand and the fork in the other. Most of the following light buffet items will be suitable for " Fork" parties even with the addition of anything soft like chicken mousse, galantine, terrines, chicken and other salads, etc.

Light buffet menu

Savoury Finger Foods To include any of the cold canapés—chipolata sausages on sticks; wrapped in bacon; prune sticks; celery branches piped with cheese spread; game chips, or gaufrette, very dry and seasoned; patties of chicken, lobster, crab, salmon; sausage rolls and any other puff pastry savoury snack; sandwiches: cut very small, brown or white bread —smoked salmon, egg and cress, tomato, ham, tongue, chicken, etc.

Sweets Charlotte Russe, jellies, trifles, bavaroise, etc. fruit salads or fresh raw fruits like strawberries. Ice creams, various flavours, but not as a rule coupes. Pastries, gateaux, biscuits

Beverages Coffee, tea, punch, iced coffee.

Supper buffets Generally speaking, a Supper Ball will begin late and a full buffet will be available. This is not served course by course, but will be rightly divided by lines or spaces in the printed menu denoting the different types of food as follows:

Shellfish Oysters, prawns.

Smoked fish and meat Smoked salmon, ham, trout, eels, etc.

Canapes Savoury finger toasts, with various spreads.

Savouries Chicken, lobster, crab, salmon patties, game chips, chipolata, celery sticks, cheese straws.

Fish Cold salmon, lobster, crab, fillets of sole, pomfret in aspic.

*Meats:*Chicken suprêmes, mayonnaise and salads; turkey roast—cold; ham—cold, decorated and jellied; mousse and cornets; cutlets in aspic; galantine, foie gras in aspic.

Salads Lettuce, Russian and all kinds. Mixed and plain.

Sandwiches Ham, tongue, chicken, turkey, smoked salmon, etc.

Bread Rolls Plain, egg and cress, etc., milk rolls.

Cold Sweets Charlottes, jelly trifle, bavaroise, cream, caramel, condes, flans. French pastries, various gteaux.

Ices Various bombes, biscuits, glacés with fruit and petit fours.

Beverages Coffee, tea, punch, iced coffee and tea.

Soups Sometimes hot turtle soup or a cold consommé (madrilene) will also be served at the commencement of the buffet, or it may be served at the end of the ball in which case it will be printed "en partant".

All the dishes will be very well decorated, making a great display, and quite often the ball will finish up with a breakfast dish such as eggs and bacon, kippers, etc., or as mentioned before, a bowl of soup such as: hot double consommé (clarified twice) or turtle soup, or very often soupe à l'oignon.

Outdoor catering Great care must be taken in selecting the menu, keeping in mind the facilities available on the spot, and what must be taken to augment them. The secret of outdoor catering is proper equipment, properly equipped vans, trained staff, and a knowledge of weather conditions and the number likely to be fed. Among the equipment will be shamianas, marquees, trestle tables, chairs, containers, calor gas equipment, trays, wash-up facilities, guarded arrangements (where necessary) for the payment of money, as well as the usual equipment.

Weddings Wedding parties follow either the ordinary sit-down meal pattern, or, more often than not, have a running buffet. The wedding cake will always be the centrepiece, and more floral displays will be arranged than usual. The flowers of the bride and bridesmaids may be laid alongside the cake. A silver salver will be ready to receive the telegrams. Particular care will be taken with the seating plan in conjunction with the parties. For the reception, sherries may be served (or cocktails) while the guests are congratulating the married couple, or sometimes after the nuptial service (which the guests may have attended) a cup of tea and biscuits may be served.

1st Course: Cocktails, smoked salmon, fruit, hors d'oeuvre or a good soup.
2nd Course: Cold salmon, roast poultry, grilled butcher's meat, cold suprme of chicken, aspics, etc., with vegetables and potatoes or salad and potatoes.
3rd Course: A very good sweet course; fruit sundaes, coupes, biscuits, bombes, with most likely an alternative of the cold sweets, flans, trifles, etc., served with fruit, and sometimes with petit fours or a course of French pastries.
4th Course: Coffee.

The cake is then cut and handed round, and the bride and groom are toasted with champagne. Then follow the reading of the telegrams and the speeches.

In buffet wedding receptions several dishes will be chosen from the Supper Ball menu—leaving out the hot soup, with fewer savouries and sandwiches, but a full range of cold meats—or a light buffet may be chosen as sufficient to meet the need, and tea will be served instead of coffee.

Cocktail parties Apart from the actual drinks which are the main item for a cocktail party, very tiny snacks (savoury), cigarettes and a well equipped bar are the other necessities. The food will be dressed attractively, but will also be handed round with the cocktails by the waiters.

The menu (never printed or shown) can be all kinds of savoury finger toasts, cocktail olives, stuffed olives, gherkins, walnuts, pickled onions, etc., very crisp, salted game chips, salted almonds, chipolata sausages, bacon rolls, prune and bacon rolls, cherry and bacon rolls, all on sticks. Stuffed sticks of celery, cheese fritters, cheese straws, very tiny savoury filled sandwiches. The fillings used for the canapés are caviar, smoked salmon, smoked ham, cooked ham, anchovies, sardines, shrimps, freshly made savoury purées for spreading, sliced egg, cheese, etc. Some of them will be spread on crisp toast, and others on thin, crisp flaky pastry or biscuits. All will be well decorated and then jellied with aspic.

Hospital catering This is better organised now than it was a few years ago—diets are in the charge of a dietitian, and catering is supervised by a catering officer. Their three main functions are to feed the staff, patients, and visitors. Staff will be provided with good canteen food or, as is most often the case, with the ordinary hospital diet, and the canteen will stock light refreshments. The food leaves the main kitchen in electric hotplate trolleys, and is sent to each ward which has an anteroom with an adjoining 'mise-en-place' of small equipment for making tea, bread and butter, light items like toast, etc., and salads. Each ward sends an order daily for the three meals with requests for full, light, fluid or special diets. The tea meal is usually prepared in this service room.

The three meals ordered from the kitchen will be breakfast, lunch, and either supper or dinner.

Normal diets, or full diets Will be well balanced normal meals of protein, carbohydrates (but with very little fatty food), vitamins, mineral salts, with emphasis on salads, fresh fruits, few spices and never shellfish or réchauffé dishes.

Breakfast: Fresh fruit juices, grapefruit, fresh fruit, cereals and porridge.
Fish: Haddock, kippers, herrings, fish cakes.
Eggs: All kinds.
Meats: Bacon, sausage, rarely other meats.
Vegetables: Confined to tomatoes, rarely potatoes.
Preserves, toast and beverages as usual.

Lunch: Fresh fruit juices, fresh fruit.
Soups: particularly consommé and broths.
Fish: Deep-poached, or steamed with simple sauces, sometimes grilled and fried.

Entrées: Stews, boiled chicken and meats, pies and hot pots, liver, heart, or roast joints.
Vegetables: Fresh and seasonable variety.
Potatoes: All kinds except the fatty ones.
Cold meats with fresh salads.
Sweets: Milk puddings, sponge puddings, blancmange, jellies, stewed fruit, tarts, ices.
Cheese: Sometimes.

Tea: Will follow a very light pattern.
Supper or dinner will follow the same pattern as for lunch but will be lighter in substance often with a farinaceous dish, cheese, egg, stuffed marrow, soup, salad, soused herring, cauliflower, sausage rolls, or the like instead of the main meat course.

Light diets Selected light dishes will be chosen from the ordinary menu and supplemented with plenty of egg dishes, broths, jellies, junket and fruit such as those shown under "Invalid Cookery".

Invalid cookery Dishes should be made to look very tempting, dainty, colourful and inviting to a poor appetite.

Breakfast: Milk, cereals, flaked haddock, steamed fish, eggs, herring roe.
Other meals:
Soups: Consommé and all the broths (sometimes strained).
Eggs: Lightly boiled, scrambled, poached and omelettes.
Fish: Steamed and boiled white fish, pie, and purées.
Meats: Boiled chicken, turkey, lamb, sweetbreads thinly sliced, minced chicken, turkey, lamb, beef, liver, steamed lamb cutlets.
Cheese dishes: Custards, semolina, welsh rarebit.
Vegetables: Boiled fresh vegetables, usually puréed, never fried, sautéed or braised.
Salads and potatoes, usually puréed, never fried or sautéed.
Cold meats: Ham, tongue, thinly sliced.
Sweets: All kinds of trifles, jellies, milk jellies, junket, egg custards, purées of fruit, baked fruit, fools, ices.

Liquid diets Milk, soda water, fresh fruit juices, consommé, beef tea, broths and glucose water.

Special diets Special diets will be the job of a certified dietitian or the doctor and should never be selected by the caterer. Special breads, sugar, jams, starches, etc., will be supplied for diabetics.

Particular care should be exercised in buying for invalids or hospitals. Only the freshest of vegetables, finest of fish and meat, newly laid eggs, pasteurized milk, etc., should be used in the kitchen.

School meals Here, proper knowledge and practice of well balanced meals is expected—body-building, nourishing, sustaining and full of vitamin content. The practice of central kitchens is gradually being superseded by kitchens on the spot. Insulated containers from central kitchens were never successful as the food never looked, smelled or tasted appetising. Great stress is laid upon "per head" quantities and "per head" costing. Diet sheets are made out in advance by school meals supervisors. Well balanced meals cooked to retain as much nourishment and flavour as possible should be stressed.

Snack bar and milk bar Three prime requisites—either a bar with stools or tables and chairs; tea and coffee-making machines and a soda bar space for the dispensing of ice-cream and soft drinks; as well as small equipment and other devices necessary for speedy service. The menu will contain light snacks: hot soups, beans, spaghetti, etc., on toast, salads and meat salads, sandwiches and filled rolls, cakes, buns and pastries. Great emphasis is given to ice-cream sundaes and soft drinks as well as tea and coffee and all kinds of milk shakes, Bovril, Horlicks, and in fact all those items called "counter lines".

Seasonal variations in diet

Planning, preparation and service of meals, be it for the family or for institutional feeding, should be based on certain fundamental principles such as nutritional requirements, money to be spent, palatability, seasonability and availability, variety and appearance of material, under which will come variety in colour, flavour, etc.

One of the most important aspects of meal planning is 'seasonal variations in diet'. While quite a number of the other principles of meal planning are based on this, very little thought and attention are given to this aspect.

Seasonal variation in diet has two interesting divisions:

1. Seasonability and availability of raw material.
2. Variations in the type of dishes depending on climatic changes.

Food should be eaten as far as possible when it is at its best. When any food is in season it is at its best nutritionally, aesthetically and from the palatability point of view, apart from the fact that it can be fitted in more easily into the budget. In other words, 'value for money' should be the aim of every caterer. Remember, however, that it is poor economy to buy goods of inferior quality because they appear to be cheap. There is a difference between buying cheap and inferior foods and buying good quality food at cheaper rates because it is in season. Among the tools that a food service manager should have to help him plan meals wisely should be a systematically arranged chart showing the seasonability of fruits, vegetables, meat and fish. In Mumbai we could organize this chart in two ways. One way is to have 3 sections:

(a) Monsoon June to October (b) Winter November to March (c) Summer March to June

Under each column you could start with vegetables, then fruit (with peak periods in brackets) and finally fish, meat and eggs.

MONSOON	WINTER	SUMMER
June–Oct.	Nov.–March	April–May
Vegetables:	*Vegetables:*	*Vegetables:*
Green leafy vegetables	Beetroot	Cabbage
Brinjal	Carrot	Chowli beans
Ridge grourd	Cauliflower	Round gourd
Snake gourd	Capsicum	Gherkin
Corn	Celery	Spinach
Radish	French beans	Yam
Ladies fingers or okra	Tomatoes	Snake gourd
Sweet potatoes	Peas	Ash gourd
Double beans	Parsley	Drumstick
Sword beans	Salad leaves	Garlic
Colocasia	Turnips	Onions
Ginger	Kohlrabi	Vegetable marrow
Green chillies	Leek	Cucumber
	Lime	Colocasia
		New radish
		Potatoes
		Bottle gourd
Fruits:	*Fruits:*	*Fruits:*
Sweet limes (Oct.)	Mandarin orange	Melon
Bananas	Sweet lime	Mango
Limes	(Feb.–March)	Pomello
Jammu plums	Grapefruit	Strawberry
Jammu apricot	Apple	Figs
Jammu peach	Pear	Grapefruit
Mango	Nasik grapes (Feb.–May)	Lime
Chikkoo	Pomegranate	Jammu Plum
Pineapple	Custard apple	Banana
Apple (Sept.–Oct.)	Loquat (Feb.–March)	Chikkoo
Mandarin orange	Wood apple	Surat guava
		Jackfruit
		Palmyra kernel
		Tender coconut

Fish is available from immediately after the monsoon, about the middle of September, to June. It is fresher and tastier in the winter months. Fresh Bombay Duck, like the Alphonso mango is a seasonal must, and is available from July to August and October to January.

The price of meat generally varies little with the season. Pork however, is cheaper from September to April, perhaps because it is susceptible to deterioration at higher temperature. Being a meat which has plenty of fat it is best avoided during the summer months. Eggs keep better during the winter months and hence are cheaper as well.

Another form of dividing foods could be to classify them item-wise, giving the source of supply, season and peak period. For example, mangoes from the Konkan area are available from March to the first week in June, with a peak period of April and May, and the ones from Gujarat are available from May to June.

Where feasible market trends must be studied thoroughly to know what is available, and to keep in touch with current prices. Experience has the greatest value but the inexperienced can learn by studying the market quotations published weekly in the papers and by actually studying the market.

Equally important is the second aspect—variations in the type of dishes depending on climatic changes. During the summer months appetites are on the decline and morale rather low. Greater care and attention has to be given to planning of meals to whet the appetite, to provide an interest in food and to maintain general health. Food in summer should be light, attractive, easy to prepare, and freshly prepared. Plenty of liquids and fruits should be included. Avoid spicy and greasy foods. Lime juice, either freshly prepared or prepared and stored in the refrigerator for not more than a week, to retain vitamin C is a must. Melon cocktails (scoop out centres, remove seeds, mix with sugar and lime juice), buttermilk flavoured lightly with green chillies (without seeds) and onions with salt added, mango fool (cook mature but unripe mangoes with sugar, mash and mix with custard, chill and serve) are all welcome changes during summer. Ice-cream and water ices or ice-fruits are great favourites with children. Scoops of ice-cream could be mixed with lemonade to make a tall fizzy drink for the grown-ups. Cold coffee and iced lemon tea could be an interesting change. Salads, particularly cucumber and cabbage, as both these vegetables are in season could be included in the menu. A French dressing or a dressing of lime juice, olive oil and salt will be preferable to rich mayonnaise or other salad dressing. A word of caution—cabbage should be shredded very fine when eaten raw, so that it does not cause indigestion and flatulence. Varieties of cold meats and salads, or cold fish with a tartare or mayonnaise sauce and salad, could make pleasant luncheon menus for those who like western preparations. Rich pilaus and biryanis, fried rice, etc., should be given a miss. A change from boiled rice could be had by having curd bhath, lime rice, etc. Cuchumbers, salads and raitas must be included.

During the monsoon, hot snacks and savouries can be introduced. Corn on the cob is another seasonal vegetable that could be introduced either roasted over a charcoal brazier (sigree) or boiled and buttered. Most of the so-called Indian vegetables are available during the rains. Some of the traditional Indian dishes such as spicy brinjal bhath, kadambom, masala stuffed ladies fingers, masala bhara mirchee, etc., could be included to provide variety.

With the abundance of fruits and vegetables available in the winter months there are plenty of opportunities to indulge in creative and interesting culinary preparations. There is no reason why this should mean expensive foods. It is more an opportunity of providing variety in colour, texture and flavour. Fish is at its best during this season. This is also the time when rich foods like biryanis and moghlai dishes are popular. See that foods that provide the essential vitamins and minerals are included to keep off the common cold and cough.

To sum up, seasonal variations in diet have two aspects. Knowing what is available in the market so that you can get the best for your money and introducing dishes that suit climatic conditions. Wise and intelligent planning and an interest in food are requisites.

23 / LOW-CALORIE DIETS

Very few people are overweight because of bodily disturbances. Most people are fat because they are sedentary in their occupation but eat as if they are vigorously active. Food, always a symbol of hospitality and good fellowship, is becoming more and more important. Alone or with others, most people love food. It reduces boredom and in times of stress and strain it acts as a palliative. When unhappiness is prolonged people can develop habits of over-eating that last a lifetime.

No one weight is right for all people of the same height, sex and age. Ideal weight depends in large measure on bone structure. Some people are short and stocky while others are tall and slender. Some have large bones and some have small bones. The following chart gives the desirable weights for men and women over 25. Weights are given according to frame, as normally dressed.

After checking the weight scale it is desirable to plan the daily calorie allowance. Science has found that moderately active adults require about 33 calories for each kg. (15 calories for each pound) of body weight, or less if they are not so active. For manual labour, allow 44 calories for each kg. (20 calories for each pound) of ideal weight. For safe weight reduction, many doctors limit weight loss to a maximum of 1 kg or

2.2 pounds a week. A man who normally eats about 2500 calories worth of food daily can cut 1000 calories from his diet and still get all the proteins, vitamins and minerals he needs. A woman who normally eats only 2000 calories worth of food can spare only 500 to 700 calories each day, which means a somewhat slower weight loss. Reducing however, should be done gradually, working from a 2000-calorie diet to a 1000-calorie diet, and should stop at a point when the person is able to perform his usual work without feeling any weakness or general debility. The following points must be kept in mind:

1. Less food, but not so very much less as to affect health.
2. Avoid too much variety and spices.
3. Avoid sugar and sweets.
4. Use less fat and avoid rich meals.
5. Milk should be taken in moderation.
6. No puddings and pastries.
7. Use plenty of green vegetables but a reduced quantity of rice and chapatties. Avoid root vegetables.

MEN

HEIGHT			WEIGHT					
with shoes on			*small frame*		*medium frame*		*large frame*	
Metres	*Feet*	*Ins.*	*Kg.**	*Lb.*	*Kg.**	*Lb.*	*Kg.**	*Lb.*
1.57	5	2	52.6–56.7	116–125	56.2–60.3	124–133	59.4–64.4	131–142
1.60	5	3	54.0–58.1	119–128	57.6–61.7	127–136	60.3–65.3	133–144
1.63	5	4	55.3–59.9	122–132	59.0–63.5	130–140	62.2–67.6	137–149
1.65	5	5	57.2–61.7	126–136	60.8–65.3	134–144	64.0–69.4	141–153
1.68	5	6	58.5–63.1	129–139	62.2–66.7	137–147	65.8–71.2	145–157
1.70	5	7	60.3–64.9	133–143	64.0–68.5	141–151	67.6–73.5	149–162
1.73	5	8	61.7–66.7	136–147	65.8–70.7	145–156	69.4–75.3	153–166
1.75	5	9	63.5–68.5	140–151	67.6–72.6	149–160	71.2–77.1	157–170
1.78	5	10	65.3–70.3	144–155	69.4–74.4	153–164	73.0–79.4	161–175
1.80	5	11	67.1–72.1	148–159	71.2–76.2	157–168	74.9–81.7	165–180
1.83	6	0	69.0–74.4	152–164	73.0–78.5	161–173	76.7–83.9	169–185
1.85	6	1	71.2–76.7	157–169	75.3–80.7	166–178	78.9–86.2	174–190
1.88	6	2	73.9–79.4	163–175	77.6–83.5	171–184	81.2–88.9	179–196
1.90	6	3	76.2–81.7	168–180	79.8–85.7	176–189	83.5–91.6	184–202

*Calculated to the nearest 100 gm.

WOMEN

HEIGHT			*WEIGHT*					
with shoes on			*small frame*		*medium frame*		*large frame*	
Metres	*Feet*	*Ins.*	*Kg.**	*Lb.*	*Kg.**	*Lb.*	*Kg.**	*Lb.*
1.49	4	11	47.2–50.4	104–111	49.9–53.5	110–118	53.1–57.6	117–127
1.52	5	0	47.6–51.3	105–113	50.8–54.4	112–120	54.0–58.5	119–129
1.55	5	1	48.5–52.2	107–115	51.7–55.3	114–122	54.9–59.4	121–131
1.57	5	2	49.9–53.5	110–118	53.1–56.7	117–125	56.2–61.2	124–135
1.60	5	3	51.3–54.9	113–121	54.4–58.1	120–128	57.6–62.6	127–138
1.63	5	4	52.6–56.7	116–125	56.2–59.9	124–132	59.4–64.4	131–142
1.65	5	5	54.0–58.1	119–128	57.6–61.2	127–135	60.3–65.8	133–145
1.68	5	6	55.8–59.9	123–132	59.0–63.5	130–140	62.6–68.0	138–150
1.70	5	7	57.2–61.7	126–136	60.8–65.3	134–144	64.4–69.9	142–154
1.73	5	8	58.5–63.1	129–139	62.2–66.7	137–147	65.8–71.7	145–158
1.75	5	9	60.3–64.9	133–143	64.0–68.5	141–151	67.6–73.5	149–162
1.78	5	10	61.7–66.7	136–147	65.8–71.7	145–155	69.0–76.7	152–166
1.80	5	11	63.1–68.0	139–150	67.1–71.7	148–158	70.3–76.7	155–169

*Calculated to the nearest 100 gm.

2000-CALORIE DIET (Non-Vegetarian)

Breakfast:

Bread	60 gm (2 oz) 2 thin slices
Egg	1
Milk	235 ml (8 oz)

Coffee or tea as desired, without sugar

Mid-morning:

Milk	175 ml (6 oz)

Noon:

Rice	85 gm (3 oz) (225 gm or 9 oz cooked weight)
Dal	30 gm (1 oz) (85 gm or 3 oz cooked weight)
Mutton	85 gm (3 oz)
Curds	85 gm (3 oz)
Vegetables (not root)	1 helping
Greens	1 helping

At 4 p.m.:

Milk	235 ml (8 oz)

Coffee or tea as desired, without sugar.

Fruit (citrus)	1 portion

Dinner:

Rice	60 gm (2 oz) (170 gm or 6 oz cooked weight)
Dal	30 gm (1 oz) (85 gm or 3 oz cooked weight)
Mutton	60 gm (2 oz)
Vegetables (not root)	1 helping
Greens	1 helping
Milk	235 ml (8 oz)
Daily allowance of oil in cooking	15 gm or ½ oz

Summary of Diet:

Carbohydrates	249 gm
Proteins	91 gm
Fat	70 gm
Calories	1996

N.B.: Skimmed milk or toned milk may be used instead of whole milk, and corresponding portions of butter could be used.

2000-CALORIE DIET (Vegetarian)

Breakfast:

Bread	60 gm (2 oz) 2 thin slices)
Milk	235 ml (8 oz)
Coffee or tea as desired, without sugar	
Banana	1

Mid-morning:

Milk	175 ml (6 oz)

Lunch:

Rice	85 gm (3 oz) (225 gm or 9 oz cooked weight)
Dal	45 gm (1½ oz) (130 gm or 4½ oz cooked weight)
Curd	85 gm
Vegetable (not root)	1 helping
Greens	1 helping

At 4 p.m.:

Milk	235 ml (8 ozs.)
Banana	1
Coffee or tea as desired, without sugar.	

Dinner:

Chapatties	60 gms. wholewheat flour (2 oz) (3 phulkas weighing 20 gms each, 12.5 cm. (5") in diameter)
Dal	45 gm (1½ oz) (130 gm or 4½ oz cooked weight)
Greens	1 helping
Vegetables	1 helping
Milk	235 ml (8 oz)
Daily allowance of butter or oil for cooking	30 gm

Summary of Diet:

Carbohydrates	291 gm
Protein	72 gm
Fat	62 gm
Calories	2013

2000-CALORIE DIET (European Non-Vegetarian)

Breakfast:

Porridge (oatmeal, semolina or dalya)	15 gm (½ oz)
Milk	175 ml (6 oz)

Egg	1
Bread	60 gm (2 thin slices)
Banana	1
Mid-morning:	
Meat extract or un-sweetened lime juice	1 cup
Lunch:	
Clear soup	150 ml (5 oz)
Mutton	85 gm (3 oz)
Potatoes	115 gm (4 oz)
Salad vegetables or greens	1 helping
Milk	150 ml
Fruit	1 portion
At 4 p.m.:	
Bread	60 gm (2 thin slices)
Butter	15 gm (½ oz)
Egg	1
or Cheese	10 gm (⅓ oz)
Milk	120 ml (4 oz)
Coffee or tea as desired, without sugar.	
Dinner:	
Clear soup or strained vegetable soup	150 ml (5 oz)
Mutton	85 gm (3 oz)
Potatoes	115 gm (4 oz)
Greens or salad	1 helping
Milk	150 ml (5 oz)
Fruit	1 portion
Bedtime:	
Milk	235 ml (8 oz)
Summary of Diet:	
Carbohydrates	216 gm
Protein	87 gm
Fat	83 gm
Calories	1954

1500-CALORIE DIET (Non-Vegetarian)

Breakfast:	
Bread	60 gm (2 thin slices)
Egg	1
Milk	170 ml (6 oz)

Coffee or tea as desired, without sugar.	
Fruit	1 portion
Mid-morning:	
Unsweetened lime juice or butter milk	150 ml (5 oz)
Lunch:	
Rice	85 gm (3 oz) (255 gm or 9 oz cooked weight)
Mutton	85 gm (3 oz)
Curd	85 gm (3 oz)
Vegetable (not root)	1 helping
Greens or salad	1 helping
At 4 p.m.:	
Milk	120 ml (4 oz)
Coffee or tea as desired, without sugar.	
Fruit	1 portion
Dinner:	
Chapaties	60 gm wholewheat flour (2 oz) (3 phulkas weighing 20 gm each. 12.5 cm. (5") diameter)
Mutton	60 gm (2 oz)
Dal	30 gm (1 oz) (85 gm or 3 oz when cooked)
Vegetables (not root)	1 helping
Greens	1 helping
Daily allowance of fat in cooking	7 to 10 gms. or ¼ oz
Summary of Diet:	
Carbohydrates	215 gm
Protein	66.5 gm
Fat	43 gm
Calories	1513

1500-CALORIE DIET (Vegetarian)

Breakfast:	
Idli or	1 (with a little chutney)
Bread	60 gm (2 thin slices)
Milk	235 ml (8 oz)
Citrus fruit	1 portion
Mid-morning:	
Unsweetened lime juice or buttermilk	150 ml (5 oz)

Lunch:

Rice	85 gm (3 oz) (255 gm or 9 oz cooked weight)
Dal	45 gm (1½ oz) (130 gm or 1½ oz cooked weight)
Curd	85 gm
Vegetables (not root)	1 helping
Greens	1 helping

At 4 p.m.:

Milk	235 ml (8 oz)

Coffee or tea as desired, without sugar.

Fruit	1 portion

Dinner:

Chapaties	60 gm wholewheat flour (2 oz) (3 phulkas weighting 20 gm each 12.5 cm. (5") in diameter).
Dal	45 gm (1½ oz)
Curd	85 gm (3 oz)
Vegetables (not root)	1 helping
Greens	1 helping
Daily allowance of fat	10 gm (⅓ oz)

If desired skimmed milk can be taken, and the extra fat used for cooking purposes.

Summary of Diet:

Carbohydrates	259 gm
Protein	60 gm
Fat	27.5 gm
Calories	1528

1500-CALORIE DIET (European Non-Vegetarian)

Breakfast:

Porridge (oatmeal, semolina or dalya)	15 gm (½ oz)
Milk	150 ml (5 oz)
Toast	60 gm (2 oz) (2 thin slices)
Butter	15 gm (½ oz)
Egg	1

Mid-morning:

Meat extract or 1 cup unsweetened lime juice.

Lunch:

Clear soup or strained vegetable soup	150 ml (5 oz)
Mutton	85 gm (3 oz)

Potatoes	60 gm (2 oz) (1 medium sized)
Vegetables (not root)	1 helping
Salad	1 helping
Fruit	1 helping

At 4 p.m.:

Bread	3 thin slices
Butter	15 gm (½ oz)
Tomato or lettuce	
Milk	150 ml (5 oz)

Coffee or tea as desired, without sugar.

Dinner:

Clear soup or strained vegetable soup	150 ml (5 oz)
Mutton	85 gm (3 oz)
Potatoes	60 gm (2 oz)
Vegetables (not root)	1 helping
Greens	1 helping
Fruits	1 portion

Summary of Diet:

Carbohydrates	168 gm
Protein	64.5 gm
Fat	61 gm
Calories	1483

1200-CALORIE DIET (Non-Vegetarian)

Breakfast:

Bread	60 gm (2 oz) (2 thin slices)
Egg	1
Milk	170 ml (6 oz)

Coffee or tea as desired, without sugar.

Mid-morning:

Unsweetened lime juice	1 cup

Lunch:

Rice	60 gm (2 oz) (180 gm or 6 oz cooked weight)
Mutton	60 gm (2 oz)
Curd	85 gm (3 oz)
Vegetables (not root)	1 helping
Greens	1 helping

At 4 p.m.:

Milk	120 ml (4 oz)

Coffee or tea as desired, without sugar.

Fruit	1 portion

Dinner:

Mutton	60 gm (2 oz)
Vegetables	1 helping
Greens	1 helping
Chapaties	60 gm (2 oz) wholewheat flour (3 phulkas of 20 gm each 12.5 cm. (5") in diameter)
Daily allowance of fat in cooking	10 gm (⅓ oz)

Summary of Diet:

Carbohydrates	166 gm
Protein	52.5 gm
Fat	39 gm
Calories	1222

1200-CALORIE DIET (Vegetarian)

Breakfast:

Bread	60 gm (2 oz) (2 thin slices)
Milk	170 ml (6 oz)

Coffee or tea as desired, without sugar.

Mid-morning:

Milk	170 ml (6 oz)

Lunch:

Rice	60 gm (2 oz) (180 gm or 6 oz cooked weight)
Dal	30 gm (1 oz) (85 gm or 3 oz cooked weight)
Curd	85 gm (3 oz)
Vegetables	1 helping
Greens	1 helping

At 4 p.m.:

Milk	120 ml (4 oz)

Coffee or tea as desired, without sugar.

Dinner:

Chapaties	60 gm wholewheat flour (2 oz) (3 phulkas weighing 20 gms. each and 12.5 cm. (5") in diameter)
Dal	30 gm (85 gm or 3 oz cooked weight)
Vegetables	1 helping
Greens	1 helping
Daily allowance of fat in cooking	10 gm (⅓ oz)

Summary of Diet:

Carbohydrates	196 gm
Proteins	48 gm
Fats	25.5 gm
Calories	1211

1200-CALORIE DIET (European Non-Vegetarian)

Breakfast:

Bread	60 gm (2 oz) (2 thin slices)
Butter	7 gm (¼ oz)
Egg	1
Milk	90 ml (3 oz)
Coffee or tea as desired, without sugar.	
Fruit	1 portion

Mid-morning:

Meat extract or 1 cup unsweetened lime juice

Lunch:

Clear soup or strained vegetable broth	150 ml (5 oz)
Mutton	85 gm (3 oz)
Potatoes	60 gm (2 oz)
Vegetables	1 helping
Greens or salad	1 helping
Fruit	1 portion

At 4 p.m.:

Milk	60 gm (2 oz)
Coffee or tea as desired, without sugar.	
Bread	60 gm (2 oz)
Butter	7 gm (¼ oz)

Dinner:

Clear soup or strained broth	150 ml (5 oz)
Potatoes	60 gm (2 oz)
Vegetables (not root)	1 helping
Greens	1 helping
Milk	150 ml
Egg	1 custard without sugar

Summary of Diet:

Carbohydrates	134 gm
Proteins	60.5 gm
Fats	49.5 gm
Calories	1221

1000-CALORIE DIET (Non-Vegetarian)

Breakfast:

Bread	30 gm (1 oz) (1 slice)
Egg	1
Milk	170 ml (6 oz)

Coffee or tea as desired, without sugar.

Mid-morning:

Unsweetened lime juice	1 cup

Lunch:

Rice	45 gm (1½ oz) (130 gm or 4½ oz cooked weight)
Mutton	115 gm (4 oz)
Curd	85 gm (3 oz)
Vegetables	1 helping
Greens	1 helping

At 4 p.m.:

Milk	120 ml

Coffee or tea as desired, without sugar.

Dinner:

Rice	30 gm (1 oz) (90 gm or 3 oz cooked weight)
Egg	1
Vegetables	1 helping
Greens	1 helping
Daily allowance of fat in cooking	10 gm (⅓ oz)

Summary of Diet:

Carbohydrates	104 gm
Protein	51 gm
Fat	42.5 gm
Calories	1000

1000-CALORIE DIET (Vegetarian)

Breakfast:

Bread	30 gm (1 oz) (1 slice)
Fruit	1 portion
Milk	170 ml (6 oz)

Coffee or tea as desired, without sugar.

Mid-morning:

Milk	170 ml (6 oz)

Coffee or tea as desired, without sugar.

Lunch:

Rice	30 gm (1 oz) (90 gm or 3 oz cooked weight)
Dal	30 gm (1 oz) (90 gm or 3 oz cooked weight)
Vegetables	1 helping
Greens	1 helping

At 4 p.m.:

Milk	170 ml (6 oz)

Coffee or tea as desired, without sugar.

Dinner:

Rice or	30 gm (1 oz) (90 gm or 3 oz cooked weight)
Chapaties	30 gm wholewheat flour (1 oz)
Dal	30 gm (1 oz) (90 gm or 3 oz cooked weight)
Curds	85 gm (3 oz)
Greens	1 helping
Daily allowance of fat in cooking	10 gm (⅓ oz)

Summary of Diet:

Carbohydrates	152 gm
Proteins	47 gm
Fats	29.5 gm
Calories	1061

1000-CALORIE DIET (European Non-Vegetarian)

Breakfast:

Bread	60 gm (2 oz) (2 thin slices)
Butter	15 gm (½ oz)
Eggs	2
Milk	120 ml (4 oz)

Coffee or tea as desired, without sugar.

Mid-morning:

Meat extract or 1 cup of unsweetened lime juice.

Lunch:

Clear soup	150 ml (5 oz)
Mutton	85 gm (3 oz)
Vegetables (not root)	1 helping
Greens or Salad	1 helping
Fruit	1 portion

At 4 p.m.:

Milk	120 ml (4 oz)

Coffee or tea as desired, without sugar.

Dinner:

Clear soup	150 ml (5 oz)
Fried fish or	85 gm (3 oz)
Steamed fish	145 gm (5 oz)
Potatoes	60 gm (2 oz)
Vegetables	1 helping
Greens	1 helping
Fruit	1 portion
Milk	120 ml

Coffee or tea as desired, without sugar.

Summary of Diet:

Carbohydrates	95 gm
Protein	55 gm
Fat	51 gm
Calories	1054

ALTERNATIVES FOR USE WITH WEIGHED DIETS

One portion of fruit yielding 10 gm of carbohydrates:

Apple (medium-sized fruit)	85 gm (3 oz)
Banana (1 small or ½ big)	60 gm (2 oz)
Figs (fresh)	60 gm (2 oz)
Grapes	85 gm (3 oz)
Grapefruit	145 gm (5 oz)
Pomelo	145 gm (5 oz)
Guava	115 gm (4 oz)
Jackfruit	60 gm (2 oz)
Ripe mango (medium size)	85 gm (3 oz)
Yellow melon (½ fruit)	170 gm (6 oz)
Watermelon	285 gm (10 oz)
Orange or sweet lime (medium-sized fruit)	115 gm (4 oz)
Papaya	115 gm (4 oz)
Peaches	145 gm (5 oz)
Chikkoo	50 gm (2 oz)
Tree tomato	115 gm (4 oz)

Substitute 60 gm (2 oz) of bread with one of the following:

1 idli
1 appam
1 dosa
upuma

} prepared from 30 gm cereal and a little chutney.

Substitute 60 gm rice with:

Bread	85 gm
or	
Chapaties prepared from	60 gm wholewheat flour (3 phulkas of 20 gm each and 12.5 cm. (5") in diameter)

Substitute 85 gm (3 oz) mutton with:

liver	85 gm (3 oz) or
fried fish	85 gm (3 oz) or
steamed or boiled fish	145 gm (5 oz) or
fried brain	85 gm (3 oz) or
cheese	45 gm (1½ oz) or
chicken	85 gm (3 oz) or
boiled brain	145 gm (5 oz)

One portion of vegetables may be: green or leafy vegetables, carrot, onion, brinjal (egg plant), drumsticks, kohlrabi, tomato, vegetable marrow, gourds, pumpkins, cauliflower, ladies fingers, green beans. Avoid peas, beans and pulses, if not specially mentioned.

24 / STILL-ROOM AND PANTRY

The still-room or pantry is an all-purpose department and is open as long as service of food and beverages is required. Its chief function is the preparation of sundry foods and beverages. It is, therefore, necessary that all the staff who work in this department are properly trained. This is necessary on two counts, firstly to see that the food and beverages are skilfully prepared, and secondly to see that the portioning is done properly, as the rate of gross profit earned in this department should be higher than the other departments. The following are some of the foods and beverages required.

Breakfast All beverages, cereals, fruit juices, fruit, toast, butter, preserves, etc.

Mid-morning: Coffee, tea, snacks, etc.

Lunch: Beverages including minerals and squashes, toast melba, salads, etc.

Afternoon tea: Complete service.

Dinner: Beverages, sundries, finger bowls, etc.

From the above, it will be seen that it is essential to have a tight control system operating here, otherwise the gross profit will not be earned.

The setting is important in kitchen planning and dining room service. It is necessary to have the still-room adjacent to the dining-room and with easy access to the kitchen.

It is not advisable to make the still-room too small, as space must be made for the following equipment:

(i) A cafe set comprising counter-type equipment for coffee, tea and milk urns.
(ii) Hot water boiler.
(iii) Self-timing toaster.
(iv) Bread and butter machine if large tea trade is done.
(v) A tea-dispenser to ensure accurate measurement of portions, thus avoiding waste.
(vi) A butter-pat machine ensures quality of portions and aids costing.
(vii) A coffee percolator or Espresso machine according to the size of demand.
(viii) Glass-washing machine so that maximum hygiene can be practised.
(ix) Two-sink (stainless steel) system for washing crockery.
(x) Linen basket for dirty linen.
(xi) Storage cupboards.
(xii) Bain-marie and hot closet for the service of hot dishes, sauces, soups, etc.
(xiii) Some establishments prefer to grind coffee as it is required. For this a small grinder is necessary.

It will readily be seen that proper control of the still-room is vital to the successful operation of the food management of a hotel or catering establishment.

25 / BUFFET SERVICE

Buffet service is again becoming increasingly popular. It was the custom years ago to have a large collection of dishes, both savoury and sweet, available on a buffet for breakfast, luncheon and supper. This custom was restricted by rationing and shortage of foodstuff.

As conditions gradually returned to normal, the buffet service returned with an increasing variety of dishes.

A buffet for breakfast is no longer in vogue as much simpler menus are used for this meal.

For lunch and supper and even dinner, the number of dishes served from a buffet are again increasing. In addition to a large variety of Indian curries, savouries and sweets, typical Western cold collations are included. A cold buffet can contain as much as 40 to 50 dishes.

1. Hors d'oeuvre: caviar, pate de foie gras, fruit cocktail, fruit juices. Lobster mayonnaise, salmon mayonnaise, aspic of crab, prawn, shrimp, scampi.

2. Cold consommé, cold salmon, fish mayonnaise, cold meats such as pressed spiced meat, brisket of beef, silverside of beef, spiced glazed tongue, roast meat, roast poultry, raised pies.
3. Prepared salads, Russian, French, Italian, etc., and separate salad material—cucumber, beetroot; mustard, vinegar, etc., for the customer to make his own dressings; salad dressings, mayonnaise; sauces such as Horseradish, Cumberland, mint; proprietory pickles and chutneys.
4. Game pie, mushroom and oyster pie, cold poultry, spring chicken, capon, cold game such as partridge, pheasant, grouse; cold meats, suckling pig.
   Boar's head, wild duck, boned turkey.
   Quails stuffed with foie gras, medallion of game.
   Asparagus, baked beans, salads.
5. Indian food: Kababs—seekh, shami; tandoori preparations; pulao rice.
   Vegetarian: dahi-bhalla, potato wada, rice, a few bhujjias, peas panir, palak panir.

26 / COOKING FUELS

Use and relative advantages of coal, coke, gas, electricity, steam and oil

In considering the types of kitchen equipment that are needed for the various processes of cooking food, namely, boiling, roasting, baking, braising, grilling, stewing and frying, we must make as much use as possible of the equipment which is indigenous to India. In the last few years, kitchen equipment has been modernized to a great extent.

The different cooking methods are:

(i) Cooking by fire.
(ii) Cooking by oil.
(iii) Cooking by gas.
(iv) Cooking by electricity.
(v) Fuel-less cooking.

Cooking by fire There are other fuels that can be used in addition to coal, for instance anthracite is a very good cooking medium and is very slow-burning; it gives off an intense and consistent heat.

Coke, which is simply coal from which the gas has been extracted, gives out intense heat, but is not steady and requires a considerable amount of draught.

Wood is widely used in India, but it is very wasteful and dirty; soft wood must be used for kindling and hard wood for burning.

Charcoal can also be used and in proportion to its weight gives more heat than the above-mentioned fuels; this also must be well ventilated.

In India a large amount of cooking is done on braziers (sigrees) and mud stoves (chulas) and on all forms of open fires.

Modern ranges for burning these types of fuel are being manufactured now. They not only help to conserve fuel but are also easier to maintain and keep clean. They are also more attractive in design and appearance. Ovens are also being attached to this equipment thus providing for roasting and baking besides top cooking.

In some parts of India bread ovens are used where the fuel is placed inside the oven and raked out again when the oven has attained the required temperature, which is maintained for considerable time by the insulation of the oven.

Cooking by oil There are two types of oil which can be used for this purpose, kerosene and heavy diesel oil. In the older type of oil burners a wick was used, but the more modern method uses an oil burner with a forced draught. Oil cooking is a clean method with very little waste. The calorific value, however, varies and is lower than some other methods.

Cooking by gas Cooking by gas is easily the most flexible and useful method for cooking; very little coal gas or town gas is available in India but large quantities of butane gas are becoming increasingly available in the main cities; this is a first-class cooking medium, as its calorific value is considerably more than normal town gas. A reasonable range of equipment is now being manufactured in India for using this medium for frying, baking and roasting of food. By means of automatic regulators the cooking process can be done at a nominal cost; in addition to this, the price compares favourably with that of other cooking fuels.

Cooking by electricity It is fortunate that electricity is readily available in India and the manufacture of electrical cooking equipment is increasing quite rapidly. A considerable range of equipment necessary for the modern kitchen can now be obtained. Hotplates, boilers, toasters, cooking ranges, skillets, rice cookers, ovens, rotisseries, etc., are some of the types. The regulation of this medium is well advanced which enables the technique of modern cookery to be practised extensively. Although the price of the cooking medium is higher per unit than the other cooking mediums, because of the construction of the cooking ovens (which require no outlet) a considerable part of the cooking can be done by conserved heat, for example, if a particular item needs 2 hours oven cooking with gas, only 1½ hours of electricity is needed, the other ½ hour to complete the process can be done by conserved heat.

Cooking Fuels

Cooking by stored heat By using anthracite in a specially designed oven, the heat produced can be used to cook for a considerable period without the replenishment of fuel and is, therefore, very economical, provided the right kind of cooking stove is used.

Sundry cooking methods There are many new methods of cooking food. High-frequency electrical cooking has been experimented with but despite the saving of time, it has been found to be too expensive. Infra-red cooking is used extensively for grilling purposes but, despite all modern methods and the harnessing of different fuels, some of the older methods are still considered to produce the best results. Thus a return to spit-roasting is becoming more and more popular.

The system of pressure cooking is now being practised extensively and a variety of these domestic appliances are manufactured in India. Its advantages are speedy preparation of food and the conservation of food juices.

Fuel-less cookers Hay-box cookery is an old fashioned method of cooking by created heat when slow cooking can be used. This form of container can also be used successfully for the storing of already cooked food.

Steam and water cooking Steam and hot water under pressure can be used if sufficient supply is available for cooking in quantity: e.g., for industrial canteens, institutions, hospitals, etc.

Characteristics	*Electricity*	*Gas*	*Oil*	*Steam*	*Solid Fuel*
1. Dependability	Fails without warning	Fails at short notice because supply cannot be easily gauged	Although supply is visible it has to be regulated constantly and carefully	Supply and pressure has to be constantly maintained	Supply can always be ensured.
2. Flexibility	Intensity can be controlled to pre-determined levels and stages	Intensity can be minutely controlled	Intensity can be moderately controlled	Little control over intensity	No control over intensity
3. Economy	Electricity charges are rather heavy when compared to cost of other fuels especially when the industry does not enjoy special concession from additional levies	Gas is relatively less expensive, especially if it is the supply from city gas pipe lines	Oil is comparatively cheap at the time of purchase but may prove costly because of the possibility of leakage, pilferage, evaporation etc.	Cost of steam will depend on what form of fuel is available for its generation	Cheapest form of fuel
4. Effect on equipment & utensils	No open flame, as result of which there is very little wear and tear on utensils and equipment	Open flame is likely to destroy the operating life-span of equipment and utensils. As a result, repairs are rather heavy, especially replacement of loose parts	Rather difficult to maintain the equipment, as it leaves behind grease which is likely to spoil utensils	Same as in electricity	Leaves soot and stains on utensils. Problem of collection and disposal of ashes. Equipment has to be replaced over a comparatively short life

(*contd*)

	Characteristics	*Electricity*	*Gas*	*Oil*	*Steam*	*Solid Fuel*
5.	Cleanliness	Exceptionally clean and hygienic	Moderately clean and hygienic	Not very clean and hygienic	Clean and hygienic	Not at all clean or hygienic
6.	Safety	Least dangerous especially because of thermostatic controls, time switches and independent circuits	Gas being a combustible element, danger of explosion of the gas cylinder is present	Fire hazards likely in storage areas	Hazard of boiler explosion unless safety-valves ensure proper pressure	Fire hazard most likely because of fierce open flame
7.	Speed	Not so quick, especially in the beginning when it takes time to heat up the equipment	Quickest to reach very high temperature	Quicker, but heat may not be consistent	Fairly quick, because cooking starts immediately	Slow but sure
8.	Installation	Relatively simple, and permits mobility in equipment as the flexible leads can be easily extended to any corner of the kitchen	Installation is not very flexible, because of supply pipelines, unless gas cylinders are used	Installation is elaborate because of the regulation of supply	Installation is complicated and does not permit mobility	Installation is no problem
9.	Storage	No problem	Unless cylinders are used, storage space is not a problem	Adequate storage space has to be properly provided for the fuel tank	Storage space has to be provided for the boiler which generates steam	Storage space is a problem

(contd)

Characteristics	Electricity	Gas	Oil	Steam	Solid Fuel
10. Ventilation	Does not heat up the kitchen and the environment and as there is a complete absence of smoke or fumes, only a provision for exhaust fans is necessary	Heats up the kitchen, and the open flame is likely to create more humidity and difficult working conditions	Same as in gas	Same as in electricity	Emanates smoke and fumes which call for special type of ventilation, viz. chimneys and close canopy, etc.
11. Initial expenditure on equipment	Very heavy	As heavy as electricity	Moderately heavy	Heavy	Comparatively negligible
12. Special features	In the best types of electric cooking equipment, every square inch of range and griddle cooking surface can be heated to a uniform controllable temperature. In consequence a maximum of the operator's time is free for other purposes. Constant watchfulness is not required	Quick, powerful heat required for instant use in case of emergency can be maintained for long periods at any temperature up to red heat. Comes in useful for crash heating	The oil cooker or oil stoves play an important part in bulk cookery of fixed table d'hote meals suitable for industrial canteens, institutions or even residential hotels operating on American Plan	It is argued that in steaming the normal loss in colour, vitamins, flavour and texture are kept down to a minimum because of the absence of water as a cooking medium	For certain types of food, perfection in taste, flavour and texture can only be achieved by means of solid fuel; e.g., tandoori chicken, charcoal broiled meat dishes etc.

27 / WESTERN CULINARY TERMS

Abats Butcher's supplies such as heads, hearts, liver, kidney, etc.

Aiguillettes Thin slices of breast of poultry cut lengthwise.

À la Meaning merely, "in the style of".

À la broche Roasted in front of a fire on a spit or in a Dutch oven.

À la carte Opposite of table d'hôte, meaning that each dish is ordered and priced individually.

À la diable The French way of saying "devilled", in other words, any very hot or highly seasoned dish.

À la français Dishes that are prepared in the French way.

Apéritif A cocktail or other drink served before a meal to stimulate the appetite.

Appetizer A titbit served before a meal or as the first course. A drink such as sherry, cocktail, etc.

Aspic A transparent savoury jelly, generally made of seasoned meat stock. It is used to garnish meat or fish, or to make moulds of meat, fish or game.

Au bleu Applied to fish cooked in fish stock with wine added.

Au four Baked in the oven.

Au gras Rich. Applied to dishes with meat in a rich gravy.

Au gratin Any dish covered with sauce, breadcrumbs or cheese and afterwards baked or grilled. The food is served from the dish in which it is cooked.

Au maigre Opposite of au gras. Applied to meatless or Lenten dishes.

Au naturel Simply-cooked food, or food served raw, such as oysters.

Baba A light yeast cake, usually soaked in rum or spirit.

Bain-marie A large shallow pan to hold water in which several small sauce-pans can be heated without their contents boiling. an alternative to the double saucepan, but often used to keep cooked food warm.

Bake To cook by dry heat, usually in an oven.

Barbecue Meat basted with a highly- seasoned sauce, e.g., lamb basted with hot red-currant sauce.

Barquette A boat-shaped pastry tartlet, filled with chicken, vegetables, oyster, fish mayonnaise, etc.

Baste To spoon melted fat or liquid over food during cooking to keep it moist.

Batter A mixture of flour and liquid such as milk, egg, etc., of such consistency that it can be beaten or stirred. Used to coat foods for frying, or as pancakes, etc. May be sweet or savoury.

Béarnaise A rich sauce, resembling a Hollandaise sauce, made from butter, egg yolk and vinegar, and flavoured with peppercorns, shallots, chervil and tarragon.

Beat To mix air with food by vigorous motion; also used to make a mixture smooth and free from lumps. A wooden spoon is best for beating thick mixtures; an egg-whisk for thin ones.

Béchamel a rich white sauce.

Beignets Pancake batter fried in deep fat or fritters of different kinds.

Beurre noir Browned butter.

Beurre manie Equal quantities of flour and butter used for thickening sauces.

Bisque A rich, thick, cream soup, usually made from shellfish, e.g. lobster.

Blanch Literally to whiten, but used here to mean dipping food into boiling water for a few moments, and then into cold, to remove skin. To blanch almonds, boiling water is poured on them to whiten them and to remove the skins.

Blend To combine two or more ingredients.

Bombe glacée A mould lined with one kind of ice cream and then filled with ice cream of a different flavouring.

Bonbon Sugar confectionery — sweets.

Bouchées Small patties of light pastry sufficient for one mouthful.

Bouillon Unclarified broth or stock made from fresh meat.

Bortsch Russian soup containing beetroot.

Bouquet garni A small bunch of mixed herbs used for flovouring soups, stews, etc. Ideally, this should consist of a sprig each of parsley, thyme, basil, marjoram, with a bay leaf and a strip of lemon peel, tied together with cotton. It must always be removed before the dish is served. When fresh herbs are unobtainable, dried herbs tied in a piece of muslin may be used instead.

Brioche Very light French rolls.

Broil to cook by exposing food directly to heat; used synonymously with "grill".

Browning A substitute added to stews and gravies to darken them.

Brûnoise fashion Cut into small dice.

Brush A thin, even coating of beaten egg or milk applied to pies, buns, etc., immediately before they are put in the oven. It gives the pastry or bun a glossy appearance and helps it to brown more quickly and deeply. Pastry brushes are sold for this purpose. Dried egg is especially useful for brushing, as a very small quantity can be mixed instead of beating a whole egg.

Café au lait coffee with milk; white coffee.

Canapés Small pieces of toast, fried bread or pastry on which light savouries are served.

Carte du jour Menu for the day.

Canneloni Small pasta rolls filled with mince (Italian).

Capon A castrated male chicken. It grows large and has tender meat.

Caramel A substance made by heating sugar until it turns dark brown. Used for coating moulds, flavouring dishes, etc.

Caramelize To heat sugar until it turns brown.

Casserole a baking dish with a well-fitting lid used for cooking stews, etc. in the oven. Usually made of fireproof earthenware or glass, or of heavy enamel. The food is usually served from the casserole.

Cassolette A kind of hot hors d'oeuvre moulded to the shape of a small drum.

Caviar Salted roe of sturgeon or similar fish.

Cèpes A kind of mushroom.

Cereals Grains such as wheat, including semolina, oats, barley, rye, rice etc.

Charlotte A sweet made of alternate layers of fruit and either breadcrumbs or slices of bread and butter.

Charlotte russe Generally a mould lined with sponge cake or sponge fingers and filled with a mixture of cream and fruit, and jelly.

Chartreuse Mould of fruit, jelly or savoury mixture.

Châteaubriand Head of the fillet of beef.

Chaud-froid A cold sauce used for coating meat, game or fish.

Cheese fondue Grated cheese melted in white wine, seasoned with pepper and flavoured at the last minute with a little kirsch.

Chiffonnade Mince of sorrel, lettuce, etc. Wash the leaves, remove veins, roll and cut into fine strips with a sharp knife.

Chinois A conical strainer.

Chipolata A kind of small sausage.

Choux A kind of pastry used for such things as cream buns and éclairs.

Chowder An American soup made with pickled pork, shellfish, fish, potatoes, and other vegetables.

Cisel Finely chopped vegetables.

Coat To cover with a thin layer.

Cochineal A red colouring matter

Compote Fruit stewed in syrup.

Concass To chop roughly, e.g., concassed tomatoes.

Condiments Spices and seasonings.

Confiture Jam or fruit preserves.

Congalaise Garnish of poached oysters and shrimps cohered with Normande sauce.

Consistency The thickness or texture of mixture, such as a cake or batter mixture.

Consommé A light-coloured clear soup.

Côtelettes Cutlets.

Coupe A cream or water ice served with fruit.

Court-bouillion A well-flavoured cooking liquor for fish.

Crackling The rind of roast pork.

Cream fat To beat fat with a wooden spoon until it is light and fluffy.

Crécy (à la) Dishes containing carrots.

Crème Anything of a creamy consistency can be described thus.
Crêpe Pancakes.
Croissants French rolls, crisp and light.
Croquettes Left-over meat, fish, poultry or game, finely minced and rolled into small sausage shapes. These are coated with egg and bread crumbs and fried a golden brown.
Croûtes Ovals or rounds of fried bread.
Croûtons Bread cut in small dice or fancy shapes and fried or toasted. Used as a garnish for serving with soup.
Cuisse Leg, e.g., cuisses de volailles, cuisses de grenouilles.
Custard A cooked or baked mixture made of milk and eggs; it may be sweetened for dessert, or it may be flavoured with cheese, fish, etc., as an entrée.
Cut and fold To mix flour very gently into a mixture.
Cutlet A small piece of meat cut usually from rib of veal or pork, mutton or lamb, usually grilled or fried.
Dariole A small cup-shaped mould.
Darne The middle slice of a fish.
Devilled The same as 'à la diable', that is, any highly seasoned dish. Often this seasoning is done with some form of curry powder.
Dice To cut into small even cubes. Cut food first into slices ½ in. thick, then into strips the same width and finally hold strips together and cut into cubes. Use a chopping board and a sharp knife.
Dieppoise A garnish for fish consisting of shrimp's tails, mussels and mushrooms.
Dissolve To melt a solid food in a liquid.
Dot To put small bits of butter, cheese, cream, etc., over the surface of a dish.
Dough A mixture of a liquid, flour, etc., kneaded together into a stiff paste or roll.
Dredge To cover with a thin sprinkling.
Dust To sprinkle lightly with fine sugar, dried milk or flour.
Duxelle A mixture of parsley, mushrooms and shallots used for flavouring sauces and purées or as a forcemeat.
Écarlate Salted meat is said to be à l'écarlate when it is covered with a coat of red jelly.
Éclair Choux pastry filled with custard or cream. Can be coated with chocolate.
Émincé Finely sliced or shredded.
Entrée A dish served in the first part of a dinner, usually a made-up dish with sauce. Or it can be the main dish of a less formal meal.
Entremets Hot or cold sweets.
Escalopes Thin slices of meat dipped in egg and breadcrumbs and then fried.

Estouffade Brown stock.

Espagnole A rich brown sauce.

Farci Any kind of stuffing.

Fennel A fragrant herb used for flavouring sauces (saunf).

Fillets Fish with bone removed. Undercuts of veal or beef. Slices from the breast of a bird.

Fillet To bone fish, etc., and cut into fillets.

Flan A pastry case made in a flat tin and afterwards filled with a sweet or savoury mixture.

Flûte A long crisp roll of bread (French) used to garnish soups or to serve with soup.

Foie gras Liver of a fat goose.

Fondant Sugar boiled to 112ºC (234ºF) and then beaten to a "fudge-like" smoothness. It can be used as an icing on any kind of sweet.

Fool A summer sweet made with sieved fruit and whipped into a frothy mixture and served with cream or custard.

Forcemeat Savoury stuffing.

Frangipane Confectioner's custard.

Frappé Sweetened fruit juice, half frozen.

Fricadelles Braised game or meat in very small pieces.

Fricassée A stew generally made with chicken, veal, rabbit or lamb thickened with white sauce to which milk has been added.

Fritters Fruit, meat, vegetables or fish coated with batter and fried, usually in deep fat.

Frosting A cooked or uncooked sugar icing used to cover and decorate cakes, etc.

Fry To cook food in very hot fat in an open frying-pan.

Furnet A kind of essence extracted from fish, game, etc.

Galantine Cooked meat that has been boned, pressed into a mould with jelly and served cold.

Galette A large quoit made from puff pastry or short pastry.

Garnish To decorate

Garniture Decoration

Gâteau This can be a cake, an ice cream, or anything made in the shape of a cake and lavishly decorated.

Gelatine A product made from refined cows' hoofs. Used for jellies. Sold either granulated or in sheets. The strength varies with each brand. Allow ½ oz. to ⅓ oz. to each pint of liquid.

Genoese A rich butter sponge used as a base for gâteaux, and as a base for savoury fingers, etc.

Giblets The heart, liver and gizzard of poultry used to make gravies, soups and pies.

Gild, gilding (i) To cover an object with beaten eggs by means of a brush. (ii) To give a golden sheen to objects by means of heat.

Glace Ice, ice-cream, icing. to make smooth or glossy with icing or jelly. Also crystallized or frozen foods.

Glaze Meat glaze is made by reducing (by boiling) stock or gravy to the consistency of jelly. It is used for improving the appearance of cold meats, etc. Sugar and water glaze is brushed over fruit pies, buns, etc., when they are taken from the oven, to improve their surface appearance. Egg-and-water glaze is brushed on to savoury pies, buns, etc., before they are put in the oven.

Goulash Hungarian meat stew, flavoured with paprika.

Haggis A kind of bag pudding, made in Scotland, from liver, sheep's head, etc., finely minced and mixed with oatmeal, herbs, etc.

Haricot A type of stew. Literally, "beans".

Hash A made-up dish of meat that has been diced or minced. Usually a way of using left-overs.

Hollandaise A rich sauce of Dutch origin made with butter or cream, egg yolks and lemon or vinegar served hot or cold with many kinds of vegetables or fish.

Hors d'oeuvre Small savoury titbits, usually cold, served as an appetizer at the beginning of a meal.

Indienne A dish served in the Indian manner.

Infusion The liquid extraction derived from steeping a substance such as coffee, tea, herbs, etc., in boiling water.

Jardinière Garnish of vegetables.

Julienne Food cut into long strips. A clear soup of this name contains finely-shredded vegetables.

Junket Milk coagulated by the addition of rennet. This makes a very light and digestible sweet. It can be served with fruit, and is a valuable nursery food.

Jus Gravy

Kebab Small pieces of meat fixed on a skewer, braised or curried.

Kedgeree Indian dish of cooked fish, often salted or smoked, with rice, eggs etc. Sometimes curried.

Kirsch A favourite Continental drink is café kirsch; this is made with half a cup of black coffee and half a cup of cherry brandy, also a cherry cordial.

Knead To work a dough lightly by bringing the outside of the dough into the centre, using the knuckles of the hand.

Kromeskies Croquettes dipped in a yeast batter and fried.

Langoustine A small variety of spiny lobster.

Liaison Mixture of eggs and cream used for thickening white sauces and soups.

Larding To place strips of fatty substance such as fat bacon on top of lean meat or on the breast of a dry bird. To run strips of fat bacon through lean meat with a larding needle.

Macaroni An Italian pasta made of flour forced through a tube.

Macaroons Small cakes made from almond paste, coconut, etc.

Macédoine A mixture, usually consisting of vegetables or fruit.

Maître d'hôtel butter A piquant sauce or butter flavoured with parsley and lemon.

Marinate To soak meat or fish in a marinade.

Majoram A lemon-scented herb.

Marzipan A sweet or icing made of almonds ground to a paste with egg.

Mask To coat a dish with sauce or line a mould with jelly.

Matignon A mixture of finely minced carrot, celery, onion, ham, thyme and crushed bay leaf used to cover joints or poultry before being roasted or cooked to impart a good flavour.

Mayonnaise A thick sauce made of egg yolks, oil and vinegar, mustard, etc. Used as a dressing for salads of all kinds.

Menu List of fare.

Meringue A mixture of stiffly beaten egg white and sugar, often used as a garnish when browned in the oven. It can be made into small sugar cakes and afterwards filled with cream.

Mignonette pepper White peppercorns, coarsely ground.

Minestrone Italian soup with many vegetables and macaroni added.

Mirepoix Roughly cut onions, carrots, celery and a sprig of thyme and bay leaf.

Mise-en-place A general name given to the elementary preparation area which is constantly resorted to during the various stages of most culinary operations.

Mocha A flavouring usually made with a coffee infusion.

Mousse A light spongy dish, made with sweetened and flavoured cream, then whipped and frozen. Can also be made with a mixture of meat, vegetables, etc., mixed with gelatine.

Mousseline Same as above but moulded in small quantities. Enough for one person at a time.

Muffin A drop batter baked in small individual moulds and eaten hot with butter.

Navarin Mutton or lamb stewed with turnips.

Noodles A flour pasta served in small fancy shapes or in thin string-like tubes. Often fried in Chinese fashion.

Nougat A sweet of a fairly rich kind made with almonds, sugar, nuts, cherries and honey.

Pailles Potato straws.

Panada A thick paste of flour and liquid or flour and butter with a little liquid used to bind together ingredients which would fall apart by themselves.

Paner To coat in egg and breadcrumbs.

Papillote Paper frills placed on chops for decorations. It also means food cooked in paper casings.

Parboil To boil food until only partly cooked.

Pare To peel.

Parfait Ice-cream served in a tall glass and decorated with a variety of nuts and fruits.

Parmesan A very hard cheese made in Italy from cow's milk. Used mainly for cooking.

Pâte Pie, pastry or raised pie, or a paste.

Paysanne To cut into even, thin pieces, triangular or round or square.

Pimento Red or green pepper pods used in salads or often as a colourful garnish.

Piquante Sharply flavoured. Usually the word is applied to mustard or a sharp sauce.

Pistachio Green-coloured nut kernels. Used as a garnish.

Plat du jour Special dish of the day.

Pluck To remove feathers from poultry and birds.

Poach To cook just below boiling point in hot liquid in an open pan.

Poêle Roast done entirely or almost entirely in butter. It is a simplified process of old cookery. The joint or poultry is first fried and coated with a thick layer of matignon, wrapped in slices of pork fat covered with butter paper or aluminium foil and cooked in the oven. It is basted with melted butter during cooking.

Potage A nourishing broth or soup.

Pot-au-feu A beef soup made with vegetables, and poured over French bread or toast.

Pot-pourri A stew of various meats and spices.

Praline Burnt almond flavouring.

Pulses Vegetables that grow in pods, e.g., peas, beans, lentils, etc.

Purée A smooth mixture obtained by rubbing cooked fruit, vegetables, etc., through a sieve.

Quenelles Forcemeat or meat, fish, game or poultry, pounded, rubbed through a sieve and formed into balls, then poached or fried.

Ragoût Well-flavoured meat stew. Thick, well-seasoned and rich.

Raising agents Substances which produce a gas when acted on by heat or other substances, and make flour mixtures rise, e.g. baking powder, baking soda, yeast.

Ramekins Individual small baking dishes.

Raspings Very fine breadcrumbs obtained by grating stale or over-dried bread on a fine grater.

Ratafia A flavouring. Tiny biscuits for trifles, etc., flavoured with almonds.

Ravioli A savoury meat mixture enclosed in dough and cooked in boiling water.

Réchauffé A re-heated dish.

Relish A highly-seasoned food used as an accompaniment.
Rissole A fried cake or meat or fish in a pastry case.
Roe Eggs of fish.
Roux A thickening for soups or sauces made with flour and fat.
Royal The name of a kind of icing.
Royale A savoury egg custard cut into cubes and used as garnish for a soup.
Sabayon Yolks of eggs and a little water cooked until creamy.
Saffron The dried stigma of the crocus flower, used for adding colour and flavour.
Salmi Partly roasted game made into a rich stew.
Sauce A pouring mixture, sweet or savoury, to serve with, and enhance the flavour of another dish.
Sauté Toss and lightly brown in shallow fat.
Scald To immerse food in boiling liquid for a short time. To heat a liquid (e.g. milk) to just under boiling point or to pour boiling water on (e.g. scald a jug).
Scallop Food baked in layers with sauce and breadcrumbs.
Score To make light cuts in a surface such as the outside of a fat piece of pork before roasting.
Sear To form a hard coating on the surface of meat by exposing it to a fierce heat.
Seasoned flour Flour flavoured with salt and pepper.
Sherbet Frozen mixture of fruit juice, egg whites, sugar, milk or water.
Shortening Fat suitable for baking is sometimes called this.
Shredded Cut in fine strips e.g., lettuce, cabbage, etc.
Sift To put dry ingredients through a fine sieve.
Simmer To cook a liquid, or food in a liquid, at a temperature just below boiling point.
Singe To brown or colour.
Skewer A long pin of wood or metal used to secure meat or poultry while cooking.
Sorbet A half-frozen water ice, served in the middle of a long dinner.
Soufflé Very light baked or steamed pudding, savoury or sweet, usually puffed up with egg whites.
Souse Fish such as herrings, pickled in vinegar and spices.
Spaghetti An Italian pasta, finer than macaroni, coarser than vermicelli.
Steam To cook in steam.
Steep To soak in a hot or cold liquid.
Stew To cook by simmering in a little liquid.
Stock Well-flavoured liquid made from meat, vegetables, fish or poultry, etc., and used as a foundation for soups, sauces, stews, etc.
Suprême A name given to the fillet of fish or breast of fowl or game.
Table d'hôte A set meal at a fixed price.

Tartare A cold, sharp, savoury sauce with a base of mayonnaise served with fried fish or a ı .eat dish.

Temperature The degree of heat, usually measured in degrees Celsius (Centigrade) or Fahrenheit as °C or °F. Thus
Temperature of boiling water = 100°C or 212°F.
Temperature of simmering water = 85°C or 185°F.
Temperature of tepid water = 26.6°C or 80°F.

Tepid The temperature of a mixture of 2 parts of cold water to 1 part of boiling water, i.e. about 26.6° or 80°F

Terrine A baked, savoury meat or game mould which is cooked in the oven, usually in an earthenware dish.

Timbale A cup-shaped mould, usually made from meat, fish or vegetables, added to a custard mixture, and finely decorated.

Tournedos Small fillet steak cut from the middle of tenderloin (nearly 65 mm. (¼") thick and about 6–7 cm. (2½ to 2⅓") in diameter.

Tranche A slice.

Trançon A slice of flat fish on the bone.

Truss To tie up or skewer a bird ready for the oven after plucking and drawing.

Tutti-frutti Mixed fruit.

Vanilla A flavouring generally used for cakes, ices or puddings.

Veloutés A rich, creamy smooth sauce.

Vermicelli A very fine Italian Pasta.

Vol-au-vent Creamed game, meat or fish served in a pastry case.

Walewska Garnish for fish or collops of lobster, slices of truffles.

Whisk To beat cream or eggs until a stiff froth is obtained.

Zest Thin outer skin of oranges and lemons.

28 / INDIAN CULINARY TERMS

Akhni or Yakhni Soup or stock.

Alu Potato.

Amriti A sweetmeat.

Atta Wholemeal flour.

Baffad A curry with meat and radish from Goa.

Baghar Tempering done after the dish has been prepared. Onions and a few spices or herbs are fried in a spoonful of fat and added to the cooked dish to improve flavour.

Baked hilsa An oily fish considered a delicacy. Smoked slightly—all bones removed and baked with anchovy essence, tomato sauce, salad oil, mustard, etc.

Balushai A round ball made of dough, slightly flattened at the centre, fried and dipped in sugar syrup.

Barfi A fudge-like sweet.

Basundi Milk sweet.

Bhajjia Slices of vegetables dipped in gram flour batter and fried crisp.

Bhaji Another term for vegetable preparations.

Bhaturas Slightly leavened bread baked on a grid and then fried. Generally served with 'Chhole', a dish prepared out of whole chickpeas.

Bhel puri Crisp fried thin rounds of dough mixed with puffed rice, fried lentil, chopped onion, herbs and chutney.

Bhindi Okra/gumbo, an Indian vegetable known as ladies fingers.

Bhujjia A North Indian vegetable preparation.

Bhurta Vegetable boiled or roasted in charcoal, peeled, mashed and sautéed with a little chopped onion and chillies.

Biryani A rich preparation of rice. Parboiled rice is put in layers with a rich meat or vegetable curry and the whole is baked till cooked.

Black pepper The berry of the pepper vine dried with the skin on.

Bombay duck A small, phosphorescent, gelatinous fish, abundant at the surface of the salt waters of Bengal and Bombay. It is prepared fresh or dried. When dried, it is toasted crisp and served.

Bonda Mashed potatoes, seasoned and formed into balls, dipped in batter and deep fried — a South Indian snack.

Brinjal Eggplant or aubergine. Also called baingan.

Cardamom A spice—the fruit of the cardamom tree. The seeds are found in a pod which is dried. It has a pleasing taste and flavour.

Cashewnut The nut of the cashew fruit. It is found outside the fruit, enclosed in a kidney-shaped shell.

Chapatti or phulka Wheatbread made of unfermented dough, round in shape and paper thin. Resembles a tortilla.

Charoli An Indian nut.

Cheera Amaranth leaves.

Chikkoo A brown Indian fruit—a cross between a fig and a russet apple. Also known as sapota.

Chiwda A mixture of nuts, fried pressed rice, fried lentils, gram preparations and spices.

Cocum A sour fruit dried and used chiefly with fish. Acid in taste.

Coriander A spice. the seed of a small herb.

Cumin A spice resembling caraway seeds.

Curry powder A mixture of various spices such as coriander, chillies, turmeric, cumin etc., roasted and powdered together.

Custard apple Resembles a leaf artichoke. A luscious custard-like fruit with hard black seeds inside.

Dahi Yoghurt or curd.

Dahibhalla Ground lentil, made into fried balls and then steeped in seasoned beaten yoghurt. Served with pulao or as a snack.

Dal Lentil. There is a large variety of lentils in India.

Dhansak Literally meaning "rice & vegetables", a Parsi speciality. It is plain fried rice served with a curry rightly called "wide mouthed" as it contains an innumerable variety of ingredients—meat, lentils, vegetables, leafy vegetables, nuts and a variety of spices.

Doodh pak Sweetmeat made of rice and milk.

Do pyaz Literally "twice onion". Ground and fried onion added to meat along with other spices. Hence Do (twice) and Pyaz (onion). It is not very hot and could form a tasty accompaniment to parathas and chapatties.

Dosa A type of savoury pancake made with fermented batter of ground lentil and rice. Cooked on a griddle. A speciality of South India.

Dum A process of cooking with heat from above as well as below.

Dum phukta A dry rich meat dish prepared by cooking meat in pressurised steam.

Drumstick A long type of bean with hard fibrous covering, resembling a drumstick.

Garam masala A mixture of cloves, cinnamon, cardamom, pepper and cumin.

Gaujas A fancy sweetmeat made of dough fried and dipped in sugar syrup.

Ghee Clarified butter or vegetable shortening processed to resemble clarified butter.

Groundnut Peanut or monkey-nut.

Guava A popular fruit used to make guava cheese, jelly and stewed fruit.

Gulab jamun Khoa or Mawa (milk evaporated to remove all moisture) is kneaded and flavoured and made into balls which are fried till golden brown and dropped immediately into hot sugar syrup.

Gustaba Large meat balls (Kofta) in a gravy of curd, mixed with ground poppy seeds, nuts and onion, and lightly spiced.

Hing Asafoetida, a strong flavouring agent. It also acts as a carminative.

Hopper A counterpart of the American hot cake. For making it, the batter is fermented by the addition of toddy, an alcoholic beverage. Cooked in seasoned earthenware pots. Its subtle and pleasing flavour would appeal to all palates. Eaten with stew.

Halwa A sweet dish made of lentils, semolina or wheat, or of vegetables such as beetroot, carrot and pumpkin, with butter, milk and sugar.

Idli A fermented batter of ground lentil and rice steamed in moulds. A speciality of South India.

Jaggery Refined and solidified molasses.

Jalebi A golden-coloured, crisp sweet filled with sugar syrup, formed in rings.

Kababs A savoury barbecue done on iron rods.

Kalia A Bengali vegetable or fish dish with spices and yoghurt.

Kesari A South Indian sweet dish made of vermicelli or semolina.

Kheema Minced meat.

Kheer A pudding-like preparation of milk with other ingredients such as rice or carrot.

Khoa Milk is boiled down till all moisture is removed, used as a base for a large number of Indian sweets.

Khorma Rich, thickened brown curry of chicken, mutton or vegetables. Poppy seeds and desiccated coconut are added along with other condiments for thickening. The meat itself is made tender by marinading in curd (yoghurt) before cooking.

Khichdi Mixture of rice and lentils.

Kofta Minced meat ball.

Laddoo A sweet ball made of gram or lentil flour, rice or semolina.

Lassi A beverage made of beaten yoghurt diluted with water; sugar or salt may be added.

Lichi A luscious Indian fruit. It looks like a bigger version of the strawberry and grows in Bengal, Dehra Dun and Delhi regions.

Lime A smaller variety of lemon. Much sharper.

Loochi Bengali version of puri.

Macher jhal A special Bengali fish curry where the fish is first fried and then curried. Mustard oil is the cooking medium used. Mackerels make excellent jhal.

Machhi Fish.

Maida Refined flour.

Maize Indian corn.

Mango A very luscious Indian fruit, which has several varieties— Dasehri, Chausa, Langara, Alfonso, etc.

Marinate To steep in a mixture of yoghurt or vinegar to soften.

Masala Indian condiments and spices.

Moilee Fish or prawn cooked in plenty of coconut milk— lightly spiced.

Murgh musallam A spicy chicken preparation.

Mattar Peas.

Mutanjan Spiced rice with mutton sweetened with sugar. It is a speciality of Kashmir.

Mulligatawny curry Chicken or mutton curry with a flavour popularised in the West as Mulligatawny soup.

Nan Indian bread made of slightly leavened dough, baked on the wall of a mud oven.

Nargisi kofta curry Minced meat, mixed with spices and egg, covers a hardboiled egg (like scotch eggs) and it is fried and dropped in a spiced curry.

Neera A non-fermented drink obtained from the coconut palm.

Pachadi Seasoned yoghurt with vegetables—served in South India.

Palak mutton or Palak chicken Meat or chicken cooked with spinach, lightly spiced and thick, without much gravy. The spinach is mashed and cooked with the meat.

Pani puri A puff of dough fried and eaten with tamarind water and sprouted gram.

Panir Cottage cheese made by curdling milk with lemon juice, curd etc., and the whey removed by straining and hanging in a muslin bag.

Papaya A luscious Indian fruit; papaw or pawpaw.

Paratha Fried bread made of unleavened wheat flour.

Payasam A South Indian milk pudding made from cereal (such as rice or vermicelli) or pulse, and sugar.

Phirnee A creamy milk pudding made of rice flour.

Pomfret a type of white fish very popular in Bombay.

Prawn malai curry Prawns cooked in spiced cream and coconut cream and baked in a coconut.

Pulao A rice dish. Rice is fried in fat and cooked in stock and water.

Pulao rice A special type of rice used in pulao — thin and long and not as starchy as ordinary rice.

Pumpkin A big, round vegetable of the squash variety.

Puri Deep-fried round wheat bread. About 5 cm. or 2 inches in diameter and puffed.

Quabarga A type of meat kabab.

Rabri Sweet, thickened milk.

Raita Vegetable, raw or parboiled, mixed with beaten and seasoned yoghurt.

Rasam A spicy soup made of lentils and tomatoes. Hot and sharp; served sometimes as an appetiser. A speciality of South India.

Rasgullas Milk is curdled by the addition of curd and lime, the casein separated from whey which is then kneaded smooth and made into balls. A piece of sugar candy is usually kept in the centre. These balls are put into clarified simmering sugar syrup and cooked.

Rava Semolina.

Reshmi chapatties Unleavened bread resembling tortillas, but as thin as silk, and about 20 to 25 cm. or 8 to 10 inches in diameter. Baked over an upturned dome-like iron vessel over live coal.

Rista A minced meat ball curry, a speciality of Kashmir.

Rogan josh A red curry with a thin gravy made from the leg of mutton cut with bones into fairly large pieces. The distinct flavour is that of saffron and nutmeg. Saffron is added just before removing from the fire. The red colour is obtained by the addition of saltpetre and rattanjog, a red coloured bark.

Sambar A preparation of lentils with one or more types of vegetables—served as a necessary accompaniment to rice in South Indian vegetarian food.

Samosa A thin pastry cone filled with boiled or spiced vegetable or minced meat and deep fried.

Sandesh Sweetened milk, condensed to solid form by slow cooking and flavoured.

Seekh kabab Minced meat and spices ground together bound with egg and fixed on to a skewer and grilled.

Sev A fried savoury resembling vermicelli. It is made of gram flour dough passed through a mould and deep fried till crisp.

Shami kabab Cutlets made with minced meat and lentil.

Shrikhand A sweet yoghurt based dish with liquid removed by straining, and flavoured with saffron and nuts.

Snake gourd Vegetable with a long snake-like shape.

Tamarind A sour fruit used for curries, chutneys, etc.

Tandoori Chicken or *Fish* Spiced meat or fish barbecued in a specially designed tandoor oven.

Toddy An alcoholic drink obtained from a variety of palm.

Turmeric A yellow spice used for imparting a characteristic flavour and colour. The root of a plant belonging to the ginger family.

Uppuma A savoury South Indian dish made out of semolina and lentils.

Vindaloo A sharp and hot curry made of pork, prawn, chicken or mutton. Originated in Goa.

Wada or *Pakora* A rissole of lentil or vegetable served as a snack.

Wark Thin foil of silver or gold which is edible.

Yellow rice Rice flavoured and coloured with saffron or turmeric.

Zarda A sweet pulao served at the end of a meal.

29 / HINDI EQUIVALENTS OF SOME WELL KNOWN ENGLISH FOOD NAMES

CONDIMENT AND NUTS

Almonds	Badam
Aniseed	Saunf
Arrowroot	Araroht
Asafoetida	Hing
Baking Powder	Pakane ka soda
Bay leaf (or *Cassia*)	Tej patta
Black pepper or *peppercorns*	Kali mirch
Basil	Goolal tulsi
Breadcrumbs	Sukhi double roti ka choora
Caraway seeds	Shahjeera
Cardamoms	Elaichi
Cashewnuts	Kaju
Cinnamon	Dalchini

Cloves	Laung
Cochineal	Gulabi rung
Coconut	Nariel
Coriander leaves	Hara dhaniya
Coriander seeds	Sukha dhaniya
Cumin	Jeera
Curry leaves	Meetha neem ke patte
Dry coconut	Copra
Dry ginger	Sonth
Fenugreek	Methi
Fennel	Hasha
Ginger	Adrak
Garlic	Lassan
Green chillies	Hari mirch
Groundnuts	Moongphalli
Jackfruit seeds	Kathal ke beej
Jaggery	Gur
Lemon rind	Nimbu ka chhilka
Mace	Javitri
Marjoram	Ban tulsi
Mango powder	Amchur
Mint leaves	Pudina
Mustard seeds	Sarson or rai
Nutmeg	Jaiphal
Onion seeds	Pyaz ke beej
Parsley	Ajmoda ka patta
Pistachio	Pista
Poppy seeds	Khuskhus
Raisins	Kishmish
Red chillies	Lal mirch
Saffron	Kesar
Sage	Seesti
Gingelly seed	Til
Sugar candy	Misri
Tamarind	Imli
Turmeric	Haldi
Tymol seeds	Ajwain
Thyme	Hasha
Vinegar	Sirka

FRUITS

Apples	Seb
Apricots	Khurmani

Banana	Kela
Fig	Anjeer
Grapes	Angoor
Guava	Amrud
Jackfruit	Kathal
Lemon	Meetha Nimbu
Mango	Aam
Olives	Zaitun
Orange	Narangi or Santra
Peaches	Arhu
Pears	Naspati
Pineapple	Ananas
Pomegranate	Anar
Sour apple	Khatte seb

VEGETABLES

Beetroot	Chukandar
Bitter gourd	Karela
Brinjal (eggplant, aubergine)	Baingan
Beans	Sem
Cabbage	Band gobi
Capsicum	Bari mirch
Carrot	Gajar
Cauliflower	Phool gobi
Celery	Ajwain ka patta
Cucumber	Kakri
Colocasia leaf	Arvi ka patta
Drumstick	Saijan ki phalli
Dry beans	Chauli or Ravaan
Elephant yam	Zamikand
Fenugreek leaves	Methi
French beans	Pharas bean (Fransi)
Fresh mint	Hara pudina
Green peas	Mattar
Ladies fingers (okra)	Bhindi
Mushrooms	Kukar moote or Guchi
Onions	Pyaz
Potatoes	Alu
Pumpkin	Kaddu
Radish	Mooli
Ridge gourd	Turai
Snake gourd	Chirchira

Spinach	Palak
Spring onion	Hara pyaz
Sprouted beans	Phuli hari chauli
Sweet potato	Shakarkand
Turnip	Shalgam
Tomato	Tamatar
White gourd	Lauki
Yam	Suran

LENTILS AND CEREALS

Barley	Jowar
Bengal gram	Channa dal
Black gram	Urad dal (or maash)
Corn	Makkai
Refined flour	Maida
Wholemeal flour	Atta or gehu-ka-atta
Green gram	Moong dal
Gram flour	Besan
Large white gram	Kabuli channa
Lentil	Masoor dal
Millet flour	Bajra atta
Red gram	Arhar dal (or tur dal)
Rice	Chawal
Sago	Sabudana
Semolina	Suji
Vermicelli	Sevian
Wheat	Gehu

30 / WORK METHODS IN FOOD PREPARATION

1. Plan all jobs before starting work.
2. Wash hands before handling food or utensils.
3. Collect all food and equipment needed before beginning a job.
4. Arrange work space and equipment conveniently.
5. Keep work area neat, clean and orderly.
6. Use French knife and board for chopping.
7. Use specially designed knives for every job—slicing, dicing, peeling, boning etc.
8. Stack empty dishes to be used for serving food.
9. Use both hands to do a job whenever possible.
10. Use scoops and ladles to portion food—this provides uniform servings.
11. Scoop size refers to number of servings yielded per quart/litre. Ladle size refers to number of ounces, grams, each one holds.

12. Use standardized quantity recipes.
13. Learn what yields are obtained from all sizes and varieties of canned foods.
14. Use accurate weighing and measuring equipment for uniform results, food cost control, and to avoid waste.
15. Fasten a large paper sack at the side of work space with cellotape for gathering waste and scraps. When sack is full, deposit it in garbage can and tape another sack to work space or keep an aluminium basin on your table and put in the garbage to transfer to the main garbage can.
16. Disposable plastic gloves are good for clean, safe food preparation.
17. In preparing lettuce for salad cups, remove core by firmly hitting stem end of head flat against counter top. Let luke-warm water run through the lettuce to loosen and separate the leaves. Chill until ready to use.
18. Carrots should not be rubbed with steel wool to remove outer skin because pieces of steel may come off in food and be eaten.
19. An egg slicer may be used to cut cooked carrots, potatoes, hard-boiled eggs, bananas and other soft foods.
20. To remove the skin from tomatoes, dip them into boiling water until the skin slips off. Cool immediately by placing them in cold water. Place tomatoes in the refrigerator until ready to use.
21. A pair of scissors in the kitchen will come in handy for cutting such foods as meats for salads, and all types of vegetables for salads.
22. Drain canned berries and fruits. Thicken and cook the juice before mixing in the fruit. This keeps the fruit in whole pieces and crisp looking.
23. Do not add salt to large quantities of milk or cream sauce until the end in order to prevent it from curdling. Use a wire beater to make smooth gravies, sauces and puddings.
24. When preparing sections of oranges or grapefruit, cover them with boiling water and allow them to stand for 5 minutes. Score through the skins lengthwise with a sharp fruit knife. Do this twice to divide the skin into quarters, then pull off the rind. This will pull off the white membrane readily, along with the rind, then fruit can be sectioned. Another method is to cut the rind away in a continuing spiral with a slight sawing motion.
25. When making gelatine for moulded salads or sweets, heat only enough liquid to dissolve the gelatine and sugar. To hasten congealing, use ice water to make up the total amount of liquid; or melt the soaked gelatine over hot water, then add remaining liquid.
26. When breaking eggs, have a paper sack ready in which to drop the shells. This saves handling them again when ready to dispose of shells. Break one egg at a time into a wet cup before adding it to others.

27. If you are cutting green beans, cut a whole handful at once on your cutting board after stringing—not 2 or 3 at a time.
28. Wrap meat in foil or plastic before storing in freezer or refrigerator —brown paper or waxed paper softens and sticks—this is especially true of minced meat.
29. Instead of stuffed pork chops—try putting on top of chops with a scoop to save time.
30. Bacon grilled on racks saves draining. Bacon cut in cubes while cold, then fried, saves chopping it.
31. Add dry milk, butter and seasonings to hot boiled potatoes, then mash. Add hot water or potato water, as needed for right consistency.
32. To prevent cheese from drying and shrinking, do not grate it too long ahead of time. After grating, keep it refrigerated.
33. Cut orange in half and then slice it. Sliced orange halves with the peel left on are simple to prepare and easy to eat.
34. When serving, use a cup-sized ladle. Using a ladle of the proper size is faster than dipping out several small spoonfuls.
35. When whipping cream, be sure to chill cream, bowl and beater. Cream will then whip in half the usual length of time.
36. Use cooking containers, such as steam table pans and casseroles, for serving foods when possible. The food will be more attractive, stay warm longer and save dish-washing, time and labour.
37. Grind such foods as cheese and meats. This will save time and give uniform results.
38. Use a food chopper to cut such foods as nuts, raisins and vegetables.
39. Dampen raisins with water and they will go through the food chopper without sticking.
40. Use a food scraper to remove food quickly from container.
41. Rub hands with a little oil before preparing pumpkin and other fuzzy vegetables. Prevents roughness and irritation of hands.
42. Soak dishes containing starch and sugar in cold water; greasy ones in hot soapy water. Saves time in cleaning; also saves changing water.
43. When cutting cakes or ice-cream, dip knife in hot water to make a smoother cut.
44. Save time by using correct tools. Measure in large containers, such as 1 litre instead of 4 single cups. Weighing is still more accurate.
45. Always work with both hands. Example: Put lettuce on two salad plates at a time, placing one leaf on each plate.
46. Use large pans for cooking bacon or meat balls and place them in the oven. This will save time watching the dish.
47. Keep two pans of one food on serving counter, so that the line will not be held up when one pan is empty.
48. Use trays or mobile trolleys to bring supplies from refrigerator or supply room.

49. Cutting boards save time in chopping foods and cleaning is made easier.
50. Arrange sequence of work so there is no break or waste of motion. Example: Preparation of apples for baking. Have washed apples placed on level with worker to the left. He picks up an apple with his left hand, cores it and places it in a pan which is placed conveniently to his right.
51. To make celery rings or crescents, cut a bunch of celery with a French knife, sweep celery into colander placed on a level lower than cutting board and wash under strong stream of water.
52. Mix all dry ingredients or liquid ingredients together before blending them into each other.
53. Grease measuring cup slightly before measuring molasses, corn syrup etc., so that nothing is wasted.
54. After using electric meat grinder, put several slices of bread through grinder. This will aid in cleaning the grinder.
55. Butter sides and bottom of pan in which noodles, spaghetti, rice or apples are cooked to prevent them from boiling over and sticking to the pan.

31 / EVALUATING A RECIPE

The following points should be checked in evaluating a recipe.

1. Is the recipe clear, concise, accurate, and readable as to:
   a. Ingredients, type or kind
   b. Amount in weights or measures
   c. Instructions for method
   d. Number of portions
   e. Serving directions.

   Examples:
   (i) Size of serving
   (ii) Garnish to use
   (iii) Serve hot or cold or with a specific accompaniment.
2. Does it produce a quality product as determined by score card? If not, why?
3. Is the product nutritious?
4. Is it economical in time, energy and material?
5. Does it eliminate, as far as possible, the factor of human error?
6. Is the recipe suited to:
   a. clientele
   b. available equipment
   c. workers
   d. type of service.
7. Is the per capita cost of the product in line with the selling price?

SAMPLE SCORE CARD FOR EVALUATION OF EACH DISH IN A CLASS

NAME:

Menu in serial order:

(1)
(2)
(3)
(4)
(5)
(6)

STANDARDS:

Menu	Appearance	Consistency (thick, thin)	Texture (tenderness) (juiciness)	Flavour		Total
				Aroma	Taste	

Comments:

Scores
Very Good : 5
Good : 4
Acceptable (fair) : 3
V Poor to poor : 0–2

Oven temperatures

In most recipes in this book, reference has been given to the oven temperature or the gas setting. This is an approximate guide only. Different makes of ovens vary and it is a fact that even the same make of oven can give slightly different results at the same temperature or setting.

If in doubt as to whether the temperature given is **exactly** right for your particular oven, do at all times refer to your own manufacturer's temperature chart. It is impossible in a general book to be exact for every oven, but you will find that the following are a good average in every case.

	Electricity		*Gas Regulo*
	°F	°C	
Cool oven	225–250	107–121	1–9
Very slow oven	250–275	121–135	½–1
Slow oven	275–300	135–149	1–2
Very moderate oven	300–350	149–177	2–3
Moderate oven	375	190	4
Moderate hot oven	400	204	5
Hot oven	425–450	218–233	6–7
Very hot oven	475–500	246–260	8–9

General temperature ranges

	°F	°C	
Very Hot oven	450–475	232–246	For bread, pastries, searing of meat
Grilling heat at source	450 and up	232	Grilling meat, fish, bacon
Hot oven	400–425	204–208	
Moderate oven	350–375	177–190	
Shallow frying/deep frying and griddling	300–375	149–190	
Slow oven	300–325	149–163	
Steam range	228–250	109–128	
Water boils at sea level	212	100	
Flour and cornflour thickened	203	95	
Simmering, poaching, stewing, braising, good for dissolving gelatine holding coffee and chocolate	185–195	85–91	

	°F	°C
Maximum for egg custard, Hollandaise sauce	185	85
Final rinse in dishwashing machine (10 seconds)	180	82
Well cooked meat, medium cooked meat (internal temp.)	160	71
Egg coagulate—yolks 76°C white 74°C	156	69
Thermotainers most food for serving	150	65
Hot fudges and other sauces; rare meat	140	60
Danger range in which food bacteria thrive if in moist non-acid food materials	45–120	7.5–49
Holding most fruits, vegetables and dairy products	40	5
Meat storage (short term)	34–36	0
Water freezer	32	0
Holding ice-cream	8–12	–22.5
Holding frozen foods	0 to –20	–29 to –18

32 / SUGGESTED MENUS

VEGETARIAN LUNCHEON (3 COURSES)

(1) Lentil soup

—

Vegetable pie with cheese sauce
Creamed spinach
or
Vegetable pulao
Palak panir, Raita,
Pickle, Papad

—

Butterscotch sponge
Fruit flan

(2) Tomato juice

—

Egg croquettes—Tomato sauce
Salad
Creamed potatoes

or Alu ki tahari
Peas panir curry, Dahi bhalla
Chutney, Pickle, Papad
—
Basundi
Fruit pie

(3) Cream of spinach soup
—
Vegetable cutlets—Tomato sauce
Salad
or
Peas Pulao
Stuffed capsicum, Pakora kadhi
Peanut chutney, Papad
Carrot kheer
Apricot sponge flan

NON-VEGETARIAN LUNCHEON (*3 COURSES*)

(1) Mulligatawny soup
—
Mutton cutlets réforme
Buttered spinach, Macaire potatoes
or
Vegetable pulao
Mutton khorma, Fried beans, Raita
Pickle, Papad
—
Coffee mousse
Fruit salad
—
Coffee

(2) Cream of vegetable soup
—
Mutton Andalouse
Scalloped potatoes
or
Moghlai biryani, Onion raita
Pickle, Papad
—
Phirnee
Blancmange
—
Coffee

(3) Melon

—

Meat and potato cutlets
Cabbage salad, Sautéed carrots
or
Tomato pulao,
Shami kababs, Dal
Green chutney, Papad

—

Caramel custard
Basundi

—

Coffee

VEGETARIAN LUNCHEON (4 COURSES)

(1) Melon cocktail
Cauliflower au gratin, Salad

—

Lentil rissoles, Tartare sauce
Creamed potatoes, French beans

—

Methi bhaji pulao
Aloo dum, Masala dal
Chutney, Pickle, Papad

—

Jalebis
Tangerine chartreuse
Coffee

(2) Minestrone soup

—

Tomato japonaise, Salad

—

Nut roast, Curry sauce
Scalloped marrow
French fried potatoes

—

Potato biryani
Vegetable khorma
Boondi raita
Pickle, Papad, Chutney

—

Rasgullas
Bavarois of fruit

—

Coffee

(3) Cream of asparagus soup

—

Mock salmon steak, Hollandaise sauce
Macaroni cheese, Salad

—

Cauliflower pulao
Vegetable kofta curry, Tomato cuchumber, Moru kulumbu
Pickle, Papad

—

Barfi
Baked apple

—

Coffee

NON-VEGETARIAN LUNCHEON (*4 COURSES*)

(1) Cream of tomato soup

—

Fish soufflé, Shrimp sauce

—

Tournedos
French beans, Sautéed carrots

—

Yakhni pulao
Cucumber raita
Pickle, Papad, Chutney

—

Neopolitan mousse
Gulab jamun

—

Coffee

(2) Prawn cocktail

—

Clear julienne soup

—

Roast loin of pork
Spiced pineapple sauce
Roast potatoes
Baked cabbage

—

Moong dal khichdi
Mutton jhal faraizi, Boondi raita
Pickle, Papad, Chutney

—

Marshmallow pudding
Chocolate sauce
Vermicelli payasam

—

Coffee

(3) Clear soup royale

—

Lobster thermidor, Salad

—

Hungarian goulash with caraway dumplings
Parsley potatoes, Green peas

—

Savoury coconut rice,
Mutton kofta curry, Cauliflower & pea raita
Pickle, Papad, Chutney

—

Carrot halwa
Baked coconut pudding

—

Coffee

BANQUET (6 COURSES)

	French	*English*
	Huîtres au naturel	Oysters
	ou	or
	Hors d'oeuvres variés	Hors d'oeuvres
	—	—
	Consommé claire	Clear soup
	—	—
	Truite meunière	Grilled trout
	—	—
	Selle de mouton	Saddle of mutton
	—	—
	Haricots verts	French beans
	Pommes parisienne	Parisian potatoes
	—	—
	Suprême de volaille Alexandra	Creamed chicken
	Pommes fondante	Fondant potatoes
	—	—
	Bavaroise au rhum	Rum bavarois
	Café	Coffee
(2)	Tortue claire	Turtle soup
	—	—

	French	*English*
	Filet de sole Veronique Sauce de raisin	Fillet of sole Grape sauce
	—	—
	Vol-au-vent aux champignons	Patty case with mushrooms
	—	—
	Dinde Rôti a l'anglais Sauce cranberry Petit pois Pommes macaire	Roast turkey Cranberry sauce Peas Macaire potatoes
	—	—
	Soufflé d'ananas	Pineapple soufflé
	—	—
	Café	Coffee
(3)	Cocktail de crevettes Potage bortsch	Shrimp cocktail Bortsch soup
	—	—
	Saumon aux anchois	Salmon with anchovy souce
	—	—
	Ris d'agneau et épinards	Lamb sweetbreads with spinach
	—	—
	Perdrix rôti Croustillers Choux de Bruxelles	Roast partridge Game chips Brussels sprouts
	—	—
	Crêpes suzette	Pancakes suzette style
	—	—
	Café	Coffee

BANQUET (6 COURSES)

(1)	Hors d'oeuvres Lucullus Langue écarlate jardinière Sauce madère	Rich variety Hors d'oeuvres Lamb's tongue with mixed vegetables, madeira sauce
	—	—
	Poularde Maryland Saucissions Asperges en branches	Chicken with sweet corn Sausages Asparagus
	—	—
	Meringue Chantilly	Chantilly meringues
	—	—
	Anges au cheval	Angels on horseback
	—	—

	French	*English*
	Café	Coffee
(2)	Cocktail de Tomate	Tomato juice cocktail
	—	—
	Saumon Poche Sauce tartare	Poached salmon Tartare sauce
	—	—
	Pigeon farcie aux champignons, Petit pois Pommes Anna Gâteaux surprise	Roast pigeon stuffed with mushrooms, Garden peas Anna potatoes Gâteaux with fruit and ice-cream
	—	—
	Foie de volaille en croute	Chicken liver on toast
	—	—
	Café	Coffee
(3)	Crème d'asperges	Cream of asparagus soup
	—	—
	Homard thermidor	Lobster thermidor style
	—	—
	Côtelettes d'agneau aux cerises, Macédoine des légumes	Lamb cutlets, Cherry sauce Macédoine of vegetables
	—	—
	Poularde estouffade Coeurs d'artichauts Pommes duchesse	Chicken estouffade style Artichokes Potatoes duchess style
	—	—
	Soufflé d'ananas	Pineapple soufflé
	—	—
	Café	Coffee

DINNER (4 COURSES)

(1)	Crabe en coquille	Dressed crab in shell
	—	—
	Rognons sauté Bercy	Sautéed kidneys in Bercy sauce
	—	—
	Poularde rôti Sauce du pain Chou-fleur au gratin Pommes persil	Roast chicken and bacon Bread sauce Cauliflower with cheese sauce Parsley potatoes
	—	—

	French	*English*
	Bombe Nesselrode	Mould of vanilla ice-cream and chestnut
	—	—
	Café	Coffee
(2)	Pamplemousse au Merachine	Grapefruit
	—	—
	Noisettes de mouton aux olives	Noisettes of mutton with olives
	Pommes Lorettes	Potatoes Lorette style
	—	—
	Caneton rôti	Roast duck
	Salade d'orange	Orange salad
	Petit pois	Garden peas
	Pommes fondantes	Fondant potatoes
	—	—
	Flan des fraises	Strawberry flan
	—	—
	Café	Coffee
(3)	Canapés de foie d'oie	Canapés of goose liver
	—	—
	Fillet de pomfret Colbert	Fillet of pomfret with Colbert butter
	—	—
	Tournedos à la Florentine	Tournedos with spinach
	—	—
	Trifle Chantilly	Fruit trifle with vanilla cream
	—	—
	Diable aux cheval	Stuffed prune with mushrooms
	—	—
	Café	Coffee

DINNER (*3 COURSES*)

	French	English
(1)	Potage Madras	Madras soup
	—	—
	Darne de saumon Daumont	Poached salmon with mushrooms
	Sauce hollandaise	Hollandaise sauce
	Haricot verts	French beans
	Pommes duchesse	Duchess potatoes
	—	—
	Pêche melba	Peaches and ice-cream
	—	—
	Café	Coffee

	French	*English*
(2)	Vol-au-vent de volaille	Chicken vol-au-vent
	—	—
	L'Agneau rôti de menthe	Roast lamb with mint sauce
	Carrottes vichy	Carrots
	Pommes macaire	Macaire potatoes
	—	—
	Crème de chocolat	Chocolate cream
	—	—
	Café	Coffee
(3)	Homard à la Newburg	Lobster Newburg style
	—	—
	Oie a l'anglaise,	Roast goose
	Sauce cranberry	Cranberry sauce
	Choux de Bruxelles	Brussels sprouts
	Pommes rôtis	Roast potatoes
	—	—
	Salade des fruits	Fruit salad
	—	—
	Café	Coffee

LOW COST BALANCED MENUS

(1) Boiled rice (parboiled)
Sag (green leafy veg.) with dal
Baingan bhagar
Curd (with reconstituted non-fat milk)

(2) Tamarind rice
Sag
Groundnut chutney
Dal payasam (reconstituted non-fat milk and jaggery)

(3) Khichdi (parboiled rice, dal and green leafy vegetables)
Dhania chutney
Tindli raita (with reconstituted non-fat milk)

(4) Tandoori chapatties
Sprouted gram koshambir
Sarson ka sag
Dahi ki chutney
(curd prepared from reconstituted non-fat milk)

(5) Bajra ki roti
Chhole
Bhathu ki bhajee
Gajar ki kheer (carrot kheer using reconstituted
non-fat milk and peanuts)

(6) Tandoori chapatties
Doodhi channa
Groundnut chutney
Palak ka raita (use reconstituted non-fat milk)

(7) Boiled rice
Sambar (with non-fat milk powder and M.P.F.)
Cheera thoran
Buttermilk (use reconstituted non-fat milk)
Boiled tapioca

(8) Dry fish and mango curry
Buttermilk (use reconstituted non-fat milk)

(9) Jackfruit (chakka) curry
Small fish curry
Thakara thoran
Buttermilk (use reconstituted non-fat milk)

(10) Boiled rice
Sambar with peanut flour
Green leafy vegetable
Curd (use reconstituted non-fat milk)

(11) Pongal
Mixed vegetable curry
Methi bhaji
Curd curry

(12) Subji bhat,
(tapioca macaroni and mixed vegetables)
Pulse chutney
Curd (use reconstituted non-fat milk)

(13) Purie (50 percent peanut flour)
Moong dal with sag
Red pumpkin bhujjia

(14) Ragi chapatties
Dal with sag
Onion cuchumber
Curd (use reconstituted non-fat milk)

(15) Ragi uppuma, Sukhi dal
Dahi ka chutney, (use reconstituted non-fat milk)
Palak ka sag

(16) Vegetable uppuma
Onion & green chilli raita
(reconstituted non-fat milk)
Amaranth sag

(17) Bhakri
Mixed dals with sag
Cucumber cuchumber
Dahi (reconstituted non-fat milk)

(18) Boiled rice
Dal with sag
Grilled dried Bombay duck

(19) Boiled rice
Egg and radish curry
Arvi (colocasia)
Amla chutney

(20) Missi roti
Gonglu bhaji (turnip leaves)
Urad dal
Dahi (reconstituted non-fat milk)

(21) Makki di roti,
Sarson ka sag
Mixed dals (Channa and urad)
Lassi (reconstituted non-fat milk)

(22) Boiled rice
Varan (green cholai or methi with tur dal)
Curd (use reconstituted non-fat milk)
Groundnut chutney

(23) Chapatties (25 per cent peanut flour)
Palak and onion bhaji
Channa dal chutney
Dahi (reconstituted non-fat milk)

(24) Besan roti
Dahi (reconstituted non-fat milk)
Onion cuchumber
Cholai bhaji

33 / WEIGHT AND VOLUME EQUIVALENTS

		Approximately
Apple (medium)	1	150 gm.
" (large)	1	200 gm.
Baking powder (level)	1 tsp.	4 gm.
Baking powder (rounded)	1	6 gm.
Banana (ripe)	1	125 gm.
" (raw)	1	160 gm.

		Approximately
Beetroot	1	150–160 gm.
Besan (level)	1 dsp.	8 gm.
" (heaped)	1 "	13 gm.
" (level)	1 tbsp.	10 gm.
" (heaped)	1 "	15 gm.
"	1 cup	95 gm.
Bitter gourd (medium)	1	60 gm.
" " (large)	1	105 gm.
Brinjal (medium size)	1	100 gm.
Buttermilk	1 cup	160 ml.
Cabbage (medium)	1	485 gm.
Capsicum (medium)	1	60 gm.
Capsicum (large)	1	80 gm.
Carrot (medium)	1	65 gm.
" (large)	1	115 gm.
Cauliflower (medium)	1	400 gm.
Celery	1 bunch	115 gm.
Chicken (standard)	1	1 kg.
" (large)	1	1.2 kg.
" (medium)	1	750 gm.
" (small)	1	500 gm.
Chauli bhaji	1 bunch	140 gm.
Chukka bhaji	1 bunch	45 gm.
Cinnamon	5 cm. (2") piece	2 gm.
Coconut (grated)	1	215 gm.
Cocum	3–4	5 gm.
Colocasia leaves	1 bunch	40 gm.
Coriander leaves	1 bunch	100 gm.
Coriander powder (level)	¼ tsp.	1 gm.
" " "	½ tsp.	2 gm.
" " "	1 tsp.	3 gm.
" " "	1 dsp.	5 gm.
Coriander seeds (level)	1 tsp.	2 gm.
" " (rounded)	1 tsp.	3 gm.
" " (level)	1 tbsp.	8 gm.
" " (rounded)	1 "	12 gm.
Cumin powder (level)	¼ tsp.	1 gm.
" " "	½ "	2 gm.
Cumin powder (level)	1 tsp.	3 gm.
" " "	1 dsp.	5 gm.

		Approximately
Cumin seeds (level)	1 tsp.	5 gm.
" " (rounded)	1 tsp.	3 gm.
" " (level)	1 dsp.	5 gm.
Curd	1 cup	175 ml.
Curry leaves	1 bunch	35 gm.
Dhania jeera powder (level)	¼ tsp.	1 gm.
" " " "	½ tsp.	2 gm.
" " " "	1 tsp.	3 gm.
" " " "	1 dsp.	5 gm.
Drumstick	1	30 gm.
Fat	1 tbsp.	25 gm.
"	1 cup	175 gm.
Fenugreek leaves	1 bunch	135 gm.
Flour (level)	1 dsp.	8 gm.
" (heaped)	1 "	15 gm.
" (level)	1 tbsp.	10 gm.
" (heaped)	1 "	20 gm.
" (heaped)	1 cup	100 gm.
Garam masala (level)	¼ tsp.	1 gm.
" " "	½ tsp.	2 gm.
" " "	1 tsp.	3 gm.
" " "	1 dsp.	5 gm.
Garlic	2 flakes	2 gm.
Garlic	1 pod	20 gm.
Ginger	2.5 cm. (1") piece	10 gm.
Ginger powder	1 tsp.	2 gm.
Green chilli	1	4 gm.
" "	5	10 gm.
Jaggery	1 tbsp.	15 gm.
"	1 cup	150 gm.
Leeks	1 bunch	70 gm.
Lettuce	1 bunch	120 gm.
Mango	1	215 gm.
Mint	1 bunch	115 gm.
Oil	1 tsp.	5 ml.
"	1 dsp.	10 ml.
"	1 tbsp.	15 ml.
"	1 cup	150 ml.
Onion (small)	1	30 gm.
" (medium)	1	65 gm.
" (large)	1	135 gm.

		Approximately
Parsley	1 bunch	30 gm.
Peppercorns	5	1 gm.
Pepper powder (level)	¼ tsp.	1 gm.
" " "	½ tsp.	2 gm.
" " "	1 tsp.	3 gm.
" " (level)	1 dsp.	5 gm.
Pomfret	1	400 gm.
Potato (medium size)	1	120 gm.
" (large)	1	165 gm.
Radish	1 bunch	105 gm.
Red chilli	1	1 gm.
" "	5	4 gm.
Red chilli powder (level)	¼ tsp.	1 gm.
" " "	½ tsp.	2 gm.
" " "	1 tsp.	3 gm.
" " "	1 dsp.	6 gm.
Red onion	2 bulbs	6 gm.
" "	1 pod	12 gm.
Red radish	1 bunch	70 gm.
Refined flour (level)	1 dsp.	10 gm.
" " (heaped)	1 "	15 gm.
" " (level)	1 tbs.	10 gm.
" " (heaped)	1 "	20 gm.
" " (heaped)	1 cup	100 gm.
Rice flour (level)	1 dsp.	10 gm.
" " (heaped)	1 "	13 gm.
" " (level)	1 tbsp.	10 gm.
" " (heaped)	1 "	15 gm.
" " (heaped)	1 cup	1.15 gm.
Salmon (medium)	1	1.5 kg.
Semolina (level)	1 dsp.	12 gm.
" (heaped)	1 "	16 gm.
" (level)	1 tbsp.	14 gm.
" (heaped)	1 "	20 gm.
" (heaped)	1 cup	135 gm.
Spinach	1 bunch	100 gm.
Sugar	1 tbsp.	25 gm.
"	1 cup	175 gm.
Suva bhaji	1 bunch	80 gm.
Tamarind (size of walnut)		20 gm.
" (size of lime)		30 gm.

		Approximately
Tomato (medium)	1	110 gm.
" (large)	1	150 gm.
Turmeric powder (level)	¼ tsp.	1 gm.
" " "	½ "	2 gm.
" " "	1 tsp.	3 gm.
" " "	1 dsp.	6 gm.
Water	1 cup	160 ml.

NAMES OF INGREDIENTS IN SEVERAL INDIAN LANGUAGES

CEREALS

Name of Foodstuff	*Botanical Name*	*Hindi*	*Tamil*	*Telugu*	*Kannada*	*Oriya*	*Marathi*	*Bengali*	*Gujarati*	*Malayalam*	*Kashmiri*	*Other Names*
Millet	Pennisetum typhoideum	Bajra	Cambu	Sazzalu	Sajje	Bajra	Bajri	Bajra	Bajri	Kamboo	Bajru	Spiked millet, Pearl millet
Barley	Hordeum vulgare	Jau	Barli arisi	Barli biyyam	Barli	Jaba dhana	Jau	Job	Jau	Yavam	Wushku	—
Buck wheat	Fagopyrum esculentum	Kootu	Kotu	—	—	—	Kuttu	Titaphapur	—	Kootu	—	—
Milo	Sorghum vulgare	Juar	Cholam	Jonnalu	Jola	Janha	Jwari	Juar	Juwar	Cholam	—	Milo
Maize	Zea mays	Makkai; Bhutta	Makka cholam	Mokka jonnalu	Kempu jola	Sukhila maka	Maka	Bhutta	Makai	Cholam	Makaa'y	—
Ragi	Eleusine coracana	Mundal; Makra	Kizh-varagu	Ragulu	Ragi	Mandia	Nachni	Madua	Ragi	Muthari; Panja-pullu	—	Kora kon; Ginger millet
Rice (raw)	Oryza sativa	Arwa chawal	Pacha arisi	Biyyam	Akki	Arua chawla	Tandool	Atap chawal	Chokha; chawal	Pachari	Tomul	—
Rice (parboiled)	Oryza sativa	Usna chawal	Puzhung-al arisi	Uppudu biyyam	Kusuba-lakki	Kala-kutta; Usuna chaula	Ukda tandool	Siddha chawal	Ukra chokha; Ukra chawal	Puzhangal ari	—	—
Rice (pressed)	Oryza sativa	Chudwa	Arisi aval	Atu kulu	Avalakki	Chuda	Pohe	Chira	Pohwa	Aval	—	—
Rice (puffed)	—	Murmura	Arisi pori	Murmurala	Kurlu	Mudhi	Murmure	Mudi	Mumra	Pori	—	—

(contd.)

Name of Foodstuff	*Botanical Name*	*Hindi*	*Tamil*	*Telugu*	*Kannada*	*Oriya*	*Marathi*	*Bengali*	*Gujarati*	*Malayalam*	*Kashmiri*	*Other Names*
Semolina	Triticum aestivum	Sooji	Ravai	Rawa	Rawa	Rawa	Rawa	Sooji	Rawa	Rawa	—	Broken wheat
Vermicelli	Triticum aestivum	Siwain	Semiya	Semiya	Semige	Simai	Shevaya	Semai	Sev	Semiya	—	—
Wheat	”	Gehun	Godumai	Godhumalu	Godhi	Gahama	Gahu	Gom	Ghau	Gothambu	Ku'nu'kh	—
Wheat flour (whole)	”	Atta	Godumai mavu	Godhuma pindi	Godihu hittu	Atta	Kaneek	Atta	Ato	Gothambumavu	—	—
Wheat flour (refined)	”	Maida	Maida mavu	Maida pindi	Godi hittu; Bili	Maida	Maida	Maida	Maida	American mavu	—	—

PULSES AND LEGUMES

Name of Foodstuff	*Botanical Name*	*Hindi*	*Tamil*	*Telugu*	*Kannada*	*Oriya*	*Marathi*	*Bengali*	*Gujarati*	*Malayalam*	*Kashmiri*	*Other Names*
Bengal gram (whole)	Cicer arietinum	Channa	Kothu Kadalai	Sanagalu	Kadale	Buta	Harbara	Chola	Channa	Kadala	Chanu	Chhole; Chick pea; Garbanzo
Split Bengal gram	”	Channa dal	Kadalai parippu	Sanaga pappu	Kadale bele	—	Harbara; Harbar yachi dal	Cholar dal	Channa dal	Kadala parippu	—	—
Split Bengal gram flour	”	Besan	Kadalai mavu	—	Kadale hittu	—	Besan	—	Besan	Kadala mavu	—	—

(*contd.*)

Name of Foodstuff	Botanical Name	Hindi	Tamil	Telugu	Kannada	Oriya	Marathi	Bengali	Gujarati	Malayalam	Kashmiri	Other Names
Split black gram	Phaseolus mungo roxb	Urud dal	Ulutham parippu	Minapa pappu	Udina bele	Biri	Uddachi dal	Mash kalair dal	Alad	Uzhunnu parippu	Maha	—
Cow peas	Vigna catjang	Lobia	Karamani	Bobbarlu	Alasande	Chani	Chavli	Barbati	Chora	Payar	—	—
Field beans	Dolichos lab lab	Val	Mochai	Chikkudu	Avare	Baragudi	Walpapdi	Sim	Wal	Val avara	—	—
Green gram (whole)	Phaseolus aureus roxb	Moong	Pasipayar	Pesalu	Hesare kalu	Mooga	Moong	Moog	Moog	Cheryparyar	Muang	—
Split green gram	Phaseolus aureus roxb	Moong dal	Payathum parippu	Pesara pappu	Hesara bele	—	Moogachi dal	Moog dal	Moog ni dal	Cheru payar parippu	—	—
Horse gram	Dolichos biflorus	Kulthi	Kollu	Ulavalu	Hurule	Kolatha	Kuleeth	Kulthi kalai	Kuleeth	Muthira	—	—
Split kesari	Lathyrus sativus	Khesari-dal; Lang dal	Khesari parippu	Lamka pappu	—	Khesari	Lakh dal	Khesari dal	Lang-ni-dal	Vattu parippu	Musur	—
Lentil	Lens esculenta	Masoor dal	Mysore parippu	Misur pappu	Masur bele	Masura	Masur dal	Masoor	Masur dal	Masur parippu	Musur	—
Moth beans	Phaseolus aconitifolius Jacq	Moth	Narippayar	—	—	—	Matki	—	Math	—	—	Aconite beans; Dew gram; Kheri
Peas	Pisum sativum	Mattar	Pattani	Batani	Batani	Matara	Vatana	Mattar	Suka vatana	Pattani	Kara	Kabuli matar

(contd.)

Name of Foodstuff	*Botanical Name*	*Hindi*	*Tamil*	*Telugu*	*Kannada*	*Oriya*	*Marathi*	*Bengali*	*Gujarati*	*Malayalam*	*Kashmiri*	*Other Names*
Kidney beans	Phaseolus vulgaris	Rajmah	—	—	—	—	Shravan-ghevda	Barbati	Phanasi	—	Raaz-maha	French-beans dry
Split red gram	Cajanus cajan	Arhar dal	Tuvaram parippu	Kanda pappu	Thugare bele	Harada	Tur dal	Arhar dal	Tuver-ni-dal	Tuvara parippu	Arhar dal	Pigeon pea
Soya bean	Glycine max merr	Bhatmas	—	—	—	—	—	Gari kalai	—	—	Muth	—

LEAFY VEGETABLES

Name of Foodstuff	*Botanical Name*	*Hindi*	*Tamil*	*Telugu*	*Kannada*	*Oriya*	*Marathi*	*Bengali*	*Gujarati*	*Malayalam*	*Kashmiri*	*Other Names*
Agathi	Sesbania grandiflora	Mar	Agathi	Avise	Agase	Agasti	—	Bak	Agathio	Agathi	—	Basna
Amaranth (spiked)	Amaranthus spinosus	Kante-wali chaulai	Mullu keerai	Mulla thota koora	Mulla dantu	Kanta neutia; Saga	Kante math	Kanta notya	Kantalo dabho	Mullan cheru cheera	—	Gendari sag
Amaranth (tender)	Amaranthus gangeticus	Chaulai sag	Thandu keerai	Thota koora	Dantu	—	Math	Notya	Choli-ni bhaji	Cheera	—	Gogta sag
Bamboo shoot (tender)	Bambusa arundinacea	Bans	Moongil kuruthu	Veduru chiguru	—	Baunsa gaja	Kalkipan	Bansber ankur	Vasani kupal	Mulan koombu (Elaya)	—	—
Bathua leaves	Chenopo-dium album	Bathua sag	—	—	Sakothina soppu	Bathua sage	Chandan bathua	Belo sag	Chilni bhaji	—	—	—
Brussel sprouts	Brassica olerocea; Var gemmifera	Choti gobi	Kalakose	—	Mara kosu	Chota bandha gobi	—	Bilati bandha kopi	—	—	Haa'kh	—

(*contd.*)

Name of Foodstuff	Botanical Name	Hindi	Tamil	Telugu	Kannada	Oriya	Marathi	Bengali	Gujarati	Malayalam	Kashmiri	Other Names
Cabbage	Brasica olerocea; Var capitata	Band gobi	Muttai-kose	Gos koora	Kosu	Bhadha kopi	Kobi	Bandha kopi	Kobi	Mutta-gove	Band gobi	—
Celery leaves	Apium graveoleus; Var dulce	Shelari	—	—	—	—	—	Pandhuni sag	—	Sellary	—	—
Chekkur manis	Sauropus androgy-nons	—	—	—	—	—	—	—	—	—	—	—
Chuka ambat	Rumex vesicarius	Chuka	Chuka keerai	Chuka koora	—	—	Ambat chuka	Chuka palang	Chuka ni-bhaji	—	O'bej	Khatti palak
Colocasia leaves	Colocasia anti quorum	Arvi-ka-sag	Seppam ilai	Chama akulu	Shamagad de yele	Sarue	Alupan	Kochu sag	Alu na patra	Chembu ila	—	—
Coriander leaves	Coriandrum sativum	Hara dhania	Kotha-malli	Kothimiri	Kotham-bari soppu	Dhania	Kothim-bir	Dhane sag	Kothmir	Kotha-malli	D'aani-wal	—
Curry leaves	Murraya koenigii	Karipatha	Karivep-pilai	Karive-paku	Karibevu	Bursunga patra	Kadhi-limb	Bursunga	Mitho limbdo	Karivep-pila	—	—
Drum-stick leaves	Moringa oleifera	Saijan patta	Murungai keerai	Muluga akulu	—	Sajnasaga	Shevaga pan	Saj'na sag	Sekta ni sing-nopalo	Muringa ila	—	—
Fenu-greek leaves	Trigonella foenum graecum	Methi sag	Venthia keera	Menth koora	Menthina soppu	Methi-saga	Methi bhaji	Methisag	Methi bhaji	Uluva ila	Methi	—
Lettuce	Lactiuca sativa	Salad	—	—	—	—	—	Salad pata	Salat	Uvar cheera	Salaa'd	—

(contd.)

Name of Foodstuff	*Botanical Name*	*Hindi*	*Tamil*	*Telugu*	*Kannada*	*Oriya*	*Marathi*	*Bengali*	*Gujarati*	*Malayalam*	*Kashmiri*	*Other Names*
Manathakkali leaves	Solanum nigram	Makoy	Manathakkali	Kaman-chi	Ganika	—	—	Kakmachi	Piludi	Manathakkali	—	—
Mint	Mentha spicata	Pudina	Pudina	Pudina	Pudina	Podana patra	Pudina	Pudina	Fudina	Pudina	Pudynu	—
Mustard leaves	Brassica campestoris var sarason	Sarson ka sag	Kadugu ilai	Ava akalu	Sasuve yele	—	Mohari cha pan	Sorisa sag	Rai ni bhaji	Kadugu ila	—	—
Parsley	Petroselinum crispum	Ajmood	—	—	—	—	—	—	—	—	—	—
Radish leaves	Raphanus sativus	Mooli ka sag	Mullangi ilai	Mullangi akula	—	—	—	Mooli sag	Mooli na patra	Mullangi ila	Mujilak	—
Shepu (Dill)	Peucedanum graveolens	Sowa sag	Satha kuppi	—	Sabsiga	—	Suva Shepu	Sowa	Suvani bhaji	Satha kuppa	—	Dill
Spinach	Spinacia oleracea	Palak	Pasalai keerai	Bachchali koora	—	Palanga saga	Palak	Palang sag	Palak	Vasala cheera	Palak	—
Tamarind leaves	Tamarindus Indicus	Imli Patte	Puli ilai	Chinta chiguru	Hunise chiguru	—	Chinche-cha-pala	Tetul patta	Amli na patra	Puli ila	—	—

ROOTS AND TUBERS

Name of Foodstuff	*Botanical Name*	*Hindi*	*Tamil*	*Telugu*	*Kannada*	*Oriya*	*Marathi*	*Bengali*	*Gujarati*	*Malayalam*	*Kashmiri*	*Other Names*
Beetroot	Beta vulgaris	Chukandar	Beet	Beet	Beet	Bita	Beet	Beet	Beet	Beet	—	—

(contd.)

Name of Foodstuff	Botanical Name	Hindi	Tamil	Telugu	Kannada	Oriya	Marathi	Bengali	Gujarati	Malaya-lam	Kashmiri	Other Names
Carrot	Daucus carotta	Gajar	Mangal mullangi	Gujjara gada	Gajjare	Gajara	Gajar	Gajar	Gajar	Karat	Gaazur	—
Colocasia	Colocasia antiquorum	Arvi	Seppan kizhangu	Chama-dumpa	Sama-gadde	Saru	Alukanda	Kochu	Alvi	Chembu	—	—
Kham-ealu	Dioscorea alata	Chupri alu	Perum valli kizhangu	Pendalamu	Anthali-ga su	—	Khand	Chupri alu	Khand	Kachil kizhangu	—	—
Lotus root	Nelumbium nelumbo	Kamal ki jadh	Thamara kizhangu	Tamara dumpa	Kamala dambu	—	—	Kamala mudh	—	Tamara kizhangu	Nadur	—
Mango ginger	Curcuma amada	Am haldi	Ma inji	Mamidi allam	Mavina hasi-sunth i	—	Ambahaldi	Amada	—	Manga inji	—	—
Onion (big)	Allium cepa	Pyaz	Venga-yam	Neerulli	Erulli	Piaja	Kanda	Pyaj	Kanda	Ulli (savala)	Gand'u	—
Onion (small) (Red onion) (Madras onion)	—	Chota pyaz	Chinna vengyam	—	—	—	—	—	—	Chuman-nulli	—	—
Potato	Solanum tuberosum	Alu	Urlai kizhangu	Alu gaddalu	Alugadda	Alu	Batata	Gol alu	Batata	Urula kizhangu	Ooli	—
Radish (white)	Raphanus sativus	Mooli	Mullangi	Mullangi	Mullangi	Mula	Mula	Mula	Mula	Mullangi	Muj	—
Sweet potato	Ipomea batatas	Shakar-kand	Sakkara vali kizhangu	Chilagada dampa	Genasu	Kanda-mu la	Ratala	Ranga alu	Sakkaria	Madura kizhangu	—	—

(contd.)

Name of Foodstuff	*Botanical Name*	*Hindi*	*Tamil*	*Telugu*	*Kannada*	*Oriya*	*Marathi*	*Bengali*	*Gujarati*	*Malaya-lam*	*Kashmiri*	*Other Names*
Tapioca (Cassava)	Manihot esculenta	Simla alu	Maravalli kizhangu	Karrapen dalamu	Maragea-nasu	Kath-kanda	—	Simla alu	—	Kappa; Mara-chini	—	—
Turnip	Brassica rapa	Shalgam	—	—	—	—	—	—	—	—	Guagu'j	—
Yam (elephant)	Amorpho-phallus	Zami-kand	Senai kizhangu	Kanda dumpa	Suvarna gadde	Hathi-khojia alu	Suran	Ol	Suran	Chena	—	—
Yam (ordi-nary)	Typhonium trilobatum	Ratula	Karumai kizhangu	Kanda	Chikka suvarna gadde	Khamba alu	Goradu	Chet kachu; Ratalu	Ratalu	Chena (sadarna)	—	—

OTHER VEGETABLES

Name of Foodstuff	*Botanical Name*	*Hindi*	*Tamil*	*Telugu*	*Kannada*	*Oriya*	*Marathi*	*Bengali*	*Gujarati*	*Malaya-lam*	*Kashmiri*	*Other Names*
Agathi flowers	Sesbania aegyptiacia	Agasth ka phool	Agathi-poo	—	—	—	—	—	—	Agathi-poo	—	—
Artichoke	Cynara scolymus	Hathi-chak	—	—	—	—	—	Hathi chak	—	—	—	—
Ash gourd	Benincasa hispida	Petha	Poosnikai	Boodeda gummadi	Buda-gumbala	Panika-kharu	Kohala	Chalku-mra	Safed koloo	Kumba-langa	Masha-a'lyal	—
Bitter gourd	Momordica charantia	Karela	Pavakkai	Kakara-kaye	Hagalkai	Kalara	Karle	Karela	Karela	Pavakka	Karel'a	—
Bottle gourd (calabash cucumber)	Lagenaria vulgaris	Lauki	Suraikai	Anapa-kaya	Sorekai	Lau	Pandhara bhopla	Lai	Doodhi	Chorakai	Zeeth	—

(contd.)

Name of Foodstuff	*Botanical Name*	*Hindi*	*Tamil*	*Telugu*	*Kannada*	*Oriya*	*Marathi*	*Bengali*	*Gujarati*	*Malaya-lam*	*Kashmiri*	*Other Names*
Brinjal (Egg plant; aubergine)	Solanum Melongena	Baingan	Kathiri-kai	Vankaya	Badane	Baigan	Vangi	Begun	Ringena	Vazhu-thananga	Waangun	—
Broad beans	Vicia faba	Bakla	Avaraikai	Pedda-chikkudu	Chappa-ra davare	Simba	—	Mokhan-sin	Fafda papdi	Avarakka	—	—
Capsicum (giant chillies)	Capsicum annuum-vargrossa	Simla mirchi	Kodami-lagai	—	—	—	Bhopli mirchie	Lanka (Bilathi)	—	Unda-mulagu	Marcha-wangum	—
Cauliflo-wer	Brassica oleracea; Var bostrytis	Phool gobi	Kavipoo	Kasu gadda	Hukosu	Phool kobi	Phool kobi	Poolkobi	Phool kobi	Kaliflo-wer	Phool gobee	—
Cluster beans	Cyamopsis tetragono-loba	Guer ki phalli	Kothava-rangai	Goruchi-kudde	Gorikayi	Guanara chhuin	Govar	Jhar sim	Govar	Kothavar	—	—
Cucumber	Cucumis sativus	Khira	Kakkari-kai	Dosakayi	Southai kayi	Kakudi	Kakadi	Sasha	Kakadi	Vellari-kka	Laa'r	—
Double beans	Faba vulgris	Chastany	—	—	—	—	—	—	Papdi	Avaraj	—	—
Drumstick	Moringa oleifera	Sajan ki phalli	Murin-gakkai	Mulaga-kada	Nurge kay	Sajna chhuin	Shevaga sheng	Sajna danta	Saragavo	Murin-gakai	—	—
French beans	Phaseolus vulgaris	Bakla	Beans	Beans	Huruli-kay	Bean	Pharas-bee	—	Fansi	French avara	Fraa'sh beans	—
Gherkins	Coccinia cordifolia	Tindli	Kovaikai	Donda-kayi	Tonde-kayi	Kundru	Tondale	Telakuch	—	Kovakai	—	—

(contd.)

Name of Foodstuff	*Botanical Name*	*Hindi*	*Tamil*	*Telugu*	*Kannada*	*Oriya*	*Marathi*	*Bengali*	*Gujarati*	*Malayalam*	*Kashmiri*	*Other Names*
Jackfruit (immature)	Artocarpus heterophyllus	Kathal	Palapinju	Panasa	Halasu (yele)	Panasakatha	Phanas	Aanchar	Kawla phanas	Idichakka; Chakka	—	—
Kohlrabi (knol khol)	Brassica oleracea var canloropa	Kohlrabi	—	—	—	Ul kabi	Nol kol	Olkopi	Nolkol	Noolkol	Mo'nd	—
Ladies fingers (Okra gumbo)	Abelmoschus esculentus	Bhindi	Vendakkai	Bendakayi	Bende	Bhendi	Bhendi	Dherash	Bhinda	Vendakka	Bhindu'	—
Leeks	Allium porrum	Lasson vilayiti	—	—	—	Rasuna (Bilati)	Khorat	Piyaj (Bilati)	—	—	Praan	—
Lotus stem	Nelumbium nelumbo	Kamalgatta	Thamarathandu	Thamarakada	—	—	—	—	—	Thamarathandu	—	—
Mango (green)	Mangifera Indica	Am	Manga	Mamidikavi	Mavinakayi	Ambu (kancha)	Kairi	Am (kancha)	Ambo keri	Panchamanga	—	—
Mogra	—	—	—	—	—	—	—	—	—	—	—	—
Onion stalks	Allium cepa	Pyaz	Vengaya thandu	Ulli kadalu	Erulli soppu	Piya sandha	Pati	Piyaz kali	Dunglina dakhadi	Ullithandu	—	—
Papaya (green)	Carica papaya	Papita	Pappalikai	Boppayai kayi	Parangi	—	Papaya	Pempe (Kancha)	Papayi	Omakaya	—	—
Parwar	Trichasanthes dioica	Parwal	—	Kommu potla	—	Potala	Parwar	Patol	Padwal	Potalam	—	—
Peas	Pisum sativum	Mattar	Pachai Pattani	Pachai battani	Batani	Matara	Vatana	Mattar	Vaana	Pattani	Mattar	—

(contd.)

Name of Foodstuff	*Botanical Name*	*Hindi*	*Tamil*	*Telugu*	*Kannada*	*Oriya*	*Marathi*	*Bengali*	*Gujarati*	*Malayalam*	*Kashmiri*	*Other Names*
Plantain (green)	Musa sapientum	Kela (hara)	Vazhakkai	Aratikayi	Balekayi	Bantala kadali	Kele	Kela (kanch)	Kela	Vazhaka	—	—
Plantain flower	Musa sapientum	Kele ka phool	Vazhai-ppu	Aratipuwu	Bale-motho	Kadali bhanda	Kel phool	Mocha	Kel phool	Vazha-poo	—	—
Plantain stem	Musa sapientum	Kele ka tana	Vazhai-thandu	Arati doota	Dindo	Kadali manja	Kelicha khunt	Thor	Kelanu thed	Vazha pindi	—	—
Pumpkin	Cucurbita maxima	Kaddu	Parangi-kkai	Gumma-dikayi	Kumbola	Kakharu	Lal bhopla	Kumra	Kohlu	Mathan	Paa'rimal	—
Rhubarb stalks	Rheum emodi	Revand-chini	Nattuire-yalinni gadda kayi	Nattu pasapu chchinna da kayi	—	—	—	Reuchini danta	—	Variyath thandu	—	—
Ridge gourd	Luffa acutangula	Tori	Pirkkan kai	Beerakai	Heerai kai	Janchi	Dodka	Jhinga	Turia	Peechinga	Turrel	Sweet gourd
Snake gourd	Trichosanthes anguina	Chach-inda	Padaval-angai	Pottakayi	Padavala	Chachinda	Padval	Chichi-nga	Pandola	Padaval-anga	—	—
Spinach stalks	Spinacea oleracea	Palak ki dandi	Pasalai thandu	Bacchala kaka	—	Palanga nada	Palak deth	Palong danta	—	Vasali-cheera thandu	—	—
Sundakai	Salanum torrum	—	Sunda-kkai	Usthikayi	Sonde kai	—	—	Titbai-gum	—	Sundakka	—	—
Sword beans	Chhavalia gladiata	Bara sem	Kattu tha-mbattam	Adavi thamma	Tumbek-kai	Maharda	Abaichi sheng	Kathsim	Taravar-dini vel	Val avara	—	—

(contd.)

Name of Foodstuff	*Botanical Name*	*Hindi*	*Tamil*	*Telugu*	*Kannada*	*Oriya*	*Marathi*	*Bengali*	*Gujarati*	*Malayalam*	*Kashmiri*	*Other Names*
Tinda (Round gourd)	Citrullus vulgaris	Tinda	—	—	—	—	—	—	Todabuch	Thinda	—	—
Tomato (green)	Lyco-persicon esculentum	Vilayathi baingan	Thakkali kai	—	Asavru dapparu chapparu badane	Kancha bilati baigana	—	Bilathi bagun	Tamatu	Pacha thakkali	Ruvaan-gan	Love apple
Vegetable marrow	Cucurbita pepo	Safed kaddu	—	—	Dilpa-sand	Golu phu-tikakuri	Kashi bhopla	Dhuldul	—	—	Kaa'shir al	Field pumpkin
Water chestnut	Trapa bispinosa	Shingara	—	Kubya-kam	—	Pani singara	Shingara	Pani phal	Shingoda	—	—	—

NUTS AND OILSEEDS

Name of Foodstuff	*Botanical Name*	*Hindi*	*Tamil*	*Telugu*	*Kannada*	*Oriya*	*Marathi*	*Bengali*	*Gujarati*	*Malayalam*	*Kashmiri*	*Other Names*
Almond	Prunaus amygdalus	Badam	Badam	Badam kayi	Madami	Badama	Badam	Badam	Badam	Badam	Baadaam	—
Cashewnut	Anacardium occidentale	Kaju	Mundiri paruppu	Jeedi pappu	Geru beeja	Lanka ambu manji	Kaju	Hijli badam	Kaju	Parangi-yandi	Kaju	—
Coconut	Cocos nucifera	Nariyal	Thengai	Kobbari	Thengini kai	Nadia	Naral	Narkel	Nariyal	Thenga	Narjeel	—

(contd.)

Name of Foodstuff	Botanical Name	Hindi	Tamil	Telugu	Kannada	Oriya	Marathi	Bengali	Gujarati	Malayalam	Kashmiri	Other Names
Gingelly seeds (Sesame seeds)	Sesamum indicum	Til	Ellu	Nuvvulu	Acchellu	Rasi	Til	Til	Tal	Ellu	—	—
Groundnut (Peanut)	Arachis hypogaea	Moongphalli	Nilakkadala	Verusanagakayi	Kadale kayi	China badam	Bhui moong	China badam	Bhoising	Nilakkadala	Moong fali	—
Jungli badam	Sterculia foetida	—	—	Yenuga badam	—	—	—	—	—	—	—	Elephant badam; Malabar badam
Linseed seeds	Linum usitatissimum	Alsi	Alivirai	Avise ginzalu	—	Pesi	Juwas	Tishi	Alsi	Cheruchana vithu	A'lish	—
Mustard seeds	Brassica nigra	Rai	Kadugu	Avalu	Sasuve	Sorisa	Mohori	Sorse	Rai	Kadugu	Aasur	—
Pistachio nut	Pistacia vera	Pista	Pista paruppu	Pista	Pista	Pista	Pista	Pesta	Pista	Pista	Jalguza	—
Safflower seeds	Carthamus tinctorius	Kardi	—	Kusuma ginzalu	—	—	—	—	—	—	—	Kusumbh seeds
Sunflower seeds	Helianthus annus	Suria muki	Surya kanthi	Poduthiru gaddu puvvu ginzalu	—	—	Surya mukhi	Suraj mukhi	—	Suryakanthi	—	—
Walnut	Juglans regia	Akhrot	Nattu akrotu kottai	Nattu akroti vithu	—	Akhoot	Akrod	Akrot	Akrot	Akrotandi (Akshodakkai)	—	—

(contd.)

FRUITS AND FRUIT PRODUCTS

Name of Foodstuff	*Botanical Name*	*Hindi*	*Tamil*	*Telugu*	*Kannada*	*Oriya*	*Marathi*	*Bengali*	*Gujarati*	*Malayalam*	*Kashmiri*	*Other Names*
Ambadal	Spondias mangifera	Amra	Mambulichi	Amratakamu	Ambate	—	—	Amra	—	Mampuli	—	Indian log plum
Apple	Malus sylvestris	Seb	Apple	—	Sebu	Seu	Sufarchand	Apel	Safarjan	Apple	Tsoonth	Tarel
Apricot	Prunus aremeniaca	Khoomani	—	—	—	—	—	—	—	—	T'ser	—
Avocado pear	Persea americana	—	—	—	—	—	—	Kulunash pati	—	—	Goshtubtang	Butter fruit
Bael fruit	Aegle mamelos	Bel	Bilwa pazham	Maredu pandu	—	—	Bel	Bel	Bil	Vilavam pazham	—	—
Banana (ripe)	Musa paradisiaca	Kela	Vazhai pazham	Arati pandu	Bale hunnu	Champa kadali	Kela	Kala	Kela	Vazhapazham	Kela	—
Bilimbi	Averrhoa bilimbi	—	—	Bilimbi kayalu	Kamaleku	Karamanga	Awala	Kamranga	—	—	—	—
Blackberry	Rubus fruiticosus	Vilaiti anchu	—	—	—	—	—	Vala jam	—	—	—	Bramble
Bread fruit	Artocarpus altilis	Madar	—	—	—	—	—	Madar	—	Kadachakka	—	—
Bullock's heart	Annona reticulata	Nona atwa	Ramsita pazam	Rama phala	Rama phala	Raja amba	Ramphal	Nona	Ramphal	Athachakka	—	—
Cape goose berry	Physalis peruviana	Rasbari	—	—	—	—	Tipari	Tepari	Popta	Kodinellikai	—	—

(*contd.*)

Name of Foodstuff	*Botanical Name*	*Hindi*	*Tamil*	*Telugu*	*Kannada*	*Oriya*	*Marathi*	*Bengali*	*Gujarati*	*Malaya-lam*	*Kashmiri*	*Other Names*
Cashew fruit	Anardium occidentale	Kaju phal	Mundiri pazham	Jeedi pandu	Geru hannu	Lanka amba	Kaju phal	Hijli badam	Kaju phal	Kasu-manga	—	—
Cherries (red)	Prunus cerasus	Gilas	—	—	—	—	—	—	—	—	Gilas	—
Currants (black)	—	Munakka	—	—	—	—	Kala bedam	—	—	—	—	—
Custard apple	Annona squamosa	Sharifa	Seetha pazham	Seetha phalam	Seetha phalam	Ata	Sitaphal	Ata	Sitaphal	Seetha pazham	—	Sugar apple
Dates	Phoenix dactylifera	Khajur	Pericham pazham	Kharjoo-rapandu	Khar-joora	Khajuri	Khajur	Khejur	Khajur	Eetha pazham	Kha'zur	—
Durian	Durio zibethinus	—	—	—	—	—	—	—	—	—	Durian pazham	—
Figs	Ficus carica	Anjeer	Atti pazham	Athi pallu	Anjura	Dimiri	Anjeer	Dumoor	Anjeer	Atti pazham	Anjeer	Guliar
Grape	Vitis vini-fera	Angoor	Draksha	Draksha	Draksha	Anjoori	Draksha	Angoor	Draksha	Mundi-ranga	Da'ch	—
Grape fruit	Citrus paradisi	Chakotra	—	—	—	—	—	Bilati batabi	Chakotra	—	Bedaana	—
Guava (country)	Psidium guajava	Amrud	Koyya pazham	Jami pandu	Seebe	Pijuli (deshi)	Peru	Payra (deshi)	Jam phal	Nattu perakka	—	—
Jackfruit	Artocarpus heterophyllus	Kathal	Pala pazham	Panasa	Halasu	Panasa	Phanas	Kanthal	Phanas	Chakka	—	—
Jambu fruit	Syzygium cumini	Jamun	Naga pazham	Neredu pandu	Neralai	Jamukoli	Jambhool	Kalajam	Jambu	Naga pazham	—	Blackberry

(*contd.*)

Name of Foodstuff	*Botanical Name*	*Hindi*	*Tamil*	*Telugu*	*Kannada*	*Oriya*	*Marathi*	*Bengali*	*Gujarati*	*Malayalam*	*Kashmiri*	*Other Names*
Lemon	Citrus limon	Bara nimbu	Periya elumicha	—	—	Kagaji lembu	Limbu	Pati lebu	Motu limbu	Poonaranga	Nyomb	—
Lemon (sweet)	Citrus limetta	Mitha neebu	Kolinchi pazham	Gaja nimma parelu	Gaja nimbe	—	—	Mitha lebu	Mitha limbu	—	—	—
Lichi	Nephelium litchi	Lichi	—	—	—	—	—	Lichu	—	—	—	—
Lime	Citrus aurantifolia	Nimbu	Elumichai	Nimma pandu	Nimbe	Gangakulia limbu	Limbu	Lebu	Kadgi limbu	Cheru naranga	Nyomb	—
Lime (sweet)	Citrus sinensis	Musambi	—	—	Musambi	—	Musambi	Musambi	—	—	—	—
Loquat	Eriobotrya japonica	Lokat	Lakota pazham	Lokat	Laquot	—	Lukat	—	—	Lakot pazham	Lakot	—
Mango (ripe)	Mangifera indica	Aam (pakka)	Mam pazham	Mamidi pandu	Mavina hunnu	Amba (pachila)	Amba (picklela)	Aam (pakka)	Keri	Mam pazham	Amb	—
Mango powder	Mangifera indica	Aam choor	—	—	—	—	—	—	—	Manga podi	—	—
Mangosteen	Garania mangostana	—	Mangusthan	—	Mangusthan	—	—	Mangustin	—	Manguseen pazham	—	—
Melon, Musk	Cucumis melo	Kharbooja	Mulam pazham	Kharbooja	—	—	Kharbooja	Kharmuj	Kharbooja	—	Kherbuz	Cantaloup
Mulberry	Morus sp.	Shahtoot	Musukottai pazham	—	—	—	—	—	—	—	Tul	—
Orange	Citrus aurantium	Narangi	Kichili pazham	Kamala pandu	Kithilai	Kamala	Santre	Kamala Lebu	Santra	—	Sangtar	—

(contd.)

Name of Foodstuff	*Botanical Name*	*Hindi*	*Tamil*	*Telugu*	*Kannada*	*Oriya*	*Marathi*	*Bengali*	*Gujarati*	*Malayalam*	*Kashmiri*	*Other Names*
Palmyra fruit	Borassus flabellifer	Tar	Nangu	Thati pandu	Thati nungu	Tala	Shindi shirani	Tal shah	Tal	Panam-nunga	—	—
Papaya (ripe)	Carica papaya	Papita	Papalli pazham	Boppayi pandu	Pharangi	Amrut bhanda	Popai	Pepe	Papaya	Omakai	—	—
Passion fruit	Passiflora edulis	—	—	—	—	—	—	Passion phal	Krishna kamal	Kireeda poochad pazham	—	Granadilla
Peach	Amygdalis persica	Arhoo	—	—	Mara sebu	Piccuu	Peach	Peach phal	Peach	Peaches pazham	Tsun'um	—
Pear	Prunus persica	Nashpati	Berikkai	Berikkai	Berikkai	Nashpati	Nashpati	Nashpatti	Naspatti	Sabariil	T'ang	Goshbub
Persimmon	Dyospyros kaki	—	—	—	—	—	—	Gav	—	Persiman	—	Kaki
Pineapple	Ananas comosus	Ananas	Anasi pazham	Anasa pandu	Ananas	Sapuri Anasianas	Ananas	Anarash	Ananas	Kayitha chakka	—	—
Pipal tree figs	Ficus religiosa	Pipar kapakua	Arasam pazham	Ravi pandu	—	—	—	—	—	—	—	—
Plum	Prunus domestica	Alubokh-ara	Alpagoda	Alpagoda	—	—	—	Khajur	—	—	Laar	Aladu
Pomegranate	Punica granatum	Anar	Matha-lam pazham	Donimma pandu	Dalimbari	Dalimba	Dalimb	Dalim	Dalamb	Matha-lam pazham	Daa'n	—
Prune	Prunus salicina	—	—	—	—	—	—	—	—	—	—	—

(*contd.*)

Name of Foodstuff	*Botanical Name*	*Hindi*	*Tamil*	*Telugu*	*Kannada*	*Oriya*	*Marathi*	*Bengali*	*Gujarati*	*Malaya-lam*	*Kashmiri*	*Other Names*
Pomelo	Citrus maxima	Chakotra	Bombili-mos	Pampara panasa	Chakkota	Batapi lembu	Papnas	Batabi jambura	Papnus	Bombili mas	—	Shaddock
Raisins	Vitis vini-fera	Kishmish	Drakshai	Kishmish	Drakshi	Kishmish	Manuka	Kismis	Khismis	Mundi-ringa	Kishmish zirish	—
Rasp-berry	—	Rushbary	—	—	—	—	—	—	—	—	—	—
Rose apple	Syzygium jambos	—	Pannir-koyya	Gulab jamun	Paneeralal hunnu	Chota pijuli	Jambhool	Jamrul	Gulab jambu	Jambakka	—	—
Sapota	Achras sapota	Sapatu	Sapota	Sapota	—	—	Chikku	—	—	Sapota	—	—
Star apple	Eugenia javanica	Jambrool	—	—	—	—	—	—	—	Jambakka	—	—
Straw-berry	Fragana vesca	—	—	—	—	—	—	—	—	—	Istabari	—
Tomato (ripe)	Lycopersican esculentum	Tamatar	Thakkali pazham	Seema vanga pandu	Chappara badane	Bilati baigana	—	—	Paka tamata	Thakkali pazham	Ruwangum	—
Tree tomato	Cyphoman-dra betacea	—	—	—	—	—	—	—	—	Mara-thakkali	—	—
Wood apple	Limonia acidissima	Kaith	Vilam pazham	Velega pandu	Bele	Kaitha	Kavith	Kothbel	Kothu	Vilam pazham	—	Kapith

(contd.)

FISH AND OTHER SEAFOODS

Name of Foodstuff	*Botanical Name*	*Hindi*	*Tamil*	*Telugu*	*Kannada*	*Oriya*	*Marathi*	*Bengali*	*Gujarati*	*Malayalam*	*Kashmiri*	*Other Names*
Anchovy (India)	Engraulis mystax	—	Poruva; Nethal	Poravallu	Manangu	—	Kati	—	—	Manangu	—	—
Bhetki	Lates calcarifer	—	Painee meen; Koduva	Pandu chapa; Pandu gappa	Koliji	Durrah	Khajura	Bhetki	—	Chemballi narimeen	—	—
Bombay Duck	Harpandon nehereus	—	Vangaravasi	Vanamttalu	Bombli	—	Bombil; Bummalo	Nahare; Lotia	—	Bummili	—	—
Catfish	Arius sona	—	Mandai kaleru	Tedijella	Mogamshede	—	Shingala	—	—	Valia etta	—	—
Catfish (fresh water)	—	—	Keluthi	Jellalu	Shede	—	—	—	—	Etta	—	—
Catfish (Pungas)	—	Pariaisi	Kovail	—	—	—	—	Pungwas	—	—	—	—
Crab	Paratephusa spinigera	Kenkra	Nandu	Pitha	Aedi	Kankada	Khekra	Nona kankara	Karachio	Gnanda	—	—
Eel	—	—	Vilangu kozhi pambu; Kotah	—	—	—	Vam; Bale	Bam	—	Pambu meen	—	—
Eel (fresh water)	—	—	Serampambu	—	—	—	Ahir	—	—	—	—	—

(contd.)

Name of Foodstuff	*Botanical Name*	*Hindi*	*Tamil*	*Telugu*	*Kannada*	*Oriya*	*Marathi*	*Bengali*	*Gujarati*	*Malayalam*	*Kashmiri*	*Other Names*
Red snapper	—	—	—	—	Kemmasu	—	Tambusa	—	—	—	—	—
Ribbon fish	Trichiurus Sp.	—	Savalai	Savallu	Pambole	Puttiah	Bala; Pitiurkti; Pitiwagti	Rupa patia	—	Thalayan	—	—
Rohu (Carp variety)	Labeo rohita	Rohu	—	—	Kanchhi	Rehu	Tambada massa	Ruce	—	—	—	—
Salmon (Indian)	Polynemus tetradactylus	—	Puzha-kkala	Budatha-maga	Vameenu; Rawasi	—	Rawas	Gurjowli	—	Bameen	—	Guchhai
Sardine	Sardinella fimbriata	Charee-addee	Sudai	Kavallu	Pedi; Erebai; Hesdi	—	Pedwa; Washi	Khaira	—	Chala mathi	—	—
Sardine oil	Sardinella longiceps	—	Pouchali	Noonak-avalla	Baige; Buthai	—	Torli; Haid	Kata	—	Nalla mathi	—	—
Sawfish	—	—	Valumin; Illupa	Yahla; Hathuthi meenu	Chakku-thatte; Morrasa	—	Kandere	Khanda-magar	—	Valu-sravu	—	—
Seer	Cybium commersoni	—	Mavalasi	Yellari; konema	Arkulai	—	Tuvar anjari	Champa	—	Ayakora	—	—
Seer (Maha-sole)	Barbustor	Naharm	Bommin kendi	Podhapo-lika	Hallaminu	Kapra	Khadchi; Masta Mahsala	Tor; Putitor	—	Meruval	—	—
Herring (giant)	—	—	—	—	—	—	Bhing	—	—	—	—	—

(*contd.*)

Name of Foodstuff	Botanical Name	Hindi	Tamil	Telugu	Kannada	Oriya	Marathi	Bengali	Gujarati	Malayalam	Kashmiri	Other Names
Herring (Indian)	Pellona brachysoma	—	—	—	—	Paunia piuce	—	—	—	Kannan mathi	—	—
Hilsa fish (Indian shad)	Clupea ilisha	Hilsa	Ullam	Palasah	Paliya	—	Pala	Hilsa	—	Paluva	—	—
Indian Whiting	Sillago sihama	—	Kellak-kan	Shorangi	Kane	—	Murdi	—	—	Poozhan	—	—
Jewfish	Psuedosci-aena coibor	—	Kothalai	Gorasolu; Gorakalu	Balde	—	Ghol	Poa	Poma	—	Kora	—
Katla	Catta catla	Katla	Theppu meenu	Botchee	—	Barkur	Tambra	Katla	—	Karakatla	—	—
Lobster (common)	Palaemon sp.	—	—	—	—	—	Shevand	Mocha chengdi	—	—	—	—
Mackerel	Rastrelliger kanagurta	—	Kumla Kanan-gathi	Kaman-godechalu	Bangada	—	Bangada	—	—	Aila	—	—
Mackerel Horse	Caraux melampygus	—	Parai; Vangadai	Pora	Thiri-jande; Parei	—	Labi	—	—	Chamba; Para Koolipara	—	—
Mango fish	Poynemus paradiseus	—	—	—	—	—	Dodywa; Rawas	Tupsee much	—	—	—	—
Mullet	Mulgil ocur	Andwari	—	—	Shevta	—	—	Elanga; Arwarik; Corsula	—	Thiruta	—	—

(contd.)

Name of Foodstuff	*Botanical Name*	*Hindi*	*Tamil*	*Telugu*	*Kannada*	*Oriya*	*Marathi*	*Bengali*	*Gujarati*	*Malayalam*	*Kashmiri*	*Other Names*
Mullet (marine)	—	—	Authumeen ;Manalai; Madavai	Bonthalu; Moyala; Kanisalu	Shevta; Pare	—	Mangin boir	Bhangon	—	Thiruta; Maalan	—	—
Pearl spot	—	Pitul-kas	Karssar; Pallinchon	Cashi-mara	—	—	—	—	—	Karimeen	—	—
Pomfret, (black)	Stromateus niger	—	Karappu vavval	Nalla sandawah	Karialonji chandratya	Bahal	Halwa	—	—	Karapu avoli	—	—
Pomfret, (silver) and Cohite pomfret	Pampus artgentus	—	Vaval; Mogang vavval	Chedu vallu; Thella chadu vallu; Pipud	Majie	Bahal	Chandava; Saranga; Pomplet	Chanda	—	Vella avoli	—	—
Prawn (marine)	Penaeus sp.	Jinga	Yera	Reyyalu	—	—	Kolbi	Chingri	—	Chem-meen; Konch	—	—
Ray	Rhinoptera sewelli	—	Attuvalan tirukkai	Belugiri tenku	Kottai thorake	—	Goval pakat	Shankush	—	Kottivalan ; Padyan theandi	—	—
Shark (fresh water)	—	Boalee; Parhin; Lanchi	Valai	Wallagh	—	—	Shivda Pari, Purram	Poli; Boyali	—	Vala	—	—
Shark (Hammer headed)	—	—	Komban sora	Sappa sorrah	Kebi-chatte	—	Zori; Kanere	Julia; Magar	—	Kannen-dodi	—	—

(*contd.*)

Name of Foodstuff	*Botanical Name*	*Hindi*	*Tamil*	*Telugu*	*Kannada*	*Oriya*	*Marathi*	*Bengali*	*Gujarati*	*Malayalam*	*Kashmiri*	*Other Names*
Shark (river)	—	—	Murden sora	Sorra	Baliai	—	Waghsheer	Hangar	—	Valiya sravu	—	—
Silver barfish	—	—	Mullu valai	Mullu vala	Karli	—	Karli; Datali	Khanda	—	Mullu vala	—	—
Silver-belly	Leiognathusinsidiator	—	Karal; Chuthumu - nan karai	Karalu	Kanai kurichi	—	Surgutta; Katali; Titaka	—	—	Thali mullen	—	—
Skate	—	—	Kachu uluwai	Walaw tankee; Nululavi	Fadka; Etti balliar	—	Lang; Pakat	Rahu	—	Varithalai	—	—
Snake-headed fish	—	Murrai; Dheri murl; Sowra	Verarlu	Sowarah	Koochina muri	—	Daku	Shol	—	Wrahl	—	—
Sole	Ophiocephalus striatus cynoglossus	Morrul	Virahi	Korrameenu	Poolikuchi	Sola	Sohr	Shol	—	Kannan	—	—
Sole (Malabar)	Semifaciatus	—	Aralu	Jerrypotoo	Nangu	—	Repti; Shivra	Kukurjibh	—	Manthal	—	—
Tuna	Thynnus macropterus	—	—	—	—	—	—	—	—	—	—	—
Turbot (Indian)	—	—	—	—	—	—	Kuppa or Gedar	—	—	Sura	—	—
White bait	Anchoviella sp.	—	—	—	—	—	Ehakas; Katai	—	—	—	—	—

(*contd.*)

OTHER FLESH FOODS

Name of Foodstuff	*Botanical Name*	*Hindi*	*Tamil*	*Telugu*	*Kannada*	*Oriya*	*Marathi*	*Bengali*	*Gujarati*	*Malaya-lam*	*Kashmiri*	*Other Names*
Beef	Bos taurus	Gai ka gosht	Mattu eraichi	Go-mamsam	Danda mamsa	Gomansa	Go-mans	Go-mango	Go-mas	Go-mamsam	—	—
Buffalo meat	Bulbus bubalis	Bhains-ka-gosht	Erumai iraichi	Barre mamsam	—	—	—	—	—	Pothirachi	—	—
Duck	Anas platyrhyncha	Bathak	Vathu	Bathu	—	—	Badak	Hansh	—	Tharavu	—	—
Egg, (duck)	—	Bathak ka anda	Vathu muttai	Bathu guddu	Bathu-motte	Bataka dimba	Badak ande	Hansher dim	Bathak nu indu	Tharavu mutta	Batakh thul	—
Egg, (hen)	—	Murgi ka anda	Kozhi mutta	Kodi guddu	Koli motte	Kukkuda dimba	Kombdi ande	Dim (murgi)	Murgi nu indu	Kozhi mutta	Kokar thul	—
Egg, (turtle)	—	Katchua ka anda	—	—	—	—	—	Jagol dim	—	Ama mutta	—	—
Fowl	Gallus bankiva murgi	Murga	Kozhi	Kodi	—	—	Kombdi	Murgi	—	Kozhi	Kuakur	Chicken
Goat meat	Capra hyrchus	Khasi ka gosht	Attiraichi	Meka mam-samu	—	—	Bakryache mans	Pantar mangso	—	Attiraichi	—	—
Grey quail	Coturnic ecoturnix	Batair	—	—	—	—	—	—	—	—	—	—
Liver (goat)	Capra hyrchus	Khasi ka jigar	Attu eeral	Meka karjamu	—	—	—	Pantar mettle	—	Attu eeral	—	—
Liver (sheep)	—	Kalija (bher)	Semmari attin eeral	Gorre karjamu	—	Mendha kalija	Kaleej	Mete (vora)	Kaleju	Semmari attin eeral	Kre'hnu maaz	—

(contd.)

Name of Foodstuff	*Botanical Name*	*Hindi*	*Tamil*	*Telugu*	*Kannada*	*Oriya*	*Marathi*	*Bengali*	*Gujarati*	*Malayalam*	*Kashmiri*	*Other Names*
Mutton	—	Bakri ka gosht	Attiraichi	Mamsamu	Mamsa	Manaisa chheli	Mans sheli	Vera mangso	Gheta nu gos	Attiraichi	Maaz	—
Pigeon	Columba livia intermedia	Kabutar	Pura	Pavu-ramu	—	—	Kabutar	Pyara	—	Pravu	Katar maaz	—
Pork	Sus cristatus wagner	Suar ka gosht	Panni iraichi	Pandi mamsamu	Handi mamsa	Ghusuri mansa	Mans (dukar)	Sukar mangso	Suvarnu imas	Panni iraichi	—	—
Turtle's meat	—	Kachua ka gosht	Amai iraichi	—	—	—	—	Jagol mangso	—	Ama iraichi	—	—
Venison	Antilope cervi capra linn	Haran ka gosht	Man iraichi	Ledi mamsamu	—	—	—	—	—	Man iraichi	—	—

MILK AND MILK PRODUCTS

Name of Foodstuff	*Botanical Name*	*Hindi*	*Tamil*	*Telugu*	*Kannada*	*Oriya*	*Marathi*	*Bengali*	*Gujarati*	*Malayalam*	*Kashmiri*	*Other Names*
Milk (buffalo's)		Bhains ka doodh	Erumai pal	Barre palu	Yemme halu	Mainsi dudha	Doodh (mhaish)	Doodh (mosher)	Bhes nu doodh	Erumai pal	Maa'shi duad	—
Milk (cow's)		Gai ka doodh	Pasum pal	Avu palu	Hansuvina halu	Gai dudha	Doodh (gay)	Doodh (garu)	Gay nu doodh	Pasum pal	Gaav duad	—
Milk (goat's)		Bakri ka doodh	Attu pal	Meka palu	Adina halu	Chheli dudha	Doodh (sheli)	Doodh (chagal)	Bakri nu doodh	Attu pal	Tshaavgi chir	—
Curds		Dahi	Thayir	Perugu	Mosaru	Dahi	Dahi	Doyi	Dahi	Thayir	Zaamut duad	Yoghurt; Sour cream

(contd.)

Name of Foodstuff	*Botanical Name*	*Hindi*	*Tamil*	*Telugu*	*Kannada*	*Oriya*	*Marathi*	*Bengali*	*Gujarati*	*Malayalam*	*Kashmiri*	*Other Names*
Butter-milk		Lassi	Moru	Majjiga	Majjige	Ghola dahi	Tak	Ghol	Chhas	Moru	Chuaku duad	—
Cheese		Paneer	Palkatti	Junnu	Ginnu	Chhena	—	Paneer	Paneer	Pal katti	Tsaama	—
Cottage cheese (chenna)		Panir	—	—	—	—	—	Chenna	—	—	—	Cottage cheese
Khoa (mawa)		Khoa	Thirattu pal	Khoa	Khoa	Kua	Khava	Khoa khir	—	Khoa	—	—
Skimmed milk		—	Kadain-tha pal	Venna theesina palu	—	Sarakadha dudha	—	Makhantan a doodh	—	Padakalanj a pal	Gurus	—
Whole milk powder		—	Pal thool	Pala podi	—	Dudha gunda	—	Goora doodh	—	Pal podi	—	—

FATS AND EDIBLE OIL

Name of Foodstuff	*Botanical Name*	*Hindi*	*Tamil*	*Telugu*	*Kannada*	*Oriya*	*Marathi*	*Bengali*	*Gujarati*	*Malayalam*	*Kashmiri*	*Other Names*
Butter		Makhan	Vennai	Venna	Benne	—	Loni	Makhan	—	Venna	Thany	—
Ghee		Ghee	Ney	Neyyi	Thuppa	—	Thup	Ghee	—	Ney	—	—
Hydroge-nated fat		—	—	—	—	—	—	—	—	—	—	Vanaspati; vegetable ghee
Vegetable cooking oil		Tel	Ennai	Noone	Enne	—	Tel	Tel	—	Enna	—	—

(contd.)

MISCELLANEOUS FOODS

Name of Foodstuff	*Botanical Name*	*Hindi*	*Tamil*	*Telugu*	*Kannada*	*Oriya*	*Marathi*	*Bengali*	*Gujarati*	*Malayalam*	*Kashmiri*	*Other Names*
Amaranth seeds	Amaranthus sp.	—	Keerai vidai	Thottakoora ginjalu	—	—	—	—	—	Cheera vithu	—	—
Arrowroot flour	Maranta arundinaua	—	Kuva mavu	Pala gunda	—	Araroot	Toukil	Tavkeel	—	Koova podi	—	—
Avocado pear	Persea drymifolia	—	—	—	—	—	—	—	—	—	—	—
Bread	—	Roti	—	—	—	—	Pao	Roti	—	—	—	Double roti
Cane sugar	Saccharum officinarum	Chini	Sarkarai	Panchadara	Sakkare	—	—	Chini	—	Panchasara	Madrar	—
Coconut (tender)	Cocos nucifera	—	Elani	Letha kobbari	Yelnee	Paida	Shahale	Dab	—	Karikku	—	—
Coconut milk	Cocos nucifera	Nariyal ka doodh	Thenga pal	Kobbari palu	Kobbae halu	—	Naralache doodh	Narikel doodh	—	Thenga pal	—	—
Coconut water	Cocos nucifera	Nariyal ka pani	Ilanir	Kobbari neeru	Thanga neeru	Paida pani	Naral pani	Daber jal	Pani nariyal	Thenga vellam	—	—
Groundnut cake	Arachis hypogaea	Chinia badam ka kali	Kadalai punnakku	Verusaraga pindi	—	—	Pend	Badamer khol	—	Kadalai punnakku	—	—
Honey	—	Shaid	Then	Thene	Ten	—	Madh	Mou	—	Then	Maanch	Makhu
Jackfruit seeds	Artocarpus heterophyllus	—	—	—	—	—	Phansachya bia	—	—	Chakka kuru	—	—

(*contd.*)

Name of Foodstuff	Botanical Name	Hindi	Tamil	Telugu	Kannada	Oriya	Marathi	Bengali	Gujarati	Malayalam	Kashmiri	Other Names
Jaggery	—	Gud	Vellam	Bellum	Bella	Guda	Gul	Gud	Gol	Vellam sarkara	Gor	—
Kittul flour	Caryota urens	Mari	Coonda-panai	Jilugu chettu	Bagani	—	Berli	—	Shiva patta	Kudappan mavu	—	Talipot flour
Mush-room	—	Tila chhatto	Kalaan	Kukka godugu	—	—	—	—	—	Koon	—	—
Papad	—	Papar	Pappa-dam	Appadam	Happala	Pappada	Pappad	Papar	Pappad	Pappa-dam	—	—
Poppy seeds	Papaver somniferum	Postdana	Khask-hasa	Gasaga-salu	—	—	Khus khus	Posto	—	—	—	—
Pumpkin seeds	Cucurbita maxima	—	—	Gummadi ginjalu	—	—	Bhoplya-chya bia	Kumdar dana	—	Mathan vithugal	—	—
Rajkeera seeds	Amaranthus paniculatus	—	—	—	—	—	—	—	—	—	—	—
Red palm oil	Elaies guinensis	—	—	—	—	—	—	—	—	—	—	—
Roselle seeds	—	—	—	—	—	—	—	—	—	—	—	—
Sago	Metroxylon sago	Sago	Javvarisi	Saggu biyyam	Sabba akki	Sagu dana	Sabu dana	Saboo	Sabu dana	Sago	Saboo dana	—
Sugar-cane juice	—	Ganneka ras	Karuppar charu	Ceraku rasam	Khabbinna halu	Akhju dorua	Usacha ras	Ikkhu raush	Sherdi-naras	Karum-bin neeru	—	—
Tamarind seed kernel	Tamarindus indicus	Imli ka biya ka gudda	Puliyam kottai	Chinta gingalu	—	—	—	Tetular bichi	—	Pulin kuru	—	—
Toddy	—	Tarail	Kallu	Kallu	Henda	Tadi	Tadi	Tari	—	Kallu	—	—

(*contd.*)

Name of Foodstuff	*Botanical Name*	*Hindi*	*Tamil*	*Telugu*	*Kannada*	*Oriya*	*Marathi*	*Bengali*	*Gujarati*	*Malayalam*	*Kashmiri*	*Other Names*
Water-melon seeds	Citrullus vulgaris	—	—	—	—	—	Kalingadbia	—	—	—	—	—
Yeast	—	—	Khadi	—	—	—	Khamir	—	Khamir	—	—	—

CONDIMENTS AND SPICES

Name of Foodstuff	*Botanical Name*	*Hindi*	*Tamil*	*Telugu*	*Kannada*	*Oriya*	*Marathi*	*Bengali*	*Gujarati*	*Malayalam*	*Kashmiri*	*Other Names*
Arisithipilli	Piper clusii	Peepal	Arisithipilli	—	—	Sarupipali	—	Pipul	—	Arisithipalli	—	—
Asafoetida	Ferula foetida	Hing	Perungayam	Inguva	Hingu	Hingu	Hing	Hing	Hing	Perungayam	Yangu	—
Cardamom	Elettaria Cardamomum	Elaichi	Elakkai	Elakkai	Yelakkai	Alaichi	Veldoda	Elaichi	Elaichi	Elathari	Aa'l budu'a aa'l	—
Chillies	Capsium annum	Mirch	Milagai	Mirapakayi	Mena sinakayi	Lanka	Mirchi	Lanka	March	Mulaka	March wangun	—
Cloves	Sijzyguim aromaticum	Lavang	Krambu	Lavangalu	Lavanga	Labang	Lavang	Labang	Lavang	Krambu	Ruang	—
Coriander	Coriandrum sativum	Dhania	Kothamalli vidai	Dhaniyalu	Kothambari	Dhania	Dhane	Dhania	Dhania; Kothmir	Kothambalari	Daaniwal	—
Cumin	Cuminum cuminum	Zira	Jeeragam	Jeelakarra	Jeerage	Jeera	Jeera	Jeera	Jiru	Jeerakam	Zyur	—
Fennel	—	Saunf	—	—	—	—	Sheopa	—	—	—	—	—

(contd.)

Name of Foodstuff	*Botanical Name*	*Hindi*	*Tamil*	*Telugu*	*Kannada*	*Oriya*	*Marathi*	*Bengali*	*Gujarati*	*Malayalam*	*Kashmiri*	*Other Names*
Fenugreek	Trigonella foenum graecum	Methi	Venthiyam	Menthulu	Menthe	Methi	Methi	Methi	Methi	Uluva	Meeth	—
Garlic	Allium sativum	Lassan	Ulipoondu	Velluli	Bellulli	Rasuna	Lasoon	Rashun	Lasan	Velulli	Ruhan	—
Ginger (fresh)	Zinziber officinale	Adrak	Inji	Allum	Shunti	Ada	Ale	Ada	Adu	Inji	—	—
Kandanthippli	Piper longum	—	Kandanthippilli	—	—	Pipali	Miri	Pipul	—	Kandathippilli	—	—
Lime peel	Citrus medica var acida	Nimbu ka chilka	Elumichomthol	Nimma thekku	Nimbe sippai	Lembri chopa	Limbsal	Lebur khosa	Limbuni chal	Cherunarangatholu	—	—
Mace	Myristica fragrans	Javithri	Jathipatri	Japathri	—	Jayitri	Jaypatri	Jayitri	Jaypatri	Jathipatri	Jalwatur	—
Nutmeg	Myristica fragrans	Jaiphal	Jathikkai	Jaji kayi	Jaijikayi	Jaiphal	Jaiphal	Jaiphal	Jaiphal	Jathikkai	Zaophal	—
Nutmeg rind	Myristica fragrans	—	Jathikai thol	—	Jajikayi thogote	Jaiphal chopa	—	Jaiphal bakal	—	—	—	—
Oregano	Trachyspermum ammi	Ajwain	Omum	Vamu	Onia	Juani	Onva	Joan	—	Ayamodakam	Jaawen	Jurani
Pepper	Piper nigrum	Kali mirch	Milagu	Miriyalu	Kari menasu	Golmarich	Mire	Golmarich	Mari	Kurumulaku	Marutus	—
Tamarind pulp	Tamarindus indica	Imli	Puli	Chintha pandu	Hunise; Hannu	Tentuli	Chinch	Tetul	Amli	Puli	Tembe'r	—
Turmeric	Curcuma domestica	Haldi	Manjal	Pasupu	Anashina	Haldi	Halad	Holud	Haldhar	Manjal	Lader	—

(*contd.*)

INDIAN COOKERY

CURRY POWDERS

1. Plain Masala
2. Garam Masala
3. Pulao Masala
4. Curry Powder (A)
   Curry Powder (B)
   Curry Powder (Hot)
   Curry Powder (Mild)
   Curry Powder (Madras)
   Curry Powder (Maharashtra)
5. Curry Paste (East Indian)
6. Dhania-jeera Powder
7. Sambar Masala (for Parsi dishes)
8. Sambar Powder (A)
   Sambar Powder (B)
   Sambar Powder (C)
9. Goda masala
10. Rasam Powder
11. Meat Masala
12. Panch Phoran
13. Panch Phoran
    Chaat Masala (1) (Rajasthan)
    Chaat Masala (2)
    Chaat Masala (3)
    Chaat Masala (4)
14. Tea Masala
15. Peri Peri Masala for Chicken and Prawns
16. Vindaloo Masala

1. PLAIN MASALA

Ingredients	*For 100*
Coriander	340 gm
Red chillies	115 gm
Turmeric	30 gm
Cumin	15 gm

Method

Roast and powder fine. Use as powder or grind into a paste.

2. GARAM MASALA

Ingredients	*Quantity*
Cardamom	15 gm
Cloves	30 gm
Cinnamon	30 gm
Peppercorns	30 gm

Method

Dry and powder.

N.B. This could be made with or without peppercorns.

3. PULAO MASALA

Ingredients	*Quantity*
Cardamom (large variety) **Cloves** **Cinnamon** **Peppercorns** **Bayleaf** **Badyani**	} 15 gm

Method

Use whole or crushed and tied in a muslin bag.

4. CURRY POWDER (A)

Ingredients	*For 100*
Coriander	340 gm
Red chillies	115 gm
Turmeric	30 gm
Peppercorns	30 gm
Cinnamon	
Cloves	30 gm
Fennel	

Method

Roast coriander, red chillies, turmeric. Powder all ingredients. Sieve and use.

CURRY POWDER (B)

Ingredients	*Quantity*
Coriander	1 kg
Split bengal gram & split red gram	500 gm
Fenugreek	1 tsp
Black pepper	20 gm
Turmeric	50 gm
Curry leaves	a few

Method

Dry in the sun and powder.

CURRY POWDER (Hot)

Ingredients	*Quantity*
Coriander	340 gm
Red chillies	115 gm
Peppercorns	60 gm
Mustard	30 gm
Cumin	15 gm
Caraway seeds	15 gm
Gingelly seeds	30 gm
Poppy seeds	30 gm
Split bengal gram	15 gm
Cloves	10 gm
Cinnamon	5 gm
Cardamom	5 gm

Method

Dry and powder fine. Sieve through a fine sieve.

CURRY POWDER (Mild)

Ingredients	*Quantity*
Coriander	300 gm
Red chillies (Sankeshwari)	30 gm
Turmeric	15–20 gm
Peppercorns	3 gm
Cinnamon	3 gm
Cloves	2 gm
Fennel	5 gm

Method

Roast lightly or dry coriander and red chillies in the sun. Grind all the ingredients together. Pass through a fine sieve. Store or use as required.

CURRY POWDER (Madras)

Ingredients	*Quantity*
Dry chillies	1.5 kg
Coriander	2 kg
Split red gram	115 gm
Split bengal gram	115 gm
Split black gram	115 gm
Cumin	115 gm
Mustard	1 tbsp
Fenugreek	1 tsp
Pepper	115 gm
Asafoetida	a pinch
Parboiled rice	115 gm
Turmeric	1 tsp
Curry leaves	1 tsp

Method

First dry all the ingredients in the sun. Roast dry all the ingredients together except chillies. Roast chillies separately. Powder chillies separately and other ingredients. Pass through a sieve and mix. Keep in air-tight tins (keeps for 1 year).

CURRY POWDER (Maharashtra)

Ingredients	*Quantity*
Coriander	60 gm
Peppercorns	10 gm
Fenugreek	10 gm

Ingredients	*Quantity*
Cumin seeds	10 gm
Whole wheat	10 gm
Bengal gram	10 gm

Method

Roast and powder. Use as desired.

5. CURRY PASTE (East Indian)

Ingredients	*Quantity*
Coriander	6 tbsp
Fennel	1 heaped tsp
Cloves	1 heaped tsp
Turmeric	1 heaped tsp
Cumin	1 heaped tsp
Fenugreek	1 heaped tsp
Black pepper	1 heaped tsp
Mustard seeds	1 tsp
(if to be used for beef, double quantity)	
Garlic	3 cloves
Onion (large)	1
Red pepper	to taste

Method

On a stone, grind turmeric first, adding enough water to make a stiff paste. Add all other ingredients by degrees, grinding very finely. Omit onion, garlic and red pepper if it is to be kept overnight.

6. DHANIA-JEERA POWDER

Ingredients	*Quantity*
Coriander	1 kg
Cumin	200 gm
Badyani	100 gm
Mustard seeds	100 gm
Red chillies	100 gm
Fenugreek seeds	50 gm
Bay leaf	50 gm
Cinnamon	75 gm
Cloves	30 gm
Saffron (nag kesar)	75 gm
Cardamom	30 gm
Nutmeg	5
Mace	30 gm
Poppy seeds	75 gm
Oil	30 ml

Method

Pick and apply oil to mustard seeds. Put in the sun for two days. On the third day, roast and powder all the spices. Mix with mustard powder, sieve and tin.

7. SAMBAR MASALA (for Parsi dishes)

Ingredients	*Quantity*
Fenugreek powder	150 gm
Mustard powder	100 gm
Turmeric powder	25 gm
Asafoetida	10 gm
Salt	100 gm
Chilli powder	300 gm
Oil	100 ml

Method

Mix together fenugreek, mustard, turmeric, asafoetida and salt. Add to hot oil and roast. When roasted, remove from fire and add chilli powder. Mix will and use as required.

8. SAMBAR POWDER (A)

Ingredients	*Quantity*
Coriander (whole)	300 gm
Split red gram	100 gm
Split bengal gram	50 gm
Split black gram (white)	30 gm
Pepper (whole)	30 gm
Fenugreek	10 gm
Red chilli (whole)	250 gm
Mustard	15 gm
Turmeric roots	2
Asafoetida	15 gm
Dry coconut	250 gm
Gingelly seeds	250 gm

Method

Clean and dry in sun or roast without any oil, all ingredients except red chillies. Remove the stems and roast red chillies lightly on a tava (skillet) with very little oil. Powder all the ingredients finely. Sieve all the powdered spices and mix together with salt to taste.

SAMBAR POWDER (B)

Ingredients	*Quantity*
Red chillies	500 gm
Coriander seeds	30 gm
Turmeric	30 gm
Fenugreek seeds	15 gm
Mustard seeds	10 gm
Asafoetida	30 gm
Split bengal gram	100 gm
Split black gram	200 gm
Split red gram	200 gm
Pepper	30 gm
Curry leaves	1 bunch
Cumin	150 gm

Method

Dry all ingredients in the sun or roast without oil individually. Powder chillies separately. Powder rest of the ingredients to a smooth mixture and pass it through a fine sieve. Add a pinch of salt and mix chilli powder according to taste. Store in an airtight container and use as required.

SAMBAR POWDER (C)

Ingredients	*For 100*
Coriander	20 gm
Red chillies	5
Split black gram	3 gm
Split bengal gram	3 gm
Fenugreek seeds	3 gm
Turmeric	¼ tsp
Asafoetida	¼ tsp

Method

Roast separately and powder all together.

9. GODA MASALA

Ingredients	*For 100*
Coriander	500 gm
Cumin	250 gm
Dry coconut	250 gm
Gingelly seeds	250 gm
Chilli powder	50 gm
Turmeric	50 gm
Asafoetida	20 gm

Ingredients	*For 100*
Cinnamon	20 gm
Cloves	10 gm
Salt	to taste

Method

Roast and powder.

10. RASAM POWDER

Ingredients	*Quantity*
Coriander	300 gm
Pepper	100 gm
Split bengal gram	25 gm
Split red gram	75 gm
Cumin	1 tbsp
Turmeric	a small piece
Red chillies	25 gm

Method

Dry and powder.

11. MEAT MASALA

Ingredients	*Quantity*
Coriander	250 gm
Red chillies (use fifty per cent of the mild variety or remove seeds)	100 gm
Cumin	5 gm
Fennel (saunf)	2 gm
Turmeric	10 gm
Pepper	10 gm
Cloves	2 gm
Cinnamon	5 gm

Method

Roast separately red chillies and coriander. Add cumin and remove from fire. Add pepper, turmeric, cloves, cinnamon and fennel. Mix well and powder fine. Bottle and use as required. As a rule of thum use 3 tablespoons level for 1 kg of meat.

12. PANCH PHORAN

Ingredients	*Quantity*
Mustard seeds	1 tsp
Cumin seeds	2 gm
Onion seeds	½ tsp

Ingredients	*Quantity*
Fenugreek seeds	¼ tsp
Fennel	1 tsp

Method

Mix all together and keep in a jar. Make more than required for a particular dish.

13. CHAAT MASALA (1) (Rajasthan)

Ingredients	
Dry mango powder or **Pomegranate seeds or** **Citric acid or** **Tartaric acid**	to taste
Powdered cloves, cinnamon, cardamom and pepper	
Red chillies and coriander (roast separately and powder)	
Rock salt	

Method

Mix all powders together and use as required.

CHAAT MASALA (2)

Ingredients

Dry mango powder
Lime juice
Coriander leaves
Green chillies and a dash of chilli powder

CHAAT MASALA (3)

Ingredients

Pepper
Salt
Rock salt
Black salt (black crystals)
Bay leaf
Cloves, cardamom, cinnamon and dry ginger.

Method

Powder together. Use as desired. Green chillies, fresh ginger, coriander and cumin can be ground with the above ingredients if desired moist.

CHAAT MASALA (4) (Gujarati / Marwari)

Ingredients	*Quantity*
Dry mango	150 gm
Rock salt	
Black salt	120 gm
Common salt	
Cumin	75 gm
Black pepper	75 gm
Coriander	30 gm
Chilli	30 gm
Dry ginger powder	25 gm
Pomegranate / Anardhana	20 gm
Tamarind	20 gm
Ajwain	10 gm
Asafoetida	5 gm
Cloves	5 gm

Method

Powder together. Use as desired.

14. TEA MASALA

Ingredients	*Quantity*
Pepper	50 gm
Dry ginger	50 gm
Cardamom	20 gm
Cinnamon	10 gm
Cloves	10 gm
Nutmeg	half

15. PERI PERI MASALA (RED MASALA)

Ingredients	*Quantity*
Vinegar	as required
Ginger	50 gm
Garlic	50 gm
Coriander seeds	5 gm
Cinnamon	5 gm
Cardamom	5 gm
Cloves	5 gm
Black peppercorns	5 gm
Red chillies (Peri Peri)	200 gm
Mace	5 gm

Method

Paste all the above ingredients together with the vinegar. No water should be used for the masala. When the paste is fine, it is ready.

16. VINDALOO MASALA

Ingredients		*Quantity*
Mustard seeds	Grind using vinegar	5 gm
Cumin		5 gm
Red chillies (remove seeds)		10 gm
Garlic		½ pod
Ginger		5 gm
Onion (small)		50 gm

Method

Mix all the ingredients together. Grind using vinegar.

CEREALS

Cereals form the major (40%) component of diets in India and in other developing countries and provide the main source of energy. The cereal group includes rice, wheat and millets such as jowar (sorghum), bajra, maize, ragi, waragu kut.

Rice and wheat constitute the staple diet of people in our country but in certain regions and in some seasons of the year, millets of various types are the staple food of many groups of people. Millets are a rich source of some important micronutrients. Hence, nutritionally, it is a sound policy to include a mixture of these cereals in our dietary pattern. Gastronomically, it enriches our food by providing variety. As most millets can be cultivated in dry regions as well as in refined and irrigated areas, addition of these to our diet is also economically significant. The new hybrid varieties are not only high yielding but have the potential for being a protein adjunct.

Rice is still the staple of a large part of our population and there are many varieties of rice found in our markets. The husk which forms 24 per cent of the weight of the whole grain is injurious to health and must be removed. The rice grain after it is husked consists of three parts—germ or embryo, the outer layer or pericarp, and the inner starchy endosperm.

In milling white rice, both the germ and the pericarp are lost. Restricted milling of rice preserves a sufficiently large portion of the Vitamin B and mineral matter and has a better storage life and cooking quality than hand-pounded rice, but to prevent mould growth, rancidity etc. expeditious distribution and use are necessary.

Washing rice leads to a considerable loss of Vitamin B. To prevent this, the condition of the rice should be such that the process of washing can be eliminated. Since this is difficult till post-harvest technology is well developed, one should at least see that stones and other extraneous substances are removed prior to washing, thereby limiting the number of washes required.

Age or maturity is a factor closely allied to cooking quality. The chemical constituents of old and new rice differ somewhat, causing variations in their cooking process. Stored and matured rice swells on cooking to about three to four times its original volume while freshly harvested rice increases only about twice.

Parboiling rice—treating paddy before it is milled—has been a practice in our country for a long time. This process retains the Vitamin B even where rice is milled normally, by the infiltration of the vitamin. This process also helps to minimise losses incurred in washing of the rice preparatory to cooking. Loss in protein is also curtailed. Although the quantum of protein is less in rice as compared with wheat and other cereals and pulses, rice protein is biologically superior to other cereals (except ragi) and pulse proteins.

Cooking rice in large quantities of water and throwing away the liquor is a wasteful practice and such practices must be replaced by the absorption method of boiling rice, where rice is added to hot water of approximately twice its volume and allowed to cook gently after it has come to the boiling point once.

Wheat and wheat products have been important economically and gradual replacement of other cereal grains (primarily rice) by wheat is taking place in the human diet. Besides being a good source of energy, wheat is also a good source of proteins, vitamins and minerals. Wholemeal (atta) is generally made by grinding the whole of the wheat to a powder. Wheat meal has some of the coarser portions of the bran removed and sometimes also the wheatgerm. Wheat meal can be of any extraction but is normally 80 to 95 per cent of the wheat. When wholemeal (atta) is sieved to make chapaties, parathas etc. some of the coarser parts of the bran are automatically removed. Wholemeal and wheat meal should be freshly milled or ground since rancidity sets in very rapidly.

The extraction rate and composition of refined flour (maida) is determined by national policy and 70 to 80 per cent extraction is quite normal for bread-making flours. Flour can also be fortified or enriched. Enrichment is the term used when the minerals and vitamins lost during milling are added to the flour to the approximate levels originally present in the wheat kernels. Fortification is the term used when additional nutrients are added to increase the protein or mineral value of the flour.

In considering the role of flour for the purpose of making bread, cakes, pastries, doughnuts, nans etc. it is the protein content of the flour which is significant, since it is from this component that gluten, the framework of flour mixtures, is formed when the flour is moistened. The ability to form gluten is a unique characteristic of wheat protein, not possessed by the proteins of other grains.

The quantity and quality of gluten varies with different varieties of wheats and flours and it is in terms of quantity and quality of the gluten obtainable from the flour that the strength of flour is determined. A flour which yields a relatively large amount of gluten with pronounced elastic and cohesive properties and water absorbing power is considered a hard or strong flour and is used for making yeast bread where the leavening action is prolonged. A flour that yields less gluten and is also less absorptive as to water is called soft or weak flour and is better suited for making cakes and pastries, nans etc. where the leavening action is more quickly accomplished.

Semolina or rawa is an intermediate process in milling flour and is mostly made up of endosperm (starch).

CEREALS

1. Boiled Rice
2. Fried Rice
3. Yellow Rice
4. Lime Rice
5. Coconut Yellow Rice
6. Coconut Rice
7. Moong Dal Khitchdi
8. Split Green Gram Khitchdi
9. Egg Rice
10. Curd Rice
11. Dahi Vermicelli
12. Bagala Bhath
13. Til Rice
14. Tamarind Rice
15. Ven Pongal
16. Vangi Bhath
17. Kadambam
18. Bisi Bele Huliyanna (Sambar bhath)
19. Alu ki Tahari
20. Alu gobi ki Tahari
21. Pea Pulao
22. Vegetable Pulao
23. Tomato Pulao
24. Tomato-Coconut Pulao
25. Tomato Bhath
26. Masala Bhath
27. Yakhni Pulao
28. Channa Pulao
29. Kutchi Biryani
30. Pukki Biryani
31. Moghlai Biryani
32. Muslim Biryani
33. Mutton Biryani
34. Coorgi Biryani
35. Chicken Biryani (A)
    Chicken Biryani (B)
36. Fish Biryani
37. Prawn Pulao (A)
    Prawn Pulao (B)
38. Vegetable Biryani
39. Khitchdi
40. Khitchdi Pulao
41. Vegetable Kitchdi Pulao
42. Sabudana Kitchdi
43. Dhansak
44. Mutanjan (Kashmiri)
45. Zarda Pulao
46. Chinese Fried Rice
    Chinese Mixed Vegetables
    Shanghai Omelette
    Capsicum Salad
    Chilli Sauce

47. Spanish Rice
48. Lampries
    Lamprey Curry
    Fricadelles
    Brinjal Pahie
    Chilli Sambol
    Cucumber Sambol
    Prawn Balachow
49. Chapaties (Standard proportions)
    Chapaties
50. Parathas
51. Stuffed Parathas
52. Satpura Parathas
53. Moghlai Parathas
54. Mooli Stuffed Parathas
55. Dhakai Parathas
56. Dal Kachories
57. Methi Thepla
58. Ragi Chapaties
59. Puris (Standard proportions)
    Puris (A)
    Puris (B)
60. Spinach Puris
61. Mango Puris
62. Banana/Pumpkin Puris
63. Dal and Peas Puris
64. Sweet Puris
65. Spicy Potato Puris
66. Cheese Puris
67. Dal Puris
68. Luchi
69. Bhakhari
70. Bhaturas (A)
    Bhaturas (B)
71. Tandoori Nan
72. Fried Nan
73. Hoppers
74. Hoppers (Quick method)
75. Pal Appam or Hoppers
76. Baki Roti
77. Vella Appam
78. Vatta Appam
79. Missie Roti (A)
    Missie Roti (B)
    Missie Roti (C)
80. Methi ki Roti
81. Rajmah Roti
82. Makki ki Roti
83. Urud Dal ki Roti or Bidhai
84. Bati
85. Bulgur Pilaff

1. BOILED RICE

Ingredients	*For 4*	*For 100*
Rice	500 gm	11 kg
Water	1 litre	22 litre
Salt	10 gm	100 gm

Method

1. Wash and soak rice. 2. Bring water to a boil. 3. Add rice and salt and simmer. 4. Cook till rice is soft and water has evaporated.

2. FRIED RICE

Ingredients	*For 4*	*For 100*
Pulao rice	500 gm	11 kg
Onions	115 gm	2.8 kg
Cloves	4	30 gm

Ingredients	For 4	For 100
Cinnamon	2–3 gm	30 gm
Cardamoms	3–4	30 gm
Star anise (Badyan)	½	30 gm
Bay leaves	1	a few
Fat	50 gm	1.25 kg
Salt	to taste	100 gm

Method

1. Slice onions. 2. Clean and soak rice. 3. Heat fat. Fry onions till crisp and golden, and remove. 4. Fry whole garam masala; when it crackles add rice and fry. 5. Add hot water in the proportion 1 : 2* and salt. When rice is cooked, finish off either in the oven or with live coal on top of the lid. Serve hot, garnished with fried onions.

N.B. Hot stock can be used instead of water.

3. YELLOW RICE

Ingredients	For 4	For 100
Pulao rice	500 gm	11 kg
Fat	50 gm	1.25 kg
Onions	115 gm	2.8 kg
Turmeric	a pinch	15 gm
Cloves, Bay leaf, Cinnamon, Cardamom, Badyan	2 gm	15 gm
Salt	to taste	100 gm
Water or Stock	1 litre	23.6 litre

Method

1. Pick, wask and soak rice. 2. Slice onions. 3. Heat fat. Fry sliced onions. Remove. 4. Fry spices. Add rice and fry. 5. Add turmeric dissolved in a little water; stir well. 6. Add hot water or stock in the proportion 1 : 2 and salt. 7. Finish off as for fried rice. 8. Serve garnished with fried onion.

N.B. Chopped coriander leaves can also be used as a garnish.

4. LIME RICE

Ingredients	For 4	For 100
Rice	500 gm	11 kg
Lime	2	10–12

*1 rice : 2 water.

Ingredients	*For 4*	*For 100*
Oil	30 gm	350 gm
Turmeric	1 tsp	15 gm
Fenugreek	1 tsp	15 gm
Split black gram	15 gm	350 gm
Split bengal gram	15 gm	350 gm
Mustard seeds	½ tsp	15 gm
Asafoetida	a pinch	10 gm
Cashewnuts	30 gm	680 gm
Peanuts	30 gm	680 gm
Curry leaves	a few sprigs	1 bunch
Salt	to taste	100 gm
Red chillies (whole)	5 gm	115 gm

Method

1. Boil rice and set aside. 2. Roast and powder fenugreek, turmeric, and black gram. Mix with rice. Add salt and lime juice. 3. Heat oil, fry nuts and remove. 4. Add curry leaves, mustard seeds, asafoetida, bengal gram and red chillies. 5. When brown, remove from fire and add to rice. Mix well. Add nuts and serve hot.

5. COCONUT YELLOW RICE

Ingredients	*For 4*	*For 100*
Rice	500 gm	11 kg
Coconut	115 gm	2.8 kg
Onions	50 gm	1.25 kg
Turmeric	a pinch	30 gm
Fat	50 gm	1.25 kg
Cinnamon **Cardamom** **Cloves & bay leaf** **Badyan**	2 gm	15 gm
Stock or water	900 ml	22 litre
Salt	10 gm	100 gm

Method

1. Clean, wash and soak rice for half an hour. 2. Scrape and grind coconut; soak in part of stock. 3. Heat fat, fry sliced onion till brown and crisp. Remove. 4. Add spices, drained rice, turmeric and fry. 5. Add hot stock, coconut milk and salt. 6. Cook till rice is tender. 7. Serve hot garnished with fried onion.

6. COCONUT RICE

Ingredients	*Quantity*
Rice	1 kg
Coconut	1½
Bengal gram	5 gm
Split black gram	5 gm
Red chillies	5 gm
Mustard seeds	1 tsp
Green chillies	2
Cashewnuts	10
Oil	50 ml
Salt	to taste

Method

1. Boil rice, adding salt. 2. Grate coconut. 3. Heat oil and fry cashewnuts and remove. 4. Fry grams and spices. 5. Mix together.

7. MOONG DAL KHICHDI

Ingredients	*For 4*	*For 100*
Pulao rice	500 gm	11 kg
Split green gram	225 gm	5.65 kg
Cinnamon	1 small piece	20 gm
Cloves	6	10 gm
Fat	55 gm	1 kg
Onions	115 gm	2 kg
Turmeric	a pinch	10 gm
Salt	10 gm	100 gm

Method

1. Wash and soak gram for half an hour. 2. Wash and soak rice for 15 minutes. 3. Heat fat, add sliced onion, spices and rice, dal, salt, turmeric and double the amount of water. 4. Stir and cover the vessel. 5. Cook gently till rice is tender, and khitchdi is soft. 6. Garnish with chopped coriander leaves as desired.

8. SPLIT GREEN GRAM KHITCHDI

Ingredients	*For 4*	*For 100*
Split green gram with skin	300 gm	7.5 kg
Rice	150 gm	3.75 kg
Cumin	2 gm	40 gm
Garam masala powder	4 gm	100 gm
Chilli powder	2 gm	50 gm
Cinnamon	2 gm	50 gm

Ingredients	*For 4*	*For 100*
Black cardamom	4 gm	100 gm
Ginger	20 gm	500 gm
Onions (optional)	60 gm	1.5 kg
Fat	100 gm	2.5 kg
Salt	to taste	100 gm

Method

1. Wash and soak split green gram and rice separately. Heat half the fat. 2. Add cumin, chilli, cinnamon, cardamom and garam masala. Fry well. 3. Add rice and split green gram. Fry again. 4. Add twice the amount of hot water and salt. Cook till both rice and gram are tender. 5. Heat remaining fat. Fry sliced ginger and onion (if used), till brown. 6. Add khitchdi, mix well and remove.

9. EGG RICE

Ingredients	*For 4*	*For 100*
Pulao rice	500 gm	11 kg
Eggs	4	100
Fat	50 gm	1.25 kg
Spring onions	50 gm	1.25 kg
Peppercorns	10 gm	250 gm
Cloves	6	15 gm
Cinnamon	a small piece	30 gm
Salt	to taste	80–100 gm

Method

1. Wash and boil the rice, adding cinnamon, cloves, salt and peppercorns. 2. Keep the rice warm till you prepare the eggs. 3. Beat the eggs well (white first and then add the yolk), chop onion with leaves. 4. Heat fat; sauté onions. Add well beaten eggs, cook for a minute or two. 5. Add rice and stir well. Remove and serve hot.

N.B. Remove cinnamon and cloves before serving the rice.

10. CURD RICE

Ingredients	*For 4*	*For 100*
Rice	400 gm	10 kg
Curds (fresh)	600 ml	15 litre
Milk	400 ml	10 litre
Salt	to taste	100 gm
Ginger	10 gm	200 gm
Green chillies	10 gm	200 gm

Ingredients	*For 4*	*For 100*
Mustard seeds	4 gm	50 gm
Asafoetida	a pinch	50 gm
Curry leaves	1 sprig	1 bunch
Oil	30 ml	500 ml

Method

1. Boil rice, adding salt. Cool slightly. 2. Mix with curds. Add boiled and cooled milk. 3. Chop green chillies and ginger fine. 4. Heat oil. Fry mustard seeds and asafoetida. 5. Add curry leaves and chopped ingredients. Sauté for 2 minutes. 6. Switch off the fire and add the rice curds mixture to the pan. 7. Mix well. Serve with pickles.

11. DAHI VERMICELLI

Ingredients	*For 4*	*For 100*
Vermicelli	200 gm	5 kg
Curds (fresh)	350 gm	8.75 kg
Salt	to taste	200 gm
Green chillies	5 gm	125 gm
Ginger	5 gm	125 gm
Mustard seeds	2 gm	50 gm
Asafoetida	2 gm	50 gm
Curry leaves	2 gm	50 gm
Red chillies	1 gm	25 gm
Oil	10 ml	250 ml

Method

1. Boil the vermicelli. 2. Mix with curds, chopped green chillies, salt and ginger. 3. Heat oil. 4. Fry mustard seeds, asafoetida, curry leaves and whole red chilli. 5. Pour over vermicelli mixture. 6. Mix well and serve with pickles.

12. BAGALA BHATH

Ingredients	*Quantity*
Vermicelli	100 gm
Curds	50 gm
Milk	50 gm
Oil	10 gm
Green chillies	3 gm
Ginger	5 gm

Ingredients	*Quantity*
Split black gram	5 gm
Mustard seeds	1 gm
Curry leaves	a few
Coriander leaves	a little
Salt	to taste

Method

1. Boil vermicelli. Mix with milk and curds. 2. Add salt, curry leaves. 3. Heat oil. Add green chillies, ginger, black gram and mustard seeds. 4. Pour over vermicelli. Mix well. Garnish with finely chopped coriander leaves.

N.B. For the tempering (Method No. 3), mustard seeds, Bengal gram, red chillies, green chillies and ginger can be used instead. Fried nuts can also be mixed with the Bagala bhath.

13. TIL RICE

Ingredients	*For 4*	*For 100*
Rice	500 gm	11 kg
Gingelly seeds	115 gm	2.8 kg
Red chillies	5 gm	115 gm
Split black gram	15 gm	350 gm
Asafoetida	a pinch	15 gm
Salt	to taste	80-100 gm
Fat	115 gm	2.8 kg
Curry leaves	1 sprig	1 bunch
Cashewnuts	15 gm	340 gm
Lime	½	6

Method

1. Boil the rice. 2. Heat fat and fry the cashewnuts to a golden brown. Remove and drain. Fry curry leaves. Remove. 3. In the same fat, fry cleaned gingelly seeds, red chillies, asafoetida and split black gram. 4. Remove and grind to a powder. 5. Mix the powdered masala, fried cashewnuts, salt, lime juice and chopped curry leaves with rice.

14. TAMARIND RICE

Ingredients	*For 4*	*For 100*
Rice	400 gm	9 kg
Tamarind	50 gm	900 gm
Split black gram	50 gm	1.5 kg
Split bengal gram	50 gm	1 kg

Ingredients	*For 4*	*For 100*
Red chillies	20 gm	750 gm
Curry leaves	a few sprigs	1½ bunch
Asafoetida	1 level tsp	20 gm
Gingelly oil	150 gm	3 kg
Turmeric	a pinch	10 gm
Salt	to taste	100-120 gm
Peppercorns	a few	20 gm
Green chillies	1	15 gm
Ginger	a small piece	5 gm
Mustard	a pinch	5 gm
Water for tamarind	200 ml (approx.)	4.5 litre

Method

1. Cook rice with salt, till just done, and cool. 2. Soak tamarind in water and extract the juice. 3. Roast black gram, bengal gram and red chillies separately and grind to a coarse powder. 4. Heat oil, add asafoetida, mustard, peppercorns, turmeric, green chillies, ginger and chopped curry leaves. 5. When mustard seeds crackle, add tamarind extract, powdered spices and salt and cook till all water evaporates and mixture thickens. 6. Mix the tamarind mixture thoroughly with the rice, cover and serve hot.

N.B. Fried cashewnuts or groundnuts can be used for garnishing.

15. VEN PONGAL

Ingredients	*For 4*	*For 100*
Rice	500 gm	11 kg
Split green gram	225 gm	5.6 kg
Cashewnuts	30 gm	680 gm
Pepper	10 gm	225 gm
Cumin	3 gm	30 gm
Ginger	10 gm	225 gm
Fat	50 gm	1.25 kg
Salt	to taste	80-100 gm
Water	1 litre (approx.)	25 litre (approx.)

Method

1. Heat fat. Fry cashewnuts till golden brown and remove. Fry whole pepper and cumin. Add gram and fry lightly. Remove. 2. Boil the water: add washed rice and fried gram. 3. When half cooked, add salt and chopped ginger. 4. When done, add cashewnuts and remaining fat. Serve with coconut chutney.

16. VANGI BHATH

Ingredients		For 4	For 100
Rice		500 gm	11 kg
Brinjals (small)		1 kg	18 kg
Split black gram	Masala	115 gm	1.5 kg
Split bengal gram	Masala	115 gm	1.5 kg
Chilli powder	Masala	2 tsp	100 gm
Turmeric	Masala	a pinch	15 gm
Mustard	Masala	2 tsp	55 gm
Asafoetida	Masala	a large pinch	30 gm
Coriander seeds	Masala	5 gm	115 gm
Pepper	Masala	a small pinch	15 gm
Cumin	Masala	½ tsp	30 gm
Salt		to taste	100-120 gm
Tamarind		30 gm	450 gm
Oil		50 ml	1.25 litre

Method

1. Cook rice. 2. Roast the masala ingredients, and powder coarsely. 3. Make a thick extraction of tamarind. 4. Wash and cut brinjals into halves. 5. Heat fat. Add brinjal, powdered spices, fry well. Add tamarind extract and salt and simmer till cooked. 6. Add the curry to the rice. Mix well and serve hot.

17. KADAMBAM

Ingredients	For 4	For 100
Rice	500 gm	11 kg
Split red gram	115 gm	2.8 kg
Split bengal gram	55 gm	1.35 kg
Tamarind	55 gm	1.35 kg
Coriander seeds	15 gm	340 gm
Asafoetida	a pinch	15 gm
Split black gram	15 gm	340 gm
Mustard seeds	a little	10 gm
Oil	15 ml	250 ml
Red chillies	5 gm	115 gm
Turmeric	a pinch	15 gm
Coriander leaves	¼ bunch	6 bunches
Curry leaves	a sprig	1 bunch
French beans	55 gm	1.35 kg
Field beans	55 gm	1.35 kg
Brinjal	55 gm	1.35 kg
Ash gourd	55 gm	1.35 kg
Cucumber	55 gm	1.35 kg

Ingredients	*For 4*	*For 100*
Green chillies	5 gm	115 gm
Potatoes	55 gm	1.35 kg
Peas	55 gm	1.35 kg
Raw bananas	55 gm	1.35 kg
Drumsticks	115 gm	2.8 kg
Ginger	15 gm	340 gm
Spring onions	55 gm	1.35 kg
Coconut	55 gm	1.35 kg
Salt	to taste	100-120 gm

Method

1. Parboil the rice and set aside. 2. Boil the bengal gram and red gram together. When almost cooked remove from fire. 3. Clean and cut all the vegetables to the desired size. Boil them with a little salt. 4. Squeeze the juice of the tamarind. Add salt to taste. Add this to the vegetables. 5. Heat oil and fry chopped onions. Add this to the vegetables with chopped ginger and slit green chillies. 6. Fry together in the same oil, the coriander seeds, black gram, red chillies, asafoetida and turmeric. 7. Powder and add to the dal. 8. Fry mustard seeds and add to the dal. 9. When all the vegetables have been cooked in tamarind juice for 5 to 10 minutes, put in the dal mixture and the rice. 10. Add grated coconut. Mix without mashing the vegetables. Cook for 10 minutes. 11. Serve garnished with coriander leaves and curry leaves.

18. BISI BELE HULIYANNA (Sambar bhath)

Ingredients	*For 4*	*For 100*
Split red gram	250 gm	5.65 kg
Rice	500 gm	11 kg
Tamarind	15 gm	340 gm
Coriander seeds	30 gm	750 gm
Red chillies	15-20 gm	340-500 gm
Split bengal gram	5 gm	115 gm
Split black gram	5 gm	115 gm
Fenugreek	a pinch	20 gm
Asafoetida	a pinch	20 gm
Coconut (grated)	½	12
Salt	to taste	80-100 gm
Mustard seeds	a pinch	15 gm
Curry leaves	a sprig	1 bunch
Cashewnuts	50 gm	1 kg
Garam masala	5 gm	115 gm
Fat for frying	15 gm	225 gm
Coriander leaves	a sprig	1 bunch

Method

1. Cook red gram till very soft. 2. Soak tamarind and extract juice. 3. Fry spices, coconut and other gram in a little fat and grind to a soft paste. 4. Add the spices, garam masala, curry leaves and washed rice to cooked gram. Add salt. 5. Add sufficient hot water to cook mixture by absorption method. 6. Garnish with chopped coriander leaves and fried cashewnuts. 7. Serve hot with clarified butter.

19. ALU KI TAHARI

Ingredients	*For 4*	*For 100*
Pulao rice	500 gm	11 kg
Potatoes	500 gm	11 kg
Coriander powder	10 gm	225 gm
Chilli powder	½ tsp	55 gm
Turmeric	a pinch	10 gm
Ginger	10 gm	225 gm
Garlic	5 gm	50 gm
Onions	115 gm	2.8 kg
Fat	50 gm	1 kg
Salt	10 gm	100 gm

Method

1. Pick, clean and soak the rice. 2. Wash, peel and cut potatoes into quarters. 3. Slice onions. 4. Crush garlic and ginger and soak in a small quantity of water. 5. Heat fat and fry onions to a golden brown colour. Remove and cool. 6. Fry the potatoes and remove. 7. Add coriander powder, turmeric and chilli powder, and fry slowly. Sprinkle garlic and ginger juice. Stir and cook for a few minutes. 8. Drain the rice and add to the contents in the pan along with the potatoes. 9. Add water enough to rise 2.5 cm. (1") above the solids. Add salt. 10. Bring to boil, then let it cook slowly. 11. When ready, unmould the rice, garnish with fried onions and a few pieces of potatoes.

N.B. Equal quantities of potatoes and cauliflower may be used instead of potatoes only.

20. ALU GOBI KI TAHARI

Ingredients	*For 4*	*For 100*
Pulao rice	500 gm	11 kg
Potatoes	225 gm	5.6 kg
Cauliflower	225 gm	5.6 kg
Fat	85 gm	1.5 kg
Turmeric	2 tsp	30 gm

Ingredients	*For 4*	*For 100*
Dry ginger powder	¼ tsp	20 gm
Chilli powder	1 tsp	55 gm
Garam masala	1 tsp	20 gm
Bay leaves	2	2 gm
Cloves	8	15 gm
Cinnamon	1 piece	10 gm
Salt	to taste	100 gm

Method

1. Peel and cut potatoes in fours. Cut cauliflower into flowerettes. 2. Pick and wash rice and let it soak for half an hour. 3. Heat fat in a pan. Add cloves, cinnamon and bay leaves. Brown. 4. Add drained rice, potatoes and cauliflower and fry well for a few minutes. 5. Add turmeric and ginger powder; stir. 6. Add hot water which should be 3.5 cm. (1½") above the rice. 7. Stir in salt and chilli powder. 8. Cover and cook till rice is done. 9. When rice is cooked and each grain is separate, sprinkle garam masala over. 10. Toss lightly and serve hot.

21. PEA PULAO

Ingredients	*For 4*	*For 100*
Pulao rice	500 gm	11 kg
Peas	500 gm	11 kg
Fat	50 gm	1.25 kg
Onions	50 gm	1.25 kg
Cardamom **Cloves** **Cinnamon** **Bay leaf**	2 gm	15 gm
Salt	10 gm	100 gm

Method

1. Wash and soak pulao rice. 2. Shell peas. 3. Drain rice, slice onions. 4. Heat fat. Fry sliced onions till golden brown. 5. Remove onions; drain. Add whole spices. 6. Add rice and fry well. Add peas, continue frying for 2–3 minutes. 7. Add stock or hot water (double the amount of rice) and salt. 8. Cover and cook. 9. Finish off as for fried rice.

22. VEGETABLE PULAO

Ingredients	*For 4*	*For 100*
Pulao rice	500 gm	11 kg
Peas	115 gm	2.8 kg
Beans	115 gm	2.8 kg

Ingredients	For 4	For 100
Carrots	225 gm	5.6 kg
Cauliflower	55 gm	1.35 kg
Tomatoes	115 gm	2.8 kg
Onions	115 gm	2.8 kg
Cardamom		
Cloves		
Cinnamon	2-3 gm	15-20 gm
Bay leaf		
Peppercorn		
Salt	to taste	80-100 gm
Fat	100 gm	2.5 kg
Vegetable stock or water	1 litre	22 litre

Method

1. Shell peas. Peel and cut carrots into long thin slices. String and cut beans also into long slices. Break cauliflower into flowerettes. Slice onions. 2. Wash and drain rice. 3. Heat fat. Fry onions till crisp and remove. 4. Fry vegetables slightly and remove. 5. Add whole spices and rice; fry well. 6. Add vegetable stock and cook. 7. When rice is three-fourths done make a well in the centre. Add vegetables, cover and cook on a slow fire with live coal on lid or covered in a slow oven. 8. Cook till rice and vegetables are tender. 9. Mix well and serve hot, garnished with fried onions.

N.B. The amount of stock or water is approximate. The exact quantity required will depend on the quality of rice and the strength of heat.

23. TOMATO PULAO

Ingredients	For 4	For 100
Pulao rice	500 gm	11 kg
Tomatoes	350 gm	8 kg
Cardamom		
Cloves	2 gm	15 gm
Bay leaf		
Coconut	½	12
Onions	30 gm	680 gm
Fat	50 gm	1.25 kg
Sultanas	15 gm	340 gm
Cashewnuts	15 gm	340 gm
Coriander leaves	½ bunch	6 bunches
Green chillies	5 gm	115 gm
Turmeric	1 tsp	15 gm
Turmeric	1 tsp	15 gm
Salt	10 gm	100 gm

Method

1. Wash and soak rice. 2. Blanch the tomatoes. 3. Grate coconut, add hot water. When cold, extract milk. 4. Grind together onions, green chillies, turmeric and coriander leaves. 5. Rub tomatoes through sieve. Mix with coconut milk, add salt. 6. Drain rice. Smear ground spices over rice. Heat fat. Fry cashewnuts. Remove. 7. Fry sultanas and remove. 8. Fry cardamoms, cloves and bay leaf. Add rice and fry well. 9. Add tomatoes and coconut milk to rice with sufficient hot water to make approximately double the quantity of rice. 10. Cover and cook till rice is tender. 11. Dry off surplus moisture by putting live coal on lid of pan or by putting the pan in the oven. 12. Serve hot, garnished with sultanas and nuts.

24. TOMATO-COCONUT PULAO

Ingredients	*For 4*	*For 100*
Pulao rice	500 gm	11 kg
Tomatoes	500 gm	12.5 kg
Coconut	½	12
Salt	to taste	80-100 gm
Cloves, Cinnamon, Pepper, Bay leaf	2–3 gm	15 gm
Fat	50 gm	1.25 kg

Method

1. Pick, wash and drain rice. 2. Grate coconut and extract coconut milk, using hot water. 3. Blanch tomatoes. Peel skin. Mash and mix with coconut milk. 4. Heat fat. Fry spices. Add rice and fry. 5. Add coconut milk mixed with tomatoes and salt. (Liquid should be approximately twice the amount of rice). 6. Cook till rice is tender and dry. 7. Serve hot.

N.B. Tuna pulao can be made by following the same recipe adding a tin of flaked tuna when rice is nearly done. Stir using handle of a spoon. Cover and finish off in the oven.

25. TOMATO BHATH

Ingredients	*For 4*	*For 100*
Rice	500 gm	11 kg
Tomatoes	1 kg	25 kg
Onions	115 gm	2.8 kg
Garlic	4 flakes	30 gm

Ingredients	*For 4*	*For 100*
Ginger	5 gm	115 gm
Peppercorns	4	15 gm
Cloves	3	5 gm
Salt	to taste	100 gm
Fat	50 gm	1.25 kg
Water	1 litre	25 litre
Coriander leaves	½ bunch	6 bunches

Method

1. Add half the water to the tomatoes. Cook for a few minutes. 2. Mash well and strain. 3. Grind ginger and garlic. Mix with tomato juice. 4. Slice onions. 5. Heat fat. Brown onions and remove half for the garnish. 6. Add cloves and peppercorns. 7. Add rice and fry well. 8. Add tomato juice and remaining water and cook the rice. Add salt. 9. Cook till done. 10. Garnish with browned onions and chopped coriander leaves.

26. MASALA BHATH

Ingredients	*For 4*
Pulao rice	300 gm
Gherkins	100 gm
Cashewnuts	25 gm
Green chilli (slit)	1
Curry leaves	a few sprigs
Coriander	10 gm
Cumin	5 gm
Gingelly seeds	5 gm
Cinnamon	a small piece
Cloves	3 or 4
Asafoetida	a pinch
Dry coconut	10 gm
Mustard seeds and cumin	a pinch
Fat	20 gm
Coconut (fresh)	20 gm
Coriander leaves	15 gm
Salt	to taste

Method

1. Pick, wash and drain rice. Keep it for half an hour. 2. Roast and powder coriander, cumin, gingelly, cinnamon, cloves, and dry coconut. 3. Wash and cut gherkins lengthwise. 4. Heat three-fourths of the fat. Add mustard seeds and cumin. 5. When they crackle, add curry leaves, asafoetida, chilli. Add gherkins. Sauté for five minutes. 6. Add rice. Fry for 5 minutes. 7. Add hot water to double the quantity of gherkin-and-rice

mixture. 8. Add spices, salt and cashewnuts. 9. Cook on slow fire, stirring occasionally. 10. When the rice is nearly done, pour remaining fat over. Cover. 11. Cook till all the water has evaporated and rice is done. Serve hot, garnished with grated coconut and chopped coriander leaves.

N.B. Instead of gherkins, brinjals, raw tomatoes, potatoes or capsicum can be added.

27. YAKHNI PULAO

Ingredients	*For 4*	*For 100*
Yakhni		
Mutton	500 gm	12.5 kg
Onions	115 gm	2.8 kg
Cinnamon	a small piece	30 gm
Cloves	6	15 gm
Garlic	a few flakes	30 gm
Ginger	a small piece	55 gm
Green chillies	5 gm	115 gm
Pulao		
Pulao rice	500 gm	11 kg
Onions	115 gm	2.8 kg
Cumin	a pinch	15 gm
Bay leaf, Cloves, Cardamom, Cinnamon	2 gm	15 gm
Curds	115 gm	2.8 kg
Salt	10 gm	100 gm
Fat	50 gm	1.25 kg
Garnish		
Hard-boiled eggs	1	25

Method

Yakhni

1. Wash and cut up meat. 2. Place all yakhni ingredients in a pan, cover with stock or water and simmer till meat is tender. 3. Let it cook and remove fat from surface.

Pulao

1. Wash and soak rice. 2. Peel and slice onions. 3. Heat fat, fry sliced onions and remove. 4. Add whole spices and fry for a few minutes. 5. Add meat from stock (yakhni) and curds. Cook for 15–20 minutes. 6. Add rice and fry. 7. Add stock and salt and cook till rice is done. 8. Remove

excess moisture by putting live coal on the lid or drying in an oven. 9. Serve hot, garnished with fried onions and hard-boiled eggs.

28. CHANNA PULAO

Ingredients	*For 4*	*For 100*
Pulao rice	500 gm	11 kg
Peas	225 gm	5.6 kg
Panir	225 gm	5.6 kg
Curry leaves	1 sprig	1 bunch
Cloves	4	10 gm
Cinnamon	5 cm. (2")	15 gm
Cardamom	2	10 gm
Green chillies	2 or 3	100 gm
Salt	to taste	100 gm
Sugar	to taste	50 gm
Fat	50 gm	1.25 kg
Sultanas	15 gm	340 gm

Method

1. Heat fat. Add sultanas and remove. 2. Add panir cubes and fry to a golden brown. Remove. 3. Add curry leaves, cloves, cinnamon and cardamom. 4. Add rice and fry for 5 minutes. 5. Add shelled peas, slit green chillies, salt, sugar and hot water (double the amount of rice) to cook rice. 6. When water is almost absorbed, put in panir pieces and sultanas. 7. Cook on slow fire till water is completely absorbed and rice is cooked.

29. KUTCHI BIRYANI

Ingredients	*For 4*	*For 100*
Mutton	500 gm	12.5 kg
Rice	400 gm	11 kg
Salt	to taste	100 gm
Onions	115 gm	2.8 kg
Curds	200 ml	5 litre
Garlic	a few flakes	30 gm
Ginger	a small piece	55 gm
Cumin	½ tsp	30 gm
Cloves **Cinnamon** **Cardamom**	2 gm	15 gm
Saffron	a pinch	10 gm
Fat	100 gm	2.5 kg
Stock	800 ml	22 litre
Salt	to taste	100 gm

Method

1. Pick, wash and soak the rice. 2. Wash and cut up the meat and soak it in curds for 20 minutes. 3. Slice the onions. 4. Soak saffron in a little warm water. 5. Grind garlic and ginger. 6. Heat fat. Fry sliced onions and remove. 7. Add meat, ground spices, cloves, cardamom and cinnamon and cumin. 8. Drain the rice. Add to meat and fry. 9. Stir in hot stock. Add salt. 10. Cover the pan tightly and cook gently. 11. When rice is three-fourths cooked pour soaked saffron into the centre. Finish cooking. 12. Serve hot, garnished with fried onions.

30. PUKKI BIRYANI

Ingredients	*For 4*	*For 100*
Soup		
Mutton	500 gm	12.5 kg
Onion	55 gm	1.35 kg
Cloves		
Cinnamon	2 gm	15 gm
Cardamom		
Garlic	6 flakes	15 gm
Ginger	5 gm	115 gm
Salt	10 gm	100 gm
Rice		
Pulao rice	400 gm	11 kg
Sultanas	15 gm	340 gm
Onions	115 gm	2.8 kg
Fat	115 gm	2.8 kg
Eggs (hard-boiled)	1	25

Method

Soup

1. Wash and cut up the meat. 2. Peel onion and leave it whole;. peel garlic and bruise ginger. 3. Put all the ingredients into the pan and cook gently till meat is tender. 4. Cool and remove fat from surface. 5. Remove meat and strain soup.

Rice

1. Pick, wash and soak rice. 2. Slice onions. 3. Fry onions till crisp, remove and put aside. 4. Add meat and brown. Then add rice and spices from the soup. Fry till all fat has been absorbed. 5. Add soup and cook till rice is tender. 6. Serve hot, garnished with fried onions and sultanas and sliced hard boiled eggs.

N.B. Proportion of soup to rice 2 : 1.

31. MOGHLAI BIRYANI

Ingredients	*For 4*	*For 100*
Pulao rice	400 gm	11 kg
Mutton	500 gm	12.5 kg
Lime	1	12
Almonds or Cashewnuts	50 gm	1.25 kg
Mint	a few sprigs	3 bunches
Fat	115 gm	2.8 kg
Coriander leaves	¼ bunch	3 bunches
Onions	115 gm	2.8 kg
Ginger	5 gm	115 gm
Green chillies (chop fine)	5 gm	115 gm
Garlic	3	flakes
Curds	225 gm	5.6 kg
Milk	100 ml	2.35 litre
Red chillies (without seeds)	4 to 5	115 gm
Turmeric	a pinch	10 gm
Cardamom, Cloves, Cinnamon, Bay leaf	2 gm	15 gm
Sweet cumin	a pinch	30 gm
Saffron	a little	10 gm
Wheat flour paste	enough to seal pan	

Method

1. Wash, clean and cut the mutton into small pieces. 2. Peel and slice the onions, coriander leaves and mint. 3. Peel ginger and garlic. 4. Grind ginger, red chillies, garlic and nuts into a fine paste. 5. Heat fat. Fry onions till golden brown and crisp. Remove. 6. Add bay leaf, ground masala, and fry. 7. Add meat; fry. 8. Add tepid water and cook with lid on till meat is tender and gravy is thick. 9. Boil rice till three-fourths cooked. 10. Add salt. 11. Strain curds with a fine piece of muslin. 12. Add powdered cloves, cinnamon, cardamom, sweet cumin, turmeric, chopped green chillies, coriander leaves and mint. Add lime juice and mix well. 13. Add curds mixture to mutton. Stir well. 14. Dissolve saffron in some milk and sprinkle over half the rice. 15. In a strong pan put in layers of rice, mutton and fried onion. Repeat till all ingredients are used up. 16. Pour remaining milk and fat over the rice. Cover pan and seal edges with wheat flour paste. 17. Place in an oven 143°C (300°F) for one hour and serve very hot.

32. MUSLIM BIRYANI

Ingredients		*For 50*
Pulao rice		4 kg
Mutton (with bones)		6 kg
Potatoes		2 kg
Cinnamon	garam masala	20 gm
Cardamom (black variety)	garam masala	20 gm
Pepper	garam masala	20 gm
Clove	garam masala	20 gm
Sweet cumin	garam masala	50 gm
Cumin		40 gm
Dried plums		250 gm
Saffron		3–5 gm
Orange colour		10 gm
Turmeric		50 gm
Coriander powder		50 gm
Chilli powder		100 gm
Hydrogenated fat		1½–2 kg
Tomatoes		500 gm
Curds		2 kg
Ginger		100 gm
Green chillies		100 gm
Limes		6
Coriander leaves		1 bunch
Garlic		¼ kg
Onions		4 kg
Bay leaf		5 gm
Salt		to taste

Method

1. Boil water (double the amount of rice) with bay leaf, one-third of sweet cumin, pepper, cloves, cinnamon, cardamom, and salt. 2. Add rice when water starts boiling. Boil for 2 minutes. Remove and drain off water into another vessel. Keep water aside. 3. Clean and cut mutton and soak in curds mixed with crushed ginger, green chillies, garlic, coriander leaves, one-third cloves, cinnamon, cardamom, and onions sliced and fried crisp till golden brown and powdered. Add quartered tomatoes. 4. Peel and quarter potatoes. Half-fry in hot fat. 5. Fry in the same fat the remaining garam masala, coriander powder and red chilli powder, one-third of the turmeric and just before removing, the cumin. 6. Pour over mutton and soak for 1 hour. 7. In a heavy bottomed pan, put in the mutton and on top the fried potatoes. Over this, place parboiled rice. 8. Add water in which rice was parboiled, pulp of dried plums, lime juice, colouring and remaining turmeric mixed together. Add salt as required. 9. Seal and

cook over a slow fire—preferably coal and with live coal on top of the lid. (it can also be done in an oven for 1 to 1½ hrs.) 10. Remove from fire and keep till ready to serve. 11. Break seal. Add saffron mixed with 1 tbs. pure ghee and 1 tbs. milk. 12. Mix well and serve hot.

33. MUTTON BIRYANI

Ingredients	*For 4*	*For 100*
Meat		
Mutton	500 gm	12.5 kg
Onions	115 gm	2.8 kg
Ginger	5 gm	115 gm
Garlic	a few flakes	30 gm
Coriander powder	15 gm	340 gm
Green chillies	3	85 gm
Chilli powder	1 tsp	50 gm
Dried coconut (copra)	50 gm	1.25 kg
Poppy seeds (ground)	10 gm	225 gm
Cloves, Cinnamon, Cardamom, Peppercorns	2 gm	30 gm
Curds	225 gm	5.6 kg
Salt	to taste	80-100 gm
Fat	50 gm	1.25 kg
Rice		
Pulao rice	400 gm	11 kg
Onions	55 gm	1.35 kg
Cloves, Cinnamon, Cardamom, Bay leaf	2 gm	30 gm
Salt	to taste	50-80 gm
Fat	50 gm	1.25 kg

Method

1. Clean and cut meat. Soak in curds. 2. Roast and powder cloves, cardamom, cinnamon, and peppercorns. 3. Grind together red chillies, half the onions, ginger, garlic and green chillies and copra. 4. Heat fat. Add sliced onions. Add ground spices and fry. Add meat. Fry well. Add ground poppy seeds. 5. Add remaining curds and salt and cook gently till meat is tender. 6. Add powdered spices. Remove from fire.

Rice

1. Slice onions. Heat fat. Fry onions and remove. 2. Add spices. When they crackle, add rice and fry for a few minutes longer. 3. Add salt and

double the quantity of hot water. 4. When rice is cooked and all moisture has evaporated, remove from fire.

Biryani

Make a layer of rice in a pan, sprinkle with saffron water, place meat layer over it and again cover with rice. Serve hot, garnished with fried onions and fried nuts.

N.B. Chopped coriander leaves and mint leaves may be added to mutton if desired.

34. COORGI BIRYANI

Ingredients	*For 4*	*For 100*
Mutton (with bones)	500 gm	12.5 kg
Green chillies	15 gm	350 gm
Coriander leaves	1 bunch	50 bunches (5 kg)
Garlic	10 gm	250 gm
Ginger	50 gm	1 kg
Coconut	50 gm	1 kg
Onions	100 gm	2.5 kg
Powdered garam masala	2 gm	50 gm
Fat	30 gm	500 gm
For Pulao		
Rice	300 gm	7.5 kg
Garam masala (whole)	2 gm	30 gm
Salt	to taste	100 gm
Fat	70 gm	1.5 kg

Method

1. Wash, clean and cut meat with bones. 2. Grind together the onions, green chillies, coriander leaves, ginger, coconut, and garlic. 3. Heat fat. Add ground masala and fry for a few minutes. 4. Add meat, salt and enough water to cook till meat is tender. 5. Add garam masala and mix well.

Pulao

1. Boil water with garam masala and salt. 2. Add washed and drained rice and simmer for 5 minutes. 3. Drain. 4. In a strong pan melt half the fat. 5. Put in rice and meat in layers. 6. Pour remaining melted fat on top, when the layers are completed. 7. Seal and keep in the oven for 10–15 minutes.

35. CHICKEN BIRYANI (A) (8 Portions)

Ingredients	*Quantity*
Chicken	1 (1 kg)

Ingredients	*Quantity*
Pulao rice	400 gm
Tomatoes	250 gm
Onions	250 gm
Garlic	50 gm
Ginger	50 gm
Green chillies	50 gm
Coriander leaves	35 gm (½ bunch)
Turmeric	2 gm
Cinnamon & cardamom	3 gm
Cloves	1
Fat (preferably pure ghee)	150 gm
Salt	20–25 gm
Water	800 ml
Lime	1

Method

1. Clean and joint chicken. 2. Put into a pressure cooker with half the water, turmeric and salt. After pressure is built up cook for 3 minutes. 3. Cool and open (10 minutes). 4. Wash and drain rice. 5. Grind together ginger and garlic. 6. Slice onions and quarter tomatoes. 7. Heat fat. Add whole gram masala. 8. Add sliced onions and sauté. 9. Add ginger and garlic and fry for ten minutes. 10. Add tomatoes, whole green chillies and chopped coriander leaves. Fry for another ten minutes. 11. Add salt. Add fried ingredients to chicken and add remaining water (hot). 12. Bring to boil. Add rice and lime juice. 13. Put lid on. When steam starts coming out put weight on and cook for 10–12 minutes over slow fire. 14. Cool slightly (10–15 minutes). Open and serve immediately.

CHICKEN BIRYANI (B)

Ingredients	*For 4*	*For 100*
For curry		
Chicken (Fryer)	1	25
Onions	225 gm	5.65 kg
Fat	100 gm	2.5 kg
Garlic	5 gm	115 gm
Coriander seeds	5 gm	115 gm
Ginger	5 gm	115 gm
Cloves **Cinnamom** **Cardamom** **Peppercorns**	2 gm	30 gm
Chilli powder	½ tsp	50 gm

Ingredients	*For 4*	*For 100*
Cumin powder	¼ tsp	30 gm
Curds	225 gm	5.65 kg
Lime	1	12
Salt	to taste	80-100 gm
Rice		
Pulao rice	400 gm	11 kg
Cloves }		
Cinnamon }		
Cardamom }	2 gm	30 gm
Bay leaf }		
Peppercorns }		
Saffron	a little	15 gm
Salt	to taste	80-100 gm
Milk	a little	

Method

1. Half boil the rice with salt and spices. 2. Remove and drain. 3. Wash and joint the chicken. 4. Grind together cloves, cinnamon, cardamom, peppercorns, chilli powder, cumin and coriander. 5. Add ground spices to chicken with chopped garlic, ginger, curds, lime juice and soak for at least half an hour. 6. Heat fat. Fry sliced onions till crisp. Remove and drain. 7. Add salt and half of the crushed fried onions to the meat. 8. Put in partially cooked rice over the meat. 9. Dissolve saffron in a little hot milk and pour over the rice. 10. Add remaining fat. 11. Seal the pan and bring to boil. Reduce the fire and cook till meat and rice are done. This can be done in the oven. 12. Serve garnished with fried onions.

N.B. Fried cashewnuts and sliced hard-boiled eggs can be used to garnish the dish. If chicken is inclined to be tough, cook chicken partially over a slow fire after marinating.

36. FISH BIRYANI

Ingredients	*For 4*	*For 100*
Pulao rice	400 gm	11 kg
Tomatoes	500 gm	12.5 kg
Coconut	½	12
Salt	to taste	80-100 gm
Cloves }		
Cinnamon }	2 gm	15 gm
Pepper }		
Bay leaf }		
Fat	50 gm	1.25 kg
Fish	500 gm	12.5 kg
Salt	10 gm	80-100 gm

Ingredients	For 4	For 100
Garlic	3 cloves	30 gm
Ginger	5 gm	115 gm
Mint leaves	a few	2 bunches
Curds	150 ml	3.25 litre

Method

1. Remove bones from fish and marinate it in curds mixed with salt, chopped garlic, ginger and mint leaves. Let it stand for one hour. 2. Prepare rice as for Tomato-Coconut Pulao. 3. When rice is three fourths done make a well in the centre, and put in the fish. 4. Finish off the cooking. Mix well and serve hot.

37. PRAWN PULAO (A)

Ingredients	For 4	For 100
Prawns	1 kg	25 kg
Peas	450 gm	11 kg
Pulao rice	400 gm	11 kg
Onions	115 gm	2.8 kg
Red chillies	2	50 gm
Cloves **Cinnamon** **Cardamom**	2 gm	15 gm
Fat	50 gm	1.25 kg
Coconut	½	12
Turmeric	a pinch	15 gm
Salt	to taste	80-100 gm

Method

1. Shell prawns. Remove intestines. Wash thoroughly, smear with turmeric and salt; keep aside. 2. Shell peas. 3. Grind together chillies, cloves, cinnamon and cardamom. 4. Scrape coconut and extract milk. 5. Wash and soak rice. 6. Heat fat. Fry sliced onions; when brown, add prepared prawns and peas. Cook with lid on for about 10 minutes. 7. Add rice and fry. 8. Add coconut milk, ground spices, salt and enough hot water (twice the amount of liquid to rice). 9. Cook till rice is done and all the water has been absorbed. Serve hot.

PRAWN PULAO (B)

Ingredients	For 4	For 100
Prawns	500 gm	12.5 kg
Tomatoes	115 gm	2.8 kg
Curds	55 gm	1.35 kg
Onions	100 gm	2.5 kg

Ingredients	*For 4*	*For 100*
Coriander powder	10 gm	225 gm
Turmeric	½ tsp	15 gm
Cumin	1 tsp	15 gm
Garam masala	½ tsp	15 gm
Chilli powder	2 tsp	85 gm
Salt	to taste	80-100 gm
Fat	50 gm	1.25 kg
Coriander leaves	a few sprigs	1 bunch
Rice		
Pulao rice	400 gm	11 kg
Fat	50 gm	1.25 kg
Cloves / **Cinnamon** / **Cardamom**	2 gm	15 gm

Method

1. Shell prawns. Remove intestines and wash well. 2. Heat fat, fry sliced onions until golden brown. 3. Add cumin and finely chopped tomatoes. 4. Fry well. Add cleaned prawns and the rest of the spices, except the garam masala. Add salt. 5. Fry for another 10 minutes adding small amounts of curds at a time. 6. Add water (small quantity) and simmer till prawns are tender and a thick gravy remains. 7. Sprinkle with garam masala and finely chopped coriander leaves.

Rice

1. Prepare rice as for fried rice. 2. Put rice and prawn curry in layers. 3. Cover and seal the lid. Keep in the oven for about 30 minutes. 4. Serve hot.

38. VEGETABLE BIRYANI

Ingredients	*For 4*	*For 100*
Rice	225 gm	5.65 kg
Split green gram	115 gm	2.8 kg
Potatoes	115 gm	2.8 kg
Carrots	115 gm	2.8 kg
Peas	115 gm	2.8 kg
Tomatoes	115 gm	2.8 kg
Onions	115 gm	2.8 kg
Coconut	½	12
Cumin	a pinch	15 gm
Chilli powder	½ tsp	30 gm
Turmeric	a pinch	15 gm
Sultanas	10 gm	250 gm

Ingredients	For 4	For 100
Cashewnuts	15 gm	350 gm
Peanuts	15 gm	350 gm
Fat	100 gm	2.5 kg
Curds	75 gm	1.8 kg
Salt	to taste	100 gm

Method

1. Grind together coconut, cumin, turmeric, chilli powder and onions and extract milk. 2. Clean and soak rice and gram. 3. Prepare vegetables and blanch tomatoes. 4. Heat fat; add peas and carrots. Cook for 5 minutes. 5. Add blanched tomatoes and salt. 6. Cook till peas and carrots are tender. 7. Boil, peel and slice potatoes. Fry in hot fat till brown. Remove. 8. Fry rice and gram—add coconut milk and vegetable stock (3 fingers above rice). 9. When rice is three-fourths done, add cooked vegetables, curds and salt. 10. Cook on a slow fire with live coal on top of the lid. When dry, remove and serve garnished with fried potatoes and fried sultanas, cashewnuts and peanuts.

39. KHITCHDI

Ingredients	For 4	For 100
Pulao rice	500 gm	11 kg
Lentil	225 gm	5.6 kg
Peas	225 gm	5.6 kg
Potatoes (small)	450 gm	11 kg
Onions	225 gm	5.65 kg
Turmeric	½ tsp	15 gm
Chillli powder	1 tsp	55 gm
Cumin	½ tsp	30 gm
Salt	to taste	100 gm
Cardamom	2-3 gm	10 gm
Cloves	2-3 gm	10 gm
Sugar	a pinch	15 gm
Fat	50 gm	1.25 kg

Method

Soak lentil and rice separately. 2. Shell peas. Peel potatoes. Slice onions. 3. Heat fat. Brown half the onions, remove and keep aside. 4. Brown remaining onions, lentil, sugar and spices. 5. Add rice and vegetables kept whole. Fry till rice begins to stick. 6. Cover with hot water to about 2.5 cm. (1") above level of solids. 7. Add salt. Cook on very slow fire. Keep live coal on lid. 8. When rice, vegetables and lentils are cooked and all moisture is absorbed, remove. Serve hot, garnished with browned onions.

40. KHITCHDI PULAO

Ingredients	*For 4*	*For 100*
Mutton	500 gm	12.5 kg
Green chillies	5 gm	115 gm
Ginger	a small piece	55 gm
Garlic	a few flakes	30 gm
Red chillies	1	10 gm
Coriander leaves	½ bunch (45 gm)	5 bunches (450 gm)
Cardamom / **Cinnamon**	2 gm	30 gm
Nutmeg	a pinch	5 gm
Onions	115 gm	2.8 kg
Fat	100 gm	2.5 kg
Rice	500 gm	11 kg
Split green gram	115 gm	2.8 kg
Turmeric	¼ tsp	15 gm
Lettuce	10 gm	225 gm (4 bunches)
Cucumber	55 gm	1.35 kg
Brinjals	115 gm	2.8 kg
Ladies-fingers	55 gm	1.35 kg
Potatoes	115 gm	2.8 kg
Coconut	½	10-12
Saffron	a pinch	10 gm
Lime	1	10-12
Salt	to taste	80-100 gm

Method

1. Clean and cut mutton into 2.5 cm. (1") pieces. 2. Grind together ginger, garlic, red chillies, half the green chilles and coriander leaves. 3. Slit remaining green chillies. Slice onions. 4. Heat fat. Fry sliced onions and then the ground spices. 5. Add slit green chillies, crushed cinnamon, cardamom and nutmeg. 6. Add meat. Fry well. 7. Add enough tepid water to cook meat dry. Add salt. 8. Cook till meat is tender. 9. Parboil the rice. 10. Boil gram with turmeric separately. 11. Clean and cut vegetables and fry in remaining fat. 12. Extract coconut milk. 13. Soak saffron in lime juice. 14. In a large pan put in rice, gram, meat and vegetables in layers. Add more salt if necessary. 15. Pour coconut milk over. Sprinkle over the saffron. 16. Finish off in the oven or as for pulao till rice is cooked.

41. VEGETABLE KHITCHDI PULAO

Ingredients	*For 4*	*For 100*
Pulao rice	500 gm	11 kg
Split green gram	115 gm	2.8 kg
Turmeric	½ tsp	15 gm
Onions	55 gm	1.35 kg
Cucumber	55 gm	1.35 kg
Lettuce	10 gm	4 bunches
Brinjals	115 gm	2.8 kg
Ladies-fingers	50 gm	1.25 kg
Potatoes	115 gm	2.8 kg
Green chillies	5 gm	115 gm
Ginger	a small piece	55 gm
Garlic	a few flakes	30 gm
Red chillies	1	10 gm
Coriander leaves	½ bunch (45 gm)	5 bunches (450 gm)
Cinnamon } **Cardamom** }	2 gm	15 gm
Coconut	½	10-12
Saffron	a pinch	10 gm
Lime	1	10-12
Fat	100 gm	2.5 kg
Salt	to taste	80-100 gm

Method

1. Parboil rice. 2. Boil gram with turmeric. 3. Prepare vegetables. 4. Grind together ginger, garlic, red chillies, half the green chillies and coriander leaves. Slit remaining green chillies. 5. Crush cardamom and cinnamon. 6. Slice onion. 7. Heat fat. Fry onion. When brown and crisp, remove. 8. Fry ground masala and green chillies. Add vegetables, crushed cinnamon, cardamom and salt. Cook covered on a slow fire without adding water till three-fourths cooked. 9. Extract coconut milk. Soak saffron in lime juice. 10. In a large pan put in rice, gram and vegetables in layers. Add more salt if necessary. 11. Sprinkle over with coconut milk and soaked saffron. 12. Finish off in the oven or as for pulao, till rice is cooked.

42. SABUDANA KHITCHDI

Ingredients	*For 4*	*For 100*
Sago	100 gm	2.5 kg
Peanuts	50 gm	1.2 kg
Lime	½	12
Sugar	4-8 gm	150-200 gm

Ingredients	*For 4*	*For 100*
Potatoes	100 gm	2.5 kg
Green chillies	4–6 gm	125 gm
Ginger	5 gm	125 gm
Curry leaves	2 gm	50 gm
Oil	30 ml	750 ml
Salt	to taste	100 gm
Coriander leaves	2 sprigs	50 sprigs

Method

1. Roast and crush peanuts coarsely. 2. Clean, wash and drain sago and keep for 2 hours. 3. Boil, peel and dice potatoes. 4. Heat oil. Add sliced green chillies, ginger and curry leaves. Sauté. 5. Add sago, peanuts, sugar and salt. Cook covered. 6. Add cubed potatoes and lime juice. 7. Stir and cook till sago is done. 8. Check for seasoning. 9. Serve hot, garnish with chopped coriander leaves.

43. DHANSAK

Ingredients	*For 4*	*For 100*
Mutton	500 gm	12 kg
Split red gram	55 gm	1.35 kg
Lentil	30 gm	680 gm
Split green gram	30 gm	680 gm
Split field beans	15 gm	340 gm
Split bengal gram	30 gm	680 gm
Onions	50 gm	1.25 kg
Red pumpkin	115 gm	2.8 kg
Fenugreek leaves	50 gm	1.25 kg
Potatoes	115 gm	2.8 kg
Mint	5 gm	115 gm
Coriander leaves	30 gm	680 gm
Green chillies	5 gm	115 gm
Red chillies	5 gm	115 gm
Cumin	½ tsp	30 gm
Dry coconut	15 gm	340 gm
Ginger	5 gm	115 gm
Garlic	a few	55 gm
Peppercorns	a few	15 gm
Turmeric	½ tsp	15 gm
Tomatoes	115 gm	2.8 kg
Brinjals	115 gm	2.8 kg
Sweet potatoes	15 gm	340 gm
Coriander-cumin powder	5 gm	115 gm
Sambar powder	5 gm	115 gm
Garam masala	2 gm	30 gm

Ingredients	*For 4*	*For 100*
Salt	to taste	80-100 gm
Fat	30 gm	750 gm

Method

1. Wash and cut the mutton into large pieces. Cut the vegetables and chop half the onion. 2. Pick and wash all the pulses. 3. Chop coriander leaves, mint leaves and green chillies. 4. Roast and grind red chillies, cumin, and coconut to a fine paste. 5. Grind ginger and garlic. 6. Into a pan put in the mutton, ginger, garlic, pulses, cut vegetables, chopped coriander, green chillies, mint leaves, turmeric, and pepper powder. 7. Add enough water and let it cook. 8. When it is done, add tomatoes and salt. 9. Remove the mutton pieces and sieve the liquid through a soup strainer. Cut mutton into smaller pieces and add to pulses. 10. Fry chopped onion, ground spices, sambar powder and garam masala. 11. Add to the mixture. If it is too thick make it thin with more water. 12. Serve with fried rice.

44. MUTANJAN (Kashmiri)

Ingredients	*For 4*	*For 100*
Mutton	1 kg	22 kg
Onions	115 gm	2.8 kg
Cloves	6-8	5 gm
Peppercorns	12	5 gm
Ginger	a small piece	50 gm
Coriander powder	5 gm	55 gm
Cinnamon	1 piece	5 gm
Limes (large)	2	20
Sugar	30 gm	500 gm
Salt	to taste	80 gm
For rice		
Pulao rice	500 gm	11 kg
Cloves	6	5 gm
Peppercorns	12	5 gm
Cardamoms	12	5 gm
Almonds	15 gm	340 gm
Saffron	3/4 tsp	10 gm
Milk	1 tsp	150 ml
Salt	to taste	80 gm
Fat	50 gm	1.25 kg

Method

1. Wash and cut meat. Put into a saucepan with onions cut into quarters, and spices tied in a muslin bag. 2. Add salt and enough water to cover meat. 3. Cook slowly till meat is tender and stock is reduced. (Meat

should simmer very slowly.) 4. Remove muslin bag and squeeze to draw out flavour. 5. Add sugar and half the lime juice. 6. Cook slowly till a syrup of one string consistency is obtained. 7. Boil rice in water in which the remaining lime juice is added. When almost cooked drain thoroughly. 8. Melt fat in a pan, add spices for rice and then rice and meat. 9. Add blanched and sliced almonds, water and saffron dissolved in milk. 10. Cook till liquid is completely absorbed and rice is tender and dry. This can be done in the middle shelf of a moderate oven.

45. ZARDA PULAO

Ingredients	*For 4*	*For 100*
Pulao rice	225 gm	5.65 kg
Clarified butter	50 gm	1.25 kg
Sugar	200 gm	5 kg
Cashewnuts	30 gm	680 gm
Pistachio nuts	15 gm	340 gm
Cream	30 gm	680 gm
Saffron	a pinch	15 gm
Silver paper		

Method

1. Wash, soak and drain rice. 2. Heat half the clarified butter and fry rice. 3. Add one and a half times the quantity of water and let it cook. 4. When three-fourths cooked, add sugar and the remaining clarified butter, cream and saffron soaked in a little milk. Cover tightly. 5. Keep in the oven or with live coal on the lid. 6. Fry nuts in fat. Add to rice. 7. Serve garnished with silver paper.

46. CHINESE FRIED RICE

Ingredients	*For 4*	*For 100*
Rice	400 gm	11 kg
Leeks	200 gm	5.6 kg
Carrots	200 gm	5.6 kg
Cabbage	200 gm	5.6 kg
Onions	200 gm	5.6 kg
Celery	50 gm	1.35 kg
Eggs	4	100
Salad oil	100 ml	2.5 litre
Tomato ketchup	100 ml	2.8 litre
Soya-bean sauce	40-50 ml	1 litre
Prawns or pork	225 gm	11 kg
Turmeric	a pinch	15 gm
Salt	to taste	80-100 gm

Method

1. Prepare fried rice and cook till three-fourths done. 2. Shell prawns. Remove intestines. Wash well, smear turmeric and salt and fry. (If pork is used boil with peppercorns and salt and cut into cubes.) 3. Shred vegetables. Heat oil. Add vegetables. Sauté. 4. Add beaten eggs and scramble. 5. Add prawns and rice. Fry for a few minutes. Add sauces. Cover and cook till done. Remove and serve hot with Shanghai omelette, capsicum salad and chilli sauce.

N.B. When fried rice is made in large quantities divide into smaller portions and mix.

CHINESE MIXED VEGETABLES

Ingredients	*Quantity*
Garlic	2
Onions	100 gm
Carrot	100 gm
Cabbage	100 gm
Cauliflower	100 gm
Oil	2 tsp
Salt	to taste
Sugar	1 tsp
Pepper	2
Lime juice	½ tsp
Soya sauce	1 tsp
Ajinomoto	½ tsp
Cornflour	1

Method

Heat oil. Fry chopped garlic. Add sliced onion and carrot sliced or in strips. Fry. Add cubed cabbage and flowerettes of cauliflower. Stir fry till half done. Add lime juice, pepper, salt and sugar. Stir well. Add cornflour blended in a little water. Stir and cook for 5 minutes. Serve hot.

SHANGHAI OMELETTE

Ingredients	*For 4*	*For 100*
Eggs	4	100
Leeks	15 gm	340 gm
Carrots	15 gm	340 gm
Flaked crab or prawns	15 gm	340 gm
Cabbage	15 gm	340 gm
Onion	15 gm	340 gm
Capscium	30 gm	680 gm
Salt	to taste	50 gm
Oil	to shallow fry	115 gm

Method

1. Wash and shred vegetables. 2. Cut up the capsicum finely. 3. Beat up eggs slightly. Add vegetables, chopped prawns, salts, capsicum and mix. Pour into hot oil and fry lightly like pancakes. Garnish rice with strips of omelette.

CAPSICUM SALAD

Ingredients	*For 4*	*For 100*
Capsicums	115 gm	5.6 kg
Salt	to taste	50-80 gm
Lime	1	25
Sugar	30 gm	680 gm

Method

1. Wash capsicums. Remove seeds. 2. Chop and mix with lime juice, sugar and salt.

CHILLI SAUCE

Ingredients	*For 100*
Red capsicums	225 gm
or Red chillies	115 gm
Garlic	450 gm
Ginger	450 gm
Sugar	450 gm
Vinegar	710 ml
Salt	to taste

Method

1. Remove seeds from capsicums or chillies. 2. Peel and chop ginger and garlic. 3. Grind together all ingredients using vinegar. 4. Mix all ingredients together.

47. SPANISH RICE

Ingredients	*Quantity*
Onions	2 (chop fine)
Bacon	2 slices (chop fine)
Tomatoes	8 medium
Table rice	300 gm raw wt. 600 gm cooked
Capsicum	Optional (deseed, wash and chop fine)

Method

Heat large fry pan. Add 1 tsp oil. When hot, add bacon and onion. Brown. Add deseeded chopped capsicum. Add the tomatoes and boiled, cooled rice. Add salt to taste. Serve hot with meat curry.

48. LAMPRIES

Ingredients	*For 10*
Rice	1 kg
Fat	50 gm
Onions (small)	115 gm
Cloves	2 gm
Cardamom	
Cinnamon	
Peppercorns	
Salt	to taste
Stock	2 litre (approx.)

Method

1. Wash and soak rice. Slice onions. 2. Heat fat. Add a third of the sliced onions and fry. 3. Add rice and fry for a few minutes longer. 4. Add stock and rest of ingredients except cardamoms. 5. When rice is half cooked add cardamoms. 6. Finish off as for fried rice. Serve packeted as given below.

LAMPREY CURRY

Ingredients		*For 10*
Good sized chicken		1
Mutton		225 gm
Pork		225 gm
Beef		225 gm
Onions (small)		55 gm
Garlic		4
Ginger		a small piece
Cinnamon		5 cm. (2") piece
Cardamoms (powdered)		10 gm
Fenugreek	roast and grind	¼ tsp
Coriander seeds		1 tsp
Cumin		½ tsp
Fennel		1 tsp
Curry leaves		1 sprig
Fat		15 gm
Coconut (grate and extract milk)		1
Lime		1

Ingredients	*For 10*
Turmeric	a pinch
Dried prawns (roasted and powdered)	115 gm
Red chillies (roasted and ground)	10 gm

Method

1. Partially boil chicken, mutton and beef and use stock for rice. 2. Cut the different boiled meats and pork into small pieces. 3. Put into pan with turmeric, ground masala, ginger, garlic, cinnamon, fenugreek, half the onions, curry leaves, coconut milk. 4. Boil until the meat is tender, adding the prawns, cardamoms and lime juice when the curry is half cooked. 5. Heat fat in a fry pan. Fry the remaining onions and curry leaves. Add the prepared curry and simmer for a few minutes longer.

FRICADELLES

Ingredients	*For 10*
Beef or mutton	500 gm
Bread slices (grated)	2
Onions (small)	10 gm
Garlic	2 cloves
Ginger	a small piece
Cinnamon / **Cloves** / **Pepper**	a few (powdered)
Lime	½
Salt	to taste
Egg	1
Breadcrumbs	55 gm
Fat to fry	

Method

1. Mince the meat finely. Powder the cinnamon, cloves and pepper. Mix the meat with finely chopped onions, ginger, garlic, grated bread, salt and lime juice. 2. Form into balls about the size of a walnut. 3. Dip in egg and breadcrumbs and deep fry.

BRINJAL PAHIE

Ingredients	*For 4*	*For 100*
Brinjals	115 gm	2.8 kg
Mustard seeds	½ tsp	55 gm
Red chillies	5 gm	115 gm
Curry leaves	1 sprig	85 gm (1 bunch)

Ingredients	For 4	For 100
Ginger	5 gm	115 gm
Cumin	1 tsp	55 gm
Vinegar	50 ml	1 litre
Cinnamon	a small piece	55 gm
Coriander	5 gm	115 gm
Sugar	a pinch	55 gm
Onions	10 gm	225 gm
Garlic	a few flakes	70 gm
Green chillies	5 gm	115 gm
Tamarind	10 gm	225 gm
Coconut	1	10
Oil	20 gm	500 ml
Turmeric	5 gm	45 gm
Salt	15 gm	80–100 gm

Method

1. Slice the brinjals lengthwise and rub over with turmeric and salt. 2. Grind together red chillies, mustard seeds, cinnamon, cumin seeds and coriander. 3. Soak tamarind in salted water. Scrape coconut. Grind and extract milk. 4. Slice garlic, ginger, green chillies and onions. 5. Heat oil. Fry brinjals and remove. 6. Mix together the brinjals, ground spices, vinegar, tamarind, curry leaves, and sliced ingredients. 7. To the hot oil add the brinjal mixture and coconut milk. 8. Simmer till brinjals are well cooked (about 15 minutes) stirring all the time. 9. Add the sugar just before removing from the fire.

CHILLI SAMBOL

Ingredients	For 10
Red chillies	30 gm
Dried prawns	55 gm
Maldive fish	115 gm
Onions (small)	115 gm
Garlic	3 cloves
Ginger	a small piece
Green chillies	2
Cinnamon	5 cm. (2") piece
Curry leaves	a small sprig
Tamarind	55 gm
Lime	½
Sugar	1½ tsp
Coconut oil	50 ml
Coconut	1

Method

1. Roast and powder red chillies. Roast and powder prawns. Pound Maldive fish. 2. Peel and slice onions, chop garlic and ginger and slit green chillies. Extract 4 cups coconut milk. 3. Squeeze tamarind in coconut milk. 4. Heat half the oil in a pan. Fry half the onions and curry leaves. 5. When onions brown, add the remaining oil. 6. When the oil is hot, add remaining ingredients except the coconut milk, tamarind, lime juice and sugar and fry for a few minutes. 7. Add the coconut milk, tamarind and lime juice and let it cook over a brisk fire. Stir well. 8. When the gravy dries up, add the sugar. Stir well and remove.

CUCUMBER SAMBOL

Ingredients	*For 10*
Cucumber	1
Onions (small)	5 gm
Ripe chillies	2
Thick coconut milk	2 tbsp
Juice of lime	½ tsp
Salt to taste	

Method

1. Peel cucumber. Remove seeds and cut into fine strips. 2. Soak in salted water. 3. After a few minutes squeeze out water. 4. Slice onions and chillies. 5. Mix all ingredients together.

PRAWN BALACHOW

Ingredients	*For 10*
Dry prawns	225 gm
Red chillies	15 gm
Ginger	1 piece
Garlic	3 flakes
Onions (small)	115 gm
Tamarind	30 gm
Lime	2
Cinnamon	5 cm (2") piece
Curry leaves	2 sprigs
Oil	50 ml
Sugar	85 gm
Coconut milk	885 ml (2 extracts)
Salt	to taste

Method

1. Roast and powder prawns. 2. Roast and grind red chillies. Grind ginger, garlic and three-fourths of the onions. 3. Slice remaining onions. 4. Mix prawns, coconut milk, ground ingredients, lime juice and curry leaves. 5. Heat oil. Brown sliced onions. Add cinnamon. Prepare an extract of tamarind, adding one cup of hot water. Add prawn mixture and let it boil, stirring frequently. 6. When cooked and gravy is thickened add salt and sugar.

Packeting of lamprey

Clean plantain leaves. Warm them to make them pliable. Put 4 tablespoons of rice on each leaf. Make a well in the centre; add 1 dessertspoon of curry. Put in a teaspoonful of balachow or chilli sambol, cucumber sambol, brinjal pahie, a piece of chicken and one or two fricadelles. Fold leaves, secure with a stick and bake in a moderate oven for 15 to 20 minutes.

49. CHAPATIES (Standard proportions)

Ingredients	*Quantity*
Wheat flour	100 gm
Water	60 gm
Salt	a pinch
Dough weight	160 gm
Wheat for rolling	5 gm
Cooked wt. (5 in all)	145 gm
Per chapati	29 gm
Diameter of chapaties	15 cm.

CHAPATIES

Ingredients	*For 4*	*For 100*
Wholewheat flour	450 gm	11 kg
Salt	10 gm	100 gm
Rice flour	30 gm	680 gm
Fat	20 gm	400–500 gm

Method

1. Sieve flour. 2. Add salt and water and make a stiff dough. 3. Sprinkle some water over and set aside for at least one hour. 4. Knead well. 5. Divide into small balls. 6. Roll out using rice flour. 7. Bake well on both sides on hot griddle. 8. Toss on hot coal. Allow them to puff. 9. Smear with melted fat and serve hot.

50. PARATHAS

Ingredients	*For 4*	*For 100*
Wholewheat flour	450 gm	11 kg
Salt	to taste	100 gm
Fat	115 gm	2.8 kg
Water to mix		

Method

1. Sieve flour. 2. Rub part of the fat into flour. 3. Add salt and water and make a dough. 4. Keep aside for at least half an hour. 5. Knead well. Divide into even sized portions. Roll out 0.75 cm. (¼") thick. Smear melted fat. 6. Sprinkle a little flour over. Fold into two and roll out into round or triangular shapes. 7. Heat griddle and bake each side of paratha for a minute. Add fat around the edges and a little on top. Turn over and fry both sides.

51. STUFFED PARATHAS

Ingredients	*For 4*	*For 100*
Wholemeat flour	115 gm	2.8 kg
Refined flour	115 gm	2.8 kg
Milk	65 ml	350 ml
Curds	15 gm	225 gm
Salt	10 gm	100 gm
Fat	30 gm	680 gm
Stuffing		
Boiled potatoes	200 gm	5.6 kg
Fresh peas or	115 gm	2.8 kg
Minced meat	200 gm	5.6 kg
Green chillies	5 gm	115 gm
Ginger	a small piece	10 gm
Garlic	2 flakes	5 gm
Salt	to taste	100 gm
Garam masala powder	a pinch	15 gm
Coriander leaves	1 sprig	5 gm
Onions	30 gm	455 gm
Fat	30 gm	115 gm

Method

1. Sieve wholewheat flour and refined flour and rub in fat. Add curds, milk, salt and water if required to make a stiff dough. 2. Keep aside for half an hour. 3. Knead well and divide into even portions. 4. Roll into even sized rounds, spread some prepared filling on one. Cover with

another. Bind edges with a little milk. 5. Put on a hot greased griddle. 6. Turn when one side is light brown. 7. Put a tsp of melted fat around. 8. Cook both sides till light brown and crisp.

Stuffing

1. Boil and chop potatoes, shell and crush peas. 2. Heat fat. Add chopped onion, garlic, ginger and green chillies. Add peas or minced meat. Cook on a slow fire. 3. When peas are cooked, add chopped potatoes and remaining ingredients. Stir till dry. Remove and use as required.

52. SATPURA PARATHAS

Ingredients	*For 8*
Wholewheat flour	500 gm
Salt	to taste
Fat for dough	115 gm
Fat to brush over after baking	115 gm
Water to make a soft dough	

Method

1. Sift flour. Add salt. 2. Prepare a soft dough with water. Set aside for one hour. Knead well. 3. Divide into even sized portions. Form into balls. 4. Roll into rounds 17.5 cm. (7") in diameter. 5. Smear with melted fat. Roll into the shape of pencils. 6. Apply fat over. 7. Press vertically lightly. Set aside for 15 minutes. 8. Roll out to 0.75 cm. (¼") thick rounds. 9. Bake on a dry griddle over slow fire. Place over live coal or over a gas flame to finish the cooking. Smear over immediately with fat. 10. Beat lightly between the palms of the hands and separate flakes. Tear into 4 to 5 pieces and serve hot.

53. MOGHLAI PARATHAS

Ingredients	*For 8*
Refined flour	500 gm
Melted fat (for dough)	115 gm
Salt	to taste
Water to make a soft dough	
Fat for frying	

Method

1. Sift flour. Add salt. Prepare a soft dough with water. Knead well. Set aside covered for one hour. 2. Divide into 8 portions. Form into balls and set aside for another 15 minutes. 3. Roll each into a round 17.5 cm. (7") in diameter. Smear over melted fat. 4. Make a cut from centre to the edge. 5. Roll from one end of the cut side in the shape of a cone to the

other end. 6. Press cone between palms. Roll out 0.75 cm. (¼") thick rounds. 7. Deep fry till golden brown. Remove and drain. Serve hot.

54. MOOLI STUFFED PARATHAS

Ingredients	*For 4*	*For 100*
Wholewheat flour	450 gm	10 kg
Radish	225 gm	5.6 kg
Chilli powder	5 gm	115 gm
Salt	10 gm	100 gm
Fat	115 gm	2.8 kg

Method

1. Rub some fat into the flour, add salt. 2. Add water and prepare a stiff dough. 3. Divide into equal portions and form into balls. 4. Roll out as for chapaties. 5. Grate radish. Remove excess moisture if any. Season. 6. Sprinkle seasoned radish on one round and cover with another; press down the edges. 7. Cook as for plain parathas.

N.B. Radish may be cut into cubes and cooked with salt but no water, over a slow fire till tender and dry and then mashed for the filling. This helps to retain flavour.

55. DHAKAI PARATHAS

Ingredients	*For 4*	*For 100*
Refined flour	450 gm	11 kg
Salt	to taste	80-100 gm
Fat	30 gm	680 gm
Fat for frying	30 gm	680 gm

Method

1. Rub part of the fat into the flour. 2. Knead to a soft dough with water. 3. Divide dough into even sized-balls. 4. Roll each ball into a round like a chapati. 5. Smear with fat and sprinkle a little flour over. 6. Cut from the centre of the round to the edge. 7. Roll from one edge to the other to form a cone. 8. Flatten and roll into a round shape. 9. Heat griddle. Bake paratha for a minute. Add melted fat round the edges and on a slow fire, fry both sides till golden brown and crisp.

56. DAL KACHORIES

Ingredients	*For 4*	*For 100*
Black gram	115 gm	2.8 kg
Wholewheat flour	225 gm	5.6 kg

Ingredients	*For 4*	*For 100*
Refined flour	225 gm	5.6 kg
Coriander	a few	85 gm
Peppercorns	a few	10 gm
Cumin powder	½ tsp	15 gm
Coriander powder	5 gm	115 gm
Red chillies powder	½ tsp	30 gm
Salt	to taste	50-80 gm
Milk or curds to mix	55 gm	1.35 kg
Oil to fry (absorption)	50 gm	1.25 kg

Method

1. Soak black gram overnight. 2. Crush next morning and remove skin. 3. Add crushed pepper, coriander and powdered masala. 4. Heat a little oil and fry gram mixture on a slow fire till cooked. 5. Add salt. 6. Make a dough with both flours and milk or curds. Knead well. 7. Divide into even sized balls, stuff with gram mixture and roll out as for stuffed parathas. 8. Fry as for puris.

57. METHI THEPLA

Ingredients	*Quantity*
Fenugreek leaves	20 gm
Wheat flour	50 gm
Jowar or bajra flour	30 gm
Chilli powder	½ tsp
Coriander powder	½ tsp
Turmeric	¼ tsp
Salt	½ tsp
Oil	10 gm

Method

1. Sieve flours together. 2. Add chilli powder, coriander powder, turmeric, salt and chopped fenugreek leaves and mix. 3. Prepare dough, adding enough water. 4. Set aside for half an hour. 5. Divide into small balls and roll out very thin. 6. Shallow fry on a hot griddle.

58. RAGI CHAPATIES

Ingredients	*For 4*	*For 100*
Atta	50 gm	12.5 kg
Ragi flour	30 gm	7.5 kg
Hot water	60 ml	3 litre

Ingredients	*For 4*	*For 100*
Fat or oil	2 tsp	340 gm
Salt	a pinch	100 gm

Method

1. Mix salt and flour. 2. Add hot water gradually and knead for 5 mintues. 3. Prepare a soft dough and divide into balls. 4. Roll out into thin chapaties and put on a hot griddle. 5. Smear with a little fat or oil and spread it evenly. 6. Cook on both sides.

59. PURIS (Standard proportions)

Ingredients	*Quantity*
Wheat flour	100 gm
Water	50 gm
Oil	5 gm
Salt	a pinch
Dough weight	115 gm
Cooked weight of puris (8 in all)	150 gm
Per puri	19 gm
Diameter of puris	10 cm (about 4")

PURIS (A)

Ingredients	*For 4*	*For 100*
Wholewheat flour	400 gm	10 kg
Oil	1 tsp	150 ml
Salt	to taste	115 gm
Fat (absorption)	30 gm	340 gm
Water		

Method

1. Sieve flour. Mix oil. Add water and salt and prepare a medium stiff dough. Knead well. Set aside for at least half an hour. 2. Knead dough again till soft. 3. Divide into even sized balls. 4. Roll out to 0.2 cm. (1⁄16") thickness and 5–10 cm. (3"–4") in diameter. 5. Fry puris gently pressing down with a flat spoon in a circular motion. 6. When puffed up turn over. Lightly brown on both sides. 7. Drain on absorbent paper and serve hot.

PURIS (B)

Ingredients	*For 4*	*For 100*
Wholewheat flour	200 gm	5 kg

Ingredients	For 4	For 100
Refined flour	225 gm	5.6 kg
Fat	55 gm	1.36 kg
Salt	to taste	50 gm
Oil or fat to fry (absorption)	30 gm	340 gm

Method

1. Prepare a stiff dough with water, salt, and both flours. Knead well. Set aside for at least half an hour. 2. Knead dough again till soft. 3. Divide into even sized balls. 4. Roll out to 0.2 cm. (1⁄16") thickness and 7.5–10 cm. (3"–4") in diameter. 5. Follow steps 5 to 7 for Puris (A).

60. SPINACH PURIS

Ingredients	Quantity (50 Puris)
Wholewheat flour	500 gm
Spinach purée	120 ml
Water	50 ml
Salt	to taste
Fat (for the dough)	30 gm
Fat for frying	1 kg

Method

1. Sieve flour and add spinach purée, water, fat and salt to prepare a medium stiff dough. Knead well. Set aside for at least half an hour. 2. Divide the dough into even sized balls. 3. Roll out puris evenly with a 10 cm. diameter approximately. 4. Fry puris in enough oil, gently pressing down with a flat spoon in a circular motion. 5. When puffed up turn over. Lightly brown on both sides. 6. Drain on absorbent paper and serve hot.

61. MANGO PURIS

Ingredients	For 8
Refined flour	115 gm
Fat	30 gm
Mango pulp	55-85 gm
Sugar	1 tsp
Oil for frying	

Method

1. Sift flour. Rub in fat. 2. Add mango pulp and make a stiff dough. 3. Divide into equal portions and roll into thin puris. 4. Deep fry. Remove and sprinkle over with sugar. Serve hot.

62. BANANA/PUMPKIN PURIS

Ingredients and method same as above but use banana pulp or cooked pumpkin instead of mango pulp. Jaggery may be used instead of sugar.

63. DAL AND PEA PURIS

Ingredients	*For 4*	*For 100*
Filling		
Peas	100 gm	2.5 kg
Lentil	150 gm	3.75 kg
Onions	50 gm	1.25 kg
Green chillies	3	75 gm
Turmeric	a pinch	15 gm
Cumin	¼ tsp	10 gm
Lime juice	few drops	3
Salt	1 tsp	80-100 gm
Water	230 gm	5.75 litre (approx.)
Covering		
Wholewheat flour	450 gm	11.8 kg
Fat	30 gm	680 gm
Salt	1 tsp	80 gm
Water to mix	260 gm	6.5 litre

Method

1. Pick and wash lentil, shell peas. Crush green chillies into small pieces. 2. Put in all ingredients except salt and cook gently till tender and all water has evaporated. 3. Add salt. Remove from fire. 4. Sift flour. Add second lot of salt. 5. Make a well in the centre. Add melted fat. Mix well. Add water and make a fairly stiff dough. Allow to stand for one hour. 6. Divide into even sized balls. Flatten. Put in a small ball of filling. Pinch the edges to enclose filling. 7. Roll out into thin puris using a little flour or rice flour to dust. 8. Fry as for puris.

64. SWEET PURIS

Ingredients	*Quantity*
Covering	
Wholewheat flour	450 gm
Fat	30 gm
Salt	1 tsp
Water to mix	260 gm
Filling	
Split green gram	250 gm

Ingredients	*Quantity*
Sugar	100 gm
Poppy seeds	2 tsp
Cumin	½ tsp
Cloves	6
Cinnamon	1 piece
Cardamom	6

Method

1. Clean and cook gram till tender and dry. 2. Roast and powder spices. 3. When gram is cooked, add powdered spices and sugar. Mix well. 4. Sift flour. Add salt. 5. Make a well in the centre. Add melted fat. Mix well. Add water and make a fairly stiff dough. Set aside for one hour. 6. Divide into even sized balls. Flatten. Put in a small ball of filling. Pinch the edges to enclose filling. 7. Roll out using a little flour or rice flour to dust. 8. Fry as for puris.

65. SPICY POTATO PURIS

Ingredients		*For 4*	*For 100*
Potatoes		225 gm	5.6 kg
Refined flour		225 gm	5.6 kg
Cumin		½ tsp	15 gm
Onions	chop fine	55 gm	1.35 kg
Coriander leaves	chop fine	¼ bunch	6 bunches
Garam masala	chop fine	½ tsp	15 gm
Salt		to taste	80-100 gm
Fat to mix		10 gm	225 gm
Fat to deep fry (absorption)		30 gm	340 gm

Method

1. Boil, peel and mash potatoes. 2. Mix thoroughly with sieved flour, cumin, garam masala, chopped onion, coriander and salt. 3. Add fat and mix well to form a dough adding a little water if necessary. 4. Divide the dough into small balls and roll them out like ordinary puris but about 0.75 cm. (¼") thick. 5. Heat fat. When smoking hot, deep fry the puris until golden brown on both sides (as for Puris A). 6. Remove and drain on absorbent paper.

66. CHEESE PURIS

Ingredients	*For 30*
Wholewheat flour	75 gm
Refined flour	75 gm

Ingredients	*For 30*
Potatoes	150 gm
Onions	50 gm
Cheese	50 gm
Ginger	a small piece
Green chillies	2
Lime	1
Fat (to rub in)	2 tsp
Salt to taste	
Oil to fry	

Method

1. Boil potatoes. Peel and mash. Chop onion, green chillies and ginger finely. 2. Heat 1 tsp oil. Sauté onion. Add chopped ingredients, salt and lime juice to taste. Mix well. Remove. 3. Add grated cheese; mix with sieved flours. Add fat and sufficient water to make a stiff dough. Knead well till smooth. Set aside at least for half an hour. Roll out into puris 7.5 cm. (3") in diameter and deep fry. Serve hot.

67. DAL PURIS

Ingredients	*For 4*	*For 100*
Covering		
Wholewheat flour	450 gm	11 kg
Salt	to taste	100 gm
Fat	30 gm	680 gm
Filling		
Black gram	225 gm	5.6 kg
Cumin	5 gm	100 gm
Cardamom	1	5 gm
Cloves	4	5 gm
Cinnamon	2.5 cm. (1") piece	10 gm
Red chillies	3 gm	85 gm
Salt	to taste	50-80 gm
Fat	15 gm	340 gm
Oil or fat for frying (absorption)	30 ml	340 ml

Method

1. Sieve flour, rub in the fat. 2. Add salt and water and prepare a soft dough. Set aside for half an hour. 3. Knead well. 4. Divide into even sized balls. 5. Press the centre of each and put in prepared gram mixture. Close the opening well. 6. Flatten and roll out into rounds of 10 cm. (4") diameter. 7. Deep fry in hot fat on a slow fire till brown.

Filling

1. Soak gram for 2 hours. Remove husk and grind to a paste. 2. Grind the spices together. 3. Heat fat. Fry ground spices and add gram paste and salt. Fry till all moisture is absorbed.

68. LUCHI

Ingredients	*For 4*	*For 100*
Refined flour	450 gm	11 kg
Fat	60 gm	1.36 kg
Salt	to taste	100 gm
Oil for frying (absorption)	30 ml	340 ml
Warm water to mix (about 60%)		

Method

1. Sieve the flour into a mixing bowl with salt. 2. Rub in the fat. 3. Add enough warm water to form a stiff dough. 4. Knead well till the dough becomes soft and smooth. 5. Divide dough into even sized balls. 6. Roll each with the help of a little dry flour, into thin rounds. 7. Deep fry in hot oil. Drain and serve hot.

69. BHAKHARI

Ingredients	*For 4*	*For 100*
Wholewheat flour	450 gm	11 gm
Sour curds	115 gm	2.8 kg
Turmeric	½ tsp	15 gm
Chilli powder	1 tsp	15 gm
Asafoetida	a pinch	50-80 gm
Salt	to taste	100 gm
Fat	50 gm	1.25 kg
Fat to fry	50 gm	1.25 kg

Method

1. Sieve flour, add salt, chilli powder, turmeric and asafoetida. 2. Rub in fat. 3. Add sour curds and mix well. Knead and leave for 1 hour. 4. Knead again. Divide into even sized balls. Roll out into rounds 13 cm. (about 5") in diameter. 5. Fry like parathas.

70. BHATURAS (A) (15 portions)

Ingredients	*Quantity*
Maida (refined flour)	1 kg
Potatoes	250 gm
Salt	10-12 gm
Fat for frying (absorption)	150 gm

Method

1. Peel the potatoes, boil and mash. 2. Sieve the flour, add mashed potatoes, salt and enough water to form a soft dough. 3. Keep aside for half an hour. 4. Roll out puris of 6" diameter. 5. Fry them in hot fat like puris and serve hot.

BHATURAS (B)

Ingredients	*For 4*	*For 100*
Refined flour	450 gm	11 kg
Yeast	5 gm	100 gm
Curds	115 gm	2.8 litre
Salt	to taste	80-100 gm
Fat to deep fry (absorption)	30 gm	340 gm

Method

1. Mix yeast in 120 ml of lukewarm water. Set aside for 10 to 15 minutes. 2. Make a dough with curds, yeast ferment, salt and flour (fairly wet). 3. Set aside for one hour. 4. Knead well. Proceed as for Bhaturas (A) steps 4 to 6.

N.B. Bread slices soaked in water and squeezed out can be mixed with flour and soda bicarbonate to prepare dough.

71. TANDOORI NAN

Ingredients	*For 40*
Refined flour	2 kg
Baking powder	3 level tbsp
Salt	1 heaped tbsp
Melted fat	100 gm
Eggs	4
Milk	225 gm
Curds	150 ml
Sugar	1 level tbsp
Gingelly seeds	30 gm
Cold water to mix	

Method

1. Sieve flour. Mix salt and baking powder. 2. Beat the eggs with sugar and milk and mix with flour. 3. Add cold water. Mix well. 4. Make a smooth dough. Add melted fat and knead well. 5. Add salt and curds and knead again. The dough should be very smooth. 6. Keep aside for 1 hour. Divide into even sized balls. Brush over with melted fat. Rest for a further 15 to 20 minutes. 7. Shape each portion with the hand thus:

8. Smear top of nan with gingelly seeds and bake in the tandoor.

72. FRIED NAN

Ingredients	*For 16*
Refined flour	500 gm
Egg	1
Milk	½ cup
Butter	60-80 gm
Salt	to taste
Gingelly seeds	1 tsp
Granulated yeast	½ tsp
Fat for frying	

Method

1. Sieve flour. Add salt. Rub in butter. 2. Add yeast to lukewarm milk. Set aside for a few mintues and add to the flour mixture. 3. Add beaten egg gradually. Knead well. 4. When the dough doubles in size, divide into even portions and roll out into oval shapes about 1.25 cm. (½") in thickness. 5. Sprinkle gingelly seeds on top. Allow the ovals to rise about double their size. 6. Deep fry in hot fat until golden brown on both sides. Drain and remove.

73. HOPPERS

Ingredients	*For 4*
Refined flour	250 gm
Rice flour	500 gm
Yeast (dry)	1 tsp
Salt	1 tsp
Sugar	1 tsp
Tepid water	350 ml
Coconut milk	200 ml
(use ½ coconut)	(2 extracts)

Method

1. Mix yeast in tepid water. 2. Add to flours with salt and sugar. 3. Mix well and leave to ferment for about 10 hours. 4. Add coconut milk. Mix well. 5. Place a fry-pan over a slow fire. Grease the pan lightly with

gingelly oil or melted butter. 6. Pour in a spoonful of the batter. Take the pan with both hands and give it a circular twist so that about 1.25 cm. (½") more of the pan is thinly coated with the batter, which, when the hopper is cooked, forms a crisp brown border. 7. Cover with a cone-shaped tight fitting lid and cook till done.

N.B. For egg hoppers, when the hopper is half done, make a slight depression in the centre and break an egg carefully into it. Cover the pan and bake till egg is cooked.

74. HOPPERS (Quick method)

Ingredients	*For 6*
Rice flour	225 gm
Refined flour	225 gm
Dry yeast	5 gm
Warm water	1 tbsp
Sugar	1 heaped tbsp
Butter	1 heaped tsp
Coconut milk (first extract)	200 ml
Coconut milk (second extract)	400 ml
Grated nutmeg	a pinch
Salt	2 tsp

Method

1. Soak yeast in warm water. 2. When yeast starts to work (it becomes frothy and bubbly), add sugar and melted butter. 3. Add the coconut milk. 4. Add the mixture gradually to the flour adding more coconut milk, if necessary to make it suitable batter for hoppers. 5. Add grated nutmeg. 6. Set aside for 1 to 2 hours. 7. Add salt just before making the hoppers. Do not stir too much. 8. Continue as for Hoppers, steps 5 to 7.

75. PAL APPAM or HOPPERS

Ingredients	*Quantity*
Rich flour	130 gm
Toddy	100 ml
Rice flour (coarse) or Semolina (sooji)	25 gm
Water	200 ml
Coconut (large)	½
Soda	a pinch
Sugar	50 gm
Salt	to taste

Method

Roast rice flour lightly without addition of fat in a deep vessel. To the coarse rice flour, add 200 ml of water and cook to porridge consistency. Add this and the toddy to the rice flour and knead to a soft dough. Leave overnight to ferment. Grate coconut and prepare 150 ml coconut milk (3/5ths of a standard cup). Add the coconut milk, sugar and salt to the rice flour dough. Cover and let it stand.

Pour a spoonful of batter in a thick iron pan (well seasoned). Set for a minute and then take the pan with both hands and give it a circular twist till about 1 cm. more of the pan is thinly coated with the batter, which, when the hopper is baked forms a crisp brown border. The inside of the hopper pan should not be washed but greased with a mixture of melted butter and gingelly oil. If the hopper sticks to the pan, fry an egg in the pan, remove, tie in soft rag and use to grease the pan by dipping in oil and rubbing over the bottom of the pan. (Serve appam with chicken stew).

76. BAKI ROTI

Ingredients	*For 4*	*For 100*
Refined flour	500 gm	5 kg
Salt	4 gm	40 gm
Melted mutton fat or marvo	100 gm	1 kg
Eggs	2	20
Iced water (to mix)	120 ml	1.2 litre

Method

1. Sieve the flour. Add salt. Make a well in the centre. 2. Break eggs into the well. 3. Mix with sufficient cold water to make a stiff dough. 4. Knead well, and set aside for half an hour. 5. Divide into even portions. Roll out thinly. 6. Spread melted fat with the hand, pulling the rolled out dough till it is as thin as paper. 7. Gather up the ends and form into a ball. 8. Roll out again into a roti 7 cm. in diameter and ½ cm. in thickness. 9. Shallow fry on a hot greased griddle or tava. 10. Turn over, to cook on both sides. 11. When cooked, shake to make flakes.

77. VELLA APPAM

Ingredients	*For 8*
Raw rice	500 gm
Sugar	1 tsp
Toddy	250 ml
Water	50 ml
Coconut	1
Salt	to taste

Ingredients	*For 8*
Cumin	1 large pinch
Garlic (optional)	2 cloves

Method

1. Wash and soak rice. Drain and dry for a little while. 2. Pound well. Roast slightly. Sieve through a fine sieve. 3. Remove the coarser powder that remains on the sieve and to it add 1 cup water. 4. Cook together till tender. 5. Add to the sifted flour with the toddy and sugar. Knead well. 6. The mixture should be of a thick batter consistency. 7. Leave overnight. 8. Next morning grind the coconut into a fine paste with cumin and garlic if used. 9. Mix with the batter; add salt to taste. 10. Set aside for one hour. 11. Heat griddle. Pour spoonfuls of mixture and spread till about 7.5 to 10 cm. (3" to 4") in diameter and 0.7 cm. (¼") thick. 12. When one side is done, turn over and bake the second side. Serve hot with fried meat (irachi olathiyathu) or meat curry.

N.B. Half a teaspoon of granulated yeast may be used instead of toddy in which case mix yeast with a cup of lukewarm water and sugar and allow it to work for about half an hour before adding to the flour.

78. VATTA APPAM

Ingredients same as for Vella Appam but add more sugar (1 to 2 tbsp). Proceed till the addition of ground coconut. Allow to rise (about 2 hours). Pour into greased pan about 20 cm. (8") in diameter and 5 cm. (2") deep. (Aluminium or brass or enamel pan may be used). Steam in steamers. Leave to cool and remove.

79. MISSIE ROTI (A)

Ingredients	*For 4*	*For 100*
Refined flour	200 gm	5 kg
Bengal gram flour	200 gm	5 kg
Spinach	100 gm	2.5 kg
Onions	100 gm	2.5 kg
Water	200 ml (approx.)	5 litre
Salt	to taste	80-100 gm
Fat to fry	100 gm	2.5 kg

Method

1. Sift together flour and gram flour. 2. Wash spinach well. Drain and chop finely. 3. Peel and chop onions finely. 4. Add chopped ingredients to the sifted flour. 5. Add salt and water. 6. Knead to a stiff dough.

7. Divide into even portions. 8. Roll out each portion thinly to an oval shape 13 cm. (about 5") long and 8 cm. (about 3") wide. 9. Apply melted fat. Sprinkle flour. Fold into two. 10. Roll tightly lengthwise and then breadthwise (this is in order to obtain flakes). 11. Press and roll using a little melted fat. 12. Bake dry on a griddle. When both sides are baked, smear a tsp of fat on the top surface. Turn over. Press down air pockets. Turn over once more and fry for a minute or two longer.

MISSIE ROTI (B)

Method and ingredients same as above except that wholewheat flour is used instead of refined flour.

MISSIE ROTI (C)

Method and ingredients same as for Missi Roti (A) except that cornflour is used instead of refined flour.

80. METHI KI ROTI

Ingredients	*For 6*
Wholewheat flour	100 gm
Bengal gram flour	50 gm
Fenugreek leaves	50 gm
Coriander leaves	15 gm
Salt	5 gm
Turmeric	a pinch
Fat	50 gm

Method

1. Sieve flour and gram flour together. Add chopped coriander and fenugreek leaves. Add salt, a pinch of turmeric and 15 gm of fat. 2. Prepare a soft dough using water. Roll into a thin chapati. Apply fat. Make into a ball. 3. Roll it again into a chapati. Bake both sides on a hot griddle. 4. Apply fat. Fry for a few minutes and remove.

81. RAJMAH ROTI

Ingredients	*For 18*
Wholewheat flour	460 gm
Kidney beans	230 gm
Green chillies	20 gm
Onions	60 gm
Salt	to taste

Ingredients	*For 18*
Coriander leaves	a few sprigs
Fat	60 gm
Cumin	a pinch

Method

1. Soak kidney beans for about 8 hours. Then cook till nicely soft. 2. Grind together cooked kidney beans, green chillies, salt and cumin. Mix with flour, keeping aside a little flour for rolling. 3. Add chopped onions and coriander leaves and make medium consistency dough. Keep aside for half an hour. Knead well. 4. Divide into even sized balls. Roll out 0.5 cm. (about ⅛″) thick. 5. Heat griddle. Bake each roti for a minute, add fat round the edge. Turn over. Bake both sides. Serve hot.

82. MAKKI KI ROTI

Ingredients	*For 14*
Maize flour (coarse)	450 gm
Salt	1½ tsp
Water	1½ tea cupful
Melted butter or ghee	30 gm

Method

1. Sieve the flour. Add salt. 2. Prepare a stiff dough by gradually adding the water. 3. Mix and knead and use at once. Separate enough dough to make one roti. Shape the roti (thick and round) on your hand. 4. Place on well-greased griddle kept over fire. Continue flattening by pressing all round with the palm of the hand, taking care not to break it. 5. Cook on both sides over a slow fire. Smear ghee and serve. Repeat for other rotis.

83. URAD DAL KI ROTI or BHIDHAI

Ingredients	*For 4*	*For 100*
Split black gram	225 gm	5.6 kg
Wholewheat flour	225 gm	5.6 kg
Coriander powder	5 gm	115 gm
Dry ginger powder	1 tsp	20 gm
Turmeric	1 tsp	20 gm
Chilli powder	1 tsp	85 gm
Salt	to taste	100 gm
Fat	10 gm	250 gm
Clarified butter	10 gm	250 gm

Method

1. Soak dal overnight. 2. Drain and grind coarsely. 3. Heat fat. Add gram, turmeric, coriander powder, ginger powder, chilli powder and salt. 4. Fry for a few minutes. 5. Cook with lid on, over gentle heat till gram is cooked. 6. Stir well. Remove and cook. 7. Mix with flour to make a stiff dough. 8. Set aside for half an hour. Divide into small balls. 9. Roll out into 1.25 cm. (½") thick chapaties and bake on a griddle over a very slow fire till it cooks through. 10. Hold over live coal for a few minutes. 11. Smear surface with clarified butter and prick with a fork to keep rotis soft. 12. Repeat process.

84. BATI

Ingredients	*For 10*
Wholewheat flour	250 gm
Curds	150 gm
Salt	a pinch
Fat	150 gm

Method

1. Sieve flour. Beat curds well. 2. Add salt and melted fat (about 30 gm) and curds to the flour. 3. Add sufficient water to make a stiff dough (as for puries). 4. Divide the dough into even sized balls, lightly flatten, press in the centre with the thumb. 5. Boil these balls in hot water for about 10–12 minutes. Remove. 6. With a sharp knife slit across in the centre of the ball without cutting through. 7. Fry these in fat till golden brown in colour. 8. Serve them piping hot with a little melted fat poured over.

85. BULGUR PILAFF

Ingredients	*For 4*	*For 100*
Bulgur wheat	225 gm	5.65 kg
Meat	250 gm	6 kg
Fat	30 gm	340 gm
Mutton stock	800 ml–1 litre	25 litre
Tomatoes	115 gm	2.8 kg
Sultanas	10 gm	250 gm
Garlic	5 gm	115 gm
Salt	to taste	80-100 gm

Method

1. Heat fat. Fry finely chopped garlic and bulgur wheat for 6 to 8 minutes. 2. Fry meat pieces cut into small cubes and add to fried bulgur. Fry well. 3. Add mutton stock, sliced tomatoes, sultanas and salt. 4. Finish off as for rice pulao.

DALS

1. Dal
2. Parsi Dal
3. Masala Dal
4. Gujarati Dal
5. Watli Dal
6. Mango Dal (Ambyachi dal)
7. Makhani Dal
8. Punjabi Dal
9. Moong Dal with Coconut
10. Moong Dal with Palak
11. Varan
12. Sukha Dal (A)
    Sukha Dal (B)
13. Moong with Coconut
14. Sambar (A)
    Sambar (B)
    Sambar (C)
    Sambar (D)
    Sambar Powder
15. Tur Dal and Vegetable Sorak
16. Brinjal Sorak
17. Vegetable and Dal Kulumbu
18. Mooli and Sprouted Moong Cuchumber
19. Rasam (A)
    Rasam (B)
    Rasam (C)
20. Lime Rasam
21. Pepper Water
22. Poondu Rasam
23. Jeera Kulumbu
24. Jeera Meera Kadhi
25. Garlic Kadhi
26. Sambaram
27. Amti
28. Alu Chhole
29. Alu Chhole (Dry)
    Alu Chhole ki Chaat
    Chutney
30. Kabuli Mattar (Dry peas)
31. Sundal Kadala
32. Doodhi Chana
33. Dalcha
34. Sprouted Chana Bhaji
35. Dalma
36. Dried Beans Usal
37. Green Gram Koshumbir
38. Red Gram with Greens
39. Sprouting of Moong
40. Sprouted Green Gram Usal
41. Padwal and Val Dalimbi
42. Rajmah

PULSES

Pulses form a nutritionally significant item of diet in India. The varieties commonly used are Bengal gram (channa), black gram (urud), red gram (arhar; tur), green gram (moong), and lentil (masoor) and the less used ones are cow pea (lobia), field bean (val), horse gram (kulthi), moth beans (moth), dried peas (kabuli mattar), rajmah, soya bean etc. Combined with cereals, they form important protein sources for vegetarians, and in low and medium cost balanced meals. If they are combined with wheat in the proportion of one part pulse to four parts wheat, biologically first class protein is obtained. The crude protein of this group ranges from 22 to 25 per cent and goes up to 40 per cent in soya bean. Split, dehusked grams are known as 'dals'

Pulses are used in a variety of preparations either as whole gram or split and dehusked or powdered. Tender seeds in green pods are eaten during the season in parts of Andhra Pradesh and Maharashtra. Plain roasted Bengal gram with roasted peanuts is given to young children, expectant and lactating mothers to improve the quality of protein in their diets. A combination of 40 parts of wheat, 10 parts of Bengal gram, 10 parts of jaggery can be used as a tasty snack, either made into balls (ladoos) or eaten as chikki.

Sprouting pulses by soaking for 12 to 24 hours, draining and then tying in a wet cloth for a further 24 hours improves their digestibility and increases the Vitamin C content as much as six times. Vitamins of the B complex group are also increased. Besides using pulses in whole form or split and dehusked for chhole, rajmah, kabuli mattar, dals, sambars etc., they are cooked in combination with green leafy and other vegetables thereby improving their total nutritive value.

Cooking pulses takes a longer time than cooking fresh vegetables as they are dehydrated. Soaking for an hour or so prior to cooking helps to speed up the process. The addition of salt increases the cooking time of pulses. Soda bicarbonate is sometimes added to reduce the cooking time but this destroys the Vitamin B content of the food.

1. DAL

Ingredients	*For 4*	*For 100*
Split red gram or lentil	225 gm	5.6 kg
Onions	55 gm	1.35 kg
Green chillies	10 gm	225 gm
Turmeric	a pinch	10 gm
Fat	30 gm	225 gm
Salt	to taste	100 gm
Tempering		
Fat	10 gm	55 gm
Curry leaves	a sprig	1 bunch
Mustard seeds	a pinch	10 gm
Whole red chillies	2-3	15 gm

Method

1. Pick and wash gram or lentil. 2. Slice onions and slit green chillies. 3. Heat fat. Sauté gram, onion, chillies, turmeric. Add enough water to cook. 4. When tender remove from fire and mash. Add more water if required. 5. Add salt and bring to boil. 6. Remove and temper with the given ingredients.

2. PARSI DAL

Ingredients	*For 4*	*For 100*
Split red gram	120 gm	3 kg

Ingredients	*For 4*	*For 100*
Turmeric	½ tsp	10 gm
Salt	2 tsp	80-100 gm
Water	4 cups	15 litre
Clarified butter(ghee)	1 tbsp	350 gm
Garlic	2 cloves	2 pods
Cumin	½ tsp	10 gm

Method

1. Cook the gram and turmeric in half the amount of water till the gram is tender. Drain and mash. Add salt and keep it aside. Heat clarified butter. Add finely chopped garlic and cumin and fry till the cumin is brown. Pour this into the prepared dal. Add the remaining water and bring to boil. This dal should be like a very thick soup. Serve hot with boiled rice.

3. MASALA DAL

Ingredients	*For 4*	*For 100*
Split red gram	225 gm	5.6 kg
Green chillies	10 gm	225 gm
Coriander leaves	½ bunch	3 bunches
Turmeric	a pinch	15 gm
Coconut	½	10
Salt	to taste	100 gm
Mustard seeds	a pinch	15 gm
Cumin	a pinch	30 gm
Tomatoes	225 gm	5.6 kg
Fat	30 gm	340 gm

Method

1. Clean and boil gram until soft. 2. Mash well. 3. Add slit green chillies, turmeric, salt and chopped tomatoes. 4. Grate and grind coconut to a fine paste. 5. When tomatoes are cooked add ground coconut. 6. Heat fat in a pan. Add mustard seeds and cumin seeds. Pour over dal. 7. Garnish with chopped coriander leaves and serve hot.

4. GUJARATI DAL

Ingredients	*For 4*	*For 100*
Split red gram	100 gm	2.5 kg
Green chillies	6 gm (3)	150 gm (75)
Ginger	5 gm	125 gm
Turmeric	1 gm	25 gm

Ingredients	For 4	For 100
Jaggery	12-15 gm	300 gm
Salt	to taste	100 gm
Cocum or	3-4	100
Tamarind	15 gm	375 gm
Water	1.25 litre	30 litre
Oil	15 ml	300 ml
To temper		
Mustard seeds	1 gm	20 gm
Fenugreek	1 gm	20 gm
Asafoetida	1 gm	20 gm

Method

1. Boil the gram in water till well cooked. 2. Mash well. 3. Add sliced green chillies, ginger, turmeric, salt, tamarind juice or cocum, and jaggery. 4. Boil for half an hour over slow fire. Remove. 5. Heat oil in a frying pan. 6. Add mustard seeds, fenugreek and asafoetida. 7. As the seeds splutter, pour over dal. 8. Mix well.

N.B. Split black gram (urad dal) can be substituted for red gram. Use 30 gm of curds beaten up in a cup of water instead of tamarind or cocum, and reduce jaggery to 10 gm

5. WATLI DAL

Ingredients	For 4	For 100
Split bengal gram	225 gm	5 kg
Cumin	10 gm	100 gm
Coriander leaves	¼ bunch	2 bunches
Green chillies	6-8	115 gm
Mustard seeds	5 gm	30 gm
Asafoetida	3 gm	20 gm
Turmeric	3 gm	20 gm
Salt	to taste	80-100 gm
Chilli powder	3 gm	30 gm
Oil	60 ml	1.4 litre

Method

1. Soak gram overnight. 2. Grind with salt, green chillies and cumin. 3. Heat oil, add mustard seeds, asafoetida, turmeric and chilli powder. 4. Add the gram mixture and water and stir well. 5. Cover the pan and let it cook, stirring occasionally. 6. When gram is cooked add the chopped coriander leaves and serve hot.

6. MANGO DAL (Ambyachi dal)

Ingredients	*For 4*	*For 100*
Split bengal gram	150 gm	4 kg
Sugar	5 gm	100 gm
Raw mango	30 gm	500 gm
Mustard seeds	5 gm	30 gm
Turmeric	a pinch	20 gm
Green chillies	2-3	115 gm
Chilli powder	a pinch	30 gm
Oil	30 ml	500 ml
Asafoetida	2 gm	20 gm
Coriander leaves	4 sprigs	2 bunches
Salt	to taste	80-100 gm

Method

1. Soak gram overnight. 2. Crush the gram coarsely. 3. Add grated raw mango, chopped chillies, sugar and salt and boil. 4. Heat oil, add mustard seeds. When they crackle, add the chilli powder, turmeric and asafoetida. 5. Mix well and serve garnished with green coriander.

7. MAKHANI DAL

Ingredients	*Quantity*
Black gram (whole)	250 gm
Kidney beans	50 gm
Onions	1
Tomato (large)	1
Ginger	2" piece
Garlic	½ pod
Green chillies	10 gm
Red chilli powder	5 gm
Turmeric	¼ tsp
Oil	30 ml
Ghee (clarified butter)	60 gm
Cumin seeds	½ tsp
Salt	to taste
Coriander leaves	

Method

1. Clean and soak gram and beans separately for at least 4 hours. 2. Boil kidney beans. When half cooked, add gram and oil and boil till both are well cooked. 3. Heat half the ghee. Add cumin seeds, sliced ginger, sliced onion and chopped garlic, and fry till golden brown. 4. Add turmeric, chilli powder and chopped tomatoes and fry till tomatoes are cooked. 5. Add gram and beans and half of the chopped coriander leaves. 6. Cook on a slow fire stirring constantly for another 20 minutes. 7. Add the

remaining ghee and remove from the fire. 8. Garnish with remaining chopped coriander leaves.

8. PUNJABI DAL (4 portions)

Ingredients	*For 4*
Rajmah	100 gm
Urad dal (black, whole)	75 gm
Channa dal	25 gm
Urad dal (split)	25 gm
Ginger	10 gm
Green chillies	10 gm
Tomatoes	150 gm
Onions	150 gm
Garam masala	a pinch
Butter	30 gm
Fat	30 gm

Method

1. Pick, wash and cook all the dals together till tender. 2. Separately heat fat. Add chopped onions. Fry till golden brown. 3. Add finely chopped tomatoes and made a smooth gravy. Cut ginger and green chillies into juliennes. 4. Add cooked dals, ginger and green chillies to the fat and cook for a few minutes. 5. Add butter and garam masala powder and serve hot.

9. MOONG DAL WITH COCONUT

Ingredients	*For 4*	*For 100*
Split green gram	115 gm	2.85 kg
Onions	30 gm	680 gm
Green chillies	10 gm	225 gm
Cumin	½ tsp	15 gm
Turmeric	a pinch	10 gm
Salt	10 gm	100 gm
Fat	30 gm	225 gm
Curry leaves	a few sprigs	30 gm
Mustard seeds	a pinch	10 gm
Coconut	30 gm	680 gm

Method

1. Roast gram on hot griddle till it starts to brown. 2. Grind green chillies and turmeric. 3. Boil gram with ground chillies and turmeric; when cooked, add salt. 4. Grind together coconut, cumin and onion to a very fine paste. 5. Add to gram and add sufficient water to make a thin gravy.

Bring to boil. 6. Remove from fire and temper with mustard seeds, curry leaves and a few slices of onion browned in the fat.

10. MOONG DAL WITH PALAK

Ingredients	*For 4*	*For 100*
Split green gram	225 gm	5.6 kg
Spinach	1 kg	25 kg
Turmeric	a pinch	15 gm
Asafoetida	a pinch	15 gm
Chilli powder	5 gm	115 gm
Oil (for tempering)	10 ml (about 1tbsp)	225 ml
Salt	to taste	100 gm

Method

1. Wash and soak gram in double the quantity of water for one hour. 2. Cook till soft. 3. Pick and wash spinach. Add to gram and cook for 10 to 15 minutes. Add salt, turmeric and chilli powder. Remove from fire. 4. Heat oil. Fry asafoetida and pour over dal. Mix well.

11. VARAN

Ingredients	*For 4*
Split red gram	120 gm
Salt	to taste
Turmeric	a pinch

Method

1. Wash and soak gram. 2. Boil the water. 3. Add gram and turmeric. 4. Cook till water is nearly finished and add salt. 5. Mix well with a ladle. (Consistency of gram should be thick.) 6. Serve hot.

12. SUKHA DAL (A)

Ingredients	*For 4*	*For 100*
Split black gram	225 gm	5.6 kg
Garlic	a few flakes	55 gm
Green chillies	5 gm (1 or 2)	115 gm
Turmeric	a pinch	10 gm
Cumin	a pinch	30 gm
Salt	to taste	100 gm
Fat	15 gm	225 gm

Method

1. Wash and soak gram for 2 hrs. Drain. 2. Heat fat. Add sliced garlic,

chopped green chillies, turmeric and cumin. Sauté. 3. Add gram. Fry for 5–10 minutes. 4. Sprinkle water, cover and cook on a very slow fire till gram is cooked. Stir occasionally and sprinkle more water if necessary. (Use water in which gram was soaked.) 5. When gram is cooked, add salt, stir and serve hot.

SUKHA DAL (B)

Ingredients	*For 4*	*For 100*
Split bengal gram	225 gm	5.6 kg
Red chillies	5 gm	115 gm
Onions	30 gm	680 gm
Curry leaves	a sprig	1 bunch
Salt	to taste	30 gm
Oil	30 ml	500 ml

Method

1. Boil gram with just enough water to cook. 2. Peel and coarsely crush onion with the red chillies. 3. Heat oil. Add crushed chillies, onion and curry leaves. Sauté. 4. Add cooked gram and salt. Stir well for a few minutes and remove.

13. MOONG WITH COCONUT

Ingredients	*For 4*	*For 100*
Green gram	225 gm	5.6 kg
Coconut	55 gm	1.35 kg
Turmeric	a pinch	15 gm
Green chillies	5 gm	115 gm
Curry leaves	a sprig	a bunch
Onions	15 gm	225 gm
Salt	to taste	100 gm (approx.)
Oil	30 ml	340 ml

Method

1. Grind together turmeric, green chillies and part of the onion. Mix well on the stone with finely grated coconut. 2. Cook green gram with just enough water till done. 3. When cooked and very little moisture is left, add coconut mixture, curry leaves and salt. 4. Cover and cook on a slow fire for a few minutes (it should be completely dry.) 5. Stir well. Remove from fire. 6. Heat oil. Add finely chopped onion. 7. When onion is browned, add gram. Stir well for a few minutes. Remove and serve hot.

14. SAMBAR (A)

Ingredients	*For 4*		*For 100*
Lentils	100 gm		1 kg
Coriander	20 gm	roast separately and powder	200 gm
Red chillies	5 gm		50 gm
Split bengal gram	3 gm		30 gm
Split black gram	3 gm		30 gm
Fenugreek	3 gm		30 gm
Asafoetida	½ tsp		20 gm
Ladies fingers	30 gm		300 gm
Onions (small)	50 gm		500 gm
Brinjal (small)	1 (50 gm)		500 gm
Drumsticks	4 (120 gm)		1.2 kg
Turmeric	¼ tsp(1 gm)		10 gm
Tamarind (to taste)	15 gm		150 gm
Salt (to taste)	10 gm		80-100 gm
To temper			
Curry leaves	1 sprig		a few sprigs
Red chillies	2 (2 gm)		10 gm
Mustard seed	a pinch (1 gm)		10 gm
Fenugreek	¼ tsp (1 gm)		10 gm
Clarified butter	1 tsp (15 gm)		100–150 gm
Onions (small)	10 gm		100 gm

Method

1. Boil dal. Add vegetables cut into even-sized pieces, and powdered spices, and cook till vegetables are tender. 2. Add tamarind juice extracted in a cup of hot water. Bring to boil. Test for seasoning and remove. 3. Heat clarified butter in a frypan. Add mustard seeds, sliced onions, broken red chillies, curry leaves and fenugreek. 4. When onions brown, pour over sambar. Stir well.

SAMBAR (B)

Ingredients	*For 4*	*For 100*
Split red gram	50 gm	1.25 kg
Red chilies	5 gm	115 gm
Coriander	5 gm	115 gm
Turmeric	a pinch	15 gm
Coconut	30 gm	680 gm
Fenugreek	a pinch	15 gm
Cumin	a large pinch	20 gm
Tamarind	20 gm	500 gm

Ingredients	For 4	For 100
Drumsticks	30 gm	680 gm
Onions (small)	30 gm	680 gm
Brinjal	30 gm	680 gm
Ladies fingers	30 gm	680 gm
Tomatoes (optional.)	30 gm	680 gm
Salt	to taste	115 gm
Split bengal gram / **Split black gram**	5 gm	115 gm
Oil	10 ml	250 ml
Asafoetida	a large pinch	30 gm
Curry leaves	a sprig	15 gm
Mustard seeds	a pinch	15 gm
Onion (small) for tempering	30 gm	225 gm
Coriander leaves	a sprig	1 bunch
Water for gram	1 litre	25 litre
Water for tamarind	120 ml	3 litre

Method

1. Roast coriander seeds, fenugreek, cumin, red chillies, bengal gram and black gram. 2. Grate coconut. Roast and grind to a fine paste with the roasted masala. 3. Clean and wash red gram. Boil till soft. 4. Add cut and prepared vegetables and spice; simmer. 5. When vegetables are cooked, add tamarind pulp. Bring to boil and remove. 6. Temper with mustard seeds, chopped onions, curry leaves and asafoetida. Sprinkle chopped coriander leaves.

SAMBAR (C)

Ingredients	For 4	For 100
Split red gram	115 gm	2.8 kg
Drumsticks	115 gm	2.8 kg
Ladies fingers	115 gm	2.8 kg
Onions	115 gm	2.8 kg
Coconut	30 gm	680 gm
Red chillies	5 gm	115 gm
Coconut oil	30 gm	115 gm
Coriander seeds	15 gm	340 gm
Turmeric	a pinch	15 gm
Mustard seeds	a pinch	15 gm
Cumin	½ tsp	30 gm
Fenugreek	a pinch	30 gm
Tamarind	15 gm	225 gm
Curry leaves	a sprig	1 bunch

Ingredients	*For 4*	*For 100*
Asafoetida	a pinch	15 gm
Salt	to taste	100 gm
Water	500 ml	12.5 litre

Method

1. Wash gram and boil in water with turmeric powder. 2. Wash and cut drumsticks and ladies fingers into even-sized pieces; slice onions. 3. When gram is cooked, add vegetables. 4. Lightly fry in a little oil, coriander seeds, cumin, fenugreek, asafoetida and three-fourths of the red chillies. After a few minutes add grated coconut. Remove from fire when coconut gets browned. 5. Grind spices and coconut to a fine paste. 6. Soak tamarind in hot water and extract juice. 7. When vegetables are cooked, add ground ingredients. Bring to a boil. Add tamarind juice and simmer for a few minutes. Remove. 8. Heat remaining oil and fry mustard seeds, broken red chilli pieces and curry leaves. When mustard seeds crackle, pour into the sambar. Mix well.

SAMBAR (D)

Ingredients	*For 4*	*For 100*
Drumsticks	2	120 (about 500 gm)
Split red gram	120 gm	1.2 kg
Turmeric	1 gm	10 gm
Tamarind	25 gm	250 gm
Sambar powder	15 gm	150 gm
Salt	10 gm	100 gm
Asafoetida	2 gm	20 gm
Curry leaves	3 gm	30 gm
Red chillies	5 gm	50 gm
Fenugreek	3 gm	30 gm
Coriander seeds	5 gm	50 gm
Split bengal gram	10 gm	100 gm
Oil	15 ml	150 ml
Mustard seeds	2 gm	20 gm

Method

1. Wash the red gram and boil with turmeric powder. Mash when tender. 2. Wash and cut drumsticks into 5 cm. pieces. 3. Soak tamarind in 3 cups of water for about half an hour, extract the juice and strain it. 4. Add to the tamarind juice, sambar powder, salt, asafoetida, curry leaves and drumsticks and boil for 20 minutes. 5. Fry red chillies, fenugreek, coriander seeds and channa dal in one teaspoon of oil and powder finely.

6. To the tamarind mixture, add this finely powdered masala and then the cooked gram. 7. Temper with mustard seeds and mix well.

SAMBAR POWDER

Ingredients	*Quantity*
Red chillies	250 gm
Coriander seeds	250 gm
Peppercorns	50 gm
Split red gram	50 gm
Dried curry leaves	50 gm

Method

1. Dry all the ingredients well in the sun. 2. Powder and store in airtight containers.

15. TUR DAL AND VEGETABLE SORAK

Ingredients	*For 10*
Split red gram	225 gm
Vegetables (potatoes, bottle gourd, brinjal)	225 gm
Coriander	2 tbsp
Cumin	½ tsp
Turmeric	¼ tsp
Onions	2
Red chillies	5
Garlic	3 cloves
Coconut	¼
Curds	1 cup
Salt	to taste
To temper	
Mustard seeds	½ tsp
Curry leaves	2 sprigs
Clarified butter	1 tbsp

Method

1. Clean and wash the gram. Wash vegetables and cut into even-sized pieces. Boil gram and vegetables. 2. Grind spices, onions and grated coconut to a fine paste. Mix in beaten curds. Add to the gram 3. Stir well and bring to a boil. Add salt. Remove. 4. Heat clarified butter in a fry-pan. Add curry leaves and mustard seeds. As seeds splutter, pour over prepared dish. Stir well. 5. Serve hot.

16. BRINJAL SORAK

Ingredients	*For 4*	*For 100*
Brinjal (large or medium)	2 to 3 (200 gm)	2 kg
Lentil	1 cup (150 gm)	1.5 kg
Onions	3 (300 gm)	3 kg
Coconut	½ (100 gm)	1 kg (5)
Cashewnuts	10-15	100 gm
Turmeric	¼ tsp	10 gm
Coriander	1 tbsp	150 gm
Oil	1 tbsp	150 ml
Mustard seeds	a few	10 gm
Asafoetida	a pinch	20 gm
Limes	2	20
Salt	to taste	100 gm

Method

1. Cut brinjal into 2.5 cm. (1") pieces and soak in water. 2. Clean dal and cook in 4 cups of water. 3. When half done, add sliced onions and brinjal. 4. Lightly roast the coconut and cashewnuts separately and remove. 5. Roast red chillies and coriander. 6. Grind together coconut, cashewnuts, red chillies and coriander. 7. Add ground spices to gram when vegetables are cooked. 8. Add salt to taste. Simmer till spices are cooked. 9. Remove. Heat fry-pan. Add oil, mustard seeds, asafoetida and curry leaves. 10. When seeds splutter, add gram mixture. Bring to boil. 11. Add lime juice to taste and remove.

17. VEGETABLE AND DAL KULUMBU

Ingredients	*For 15*
Split red gram	225 gm
Brinjal (1 large)	225 gm
Potatoes (2 medium)	225 gm
Tomatoes	2
Peanuts	½ cup
Coriander seeds	1 tbsp
Cumin	½ tsp
Peppercorns	a few
Fenugreek	a few
Turmeric	¼ tsp
Split bengal gram	1 tbsp
Split black gram	1 tbsp
Red chillies	6-8
Tamarind	size of a lime

Ingredients	*For 15*
Oil	1 tbsp
Mustard seeds	a few
Asafoetida	a pinch
Curry leaves	a few
Salt	to taste

Method

1. Clean red gram and boil with peanuts in 4 cups of water. 2. Clean and cut brinjal, potatoes and tomatoes. 3. Add to the cooked red gram and peanuts, and simmer till done. 4. Roast coriander, cumin, peppercorns, fenugreek, bengal gram, black gram and red chillies separately. 5. Grind together with tamarind to form a fine paste. 6. Heat oil. Add mustard seeds, curry leaves and asafoetida. 7. As seeds splutter, add ground spices and fry for about 5 minutes. 8. Add cooked red gram, vegetable mixture, salt to taste and more water, if desired. 9. Simmer for 10 to 15 minutes. 10. Serve hot with boiled rice and spinach.

18. MOOLI AND SPROUTED MOONG CUCHUMBER

Ingredients	*For 15*
Green radish leaves	1 bunch
Sprouted green gram	100 gm
Lime	1
Green chillies	10 gm
Peanut flour (roast peanuts and powder)	10 gm
Onions	20 gm
Oil	15 ml
Mustard seeds	a pinch
Salt	to taste

Method

1. Wash and chop radish leaves finely. Chop onion. 2. Steam sprouted gram for about 5 minutes. 3. Mix with radish leaves. 4. Add salt and peanut flour. 5. Heat oil, add mustard seeds. When they crackle, pour over the radish and gram mixture. 6. Add lime juice and mix well and serve.

19. RASAM (A)

Ingredients	*For 4*	*For 100*
Split red gram	30 gm	680 gm
Tamarind	10 gm	225 gm
Coriander leaves	¼ bunch	1 bunch
Masala		
Red chillies	2 or 3	55 gm
Asafoetida	a pinch	5 gm

Ingredients	*For 4*	*For 100*
Coriander	5 gm	115 gm
Peppercorns	a few	30 gm
Cumin	a pinch	5 gm
Garlic	1 flake	5 gm
Salt	15 gm	100 gm
Tempering		
Oil	15 ml	115 ml
Red chillies	1	6
Mustard seeds	1 tsp	10 gm
Curry leaves	1 sprig	1 bunch

Method

1. Cook gram in water till tender. 2. Squeeze tamarind in a little water. 3. Roast and pound spices. 4. Mix together the liquid in which the gram was cooked, part of the gram mashed up, pounded masala, tamarind juice and salt to taste. 5. Bring to boil. 6. Remove and temper with mustard seeds, whole red chillies and curry leaves.

RASAM (B)

Ingredients	*For 4*	*For 100*
Split red gram	30 gm	680 gm
Tomatoes	115 gm	2.8 kg
Lime	1	6
Curry leaves	a few	1 bunch
Coriander leaves	½ bunch	2 bunches
For tempering		
Mustard seeds	1 tsp	10 gm
Black gram	2 gm	30 gm
Cumin	a pinch	5 gm
Red chillies	2	5 gm
Asafoetida	a pinch	5 gm
Oil	10 ml	200 ml
Salt	to taste	100 gm
Green chillies	5 gm	115 gm

Method

1. Boil the gram till tender; remove the water. 2. Cut tomatoes, slit green chillies and chop coriander leaves. 3. Add tomatoes, green chillies, coriander leaves and curry leaves to gram water. Boil. 4. Heat oil; add all the ingredients for tempering. 5. When spices crackle add to boiling rasam. Add salt and boil for 5–10 minutes. 6. Remove from heat and add lime juice.

RASAM (C)

Ingredients	*For 4*	*For 100*
Lentil	30 gm	680 gm
Oil	10 ml	200 ml
Onions	15 gm	340 gm
Garlic	1 flake	15 gm
Red chillies	2-3	10 gm
Coriander seeds	10 gm	225 gm
Turmeric	a pinch	5 gm
Mustard seeds	a pinch	5 gm
Cumin	a pinch	5 gm
Fenugreek	5-6	3-5 gm
Peppercorns	6	5 gm
Tamarind	15 gm	225 gm
Water	1 litre	14.75 litre
Curry leaves	a few sprigs	1 bunch
Salt	to taste	100 gm

Method

1. Boil lentil in water till soft. 2. Chop onion. Slice garlic, crush coriander. 3. Heat oil and fry lightly onion, garlic, coriander, whole red chillies, turmeric, mustard seeds, cumin, fenugreek, peppercorns, and curry leaves. 4. Drain off 1 cup liquid for 4, and 4 litres for 100, from the boiled lentil. Soak tamarind. Squeeze out pulp into liquid. 5. Add the boiled lentil, tamarind pulp and salt. 6. Bring to boil and simmer for 10-15 minutes. 7. Strain and serve hot.

20. LIME RASAM

Ingredients	*For 4*
Water	3 cups
Lime	½-1
Garlic	a small clove
Ginger	a small piece
Cumin	a small pinch
Coriander seeds	½ tsp
Turmeric	a small pinch
Coriander leaves	a few sprigs
Salt	to taste
For tempering	
Asafoetida	a small pinch
Curry leaves	1 sprig
Red chilli	1
Mustard seeds	a few
Oil	½ tsp

Method

1. Crush together garlic, ginger, cumin and coriander seeds. 2. Mix with lime juice, water, salt, turmeric and coriander leaves. 3. Bring to a boil. Simmer for a few minutes. Remove from fire. 4. Heat oil, add curry leaves, broken red chilli, asafoetida and mustard seeds. As seeds crackle, pour rasam into the pan. Reheat and remove.

21. PEPPER WATER

Ingredients	*For 4*	*For 100*
Water	600 ml	14.75 litre
Coriander	10 gm	225 gm
Cumin	a pinch	15 gm
Peppercorns	6	15 gm
Mustard seeds	a pinch	10 gm
Garlic	6 flakes	10 gm
Tomatoes (optional)	6 (about)	1 kg
Onions (small)	4	60 gm
Asafoetida	a pinch	10 gm
Tamarind	10 gm	225 gm
Salt	to taste	100 gm
For tempering		
Oil	15 ml	200 ml
Curry leaves	1 sprig	1 bunch
Red chillies	1-2	10 gm
Onion (small)	1	10 gm

Method

1. Roast asafoetida, cumin, peppercorns, garlic, onion and coriander. Crush. 2. Soak tamarind in a little hot water. Squeeze and mix in the water. Add crushed ingredients and tomatoes, if desired. 3. Add salt to taste and simmer for 10 minutes. Strain. 4. Heat oil in another pan. Add sliced (small) onion, curry leaves and whole red chilli. Fry for a minute or two. 5. Add pepper water. Bring to boil and remove.

22. POONDU RASAM

Ingredients	*Quantity*
Peppercorns	¾ tsp (2 gm)
Red chillies	3
Split bengal gram	1 tsp (4 gm)
Cumin	¾ tsp (2 gm)
Tamarind	size of 1 lime (10 gm)

Ingredients	*Quantity*
Piper longum (Kandan thippali)	¼ tsp (2 gm)
Garlic	6-7 flakes (10 gm)
Mustard seeds	½ tsp (2 gm)
Curry leaves	a few (1 sprig)
Oil	2 tsp (10 ml)
Water	500 ml

Method

1. Grind curry leaves, garlic and cumin finely. 2. Soak tamarind in 1 cup hot water. Squeeze out pulp. 3. Heat oil and add mustard and 2 broken red chillies. 4. Add tamarind pulp. Cook till tamarind flavour disappears. 5. Add ground ingredients, red chillies, gram, piper longum and ½ litre water.6. Bring to boil and cook till garlic is cooked. Add a little powdered cumin before removing.

23. JEERA KULUMBU

Ingredients	*Quantity*
Mangoes (unripe)	2
Chilli powder	½ tsp
Salt	to taste
Cumin	1 tsp
Oil	1 tbsp
Mustard	a pinch
Fenugreek	a pinch
Curry leaves	a few

Method

1. Heat oil; add mustard seeds, fenugreek and curry leaves. 2. As seeds splutter, add mango cut into 2.5 cm. × 0.75 cm. (1" × ¼") pieces. 3. Add chilli powder and salt. Fry for a few minutes. 4. Add 2-3 cups water and simmer till mangoes are cooked. 5. Roast and powder cumin and add to the mangoes just before removing from the fire.

24. JEERA MEERA KADHI

Ingredients	*For 8*
Coconut	1 (225 gm)
Cumin	½ tsp (5 gm)
Peppercorns	2–3
Tamarind	10 gm
Red chillies	2–3 (3 gm)
Garlic	10 flakes (5–7 gm)
Coriander	½ tsp (5 gm)

Ingredients	*For 8*
Clarified butter	1 tbsp
Salt	to taste
pomegranate rind	

Method

1. Heat half of the clarified butter. Add peppercorns, 2 flakes of garlic, coriander, cumin. Fry lightly. Remove. 2. Add half of the remaining clarified butter and fry pomegranate rind and red chillies. 3. Mix fried ingredients with coconut and salt and grind well. Heat the remaining clarified butter. Fry sliced garlic till golden brown and pour over the ground ingredients. Mix well. 4. Serve with wet khitchdi or soft boiled rice.

25. GARLIC KADHI

Ingredients	*For 4*	*For 100*
Coconut	½	12
Red chillies (Sankeshwari)	2	50 gm
Peppercorns	1 gm (5)	25 gm
Garlic	4 gm	50 gm
Cocum	5 gm	75 gm
Salt	to taste	100 gm
Coriander leaves	2 sprigs	½ bunch

Method

1. Grind together coconut, red chillies, peppercorns and cocum. 2. Add 1 cup water. Keep aside for about 10 minutes and extract juice. 3. Add salt and chopped coriander leaves.

26. SAMBARAM

Ingredients	*For 8*
Buttermilk	6 cups
Ginger	1.25 cm. (½" piece)
Green chillies	3-4
Garlic	2 flakes
Red onions or	4
Medium-sized onion	1 (65 gm)
Cumin	a large pinch
Turmeric	1 tsp
Lime leaf	¾
Curry leaves	a few
Salt	to taste

Method

1. Add salt and curry leaves to buttermilk. 2. Crush remaining ingredients on a grinding stone and tie in a muslin bag. Steep in the buttermilk. 3. With a spoon, press the bag a few times to extract flavour. 4. Set aside for 2 to 3 hours. 5. Strain and serve in Pony tumblers. If desired, a small piece of lime leaf can be floated on top.

27. AMTI

Ingredients	*For 4*	*For 100*
Split red gram	150 gm	3 kg
Onions	50 gm	1 kg
Mustard seeds	2 gm	50 gm
Turmeric	2 gm	10 gm
Chilli powder	2 gm	50 gm
Green chillies	4	115 gm
Tamarind	4 gm	100 gm
Jaggery (to taste)	2 gm	50 gm
Garam masala*	2 gm	50 gm
Oil	30 ml	500 ml
Salt	(a) 2 litre	(a) 50 litre
Water	(b) 1.5 litre	(b) 35 litre

Method

1. Clean, wash and soak the gram for half an hour and cook till soft. [Water amount (a) if chapaties are to be served with Amti; otherwise as given in (b)]. 2. Heat oil and add mustard seeds; when they crackle, add slit green chillies and chopped onion. When the onion is tender, add chillies and chopped onion. When the onion is tender add chilli powder, turmeric and garam masala. 3. Add the cooked gram, bring to boil, add tamarind juice, jaggery, and salt.

28. ALU CHHOLE

Ingredients	*For 4*	*For 100*
Bengal gram	225 gm	5.65 kg
Soda bicarbonate	1 tsp	15 gm
Large cardamom	1	30 gm
Cinnamon powder	½ tsp	15 gm
Cumin powder	½ tsp	15 gm
Pepper powder	½ tsp	15 gm
Clove powder	½ tsp	15 gm
Coriander powder	½ tsp	15 gm

*See Curry Powders.

Ingredients	*For 4*	*For 100*
Turmeric	⅛ tsp	10 gm
Chilli powder	½ tsp	15 gm
Green chillies	3	85 gm
Tamarind	30 gm	680 gm
Onions	55 gm	1.35 kg
Tomatoes	55 gm	1.35 kg
Potatoes	115 gm	2.8 kg
Coriander leaves	2 sprigs	2 bunches
Fat	15 gm	250 gm

Method

1. Wash and soak gram overnight with soda bicarbonate. 2. Cook gram till tender. 3. Add powdered cardamom, cinnamon, cumin, cloves, pepper, coriander and cool. 4. Heat half of the fat. Fry sliced onion, turmeric and chilli powder. 5. Add gram, tomatoes and whole green chillies. 6. Continue cooking and mash gram. 7. Just before removing from the fire add tamarind juice and salt. 8. Boil potatoes and slice. 9. Fry half of the sliced potatoes and add to the gram. 10. Serve garnished with boiled and sliced potatoes and chopped coriander leaves.

29. ALU CHHOLE (Dry)

Ingredients	*For 4*	*For 100*
Small bengal gram	225 gm	5.65 kg
Soda bicarbonate	1 tsp	15 gm
Large cardamom	1	30 gm
Cinnamon powder	½ tsp	15 gm
Cumin powder	½ tsp	15 gm
Pepper powder	½ tsp	15 gm
Clove powder	½ tsp	15 gm
Coriander powder	1 tsp	30 gm
Turmeric	⅛ tsp	10 gm
Chilli powder	½ tsp	15 gm
Pomegranate seeds	1 tsp	30 gm
Onions	55 gm	1.35 kg
Green chillies	5 gm	115 gm
Tomatoes	115 gm	2.8 kg
Potatoes	115 gm	2.8 kg
Salt	to taste	80-100 gm
Fat	15 gm	250 gm

Method

1. Wash and soak the gram overnight with soda bicarbonate. 2. Boil gram till it is tender. 3. Fry sliced onion. Add spices and pomegranate seed

powder. 4. Add gram and stir lightly. The gram should be coated with spices. 5. Add salt. Remove from fire. 6. Boil potatoes. Peel and cut them into fingers. 7. Serve gram in the centre, with potato fingers round and green chillies sticking up from the gram. The gram should also be garnished with slices of tomatoes.

ALU CHHOLE KI CHAAT

Ingredients	*For 8*
Alu Chhole	
Kabuli channa	2 katoris
Soda	½ tsp
Masala (ground)	
Red chillies which give bright red colour and are less hot	8-10
Coriander seeds (lightly roasted)	1–1½ tbsp
Turmeric powder	¾ tsp
Green chillies	3-4
Ginger	a piece
Onions	2
Mace	a pinch
Pure ghee enough to cook the masala	
Anardana (ground)	2-3 tsp
Garam masala	1½–2 tsp
Jeera (roasted)	Powdered
Clove	Powdered
Big Cardamom	Powdered
Cinnamon	Powdered
Boiled potatoes	4

Method

1. Boil the channa in the soda water in which it is soaked overnight. Drain the water. 2. Cook the finely ground masala. Add the ground anardana. 3. Mix the channa with the masala and keep it on slow fire, sprinkling water if necessary. 4. Add the garam masala last and stir. Remove from fire. 5. Take a little ghee in a pan or tawa, add a little chilli powder (red) and brown the thick roundels of boiled potatoes. 6. Arrange on top of chhole and at the base. 7. Sprinkle chopped coriander leaves.

CHUTNEY

Ingredients	*For 8*
Tamarind pulp	1 cup
Black khajur paste	½ cup

Ingredients	*For 8*
Jaggery	a little
Dry ginger powder	a little
Red chilli powder	a little
Jeera	
Saunf (roasted and grounded)	a little
Salt (black)	a little
Raisins	a few
Mint leaves (chopped)	

Method

Cook on slow fire the pulp and the paste. Add the gur. Add the other ingredients. Cook till the distinct flavour is obtained and the chutney has a blackish brown colour. (Strips of boiled dry khajur may be added)

30. KABULI MATTAR (Dry peas)

Ingredients	*For 4*
Dry peas	115 gm
Lime	½ to 1
Green chillies	15 gm
Coriander leaves	½ bunch
Ginger	a small piece
Chilli powder	½ tsp
Garam masala powder	a pinch
Cumin powder	a pinch
Salt	to taste

Method

1. Wash and soak peas overnight, preferably with a pinch of soda. 2. Cook in the same water till soft. 3. Mash roughly, add lime juice, salt, finely chopped green chillies, coriander leaves and ginger, chilli powder, garam masala powder and cumin powder. Mix well and serve.

31. SUNDALL KADALA

Ingredients	*For 8*
Bengal gram	500 gm
Coconut	112 gm
Red chillies	5-6
Oil	15 ml
Salt	to taste

Method

1. Soak the gram overnight. 2. Boil till the skin separates. 3. Slice coconut into fine slices. 4. Heat oil in a fry pan. 5. Add broken red chillies and

coconut pieces. 6. When coconut starts browning, add boiled gram and salt. 7. Fry well. 8. Remove and serve hot.

32. DOODHI CHANA

Ingredients	*For 4*	*For 100*
Split bengal gram	225 gm	5.65 kg
Bottle gourd	225 gm	5.65 kg
Onions	50 gm	1 kg
Chilli powder	1 tsp	50 gm
Coriander powder	1 tsp	50 gm
Turmeric	½ tsp	20 gm
Ginger	5 gm	115 gm
Green chillies	3	100 gm
Garam masala	1 tsp	30 gm
Tomatoes	50 gm	1.5 kg
Fat	15 gm	250 gm
Lime	¼	4
Coriander leaves	a few sprigs	2 bunches
Salt	to taste	100 gm
To temper		
Fat	10 gm	200 gm
Asafoetida	a small pinch	½ tsp
Ginger	a small pinch	10 gm
Garlic	1 flake	5 gm
Red chilli	1	5
Cumin	a pinch	5 gm

Method

1. Heat fat and fry onion till golden brown. 2. Add chilli powder, coriander powder, turmeric, chopped ginger, slit green chillies and finely chopped tomatoes. Saute for 3 to 5 minutes. 3. Add gram and sauté. Add double the amount of water. 4. Dice gourd and add to gram when it is three-fourths done. 5. When cooked, add roasted and powdered garam masala and salt. 6. Mix lime juice. Remove pan from fire. 7. Heat fat for tempering . Add whole red chillies, sliced ginger, crushed garlic and cumin. Fry . 8. Pour over gram, mix well.

33. DALCHA

Ingredients	*For 4*	*For 100*
Split bengal gram	150 gm	3 kg
Bottle gourd	250 gm	5 kg
Oil	35 ml	700 ml
Tamarind	25 gm	500 gm

Ingredients	*For 4*	*For 100*
Onions	75 gm	1.5 kg
Curry leaves	1 sprig	1 bunch
Chilli powder	10 gm	200 gm
Turmeric	2 gm	40 gm
Salt	to taste	100 gm
Ginger	5 gm	100 gm
Garlic	5 gm	100 gm
Cumin	2 gm	40 gm

Method

1. Soak gram overnight. Boil the gram with turmeric till cooked. 2. Extract tamarind juice. Slice onions and grind ginger and garlic. 3. Heat oil, add cumin and whole red chillies. Add ginger-garlic paste, onions and fry well. 4. Then add the gourd cut into big pieces. Add a little water and cook for a few minutes. 5. Finally, add tamarind juice, the cooked gram and salt and simmer for 10 minutes. Serve hot.

34. SPROUTED CHANA BHAJI

Ingredients	*For 4*	*For 100*
Sprouted bengal gram	225 gm	5.6 kg
Chilli powder	5 gm	115 gm
Turmeric	a pinch	30 gm
Onions	115 gm	2.8 kg
Green chillies	5 gm	115 gm
Coriander leaves	½ bunch	6 bunches
Fat	30 gm	500 gm
Garam masala	5 gm	115 gm
Lemon	1	12
Salt	to taste	100 gm

Method

1. Boil sprouted gram in just enough water to cook it. 2. When half cooked add chilli powder, turmeric, and garam masala . 3. When gram is cooked and no water remains, add salt. 4. Chop onions finely and slice green chillies. 5. In a big pan heat fat. Add onions. When browned add green chillies and cooked gram. 6. Fry together for a few minutes. 7. Remove from fire and serve garnished with chopped coriander leaves and a slice of lemon.

35. DALMA

Ingredients	*For 4*	*For 100*
Split green gram	225 gm	5.6 kg

Ingredients	For 4	For 100
Potatoes	115 gm	2.8 kg
Brinjal	115 gm	2.8 kg
Drumsticks	115 gm	2.8 kg
Green banana	115 gm	2.8 kg
Oil	15 ml	250 ml
Red chillies (whole)	5 gm	115 gm
Turmeric	a pinch	10 gm
Cumin	5 gm	115 gm
Onions	115 gm	2.8 gm
Salt	to taste	100 gm

Method

1. Wash and cook the gram. 2. When gram is cooked, add prepared vegetables, turmeric and salt. 3. When vegetables are tender, remove. 4. Temper with whole chillies, sliced onions and cumin. Serve hot.

36. DRIED BEANS USAL

Ingredients	For 4	For 100
Dried beans	115 gm	2.8 kg
Onions	115 gm	2.8 kg
Turmeric	3 gm	20 gm
Red chillies	3 gm	20 gm
Oil	15 ml	250 ml
Mustard seeds	a pinch	15 gm
Asafoetida	a pinch	15 gm
Tamarind	10 gm	225 gm
Green chillies	2-3	115 gm
Grated coconut	30 gm	2
Coriander leaves	a few sprigs	1 bunch
Goda masala or	5 gm	100 gm
Coriander-cumin powder	3-5 gm	75-100 gm
Jaggery	10 gm	115 gm
Salt	to taste	80-100 gm

Method

1. Soak the beans overnight. Drain. Hang in a piece of muslin to sprout (about 12 hrs). 2. Boil in the same water in which they were soaked, with green chillies, until tender. 3. Heat oil. Add mustard seeds, as they crackle, add chopped onions. When onions are golden brown add turmeric, red chillies, asafoetida, and goda masala or coriander-cumin powder. 4. Add boiled beans and cook for 10 to 15 minutes. 5. Add

tamarind, jaggery and salt. 6. When cooked, serve hot, garnished with grated coconut and coriander leaves.

37. GREEN GRAM KOSHUMBIR

Ingredients	*For 4*	*For 100*
Split green gram	50 gm	1.3 kg
Green chillies	2	55 gm
Ginger	5 gm	115 gm
Lime	½	10–12
Coconut	30 gm	680 gm
Coriander leaves	1 bunch	12 bunches
Salt	to taste	80–100 gm
Tempering		
Split black gram	¼ tsp	30 gm
Mustard	¼ tsp	30 gm
Red chillies	1	30 gm
Fat	1 tsp	50 gm

Method

1. Soak the green gram overnight in sufficient water. Drain 2. Grate coconut, chop chillies, ginger and coriander leaves fine. 3. Mix all the ingredients together. 4. Add the tempering. Serve chilled.

38. RED GRAM WITH GREENS

Ingredients	*For 4*	*For 100*
Split red gram	50 gm	1.3 kg
Greens	200 gm	5 kg
Tamarind	lime-sized ball	225 gm
Green chillies	2	85 gm
Curry leaves	1 sprig	1 bunch
Salt	to taste	80–100 gm
Tempering		
Split black gram	½ tsp	30 gm
Mustard	½ tsp	30 gm
Red chillies	2	50 gm
Fenugreek	¼ tsp	15 gm
Fat or oil	1 tbsp	115 gm
Asafoetida	a pinch	10 gm
Rice flour	1 tsp	30 gm

Method

1. Cook red gram in water. 2. Chop greens and green chillies. 3. Extract

tamarind juice. 4. Add the gram, greens and tamarind extract to the tempering along with salt and boil well. 5. Serve hot.

39. SPROUTING OF MOONG

Ingredients	*Quantity*
Whole moong	100 gm
Weight after sprouting	240 gm
Time for sprouting	48 hrs

Method

Clean and wash moong. Soak in enough water to cover moong. Keep for 24 hours. Tie in a muslin cloth and hang for a further 24 hours. Open and use as required. If longer sprouts are required spread on a towel, sprinkle with water and leave till the sprouts grow.

N.B. Sprouting increases Vitamin C content by approx 20%. Steam or cook quickly for use.

40. SPROUTED GREEN GRAM USAL

Ingredients	*For 4*
Green gram (sprouted)	50 gm
Green chillies	2
Grated coconut	30 gm
Lime	1
Oil	1 tsp
Mustard seeds	a few
Ginger	6 gm
Red chillies	2

Method

1. Grate coconut, chop green chillies, ginger and coriander leaves finely. 2. Mix all the ingredients together. Add tempering and sauté for some time. Serve chilled.

To sprout gram

3. Soak gram for 24 hours. Spread on a damp blanket covered with a moist cloth or hang in a muslin bag. 4. In 2 to 3 days, gram will germinate with 1 cm. (½") of sprout. The germinated gram should be consumed raw or after cooking for minimum period.

41. PADWAL AND VAL DALIMBI

Ingredients	*For 4*
Sprouted field beans (whole)	75 gm
Snake gourd	225 gm

Ingredients	*For 4*
Chilli powder	5 gm
Salt	to taste
Coriander-cumin powder	5 gm
Mustard seeds	a pinch
Asafoetida	a pinch
Turmeric	a pinch
Oil	10 gm
Jaggery	a little
Grated coconut	15 gm
Coriander leaves	15 gm

Method

1. Sprout the field beans and soak them in warm water for two hours and skin. 2. Heat fat. Add mustard seeds. When they crackle, add asafoetida and turmeric. 3. Add field beans and water and cook till three-fourths done. 4. Wash and cut the snake gourd into two pieces and then cut into slices. 5. Add to the field beans. Add chilli powder, jaggery and salt. 6. Cook till snake gourd is done. 7. Garnish with grated coconut and coriander leaves and serve hot.

42. RAJMAH

Ingredients	*Quantity*
Kidney beans	250 gm
Onions	250 gm
Ginger	10 gm
Garlic	30 gm
Cumin seeds	a pinch
Tomatoes	250 gm
Fat	60 gm
Salt	to taste.
Turmeric powder	½ tsp
Coriander powder	1 tsp
Green chillies	3
Chilli powder	1 tsp
Garam masala	½ tsp

Method

1. Wash, soak and boil kidney beans. 2. Chop onions fine. Blanch tomatoes and purée them. 3. Grind ginger and garlic. 4. Heat fat. Add cumin. Fry onions. 5. Add ginger, garlic and fry till golden brown. 6. Add turmeric powder, coriander powder, chilli powder and slit green chillies. Fry. 7. Add tomato purée. Cook for 7 minutes. 8. Add kidney beans and cook till gravy is thick. 9. Finish with ½ tsp garam masala and chopped coriander.

VEGETABLES

1. Onion Cuchumber
2. Tomato Cuchumber
3. Panchamrut
4. Cabbage Salad (Indian)
5. Carrot Salad
6. Cucumber Cuchumber
7. Bhindi
8. Fried Ladies Fingers
9. Fried Bhindi
10. Bhindi Fried in Batter
11. Fried Beans
12. Fried Chauli Beans
13. Fried Tindli
14. Green Beans
15. Beans Foogath
16. Cabbage Foogath
17. Chauli Bean Foogath
18. Green Tomato or Billing Foogath
19. Drumstick Flower Peera
20. Cabbage Thoran
21. Papaya Thoran
22. Cheera Thoran (Amaranth thoran)
23. Vazhakkai Thoran (Banana with coconut)
24. Chembu Curry (Arvi curry)
25. Kappa Curry (Tapioca with coconut)
26. Chakka Curry (Jackfruit with coconut)
27. Onion Bhaji
28. Cauliflower Fried
29. Cauliflower Bhujjia (A)
    Cauliflower Bhujjia (B)
    Cauliflower Bhujjia (C)
30. Cauliflower and Potato Bhujjia
31. Cauliflower and Peas Curry
32. Doi Phool Gobi
33. Sukhi Gobi
34. Cabbage Bhujjia
35. Cabbage and Potato Bhujjia
36. Tomato and Onion Bhujjia
37. Potato and Tindli Bhujjia
38. Tomato Bhurta
39. Chinese Vegetables
40. Tomato Mahasha
41. Tomato Ambal
42. Tomatochen Sar
43. Batata ne Tomatoes
44. Mixed Vegetable Bhujjia
45. Panch Phoorner Charchari (Bengali)
46. Shuktoni
47. Phulkapir Dalna
48. Brinjal Pahie
49. Bagara Baingan
50. Brinjal Vella Khorma
51. Navrattan Korma
52. Brinjal Curry
53. Brinjal and Potato Curry
54. Brinjal Bhurta
55. Bhaja Maslar Tarkari
56. Stuffed Brinjals (Maharashtrian)
57. Stuffed Brinjals
58. Stuffed Round Gourd
59. Cheese Ball Curry
60. Cheese Kofta Curry
61. Panir
62. Palak Panir
63. Peas Panir Curry
64. Alu Panir Khorma
65. Panir Kofta Curry
66. Methi Panir
67. Cashew Potato Curry
68. Cashew Masala
69. Mukandwadi
70. Padval Ulathiyathu
71. Stuffed Padval
72. Snake Gourd Caldeen
73. Fried Suran
74. Fried Karela or Pavakka Ulathiyathu
75. Potato Stuffed Karela

76. Masala Karela
77. Vegetable Stuffed Karela
78. Pavakkai Varatharacha Curry (Bitter gourd curry)
79. Potato Bhaji(A)
    Potato Bhaji (B)
    Potato Bhaji (C)
80. Puri ka Alu
81. Batate Sukhe
82. Alu Mattar
83. Alu Dum
84. Potato Bhurta (Alu bhurta)
85. Alu Methi
86. Batata Kut
87. Spicy Potatoes
88. Batata Chilli Fry
89. Batata Thilsane
90. Batata Kosambri
91. Bhanap Batata
92. Ras Batata
93. Highly Spiced Chouchou
94. Batata Hooman
95. Til Alu Dum
96. Potato Ambat
97. Stuffed Vegetable Shak
98. Sweet Potato Curry
99. Sweet Potato Puli Kulumbu
100. Alu Muckala Potatoes
101. Alu Palak
102. Mixed Vegetable Curry
103. Vegetable Moilee
104. Vegetable Hussainy Curry
105. Vegetable Curry (A)
     Vegetable Curry (B)
106. Vegetable Patia
107. Vegetable Khorma
108. Dahi Khorma
109. Vegetable Do Pyaz
110. Vegetable Indad
111. Vegetable Vindaloo
112. Vegetable Makhanwala
113. Lagan Sala
114. Sarson ka Sag (Mustard greens)
115. Mooli Sag
116. Palak Sag
117. Sag Bhaji (A)
     Sag Bhaji (B)
118. Amaranth Sauté (Cheera vazhattiathu)
119. Amaranth Sauté (Cholai Bhaji)
120. Oondhiu
121. Doodhi Kofta Curry
122. Potato Kofta Curry
123. Vegetable Kababs (A)
     Vegetable Kababs (B)
124. Vegetable Chops
125. Masala Bhara Mirchi
126. Vegetable Cutlets (Indian)
127. Stuffed Capsicums (A)
     Stuffed Capsicums (B)
128. Doodhi Pachadi
129. Ginger Pachadi
130. Vellari Pachadi
131. Uppumanga Pachadi
132. Curd Pachadi
133. Ladies Finger Raita
134. Onion Raita
135. Cauliflower and Peas Raita
136. Cucumber Raita
137. Boondi Raita
138. Mint Raita
139. Palak Raita.
140. Tomato Raita
141. Brinjal Raita
142. Potato Raita
143. Banana Raita
144. Banana Chaat
145. Kadhi
146. Pakoda Kadhi
147. Bhindani Kadhi
148. Palak Ki Kadhi
149. Palak Pakoda Kadhi
150. Moru Kulumbu
151. Gatta Curry
152. Dahi Bhalla
153. Curd Curry
154. Moru Kachiyathu
155. Ginger Curry

156. Vellari Red Curry
157. Citron (Lime) Curry
158. Vellari Moru Curry
159. Mango Marrow Puliserry
160. Avial
161. Panchang Curry
162. Kalan
163. Olan
164. Erussery
165. Vegetable Koottu Curry
166. Mango Sorak
167. Ash Gourd Bhurta

1. ONION CUCHUMBER

Ingredients	*For 4*	*For 100*
Onions	225 gm	5.6 kg
Coriander leaves	¼ bunch	6 bunches
Green chillies	5 gm	115 gm
Lime	15 gm	12
Salt	to taste	80-100 gm

Method

Slice the onions into moderately sized strips. Chop coriander leaves and green chillies and mix with onion, lime juice and salt.

2. TOMATO CUCHUMBER

Ingredients	*For 4*	*For 100*
Tomatoes	225 gm	5.65 kg
Capsicum	115 gm	2.75 kg
Onions	55 gm	1.35 kg
Lime	half	10
Salt	to taste	100 gm

Method

1. Chop all ingredients into very fine pieces. 2. Add lime juice and salt.

3. PANCHAMRUT

Ingredients	*For 4*
Peanuts(1)	75 gm
Cashewnuts	50 gm
Dry coconut	100 gm
Gingelly seeds	15 gm
Peanuts (2)	15 gm
Tamarind	5 gm
Jaggery	10 gm
Cumin powder	5 gm
Mustard seeds	a pinch

Ingredients	*For 4*
Turmeric	a pinch
Cumin	a pinch
Asafoetida	a pinch
Oil	10 ml
Salt	to taste

Method

1. Soak first lot of peanuts for one hour and remove the skin. 2. Chop cashewnuts in big pieces. dice the dry coconut. 3. Soak tamarind and take out the pulp. 4. Roast gingelly seeds and remaining peanuts and pound together. 5. Heat oil; add mustard seeds. 6. When they crackle, add cumin, asafoetida and turmeric. 7. Add skinned peanuts, cashewnuts and dry coconut. 8. Sauté for two minutes. Add tamarind pulp and all other ingredients. 9. Cook on a slow fire for about half an hour. Serve hot.

4. CABBAGE SALAD (Indian)

Ingredients	*For 4*	*For 100*
Cabbage (fresh)	225 gm	5.65 kg
Onions	55 gm	1.35 kg
Green chillies	5 gm	115 gm
Coriander leaves	½ bunch	4 bunches
Salad oil	30 ml	500 ml
Lime	1	12
Salt	to taste	50-100 gm

Method

1. Shred cabbage fine. Chop green chillies, onions and coriander leaves. 2. Mix all ingredients together.

5. CARROT SALAD

Ingredients	*For 4*
Grated carrot	1
Green chilli (chopped)	1
Leaves and bulb of small red onion (chopped)	1
Coconut milk	1 tbsp
Salt	to taste

Method

1. Mix all ingredients together.

6. CUCUMBER CUCHUMBER

Ingredients	*For 4*	*For 100*
Cucumber	225 gm	5.65 kg
Onions	55 gm	1.35 kg
Green chillies	2	100 gm
Salt	to taste	80-100 gm
Lime	1	12
Coriander leaves	½ bunch	6 bunches

Method

1. Wash all ingredients. Peel cucumber and onion. Chop finely, cucumber, onion, green chillies and coriander leaves. 2. Mix prepared ingredients together. Add salt and lime juice. mix well. Serve fresh.

7. BHINDI

Ingredients	*For 4*	*For 100*
Ladies fingers (okra)	450 gm	11 kg
Salt	1 tsp	80 gm
Turmeric	¼ tsp	15 gm
Chilli powder	½ tsp	50 gm
Green chillies	2	50 gm
Coriander powder	1 tsp	100 gm
Oil	50 ml	1.25 litre

Method

1. Wipe and chop ladies fingers into small pieces, Chop green chillies. 2. Add ladies fingers and the spices. Stir, keep covered. 3. Cook over gentle heat for about 25 minutes.

8. FRIED LADIES FINGERS

Ingredients	*For 4*
Ladies fingers (okra)	10
Red chillies	5
Peppercorns	10
Garlic	1 flake
Red onions	2
Turmeric	¼ tsp
Salt	to taste
Oil	2 tsp

Method

1. Wipe ladies fingers with a wet cloth. 2. Cut into 2.5 cm. (1") lengths.

3. Grind together all spices 4. Heat 1 tsp oil. Fry ladies fingers. 5. Add ground spices and salt. Mix well. 6. Add just enough water to cook dry. Remove and fry in remaining oil.

9. FRIED BHINDI

Ingredients	*For 4*	*For 100*
Ladies fingers	225 gm	5.6 kg
Fat (absorption)	30 gm	500 gm
Chilli powder	10 gm	55 gm
Salt	10 gm	100 gm

Method

1. Wash and cut ladies fingers into fine rounds. 2. Heat fat and deep fry ladies fingers. 3. Remove from fat and while still hot sprinkle with chilli powder and salt.

10. BHINDI FRIED IN BATTER

Ingredients	*For 4*	*For 100*
Ladies fingers	450 gm	11 kg
Red chillies	5 gm	115 gm
Pepper	½ tsp	30 gm
Turmeric	½ tsp	30 gm
Cinnamon	1 small piece	30 gm
Salt	to taste	50 gm
Batter		
Bengal gram flour	30 gm	680 gm
Soda bicarbonate	a pinch	10 gm (about)
Salt	to taste	50 gm
Oil to fry (absorption)	30 ml	500 ml

Method

1. Wipe ladies fingers with a damp cloth and slitre 2. Grind together red chillies, pepper, turmeric, cinnamon and salt. 3. Stuff ladies fingers with ground spices. 4. Prepare a thick batter with gram flour, water, salt and soda. 5. Heat oil. 6. Dip ladies fingers in batter and deep fry. 7. Remove and drain on absorbent paper.

11. FRIED BEANS

Ingredients	*For 4*	*For 100*
French beans	225 gm	5.6 kg
Salt	10 gm	100 gm

Ingredients	*For 4*	*For 100*
Red chillies	5 gm	115 gm
Oil	15 ml	250 ml
Onions	10 gm	115 gm

Method

1. String beans and cut into small pieces. 2. Crush chillies coarsely. 3. Mix together chillies, beans, salt and enough water to cook the beans. 4. Heat oil. Fry chopped onions; when brown, add cooked beans. Fry well and remove.

12. FRIED CHAULI BEANS

Ingredients	*For 4*	*For 100*
Chauli beans	225 gm	5.6 kg
Salt	to taste	50-80 gm
Fat or oil	30 gm	500 gm
Red chillies	5 gm	115 gm
Onion	10 gm	225 gm

Method

1. String and cut beans into small pieces. 2. Crush chillies. 3. Add chillies to beans, add salt and just enough water to cook. 4. Cook on a slow fire with lid partially off. 5. When water has evaporated and beans are cooked, remove. 6. Heat fat. Fry sliced onions. Add beans and sauté.

13. FRIED TINDLI

Ingredients	*For 4*	*For 100*
Gherkins	115 gm	2.8 kg
Mustard seeds	a pinch	30 gm
Chilli powder	1 level tsp	85 gm
Turmeric	a pinch	15 gm
Cumin powder	a large pinch	30 gm
Salt	to taste	50 gm
Sugar	½ tsp	30 gm
Oil	20 ml	400 ml

Method

1. Wash and drain gherkins. 2. Cut lengthwise into 8 to 10 pieces. 3. Heat oil. Add mustard seeds. When they crackle add gherkins and sauté. 4. Cover and cook over a slow fire (no water should be added) till tender. Stir now and then. 5. Remove lid. Add salt, turmeric, cumin powder and chilli powder. Mix well. Cook for a further 5 minutes. 6. Add sugar. Mix well and remove.

14. GREEN BEANS

Ingredients	*Quantity*
French beans	100 gm
Mustard seeds	1 gm
Urad dal	2 gm
Red chillies	2 gm
Raw tomatoes	25 gm
Salt	5 gm/to taste
Oil	10 ml

Method

1. Cut beans into small pieces. 2. Heat oil. Add mustard seeds, urad dal, red chillies and beans, and salt. 3. Cook on slow fire for 10–15 minutes. 4. Add raw tomatoes and remove immediately.

15. BEANS FOOGATH

Ingredients	*For 4*	*For 100*
French beans	450 gm	11 kg
Onions	55 gm	1.35 kg
Green chillies	5 gm	115 gm
Mustard seeds	a pinch	15 gm
Oil	30 ml	500 ml
Coconut	55 gm	1.35 kg
Salt	to taste	100 gm
Curry leaves	1 sprig	1 bunch

Method

1. Wash, string and cut beans into fine round pieces. 2. Chop onion and green chillies. 3. Heat oil, Add mustard seeds. 4. When mustard seeds crackle, add chopped onion, green chillies, and curry leaves. Sauté. 5. Add sliced beans, salt and enough water to cook beans. 6. Cook till beans are done and all water has evaporated. 7. Add grated coconut, cook a little longer, stir well and remove from fire. Serve hot.

16. CABBAGE FOOGATH

Ingredients	*For 4*	*For 100*
Cabbage	455 gm	11 kg
Onions	55 gm	1.35 kg
Green chillies	5 gm	115 gm
Mustard seeds	a pinch	15 gm
Oil	30 ml	500 ml
Coconut	55 gm	1.35 kg

Ingredients	For 4	For 100
Salt	to taste	100 gm
Curry leaves	1 sprig	1 bunch

Method

1. Shred cabbage fine. 2. Chop onion and green chillies. 3. Heat oil, add mustard seeds. 4. When mustard seeds crackle, add chopped onion, green chillies and curry leaves. Sauté. 5. Add cabbage and salt. 6. Cook on a slow fire till cabbage is tender. Stir constantly and sprinkle a little water if necessary. 7. Add grated coconut, cook a little longer, stir well, remove from fire and serve hot.

17. CHAULI BEAN FOOGATH

Ingredients	For 4	For 100
Chauli beans	225 gm	5.65 kg
Coconut	50 gm	1.25 kg
Green chillies	5 gm	115 gm
Cumin	a small pinch	15 gm
Turmeric	a pinch	10 gm
Mustard seeds	a pinch	10 gm
Onions	5 gm	115 gm
Curry leaves	a few sprigs	1 bunch
Oil	15 ml	250 ml
Salt	to taste	50 gm

Method

1. Wash and cut beans into fine round pieces. 2. Add salt and just enough water to cook the beans. 3. Boil till beans are tender and all the water has evaporated. 4. Grind chillies, cumin and turmeric; mix well with finely grated coconut. 5. Make a well in the centre of the cooked beans. Add coconut. Cover and cook on a very slow fire till quite dry. Stir and remove. 6. Temper with fried mustard seeds.

18. GREEN TOMATO OR BILLING FOOGATH

Ingredients	For 4	For 100
Green tomato or Billing (fresh and hard)	225 gm	5.5 kg
Coconut	½	12
Onions	225 gm	5.5 kg
Green chillies	10-15 gm	250-340 gm
Curry leaves	a few sprigs	1 bunch
Fresh coconut oil	15 ml (1 tbsp)	250 ml
Salt	to taste	100 gm

Method

1. Wash and slice tomatoes (they should be hard and green). 2. Chop green chillies and slice onions. 3. Grate coconut fine. 4. Mix all ingredients together. Add salt and curry leaves. Cook over a slow fire. 5. When tomatoes are cooked and mixture is dry, add fresh coconut oil. Stir well and remove from fire.

Variations: Red onions, finely sliced ladies fingers, capsicum, bitter gourd can be prepared similarly but add cocum to taste.

19. DRUMSTICK FLOWER PEERA

Ingredients	*For 8*
Drumstick flowers	500 gm
Onions	200 gm (2)
Onions (small)	2
Capsicum	10
Green chillies	6 gm
Boiled & minced meat	100 gm
Coconut	¼
Ginger	4 gm
Green tomatoes	2
Salt	to taste
Mustard seeds	4 gm
Raw rice	5 gm
Fat or oil	15 gm
Egg	1
Curry leaves	a few

Method

1. Wash the drumstick flowers and keep in a basket and drain. Clean and cut vegetables into fine slices and keep separately. Heat fat in a pan. Add rice and mustard seeds. 3. When they splutter, add finely chopped small onions. 4. When this turns brown add the flowers and stir. 5. Then add the capsicum, chillies, sliced big onions and ginger. Stir for two more minutes. 6. Add green tomatoes and cover with the lid. 7. When the mixture is almost dry, add minced meat and coconut. Steam for a minute or two. 8. Open the lid, stir it with a fork and add beaten egg. 9. When the egg is cooked, add curry leaves and serve with rice or chapaties.

20. CABBAGE THORAN

Ingredients	*For 4*	*For 100*
Cabbage	150 gm	3.75 kg
Coconut	100 gm	2.5 kg

Ingredients	For 4	For 100
Green chillies	1 big or 2 small	75 gm
Onions	10 gm (a small piece)	250 gm (2 large)
Turmeric	a large pinch	15 gm
Garlic	2 flakes	15 gm
Salt	to taste	80-100 gm
Curry leaves	2 sprigs	1 bunch
To temper		
Oil	15 ml	250 ml
Onions (small)	5 gm	30 gm
Rice	1 tsp	50 gm

Method

1. Wash and shred cabbage fine, like grated coconut. 2. Grate coconut fine. 3. Crush well green chillies, onion and garlic. 4. Add coconut and turmeric and mix while grinding till well belended. 5. Cook cabbage with salt and water if desired to cook it dry but crisp. 6. Add coconut mixture and curry leaves. Do not mix. Cover and cook for about 3 minutes on a slow fire to allow steam to go through coconut mixture and curry leaves. 7. Stir with the handle of a wooden spoon to mix. 8. Remove from fire after about 2-3 minutes. It should be completely dry . 9. Heat oil. Add finely chopped onion. When it browns add rice. 10. When rice puffs up add cabbage thoran. Fry for about 2 to 3 minutes. Remove. Serve hot or cold.

Variations: Runner beans, french beans, papaya, brinjal, snake gourd and papdi can be prepared in the same manner. Mustard seeds may be substituted for rice for tempering, if desired.

21. PAPAYA THORAN

Ingredients	For 8
Papaya (raw, medium-sized)	1
Coconut	1
Garlic	2 cloves
Onions	3
Green chillies or a few kanthari	3
Turmeric	¼ tsp
Curry leaves	a few
Rice	1
Oil	1 tbsp
Salt	to taste

Method

1. Peel papaya. Cut into two. Remove seeds. Wash well. Cut into

quarters. Chop fine (slit lengthwise and then cut across to chop fine) or grate on the medium grater. 2. Grate coconut fine. Grind together garlic, onions and turmeric. Grind green chillies coarsely (if kanthari is used grind fine). 3. Mix together the ground ingredients and coconut. In a thick-bottomed pan put the chopped papaya and salt and cook covered till moisture evaporates. 4. Put the ground ingredients with the coconut in the centre of the pan and cover with cooked papaya. Allow the steam to come through for a couple of minutes. 5. Check for salt and stir using the handle of a ladle. Remove from fire. 6. Heat oil in a frying pan. Add rice and curry leaves. When the rice puffs up, add papaya mixture and stir well. Remove and serve hot with rice and curry.

22. CHEERA THORAN (AMARANTH THORAN)

Ingredients	*For 4*	*For 100*
Amaranth (cheera cholai)	225 gm	5.6 kg
Coconut	115 gm	2.8 kg
Red onions	1 bulb	60 gm
Garlic	2 flakes	15 gm
Green chillies	5	115 gm
Split black gram	1 tsp	30 gm
Oil	15 ml	250 ml
Salt	to taste	80-100 gm

Method

1. Wash and drain Amaranth leaves (use stems if they are very tender). 2. Grate coconut fine. 3. Grind onion and garlic fine. Crush the green chillies well. Add coconut and mix well while grinding. 4. Chop leaves into fine pieces. 5. Heat oil. Add black gram. When gram browns, add chopped leaves and sauté for 2–3 minutes. 6. Add salt and ground ingredients. Cover and cook for 5 minutes. Mix well on fire. Remove.

N.B. A variety of edible leaves can be prepared in the same way.

23. VAZHAKKAI THORAN (BANANA WITH COCONUT)

Ingredients	*For 8*
Raw bananas	500 gm
Coconut	½
Green chillies	10 gm
Turmeric	½ tsp
Garlic	2 flakes
Red onions	1
Curry leaves	2 sprigs
Salt	to taste

Ingredients	*For 8*
To temper	
Coconut oil	15 ml
Red onions	2

Method

1. Peel and cut bananas into cubes. Wash well. 2. Add just enough water to cook it nearly dry. Add salt . Cook. 3. Grind together green chillies, turmeric, coconut, garlic and onion. 4. Add ground ingredients to cooked banana. Allow steam to pass through. 5. Mix well. Add curry leaves and remove from fire. 6. Heat oil in a fry pan. Add sliced onions. When they brown, add banana mixture. Stir well for 2–3 minutes.

24. CHEMBU CURRY (ARVI CURRY)

Ingredients	*For 8*
Colocasia	500 gm
Cocum	5 gm
Coconut	½
Turmeric	1 tsp
Green chillies or kanthari	10 gm
Garlic	3 flakes
Red onions	1
Curry leaves	2 sprig
Coconut oil (fresh)	30 ml
Salt	to taste

Method

1. Peel colocasia. Wash well. 2. Put into cold water and bring to boil. Drain . 3. Add salt, washed cocum and just enough water to cook colocasia. 4. Grind together to a fine paste coconut, green chillies, turmeric, garlic and onion. 5. When colocasia is cooked and moisture nearly dry, add ground ingredients. Mix well with the handle of a wooden spoon and stir over fire for about 2 minutes. 6. Add curry leaves and fresh coconut oil. Remove from fire.

25. KAPPA CURRY (TAPIOCA WITH COCONUT)

Ingredients	*For 8*
Tapioca	500 gm
Coconut	1
Green chillies or kanthari	10 gm
Turmeric	1 tsp
Garlic	2 flakes
Red onions	1

Ingredients	*For 8*
Salt	to taste
Curry leaves	2 sprigs
Coconut oil	30 ml
To temper	
Red onions	1
Split black gram	1 tsp

Method

1. Peel and dice tapioca. Wash well. 2. Put into cold water. Bring to boil. Drain. 3. Add salt and a little cold water and reheat. 4. Grind together coconut, green chillies, turmeric, garlic and red onion. 5. Add ground ingredients to tapioca. Mix well. 6. Remove from fire and add the curry leaves. 7. Heat oil in a fry pan. Add sliced onion and split black gram. When they brown, add tapioca preparation. Stir well for 2 to 3 minutes. Remove.

26. CHAKKA CURRY (JACKFRUIT WITH COCONUT)

Ingredients	*For 8*
Jackfruit (raw, medium-sized)	1
Cumin (optional)	a pinch
Red onions	2
Coconut	1
Turmeric	1 tsp
Green chillies	10–15 gm
Salt	to taste
Curry leaves	a few sprigs
To temper	
Coconut oil	30 ml
Red onions	1
Mustard seeds	1 tsp
Garlic	4 flakes

Method

1. Cut jackfruit into quarters. Cut off the white pith on top. 2. With oiled hands, separate fruit, remove seeds and slice into thin, long pieces. 3. In a big strong pan, put in the prepared jackfruit. Add salt and sprinkle a little water over. 4. Cover tightly and cook quickly. 5. Grind together cumin, green chillies, turmeric and onions. Add coconut and grind coarsely. 6. Make a well in the centre of the jackfruit. Add ground paste. Cover with the jackfruit and allow steam to pass through. Stir with the handle of a wooden spoon and mix well. Add curry leaves. 7. Heat oil. Add sliced onion. When brown add mustard seeds and garlic. 8. When seeds crackle add jackfuit curry. Stir well for 2 or 3 minutes.

27. ONION BHAJI

Ingredients	*For 4*	*For 100*
Onions	450 gm	11 kg
Salt	to taste	80 gm
Turmeric	½ tsp	15 gm
Chilli powder	½ tsp	15 gm
Coriander powder	1 tsp	85 gm
Cumin	a pinch	15 gm
Ginger	5 gm	115 gm
Vinegar or lime juice	1 tsp	30-50 ml
Fat	30 gm	500 gm

Method

1. Heat fat. Add cumin. 2. Add sliced onions, sliced ginger, dry spices and salt. 3. Cook on a slow fire for about 20 minutes. 4. Add vinegar or lime juice. Continue cooking for a further 5 minutes.

28. CAULIFLOWER FRIED

Ingredients	*For 4*	*For 100*
Cauliflower	450 gm	11 kg
Refined flour	30 gm	680 gm
Milk	150 ml	3.25 litre
Cheese	50 gm	1 kg
Eggs	2	50
Butter	30 gm	680 gm
Salt	to taste	80-100 gm
Chilli powder	½ tsp	50 gm
Oil to fry		

Method

1. Wash and parboil cauliflower in salted water. 2. Cut into flowerettes. 3. Make a smooth batter with flour, egg yolk, milk and salt. 4. Add grated cheese, melted butter and chilli powder. Stand for half an hour. 5. Add stiffly beaten whites of eggs. 6. Dip cauliflower in batter and deep fry.

29. CAULIFLOWER BHUJJIA (A)

Ingredients	*For 4*	*For 100*
Cauliflower	450 gm	11 kg
Onions	55 gm	1.36 kg
Dry mango powder	½ tsp	30-45 gm
Mustard seeds or cumin	½ tsp	15 gm
Turmeric	½ tsp	15 gm

Ingredients	*For 4*	*For 100*
Garlic	3 flakes	30 gm
Ginger	a small piece	100 gm
Green chillies	2	200 gm
Fat	15 gm	340 gm
Salt	to taste	100 gm

Method

1. Break cauliflower into small sprigs and wash. 2. Slice onion, half the garlic, ginger, chillies and grind remainder. 3. Heat fat. Add mustard seeds or cumin. When seeds crackle, add turmeric and sliced ingredients and fry well. Add ground spices and cauliflower. Add salt. 4. Cook mango powder. Stir well and remove.

N.B. Tomatoes may be substituted for mango powder, in which case, cook for a further 5–10 minutes after adding tomatoes.

CAULIFLOWER BHUJJIA (B)

Ingredients	*For 4*	*For 100*
Cauliflower	450 gm	11 kg
Curds (beaten)	1 tbsp	340 ml
Fat	15 gm	340 gm
Turmeric	¼ tsp	15 gm
Salt	to taste	80 gm
Chilli powder	1 tsp	85 gm
Cumin	a pinch	15 gm
Mustard seeds	a pinch	15 gm
Asafoetida (optional)	a pinch	10 gm

Method

1. Cut cauliflower into flowerettes. 2. Heat fat. Add mustard seeds and cumin. 3. When mustard seeds and cumin crackle, add cauliflower, chilli powder, turmeric and salt. 4. Cook covered on a very slow fire (a little water may be sprinkled, if necessary). 5. When cauliflower is cooked add beaten curds. Mix well and remove.

N.B. Asafoetida may be fried with mustard and cumin if desired.

CAULIFLOWER BHUJJIA (C)

Ingredients	*For 4*	*For 100*
Cauliflower	450 gm	11 kg
Ginger	5 gm	115 gm
Raisins	15 gm	340 gm

Ingredients	*For 4*	*For 100*
Salt	to taste	80 gm
Fat	30 gm	500 gm
Cumin	a pinch	15 gm
Mustard seeds	a pinch	15 gm
Sugar	½ tsp	30 gm
Lime	¼	6

Method

1. Heat fat. Add mustard and cumin. 2. When they crackle add chopped ginger. Fry well. 3. Add cauliflower, raisins and salt. Sauté. 4. Add enough water to cook cauliflower. 5. Cook till tender. Add sugar and lime juice. Remove.

30. CAULIFLOWER AND POTATO BHUJJIA

Ingredients	*For 4*	*For 100*
Cauliflower	450 gm	11 kg
Potatoes	225 gm	5.65 kg
Onions	115 gm	2.8 kg
Coriander powder	1 tsp	85 gm
Chilli powder	1 tsp	85 gm
Turmeric	½ tsp	10 gm
Green chillies	1	10 gm
Lime	½	10
Fat	50 gm	1.25 kg

Method

1. Peel and cut potatoes into fours. Cut cauliflower into large pieces. 2. Heat fat. Fry coriander powder, chilli powder and turmeric. Add sliced onions, prepared vegetables and whole green chillies. 3. Add enough water to cook. 4. When vegetables are well cooked and dry, add lime juice and remove.

31. CAULIFLOWER AND PEA CURRY

Ingredients	*For 4*	*For 100*
Cauliflower	225 gm	5.65 kg
Peas	225 gm	5.65 kg
Onions	30 gm	680 gm
Chilli powder	1 tsp	85 gm
Coriander powder	1 tsp	85 gm
Turmeric	½ tsp	15 gm
Tomatoes	115 gm	2.8 kg

Ingredients	*For 4*	*For 100*
Salt	to taste	100 gm
Fat	30 gm	340 gm
Coriander leaves	a few sprigs	1 bunch

Method

1. Wash and cut the cauliflower. 2. Heat fat. Fry chopped onion till transparent. Add chilli powder, turmeric and coriander powder. Fry for a few minutes. 3. Add cauliflower and shelled peas. Fry for 5 minutes. 4. Add chopped tomatoes and a little stock or water and salt. 5. Cook on a very slow fire till vegetables are well cooked. 6. Serve hot, garnished with coriander leaves.

32. DOI PHOOL GOBI

Ingredients	*For 4*	*For 100*
Cauliflower	450 gm	11 kg
Curds	225 gm	5.6 kg
Onions	225 gm	5.6 kg
Garlic	4 flakes (1") piece	15 gm
Cloves	2	5 gm
Cardamom	2	5 gm
Cinnamon	2 cm. (2") piece	10 gm
Salt	to taste	100 gm
Sugar	to taste	30 gm
Fat	30 gm	500 gm

Method

1. Wash and cut cauliflower into flowerettes. 2. Slice half the onions and grind the remaining half with garlic and ginger. 3. Beat the curds and mix it with half of the ginger paste, Salt and sugar. 4. Coat the pieces of cauliflower thoroughly with the curds paste, stuffing the mixture well into the crevices. 5. Heat fat. Fry sliced onions. Add cloves, cardamom and cinnamon and the remaining ginger paste. Fry for 5 minutes. 6. Add the pieces of cauliflower and fry gently. 7. Sprinkle with a little water. Cover and let simmer. 8. Add fat at short intervals to prevent sticking.

33. SUKHI GOBI

Ingredients	*For 4*	*For 100*
Cauliflower	450 gm	11 kg
Asafoetida	a pinch	10 gm
Ginger	2.5 cm. (1") piece	100 gm
Curds	150 ml	3.75 litre

Ingredients	For 4	For 100
Coriander powder	5 gm	115 gm
Turmeric	¼ tsp	15 gm
Garam masala	2 tsp	50 gm
Chilli powder	1 tsp	85 gm
Onions	50 gm	1 kg
Salt	to taste	100 gm
Fat	30-50 gm	1 kg

Method

1. Wash and cut cauliflower into flowerettes. 2. Heat fat and fry finely sliced onion to a golden brown. 3. Add asafoetida and crushed ginger. 4. Fry for a few minutes. Add cauliflower, salt, coriander and turmeric. Fry for 5 minutes. 5. Cover and cook gently. Occasionally remove lid and stir to prevent burning. 6. When the cauliflower is nearly done add chilli powder and garam masala. 7. Add curds a little at a time and keep on cooking till cauliflower is tender and mositure from curds evaporates.

34. CABBAGE BHUJJIA

Ingredients	For 4	For 100
Cabbage	450 gm	12.5 kg
Onions	55 gm	1.35 kg
Chilli powder	½ tsp	50 gm
Turmeric	¼ tsp	15 gm
Green chillies	3	200 gm
Salt	to taste	100 gm
Lime	¼	8
Coriander leaves	a few sprigs	1 bunch
Mustard seeds	a pinch	10 gm
Asafoetida	a pinch	10 gm
Oil	30 ml	500 ml

Method

1. Clean, wash and shred cabbage. 2. Slice onion; chop green chillies. 3. Heat oil. Add mustard seeds and when they crackle add asafoetida. 4. Add onion. Fry lightly. Add cabbage, spices and salt . 5. Cook on slow fire for about 10 minutes. Add lime juice and chopped coriander leaves.

35. CABBAGE AND POTATO BHUJJIA

Ingredients	For 4	For 100
Cabbage	250 gm	5.6 kg
Potatoes	250 gm	5.6 kg

Ingredients	*For 4*	*For 100*
Onions	60 gm	1.35 kg
Fat or oil	30 gm	340 gm
Cumin/Mustard seeds	a pinch	15 gm
Green chillies	5 gm	115 gm
Lime	½	8
Salt	10 gm	100 gm

Method

1. Prepare vegetables. 2. Heat fat. Add cumin and sliced onions. 3. When slightly brown, add prepared vegetables, green chillies and salt. 4. Add enough water to cook. Cook till soft and dry. 5. Add lime juice and remove.

N.B. Mustard seeds may be used instead of cumin.

36. TOMATO AND ONION BHUJJIA

Ingredients	*For 4*	*For 100*
Tomatoes	450 gm	11 kg
Onions	225 gm	5.65 kg
Green chillies	2-3	225 gm
Cumin	a little	55 gm
Salt	to taste	80-100 gm
Fat	15 gm	250 gm

Method

1. Heat fat and fry cumin. 2. When they crackle, add chopped chillies, onions and quartered tomatoes. Add salt. 3. Cook on a slow fire till bhujjia is dry and vegetables cooked.

37. POTATO AND TINDLI BHUJJIA

Ingredients	*For 4*	*For 100*
Gherkins	200 gm	5 kg
Onions	50 gm	1.25 kg
Potatoes	100 gm	2.5 kg
Mustard seeds	a pinch	10 gm
Turmeric	¼ tsp	30 gm
Chilli powder	¼ tsp	30 gm
Salt	to taste	80-100 gm
Oil	20 ml	500 ml

Method

1. Slice gherkins and onion. 2. Cut potatoes into thin fingers. 3. Heat oil. Add mustard seeds and turmeric. 4. Add onion, gherkins, potatoes and cook. 5. Add salt and chilli powder and mix well.

38. TOMATO BHURTA

Ingredients	*For 4*	*For 100*
Tomatoes	450 gm	11 kg
Green chillies	3	200 gm
Onions	55 gm	1.35 kg
Garlic	3 flakes	30 gm
Cumin	¼ tsp	30 gm
Fat	15 gm	340 gm
Coriander leaves	a few	1 bunch
Salt	to taste	80-100 gm

Method

1. Wash and wipe the tomatoes. 2. Roast tomatoes and onion in hot ash (10 minutes) or bake in an oven. 3. Peel tomatoes, chop fine. Chop onions. 4. Heat fat. Add cumin, chopped onion, chopped garlic and green chillies. 5. Add tomatoes and salt; cook for a few minutes. 6. Serve hot, garnished with coriander leaves.

39. CHINESE VEGETABLES (MIXED VEGETABLES)

Ingredients	*Quantity*
Garlic	2 flakes
Onions	100 gm
Carrots	100 gm
Cabbage	100 gm
Cauliflower	100 gm
Oil	2 tsp
Salt	to taste
Sugar	1 tsp
Pepper powder	2 pinches
Lime juice	½ tsp
Soya sauce	1 tsp
Ajinomoto (optional)	a pinch
Cornflour	1 tbsp

Method

Heat oil, fry chopped garlic, after some time add cut onion, cut carrot and fry for sometime then add cut cabbage, cauliflower. Fry till it is half cooked. Then add lime juice, pepper powder, salt and sugar. Stir. Lastly add cornflour mixed with water. Stir well. Cook it for 5 minutes and remove.

40. TOMATO MAHASHA

Ingredients	*For 4*	*For 100*
Tomatoes (even-sized medium ripe)	500 gm	12.5 kg
Onions	100 gm	2.5 kg
Lentil	225 gm	5.6 kg
Green chillies	2	200 gm
Potatoes	225 gm	5.6 kg
Fat	50 gm	1.35 kg
Salt	to taste	100 gm
Refined wheat flour (for paste)	15 gm	340 gm

Method

1. Cut tops off tomatoes and scoop out pulp. Sprinkle with salt and place inverted on racks. 2. Boil and mash lentil and potatoes. 3. Chop onions and chillies. 4. Heat part of the fat and fry onions. 5. Mix together onions, chillies and salt with mashed lentil and potatoes. 6. Cool mixture and fill tomatoes. 7. Firmly press down stuffing. Put tops of tomatoes on, like lids, and seal with flour and water paste. 8. Heat fat. Fry the tomatoes first on sealed side. When browned, turn and fry all over. Cook covered till tomatoes are quite soft.

41. TOMATO AMBAL

Ingredients	*For 4*	*For 100*
Tomatoes	450 gm	11 kg
Mustard oil	30 ml	500 ml
Jaggery	15 gm	340 gm
Turmeric	½ tsp	15 gm
Salt	to taste	80-100 gm
Mustard seeds	¼ tsp	30 gm

Method

1. Wash and cut tomatoes into quarters. 2. Heat oil, add mustard seeds. 3. When mustard seeds crackle add tomatoes. 4. Fry for a minute or two. Add jaggery, turmeric and salt. 5. Cover and cook gently till tomatoes are cooked and gravy thickens.

N.B. For tomato-brinjal ambal, use equal quantities of brinjals and tomatoes. Cut brinjals into quarters lengthwise and fry well before adding tomatoes.

42. TOMATOCHEN SAR

Ingredients	*For 4*	*For 100*
Tomatoes	115 gm	2.8 kg
Lentil	115 gm	2.8 kg
Water	1 litre	25 litre
Red chillies	5 gm	115 gm
Garlic	3 cloves	30 gm
Ginger	5 gm (1 cm. piece)	115 gm
Coriander leaves	a few	1 bunch
Turmeric	¼ tsp	15 gm
Mustard seeds	¼ tsp	15 gm
Cumin	¼ tsp	15 gm
Garam masala	a pinch	10 gm
Curry leaves	a few	1 bunch
Salt	to taste	100 gm
Fat	15 gm	340 gm

Method

1. Boil together lentil and tomatoes till tender. 2. Heat fat. Fry red chillies broken into small pieces. 3. Add mustard seeds, cumin and curry leaves. 4. When mustard seeds crackle add ground ginger and garlic, turmeric, tomato mixture and salt. 5. Bring to boil. Add garam masala and chopped coriander leaves and remove.

43. BATATA NE TOMATOES

Ingredients	*For 4*	*For 100*
Potatoes	225 gm	5.6 kg
Tomatoes	115 gm	2.8 kg
Coriander leaves	a few	3 bunches
Green chillies	10 gm	250 gm
Ginger	5 gm (1 cm. piece)	115 gm
Turmeric	½ tsp	30 gm
Chilli powder	2-3 gm (1 tsp)	85 gm
Mustard seeds	½ tsp	15 gm
Sugar	1 tsp	30 gm
Salt	to taste	100 gm
Fat	30 gm	500 gm

Method

1. Heat fat. Fry mustard seeds. 2. Add peeled and diced potatoes and fry. 3. Add a little water and cook till potatoes are nearly done and water

has been absorbed. 4. Add tomatoes and remaining ingredients. 5. Cook on slow heat until tomatoes are well mashed up.

44. MIXED VEGETABLE BHUJJIA

Ingredients	*For 4*	*For 100*
Potatoes	225 gm	5.65 kg
Cabbage	115 gm	2.8 kg
Peas	115 gm	2.8 kg
Tomatoes	115 gm	2.8 kg
Onions	115 gm	2.8 kg
Turmeric	½ tsp	15 gm
Cumin	½ tsp	15 gm
Ginger	10 gm	225 gm
Garlic	3 flakes	30 gm
Dry mango powder or pomegranate seeds or lime	to taste	30-50 gm
Fat	30 gm	500 gm
Salt	to taste	80-100 gm

Method

1. Wash and prepare vegetables. 2. Heat fat. Fry spices. Add vegetables and salt. Saute and mix well. 3. Cover the pan with a well-fitting lid. 4. Cook gently, shaking the pan frequently to prevent burning. Add water if necessary. Cook till all vegetables are properly cooked. 5. Add mango powder or pomegranate seeds or lime juice and remove.

N.B. Any other combination of vegetables may be used. Potatoes may be parboiled in jackets and then added to quicken the cooking process.

45. PANCH PHOORNER CHARCHARI (Bengali)

Ingredients	*For 4*	*For 100*
Potatoes	225 gm	5.6 kg
Brinjals	115 gm	2.8 kg
Red pumpkin	115 gm	2.8 kg
Peas	115 gm	2.8 kg
Green chillies	10 gm	250 gm
Onion seeds, Mustard seeds, Cumin, Fenugreek, Fennel	5 gm	115 gm
Curry leaves	a sprig	1 bunch

Ingredients	For 4	For 100
Sugar	1 tsp	30 ml
Oil	15 ml	250 ml
Salt	to taste	80-100 gm
Red chillies	1	10

Method

1. Peel and cut potatoes and pumpkin into 2.5 cm. (1") cubes. Cut brinjals into even-sized pieces. Shell peas. 2. Heat fat. Fry red chillies broken into small pieces, and slit green chillies, mixed spices and curry leaves. Add vegetables and sauté. 3. Add sugar, salt and enough water to cook vegetables. Cover. 4. Let it simmer till vegetables are tender and water is absorbed.

46. SHUKTONI

Ingredients	For 8
Chauli beans	10 gm
Brinjals	2
Potatoes	150 gm (2 medium)
Drumsticks	30 gm
Broad beans	100 gm
Radish	2 gm (1 slice)
Peas	100 gm
Bitter gourd	50 gm (2)
Ginger	5 gm (2.5 cm. piece)
Turmeric powder	1 gm (¼ tsp)
Mustard seeds	2 gm
Milk	20 ml
Salt	5-7 gm (to taste)
Sugar	2 gm
Fat	30 gm
Dry mixed spices	
Fenugreek	a pinch
Onion seeds	a pinch
Fennel	a pinch
Cumin	a pinch
Mustard seeds	a pinch

Method

1. Cut beans, brinjals, peeled potatoes, radish and bitter gourd into long pieces and fry separately. 2. Cut drumsticks into long pieces and shell peas. 3. Grind ginger, mustard seeds and turmeric to a smooth paste.

4. Heat fat, fry dry mixed spices and curry leaves. Add vegetables and fry a little. 5. Add ground spices, salt, sugar and enough water to cook the vegetables. Cover and simmer till vegetables are tender. 6. Add milk and cook till the gravy becomes thick.

47. PHULKAPIR DALNA

Ingredients	*For 8*
Cauliflower	500 gm
Potatoes	250 gm
Green peas	125 gm
Turmeric	6 gm
Red chillies	6 gm
Coriander	15 gm
Salt	10 gm
Mustard oil	50 ml
Cumin	6 gm
Curds	25 gm
Sugar	5 gm
Garam masala	5 gm
Fat	1 tbsp

Method

1. Grind turmeric, cumin, chillies, coriander to a paste. 2. Peel and cut potatoes into squares and wash well. Cut the cauliflower into flowerettes and wash. 3. Heat oil and fry the cauliflower. Add the ground spices and potatoes and fry well. 4. Add the green peas and enough water just to cover the vegetables. 5. Add some curds, sugar and salt. When the vegetables are cooked, remove from fire. 6. Add a tbsp of fat and garam masala powder.

48. BRINJAL PAHIE

Ingredients	*For 4*	*For 100*
Brinjals	225 gm	5.6 kg
Mustard seeds	½ tsp	55 gm
Red chillies	5 gm	115 gm
Curry leaves	1 sprig (1 bunch)	85 gm
Ginger	5 gm	115 gm
Cumin	1 tsp	55 gm
Vinegar	50 ml	1 litre
Cinnamon	a small piece	55 gm
Coriander	5 gm	115 gm
Sugar	a pinch	55 gm

Ingredients	*For 4*	*For 100*
Onions	10 gm	225 gm
Garlic	a few flakes	70 gm
Green chillies	5 gm	115 gm
Tamarind	10 gm	225 gm
Coconut (extract milk)	1	10
Oil	30 ml	500 ml
Turmeric	5 gm	45 gm
Salt	15 gm	100 gm

Method

1. Slice the brinjals lengthwise and rub over with turmeric and salt. 2. Grind together red chillies, mustard seeds, cinnamon, cumin and coriander. 3. Soak tamarind in salted water. 4. Slice garlic, ginger, green chillies and onion. 5. Heat oil; fry brinjals and remove. 6. Mix together the brinjals, ground spices, vinegar, tamarind, and curry leaves. 7. To hot oil add the brinjal mixture and coconut milk. 8. Simmer for 15 minutes, stirring all the time. The brinjals must be well cooked and mashed up. 9. Add the sugar just before removing from the fire.

49. BAGARA BAINGAN

Ingredients	*For 4*	*For 100*
Brinjals	450 gm	11 kg
Red chillies	5 gm	115 gm
Coconut	115 gm	2.70 kg
Coriander seeds	15 gm	340 gm
Garlic	5 gm	115 gm
Gingelly seeds	5 gm	115 gm
Onions	225 gm	5 kg
Tamarind	115 gm	2 kg
Jaggery	5 gm	55 gm
Mustard seeds	a pinch	30 gm
Turmeric	a pinch	30 gm
Curry leaves	a sprig	1 bunch
Gingelly oil	30 ml	500 ml
Salt	to taste	100 gm
Green chillies	5 gm	115 gm
Fat	30 gm	500 gm

Method

1. Wash brinjals, breaking the stem; cut them lengthwise in quarters. 2. Heat the oil and fry brinjals till the skin gets a brownish colour. 3. Remove and keep aside. 4. In the same oil fry the coriander seeds,

chillies and onions. Grind fried spices with coconut and garlic. 5. Roast gingelly seeds separately and powder. 6. Soak tamarind and extract pulp. 7. Add to ground spices. 8. To the remaining oil add chopped green chillies and turmeric and the tamarind mixture. Fry masala well . 9. Add brinjals and gingelly powder. 10. Cover and cook till gravy thickens. 11. Add jaggery and salt. 12. When gravy is quite thick remove from fire. 13. In another pan heat fat. Add mustard seeds and curry leaves. 14. When mustard seeds crackle pour over the curry. Mix well and serve.

50. BRINJAL VELLA KHORMA

Ingredients		*For 8*
Tender brinjals		500 gm
Tomatoes		250 gm
Onions (large)	grind to a fine paste	1
Green chillies		6-10
Garlic		½ pod
Ginger		2.5 cm. (1") piece
Coconut		½ (grind separately)
Cloves	crush	3
Cinnamon		2.5 cm. (1") piece
Cardamoms		3
Oil		50 ml
Salt		to taste
Lime or		1
Curds		2 tbsp
Mint leaves for garnishing		

Method

1. Heat oil. Fry ground masala. 2. Add crushed spices and fry well. 3. Add chopped tomatoes. Fry for 5 minutes; 4. Add brinjals slit into 4 and continue frying for a further 5–10 minutes. Add salt. 5. Add ground coconut. Cook till brinjals are done. 6. Add lime juice or curds. Mix well. Remove. Garnish with mint.

51. NAVRATTAN KORMA

Ingredients	*Quality*
Potato diced	150 gm
Carrot	100 gm
Beans	100 gm
Cauliflower (cubes)	150 gm
Makhna	25 gm
Paneer	100 gm
Garlic paste	25 gm

Ingredients	*Quality*
Chopped green chilli	2 tsp
Green cardamom powder	1 tsp
Fresh cream	200 gm
Broken cashew paste	150 gm
Cherry	½ cup
Kismis	2 tbsp
Bayleaf	4
Salt	to taste
Refined oil	150 gm
Pomegranate (red)	50 gm
Saffron (optional)	2 tsp

Method

1. Heat oil until smoking point, add garlic paste and bayleaf. Add cashew paste, sauté for 15 minutes on slow fire. Add water. Bring to boil. Add cardamom powder and fresh cream. Keep aside. 2. Boil above mixed vegetables with a little water. Cook till tender. 3. Heat fresh cream and cooked vegetables. Add cashew gravy and mix it. Finish with saffron mixed in a little milk if used. 4. Garnish with dry cherry and sautéd kismis.

52. BRINJAL CURRY

Ingredients	*For 4*	*For 100*
Brinjals	250 gm	5.6 kg
Coconut (3 extracts)	¼ 6	
Red chillies	6	150 gm
Turmeric	¼ 25 gm	
Pepper	½ tsp	50 gm
Salt	to taste	50-80 gm
Garlic	2 flakes	20 gm
Onions	15 gm	340 gm
Oil	30 ml	750 gm
Mustard seeds	½ tsp	10 gm
Ginger	1.25 cm. (½") piece	75 gm
Green chillies	3	75 gm
Onions	50 gm	1.25 kg
Vinegar	15 ml	(to taste)

Method

1. Wash and cut brinjals into 5 cm. (2") pieces or keep whole but slit if small variety is used. 2. Grind to a smooth paste red chillies, turmeric, pepper, salt, garlic and 50 gm of onion. 3. Apply mixture to brinjals and

set aside for 10–15 minutes. Wipe off masala from brinjals. 4. Heat oil. Fry brinjals till skin shrinks. Remove. To the same oil, add mustard seeds, sliced ginger, 15 gm onion and green chillies. 5. Fry well. Add masala removed from brinjal. Add 2nd and 3rd extract of coconut milk. Bring to boil. Add vinegar and when liquid boils, quickly add brinjals . 9. Leave pan uncovered and continue to boil briskly till gravy becomes thick. When gravy is thick, add first extract (thick) of coconut milk and remove.

53. BRINJAL AND POTATO CURRY

Ingredients	*For 4*	*For 100*
Brinjals	450 gm	11 kg
Potatoes	225 gm	5.6 kg
Tomatoes	225 gm	5.6 kg
Spring onions	115 gm	2.8 kg
Turmeric	½ tsp	30 gm
Chilli powder	½ tsp	30 gm
Sweet oil	100 ml	2.5 litre
Salt	to taste	80-100 gm

Method

1. Wash and cut brinjals into quarters. 2. Chop tomatoes and onions. 3. Peel and cut potatoes into cubes. 4. Heat oil. Fry brinjals. 5 Add turmeric, chilli powder, remaining vegetables and salt. 6. Cook on a very slow fire, covered, till all vegetables are well cooked. 7. Stir occasionally to see that the curry does not burn.

54. BRINJAL BHURTA

Ingredients	*For 4*	*For 100*
Brinjals	225 gm	5.6 kg
Onions	115 gm	2.8 kg
Green chillies	5 gm	115 gm
Turmeric	a pinch	10 gm
Chilli powder	a pinch	10 gm
Cumin powder	a pinch	10 gm
Garlic	2 flakes	15 gm
Oil	10 ml	200 ml
Salt	10 gm	200 gm
Coriander leaves	a few sprigs	1 bunch

Method

1. Roast brinjals in hot ash or on hot tava or griddle. 2. Remove skin and mash. 3. Slice a small portion of the onions; chop remaining onions fine.

4. Chop green chillies, and garlic. 5. Heat fat and fry sliced onions. Add mashed brinjals, turmeric, cumin powder, chilli powder, salt and garlic. Cook for a few minutes. 6. Remove from fire, and chopped onion, green chillies and coriander leaves. Mix well.

N.B. Curds can be used for this bhurta.

55. BHAJA MASLAR TARKARI

Ingredients	*For 2*
Brinjals	100 gm
Curds	100 gm
Green chillies	10 gm (5)
Red chilli	1
Mustard seeds	½ tsp
Cumin	½ tsp
Fenugreek	½ tsp
Salt	1 tsp
Sugar	1 tsp
Fat	30 gm

Method

1. Roast mustard seeds and cumin and powder. 2. Cut brinjals lengthwise and slit green chillies. 3. Heat fat; fry fenugreek seeds and broken red chilli. 4. Add brinjals and fry well. Mix sour curds with half a cup of water, sugar, salt and green chillies and add to the brinjal mixture. 5. Cover and cook till brinjals are tender and gravy is thick. Add powdered spices, mix well and remove from fire.

56. STUFFED BRINJALS

Ingredients	*For 4*	*For 100*
Brinjals	225 gm (2)	5.6 kg (50)
Filling		
Potatoes	115 gm	2.8 kg
Peas	115 gm	2.8 kg
Carrots	115 gm	2.8 kg
Onions	55 gm	1.36 kg
Green chillies	5 gm	115 gm
Coating		
Bengal gram flour	55 gm	455 gm
Base		
Potatoes	225 gm	5.65 kg
Butter	15 gm	340 gm

Ingredients	*For 4*	*For 100*
Garnish		
Tomatoes	10 gm	225 gm
Fat to fry (absorption)	30 gm	340 gm
Salt	to taste	100 gm

Method

1. Parboil brinjals. Cut into two, lengthwise. Scoop out centre. 2. Dice vegetables and onions. Shell peas. Chop green chillies. Boil vegetables and chillies in just enough water to cook. Add salt. 3. Heat a little fat. Sauté scooped centres of brinjals. Add vegetables and mix well. 4. Stuff brinjals with filling. 5. Prepare a batter with gram flour and water. Add salt . 6. Coat brinjals and deep fry. Remove and drain. 7. Boil and mash potatoes. 8. Pipe a border of mashed potatoes on a flat dish. Arrange brinjals in the centre. Decorate with strips of tomatoes.

57. STUFFED BRINJALS (Maharashtrian)

Ingredients		*For 4*	*For 100*
Brinjals (long variety)		450 gm	11 kg
Onions		115 gm	2.8 kg
Mustard seeds		½ tsp	15 gm
Tamarind		5 gm	250 gm
Coconut		115 gm (½)	2.8 kg (12)
Salt		to taste	100 gm
Fat		30 gm	500 gm
Curry leaves		2 sprigs	1 bunch
Red chillies	spices for frying	8	150 gm
Coriander	spices for frying	10 gm	250 gm
Cumin	spices for frying	½ tsp	15 gm
Fenugreek	spices for frying	½ tsp	15 gm
Turmeric	spices for frying	½ tsp	15 gm
Oil to fry		15 ml	250 ml

Method

1. Fry spices in a little hot oil. 2. Grind spices with tamarind and salt. When well ground, grind coconut and mix. 3. Slit brinjals into four pieces, up to three-fourths of the ground spices. 5. In a shallow pan heat fat. Add mustard seeds and curry leaves . 6. When mustard seeds crackle, add chopped onions and fry till golden brown. 7. Place the brinjals in the vessel and add remaining spices with a little water. 8. Cover and cook on slow fire turning brinjals occasionally to ensure even cooking. 9. When brinjals are cooked and gravy is thickened, remove.

58. STUFFED ROUND GOURD

Ingredients	*For 4*	*For 100*
Medium-sized round gourd (tinda)	500 gm (4)	12.5 kg (100)
Coriander powder	10 gm	200 gm
Chilli powder	1 tsp	85 gm
Turmeric	½ tsp	15 gm
Coriander leaves	a few sprigs	2 bunches
Lime	½	10
Coconut	30 gm	680 gm
Mawa	60 gm	1.36 kg
Sugar	a pinch	10 gm
Garam masala	a pinch	15 gm
Oil	100 ml	1 lit
Salt	to taste	100 gm

Method

1. Wash the gourd and peel. 2. Cut a slice off at the stem end. Scoop out the seeds. 3. Rub inside with salt and set aside. 4. Mix together coriander powder, chilli powder, turmeric, chopped coriander leaves, lime juice, grated coconut, mawa, garam masala, sugar and salt. 5. Stuff the gourds with the prepared mixture. 6. Put the top slices back. Fix with toothpicks. 7. Cook in a moderate oven, using oil to baste, till soft. Serve hot.

N.B. Kohlrabi can also be used instead of round gourd.

59. CHEESE BALL CURRY

Ingredients	*For 4*
Cheese	225 gm
Refined flour	115 gm
Eggs	4
Salt and pepper	to taste
Oil for frying	
Gravy	
Onions	60 gm
Garlic	2 flakes
Ginger	a small piece
Tomato pureé	30 ml
Chilli powder	½ tsp
Dried plums	15 gm
Fat	60 gm

Ingredients	*For 4*
Turmeric	a pinch
Coriander leaves	a few

Method

Cheese Balls

1. Sieve flour, salt and pepper. Add finely grated cheese. 2. Beat egg yolks and add to dry ingredients. Mix well. 3. Let the mixture stand for at least ½ hour. 4. Heat oil. While oil is heating beat egg whites stiff and fold into the mixture lightly but thoroughly. 5. Put teaspoonfuls of the mixture into the hot oil. 6. Remove as they turn a light golden brown colour. 7. Drain on absorbent paper.

N.B. Do not allow to fry too long or else the cheese balls become tough.

Gravy

1. Grind together onions, garlic, ginger, chilli powder and turmeric 2. Heat fat. Add ground spices. 3. Add tomato pureé, plums and a little water. Simmer for 5 minutes. 4. Add fried cheese balls and simmer for another 2–3 minutes. 5. Serve hot garnished with chopped coriander leaves.

60. CHEESE KOFTA CURRY

Ingredients	*For 4*	*For 100*
Cheese	115 gm	2.8 kg
Bengal gram flour	60 gm	1.36 kg
Turmeric	1/8 tsp	10 gm
Chilli powder	¼ tsp	15 gm
Ginger	a small piece	55 gm
Coriander powder	10 gm	250 gm
Green chillies	10 gm	250 gm
Onions	115 gm	2.8 kg
Tomatoes	225 gm	5.6 kg
Cumin	a pinch	15 gm
Curds	1 tbsp	500 ml
Soda bicarbonate	a pinch	10 gm
Salt	to taste	100 gm
Oil	30 gm	500 gm
Coriander leaves	a few sprigs	1 bunch

Method

1. Grind together to a fine paste the turmeric, chilli powder and coriander powder. 2. Heat oil. Add cumin, chopped onions, green chillies and

ginger. Saute. 3. Add ground spices and fry. 4. Add chopped tomatoes and salt to taste. Simmer, adding a little water if necessary. 5. Cut cheese into cubes. 6. Prepare a thick batter with gram flour, soda, salt and water. 7. Dip cheese in the batter and deep-fry. 8. Drain and put into prepared curry. Cook for a few minutes. 9. Add beaten curds. Do not boil after adding curds but mix well. 10. Serve hot, garnished with a pinch of finely chopped coriander leaves.

61. PANIR

Ingredients	*For 4*	*For 100*
Milk	950 ml	15 litre
Sour curds or	55 gm	225 gm
Lime juice or	1 tbsp	10-12
Vinegar	1 tsp	2 tsp
Crushed peppercorns	a few	15 gm
Coriander leaves	a few sprigs	1 bunch

Method

1. Bring milk to boiling point. 2. Add crushed peppercorns, coriander leaves and beaten curds or vinegar or lime juice, stirring the milk slowly, 3. Stir till whey separates. 4. Pour the whole into a clean muslin bag, tie loosely and hang till most of the liquid drains off. 5. Keep the bag under a heavy weight for half an hour. 6 . Cut into cubes to be used in the preparation of the curry.

62. PALAK PANIR

Ingredients	*For 4*	*For 100*
Spinach	455 gm	11.3 kg
Fenugreek leaves	¼ bunch	5 bunches
Cottage cheese (panir)	115 gm	2.8 kg
Ginger	a small piece	55 gm
Garlic	a few flakes	30 gm
Green chillies	5 gm	115 gm
Chilli powder	5 gm	115 gm
Coriander leaves	30 gm	500 gm
Fat	30 gm	500 gm
Salt	to taste	80-100 gm

Method

1. Cut panir into cubes. 2. Heat fat. Fry panir till pale brown and remove. 3. Grind together chilli powder, garlic and ginger. 4. Fry spices and whole green chillies. 5. Add washed and chopped spinach and fenugreek leaves. Sauté. 6. Add salt. Cook quickly for a few minutes. Add water if

necessary. Cover and cook on a slow fire till spinach and fenugreek leaves are cooked. Mash well. 7. Add panir cubes. Bring to boil and remove. Garnish with chopped coriander leaves.

63. PEAS PANIR CURRY

Ingredients	*For 4*	*For 100*
Fresh peas	450 gm	11 kg
Cottage cheese(panir)	115 gm	2.8 kg
Coriander powder	5 gm	115 gm
Chilli powder	½ tsp	50 gm
Turmeric	a pinch	15 gm
Garam masala	⅛ tsp	15 gm
Onion	55 gm	1.36 kg
Fat	30 gm	500 gm
Garlic	3 flakes	20 gm
Ginger	a small piece	60 gm
Tomatoes	225 gm	5.65 kg
Salt	to taste	100 gm
Blanched almonds or Cashewnuts	30 gm	680 gm
Curds	30 gm	750 gm
Coriander leaves	a few sprigs	1 bunch

Method

1. Grind together onion, coriander powder, chilli powder, turmeric, ginger and garlic to a fine paste. 2. Grind almonds, or cashewnuts separately. 3. Heat fat. Fry panir cubes till light brown and remove. 4. In the same fat fry spices. Add peas and fry. 5. Add tomato pulp, salt and a small quantity of water. 6. Cook till peas are soft. Add fried cottage cheese. Simmer. 7. Add the ground nuts and beaten curds. Mix well. Bring to boil and serve hot garnished with chopped coriander leaves.

64. ALU PANIR KHORMA

Ingredients	*For 10*
Potatoes	450 gm
Cottage cheese (panir)	115 gm
Coconut	55 gm
Ginger	5 gm
Green chillies	5 gm
Coriander leaves	1 bunch.
Onions	115 gm
Fennel	1 tsp

Ingredients	*For 10*
Cardamom cloves and cinnamon	5 gm
Salt	to taste
Fat	55 gm
Lime	½

Method

1. Wash and dice potatoes and boil. Grind together ginger, chillies, coriander leaves, fennel and half the onions. 2. Roast and powder cardamom cloves and cinnamon. Grate coconut and extract milk. 3. Heat fat and fry remaining onions. Add the powdered spices and the ground spices. 4. Add cooked potatoes and fry well. Fry panir cubes till light brown. 5. Add fried panir to potatoes. Add coconut milk and bring to boil. 6. Serve, adding salt and lime juice to taste.

65. PANIR KOFTA CURRY

Ingredients	*For 8*
Milk	2 litre
Sour curds	100 gm (¾ cup)
Ginger	2.25 cm. (1")piece
Green chillies	2
Onions (small)	6–10
Salt	to taste
Fat	to
Curry	
Coriander powder	15 gm
Red chillies	3–5
Turmeric	a pinch
Dry coconut	30 gm
Garlic	a few flakes
Tomatoes	2 (225 gm)
Lime (optional)	½
Onions	55 gm
Fat	to
Salt	to taste

Method

For Panir Koftas

1. Boil milk. Add curds. Set aside. 2. When the milk separates strain in muslin cloth. Keep aside the whey. Tie up the muslin and hang it till all moisture is removed. 3. Knead on a marble slab to smooth out. 4. Add

minced (or finely chopped) onions, green chillies, ginger and salt. 5. Form into balls and fry.

For Curry

1. Slice onions. Grind spices and garlic with coconut. 2. Blanch to matoes. Heat fat. Fry sliced onions and spices. 3. Add blanched tomatoes. Bring to boil. 4. Add salt and enough panir whey for gravy. 5. When spices are cooked and gravy is fairly thick add panir koftas. 6. Add a few drop of lime juice if desired and remove from fire.

N.B. If desired, red chillies can be reduced.

66. METHI PANIR

Ingredients	*For 4*
Cottage cheese (panir)	225 gm (prepared from 2.5 litre milk)
Onions	30 gm
Fenugreek leaves	115 gm
Chilli powder	2 tsp
Garam masala	1 ½ tsp
Turmeric	½ tsp
Coriander seeds	2 tsp
Lime juice	1 tsp–1½ tsp (to taste)
Salt	to taste
Water	150 ml
Fat	100 gm

Method

1. Chop fenugreek leaves after removing root and part of stem attached to root. 2. Wash and apply 2 tsp salt and keep aside for an hour. 3. Squeeze out water from the leaves and wash them thoroughly (3–4 washings). 4. Grind fenugreek leaves. 5. Heat fat (50 gm) and fry onions. 6. Add ground fenugreek leaves, and spices (except garam masala) and fry. 7. Fry cubes of panir in remaining fat. Add fried panir and water to fenugreek. Cover. Cook till gravy is thick. Add garam masala and lime juice and remove from the fire.

67. CASHEW POTATO CURRY

Ingredients	*For 4*	*For 100*
Potatoes	125 gm (2 medium)	3.25 kg

Ingredients	For 4	For 100
Cashewnuts	75 gm	1.8 kg
(Preferably green tender ones)		
Red chillies	2	50 gm
Turmeric	¼ tsp	25 gm
Coriander	1 tbsp	200 gm
Cumin	a pinch	25 gm
Lime	½ 12	
Onions	2 (200 gm)	6 kg
Green chillies	2	50 gm
Ginger	10 gm	250 gm
Garlic	4 cloves	50 gm
Coconut	½	12
Oil	2 tbsp	625 ml
Curry leaves	1 sprig	1 bunch
Curry leaves	1 sprig	1 bunch
Mustard seeds	a pinch	10 gm
Salt	to taste	100 gm

Method

1. Peel and cut potatoes into 5 cm. (2") pieces. Soak cashewnuts in hot water. 2. Grate coconut. Extract coconut milk from three-fourths of the coconut (twice). 3. Boil cashewnuts and potatoes in the second extraction of coconut milk. 4. Grind to a fine paste the remaining coconut, red chillies, coriander, turmeric and cumin. 5. Slice onions and slit green chillies. Slice ginger and garlic. 6. Heat the oil. Add mustard and curry leaves. When seeds splutter add ground spices and sliced ingredients. Cook till onions are soft. 7. Add cooked vegetables, lime juice and salt. Simmer for 10 minutes. 8. Add the first extraction of coconut milk and simmer for 5 minutes. Test for seasoning and remove.

N.B. Instead of potatoes, mushrooms or drumsticks may be used.

68. CASHEW MASALA

Ingredients	For 10
Tender or dried cashewnuts	200 gm
Red chillies	5-6
Peppercorns	a few
Cumin	a pinch
Fennel	a pinch
Turmeric	a large pinch
Garam masala	¼ tsp
Garlic	2 flakes

Ingredients	*For 10*
Onion	a small piece
Coconut	½
Curry leaves	a few
Salt	to taste
Fat	1 tbsp

Method

1. Soak cashewnuts in hot water for 2 to 3 hours. 2. Grind the spices with onion and garlic. 3. Mix with soaked cashewnuts and cook till half done. 4. Slice coconut and cut slices into ½ cm. (¼") pieces. 5. Add coconut and salt to cashewnuts and cook till cashewnuts are tender and hardly any liquid remains. 6. Heat fat. Add curry leaves. 7. Add prepared cashews. Sauté and remove. Serve hot.

69. MUKANDWADI

Ingredients	*For 4*	*For 100*
Wholewheat flour	225 gm	5.6 kg
Split bengal gram	115 gm	2.8 kg
Onions	60 gm	1.36 kg
Garlic	2 flakes	15 gm
Ginger	a small piece	30 gm
Tomato pureé	30 ml	680 ml
Chilli powder	½ tsp	50 gm
Dried plums	15 gm	340 gm
Fat	60 gm	1 kg
Turmeric	a pinch	15 gm
Coriander leaves	a few	1 bunch

Method

1. Make a stiff dough with wheat flour. Set aside for half an hour. 2. Wash dough under a running tap in a muslin bag to separate gluten from starch. Catch starch liquid in a bowl. 3. When all the starch has been removed, flatten gluten between the palms. 4. Cook along with gram, chilli powder and turmeric in the starch water till gram is cooked. 5. Remove. Cut into cubes and fry in fat. Keep these wadi aside.

Curry

1. Grind together onion, garlic and ginger. 2. Heat remaining fat. Add ground spices. 3. Add tomato pureé, dried plums and the liquid in which the gram is cooked. Simmer for 5 minutes. 4. Add gram and fried wadi. Simmer for another 2–3 minutes. 5. Serve hot garnished with chopped coriander leaves.

70. PADVAL ULATHIYATHU

Ingredients	*For 4*	*For 100*
Snake gourd (tender)	225 gm	5.6 kg
Red chillies	3	8.5 gm
Salt	to taste	50-80 gm
Oil	30 ml	500 ml

Method

1. Wash gourd. Cut into 3.5 cm. (1 ½") pieces. Cut into half and remove seeds and white pith. 2. Slice into fingers about 0.25–0.5 cm. (⅛"–¼") thick. 3. Crush red chillies. 4. Mix gourd pieces, chillies and salt and barely cover with water. 5. Cook till gourd is tender and no moisture remains. 6. Heat oil. Fry cooked gourd.

N.B. Raw bananas, kurkas, chauli beans etc., can be prepared in the same manner.

71. STUFFED PADVAL

Ingredients	*For 4*	*For 100*
Snake gourd (tender)	450 gm	11 kg
Onions	55 gm	1.35 kg
Potatoes	225 gm	5.6 kg
Green chillies	10 gm	250 gm
Ginger	a small piece	30 gm
Turmeric	a pinch	15 gm
Mustard seeds or Fenugreek seeds	a pinch	15 gm
Salt	to taste	80-100 gm
Lime	½	10
Bengal gram flour	30 gm	340 gm
Water	600 ml	14.75 litre
Oil to fry (absorption)	30 ml	340 ml

Method

1. Wash and steam gourd, whole or cut into half, until half cooked. 2. Cut into 5 cm. (2") pieces. Remove seeds. Apply salt and set aside. 3. Boil potatoes. Peel and dice. 4. Chop onion, green chillies and ginger. 5. Heat a little oil. Add mustard seeds; when they crackle, add chillies, onion, ginger, turmeric, potatoes and salt. Mix well. 6. Add lime juice. Mix again and remove. 7. Stuff gourd with potato stuffing. 8. Prepare a batter with gram flour, salt and water. 9. Dip gourd in batter and deep fry in hot oil.

72. SNAKE GOURD CALDEEN

Ingredients	*For 4*
Snake gourd (tender)	115 gm
Salt	to taste
Coconut	½
Coriander	5 gm
Cumin	a pinch
Turmeric	a pinch
Ginger	2.5 cm. (1") piece
Green chilli	1
Cinnamon	2.5 cm. (1") piece
Oil	150 ml
Onion	15 gm

Method

1. Wash and cut snake gourd into 5 cm. by 2.5 cm. (2″ × 1″) pieces. Parboil with a little salt and water. 2. Grind to a fine paste, coconut, coriander, cumin, turmeric, ginger, green chilli and cinnamon,. 3. Heat oil. Add sliced onion. Sauté. Add ground ingredients and fry for a few minutes more. 4. Add snake gourd pieces, a cup of water and more salt if desired. Cook till gravy is thick and gourd is tender.

73. FRIED SURAN

Peel and wash elephant yam (suran). Grate on a medium-sized grater and put into salted water. Drain. Heat oil in a deep fry pan. Fry crisp. Mix chilli powder and more salt if desired, while still hot. Cool and tin and use as desired.

74. FRIED KARELA or PAVAKKA ULATHIYATHU

Ingredients	*For 4*	*For 100*
Bitter gourd	225 gm	5.65 kg
Green chillies	10 gm	250 gm
Coconut (fresh)	55 gm (¼)	1.36 kg (6)
Salt	to taste	80-100 gm
Coconut oil	15 ml	340 ml

Method

1. Wash and dry gourd. Slit and remove seeds and pulp. 2. Cut into fine slices or roundels. 3. Slit green chillies. 4. Cut coconut into 0.75 cm (¼") pieces. 5. Cook together gourd, green chillies and coconut with salt and just enough water to cook gourd dry. 6. Cook over gentle heat till gourd

is done and water evaporated. 7. Heat oil in a fry pan. Add cooked gourd and fry till gourd is fairly crisp.

75. POTATO STUFFED KARELA

Ingredients	*For 4*	*For 100*
Bitter gourd (medium sized)	340 gm (4)	8.5 kg (100)
Potatoes	150 gm	3.7 kg
Chilli powder	5 gm	115 gm
Garam masala	2 tsp	50 gm
Tamarind	15 gm	340 gm
Salt	15 gm	120 gm
Fat	15 gm	250 gm

Method

1. Salt bitter gourds. Remove seeds and pulp. 2. Smear inside and out with salt and set aside . 3. Boil potatoes. Peel and dice. 4. Mix with chilli powder, garam masala and tamarind pulp. 5. Stuff bitter gourds with prepared stuffing 6. Tie. 7. Heat fat. Fry gourds lightly. Cover and cook on a slow fire till gourds are well cooked.

76. MASALA KARELA

Ingredients	*For 4*	*For 100*
Bitter gourd	450 gm	11 kg
Red chillies	5 gm	115 gm
Peppercorns	a few	15 gm
Mustard	1 tsp	20 gm
Tamarind	10 gm	250 gm
Garlic	5 gm	30 gm
Ginger	1 cm. (½") piece	50 gm
Onions	115 gm	2.8 kg
Green chillies	2	50 gm
Vinegar	15 ml	250 ml
Mustard oil	15 ml	250 ml
Jaggery	15 gm	250 gm
Salt .	to taste	100-120 gm

Method

1. Slit gourds from one side. Remove seeds and pulp. 2. Cut into thin slices. Boil in salted water until half cooked. 3. Remove and drain. 4. Grind together the red chillies, peppercorns, half the mustard, tamarind and garlic to a fine paste. 5. Finely slice onions, green chillies and ginger. 6. Heat mustard oil. Add remaining mustard and then sliced masala, gourd masala, vinegar and salt. 7. Add sufficient water to cook

gourd dry. 8. Cook till gourd is tender. 9. Add powdered jaggery. Cook till water is completely dried up. 10. Keep overnight and serve the next day.

N.B. After cutting gourd into thin slices apply salt and place in a flat plate to dry in the sun.

77. VEGETABLE STUFFED KARELA

Ingredients	*For 4*	*For 100*
Bitter gourd (medium size)	340 gm (4)	8.5 kg (100)
Tamarind	a little	30 gm
Potatoes	225 gm	5.6 kg
Cauliflower	115 gm	2.8 kg
Onions	115 gm	2.8 kg
Turmeric	1 tsp	15 gm
Coriander powder	5 gm	115 gm
Chilli powder	1 tsp	85 gm
Garam masala	1 tsp	30 gm
Lime	1	12
Egg	1	6
Salt	to taste	80-100 gm
Fat	50 gm	1 kg

Method

1. Slit gourds from one side. Remove seeds and pulp carefully without breaking the gourds. 2. Rub inside and out with salt and let them stand for 5 to 6 hours. 3. Wash well under running water. 4. Boil the gourds in salted water to which has been added the tamarind pulp. 5. Cook till half done. Remove, drain and dry completely. 6. Heat part of the fat. Add finely sliced onions. Fry till golden brown. 7. Add the spices. Fry. 8. Add boiled mashed potatoes and boiled cauliflower and salt. 9. Add lime juice. Keep frying till well browned. 10. Stuff gourd. Tie with a thread. 11. Heat remaining fat. 12. Dip prepared gourd in beaten egg. Fry till light brown.

78. PAVAKKAI VARATHARACHA CURRY (BITTER GOURD CURRY)

Ingredients	*For 8*
Bitter gourds (big)	2
Green chillies	4
Salt	to taste
Red chillies	10
Coriander seeds	2 tbsp

Ingredients	*For 8*
Turmeric	1.25 cm. (½") piece
Red onion (a)	1
Garlic (a)	2 flakes
Tamarind	ball, the size of a lime (3.5 cm. diameter)
Medium sized coconut	1
Red onion (b)	1
Garlic (b)	1 flake
Curry leaves	a few sprigs
For tempering	
Oil	2 tbsp
Mustard seeds	½ tsp
Onion	1

Method

1. Wash and dry gourds. Cut lengthwise. Remove seeds and cut into pieces 0.75 cm. by 3.75 cm. (¼" × 1½"). 2. Parboil with salt and slit green chillies, till cooked dry. 3. Roast well and grind red chillies, coriander seeds and turmeric along with red onion(a) and garlic (a). 4. Soak tamarind in 1 cup water. 5. Mix ground ingredients of (3) above with tamarind pulp and add to bitter gourd. Add more salt if desired. Simmer till thick gravy remains. 6. Grate coconut fine and roast with red onion (b), garlic (b) and curry leaves till well browned. Grind to a fine paste. 7. Mix with 1 cup of water and add to bitter gourd. Taste to ensure that the dish has enough salt and sourness. 8. Bring to boil. 9. Heat oil: add mustard seeds. 10. When seeds crackle, add small onion (sliced), and brown. 11. Add prepared bitter gourd and remove.

Variations: Elephant yam, snake gourd, brinjals etc., can be used instead of bitter gourd.

79. POTATO BHAJI (A)

Ingredients	*For 4*	*For 100*
Potatoes	225 gm	11.3 kg
Onions	85 gm	2 kg
Coriander leaves	a small bunch	6 bunches
Green chillies	10 gm	250 gm
Tamarind	5 gm	115 gm
Mustard seeds	½ tsp	10 gm
Asafoetida	a pinch	10 gm
Coconut oil	15 ml	340 ml

Ingredients	*For 4*	*For 100*
Salt	to taste	80-100 gm
Curry leaves	1 sprig	½ bunch

Method

1. Wash, boil, peel and cut potatoes into cubes. 2. Add tamarind pulp, green chillies and onions. Mix well. 3. Heat oil in a pan. Fry mustard seeds, asafoetida and curry leaves. 4. Remove pan from fire. Add prepared potatoes and salt. Mix well. Garnish with chopped coriander leaves.

POTATO BHAJI (B)

Ingredients	*For 4*	*For 100*
Potatoes	450 gm	11 kg
Onions	225 gm	5.6 kg
Cumin	¼ tsp	15 gm
Turmeric	a pinch	15 gm
Chilli powder	5 gm	115 gm
Coriander powder	10 gm	225 gm
Salt	to taste	100 gm
Fat	30 gm	455 gm
Curds	115 gm	2.8 kg

Method

1. Boil and peel potatoes; cut into small pieces. 2. Peel and chop onions. 3. Heat fat; add cumin and turmeric; fry for 3–5 minutes. 4. Add chopped onions and fry till golden brown. 5. Mix together curds, chilli powder, coriander powder and salt. 6. Add to browned onions; cook covered for a few minutes. 7. Add potatoes, simmer for 10 minutes and serve hot.

POTATO BHAJI (C)

Ingredients	*For 4*	*For 100*
Potatoes	225 gm	5.6 kg
Onions	115 gm	2.8 kg
Green chillies	5 gm	115 gm
Turmeric	a pinch	15 gm
Salt	10 gm	100 gm
Tomatoes	115 gm	2.8 kg
Fat	10 gm	225 gm
Mustard seeds	a pinch	15 gm
Curry leaves	a sprig	1 bunch

Method

1. Peel potatoes and cut into quarters. 2. Slice onions and green chillies. 3. Heat fat. Sauté onions, green chillies and potatoes. Add turmeric and continue frying for a few minutes. 4. Add chopped tomatoes, salt and enough water to cook potatoes. 5. When potatoes are soft and gravy is thick remove and temper with mustard seeds and curry leaves fried in oil. 6. Serve hot with puries or as a vegetable.

80. PURI KA ALU

Ingredients	*For 4*	*For 100*
Potatoes	500 gm	12 kg
Tomatoes	125 gm	3 kg
Poppy seeds	25 gm	600 gm
Ginger	2½ gm	60 gm
Curds	75 ml	2 litre
Cumin powder	1 gm	50 gm
Turmeric	1 gm	50 gm
Coriander powder	3 gm	150 gm
Chilli powder	2 gm	100 gm
Bay leaf	½ gm	20 gm
Cardamoms (black)	1	50 gm
Salt	to taste	100 gm
Fat	25 gm	100 gm

Method

1. Boil potatoes, peel and cube. 2. Heat fat. Add chopped ginger, chopped tomatoes. 3. Fry well till almost dry. 4. Add ground poppy seeds. Fry again. 5. Add curds. Mix well and cook till fat floats on top. 6. Add cumin powder, coriander powder, turmeric powder, chilli powder, bay leaf, black cardamoms and salt to taste. Fry well. 7. Add boiled and cubed potatoes and a little hot water. Simmer till well blended. 8. Remove. Serve hot with puries.

81. BATATE SUKHE

Ingredients	*For 4*	*For 100*
Potatoes	450 gm	11 kg
Grated coconut	½	10
Coconut oil	15 ml	250 ml
Red chillies	5 gm	115 gm
Turmeric	½ tsp	10 gm
Coriander seeds	10 gm	250 gm
Fenugreek	¼ tsp	5 gm

Ingredients	*For 4*	*For 100*
Split black gram	1 tsp	30 gm
Onions	85 gm	2 kg
Tamarind	10 gm	250 gm
Salt	to taste	80-100 gm

Method

1. Wash, boil, peel and cut potatoes into small cubes. 2. Roast coriander seeds, fenugreek, split black gram and red chillies. 3. Grind coconut and turmeric along with roasted spices. 4. Heat half the oil. Fry potatoes, add ground spices, tamarind pulp and salt and cook on a slow fire till the spices are cooked and gravy is thick. Remove from fire. 5. Heat remaining oil. Add finely chopped onions. When well fried, pour over potatoes.

82. ALU MATTAR (6 portions)

Ingredients	*Quantity*
Potatoes	450 gm
Peas	450 gm
Onions	250 gm
Ginger	10 gm
Garlic	30 gm
Turmeric	a pinch
Chilli powder	5 gm
Coriander powder	10 gm
Cumin powder	a small pinch
Tomatoes	225 gm
Curds	60 ml
Cashewnuts	15 gm
Garam masala	a pinch
Fat	100 gm

Method

1. Chop onions. Grind ginger and garlic into a smooth paste. 2. Boil potatoes. Peel and cut into quarters. 3. Shell peas. 4. Fry peas and potatoes. Remove. 5. Fry onions, ginger-garlic paste and spices (chilli powder, turmeric, coriander and cumin). 6. Add blanched tomatoes and simmer till spices are cooked. 7. Add well beaten curds, potatoes and peas and water, if required, and simmer till gravy is thick. 8. Add garam masala powder and remove.

N.B. If tomatoes are sour, reduce the quantity of curds to 30 ml

83. ALU DUM

Ingredients	*For 4*	*For 100*
Potatoes	450 gm	11 kg
Peas	220 gm	5.6 kg
Onions	50 gm	1.35 kg
Green chillies	5 gm	115 gm
Salt	to taste	80-100 gm
Fat	50 gm	1.25 kg
Lime juice	½ lime	6 limes
Curry		
Tomatoes	220 gm	5.6 kg
Onions	30 gm	680 gm
Turmeric	a pinch	10 gm
Chilli powder	5 gm	115 gm
Stuffing		
Peas	220 gm	5.6 kg
Onions	50 gm	1.35 kg
Green chillies	5 gm	115 gm
Salt	to taste	80-100 gm
Fat	50 gm	1.25 kg
Lime juice	½ lime	6 limes

Method

1. Boil potatoes in jackets. 2. Peel. Cut into half lengthwise. 3. Scoop out centre, leaving 1.25 cm. (½") thick walls. 4. Stuff with prepared stuffing. 5. Put the halves together and secure with toothpicks. 6. Fry till light brown. Put into curry and cook for 15 to 30 minutes. Serve hot, garnished with chopped coriander leaves.

Curry

7. Heat a little fat. Add chopped onion, chilli powder, turmeric and tomato pureé.

Stuffing

1. Heat fat. Add chopped onion and green chillies and sauté. 2. Add peas and cook on slow fire till peas are tender. 3. Add scooped out potatoes, salt and lime juice and mix well.

84. POTATO BHURTA (ALU BHURTA)

Ingredients	*For 4*	*For 100*
Potatoes	220 gm	5.6 kg
Onions	50 gm	1.36 kg

Ingredients	*For 4*	*For 100*
Green chillies	5 gm	115 gm
Lime	1	12
Fat	30 gm	500 gm
Mustard seeds	½ tsp	30 gm
Chilli powder	1 tsp	30 gm
Salt	10 gm	100 gm
Coriander leaves	a few sprigs	½ bunch

Method

1. Boil potatoes. Peel and mash. 2. Chop green chillies and onions. 3. Heat fat. Add mustard seeds. When they crackle remove pan from fire and add chilli powder. 4. Add chopped onion, green chillies, mashed potatoes, salt and lime juice. Mix well. 5. Serve garnished with coriander leaves.

85. ALU METHI

Ingredients	*Quantity*
Potatoes	500 gm
Onions	120 gm
Fat	50 gm
Fenugreek leaves	a small bunch
Turmeric	¼ tsp
Tomatoes	115 gm
Curds	50 ml
Garlic	2-4 flakes
Salt	to taste

Method

1. Wash, peel and quarter potatoes and place in cold water. 2. Heat fat. Brown chopped onions slightly. Clean and chop fenugreek leaves. 3. Add turmeric and fenugreek leaves and continue frying. 4. Add curds, chopped garlic, potatoes, salt and sufficient water to cook potatoes. 5. Add finely chopped tomatoes and cook for a few minutes longer.

86. BATATA KUT

Ingredients	*For 4*	*For 100*
Potatoes	225 gm	5.6 kg
Red chillies	5-8 gm	80-100 gm
Fenugreek	½ tsp	15 gm
Mustard seeds	1 tsp	15 gm
Tamarind	5 gm	115 gm
Asafoetida	a pinch	15 gm

Ingredients	For 4	For 100
Oil	50 ml	1.25 litre
Salt	to taste	80-100 gm

Method

1. Wash potatoes thoroughly. 2. Peel and cut into strips 1.25 cm. (½") in length. 3. After squeezing out all water, apply salt and set aside for 10 minutes. 4. Fry the potato pieces in oil till golden and set aside. 5. Roast red chillies, fenugreek, mustard and asafoetida in a little oil. 6. Grind along with tamarind to a fine, thick paste. 7. Mix ground spices to fried potatoes and serve immediately so that potatoes remain crisp.

87. SPICY POTATOES

Ingredients	For 4	For 100
Potatoes	450 gm	11 kg
Onions	225 gm	5.6 kg
Chilli powder	2 tsp	115 gm
Tamarind	5 gm	115 gm
Coconut oil	60 ml	1.5 litre
Grated coconut	1 tbsp	2 coconuts
Salt	to taste	80-100 gm

Method

1. Boil, peel and cut potatoes into square pieces. 2. Fry chopped onions in coconut oil till light brown. 3. Add potatoes to fried onions. Add salt. 4. Grind chilli powder, tamarind and grated coconut to a fine paste using water. 5. Add ground spices to potatoes and cook in a slow fire till gravy is thick.

88. BATATA CHILLI FRY

Ingredients	For 4	For 100
Potatoes	225 gm	5.6 kg
Red chillies	5 gm	115 gm
Grated coconut	1 tbsp	2 coconuts
Tamarind	5 gm	115 gm
Jaggery	1 small piece	15 gm
Garlic	1 small piece	15 gm
Coconut oil	15 ml	250 ml

Method

1. Boil and peel potatoes and cut into 2.5 cm (1") cubes. 2. Grind chillies, grated coconut and tamarind. 3. Add ground spices, salt and jaggery (with sufficient water to cover potatoes) to the potato cubes. 4. Keep on

fire. Bring to boil and simmer for 5 to 10 minutes. 5. Fry crushed garlic in oil. 6. Remove potatoes from fire and add fried garlic with the oil in which it was fried. 7. Stir well and serve hot.

89. BATATA THILSANE

Ingredients	*For 4*	*For 100*
Potatoes	225 gm	5.6 kg
Red chillies	4	85 gm
Coconut oil	15 ml	340 ml
Garlic	8 cloves	30 gm
Tamarind	5 gm	115 gm
Salt	to taste	10 gm

Method

1. Peel and cut potatoes into thin pieces 3.75 cm. (1½") long, 2. Wash thoroughly. Drain and add salt and tamarind pulp. 3. Heat oil. Add slightly crushed garlic and when golden brown add broken red chillies. 4. Stir well. Then add the potatoes and keep on a low fire. 5. Sprinkle water and let potatoes cook well. 6. Remove when dry.

90. BATATA KOSAMBRI

Ingredients	*For 4*	*For 100*
Potatoes	225 gm	5.6 kg
Onions	100 gm	2.5 kg
Grated coconut	55 gm (¼)	1.35 kg (6)
Salt	to taste	100 gm
Lime	1	25
Coriander leaves	1 small bunch	12 bunches
Green chillies	3	115 gm

Method

1. Wash, boil, peel and cut potatoes into cubes. 2. Chop onions, chillies and coriander leaves. 3. Add grated coconut, chopped ingredients, lime juice and salt to the potato pieces. Mix well.

91. BHANAP BATATA

Ingredients	*For 4*	*For 100*
Young potatoes (small and round)	450 gm	11 kg
Red chillies	10 gm	225 gm
Tamarind	5 gm	115 gm
Groundnut oil	60 ml	1 litre
Salt	to taste	80-100 gm

Method

1. Wash, boil and peel the potatoes. 2. Heat oil and fry potatoes. 3. Grind chillies and tamarind. 4. When potatoes are fried, add chillies, tamarind, salt and enough water to make a thick gravy. 5. Reduce fire and cook potatoes till gravy is thick.

92. RAS BATATA

Ingredients	*For 4*	*For 100*
Potatoes	115 gm	2.8 kg
Onions	115 gm	2.8 kg
Cauliflower	115 gm	2.8 kg
Tomatoes	225 gm	5.6 kg
French beans	115 gm	2.8 kg
Peas	115 gm	2.8 kg
Bottle gourd	115 gm	2.8 kg
Carrots	115 gm	2.8 kg
Green chillies	10 gm	250 gm
Peppercorns	6	15 gm
Cinnamon	1.25 cm. (½") piece	10 gm
Cloves	6	5 gm
Coconut	115 gm (½)	12
Salt	to taste	100 gm

Method

1. Wash and cut vegetables, green chillies, and potatoes, and boil. 2. Crush the pepper, cinnamon cloves and salt and add to vegetables. 3. When vegetables are properly cooked, add thick coconut milk and keep on fire till it boils. 4. Lower heat and let the curry simmer.

93. HIGHLY SPICED CHOUCHOU

Ingredients	*For 4*	*For 100*
Potatoes	225 gm	5.6 kg
French beans	115 gm	2.8 kg
Carrots	115 gm	2.8 kg
Brinjal	115 gm	2.8 kg
Red chillies	10 gm	250 gm
Fenugreek	¼ tsp	15 gm
Mustard seeds	½ tsp	15 gm
Turmeric	½ tsp	15 gm
Asafoetida	a pinch	10 gm
Salt	to taste	100 gm

Ingredients	*For 4*	*For 100*
Lime (juice)	½ to 1	12 to 15
Groundnut oil	50 ml	1.25 litre

Method

1. Boil and peel the potatoes. 2. Wash other vegetables and cut them in longish strips. 3. Heat groundnut oil (setting aside a little for roasting spices) in a pan and add turmeric powder, vegetable strips. potatoes and salt and cook on a very low fire, stirring at intervals. 4. In a separate vessel, heat remaining oil and roast chillies, fenugreek. mustard seeds and asafoetida. 5. Grind the roasted spices (using a little water) into a thick paste. 6. Add the spices to vegetables when they are tender and simmer for another 10 minutes. 7. Remove from the fire and add lime juice and mix.

94. BATATA HOOMAN

Ingredients	*For 4*	*For 100*
Potatoes	225 gm	5.6 kg
Coconut	½	10
Red chilles	4	115 gm
Tamarind	5 gm	115 gm
Salt	5 gm	115 gm
Asafoetida	a pinch	10 gm
Coconut oil	15 ml	250 ml

Method

1. Wash, boil, peel and cut potatoes into large pieces. 2. Grind into a fine paste, chillies, tamarind and grated coconut. 3. Add ground spices to the potatoes with enough water to barely cover solids. Add salt . 4. Bring to boiling point. Reduce heat and simmer till spices are cooked. 5. Remove from fire. Mix asafoetida in a little water. Add to curry along with fresh coconut oil. Mix well.

95. TIL ALU DUM (2 big portions)

Ingredients	*Quantity*
Potatoes (boil, peel and cube)	250 gm
Gingelly seeds (roast and powder)	650 gm
Salt	to taste
For tempering	
Oil	50 ml
Fenugreek seeds	5 gm
Green chillies	10 gm

Ingredients	*Quantity*
Turmeric	¼ tsp
Asafoetida	1 tsp
Timur (optional)	1 tsp

Method

1. Mix together cubed potatoes, roasted and powdered gingelly (sesame) seeds and salt. 2. Heat oil, add fenugreek seeds. 3. As they splutter, add green chillies, turmeric and asafoetida. 4. Mix well and pour over potato mixture.

96. POTATO AMBAT

Ingredients	*For 4*	*For 100*
Split red gram	115 gm	2.8 kg
Potatoes	225 gm	5.6 kg
Onions	115 gm	2.8 kg
Coconut	½	10
Red chillies	4	115 gm
Fenugreek	½ tsp	5 gm
Tamarind	10 gm	250 gm
Salt	to taste	80-100 gm
Oil	30 ml	500 ml

Method

1. Wash and boil the gram. (If gram is soaked for a couple of hours it will boil more easily.) 2. Peel and cut potatoes into large pieces. 3. When gram is half cooked add potatoes. 4. Boil till potatoes are soft. Add salt. 5. Roast fenugreek using a little oil. 6. Grind together coconut, red chillies, roasted fenugreek and tamarind to a fine paste. 7. Add ground spices to gram and potatoes with sufficient liquid to barely cover solids. 8. Boil till spices are cooked. Remove. 9. Heat oil. Fry finely chopped onions. When golden brown pour over ambat and mix well.

97. STUFFED VEGETABLE SHAK

Ingredients	*Quantity*
Potatoes	1 kg
Brinjals (small round variety)	500 gm
Sweet potatoes	250 gm
Yam (Zaminkhand, purple variety)	250 gm
The stuffing	
Fresh coconut	½
Coriander leaves	½ bunch

Ingredients	*Quantity*
Gram flour	2 tsp
Coriander-cumin powder	2 tbsp
Salt	to taste
Ginger	2.5 cm. (1")piece
Green chillies	6-8
Turmeric	½ tsp
Asafoetida	a pinch
Oil	1 cup

Method

1. Grind coconut. 2. Chop the coriander leaves, ginger and green chillies. 3. Mix all the spices and coconut together with salt. 4. Add 2 tbsp oil and mix well. 5. Peel potatoes, sweet potatoes and yam. 6. Slit vegetables into four. 7. Stuff with prepared masala. 8. Bind together. 9. Heat ¾ cup oil in a pan. 10. Add the vegetables 11. Stir well. Cook over extremely slow fire for 1 ½ hours, keeping a little water on the lid of the pan to prevent burning. 12. The vegetables and spices should be well cooked. 13. Test for salt and remove.

98. SWEET POTATO CURRY

Ingredients	*Quality*
Sweet potatoes (large)	2
Onions	4
Cumin	½ tsp
Mustard seeds	¾ tsp
Curry leaves	one sprig
Garlic	2 flakes
Red chillies (powdered)	4
Turmeric	½ tsp
Oil	30 ml
Salt	to taste

Method

1. Heat oil. Add mustard, cumin and curry leaves. 2.When seeds crackle, add chopped onions and allow to brown. 3. Add sweet potatoes, chilli powder, turmeric, salt, and enough water to cook. 4. Cook till done and gravy is thick.

N.B. Milk may be added instead of water if available or at least a small quantity of milk can be added towards the end to make the curry more tasty. Yam, potatoes or egg and potatoes can be used instead of sweet potatoes.

99. SWEET POTATO PULI KULUMBU

Ingredients	*Quantity*
Large sweet potatoes	2 (450 gm)
(plantains, yams, or brinjals can also be used)	
Tamarind	size of an orange
Onions	1
Chilli powder	2 tsp
Turmeric	¼ tsp
Salt	to taste
Water	1 litre
Tempering	
Oil	15 ml
Mustard seeds	1 tsp
Curry leaves	a few

Method

1. Soak tamarind in a cup of warm water. 2. Squeeze out the pulp. 3. Peel sweet potatoes, cut into cubes and put into the tamarind pulp. 4. Add chopped onion, chilli powder, turmeric, salt and water. Boil down to half its volume. 5. Heat oil. Add mustard seeds and curry leaves. 6. When they crackle, pour over the curry. Mix well.

100. ALU MUCKALA POTATOES

Ingredients	*Quantity*
Potatoes (old) (oblong in shape and with smooth skin)	1 kg
Oil	340 ml (approx.)
Turmeric	½ tsp
Salt	to taste

Method

1. Peel and wash potatoes and let them drain in a colander. 2. Put water to boil in a pan with ½ tsp turmeric and 1 tbsp salt . 3. When water starts boiling, put in the potatoes (do not cover) and let the water boil up again with the potatoes in it. 4. Take off the fire immediately and drain the potatoes in a colander after this parboiling 5. Take oil in a pan enough to cover potatoes and heat it on a brisk fire. 6. Take off fire, put in potatoes and put back on a brisk fire, cooking for a few minutes, until a slight crust forms—stirring now and again. 7. Then put on a slow fire and let them redden, gradually stirring until a crust forms. 8. When ready, if you do not want potatoes to absorb oil, turn into a clean dry pan with some salt in it. The oil can be used again if bottled when cool.

101. ALU PALAK

Ingredients	*For 4*	*For 100*
Spinach	225 gm	5.6 kg
Fenugreek leaves	$\frac{1}{4}$ bunch	6 bunches
Potatoes	225 gm	5.6 kg
Ginger	10 gm	225 gm
Garlic	a few flakes	30 gm
Green chillies	5 gm	115 gm
Chilli powder	5 gm	115 gm
Coriander leaves	a few	30 gm
Fat	30 gm	500 gm
Salt	10 gm	100 gm

Method

1. Peel and cut potatoes into quarters. 2. Heat fat and fry potatoes. Remove. 3. Grind together chilli powder, garlic and ginger. 4. Fry masala and whole green chillies. 5. Add washed and chopped spinach and fenugreek leaves. 6. Sauté. Add potatoes and salt and cook covered on a slow fire till potatoes are tender and the leaves are mashed up. Garnish with coriander leaves.

N.B. Sprinkle a little water if required.

102. MIXED VEGETABLE CURRY

Ingredients	*For 4*	*For 100*
Kidney beans	100 gm	2.5 kg
Cauliflower	115 gm	2.8 kg
Potatoes	115 gm	2.8 kg
Onions	30 gm	680 gm
Carrots	30 gm	680 gm
Peas	115 gm	2.8 kg
Tomatoes	115 gm	2.8 kg
Chilli powder	5 gm	115 gm
Coriander powder	10 gm	225 gm
Turmeric	a pinch	15 gm
Garlic	a few flakes	30 gm
Ginger	5 gm	115 gm
Green chillies	5 gm	115 gm
Dry coconut	10 gm	225 gm
Tamarind or	10 gm	225 gm
Dry mango powder	to taste	30 gm
Oil	30 ml	500 ml

Method

1. Wash and soak kidney beans. Boil in the same liquid till tender. 2. Prepare vegetables. 3. Slice onions and slit green chillies. 4. Grind together coriander powder, chilli powder, turmeric, garlic, ginger and dry coconut. 5. Heat oil. Fry spices. 6. Add prepared vegetables except tomatoes, sliced onion and green chillies. Fry for 5 minutes. 7. Add chopped tomatoes and sliced ingredients, salt and a little water if necessary and cook on a slow fire till vegetables are cooked. Add kidney beans and simmer. 8. Soak tamarind in a small quantity of water, strain and add to cooked vegetables. Or add dry mango powder. 9. Bring to boil, simmer for a few minutes and remove.

103. VEGETABLE MOILEE

Ingredients	*For 6*	*For 100*
Peas	200 gm	4 kg
Potatoes	250 gm	5 kg
Cauliflower	100 gm	2 kg
Carrots	100 gm	2 kg
Tomatoes	150 gm	3 kg
Onions	200 gm	4 kg
Green chillies	6-8 gm	150 gm
Ginger	10 gm	200 gm
Turmeric	10 gm	200 gm
Coconut	1	10
Salt	5-10 gm	100 gm
Lime	½–1	10
Oil	50 ml	1 kg

Method

Peel and quarter potatoes. Wash cauliflower and break in floweretts with the leaves. Peel carrots and cut into 1" pieces. Shell peas. Peel and slice onions and ginger. Slit green chillies. Grate coconut and prepare three extractions, thick, medium and thin. Extract lime juice. Heat oil. Sauté onions, green chillies and ginger and cook till onion is tender. Add turmeric and potatoes. Sauté for a few minutes. Add third extraction of coconut milk. Cook gently till potatoes are ¾th done. Add carrots, cauliflower, peas and salt. Simmer till vegetables are cooked. Add chopped tomatoes and second extraction of coconut milk. Simmer. Add lime juice and test for seasoning. Add first extraction of coconut milk. Remove from fire and mix gently.

104. VEGETABLE HUSSAINY CURRY

Ingredients		For 4	For 100
Potatoes		450 gm	11 kg
Carrots		115 gm	5.65 kg
Beans		115 gm	2.8 kg
Peas		225 gm	2.8 kg
Milk		600 ml	14.75 litre
Green chillies		5 gm	115 gm
Garlic		a few flakes	55 gm
Ginger		5 gm	115 gm
Onions		115 gm	2.8 kg
Tomatoes		225 gm	5.65 kg
Cumin	grind together	a pinch	20 gm
Coriander	grind together	5 gm	115 gm
Red chillies	grind together	3 gm	85 gm
Turmeric	grind together	a pinch	15 gm
Coriander leaves		a few	1 bunch

Method

1. Boil and mash potatoes . 2. Boil vegetables. 3. Prepare panir with milk and cut into cubes. 4. Follow method 3 to 10 of Hussainy Curry (Recipe 26 in meat section).

105. VEGETABLE CURRY (A)

Ingredients	For 4	For 100
Potatoes	225 gm	5.6 kg
Pumpkin	225 gm	5.6 kg
Onions	115 gm	2.8 kg
Peas	115 gm	2.8 kg
Vinegar	30 ml	340 gm
Sugar	1 tsp	30 gm
Green chillies	30 gm	115 gm
Turmeric	a pinch	10 gm
Cumin	a pinch	30 gm
Ginger	a small piece	55 gm
Garlic	a few flakes	30 gm
Salt	to taste	100 gm
Oil	30 ml	500 ml

Method

1. Peel and cut potatoes and pumpkin into cubes. Shell peas. Peel and slice onions. 2. Slit green chillies, grind the rest of the spices. 3. Heat oil. Fry pumpkin and potato cubes. Remove. 4. Add sliced onions and

ground spices. Fry well. 5. Add peas, a little water, salt and green chillies. Bring to boil and add potatoes. 6. When nearly cooked add pumpkin. Simmer till ready. 7. Add vinegar and sugar. Bring to boil. Remove and serve hot.

VEGETABLE CURRY (B)

Ingredients	*For 4*	*For 100*
Potatoes	225 gm	5.6 kg
Beans	115 gm	2.8 kg
Cabbage	225 gm	5.6 kg
Tomatoes	225 gm	5.6 kg
Carrots	115 gm	2.8 kg
Onions	115 gm	2.8 kg
Fat	50 gm	1.25 kg
Coriander leaves	¼ bunch	6 bunches
Pomegranate seeds	5 gm	115 gm
Chilli powder	10 gm	225 gm
Coriander powder	5 gm	115 gm
Turmeric	a pinch	15 gm
Salt	to taste	80-100 gm

Method

1. Prepare vegetables. Blanch tomatoes. Slice onions. 2. Fry sliced onions. Add spices and fry well. 3. Add vegetables (except tomatoes), salt and water and cook. 4. When vegetables are half done, add tomatoes and pomegranate seeds. Cook till vegetables are tender and gravy is thick. Garnish with coriander leaves.

106. VEGETABLE PATIA

Ingredients	*For 4*	*For 100*
Cherry tomatoes	55 gm	1.35 kg
Brinjal	115 gm	2.8 kg
Drumsticks	225 gm	5.6 kg
Cauliflower	115 gm	2.8 kg
Potatoes	225 gm	5.6 kg
Green chillies	10 gm	200 gm
Coriander leaves	½ bunch	4 bunches
Cumin	a pinch	15 gm
Garlic	a few flakes	30 gm
Bengal gram flour	1 tsp	75 gm
Coconut	½	10

Ingredients	*For 4*	*For 100*
Coriander powder	5 gm	115 gm
Turmeric	a pinch	10 gm
Onion	55 gm	1.35 kg
Sweet oil	15 ml	250 ml
Tamarind	10 gm	225 gm
Curry leaves	1 sprig	1 bunch
Salt	to taste	100 gm
Coriander leaves (for the garnish)	a few	

Method

1. Prepare vegetables. 2. Chop onion, Grind coconut, green chillies, coriander leaves, garlic, cumin and coriander powder to a fine paste. 3. Soak tamarind in warm water and strain it. 4. Heat oil; fry chopped onion till light brown. 5. Add ground spices, turmeric, gram flour and curry leaves. 6. Cook for a few minutes. 7. Add water and bring to boil. 8. Put in the vegetables. Add salt and cook till tender. 9. Add tamarind juice and cherry tomatoes. Cook for a few minutes longer. Serve hot, garnished with coriander leaves.

107. VEGETABLE KHORMA

Ingredients	*For 4*	*For 100*
Potatoes (boiled)	450 gm	11 kg
Cabbage	115 gm	2.8 kg
Peas	200 gm	5 kg
Beans	115 gm	2.8 kg
Coconut	55 gm	6
Ginger	5 gm	115 gm
Green chillies	5 gm	115 gm
Coriander leaves	1 bunch	15 bunches
Onions	115 gm	2.8 kg
Fennel	1 tsp	75 gm
Cardamom, Cloves, Cinnamon	2 gm	50 gm
Salt	to taste	100 gm
Fat	50 gm	1.25 kg
Lime	½ 8	

Method

1. Peel potatoes and cut into cubes. 2. Wash and dice remaining

vegetables. 3. Sauté vegetables in a little oil. 4. Add water to cook vegetables. 5. Grind together ginger, green chillies, coriander leaves, fennel, half the onions and grated coconut. 6. Roast and powder garam masala. 7. Heat fat and fry remaining sliced onions. 8. Add garam masala and ground ingredients. Sauté. 9. Add potatoes and vegetables, and a little hot water and cook for 5 minutes. 10. Add salt and lime juice. 11. Mix well and serve hot.

108. DAHI KHORMA

Ingredients	*Quantity*
Curds	2 cups
Green chillies	6
Split bengal gram	25 gm
Split black gram	25 gm
Cashewnuts	8
Cumin	10 gm
Coconut	½
Green peas	225 gm
Potatoes	225 gm
Cauliflower	225 gm

Method

1. Boil potatoes till soft; peel and cut into cubes. 2. Shell peas and steam or boil. 3. Wash cauliflower, cut into small pieces and steam or boil. 4. Grind the grams, cumin, coconut and green chillies into a fine paste. 5. Add all the vegetables to the paste. Add curds and cook over a slow fire (simmering point) for 5 minutes. 6. Fry cashewnuts and use for garnishing.

109. VEGETABLE DO PYAZ

Ingredients	*For 4*	*For 100*
Cauliflower	225 gm	5.65 kg
Fresh peas	115 gm	2.8 kg
White pumpkin	225 gm	5.65 kg
Broad beans	225 gm	5.65 kg
Tomatoes	225 gm	5.65 kg
Onions	225 gm	5.65 kg
Kashmiri red chillies (without seeds)	10 gm	225 gm
Coriander powder	10 gm	225 gm
Turmeric	a pinch	15 gm
Cumin	a pinch	10 gm

Ingredients	*For 4*	*For 100*
Ginger	10 gm	225 gm
Garlic	a few cloves	15 gm
Mustard seeds	a pinch	10 gm
Salt	10 gm	100 gm
Oil	30 ml	500 ml

Method

1. Prepare the vegetables. 2. Grind together ginger, red chillies, coriander powder, turmeric, cumin, garlic, mustard seeds and half the onions. 3. Slice remaining onions. 4. Heat fat and fry the onions till golden brown. Remove. 5. Fry ground spices and vegetables. 6. Add browned onions, salt and water. Cook till vegetables are tender and gravy is thickened.

110. VEGETABLE INDAD

Ingredients	*For 4*	*For 100*
Potatoes	255 gm	5.6 kg
Carrots	115 gm	2.8 kg
Radish	225 gm	5.6 kg
Tomatoes	115 gm	2.8 kg
Cauliflower	225 gm	5.6 kg
Cumin	a pinch	30 gm
Red chillies (without seeds)	2 gm	50 gm
Green chillies	5 gm	115 gm
Turmeric	a pinch	10 gm
Onions	115 gm	2.8 kg
Ginger	a small piece	30 gm
Garlic	3 flakes	15 gm
Vinegar	15 ml	340 ml
Fat	15 gm	340 gm
Cloves } **Cinnamon** }	2 gm	50 gm
Salt	to taste	80-100 gm

Method

1. Clean and cut vegetables and boil with cinnamon cloves and salt. 2. Grind turmeric, red chillies, garlic, ginger and cumin, using vinegar. Slit green chillies. 3. Grind onions coarsely. 4. Heat fat. Fry ground spices, add vegetables, remaining vinegar, water and slit green chillies. Simmer for 10 minutes.

111. VEGETABLE VINDALOO

Ingredients	*For 4*	*For 100*
Kohlrabi	225 gm	5.6 kg
Radish	115 gm	2.8 kg
Potatoes	225 gm	5.6 kg
Carrots	115 gm	2.8 kg
Tomatoes	115 gm	2.8 kg
Onions	115 gm	2.8 kg
Ginger	a small piece	30 gm
Garlic	a few flakes	15 gm
Red chillies (without seeds)	5 gm	115 gm
Mustard seeds	½ tsp	30 gm
Turmeric	a pinch	10 gm
Vinegar	30 ml	590 ml
Salt	to taste	80-100 gm
Fat	30 gm	500 gm

Method

1. Prepare vegetables. 2. Grind spices using vinegar. 3. Heat fat; fry spices. 4. Add vegetables and remaining vinegar. Add salt. 5. Cook till vegetables are tender.

112. VEGETABLE MAKHANWALA (4 portions)

Ingredients	*Quantity*
Carrots	100 gm
Cauliflower	150 gm
Green peas (shelled)	100 gm
French beans	100 gm
Butter	200 gm
Tandoori masala	
Kashmiri red chillies	5 gm
Ginger	5 gm
Garlic	5 gm
Garam masala	a pinch
Lime	1
Curds	250 gm
Tomato ketchup	30 ml
Cream	75 ml
Coriander leaves	¼ bunch

Method

1. Parboil the vegetables separately and keep the water. 2. Prepare

marinade by grinding together ginger, garlic and red chillies and mix with the curds. Add garam masala and lime. 3. In a shallow pan, melt the butter and after it melts, add the marinade and fry very well till the oil separates from the masala. 4. Add the water which was kept aside and add the vegetable to it. 5. Cook for some time till the gravy is thick. Add chopped coriander leaves, tomato ketchup and top with cream. 6. Sprinkle with garam masala and serve hot. Garnish with coriander leaves.

113. LAGAN SALA

Ingredients	*Quantity*
Sweet potatoes	115 gm
Potatoes	115 gm
Elephant yam	115 gm
Carrots	115 gm
Shelled green peas (boiled)	225 gm
Banana cut up into small cubes and fried (optional)	1
Turmeric	¼ tsp
Chilli powder	1 tsp
Vinegar	½ cup
Onions (finely chopped)	450 gm
Fat	225 gm
Large tomato (finely chopped)	1
Small whole tomatoes	a few
Sugar	1½ tsp
Salt	to taste

Method

1. Cut sweet potatoes, potatoes, elephant yam and carrots into small cubes and fry separarely. 2. Fry onions till light brown. 3. Add chopped tomato and cook for a few minutes. 4. Add turmeric and chilli powder and all the fried vegetables, green peas and whole tomatoes. 5. Mix well together. Cover and cook for another 2 to 3 mins. 6. Add sugar, salt and vinegar. Simmer for 5 minutes and serve hot. 7. Add 2 to 3 whole green chillies if desired.

114. SARSON KA SAG (MUSTARD GREENS)

Ingredients	*Quantity*
Mustard greens	750 gm
Spinach	250 gm
Chilli powder	1 heaped tsp

Ingredients	Quantity
Ginger	1 small piece
Onions	50 gm (1 small)
Salt	to taste
Ghee	60 gm
(Clarified butter or fat)	

Method

1. Wash and clean mustard greens and spinach. 2. Cut finely and put into a pan with a cup of water. Add chilli powder and half the ginger finely chopped. 3. Cook over a very slow fire till done. 4. Mash well. Add salt. 5. In another vessel, heat the clarified butter. Add sliced onion and remaining sliced ginger. Brown. Add greens and mix well. Serve hot with makki ki roti.

115. MOOLI SAG

Ingredients	Quantity
White radishes and tender leaves of white radishes	250 gm
Ginger	2.5 cm. (1") piece
Chilli powder	½ tsp
Oil or fat	½ tsp
Salt	to taste
Lime	½

Method

1. Heat oil. Add finely chopped ginger, chilli powder and finely chopped radishes and leaves. 2. Mix well. Add salt and just sufficient water to cook dry. 3. Cook over a slow fire till done. Add lime juice and remove.

116. PALAK SAG

Ingredients	For 4	For 100
Spinach	450 gm	11 kg
Ginger	10 gm	225 gm
Garlic	2 flakes	15 gm
Green chillies	5 gm	115 gm
Chilli powder	½ tsp	85 gm
Coriander leaves	a few	3 bunches
Fat to fry	115 gm	1.25 kg
Brinjal	30 gm	680 gm

Ingredients	*For 4*	*For 100*
Coriander	a few seeds	15 gm
Asafoetida	a little	10 gm

Method

1. Clean spinach and wash well. 2. Clean and slice garlic, ginger, green chillies; chop coriander leaves and cut brinjal. 3. Put all prepared ingredients and chilli powder into a pan. Add salt and a little water and cook till vegetables are done and water evaporates. 4. Heat fat in a fry pan. Add powdered asafoetida, coriander and mashed spinach. 5. Fry well, Remove and serve hot.

117. SAG BHAJI (A)

Ingredients	*For 4–6*	*For 20*
Spinach	½ bunch	1 bunch
Potato (large)	1	2
Onions	1 (small)	1
Diced carrot	½ cup	1 cup
Tomatoes (large)	2	4
Split bengal gram	¼ cup	½ cup
Brinjal (small)	1	1
Fenugreek leaves	½ bunch	1 bunch
Dill	½ bunch	1 bunch
Fat for frying		
Masala		
Ginger	1 cm. (½") piece	2.5 cm. (1") piece
Green chillies	2	4
Cardamom (large)	½	1
Garlic	4 cloves	8 cloves
Cumin	½ tsp	1 tsp
Mint leaves	a few	1 tsp
Garam masala powder	1 tsp	2 tsp
Coriander leaves	¼ bunch	½ bunch

Method

1. Soak gram for 2 hours. 2. Clean all leaves and chop finely. 3. Cut potatoes, onion, brinjal and carrot into small pieces. 4. Put soaked gram, the different leaves and vegetables and cook over a very slow fire till vegetables are well cooked. 5. Using a churner, mash up all the ingredients. In a large fry-pan, heat about 50 gm of fat. 6. Lightly fry

the ground spices. Add vegetables and fry over low heat till the mixture is fairly dry. 7. Sprinkle garam masala powder, chopped mint and coriander leaves. 8. Serve hot.

SAG BHAJI (B)

Ingredients	*Quantity*
Spinach	1 bunch
Chuka	1 bunch
Dill	¼ bunch
Fenugreek leaves	¼ bunch (leaves only)
Coriander leaves	¼ bunch
Split bengal gram	85 gm
Carrot (medium)	1
Potato (medium)	1
Bottle gourd	size of 1
Onions (medium)	1
Green chillies	2
Tomatoes (medium)	2
Garlic	6 flakes
Ginger	a small piece
Salt	to taste
Oil	1 tbsp
Clarified butter	1 tbsp

Method

1. Slice onion, chop green chillies, garlic and ginger. 2. Wash and cut all the other vegetables. 3. Wash and soak bengal gram for 2 to 3 hours. 4. Heat oil, sauté garlic, ginger and green chillies. 5. Add all the leafy vegetables, carrot, potato and bottle gourd. Place drained gram on top, chopped tomatoes and salt. 6. Cover pan and cook over slow fire till gram is cooked. 7. Churn well to mash and test for seasoning. 8. Consistency should be thick but not dry. Reheat. Pour clarified butter over and serve.

N.B. If chuka is not available, add one more tomato.

118. AMARANTH SAUTE (CHEERA VAZHATTIATHU)

Ingredients	*For 4*	*For 100*
Amaranth leaves	450 gm	11 kg
Small red onion	115 gm	2.8 kg
Green chillies	10 gm	250 gm
Salt	to taste	80 gm
Oil	20 ml	400 ml

Method

1. Wash and drain leaves. 2. Peel and slice onions and slit green chillies. 3. Chop leaves. 4. Heat oil. Add onions and green chillies, sauté for one to two minutes. 5. Add leaves and salt. Cover and cook for two to three minutes. Mix well and remove.

119. AMARANTH SAUTE (CHOLAI BHAJI)

Ingredients	*Quantity*
Amaranth	115 gm
Onions	1 medium sized
Garlic	1 clove
Salt	to taste
To temper	
Oil	1 tsp
Mustard seeds	a pinch
Split black gram	1 tsp
Red chilli	1

Method

1. Heat oil. Add broken red chilli, gram and mustard seeds. 2. As seeds crackle, add chopped onion, garlic and green leaves. 3. Add salt and just sufficient water (about a tbsp) to cook leaves dry. 4. Cook over a slow fire till leaves are dry.

120. OONDHIU

Ingredients	*Quantity*
Yam	115 gm
Potatoes	340 gm
Sweet potatoes	225 gm
Small brinjal	225 gm
Ripe rajeli bananas	3
Fenugreek leaves	1 bunch
Soda bicarbonate	a pinch
Sugar	2 tsp
Lime	1
Coconut	½ (115 gm)
Coriander leaves	1 bunch
Garlic	30 gm
Double beans	115 gm
Field beans	115 gm
Bengal gram flour	115 gm

Ingredients	*Quantity*
Chilli powder	2 tsp
Turmeric	½ tsp
Green chillies	5-10 gm
Ginger	½ inch piece
Asafoetida	¼ tsp
Gingelly oil	120 ml
Salt	to taste

Method

1. Peel yam, potatoes and sweet potatoes. 2. Cut yam and sweet potatoes into 2.5 cm. (1") cubes. 3. Remove stems from brinjals. Cut bananas into 2 pieces each without removing skin. 4. Slit potatoes, brinjals and bananas into quarters up to half way down their lengths. 5. Clean fenugreek leaves. Sprinkle with salt (this removes bitterness) and set aside. 6. Clean double beans. 7. Mix salt, a pinch of turmeric, chilli powder, a little oil, fenugreek leaves and the gram flour. 8. Add water little by little to form a stiff paste. 9. Make balls of this paste. Fry till brown and set aside. 10. Mix together grated coconut, chopped coriander leaves, garlic, ground ginger, green chillies, sugar, soda bicarbonate and asafoetida. Mix well. 11. Divide into three portions. Stuff slit brinjals, potatoes and bananas with 2 portions. 12. Smear yam and sweet potatoes with remaining third, setting aside about 1 tsp of the spices. 13. Heat oil in a shallow pan. 14. When hot, add spices. Fry well. 15. Add 300 ml of water. When the liquid boils. add double beans, field beans and a pinch of soda. Cook for a few minutes. 16. Add stuffed brinjals. Cook for 10 minutes. 17. Add potatoes, sweet potatoes and yam cubes. 18. When nearly done, add fried gram balls and stuffed bananas. 19. Cook till done.

121. DOODHI KOFTA CURRY (2 koftas each)

Ingredients	*For 4*	*For 100*
Bottle gourd	225 gm	5.6 kg
Onions	30 gm	750 gm
Bengal gram flour	30 gm	750 gm
Green chillies	2 to 3	75 gm
Ginger	5 gm	115 gm
Coriander leaves	¼ bunch	6 bunches
Oil to fry koftas and for gravy	50 ml	1 litre
Gravy		
Tomatoes	200 gm	5 kg
Onions	100 gm	2.5 kg
Red chilli powder	5 gm	115 gm

Ingredients	*For 4*	*For 100*
Turmeric	a pinch	20 gm
Coriander powder	10 gm	250 gm
Cumin	a pinch	20 gm
Garam masala	a pinch	20 gm
Salt	to taste	100 gm

Method

1. Peel and grate bottle gourd. Remove excess moisture by squeezing. (Reserve the liquid.) 2. Chop fine the green chillies, ginger, coriander leaves and onion. 3. Mix with grated gourd, gram flour and salt. Form into even sized balls. 4. Heat oil. Deep fry koftas and set aside.

To prepare gravy

5. Grind spices to a fine paste. Slice onions. Chop tomatoes. 6. Heat oil. Add sliced onions and fry well. Add ground spices and fry till oil separates from spices. 7. Add chopped tomatoes, salt, liquid from the grated gourd and water (about 300 ml or 1 glass for 4 portions). Bring to boil. 8. Simmer till gravy is thick. Add fried koftas. 9. Bring to boil. Check for seasoning and remove. Serve hot.

122. POTATO KOFTA CURRY

Ingredients	*Quantity*
Koftas	
Potatoes	500 gm
Onions (a)	50 gm
Green chilli	1
Coriander leaves (a)	a few
Salt	to taste
Bengal gram flour	50 gm
Water	1 cup
Oil to fry	
Green chutney	
Coriander leaves (b)	½ bunch
Small onions(b)	5
Cumin	a pinch
Coconut (a)	1 tbsp
Lime juice	to taste
Salt	to taste
Curry	
Chilli powder	1 tsp (level)
Coriander powder	1 dsp (level)

Ingredients	*Quantity*
Turmeric	¼ tsp
Garlic	4 flakes
Onion (c)	¼ (25 gm)
Coconut (b)	½
Poppy seeds	50 gm
Onion (d)	1 (sliced)
Tomatoes (2 medium)	150 gm
Oil	1 tbsp
Coriander leaves (c)	a few

Method

1. Peel potatoes. Boil in salted water. Drain and dry. Mash. 2. Add chopped onion (a), coriander leaves (a), green chilli and salt. 3. Shape into balls. Press down in centre. 4. Grind chutney ingredients to a fine paste. 5. Stuff kofta balls with prepared chutney. Close. Dip in gram flour batter and deep fry. 6. Grind to a fine paste: chilli powder, coriander powder, turmeric, garlic, and onion(c) 7. Grind coconut (b) and poppy seeds separately. 8. Heat oil. Add sliced onion (d) and fry till golden brown. 9. Add ground spices. Fry well over slow fire. 10. Add chopped tomatoes. Cook for another 10 minutes, adding more water as desired. 11. Add poppy seeds mixed in 1 cup water. Simmer for 5 minutes. 12. Add ground coconut mixed in another cup of water . Bring to boil. 13. Add salt. Check for seasoning. Add fried koftas. Boil for 2 minutes. 14. Add chopped coriander leaves (c) and remove.

123. VEGETABLE KABABS (A) (15 Kababs)

Ingredients	*Quantity*
Potatoes	100 gm
Carrots	100 gm
Beans	100 gm
Cauliflower	100 gm
Onions	100 gm
Split Bengal gram	50 gm
Coriander leaves	¼ bunch
Cumin powder	1 gm
Cloves	1 gm
Cinnamon	1 gm
Green chillies	20 gm
Egg	1
Lime	¼
Oil(absorption)	50 gm
Salt	10 gm

Method

1. Boil gram. 2. Peel potatoes and boil. 3. Chop fine, carrots, cauliflower and beans. 4. Chop onions and green chillies fine too. 5. Heat 1 tbsp oil. Add onions and green chillies. Sauté. Add finely chopped vegetables . 6. Stir constantly till cooked. 7. Add mashed gram (dal) and potatoes. 8. Add powdered cumin cloves and cinnamon. Mix well on the fire. 9. Remove. 10 . Add salt and chopped coriander leaves and egg. Mix well. 11. Add lime juice. 12 . Shape like shammi kababs and fry in hot oil.

VEGETABLE KABABS (B)

Ingredients	*For 4*	*For 100*
Potatoes	225 gm	5.65 kg
Carrots	225 gm	5.65 kg
Onions	115 gm	2.8 kg
Peas	225 gm	5.65 kg
Green chillies	5 gm	115 gm
Bengal gram flour	10 gm	250 gm
Coriander leaves	10 gm	250 gm
Lime	1	20
Fat (absorption)	50 gm	1 kg
Salt	to taste	100 gm

Method

1. Boil and mash vegetables. 2. Chop onions, green chillies and coriander leaves. 3. Heat a little fat and sauté onions and green chillies. 4. Add mashed vegetables, lime juice and salt to taste. 5. Make into balls, dip in gram flour batter and deep fry to a golden brown.

124. VEGETABLE CHOPS

Ingredients	*For 4*	*For 100*
Potatoes	225 gm	5.65 kg
Bread	115 gm	2.8 kg
Lime	¼	6
Mixed vegetables or peas	250 gm	5.65 kg
Onions	55 gm	1.35 kg
Capsicum	30 gm	680 gm
Pepper	1 tsp	30 gm
Salt	to taste	100 gm
Fat	50 gm	1.25 kg
Macaroni (dry)	10 gm	250 gm

Method

1. Boil potatoes. Peel and mash when still hot. 2. Soak bread in water. Squeeze out moisture and mix with potatoes. Add lime juice and salt. Shell peas or prepare mixed vegetables. 3. Chop onion and capsicum fine. 4. Heat a little fat. Add onion; fry till transparent. Add capsicum, peas (or mixed vegetables), salt and pepper. 5. Cook in just sufficient water to cook vegetables dry. Remove and mash. 6. Divide potatoes and filling into even portions. 7. Shape potatoes into cups and stuff with filling. Bind the edges together and shape it like a chop. Stick a piece of macaroni in to resemble a bone. 8. Shallow fry on thick griddle till crisp and brown. Pour a little fat from the sides to fry crisp.

125. MASALA BHARA MIRCHI

Ingredients	*For 4*	*For 100*
Capsicum or big green chillies	340 gm (4 large)	8 kg (100 large)
Bengal gram	30 gm	680 gm
Onions	55 gm	1.35 kg
Grind		
Garlic	a few flakes	30 gm
Ginger	a small piece	55 gm
Green chillies	5	115 gm
Coriander leaves	½ bunch	10 bunches
Turmeric	a pinch	15 gm
Chilli powder	a pinch	15 gm
Salt	to taste	80-100 gm
Fat	50 gm	1.25 kg

Method

1. Soak gram overnight. 2. Slit capsicums lengthwise. Remove seeds. 3. Slice onion, grind spices. 4. Mix together gram, sliced onion and ground spices and lightly fry in a little fat. 5. Stuff capsicums with the fried filling. 6. Heat remaining fat. Place capsicums neatly in it. Cover and cook over a slow fire. Sprinkle water occasionally if necessary. 7. Cook till tender. Add a little more fat and finish cooking.

126. VEGETABLE CUTLETS (Indian)

Ingredients	*For 4*	*For 100*
Potatoes	450 gm	11 kg
Carrots	115 gm	2.72 kg
Peas	115 gm	2.72 kg

Ingredients	For 4	For 100
Onions	55 gm	1.3 kg
Lime	1	6
Ginger	5 gm	115 gm
Green chillies	5 gm	115 gm
Refined flour	5 gm	115 gm
Salt	to taste	100 gm
Eggs	1	12
Breadcrumbs	55 gm	455 gm
Fat (absorption)	30 gm	500 gm

Method

1. Boil potatoes and mash. 2. Boil vegetables and chop fine. 3. Chop green chillies, ginger and onion fine. 4 Mix spices, vegetables and potatoes together. 5. Add lime juice and salt. 6. Shape into cutlets. Dip in flour, then egg and breadcrumbs and deep fry.

127. STUFFED CAPSICUMS (A)

Ingredients		For 4	For 100
Capsicums (large)		4 (450 gm)	100 (11 kg)
Potatoes		450 gm	11 kg
Onions		35 gm	1.36 kg
Cinnamon	roast		
Cloves	and	5 gm	45 gm
Cardamom	powder		
Worcester sauce		120 ml	1.5 litre
Fat		30 gm	500 gm
Salt		10 gm	100 gm

Method

1. Slice tops of capsicums. 2. Remove seeds and wash. 3. Apply salt inside and keep upside down on a rack. 4. Boil potatoes. Peel and dice. Chop onion. 5. Heat fat and fry onion, add diced potatoes and spices and salt and sauté. 6. Fill capsicums with potato mixture. 7. Arrange on a baking tray. Pour Worcester sauce over and bake in a slow oven till capsicums are tender.

STUFFED CAPSICUMS (B)

Ingredients	For 4	For 100
Capsicums (large)	450 gm	11 kg
Potatoes	450 gm	11 kg

Ingredients	For 4	For 100
Green chillies	4-5	55 gm
Cheese	30 gm	680 gm
Coriander leaves	¼ bunch	1 bunch
Turmeric	a pinch	10 gm
Fat	30 gm	500 gm
Mustard seeds	a few	5 gm
Lime	½	12
Salt	to taste	100 gm

Method

1. Slice the top of capsicums. 2. Remove seeds, wash, apply salt on the inside and keep upside down on a rack. 3. Boil and chop potatoes; temper with mustard seeds. Add chopped green chillies, coriander leaves, turmeric and salt to taste. 4. Mix well, add lime juice. 5. Stuff capsicums with prepared stuffing. Top with cheese. 6. Heat fat in a frying pan and cook capsicums on a very slow fire till soft. 7. Serve hot.

128. DOODHI PACHADI

Ingredients	For 4	For 100
Bottle gourd	450 gm	11 kg
Onions	115 gm	1.36 kg
Ginger	5 gm	115 gm
Green chillies	5 gm	115 gm
Curds	225 gm	5.65 kg
Salt	10 gm	100 gm
For tempering		
Mustard seeds	a pinch	10 gm
Curry leaves	1 sprig	1 bunch
Onions	5 gm	115 gm
Red chilli	1	10
Oil	15 ml	250 gm

Method

1.Wash, peel and dice the gourd. 2. Chop ginger, slit green chillies and slice onions. 3. Cook all ingredients with just enough water to cook the vegetable. 4. Remove from fire, add beaten curds and salt. 5. Heat oil. Add mustard seeds, curry leaves, sliced onion and whole red chillies. When seeds crackle, pour over gourd and curds mixture. Mix well.

129. GINGER PACHADI

Ingredients	*Quantity*
Ginger	15 gm
Green chillies	5 gm (1 to 2)
Mustard seeds	5 gm
Onions	30 gm
Curds (fresh)	250 ml
Coconut	¼
Curry leaves	a sprig
Salt	to taste
Oil	10 ml
Tempering	
Oil	10 to 15 ml
Mustard seeds	1 pinch
Onions	1
Curry leaves	1 sprig

Method

1. Grate coconut and grind to a paste with mustard seeds. 2. Slice ginger, soak in water for one hour. 3. Chop green chillies and onion fine. Cook together in very little water, ginger, green chillies and onion. 4. Beat curds well, add the ground ingredients and the cooked ingredients. Mix well. Add salt to taste. 5. Heat oil, add sliced onion and as it browns, add the mustard seeds. When they crackle, add curry leaves and pour over pachadi. Mix.

130. VELLARI PACHADI

Ingredients	*Quantity*
Veg. marrow (cucumber)	1 (400 gm)
large, yellow/orange variety	
Coconut	200 gm
Green chilli	1
Red onions (small)	3
Garlic	2 flakes
Cumin (optional)	½ tsp
Mustard seeds	5 gm
Curds	150 ml
Salt	to taste
For tempering	
Oil	15 ml
Curry leaves	1 sprig

Ingredients	*Quantity*
Mustard seeds	1 pinch
Small onion	1

Method

1. Peel, remove seeds and cut cucumber into small cubes. 2. Peel and slice onions and garlic. 3. Boil together the above three ingredients with a little salt. 4. Grind to a fine paste green chillies, coconut and cumin if used. 5. Beat curds till smooth. Add boiled vegetables, finely crushed mustard. 6. Check for seasonings and bring to boil. 7. Heat oil, add sliced onions and curry leaves. 8. When onions brown, add mustard seeds and as the seeds crackle pour over pachadi. Mix well.

131. UPPUMANGA PACHADI

Ingredients	*Quantity*
Medium sized salted mangoes (uppumanga)	4
Green chillies	6
Small onions	100 gm
Coconut	½
Liquid from salted mangoes or the brine in which the salted mangoes are put	to taste
To temper	
Curry leaves	1 sprig
Oil	1 tbsp
Small onion	1
Mustard seeds	a large pinch

Method

1. Slice salted mangoes with a stainless steel knife and cut into small cubes. 2. Put into a cooking vessel along with mango seeds. 3. Finely slice onions. Slit 2 green chillies and add along with onions to the mangoes. 4. Grate coconut and prepare first and second extraction of coconut milk. 5. Add the second extraction of coconut milk to the brine and mix with the mangoes. 6. Heat slowly to simmering point. Remove from fire. 7. Heat oil in a fry pan. Add sliced onions. As they brown, add mustard seeds and curry leaves. 8. When the mustard seeds splutter, pour into the pachadi. Add the first extraction of coconut milk. Mix well.

132. CURD PACHADI

Ingredients	*For 4*	*For 100*
Sour curds	225 gm	5.6 kg
Green chillies	10 gm	225 gm
Coconut	55 gm	1.36 kg
Ginger	15 gm	340 gm
Coconut oil	15 ml	250 ml
Mustard seeds	1 tsp	30 gm
Curry leaves	a few	1 bunch
Salt	to taste	100 gm

Method

1. Grate and grind coconut to a fine paste. 2. Chop green chillies and ginger. 3. Beat curds well. Add ground coconut, green chillies and ginger. Add salt; mix well. 4. Heat oil. Add curry leaves and mustard seeds. When the mustard seeds crackle add to the curds mixture. Mix well.

133. LADIES FINGER RAITA

Ingredients	*For 4*	*For 100*
Curds	225 ml	5.3 ml
Ladies fingers	115 gm	2.72 kg
Greeen chillies	5 gm	115 gm
Onions	10 gm	225 gm
Salt	15 gm	100 gm
Oil	15 gm	250 gm

Method

1. Beat curds well with salt. 2. Chop ladies fingers, green chillies and onion. 3. Heat oil and fry chopped ingredients till crisp. 4. Add to beaten curds and serve at once.

134. ONION RAITA

Ingredients	*For 4*	*For 100*
Curds	225 gm	5.6 kg
Onions	115 gm	2.8 kg
Green chillies	5 gm	115 gm
Coriander leaves	¼ bunch	4 bunches
Cumin(optional)	a pinch	30 gm
Salt	to taste	100 gm

Method

1. Peel and slice onions. Chop green chillies and coriander leaves.

2. Roast and powder cumin if used. 3. Beat curds and mix all ingredients together.

135. CAULIFLOWER AND PEAS RAITA

Ingredients	*For 4*	*For 100*
Cauliflower	115 gm	2.8 kg
Peas	115 gm	2.8 kg
Curds	225 gm	5.6 kg
Chilli powder	5 gm	115 gm
Salt	to taste	100 gm

Method

1. Wash and cut cauliflower into fairly small pieces. 2. Shell peas. 3. Boil vegetables in salted water. Remove and drain. 4. Beat curds with salt. 5. Add boiled vegetables and sprinkle chilli powder to form a pattern.

136. CUCUMBER RAITA

Ingredients	*For 4*	*For 100*
Cucumber	55 gm	1 kg
Green chillies	5 gm	75 gm
Coriander leaves	5 gm	115 gm
Curds	225 ml	5.65 litre
Salt	to taste	100 gm

Method

1. Peel and grate the cucumber. 2. Beat the curds. 3. Add green chillies and coriander leaves. 4. Add salt.

N.B. Add grated coconut to improve flavour.

137. BOONDI RAITA

Ingredients	*For 4*	*For 100*
Batter		
Bengal gram flour	55 gm	1.36 kg
Chilli powder	1 tsp	75 gm
Cumin powder	a pinch	15 gm
Fat to fry (absorption)	30 gm	750 gm
Raita		
Curds	225 gm	5.6 kg
Crushed cumin or		
Ground mustard	1 pinch	10 gm

Ingredients	*For 4*	*For 100*
Coriander leaves	¼ bunch	1 bunch
Salt	to taste	100 gm

Method

1. Make a thick batter with gram flour, water and spices. 2. Heat fat. Pour batter into it through a perforated spoon to make boondis; fry till crisp. Remove and drain. Dip boondis in hot water and take out immediately. When cold, put into beaten curds to which cumin, salt and chopped coriander leaves have been added.

138. MINT RAITA

Ingredients	*For 100*
Mint	6 bunches (510 gm)
Green chillies	30-45 gm
Curds	5 kg
Salt	to taste

Method

1. Pick leaves of mint. Wash and grind with salt and green chillies. 2. Add to curds and beat well.

139. PALAK RAITA

Ingredients	*For 4*	*For 100*
Curds	225 gm	5.6 kg
Spinach	115 gm	2.8 kg
Green chillies	5 gm	115 gm
Salt	to taste	100 gm
For tempering		
Cumin	½ tsp	50 gm
Mustard	½ tsp	50 gm
Fenugreek	½ tsp	50 gm
Whole red chillies	2 or 3	50 gm
Oil	15 ml	500 ml

Method

1. Pick and wash spinach. Steam. 2. Beat curds and mix with steamed spinach and chopped green chillies. Add salt. 3. Heat oil. Add red chillies, mustard, cumin and fenugreeek. When seeds crackle pour over spinach and curds mixture. Mix well.

140. TOMATO RAITA

Ingredients	*For 4*	*For 100*
Curds	225 gm	5.65 kg
Tomatoes	115 gm	2.8 kg
Onions	50 gm	1.15 kg
Salt	10 gm	80-100 gm
Green chillies	10 gm	250 gm
Chilli powder	a pinch	30 gm
Coriander leaves	a few sprigs	a bunch

Method

1. Chop tomatoes, onion and green chillies very fine. 2. Add to beaten curds. Add salt and mix well. 3. Turn into a bowl and garnish with chilli powder and finely chopped coriander leaves.

141. BRINJAL RAITA

Ingredients	*For 4*	*For 100*
Brinjal	115 gm	2.8 kg
Curds	225 gm	5.6 kg
Chilli powder	5 gm	115 gm
Garam masala	a pinch	30 gm
Cumin	a pinch	30 gm
Salt	to taste	100 gm (approx.)
To temper		
Mustard seeds	a pinch	30 gm
Red chillies	15 ml	500 ml
Oil	15 ml	500 ml

Method

1. Place brinjal on live coals or grill and roast, turning frequently. 2. When skin turns black and the brinjal is soft inside, remove and peel. 3. Mash well and add to beaten curds. 4. Add salt and spices and mix. 5. Heat oil. Add mustard seeds and whole red chillies. When the seeds crackle, pour over brinjal mixture, and mix well.

142. POTATO RAITA

Ingredients	*For 4*	*For 100*
Potatoes	115 gm	2.8 kg
Curds	225 ml	5.6 litre
Chilli powder	5 gm	115 gm

Ingredients	*For 4*	*For 100*
Onions	15 gm	450 gm
Salt	to taste	100 gm

Method

1. Boil potatoes till tender. Peel and chop. 2. Beat curds with chilli powder, salt and chopped onion. 3. Add chopped potatoes.

N.B. Powdered cumin or chopped coriander leaves can be used as garnish.

143. BANANA RAITA

Ingredients	*For 10*
Bananas (ripe)	6 (75 gm each)
Fresh curds (thick and slightly sweet)	1 cup (260 gm)
Grated coconut	120 gm
Green chillies	2
Salt	to taste
Curry leaves	1 sprig
Mustard seeds	a pinch
Oil	20 ml

Method

1. Peel and slice bananas into rounds. Mix with lightly beaten curds, grated coconut and salt to taste. 2. Heat oil. Add curry leaves, green chillies and mustard seeds. When the seeds crackle, pour over banana and curds mixture. Mix well.

144. BANANA CHAAT

Ingredients	*Quantity*
Ripe bananas	6
Salt	to taste
Sour lime	2
Spices (black salt, cumin, mango powder, pepper powder, cloves, cardamom powder, chilli powder)	1 tbsp

Method

1. Peel and slice bananas. 2. Mix with the powdered spices moistened with lime juice. 3. Add salt to taste.

145. KADHI

Ingredients	*For 4*	*For 100*
Curds	225 gm	2.75 kg
Water	360 ml	8.5 litre
Bengal gram flour	20 gm	450 gm
Curry leaves	a sprig	1 bunch
Turmeric	a pinch	20 gm
Cumin and fenugreek	1 tsp	75 gm
Fat	10 gm	225 gm
Green chillies	5 gm	115 gm
Ginger	5 gm	115 gm
Garlic	5 gm	115 gm
Salt	10 gm	100 gm
Sugar (optional)	10 gm	100 gm
Coriander leaves	a few sprigs	1 bunch

Method

1. Add enough water to curds and beat well. 2. Strain to remove butter, leaving buttermilk. 3. Make a paste with a little cold buttermilk and gram flour. 4. Add salt and turmeric to remaining buttermilk and heat without boiling. 5. Add gram flour paste, stirring all the time. 6. Grind green chillies, ginger and garlic together. 7. Add curry leaves and ground spices and cook to the right consistency. 8. Heat fat. Add cumin and fenugreek. When seeds crackle, pour over kadhi. Garnish with chopped coriander leaves.

146. PAKODA KADHI

Ingredients	*For 4*	*For 100*
Pakodas		
Bengal gram flour	55 gm	1.35 kg
Onions	55 gm	1.35 kg
Green chillies	5	115 gm
Turmeric	a pinch	10 gm
Water	30 ml	1-1.8 litre
Salt	a pinch	100 gm
Chilli powder	5 gm	115 gm
Oil to fry (absorption)	30 ml	500 ml
Soda bicarbonate	a pinch	10 gm
Kadhi		
Curds	225 gm	5.6 kg

Ingredients	*For 4*	*For 100*
Bengal gram flour	20 gm	455 gm
Curry leaves	a sprig	1 bunch
Turmeric	a pinch	10 gm
Cumin and fenugreek	1 tsp	75 gm
Fat	10 gm	115 gm
Green chillies	5 gm	115 gm
Ginger	5 gm	115 gm
Garlic	2 to 3 flakes	75 gm
Salt	10 gm	100 gm
Oil	10 ml	200 ml

Method

Kadhi

Follow step 1 to 8 of previous recipe for Kadhi.

Pakodas

1. Chop onion and chillies. 2. Mix together all ingredients for pakodas except oil and soda. 3. Let batter stand for one hour. 4. Add soda. 5. Drop teaspoons of batter into hot oil. 6. When light brown, remove and put into prepared kadhi.

147. BHINDANI KADHI

Ingredients	*For 4 to 6*
Ladies fingers (slit in half vertically)	225 gm
Buttermilk	225 ml
Turmeric powder	1 tsp
Bengal gram flour	1 tsp
Ginger (chop fine)	1.25 cm. (½") piece
Green chillies	to taste
Coriander leaves	a few
Salt	to taste
Fat	2 tsp

Method

1. Make a paste of the gram flour with a spoonful of buttermilk. 2. Add remaining buttermilk, turmeric, ginger, green chillies, coriander leaves and salt. 3. Heat gently till the mixture thickenes. Meanwhile, cut ladies fingers into 2.5 cm. (1") pieces. Season. Fry in hot fat. 4. Add to buttermilk mixture and continue cooking for another 10 minutes.

148. PALAK KI KADHI

Ingredients	*For 100*
Spinach	5.6 kg
Bengal gram flour	500 gm
Curds	5.6 kg
Green chillies	200 gm
Split Bengal gram	200 gm
Peanuts	200 gm
Cumin	15 gm
Turmeric	15 gm
Fat	500 gm
Sugar	100 gm
Salt	100 gm

Method

1. Soak gram for 2–3 hours. Shell and soak peanuts. 2. Cook spinach with the gram and shelled and soaked peanuts. 3. Mash the mixture well. 4. Add gram flour to the mixture and mix it properly. 5. Beat curds, add water to make thick buttermilk. 6. Add to the spinach mixture and cook till it boils. 7. Heat fat, add slit green chillies and cumin. When the seeds crackle, add turmeric and pour the tempering over the spinach and buttermilk mixture. 8. Add salt and sugar. Cook for five minutes more. 9. Serve hot.

149. PALAK PAKODA KADHI

Ingredients	*For 4*	*For 100*
Bengal gram flour	170 gm	4 kg
Curds	225 gm	5.6 kg
Water	300 ml	7.5 litre
Spinach	225 gm	5.6 kg
Turmeric	½ tsp	50 gm
Asafoetida	½ tsp	50 gm
Cumin	½ tsp	50 gm
Fennel	½ tsp	50 gm
Cloves	4	50 gm
Soda bicarbonate	½ tsp	10 to 15 gm
Salt	5 gm	115 gm
Chilli powder	to taste	100-120 gm
Fat to fry (absorption)	30 gm	500 gm
Fat for kadhi	15 gm	250 gm

Method

1. Prepare a thick batter with three-fourths of the gram flour, soda

bicarbonate, half the chilli powder and salt and water. 2. Heat fat in a deep fry-pan (karai) and fry spoonfuls of batter. 3. Turn over when one side is cooked. When golden yellow, remove and drain. 4. Wash spinach thoroughly. Chop fine. 5. Dissolve asafoetida in a little water. 6. Heat fat for kadhi in a pan. 7. Add asafoetida, cumin, mustard seeds, fennel and cloves. 8. When well browned, add spinach. 9. Cover and cook till spinach is done. 10. Mix the remaining gram flour with beaten curds, turmeric and salt, remaining chilli powder and water. Beat till smooth. 11. Stir in this mixture with spinach and allow to simmer. 12. When it starts bubbling, stir. Cook for about 10 to 15 minutes. 13. Add fried pakodas. Stir lightly. Cook for another 5 to 10 minutes and remove.

150. MORU KULUMBU

Ingredients	*For 20*
Buttermilk	½ litre
Coconut	½
Turmeric	1 tsp
Green chilli	6-7
Ginger	2.5 cm. (1") piece
Cumin	2 tsp
Bengal gram flour	1 tbsp
Salt	to taste
Any vegetable (potatoes, pumpkin, green leaves or fried ladies fingers)	250 gm
Oil	1 tbsp
Asafoetida	a pinch
Curry leaves	1 sprig
Mustard seeds	a pinch
Split black gram	1 tsp

Method

1. Grate coconut and grind to a fine paste with green chillies, cumin and ginger. 2. Mix all the ingredients down to gram flour with buttermilk. 3. Add salt and vegetable. Heat, stirring all the time, and as the mixture comes to a boil, remove. 4. Heat oil. Add black gram and as it browns, add mustard seeds. When seeds crackle add asafoetida and curry leaves. 5. Pour over the vegetable and curds mixture. Stir well.

151. GATTA CURRY

Ingredients	*Quantity*
Bengal gram flour	150 gm
Salt (to taste)	a pinch

Ingredients	*Quantity*
Curds	10 gm
Fat	2 tbsp
Turmeric	a pinch
Coriander powder	20 gm
Chilli powder	to taste
Cumin	1 tsp
Oregano	5 gm

Method

1. Sieve gram flour. Add a pinch each of salt, chilli powder, oregano and a little fat. 2. Make a hard dough using water. Then roll it out into round, long sticks. 3. Boil in hot water for about 15 minutes. 4. Remove and cut them into short 1.25 cm. (or ½" length) pieces (gatta) with a knife. 5. Fry lightly in hot fat. 6. Beat curds well with a little water; add turmeric, coriander powder and salt. 7. Heat a little fat in a pan; add cumin. 8. When the cumin is browned add chilli powder and beaten curds mixture and fried "gatta". 9. Keep on stirring. Remove when the gravy starts thickening . Serve hot.

152. DAHI BHALLA

Ingredients	*For 4*	*For 100*
Split black gram	225 gm	5.6 kg
Fat to fry (absorption)	30 gm	500 gm
Green chillies	10 gm	200 gm
Onions	55 gm	1.35 kg
Soda bicarbonate	a pinch	10 gm
Curds	1.5 litre	35 litre
Chilli powder	2 gm	50 gm
Cumin powder	a pinch	20 gm
Salt	5-10 gm	100 gm
Coriander leaves	a few	1 bunch

Method

1. Soak gram for 12 hours. 2 Grind well and add salt, chopped green chillies, onion and soda. Beat well to enclose air. 3. Make it into round flat cakes 5 cm. in diameter and 1.25 cm. thick and fry in deep hot fat. 4. Soak fried bhallas in salted hot water for 15 minutes immediately after removing from fry pan. 5. Squeeze out water gently by pressing bhallas in between the palms of both hands. 6. Put into curds beaten up with salt, chilli powder and cumin powder. Garnish with coriander leaves.

153. CURD CURRY

Ingredients	*For 4*	*For 100*
Curds	225 gm	5.6 kg
Green chillies	5 gm	115 gm
Garlic	1 flake	30 gm
Ginger	5 gm	115 gm
Onions	115 gm	2.8 kg
Coriander leaves	¼ bunch	8 bunches
Salt	to taste	80-100 gm
Cumin	¼ tsp	20 gm
Chilli powder	½ tsp	50 gm
Coriander powder	1 tsp	85 gm
Turmeric	½ tsp	50 gm
Fat	15 gm	250 gm

Method

1. Beat curds till smooth. Add salt. 2. Chop onions. 3. Grind ginger and garlic and slice green chillies. 4. Heat fat. Fry onions, ground garlic and ginger, chilli powder, coriander powder and turmeric. Fry well. 5. Add green chillies and cumin. Fry for a minute or two longer. 6. Remove. Cool a little. Add beaten curds. Mix well. Return to fire and heat for a few minutes stirring all the time. Garnish with chopped coriander leaves.

154. MORU KACHIYATHU

Ingredients		*Quantity*
Buttermilk (sour)		1 litre
Curry leaves		2-3 sprigs
Coconut	grind together	¼
Red chillies or	grind together	2
Small green chillies	grind together	5–6
Turmeric	grind together	¼ tsp
Cumin	grind together	a pinch
Small onion	grind together	1
Green chillies (slit)		2
Ginger (slice)		a small piece
Salt		to taste

Tempering

Coconut oil	15 ml
Red onion	1
Red chillies	2
Mustard seeds	1 tsp
Fenugreek	1 tsp
Curry leaves	1 sprig

Method

1. Soak curry leaves in buttermilk. 2. Heat oil in a large pan. Add sliced onion, broken red chillies, mustard seeds, fenugreek and curry leaves. 3. When seeds crackle, add ground ingredients, slit green chillies and sliced ginger. Stir well. 4. Add buttermilk and salt and cook without allowing to boil till steam starts rising. Stir all the time. 5. Remove from fire and stir occasionally till cool.

155. GINGER CURRY

Ingredients	*For 4*	*For 100*
Ginger	30 gm	680 gm
Green chillies	2	50 gm
Coconut	30 gm	680 gm
Salt	to taste	100 gm
Coconut oil	20 ml	400 ml
Mustard seeds	a pinch	30 gm
Red chillies	15 gm	340 gm
Fenugreek	2-3 gm	50 gm
Tamarind	10-15 gm	250-340 gm
Molasses or sugar	5 gm (about)	100 gm
Curry leaves	a few	1 bunch

Method

1. Peel and chop the ginger finely and soak in a little hot water. 2. Chop the green chillies. 3. Slice and chop coconut into small pieces. 4. Drain ginger. Put ginger, chillies, curry leaves, coconut into a pan. Add a little water and salt. Cook over a slow fire till dry. 5. Roast red chillies and fenugreek seeds and powder fine. 6. Soak tamarind in a little hot water. 7. Heat oil in a pan. Add mustard seeds; when they crackle add cooked ginger mixture. Sauté. 8. As the mixture turns reddish brown, remove from fire. Add red chilli and fenugreek powder. 9. Add tamarind water. Return to fire. Add salt. 10. Add molasses and bring to boil. Simmer for a few minutes. Remove from fire.

156. VELLARI RED CURRY

Ingredients	*For 4*	*For 100*
Cucumber (large orange variety)	225 gm	5.6 kg
Red chillies	20 gm	400-500 gm
Coconut oil	15 ml	250 gm
Mustard seeds	½ tsp	15 gm
Tamarind	10 gm	250 gm

Ingredients	*For 4*	*For 100*
Fenugreek	½ tsp	50 gm
Turmeric	¼ tsp	10 gm
Water	600 ml	14 litre
Salt	to taste	100 gm

Method

1. Roast red chillies and fenugreek seeds. Powder fine. 2. Peel and cut cucumber into 2 inch cubes. 3. Soak tamarind in water; extract pulp. 4. Heat oil. Add mustard seeds and then powdered spices and turmeric. Fry well. 5. Add tamarind, water, salt and cucumber pieces. 6. Bring to boil. Simmer till cucumber is cooked.

157. CITRON (LIME) CURRY

Ingredients	*For 4*	*For 100*
Citron (vadukapuli naranga)	1	5
Onions	50 gm	250 gm
Green chillies	4 gm	20 gm
Chilli powder	10 gm	50 gm
Mustard seeds	5 gm	25 gm
Ginger	10 gm	50 gm
Vinegar	15 ml	75 ml
Salt	to taste	100 gm
Til oil	150 ml	750 ml

Method

1. Boil some water. Add salt and immerse citron. Leave it for 5 minutes. 2. Remove and wipe well. Cut into 1 cm. pieces. 3. Heat oil. Add mustard seeds. 4. As seeds crackle, add chopped onion, green chillies and ginger. Sauté. 5. Add red chilli powder. Fry for 2 minutes longer. 6. Add citron pieces. Add salt and vinegar. Bring to boil. 7. Cook for a further 10 minutes and remove.

158. VELLARI MORU CURRY

Ingredients	*For 4*	*For 100*
Cucumber (large orange variety)	225 gm	5.6 kg
Fresh coconut	115 gm (½)	10-12
Green chillies	10 gm	250 gm
Turmeric	⅛ tsp	10 gm
Cumin	a pinch	10 gm
Small onions	2	30 gm

Ingredients	*For 4*	*For 100*
For tempering		
Red chilli	1	20 gm
Mustard seeds	1 tsp	15 gm
Onion (small)	1	20 gm
Curry leaves	1 sprig	1 bunch
Coconut oil	15 ml	250 ml
Salt	to taste	100 gm
Curds (sour)	150 ml	3.75 litre

Method

1. Wash and peel cucumber; cut into 2.5 cm. (1") pieces. 2. Slit green chillies. 3. Mix together green chillies, half the turmeric, cucumber pieces, salt and enough water to cover vegetable. 4. Simmer till tender . 5. Grind together coconut, remaining turmeric, onion and cumin to a very fine paste. 6. Mix together ground ingredients with beaten curds and a little water if thick. 7. When cucumber is cooked, add curds mixture. 8. Heat to simmering point over gentle heat, stirring gently. Do not allow to boil. 9. Remove from fire when quite hot. 10. In a fry pan heat oil. Add sliced onion, whole red chilli and curry leaves. When onion browns, add mustard seeds. When seeds crackle pour over curry. Stir well.

N.B. Do not cover till cooked. This curry can be kept for two days at room temperature.

159. MANGO MARROW PULISERRY

Ingredients	*For 10*
Vegetable marrow (mature)	½
Raw green mango	1
Turmeric	½ tsp
Salt	to taste
Coconut	1
Green chillies	3
Parboiled rice	1 dsp
Buttermilk	750 ml
Oil	15 ml
Red chilli	1
Curry leaves	a few sprigs
Mustard seeds	1 tsp

Method

1. Peel marrow and mango and cut into even-sized pieces. Add turmeric and salt and add just sufficient water to cook dry. 2. Grate and grind

coconut, rice and green chillies and mix well with buttermilk. 3. Pour this mixture into the pan. Test for salt, adding more if needed, and bring to a boil. Remove. 4. Heat oil. Add curry leaves, mustard seeds and broken red chilli. When seeds crackle, pour over puliserry and mix well.

N.B. Instead of coconut, bengal gram flour can be used, in which case simmer mixture for 10 minutes.

160. AVIAL

Ingredients	*For 4*	*For 100*
Drumsticks	225 gm	5.6 kg
Potatoes	115 gm	2.8 kg
Brinjal	115 gm	2.8 kg
Elephant yam	115 gm	2.8 kg
Plantain(raw)	115 gm	2.8 kg
Chauli beans	115 gm	2.8 kg
Coconut	115 gm (½)	2.8 kg (12)
Coconut oil	50 ml	1.25 litre
Green chillies	5 gm	115 gm
Turmeric	a pinch	15 gm
Cumin	a pinch	15 gm
Curds or Mangoes	115 gm	2.9 kg
Curry leaves	a sprig	1 bunch
Salt	to taste	100 gm

Method

1. Wash and peel vegetables and cut them into long pieces. 2. Grind together coconut, chillies and cumin to a fine paste. 3. Beat the curds well. 4. Boil vegetables in sufficient water with turmeric and salt. 5. Add ground ingredients, beaten curds and curry leaves. Bring to boil. Pour fresh coconut oil and remove from fire. Serve hot.

161. PAZHAMANGA CURRY

Ingredients	*Quantity*
Ripe mangoes	5 small or 2 large
Green chillies	3
Turmeric	½ tsp
Red onion (small)	1
Coconut	½
Cumin seeds	¼ tsp
Buttermilk	300 ml (1 glass)
Curry leaves	1 sprig

Ingredients	Quantity
Salt	to taste
For tempering	
Red chilli	1
Mustard seeds	a pinch
Coconut oil	15 ml

Method

Peel the mangoes. If small, keep whole and if large, cut into pieces. Grind together green chillies and turmeric. Mix with mangoes. Put into a pan. Cover with water. Add salt and cook till fairly dry. Grind together into a fine paste, grated coconut, cumin seeds and red onion. Mix with buttermilk, and add to mangoes with curry leaves. Cook, without allowing it to boil, for a few minutes. Remove from the fire. Check for seasoning. Heat oil. Add broken red chillies and mustard seeds. When they crackle pour over the curry and mix well. If the mangoes are sweet, sour buttermilk or curds can be used.

162. KALAN

Ingredients	For 4	For 100
Cooking bananas, or Raw elephant yam	225 gm	5.6 kg
Chilli powder	1 level tsp	100 gm
Turmeric	½ tsp	50 gm
Salt	to taste	100 gm
Coconut	100 gm (about ½)	2.5 kg (about 10)
Peppercorns (optional)	a few	30 gm
Small red onion	5 gm	115 gm
Cumin	a pinch	20 gm
Curds	225 gm	5.6 kg
Curry leaves	3 sprigs	1 bunch
Tempering		
Oil	30 ml	500 ml
Fenugreek	a pinch	10 gm
Mustard seeds	a pinch	10 gm
Red chillies (broken)	3	50 gm
Curry leaves	1 sprig	1 bunch

Method

1. Peel and slit bananas and then cut into 2.5 cm. (1") pieces. 2. Mix

together bananas, chilli powder, half the turmeric, part of the salt and enough water to cook bananas fairly dry. 3. Grind together to a very fine paste, coconut, peppercorns, rest of turmeric and cumin. 4. When bananas are cooked, add ground ingredients, well beaten curds and more salt. 5. Simmer, stirring occasionally, till the mixture becomes quite thick (10 to 15 minutes). 6. Remove from fire. Add whole fresh curry leaves. 7. Heat oil. Add fenugreek, mustard seeds and broken red chillies. When seeds crackle, add curry leaves and sliced onion. When onion browns pour over and mix well.

163. OLAN

Ingredients	*For 4*	*For 100*
Ash gourd	225 gm	5.6 kg
Haricot beans (red)	115 gm	2.8 kg
Green chillies (slit)	10 gm	250 gm
Small onions (sliced)	30 gm	680 gm
Coconut	55 gm	1.36 kg
Coconut oil	15 ml	250 ml
Curry leaves	2 sprigs	1 bunch
Cumin powder	a pinch	10 gm
Salt	to taste	80-100 gm

Method

1. Peel and cut ash gourd into cubes. 2. Boil the ash gourd with chilles, curry leaves and onions, salt and powdered cumin. 3. Soak beans overnight. Boil till tender. 4. Scrape coconut and extract milk. 5. Add cooked beans and coconut milk to ash gourd. Bring to boil. 6. Add fresh coconut oil. Mix well and remove. Serve hot.

164. ERUSSERY

Ingredients	*For 4*	*For 100*
Raw bananas or Red pumpkin	225 gm	5.6 kg
Green chillies	5 gm	115 gm
Turmeric	1 tsp	15 gm
Coconut	1 (225 gm)	25 (5.6 kg)
Mustard seeds	1 tsp	15 gm
Cumin	½ tsp	10 gm
Red onions	5	30 gm
Coconut oil	15 ml	250 ml

Ingredients	*For 4*	*For 100*
Curry leaves	2 sprigs	1 bunch
Salt	to taste	100 gm

Method

1. Peel and cut bananas into pieces 2.5 cm. (1") long and 0.75 cm. (¼") thick. 2. Wash well in a little buttermilk to remove stains. 3. Grind together green chillies and turmeric. 4. Smear on banana pieces. Add salt, water and curry leaves and cook till bananas are tender and water almost dried up. 5. Grind together half the grated coconut and cumin to a smooth paste. Add to bananas. 6. Heat without boiling, stirring all the time. Remove. 7. Heat coconut and sliced onions. When nearly brown, add mustard seeds. 9. When mustard seeds crackle, add curry. 10. Mash bananas. Bring to boil and remove.

N.B. If pumpkin is used, peel and cook with turmeric till dry. Coarsely grind green chillies and add.

165. VEGETABLE KOOTTU CURRY

Ingredients	*Quantity*
Split bengal gram	50 gm
Elephant yam	100 gm
Ash gourd	100 gm
Pepper	10 gm
Salt	to taste
Turmeric	¼ tsp
Coconut	½
Red chillies	5
To temper	
Coconut	½
Mustard seeds	3 gm
Oil	30 ml
Curry leaves	1 sprig
Split black gram	10 gm
Jaggery	1 small piece

Method

1. Cook bengal gram in 3 times its volume of water. Peel and cut yam and ash gourd into 0.75 cm. (¼") pieces. 2. Add the vegetables, pepper, salt and turmeric and 1 cup of water to the cooked gram and cook till vegetables are done. 3. Meanwhile, grind to a fine paste the coconut and chillies and add to the cooked vegetables and gram. Bring to a boil and remove. 4. Heat oil. Fry grated coconut, mustard seeds, curry leaves and

black gram till brown. Add, with grated jaggery, to the curry. 5. Mix well. Keep covered for a few minutes. Serve hot.

166. MANGO SORAK

Ingredients	*For 10*
Kashmiri chillies	10
Coconut	½
Tamarind (optional)	a little
Turmeric	a small piece
Green mangoes	1-2
Oil	4 tbsp
Onions	1-2

Method

1. Grind chillies with turmeric and when the mixture is half ground, add tamarind (if used) and grind to a fine paste. 2. Peel and slice the mangoes and apply a little salt to the slices. 3. Grate coconut and extract milk. Slice onion. 4. Heat oil and fry sliced onion till brown; add ground masala and fry for a little while; add coconut milk and a little water if desired. 5. When the curry starts boiling, add mango slices and cook till the mango slices are done. Add a little salt if desired.

167. ASH GOURD BHURTA

Ingredients	*Quantity*
Ash gourd	500 gm
Oil	15 ml
Onions	200 gm
Green chillies	4
Lime juice	1 tsp
Coriander leaves	a few sprigs
Salt	to taste

Method

1. Peel and cut gourd into cubes. Cook over a slow flame, adding just enough water to cook dry, till tender. Mash gourd. 2. Heat oil. Add chopped onions and green chillies and sauté. Add gourd and salt and mix well. Fry for 5 minutes more. 3. Remove pan from fire. Add lime juice and chopped coriander leaves.

N.B. If desired, a little roasted cumin powder could be added in which case add this before adding the lime juice.

EGGS

1. Egg and Potato Curry
2. Egg and Vegetable Curry
3. Masalyachi Andi
4. Egg and Dal Curry
5. Egg and Dal Cutlets
6. Egg Curry (S. Indian)
7. Omelette Curry
8. Egg and Vegetable Moilee
9. Egg stew
10. Egg Baffat
11. Ceylon Egg Curry (A)
    Ceylon Egg Curry (B)
12. Egg and Methi Bhaji Curry
13. Egg Patties
14. Egg Indad
15. Scrambled Egg with Coconut
16. Scrambled Egg with Methi Bhaji
17. Egg on Potatoes
18. Egg on Tomatoes
19. Bindhu Pur Edu (Egg on ladies fingers)
20. Egg Kalia
21. Tomato Egg Mould

1. EGG AND POTATO CURRY

Ingredients	*For 4*	*For 100*
Eggs	4	100
Potatoes	225 gm	5.6 kg
Onions	115 gm	2.8 kg
Red Chillies	5 gm	120 gm
Coriander	10 gm	250 gm
Turmeric	1 gm	25 gm
Coconut	½	10
Cinnamon cloves	½ gm	10 gm
Green chillies	2	50
Ginger	2 gm	50 gm
Curry leaves	1 sprig	1 bunch
Salt	5 gm	100 to
Vinegar	10 ml	250 ml
Oil	30 ml	750 ml

Method

1. Hard-boil eggs. Crack and cool in water. Shell and keep aside. 2. Peel potatoes. Quarter and immerse in cold water. 3. Slice onions. Chop ginger, grate coconut. 4. Roast red chillies, coriander and turmeric and grind to a fine paste. 5. Grind coconut also to a smooth paste. 6. Heat half of the oil. Sauté sliced onions leaving aside a few slices for tempering. 7. Add ginger, whole green chillies and ground spices. When well fried, add ground coconut and fry for 2 minutes. 8. Add potatoes, water and salt and cook till potatoes are tender. 9. Add eggs, cut into halves and vinegar. Remove from fire. 10. Heat remaining oil in a fry pan. Brown onions, crushed cloves and cinnamon. Add curry leaves and pour over curry.

2. EGG AND VEGETABLE CURRY

Ingredients	*For 4*	*For 100*
Eggs	4	100
Potatoes	225 gm	5.6 kg
Beans	115 gm	2.8 kg
Cabbage	225 gm	5.6 kg
Tomatoes	225 gm	5.6 kg
Carrots	115 gm	2.8 kg
Onions	115 gm	2.8 kg
Fat	50 gm	1.25 kg
Coriander leaves	¼ bunch	6 bunches
Pomegranate seeds	5 gm	115 gm
Chilli powder	10 gm	225 gm
Coriander powder	5 gm	115 gm
Turmeric	a pinch	15 gm
Salt	to taste	80–100 gm

Method

1. Prepare vegetables. Blanch tomatoes. Slice onions. 2. Fry sliced onions. Add spices and fry well. 3. Add vegetables (except tomatoes), salt and water, and cook. 4. When vegetables are half done, add tomatoes and pomegranate seeds. Cook till vegetables are tender and gravy is thick. 5. Add shelled halved hard-boiled eggs. Simmer for about 5 minutes longer.

3. MASALYACHI ANDI

Ingredients	*For 4*	*For 100*
Eggs	4	100
Onions	100 gm	2.5 kg
Coconut	50 gm (¼)	1.35 kg
Chilli powder	2–3 gm	85 gm
Peppercorns	3	10 gm
Cloves	3	15 gm
Cinnamon	1.25 cm. (½") piece	15 gm
Salt	to taste	100 gm
Fat	30 gm	500 gm

Method

1. Hard-boil and shell eggs. 2. Grind to a fine paste coconut, chilli powder, peppercorns cloves, cinnamon and salt. 3. Slit eggs length wise and stuff with ground spices. Tie with threads. 4. Heat fat. Add sliced onions and brown. 5. Add remaining spices and a little water and simmer till spices are cooked. 6. Add eggs and bring to boil. Remove.

4. EGG AND DAL CURRY

Ingredients	*For 4*	*For 100*
Eggs	4	100
Lentil	115 gm	1.35 kg
Red chillies	5 gm	115 gm
Cumin	a pinch	30 gm
Poppy seeds	5 gm	115 gm
Coriander	5 gm	115 gm
Onions	10 gm	225 gm
Tamarind	a little	225 gm
Fresh coconut	115 gm	2.8 kg
Salt	to taste	100 gm
Oil	15 ml	250 ml

Method

1. Hard-boil eggs; shell and cut into halves. 2. Wash and boil lentil in a little water till cooked. Add salt. 3. Grate coconut and extract thick and thin milk. 4. Roast red chillies, cumin, poppy seeds and coriander. Add tamarind and grind. 5. Slice onion. 6. Heat fat. Fry sliced onion and spices. 7. Add thin extraction of coconut milk and spices. Simmer. 8. When well cooked, add thick extraction of coconut milk and hard-boiled eggs. Bring to boil and remove from fire.

5. EGG AND DAL CUTLETS

Ingredients	*For 4*	*For 100*
Eggs	4	100
Split bengal gram	225 gm	5.6 kg
Pumpkin (white)	115 gm	2.8 kg
Onions	55 gm	1.35 kg
Turmeric	a pinch	10 gm
Green chillies	5 gm	115 gm
Bengal gram flour	55 gm	1.35 gm
Fat for frying (absorption)	30 gm	500 gm
Eggs	2	50

Method

1. Pick and wash the gram. 2. Chop onion and chillies. Peel and cut pumpkin. 3. Boil gram, pumpkin, green chillies and onion in very little water. 4. When gram is cooked, remove from fire and mash to a pulp. 5. Hard-boil eggs and divide into quarters. 6. Divide gram mixture into balls. Place a quarter of egg in the centre and shape. 7. Coat with gram flour batter and deep fry to a golden brown colour.

6. EGG CURRY (S. Indian)

Ingredients	*For 4*	*For 100*
Eggs (duck's or hen's)	4	100
Potatoes	225 gm	5.65 kg
Onions	115 gm	1.35 kg
Red chillies	5 gm	115 gm
Coriander	10 gm	225 gm
Turmeric	a pinch	15 gm
Coconut	½ (115 gm)	12 (2.8 kg)
Cinnamon	a small piece	15 gm
Cloves	2 to 3	5 gm
Oil	30 ml	500 ml
Vinegar	1 tsp (to taste)	100 ml (to taste)
Salt	to taste	80-100 gm
Green chillies (optional)	2	50 gm
Ginger	a small piece	50 gm
Curry leaves	1 sprig	1 bunch

Method

1. Hard-boil eggs. Crack and cool in water. Shell and keep aside. 2. Peel potatoes. Quarter and steep in cold water. 3. Slice onions. 4. Roast red chillies, coriander and turmeric. Grind to a fine paste. 5. Chop ginger. 6. Grate coconut. Take out two extractions of coconut milk; the first extract thick and the second extract thin. 7. Heat half the oil. Sauté sliced onions leaving aside a few slices for tempering. 8. Add spices and fry. 9. Add potatoes, chopped ginger, whole green chillies and the second extract of coconut milk and salt. Cook till potatoes are tender. 10. Add eggs cut into halves and the thick extract of coconut milk. 11. Add vinegar and remove from fire. 12. Heat remaining oil. Add onions, curry leaves, crushed cinnmon and cloves. 13. When onions are browned pour over curry. Stir well.

7. OMELETTE CURRY

Ingredients as above. Prepare omelette with eggs. Cut into 5 cm. (2 inch) slices and add to prepared curry instead of hard-boiled eggs.

8. EGG AND VEGETABLE MOILEE

Ingredients	*For 4*
Eggs	4
Potatoes	250 gm
Cauliflower	100 gm

Ingredients	*Quantity*
Carrots	100 gm
Tomatoes	150 gm
Onions	200 gm
Green chillies	6 gm (2)
Ginger	10 gm
Turmeric	2-3 gm
Coconut	1
Salt	3-5 gm
Lime	½ to 1
Oil	15 ml

Method

1. Hard-boil the eggs. Crack and put into water. 2. Peel potatoes and quarter. Wash cauliflower and break into flowerettes with the leaves. 3. Peel carrots and cut into 2.5 cm. (1") pieces. 4. Peel and slice onions and ginger. Slit green chillies. 5. Grate coconut and prepare three extractions, thick, medium and thin. Extract lime juice. 6. Heat oil, sauté onions, green chillies and ginger and cook till the onion slices are tender. 7. Add turmeric and potatoes. Sauté for a few minutes. 8. Add third extraction of coconut milk and cook gently till potatoes are three-fourths done; 9. Add carrots, cauliflower and salt. Simmer for a further 5–10 minutes. 10. Add chopped tomatoes and second extract of coconut milk. Simmer. 11. Add lime juice and test for seasoning . 12. Now add shelled eggs cut into halves. Bring to boil. 13. Add first extract of coconut milk. Turn off the fire and mix gently.

9. EGG STEW

Ingredients	*For 4*	*For 100*
Eggs	4	100
Potatoes	225 gm	5.6 kg
Onions	115 gm	2.8 kg
Green chillies	6	50 gm
Ginger	5 gm	100 gm
Peppercorns	1 gm	25 gm
Tomatoes	100 gm	2.5 kg
Salt	to taste	80-100 gm
Coconut	½	12
Fat/oil	10 gm	250 gm
Vinegar	to taste	to taste
For tempering		
Cloves	cinnamon	2 gm
Mustard seeds	½ gm	10 gm

Ingredients	*For 4*	*For 100*
Small onion	5 gm	100 gm
Oil	10 gm	50 gm
Vinegar	to taste	to taste

Method

Hard-boil eggs. Crack and cool in cold water. Shell and cut into halves. Grate coconut and prepare three extractions, thick, medium and thin. Slit green chillies and slice onions and ginger. Heat fat. Sauté onions, ginger and green chillies. Add third extract of coconut milk, peppercorns and peeled and quartered potatoes. When potatoes are cooked, add second extract of coconut milk and quartered tomatoes. Bring to boil. Add eggs and the first extract of coconut milk and vinegar as desired. Remove from fire. Heat oil in a fry pan. Add mustard seeds and curry leaves. When the seeds crackle, add finely chopped onions, crushed cinnamon and cloves. As the onions brown, pour over the stew. Mix well.

N.B. If desired a little rice flour or refined flour can be mixed with cold water and added to the stew to thicken the gravy.

10. EGG BAFFAT

Ingredients	*For 4*	*For 100*
Eggs	4	100
Potatoes	225 gm	5.65 kg
Red chillies	5 gm	115 gm
Cumin	1/4 tsp	15 gm
Turmeric	a pinch	15 gm
Coriander	10 gm	225 gm
Onions	115 gm	2.8 kg
Green chillies	2	100 gm
Ginger	5 gm	115 gm
Vinegar	10 ml	225 ml
Salt	to taste	80-100 gm
Fat	30 gm	500 gm
Garlic	2 clove	15 gm

Method

1. Hard-boil eggs. Shell and cut into halves. 2. Boil potatoes. Peel and quarter. 3. Grind together red chillies, cumin, turmeric and coriander. 4. Slice onions. Green chillies, ginger and garlic. 5. Heat fat in a pan. Fry half the onions. 6. Add spices and fry for 2–3 minutes. 7. Add remaining onions and other sliced ingredients, water, salt and vinegar. 8. Bring to boil and simmer till spices and onions are cooked. 9. Add potatoes and eggs. Bring to boil and remove.

N.B. White radish may be used instead of potatoes in which case boil radish with lime and water. Coconut milk may be added instead of water. Follow directions for mutton baffat.

11. CEYLON EGG CURRY (A)

Ingredients	*For 4*	*For 100*
Eggs	4	100
Small onions	55 gm	1.35 kg
Green chillies	1	50 gm
Turmeric	¼ tsp	15 gm
Ginger	5 gm	115 gm
Garlic	1 clove	20 gm
Curry leaves	2 sprigs	1 bunch
Fenugreek	¼ tsp	15 gm
Cinnamon	a small piece	15 gm
Lime	½	12
Coconut	½	12
Salt	to taste	80-100 gm

Method

1. Hard-boil the eggs, crack, cool in water. Shell and cut into halves. 2. Grate coconut. Grind and make a thick and a thin extraction. 3. Slit green chillies. Slice onions, chop ginger. 4. In a pan put together all the ingredients except eggs, thick coconut milk and lime juice. 5. Boil until all ingredients are cooked. 6. Add thick coconut milk and lime juice and stir well. 7. Add eggs. Simmer for a few minutes longer, stirring all the time.

N.B. The gravy by itself is known as coconut soup or kirihothi.

CEYLON EGG CURRY (B)

Ingredients	*For 4*	*For 100*
Eggs	4	100
Small onions	30 gm	680 gm
Garlic	2 flakes	10 gm
Ginger	5 gm	115 gm
Cinnamon	2.5 cm. (1") piece	15 gm
Coriander	5 gm	115 gm
Red chillies	5 gm	115 gm
Fennel	½ tsp	50 gm
Cumin	a pinch	10 gm
Fenugreek	a few seeds	10 gm

Ingredients	*For 4*	*For 100*
Lime	½	12
Coconut	½	12
Fat	15 gm	250 gm
Turmeric	¼ tsp	15 gm
Salt	to taste	80-100 gm
Curry leaves	a sprig	1 bunch

Method

1. Hard-boil eggs, crack, cool in water. Shell. 2. Prick with a stout pin and smear over with salt and turmeric. 3. Grate and extract medium strength coconut milk. 4. Slice onions, chop ginger and garlic. 5. Roast cumin and fennel, and powder. 6. Grind together red chillies and coriander. 7. Heat fat. Fry eggs and remove. Add half the sliced onions and fry. 8. Add all the ingredients except lime juice and eggs. 9. Boil until gravy is thick, stirring now and then. 10. Add the eggs and the lime juice; simmer for a few minutes longer.

12. EGG AND METHI BHAJI CURRY

Ingredients	*For 4*	*For 100*
Eggs	4	100
Fenugreek leaves	12 bundles	300 bundles
Onions	115 gm	2.8 kg
Ginger	5 gm	115 gm
Green chillies	2	50 gm
Garlic	3 flakes	20 gm
Coconut	½	12
Red chillies	5 gm	115 gm
Cumin	½ tsp	50 gm
Mustard	½ tsp	50 gm
Turmeric	¼ tsp	20 gm
Peppercorns	4	15 gm
Fat	30 gm	500 gm
Salt	to taste	80-100 gm

Method

1. Hard-boil eggs, crack, cool in water and shell. 2. Cut off roots of fenugreek leaves. Wash and chop leaves. 3. Slice half the onions, green chillies, ginger and garlic. 4. Grate coconut. Grind and extract thick and thin extractions of milk. 5. Grind red chillies, cumin, mustard, turmeric, perppercorns, and half the remaining onions. 6. Mix together the sliced ingredients, fenugreek leaves, second extraction of coconut milk, ground ingredients and salt. 7. Boil till leaves are cooked. 8. Heat fat and fry

remaining onions. Add to the curry. 9. Lastly add thick extraction of coconut milk and halved eggs. Bring to boil and remove from fire.

13. EGG PATTIES

Ingredients	*For 4*	*For 100*
Eggs	4	100
Onions	115 gm	2.8 kg
Green chillies	5	115 gm
Ginger	5	115 gm
Coriander leaves	½ bunch	3 bunches
Salt	to taste	50 gm
Fat	10 gm	200 gm
Covering		
Refined flour	115 gm	2.8 kg
Fat	30 gm	500 gm
Rice flour	15 gm	340 gm
Salt	a pinch	30 gm

Method

1. Hard-boil eggs. Crack and cool in water. Shell and chop into small pieces. 2. Chop fine the green chillies onions. ginger and coriander leaves. 3. Sauté in a small quantity of hot fat. Remove, add eggs and salt. 4. Prepare a dough with flour, salt and water. Let it stand for at least 1 hour. 5. Knead dough well. Roll out into large chapaties, smear with fat, sprinkle a little rice flour over. 6. Fold serveral times. Roll out thinly; cut into squares or circles. 7. Fill with prepared stuffing. Turn over and seal edges with water. 8. Deep fry and serve hot.

14. EGG INDAD

Ingredients	*For 4*	*For 100*
Eggs	4	100
Potatoes	225 gm	5.65 kg
Red chillies	3	85 gm
Cumin	½ tsp	15 gm
Turmeric	a pinch	15 gm
Green chillies	15 gm	85 kg
Onions	115 gm	115 gm
Ginger	5 gm	115 gm
Garlic	3 flakes	20 gm
Vinegar	to taste	80-100 gm
Fat	15 gm	250 gm
Sugar	1 tsp	30 gm

Method

1. Hard-boil the eggs, crack and cool in water, shell and cut into halves. 2. Boil potatoes in their jackets. Peel and quarter. 3. Grind the spices and half the onions. 4. Heat fat. Add remaining onions sliced, and ground spices. Fry well. 5. Add water, salt, sugar and vinegar. Bring to boil. 6. Add eggs and potatoes. Simmer for a few minutes longer. Remove and serve hot.

15. SCRAMBLED EGG WITH COCONUT

Ingredients	*For 4*	*For 100*
Eggs	4	100
Coconut	½	12
Red chillies	3	85 gm
Small onions	30 gm	680 gm
Oil	15 ml	250 ml
Salt	to taste	50 gm

Method

1. Grate coconut; crush red chillies. Slice onions. 2. Break eggs. Beat well. Add coconut, onions, chillies and salt . 3. Heat oil in a fry pan. Add egg mixure. As it starts setting, stir. Remove when cooked and serve immediately.

16. SCRAMBLED EGG WITH METHI BHAJI

Ingredients	*For 4*	*For 100*
Eggs	4	100
Fenugreek leaves	8 bunches	200 bunches
Small onions	30 gm	680 gm
Green chillies	10 gm	200 gm
Ginger	5 gm	115 gm
Garlic	a few flakes	20 gm
Turmeric	a pinch	15 gm
Lime juice	½	12
Sugar	1 tsp	30 gm
Fat	30 gm	500 gm

Method

1. Hear fat. Sauté sliced onion. 2. Add washed and chopped fenugreek leaves, green chillies, ginger, peeled and chopped garlic and turmeric. 3. Fry for a few minutes. Add lime juice and sugar 4. Spread in a shallow pan. Beat eggs well and pour over fenugreek leaves. 5. Cover and cook on gentle heat till the eggs set. 6. Serve hot, cut into pieces.

N.B. The small variety of fenugreek leaves should be used.

17. EGG ON POTATOES

Ingredients	*For 4*	*For 100*
Eggs	4	100
Potatoes	450 gm	11 kg
Salt	to taste	100 gm
Fat	50 gm	1.25 kg

Method

1. Peel and cut potatoes into thin roundels. 2. Heat fat. Sauté potatoes. Add salt. 3. Cover and cook over gentle heat till potatoes are cooked. 4. When cooked, spread onto a shallow pan. 5. Make dents. Break eggs one at a time into a wet cup. Pour one into each dent. 6. Cook covered over gentle heat till eggs set. 7. Serve hot with tomato sauce.

18. EGG ON TOMATOES

Ingredients	*For 4*	*For 100*
Tomatoes	500 gm	12.5 kg
Onions	225 gm	5.6 kg
Ginger	1.25 cm. (½") piece	85 gm
Jaggery	10 gm	250 gm
Chilli powder	1 tsp	100 gm
Eggs	4	100
Fat	30 gm	500 gm

Method

1. Blanch and chop tomatoes. Peel and chop onions. 2. Grind ginger. 3. Heat fat. Brown chopped onions. Add all ingredients except eggs and jaggery and cook till sauce thickens. 4. Add jaggery. Mix well and cook for 5 minutes. 5. Spread the pulp in a shallow pan or pie dish. 6. Make slight dents. Break eggs one at a time into wet cups and pour one in each dent. 7. Cover and cook with live coal on top of lid, or in an oven, till eggs are fairly hard.

19. BINDHU PUR EDU (EGG ON LADIES FINGERS)

Ingredients	*For 4*	*For 100*
Ladies fingers	450 gm	11 kg
Onions	115 gm	2.8 kg
Chilli powder	1 tsp	100 gm
Garam masala	1 tsp	85 gm
Turmeric	¼ tsp	30 gm
Lime juice	½	12

Ingredients	*For 4*	*For 100*
Tomatoes	55 gm	1.35 kg
Eggs for mixing	2	50
Eggs for frying	4	100
Salt	to taste	80-100 gm
Fat	30 gm	500 gm

Method

1. Wipe ladies fingers with a wet cloth. 2. Chop ladies fingers, onions and tomatoes. 3. Heat half the fat. Fry onions. Add ladies fingers and tomatoes. 4. Add all the spices and seasonings except lime juice. 5. Cook for 15 to 20 minutes. 6. Beat eggs and mix with ladies fingers. 7. Remove from fire and spread in a pyrex pie dish. Sprinkle lime juice. 8. Fry remaining eggs. Place on top of prepared vegetables. Bake for 5 to 10 minutes.

20. EGG KALIA

Ingredients	*Quantity*
Eggs	8
Potatoes	500 gm
Onions	225 gm
Peas	115 gm
Oil	100 ml
Coriander	10 gm
Ginger	2.5 cm. (1") piece
Salt	to taste
Turmeric	½ tsp
Cumin	¼ tsp
Pepper	¼ tsp
Garam Masala	¼ tsp
Cloves, cinnamon, cardamom	
Curry leaves	a few
Red chillies	3
Fat	1 tbsp

Method

1. Hard-boil, cool and shell eggs. Cut into halves. Peel and qurter potatoes; peel and slice onions. 2. Heat oil. Brown eggs and onions separately. Remove. Add potatoes and peas to oil and then the coriander, pepper, cumin, ginger, garam masala, turmeric and two red chillies ground to a fine paste. Add hot water and salt. 3. Cook till potatoes are done. Add onions and eggs. Heat fat, add the remaining red chilli and curry leaves. Pour over curry and mix well.

21. TOMATO EGG MOULD

Ingredients	*Quantity*
Tomatoes	4
Onions	225 gm (1 large)
Green chillies	10 gm (2-3)
Cumin	a little
Salt	to taste
Fat	10 gm
Cornflour	1 tbsp
Milk	1 tbsp
Breadcrumbs (fresh)	1 tbsp
Eggs (hard-boiled)	4

Method

1. Heat fat and fry cumin. When the seeds crackle, add chopped chillies, onions and quartered and skinned tomatoes. Add salt to taste and cook on a very slow fire till vegetables are cooked and dry. 2. Add the cornflour blended with milk. Stir until it thickens. Add the eggs (chopped finely), and then the breadcrumbs. 3. Put into a mould rinsed with cold water and refrigerate. When set, serve with a salad.

FISH

1. Masala Fried Fish (A)
   Masala Fried Fish (B)
   Masala Fried Fish (C)
2. Fish Fry (Punjabi)
3. Fish Fingers (Punjabi)
4. Fish Fry (Malayalee)
5. Fish Fry (Goan)
6. Fish Cutlets (Indian)
7. Jinga Cutlets
8. Fish Curry (Green)
9. Macher Kofta Curry
10. Goan Fish Curry (A)
    Goan Fish Curry (B)
    Goan Fish Curry (C)
11. Mahe Kalia (Hyderabad)
12. Hyderabadi Fish Curry
13. Fish Moilee
14. Palaanum
15. Meen Thullichathu
16. Pollicha Meen
17. Fish Smore
18. Macher Jhal
19. Fish Patiya
20. Bengal Fish Curry
21. Shorshebata Jholer Mach (Bengali)
22. Machchalika Kalia
23. Patra ni Machhi
24. Tuna Appam
25. Fish in Tomato Sauce
26. Dahi Machi (A)
    Dahi Machi (B) (Bengali)
27. Baked Curried Fish
28. Baked Stuffed Fish
29. Fish in Sauce (Parsi style)
30. Fish Bambloe or Bombay Duck
31. Grilled Fish
32. Sour Fish

33. Tamarind Fish
34. Meen Pada
35. Fish Tomato (Punjabi)
36. Fish with Coconut (Meen peera)
37. Malayalee Fish Curry (Meen vevichathu)
38. Kannan and Manga
39. Fish Stew (Malayalee)
40. Fish Stew (White)
41. Fried Fish Curry (Malabar)
42. Baked Fish Curry (Malayalee) (Pollicha meen)
43. Fish Curry (Maharashtra)
44. Malabar Fish Moilee
45. Malabar Fish/Prawn Curry
46. Fish Curry (Madras)
47. Fish Vindaloo (East Indian)
48. Guisado
49. Prawn Curry
50. Prawn and Tomato Curry
51. Malai Prawn Curry
52. Prawn Vindaloo
53. Prawns in Garlic Chilli Sauce
54. Prawn Do-Pyaz
55. Prawn Coconut Curry (Konju vevichathu)
56. Goan Prawn (or fish) Curry with Mangoes
57. Prawn Caldeen (A)
    Prawn Caldeen (B)
58. Prawn Temperado
59. Masala Prawns
60. Prawn Fry
61. Lobster Curry (A)
    Lobster Curry (B)
62. Lobster Masala
63. Crab Curry (A)
    Crab Curry (B)
64. Crab Pulao
65. Oyster Lonevas

1. MASALA FRIED FISH (A)

Ingredients	*For 4*	*For 100*
Fish (pomfret, salmon, mackerel etc.)	500 gm	12.5 kg
Ginger	5 gm	115 gm
Garlic	a few flakes	55 gm
Red chillies	5 gm	115 gm
Tamarind	10 gm	225 gm
Cumin	a pinch	30 gm
Salt	15 gm	100 gm
Oil	30 ml	500 ml

Method

1. Clean and wash fish. Cut into slices; if small fish, keep whole, but make gashes. 2. Grind together the spices and salt. 3. Smear fish with this paste. 4. Keep aside for a while. 5. Shallow fry till cooked. Serve hot.

MASALA FRIED FISH (B)

Ingredients	*For 4*	*For 100*
Pomfret	500 gm	12.5 kg
Oil for frying	50 ml	1.25 litre

Ingredients	*For 4*	*For 100*
Masala		
Kashmiri chillies	10 gm	255 gm
Ginger	a small piece	55 gm
Garlic	6 flakes	55 gm
Cumin	a pinch	30 gm
Mustard seeds	a small pinch	15 gm
Cinnamon	a small piece	5 gm
Cloves	2	5 gm
Peppercorns	6	15 gm
Tamarind	10 gm	225 gm
Onion	15 gm	340 gm
Salt	to taste	100 gm
Vinegar	20 ml	200 ml

Method

1. Wash, scale and trim the fins of the fish. 2. Remove the intestines and bones. 3. Wash again in vinegar. Make gashes on the fish. 4. Grind the spices and salt and stuff the fish; smear outside as well. 5. Tie up with a piece of twine. Allow to stand for a while to let fish absorb the spices. 6. Shallow fry and serve hot.

MASALA FRIED FISH (C)

Ingredients	*For 4*	*For 100*
Fish	500 gm	12.5 kg
Turmeric	a pinch	10 gm
Green chillies	5 gm	115 gm
Coriander	5 gm	115 gm
Coconut	¼	6
Onions	55 gm	1.36 kg
Garlic	2 flakes	15 gm
Coriander leaves	¼ bunch	6 bunches
Tomato sauce	55 gm	1.36 kg
Curds	115 gm	2.8 kg
Salt	to taste	100 gm
Oil	30 ml	500 ml

Method

1. Clean and cut fish into pieces. Wash well. 2. Grind together coconut, coriander, turmeric and green chillies. 3. Chop garlic and coriander leaves, slice onions. 4. Heat a little oil in a pan and slightly shallow fry the fish. 5. Remove fish. Add more oil and put in ground spices, chopped

ingredients and tomato sauce. 6. Fry well. Add beaten curds and pieces of fish and cook covered, on a slow fire till ready.

2. FISH FRY (Punjabi)

Ingredients	*For 4*	*For 100*
Fish (fresh-water)	500 gm	12.5 kg
Onions	100 gm	2.5 kg
Ginger	5 gm	115 gm
Cumin	1 tsp	100 gm
Garlic	3 to 4 flakes	85 gm
Turmeric	½ tsp	20 gm
Chilli powder	1 tsp	100 gm
Salt	1 tsp	80-100 gm
Dry mango powder	1 tsp	80-100 gm
Garam masala	½ tsp	50 gm
Fat to fry (absorption)	30 gm	750 gm

Method

1. Scale and clean fish skin and remove bones. Wash well. 2. Cut into 7.5 cm. × 3.5 cm. (approx 3" × 1½") pieces. 3. Grind spices (onions to garam masala) and smear over the fish. 4. Set aside for about 3 hours. 5. Deep fry lightly. Remove and drain. 6. When about to serve, deep fry again. Serve with tamarind or mint chutney.

3. FISH FINGERS (Punjabi)

Same as above. Cut into finger lengths. Fry as above and serve on toothpicks with chutney.

4. FISH FRY (Malayalee)

Ingredients	*For 4*	*For 100*
Pomfret or Mullet or Salmon or Mackerel	500 gm	12.5 kg
Red chillies	10 gm	250 gm
Peppercorns	a few	30 gm
Turmeric	½ tsp	20 gm
Garlic	a few flakes (4)	100 gm
Red onions	4 bulbs	100 gm
Salt	to taste	100 gm
Coconut oil	30 ml	500 ml

Method

1. Clean fish. 2. Wash thoroughly in several rinses of water. A little lime juice can be mixed in the last rinse. Drain thoroughly. 3. Grind onions, red chillies, peppercorns, turmeric, garlic and salt. 4. Smear on fish; set aside for half an hour. 5. Heat a small quantity of oil in a frying pan. 6. Shallow fry fish on both sides till brown and fairly crisp. 7. Drain each piece on the side of the frying pan away from direct heat for about 2 to 3 minutes before removing.

5. FISH FRY (Goan)

Ingredients	*For 4*	*For 100*
Small fish	500 gm	12.5 kg
Onions	225 gm	5.6 kg
Turmeric	a pinch	15 gm
Dry chillies	5 gm	115 gm
Mustard seeds	5 gm	115 gm
Cumin	3 gm	85 gm
Garlic	5 gm	115 gm
Oil	15 ml	250 ml
Salt	to taste	100 gm

Method

1. Clean and wash the fish, smear with turmeric and salt. 2. Grind mustard seeds, cumin, garlic, half the onions and chillies to a fine paste. 3. Chop remaining onions. 4. Heat oil. Fry chopped onions. Add fish and fry. 5. Add ground spices and a little water. 6. Cover and simmer till fish is cooked (about 15–20 minutes).

6. FISH CUTLETS (Indian)

Ingredients	*For 4*	*For 100*
Fish (pomfret, jew fish, salmon, etc.)	500 gm	12.5 kg
Bread	2 slices	1.35 kg
Lime	¼	6
Green chillies	5 gm	115 gm
Onions	200 gm	5 kg
Egg	1	12
Salt	to taste	80-100 gm
Breadcrumbs	30 gm	340 gm
Oil for frying (absorption)	30 ml	500 ml
Cucumber	30 gm	680 gm
Tomatoes	55 gm	1.36 kg
Coriander leaves	a few	½ bunch

Method

1. Clean, wash and boil fish. Flake fish. 2. Chop onions and chillies fine. 3. Soak bread in water. 4. Squeeze out water from bread. 5. Mix all ingredients. Add salt. 6. Shape into cutlets. Coat with egg and breadcrumbs and deep fry. 7. Garnish with chopped coriander leaves, sliced cucumber and tomatoes.

7. JINGA CUTLETS

Ingredients	*For 4*	*For 100*
Large prawns	500 gm	12.5 kg
Onions	200 gm	5 kg
Garlic	4 flakes	100 gm
Ginger	1 inch piece	115 gm
Green chillies	10 gm	250 gm
Salt	to taste	100 gm
Egg	1	10
Breadcrumbs	30 gm	680 gm
Fat to fry	60 gm	1 kg

Method

1. Shell prawns. Remove intestines and wash well. 2. Grind together onions, garlic, ginger, green chillies and salt, to a fine paste. 3. Smear paste on prawns. 4. Marinade for half an hour. 5. Dip prawns in egg. Cover with bread crumbs and shallow fry in hot fat till crisp and brown.

8. FISH CURRY (Green)

Ingredients	*For 4*
Fish	450 gm
Ginger	½ inch
Garlic	8-9 cloves
Turmeric	¼ tsp
Coriander leaves	1 bunch
Salt	to taste
Coconut	30 gm
Cumin	¼ tsp
Fennel	¼ tsp
Green chillies	4-5
Lemon	½
Oil	30 ml

Method

1. Clean and cut fish. Wash again. Apply salt. 2. Grind coconut, cumin,

fennel, three-fourths of the garlic, ginger, turmeric and green chillies. When almost done, add coriander. 3. Add juice of ½ lemon. 4. Heat oil and fry 2–3 cloves of crushed garlic, add spices, water and a little salt. Cook till required amount of gravy remains. 5. Add fish; simmer till fish is cooked. 6. Serve with lemon.

9. MACHER KOFTA CURRY

Ingredients	*For 4*	*For 100*
Fish	500 gm	12.5 kg
Coconut	115 gm	2.8 kg
Tomato Sauce	1 tbsp	340 ml
Potatoes	340 gm	8.5 kg
Bread	30 gm	680 gm
Milk	75 ml	1.5 litre
Onions	250 gm	5.6 kg
Ginger	5 gm	115 gm
Green chillies	3	85 gm
Turmeric	½ tsp	50 gm
Cumin powder	½ tsp	50 gm
Coriander powder	½ tsp	50 gm
Chilli powder	¼ tsp	25 gm
Cloves	2	5 gm
Cardamom	1	a few
Cinnamon	2.5 cm (1") piece	15 gm
Curry leaves	1 sprig	1 bunch
Salt	to taste	100 gm
Sugar	to taste	50 gm
Fat	30 gm	500 gm
Fat or oil to fry koftas		

Method

1. Clean and steam fish. Remove bones and skin and mash. 2. Chop chillies fine. Grind half the onions with the ginger. Slice remaining onions. Grate coconut. 3. Boil and mash a third of the potatoes and dice the remaining. 4. Mix fish, coconut, chopped chillies, half of the ground onions, tomato sauce, mashed potatoes, bread soaked in milk and salt. 5. Form into small balls. Fry till brown and keep aside. Fry potato cubes till light brown. 6. Drain and keep aside. 7. Fry curry leaves cloves, cardamom and cinnamon. 8. Add sliced onions and fry till golden brown. 9. Add remaining ground onions, ginger and the rest of the spices. 10. Add salt, sugar, fried potatoes and enough water to cover solids. Cook till potatoes are tender. 11. Put in fish balls. Bring to boil and remove.

10. GOAN FISH CURRY (A)

Ingredients	*For 4*	*For 100*
Fish	500 gm	12.5 kg
Onions	50 gm	1.25 kg
Red chillies	5-10 gm	115-250 gm
Turmeric	½ tsp	50 gm
Cumin	½ tsp	50 gm
Coriander	10 gm	225 gm
Coconut	115 gm	2.8 kg
Tomatoes	55 gm	1.35 kg
Green chillies	5 gm	115 gm
Curry leaves	1 sprig	1 bunch
Tamarind	10 gm	225 gm
Salt	10 gm	100 gm
Oil	15 ml	500 ml

Method

1. Chop onions, Roast and grind red chillies, turmeric, cumin and coriander. 2. Grind coconut to a fine paste and mix with spices. 3. Heat oil. Fry onions, add coconut paste and slit green chillies. 4. Fry for 2 to 3 minutes; add chopped tomatoes and sufficient water. 5. Soak tamarind in a little water to extract pulp. 6. Clean and cut fish into slices, wash well; smear with salt and a little turmeric. 7. Add fish to simmering gravy. 8. Add tamarind extract, curry leaves and salt and simmer till fish is cooked.

GOAN FISH CURRY (B)

Ingredients	*For 6*
Fish (salmon, jew fish or hilsa)	300 gm
Kashmiri chillies	8-10
Turmeric	¼ tsp
Tamarind	a lemon-sized ball
Coconut	½
Dry mango pieces	2-3
Salt	to taste

Method

1. Clean and slice fish. Apply salt and set aside. 2. Remove seeds from chillies and grind with turmeric. 3. When half done, add tamarind and grind to a fine paste. 4. Grate coconut and extract the milk (3 times). Mix with ground spices. 5. Add a little water if too thick. Put the mixture into a pan, add the dry mango pieces and bring to boil. 6. When liquid starts boiling, add fish and cook till done.

GOAN FISH CURRY (C)

Ingredients	*For 6*
Fish (salmon, jew fish or hilsa)	300 gm
Kashmiri chillies	8-10
Turmeric	¼ tsp
Coriander seeds	1 dsp
Coconut	½
Tamarind	walnut size
Dry mango pieces	2-3
Salt	to taste

Method

1. Clean and slice fish. Apply salt and set aside for half an hour. 2. Grind together the Kashmiri chillies (seeds removed), turmeric, coriander seeds and grated coconut. 3. When half done, add tamarind and grind to a fine paste. 4. Mix ground ingredients with sufficient water to cook fish and leave a gravy. 5. Add dry mango pieces. Bring to boil. 6. When it starts boiling, add fish and simmer till fish is cooked.

11. MAHE KALIA (Hyderabad)

Ingredients	*For 4*	*For 100*
Mackerel	500 gm	12.5 kg
Gingelly seeds (til)	15 gm	350 gm
Groundnut	20 gm	500 gm
Dry coconut (copra)	20 gm	500 gm
Tamarind	15 gm	350 gm
Onions	100 gm	2.5 kg
Mustard	2 gm	50 gm
Cumin seeds	1 gm	25 gm
Red chillies	20 gm	500 gm
Ginger	10 gm	250 gm
Garlic	10 gm	250 gm
Turmeric	1 gm	25 gm
Salt	to taste	100 gm
Curry leaves	a few	1 bunch
Oil	50 ml	1 litre

Method

1. Clean the fish. Make gashes and keep whole. 2. Soak tamarind in a cup of water. 3. Roast and grind til, groundnut, chillies and copra. 4. Grind ginger and garlic separately. 5. Heat oil. Add mustard and cumin. 6. As they start to crackle, add curry leaves and sliced onions, and then roasted and ground spices, turmeric and ginger-garlic paste. 7. Fry well, sprinkling a little water occasionally if desired. 8. Squeeze

out the tamarind juice. Strain and add. 9. Simmer for 10 minutes. 10. Add salt. Add fish and more water if desired. 11. Simmer till the fish is cooked. 12. Dish out carefully. 13. The gravy should be of pouring consistency.

12. HYDERABADI FISH CURRY

Ingredients	*For 4*	*For 100*
Pomfret or other large fish	500 gm	12.5 kg
Gingelly seeds (sesame)	20 gm	400 gm
Cumin	10 gm	250 gm
Coriander seeds	20 gm	400 gm
Dry coconut	½	10
Onions	250 gm	5.6 kg
Curry leaves	a few sprigs	2 bunches
Tamarind	30 gm	680 gm
Sweet oil	50 ml	1.25 litre
Red chillies	3	85 gm
Asafoetida	a pinch	10 gm
Coriander leaves	a few sprigs	1 bunch
Salt	to taste	100 gm

Method

1. Clean and cut fish into slices. 2. Bake onions in the oven or in hot ash. 3. Roast together coriander seeds, red chillies, cumin, gingelly (sesame) seeds and grated dry coconut. 4. Grind the masala with the onions to a thick paste. 5. Soak tamarind in hot water. Squeeze out pulp. 6. Heat oil. Add a few seeds of cumin, asafoetida, curry leaves. 7. Remove pan from fire. Add ground paste. 8. Return to fire. Fry well. 9. Add tamarind pulp and salt. Cook for 10 minutes. 10. Add sliced pieces of fish. 11. Cook till fish is done. 12. Serve garnished with chopped coriander leaves.

13. FISH MOILEE

Ingredients	*For 4*	*For 100*
Pomfret, salmon, jew fish, mullet etc.	500 gm	12.5 kg
Onions	55 gm	1.35 kg
Ginger	10 gm	250 gm
Salt	to taste	100 gm
Coconut	1	20
Curry leaves	1 sprig	1 bunch
Garlic	a few flakes	55 gm
Green chillies	10 gm	250 gm

Ingredients	*For 4*	*For 100*
Vinegar	10 ml	250 ml
Lime	1 (large)	7
Water	115 ml	5.6 litre
Potatoes	225 gm	5.6 kg
Turmeric	a large pinch	30 gm
Oil	15 ml	250 ml

Method

1. Clean, wash in several rinses of cold water and cut fish. 2. Peel and slice garlic, ginger and onions; slit green chillies. Make two extracts of coconut milk. Heat oil, sauté sliced onions. Add turmeric and cook for 2 to 3 minutes. 4. Add garlic, ginger, curry leaves, green chillies, fish and potatoes. 5. Add second extract of coconut milk and salt and cook gently. 6. When ready add the thick first extract of coconut milk. 7. Bring to boiling point. 8. Add lime juice and vinegar. Serve hot.

14. PALAANUM

Ingredients	*For 12*
Coconuts	2
Fish or prawns	1 kg
Onions	340 gm
Turmeric	¼ tsp
Fenugreek	1 tsp
Green chillies	6-8
Ginger	2.5 cm. (1") piece
Salt	to taste
Curry leaves	1 sprig
Lime	1

Method

1. Grate coconut. Extract coconut milk, the first extraction thick, the second with 150 ml of water, and the third with 300 ml of water. Set aside. 2. Scale, clean and wash fish well. (Shell and wash prawns. Remove intestines.) Cut into 2.5 cm. (1") slices. Slice onions. 3. Put into a pan the second and third extractions of coconut milk, turmeric, fenugreek, slit green chillies, sliced onions, ginger, fish, salt and curry leaves. Bring to boil and simmer till fish is done. 4. Add first extraction of coconut milk and lime juice. Remove from fire.

15. MEEN THULLICHATHU

Ingredients	*For 6*
Small fish	250 gm
Green chillies	10 gm

Ingredients	*For 6*
Ginger	2.5 gm (½") piece
Onions	100 gm
Oil	15 ml
Coconut	½
Vinegar and salt	to taste
Curry leaves	1 sprig

Method

1. Clean fish and keep whole. 2. Slice onions, ginger and slit green chillies. 3. Grate coconut and prepare three extractions. 4. Heat oil. Sauté onions, ginger, green chilies and curry leaves. 5. Add third extraction of coconut milk and salt. Bring to boil. 6. Add fish. Allow to simmer. As liquid evaporates, add second extraction, simmer till fish is cooked. 7. Add vinegar and first extraction of coconut milk and remove.

16. POLLICHA MEEN

Ingredients	*For 6*
Karmeen (pearl spot) or small black pomfret or take medium size mackerel	1 kg
Small red onions	100 gm
Concassed tomatoes	30 gm
Turmeric	2 gm
Red chillies (Bydagi red or Kashmiri with seeds removed)	20 gm
Ginger	5 gm
Garlic	10 gm
Green chillies	2 no.
Curry leaves	1–2 springs
Green chillies (split)	2 nos.
Vinegar or Kudampuli (Cocum/garcina)	to taste
Water	as required
Salt	to taste
Coconut oil	50 ml
Banana leaves	

Method

1. Soak strips of kudampuli in about 30 ml water descale and remove sliminess on the skin of fish using the blunt part of knife or brick pumice stone. 2. Wash well in several rinses of cold water using lime juice or vinegar to remove fishy odour. Drain. 3. Make gashes on the fish keeping them whole. 4. Apply a mixture of kudampuli, water, or vinegar. Set aside for about 15 minutes. 5. Grind red chillies to a smooth paste and

finely chop ginger and garlic. 6. Heat a teaspoon of oil, add ginger garlic, split curry leaves, red chilly paste, concassed tomatoes and salt. 7. Cook for a few minutes. 8. Remove and apply liberally on both sides and the inside of the fish. 9. Wilt banana leaves and line a strong bottomed pan or fry pan. 10. Add the remaining oil and when hot, arrange fish on the leaf. 11. Fold over the leaf and cook covered for about 10 minutes or until the fish is cooked. 12. Serve hot in the banana leaf with slices of bread.

17. FISH SMORE

Ingredients	*For 4*	*For 100*
Pomfret, salmon seer or beckti	500 gm	12.5 kg
Turmeric	a pinch	20 gm
Onions	30 gm	455 gm
Garlic	2 cloves	50 gm
Ginger	a small piece	55 gm
Cinnamon	2.5 cm. (1") piece	20 gm
Vinegar	50 ml	590 ml
Curry leaves	a sprig	1 bunch
Coriander	10 gm	225 gm
Red chillies	5 gm	115 gm
Cumin	a pinch	20 gm
Fennel	a pinch	20 gm
Pepper	a pinch	20 gm
Salt	to taste	100 gm
Oil	30 ml	500 ml
Coconut	½	8 to 10

Method

1. Roast and powder coriander, red chillies, cumin and fennel. 2. Clean and slice fish. Wash well. 3. Rub over with pepper, salt and turmeric. 4. Heat oil. Lightly fry the fish. 5. Grate coconut and extract milk. 6. Peel and slice onions, garlic and ginger. 7. Put all the ingredients into the pan with the fish and allow to simmer till fish is cooked.

18. MACHER JHAL

Ingredients	*For 4*	*For 100*
Mackerel	4 (500 gm)	100 (12.5 kg)
Ginger	5 gm	115 gm
Garlic	a few flakes	50 gm
Onions	115 gm	2.72 kg
Red chillies (a) (without seeds)	5 gm	115 gm
Coriander	10 gm	225 gm
Poppy seeds	5 gm	115 gm

Ingredients	*For 4*	*For 100*
Green chillies	a few	50 gm
For tempering		
Mustard seeds	a pinch	50 gm
Fenugreek	a pinch	20 gm
Red chillies (b)	1	20 gm
Cumin	a pinch	20 gm
Mustard oil	30 ml	750 ml
Lime	1	6
Jaggery or sugar (to taste)	3-5 gm	55 gm
Salt	to taste	100 gm

Method

1. Grind together ginger, garlic, onions, red chillies (a), coriander, poppy seeds and green chillies. 2. Clean and wash the fish. Salt lightly. 3. Heat mustard oil and fry well. 4. Remove. Pour off excess oil. 5. Add all ingredients for tempering except lime, sugar or jaggery. 6. When mustard seeds crackle, add ground spices and fry well. 7. Add very little water, salt and sugar or jaggery. 8. Cover and let it simmer till spices are cooked. 9. When gravy is fairly thick add fish and simmer for 5 to 10 minutes. 10. Remove and serve hot with slices of lime.

19. FISH PATIYA

Ingredients	*For 4*	*For 100*
Pomfret or mullets	500 gm	12.5 kg
Onions	55 gm	1.36 kg
Sweet oil	30 ml	500 ml
Brinjal	115 gm	2.8 kg
Drumsticks	115 gm	2.8 kg
Bengal gram flour	5 gm	115 gm
Coriander leaves	½ bunch	4 bunches
Green chillies	5 gm	115 gm
Garlic	a few flakes	50 gm
Turmeric	a pinch	20 gm
Cumin	a pinch	20 gm
Jaggery	3-5 gm	55 gm
Cherry tomatoes	115 gm	2.8 kg
Salt	to taste	100 gm
Coriander-cumin powder	1 tsp	30 gm
Chilli powder	2 to 5 gm	115 gm
Tamarind	10 gm	225 gm
Coconut	1	10

Method

1. Clean, wash and cut fish into slices. 2. Apply salt and leave aside.

3. Grind chilies, garlic, cumin, and coriander leaves. 4. Grate coconut, add a little warm water and extract milk. 5. Soak tamarind and squeeze out pulp. 6. Soak jaggery in tamarind pulp. 7. Peel and finely chop onions. 8. Cut brinjals lengthwise. 9. Peel and cut drumsticks. 10. Heat fat and fry onions till golden brown. 11. Add ground spices and the gram flour; stir well. 12. Add turmeric, coriander, cumin powder and chilli powder, and fry. 13. Add brinjals and drumsticks and enough water to cook them. 14. When vegetables are cooked, add tamarind pulp and coconut milk. Bring to boil. 15. Add fish and cherry tomatoes; simmer till fish is cooked. Remove from fire.

20. BENGAL FISH CURRY

Ingredients	*For 4*	*For 100*
Fish	500 gm	12.5 kg
Red chillies	5 gm	115 gm
Turmeric	a pinch	20 gm
Tomatoes	225 gm	5.6 kg
Coriander leaves	¼ bunch	6 bunches
Cloves, **Cinnamon**, **Cardamom**, **Cumin** } roast and powder	5 gm	115 gm
Onions	450 gm	11 kg
Curds	55 gm	2.8 kg
Chilli powder	¼ tsp	25 gm
Mustard seeds	a pinch	20 gm
Garlic	2 cloves	20 gm
Salt	to taste	100 gm
Mustard oil	50 ml	1.25 litre

Method

1. Roast and grind together cloves, cinnamon, cardamom and cumin. 2. Clean, wash and cut fish. 3. Grind together chillies, turmeric and part of the salt. 4. Smear fish with ground spices; shallow fry. 5. Chop coriander leaves. Grind together chilli powder, turmeric, roasted spices, mustard seeds and half the onions. 6. Slice remaining onions and garlic. 7. Heat oil, fry sliced onions and garlic, add ground spices and fry. 8. Add sliced tomatoes and fry gently till they are cooked. 9. Crush the tomatoes. Add well-beaten curds, simmer for 10 to 15 minutes. Add fried fish. Continue simmering for another 10 to 15 minutes. Garnish with chopped coriander leaves and serve.

21. SHORSHEBATA JHOLER MACH (Bengal)

Ingredients	*For 4*	*For 100*
Pala (Hilsa) fish	1 kg	10 kg
Mustard	60 gm	500 gm
Green chillies	16-20 gm	200 gm
Turmeric	3 gm	30 gm
Salt	to taste	100 gm
Mustard oil	50 ml	500 ml
Green chillies (whole)	8-10 gm	100 gm

Method

1. Clean and slice fish. 2. Apply turmeric and salt. Fry lightly (shallow fry). 3. Clean and soak mustard. Grind to a fine paste. 4. Grind green chillies and turmeric. Mix with mustard paste. 5. Heat oil till the smoke comes up. 6. Add a little water to the mustard paste. Add to the hot oil. Fry over a slow fire, adding a little water every now and then to allow the paste to cook well. 7. Add the whole green chillies and salt. 8. Add 3–4 cups of water. Allow it to come to a boil twice. 9. Add fish and simmer. Taste and remove.

22. MACHCHALIKA KALIA

Ingredients	*For 4*	*For 100*
Fish	500 gm	12.5 kg
Cauliflower	115 gm	2.8 kg
Peas	225 gm	5.6 kg
Potatoes	225 gm	5.6 kg
Onions	115 gm	2.8 kg
Ginger	2.5 cm. (1") piece	115 gm
Garlic	4 cloves	50 gm
Cardamoms	2	10 gm
Cinnamon	1 stick	20 gm
Cloves	5	10 gm
Turmeric	a pinch	20 gm
Chilli powder	5 gm	115 gm
Curds	115 gm	2.8 kg
Fat	100 gm	2.5 kg
Salt	to taste	100 gm

Method

1. Slice half the onions and grind the other half with garlic and ginger. 2. Clean, wash and cut the fish. Apply salt and set aside. 3. Prepare the vegetables. 4. Roast and powder cardamom cloves and cinnamon (garam masala). 5. Heat fat. Fry fish. Remove. 6. Fry vegetable separately. Remove. 7. Brown sliced onions; add turmeric and chilli powder, ground

spices and fried vegetables. Add beaten curds and salt and cook on moderate fire stirring occasionally, till curds is well absorbed. 8. Add water. Bring to boil and add fish. 9. Simmer till vegetables and fish are cooked. 10. Sprinkle garam masala and remove from fire. Serve hot.

23. PATRA NI MACHHI

Ingredients	*For 4*	*For 100*
Pomfret	455 gm	12.8 kg
Fresh coconut	½ (115 gm)	12 (3.8 kg)
Green chillies	5 gm	115 gm
Coriander leaves	1 bunch	20 bunches
Cumin	1	20
Salt	10 gm	100 gm
Sugar	a pinch	20 gm
Garlic	a few flakes	20 gm
Vinegar	115 ml	590 ml
Fat	50 gm	1.25 kg

Method

1. Clean and slice fish, wash well. 2. Grind together coconut, green chillies, garlic, cumin, coriander leaves, salt and sugar. Add lime juice. 3. Wipe slices with a dry cloth and coat with ground ingredients. 4. Wrap in banana leaves. 5. Heat together vinegar and fat. 6. Immerse fish in the heated vinegar and fat. 7. Cover with a lid and put live coal and top or place in warm oven. 8. Cook gently till fish is tender.

24. TUNA APPAM

Ingredients	*Quantity*
Tuna	1 tin
Coconut (grated)	½
Green chillies	10 gm
Small onions	30 gm
Tomato	½
Pepper	a large pinch
Salt	to taste
Eggs	2
Oil	1 tbsp

Method

1. Chop onions and green chillies fine. 2. Open the tin of tuna. Put into a dish. Flake. 3. Mix together grated coconut, chopped tomato, green chillies, onions, oil and pepper. 4. Break eggs and mix and blend with the mixture. Add the tuna. Add salt to taste. 5. Take 2 or 3 banana leaves. Hold over the fire to fade them slightly. 5. Place mixture on

banana leaf. Wrap one over the other. 7. Tie together and bake for 45 minutes. 8. Remove and place under the grill for about 5 minutes on both sides. 9. Open and serve in a plate in the banana leaf itself.

N.B. Tuna appam can be roasted in hot ash, if desired.

25. FISH IN TOMATO SAUCE

Ingredients	*For 4*	*For 100*
Fish (preferably salmon)	500 gm	12.5 kg
Coconut	½	12
Tomato sauce	115 gm	2.8 kg
Fat	50 gm	1.25 kg
Butter	30 gm	680 gm
Green chillies	2-3	115 gm
Ginger	a small piece	50 gm
Mustard	a pinch	10 gm
Coriander leaves	¼ bunch	6 bunches
Salt	to taste	100 gm

Method

1. Grind together green chillies, ginger, mustard, coriander leaves and salt. 2. Clean and cut fish, wash well. 3. Smear fish with ground ingredients. 4. Heat a little fat. Fry fish lightly. Remove. 5. Add more fat and remaining spice. Mix well. 6. Put fish in a pan, pour over the fat and spices, thick coconut milk and tomato sauce. 7. Add butter and allow to cook until tender. 8. Serve hot, garnished with peas or fried potatoes.

26. DAHI MACHI (A)

Ingredients	*For 4*	*For 100*
Fish	500 gm	12.5 kg
Curds	225 gm	5 kg
Cloves, **Cinnamon**, **Cardamom**, **Cumin** } powder	5 gm	115 gm
Onions	115 gm	2.9 kg
Turmeric	a pinch	20 gm
Ginger	a small piece	55 gm
Salt	to taste	100 gm (approx.)
Mustard oil	15 ml	250 ml

Method

1. Powder cloves, cinnamon, cardamom and cumin. 2. Cut fish and soak in curds for half an hour. 3. Slice half the onions and grind remaining

half with ginger to a fine paste. 4. Heat oil and brown onions. Add ground ingredients. Fry well. 5. Add remaining ingredients and cook till fish becomes tender.

DAHI MACHI (B) (Bengali)

Ingredients	*Quantity*
Rohu	1 kg
Curds	1½ cup
Turmeric	3 tsp
Red chilli powder	1 tbsp
Onions	3
Ginger	5 cm. (2") piece
Salt	to taste
Garlic	1 pod
Bay leaves, cardamom, cinnamon and cloves	about 2 gm
Fat	2 tbsp
Green chillies	5

Method

1. Clean and cut rohu fish or any fresh water fish into large pieces. 2. Apply salt and 1¼ tsp turmeric. 3. Set aside for half an hour. 4. Shallow fry in hot oil and remove. 5. Mix together the curds, the remaining turmeric, chilli powder, 2 onions coarsely ground, and finely ground ginger and garlic. 6. Soak fish in the curds mixture. 7. Heat fat. Fry remaining onion. 8. Add whole cardamom, cinnamon cloves, bayleaf and green chillies. 9. Then add the fish soaked in curds mixture and allow to simmer for about 10–15 minutes.

27. BAKED CURRIED FISH

Ingredients	*For 4*	*For 100*
Fish	500 gm	12.5 kg
Tomatoes	450 gm	11 kg
Onions	115 gm	2.8 kg
Ginger	a small piece	55 gm
Red chillies	5 gm	115 gm
Garlic	3 cloves	50 gm
Salt	to taste	100 gm
Mustard oil	30 ml	500 ml

Method

1. Clean, wash and cut fish into pieces. Salt and set aside. 2. Grind together ginger, red chillies and garlic. 3. Chop onions. 4. Heat oil. Fry chopped onions. Add spices and fry. 5. Add water and boil for 1 minute.

Add salt. 6. Keep fish in a pyrex dish, cover with diced tomatoes. 7. Pour hot sauce over and bake till cooked.

28. BAKED STUFFED FISH

Ingredients	*For 6*
Pomfret	1 (500-600 gm)
Salt	to taste
Lime	½
Stuffing	
Coconut	½
Green chillies	6
Onions	1
Coriander leaves	½ bunch
Lime	½
Garlic	2 cloves
Ginger	1.25 cm. (½") piece
Cumin	1 pinch
Salt	to taste
Fat	30 gm

Method

1. Remove scales and fins of pomfret. Slit belly and remove intestines and black membrane. Remove centre bone by filleting from belly side only. 2. Apply salt and lime juice and wash well in several changes of cold water. 3. Grind together ingredients for stuffing and stuff fish. Keep a little aside to apply over fish. Stitch open ends or tie with string. 4. Apply ground paste over fish and put into baking tin with melted fat and keep in an oven at 175°C (350°F). 5. Baste frequently and turn once during cooking. Remove string and serve hot.

29. FISH IN SAUCE (Parsi style)

Ingredients	*For 4*	*For 100*
Pomfret	500 gm	12.5 kg
Cherry tomatoes	55 gm	1.35 kg
Chilli powder	1 tsp	100 gm
Garlic	½ pod	100 gm
Salt	to taste	80–100 gm
Sugar	½ tsp	50 gm
Refined flour	30 gm	450 gm
Fat	50 gm	1.25 kg
Onions	225 gm	2.8 kg
Cumin	½ tsp	50 gm

Ingredients	*For 4*	*For 100*
Coriander leaves	¼ bunch	6 bunches
Green chillies	5 gm	115 gm
Eggs	2	50
Vinegar	50 ml	1 litre
Cinnamon	1.75 cm. (½″ piece)	20 gm

Method

1. Clean, wash and cut pomfret into slices. Apply salt and set aside. 2. Chop onions, coriander leaves and green chillies finely. 3. Grind cumin, cinnamon and garlic. 4. Wash tomatoes. 5. Heat fat, sauté onions. Add ground spices and fry. Add chilli powder and chopped ingredients. 6. Add flour, stir well. Add hot water to form a thick sauce. Cover with the lid and bring to boil. 7. When it starts boiling add fish. 8. When fish is cooked add whole tomatoes and remove. 9. When the sauce cools add eggs beaten with vinegar and sugar. 10. Reheat but do not boil, to prevent curdling. Serve hot.

30. FISH BAMBLOE or BOMBAY DUCK

Ingredients	*For 4*	*For 100*
Bombay Duck (fresh)	500 gm	12.5 kg
Chilli powder	5 gm	115 gm
Turmeric	¼ tsp	20 gm
Cumin powder	½ tsp	40 gm
Salt	to taste	80-100 gm
Tamarind pulp	15 gm	225 gm
Vinegar	10 ml	250 ml
Oil	30 ml	500 ml

Method

1. Clean fish, open them. Centre bones may be removed or left on as desired. Wash thoroughly. 2. Keep between flat plates with weight on top to remove excess liquid. Dry on cloth. 3. Grind together spices with tamarind pulp, vinegar and salt. 4. Rub into the fish. Let it stand for one hour. 5. Shallow fry.

31. GRILLED FISH

All types of fish may be grilled. They are generally grilled with the bones on; if fish is large, gashes are made. Clean, wash and rub in a mixture of chilli powder, turmeric, pepper, garlic and salt ground together. Smear on fish; let it stand for 1 hour. Dot the fish with butter and grill. Serve with slices of lime.

32. SOUR FISH

Ingredients	*For 4*	*For 100*
Fish (pomfret, salmon, mullet etc.)	500 gm	12.5 kg
Curds	225 gm	5.65 kg
Lime juice	2	limes
Sugar	½ tsp	50 gm
Big cardamom powder	1 tsp	50 gm
Turmeric	½ tsp	50 gm
Onions (finely chopped)	115 gm	2.8 gm
Fat	50 gm	1.25 kg
Ginger (slice finely)	10 gm	250 gm
Coriander powder	5 gm	115 gm
Cumin powder	½ tsp	50 gm
Chilli powder	1 tsp	100 gm
Salt	to taste	80-100 gm

Method

1. Put all ingredients together and cook on a slow fire till fish is cooked.

33. TAMARIND FISH

Ingredients	*Quantity*
Pomfret or any other suitable fish	1.35 kg
Red chillies	55 gm
Turmeric	30 gm
Garlic	30 gm
Tamarind	450 gm
Cumin	15 gm
Ginger	115 gm
Vinegar	1.2 litre
Salt	to taste

Method

1. Clean and cut fish into slices. 2. Cover with plenty of salt and keep aside for 24 hours turning it over 3 or 4 times so that fish is well salted. 3. Cover tamarind with vinegar and let it soak for 5–6 hours. Let it marinate thoroughly and then squeeze all the pulp out of it. 4. Strain through a sieve. 5. Grind chillies, turmeric and cumin seeds into a thickish paste using vinegar. 6. Slice ginger and garlic. 7. Remove fish from brine and wipe each piece thoroughly dry. 8. Rub both sides of the fish with curry paste. 9. Into a wide mouthed jar, pour sufficient tamarind pulp to cover the bottom. 10. Scatter over it a few pieces of ginger and garlic. 11. Place a piece of fish on top of this. Scatter a little more ginger and garlic. Cover with tamarind pulp. 12. Repeat process

till all the fish is used up. 13. If any of the ingredients are left over, pack them well into the jar. 14. Add enough fresh vinegar to cover the lot. 15. Seal the jar and stand the jar in the sun daily for 2–3 weeks. Shake the jar as often as possible during this period. 16. Keep the jar well covered and fry desired quantity when required.

34. MEEN PADA (20 pieces)

Use Indian salmon (rawas) or a similar fish. Cut fish into 1.75 cm. by 2.5 cm. (approx 1" × ½") pieces after scaling. Do not wash. Rub over well with salt and set aside at room temperature for 3 days. After 3 days there will be an amount of liquid extracted. Wash fish in the same liquid and wipe dry with a clean, absorbent duster. Keep in the sun to dry for 2 days.

Ingredients		*Quantity*
Tamarind		size of an egg
Chilli powder	grind	6 tbsp
Turmeric	together in	1 tsp
Cumin	vinegar	1 heaped tbsp
Garlic		3 pods

Squeeze pulp and juice out of tamarind using vinegar

Method

1. Take pieces of fish and wash in weak vinegar. 2. Squeeze pulp and juice out of tamarind using vinegar. Add to the ground ingredients a tsp of salt and the tamarind juice. 3. Dip each piece of fish individually in this mixture and place in layers in an earthenware jar. Pour remaining spices on top. 4. Place 1 tbsp pepper and 1 tsp salt on the top. Close jar with a lid. Cover with plastic and set aside. It will be ready for use in a week. When needed take out pieces and fry.

N.B. Water should not be used at any time. If vinegar is very strong use a little less tamarind. If carefully preserved, this fish will last for over a year.

35. FISH TOMATO (Punjabi)

Ingredients	*For 4*	*For 100*
Fish	500 gm	12.5 kg
Tomatoes	500 gm	12.5 kg
Green chillies	3	85 gm
Onions	100 gm	2.5 kg
Ginger	5 gm	115 gm
Cumin	½ tsp	50 gm

Ingredients	*For 4*	*For 100*
Garlic	3 to 4 flakes	55 gm
Turmeric	½ tsp	50 gm
Chilli powder	1 tsp	100 gm
Salt	1 tsp	80-100 gm
Dry mango powder	1 tsp	100 gm
Garam masala	½ tsp	50 gm
Fat to fry		

Method

1. Scale and clean fish. Skin and bone. 2. Cut into 7.5 cm. × 3.75 cm. (3" × 1½") pieces. 3. Grind the spices, smear over fish and set aside. 4. Fry lightly. 5. Blanch and pulp tomatoes. 6. Put fish in a pan with tomatoes, whole green chillies and more salt if required. 7. Cook on a slow fire for about 15 to 20 minutes. The gravy should be very thick. Serve hot.

36. FISH WITH COCONUT (MEEN PEERA)

Ingredients	*For 4*	*For 100*
Small variety of fish	500 gm	12.5 kg
Coconut	1 (225 gm)	20 (5 kg)
Green chillies	30 gm	680 gm
Garlic	6 flakes	30 gm
Small red onions	10 gm	250 gm
Turmeric	¼ tsp	10 gm
Ginger	½ inch piece	50 gm
Cocum (kudampuli)	15-20 gm	300-340 gm
Curry leaves	1 sprig	1 bunch
Coconut oil	15 ml	250 ml

Method

1. Clean fish. Keep them whole if they are very small, if not cut into 1.25 cm. (½") pieces. 2. Grate coconut into fine pieces. 3. Grind together turmeric, a few onions and garlic. Mix with coconut on the stone itself. 4. Chop green chillies and ginger (ginger must be chopped fine) and slice remaining onions. 5. Soak cocum. 6. In a stainless steel pan, first put in the curry leaves and half the cocum broken into pieces. 7. Mix together coconut mixture, fish, remaining cocum and chopped and sliced ingredients. 8. Put into prepared pan. 9. Add water to three-fourth level of fish mixture. Add salt. 10. Bring to boil quickly. Reduce heat and simmer, till fish is cooked and moisture evaporated. 11. Pour fresh coconut oil over fish. Test for seasoning and remove. 12. Cool and cover. This can be kept for 2 days.

N.B. Prawns, cray fish and lobster can be prepared in the same way. Increase quantity of water as these require more cooking time.

37. MALAYALEE FISH CURRY (MEEN VEVICHATHU)

Ingredients	*For 4*	*For 100*
Large fish like pomfret, mullet, beckti, hilsa, salmon, etc.	500 gm	12.5 kg
Red chillies	20 gm	400-450 gm
Coriander	½ tsp	50 gm
Turmeric	a small piece or ¼ tsp powder	20 gm
Small red onions	4 bulbs	50 gm
Garlic	4 flakes	50 gm
Ginger	1.25 cm. (½") piece	50 gm
Curry leaves	2 sprigs	1 bunch
Cocum (kudampuli)	15-20 gm	300-340 gm
Salt	to taste	100-120 gm
Coconut oil	30 ml	500 ml

Method

1. Clean and cut fish into 2.5 cm. (1") slices or steaks. 2. Roast or dry heat red chillies, coriander and turmeric. 3. Powder fine and grind to a smooth paste with onions and garlic. 4. Soak cocum in a little water. 5. Chop ginger into fine pieces. 6. In a heavy bottomed stainless steel pan, first put in curry leaves and half the cocum broken into small pieces. 7. Mix together ground paste, fish and salt. 8. Arrange in the stainless steel pan with the remaining cocum pieces and chopped ginger. 9. Pour water to three-fourth level of fish. 10. Bring to boil on a quick fire and simmer till fish is tender. 11. Pour fresh coconut oil over and remove from fire. 12. Cool and cover. This can be kept for 2 days. If kept for longer period, reheat with a little water and a pinch of salt each day.

38. KANNAN AND MANGA

Ingredients	*For 4*
Snakeheaded fish or murral	500 gm
Red chillies	10 to 15
Turmeric	1 tsp
Coconut	½
Onions	200 gm
Garlic	10 cloves
Ginger	5 cm. (2") piece

Ingredients	*For 4*
Oil	30 ml
Salt	to taste
Raw mango	1
Vinegar	1 tbsp
Mustard seeds	1 tsp
Curry leaves	1 sprig

Method

1. Clean and slice fish. Chop and crush onions, garlic and ginger. Grind together to a fine paste, the chillies and turmeric. Peel and slice mango. 2. Grate coconut and extract milk (4 extractions). 3. Heat oil. Add mustard seeds and curry leaves. As seeds crackle, add crushed ingredients and sauté. Add ground spices and fry well. 4. Add the second, third and fourth extractions of coconut milk, salt vinegar and sliced mango. 5. Bring to boil. Add prepared fish. Simmer till fish is cooked and gravy is thick. 6. Add the first extract of coconut milk. Test for seasoning and remove.

39. FISH STEW (Malayalee)

Ingredients	*For 4*	*For 100*
Pomfret or other fish	500 gm	12.5 kg
Coriander	10 gm	250 gm
Cloves	6	5 gm
Oil	15 ml	250 ml
Ginger	10 gm	250 gm
Green chillies	20 gm	500 gm
Coconut	½ (115 gm)	10 (2.2 kg)
Vinegar	15 ml	375 ml
Salt	to taste	100 gm
Curry leaves	a few sprigs	3 bunches
To temper		
Red onion	5 gm	115 gm
Mustard seeds	a pinch	10 gm
Oil	15 ml	250 ml

Method

1. Clean and slice fish. 2. Lightly roast coriander and cloves and grind to a smooth paste. 3. Peel and slice ginger. Slit green chillies. Make three extractions of coconut milk (thick, medium, thin) 4. Heat oil. Lightly fry ground spices. Add third extraction of coconut milk, green chillies, ginger, fish salt, curry leaves and vinegar. 5. Cook till gravy is thick. Add second

extract of coconut milk. Simmer for 10 minutes. 6. Test for seasoning. Add first extract of coconut milk, remove and temper. 7. To temper, heat oil. Fry sliced onions; when nearly brown add mustard seeds. 8. When seeds crackle pour over fish. Serve hot or cold.

40. FISH STEW (White)

Ingredients	*For 4*	*For 100*
Salmon or pomfret	500 gm	12.5 kg
Onions	225 gm	5.6 kg
Green chillies	15 gm	340 gm
Ginger	10 gm	250 gm
Coconut	½	12
Tomatoes	115 gm	2.8 kg
Vinegar	15 ml	340 ml
Curry leaves	2 sprigs	1 bunch
Salt	to taste	80-100 gm
To temper		
Cloves	4	10 gm
Red onions	2 bulbs	10 gm
Oil	30 ml	500 ml

Method

1. Clean and cut fish into neat pieces. 2. Grate coconut and make three extractions of milk (thick, medium, thin). 3. Slice onions lengthwise. Slit green chillies, slice ginger. 4. In a pan arrange fish and onions, chillies and ginger and curry leaves in layers. 5. Add salt, quartered tomatoes, vinegar and third extraction of coconut milk. 6. Bring to boil and simmer. When liquid is nearly dry add second extraction of coconut milk. 7. Bring to boil and simmer for a few minutes. Check for salt. 8. Add first extraction of coconut milk and remove. 9. Heat oil. Add finely sliced onions and crushed cloves. 10. When they brown, pour over stew. Mix well.

41. FRIED FISH CURRY (Malabar)

Ingredients	*Quantity*
Pomfret or any other suitable fish like pearl spot (karimeen)	500 gm
Red chillies	5 gm
Salt	10 gm
Oil to fry	30 ml
Onions	225 gm
Green chillies	20 gm
Ginger	10 gm

Ingredients	*Quantity*
Curry leaves	2 sprigs
Coconut	1
Vinegar	15 ml
Tempering	
Oil	15 ml
Small red onion	1
Cloves	1
Mustard seeds	a pinch

Method

1. Clean and slice fish. Gash slices. 2. Grind together salt and red chillies. 3. Smear over fish. Set aside for half an hour. 4. Heat oil in a shallow fry pan. Fry fish. 5. Peel and slice onions and ginger and slit green chillies. 6. Grate coconut and make three extractions (thick, medium and thin). 7. In a pan put sliced onion, ginger, curry leaves and green chillies. Add third extraction of coconut milk and salt to taste. Cook till onions are tender. 8. Add fried fish, second extraction of coconut milk and vinegar. Simmer. 9. When gravy is thick add first extraction of coconut milk. Bring to boil and remove. 10. Heat oil for tempering. Add sliced onions, crushed cloves and mustard seeds. When seeds splutter pour over fish curry. Mix well.

42. BAKED FISH CURRY (Malayalee) (POLLICHA MEEN)

Ingredients	*For 4*	*For 100*
Mackerel or pomfret	500 gm	12.5 kg
Red chillies	5 gm	115 gm
Fennel	1 tsp	50 gm
Salt	to taste	100 gm
Water	15-30 ml	340-680 ml
Vinegar	30 ml	680 ml
Banana leaves		
Oil	15 ml	250 ml

Method

1. Clean fish. Keep mackerel whole but cut pomfret into large pieces. 2. Make gashes in the fish. 3. Grind together red chillies, fennel and salt. 4. Smear over fish. 5. Apply oil on banana leaves. Line a pan with these leaves. Place fish over. 6. Add vinegar, cover with banana leaves and put lid on. Put live coal on lid. Cook over gentle heat till fish is cooked.

N.B. This dish can also be prepared in the oven in a covered dish.

43. FISH CURRY (Maharashtra)

Ingredients	*For 4*	*For 100*
Fish	500 gm	12.5 kg
Red chillies (use Sankeshwari or Kashmiri chillies)	10 gm	250 gm
Green chillies	5 gm	100 gm
Onions	100 gm	2.5 kg
Coconut	½	12
Curry powder (Maharashtra)	10 gm	250 gm
Turmeric	2 gm	50 gm
Oil	15 ml	300 ml
Salt	to taste	100 gm
Cocum or tamarind	5 pieces	125 pieces
Coriander leaves	1 bunch	a few

Method

1. Clean fish and slice. 2. Gind red chillies, slice onions, slit green chillies. 3. Soak tamarind in water and squeeze out the pulp. Strain. 4. Grate the coconut. Prepare two extractions of the coconut milk—the first thick (about 1 cup), and the second thin (about 2 cups). 5. Heat oil. Sauté onions and slit green chillies. 6. Add ground chillies, curry powder, and turmeric mixed with a little water. Fry well till the oil floats on top. 7. Add the second extraction of coconut milk, cocum or tamarind juice, fish and salt to taste. 8. Simmer till the fish is done. 9. Add the first extraction of coconut milk. 10. Check for seasoning. 11. Bring to a boil. Add chopped coriander leaves and remove.

44. MALABAR FISH MOILEE

Ingredients	*Quantity*
Pomfret or	1
Rawas--Ind. Salmon, Karimeen (pearl spot)	500 gm
Oil	30 ml
Rice	50 gm
Garlic (peeled and roasted slightly)	2 cloves
Ginger	2" piece
Green chillies	3 to 5
Cumin	5 gm (1 level tsp)
Turmeric	1 tsp
Salt	to taste
Coconut	1

Ingredients	*Quantity*
Tomatoes (wash, quarter and deseed)	2
Red chillies (deseeded)	10

Method

1. Clean, wash and remove the slime on the skin of the fish with the blunt part of the knife or by scrubbing. Remove entrails. Wash thoroughly. 2. Apply the ground chilli mixed with a little turmeric, salt and vinegar or lime on the fish inside and out. Cut into large slices (darne) or debone and cut into chunky cubes. 3. Roast rice without browning. Grind together with roasted garlic, ginger, green chillies, cumin and turmeric. Mix in grated coconut. Add one cup of warm water. Extract the milk and set aside. Add two to three cups of water and prepare a second extract. 4. Heat oil in a moilly pan (chatty or heavy-bottomed stainless steel pan). Fry fish lightly, add the second extract and heat till it simmers. Add the fish and simmer till done. 5. Add the quartered tomatoes, one broken red chilly, curry leaves and vinegar or lime juice. Simmer for a minute or two. Check for seasoning and remove.

45. MALABAR FISH/PRAWN CURRY

Ingredients	*Quantity*
Pomfret or	1 kg
Prawns	32
Coconut	½
Whole red chillies (non pungent red variety)	10 gm
Coriander seeds	25 gm
Fenugreek	2 gm (a pinch)
Tamarind	size of a lemon
Cumin	2 gm (a pinch)
Onions (small shallots)	100 gm
Curry leaves	2 sprigs
Green chillies	2 to 4
Ginger	½" piece
Salt	to taste

Method

1. Clean fish thoroughly using the blunt edge of the knife to remove the slime. Remove entrails. Rinse in several rinses of cold water. Slice into curry thick slices. Marinade in salt and vinegar solution. If prawns are used shell, devein and wash thoroughly. 2. Grind together the grated coconut, coriander seeds, red chilli, dry roasted fenugreek and cumin and

40 gm of the onion to a fine paste. 3. Sieve the ground ingredients, adding a little water, through a fine sieve. 4. Soak tamarind, extract pulp and add to the ground and sieved ingredients. 5. In a strong bottom pan heat about 10 ml oil. Saute julienne of ginger, whole green chilli and curry leaves. Add the spice extraction. Allow to boil. Simmer for a few minutes (to remove the raw flavour). Add fish, and simmer for about 10 minutes. 6. To temper: Brown a few slices of the small onion (shallots). Add a sprig of curry leaves. When onions are brown pour over curry. Mix well.

46. FISH CURRY (Madras)

Ingredients	*For 4*	*For 100*
Pomfret or surmai or mullet	1 (500 gm)	12.5 kg
Red chillies (use Sankeshwari or Kashmiri chillies)	10 gm	250 gm
Coriander seeds	10 gm	250 gm
Turmeric	2 gm	50 gm
Oil	50 ml	500 ml
Coconut	½	12
Green chillies	4-6 gm	120 gm
Peppercorns	½ tsp	30 gm
Cumin seeds	1 gm	25 gm
Garlic	4-6 gm	120 gm
Onions	250 gm	6 kg
Tamarind	size of lemon	350 gm
Fenugreek seeds	5 gm	100 gm
Tomato	150 gm	100 gm
Salt	150 gm	3.75 kg
Curry leaves		

Method

1. Clean and slice the fish. 2. Grate coconut. Set aside 1 tbsp for grinding and prepare two extractions of coconut milk with the remaining—the first thick (1 cup) and the second thin (2 cups). 3. Grind red chillies, coriander and turmeric to a fine paste. 4. Grind coconut separately and one onion. Slice the remaining onions. 5. Grind together garlic, peppercorns and cumin seeds. 6. Soak tamarind in 1 cup of water. Squeeze out pulp, strain. 7. Chop tomato. 8. Heat oil. Add fenugreek, curry leaves, sliced onions. Sauté. Add the first lot of ground ingredients. Fry well. 9. Add ground coconut, onion, garlic, peppercorns and cumin seeds. Sauté. 10. Add second extraction of coconut milk, tamarind juice and salt. Bring to a boil. 11. Add fish. Simmer till the fish is done.

12. Add first extract of coconut milk. Test for seasoning. Bring to boil and remove.

47. FISH VINDALOO (East Indian)

Ingredients	*Quantity*
Pomfret or surmai or ghol fish	1
Red chillies (use Sankeshwari or Kashmiri chillies)	
Cumin seeds	2 gm
Garlic	20 gm
Ginger (optional)	10 gm
Turmeric	2 gm
Salt	to taste
Vinegar	8 ml (1 tbsp)
Oil for frying fish and for curry	30 ml

Method

1. Clean, wash and slice the fish. 2. Grind to a fine paste the chillies, cumin seed, garlic, turmeric and ginger, if used. 3. Smear on the fish and keep aside for 5–10 minutes. 4. Heat oil. Fry fish lightly on both sides. Remove. 5. In a pan, heat the remaining oil. Fry the remaining spices. 6. Add about 2 cups of water (to form a thick gravy). Bring to a boil. 7. Add fish, salt and vinegar. 8. Simmer till the fish is done. Taste and remove.

48. GUISADO

Ingredients	*For 4*	*For 100*
Clams, prawns or oysters	500 gm	12.5 kg
Garlic	10 gm	250 gm
Onions	150 gm	3.75 kg
Tomatoes	250 gm (2)	6.25 kg
Oil	50 ml	1 litre
Turmeric	1 gm	20 gm
Pepper powder	2 gm	50 gm
Vinegar	30 ml	750 ml
Water	240 ml	6 litre
Salt	to taste	100 gm

Method

1. Clean fish. Wash well. 2. Finely chop onions and garlic. Heat oil and fry. 3. Add chopped tomatoes and fry for another 5–10 minutes. 4. Add

shell fish. 5. Close lid and cook for 10 minutes. 6. Add water, turmeric, black pepper, vinegar and salt. 7. Cover and cook for a further 15 minutes.

49. PRAWN CURRY

Ingredients	*For 4*	*For 100*
Prawns	500 gm	12.5 kg
Red chillies	5 gm	115 gm
Peppercorns	a few	30 gm
Mustard seeds	1 tsp	30 gm
Cumin	1 tsp	30 gm
Tamarind	10 gm	225 gm
Coriander	15 gm	340 gm
Onions	55 gm	1.35 kg
Garlic	6 flakes	30 gm
Coconut	1	8
Salt	to taste	100 gm
Curry leaves	1 sprig	1 bunch
Oil	15 ml	250 ml

Method

1. Shell prawns, remove intestines by slitting back of the prawns. Wash well. 2. Grind spices with coconut. 3. Heat oil. Fry curry leaves. Add spices, and fry well. Add salt, tamarind pulp and water. 4. When liquid starts to simmer, add prawns. 5. Continue simmering till done.

50. PRAWN AND TOMATO CURRY

Ingredients	*For 4*	*For 100*
Prawns	500 gm	12.5 kg
Garlic	a few flakes	30 gm
Onions	115 gm	2.75 kg
Ginger	10 gm	225 gm
Chilli powder	5 gm	115 gm
Coriander powder	15 gm	340 gm
Tomato	115 gm	2.75 kg
Coconut	½	12
Curry leaves	1 sprig	1 bunch
Green chillies	5 gm	115 gm
Vinegar	5 ml	100 ml
Salt	10 gm	100 gm
Oil	15 ml	250 ml

Method

1. Shell prawns and remove intestines, wash well. 2. Rub some salt on prawns. Keep aside. 3. Grind garlic, ginger, and green chillies. 4. Heat oil, fry chopped onions, ground garlic and ginger, chilli powder, coriander powder and curry leaves. 5. Add prawns and chopped tomatoes, cook on a slow fire. 6. Grate coconut and extract milk (thick). 7. When prawns are cooked, add vinegar and coconut milk. Bring to boil and remove. 8. Serve hot with rice.

51. MALAI PRAWN CURRY

Ingredients		*For 4*	*For 100*
Prawns		500 gm	12.5 kg
Onions		115 gm	2.8 kg
Ginger		a small piece	100 gm
Turmeric		¼ tsp	20 gm
Cardamom	roast and powder		
Cloves	roast and powder	1 tsp	100 gm
Cinnamon	roast and powder		
Sugar		1 tsp	100 gm
Coconut		½	12
Black treacle		1 tbsp	225 ml
Salt		a pinch	100 gm
Oil		50 ml	1.25 litre

Method

1. Shell prawns. Remove intestines and wash well. 2. Season and fry prawns, set aside. 3. Grind together half the onions and ginger to a fine paste. Slice the remaining onions. 4. Grate coconut and extract coconut milk. 5. Roast and powder garam masala. 6. Heat oil, fry the sliced onions. Add ground ingredients and turmeric and fry. Add garam masala, coconut milk, salt, sugar, treacle and prawns. Cook till prawns are done.

52. PRAWN VINDALOO

Ingredients	*For 4*	*For 100*
Prawns	500 gm	12.5 kg
Potatoes	225 gm	5.65 kg
Tomatoes	225 gm	5.65 kg
Cumin	5 gm	115 gm
Mustard seeds	5 gm	115 gm
Garlic	a few flakes	30 gm
Ginger	a small piece	55 gm
Red chillies	5 gm	115 gm

Ingredients	For 4	For 100
Turmeric	a pinch	15 gm
Onions	115 gm	2.8 kg
Vinegar	30 ml	590 ml
Salt	to taste	100 gm
Oil	30 ml	500 ml

Method

1. Shell prawns. Remove intestines and wash in several rinses of water. Boil potatoes, peel and quarter. 2. Grind spices using vinegar. Smear over prawns and keep aside for 1–2 hours. 3. Heat oil. Fry sliced onions. Remove. 4. Fry prawns. Add remaining vinegar and cook on gentle heat. 5. When half cooked, add chopped tomatoes, fried onions and potatoes. Cook gently adding salt and a little water if necessary. 6. Remove when prawns and vegetables are tender.

53. PRAWNS in GARLIC CHILLI SAUCE

Ingredients	For 6
Prawns	500 gm
Turmeric	¼ tsp
Garlic	5 flakes
Ginger	1.25 cm.
Cumin	1½ tsp
Red chillies	7 to 8
Tomatoes	250 gm
Vinegar	50 ml
Oil	1 tbsp
Salt	to taste

Method

1. Clean prawns. 2. Grind spices using vinegar. Heat oil. Fry spices. Add prawns and blanched tomatoes and salt. 4. Bring to boil. Simmer till done. 5. Add vinegar as desired before removing.

54. PRAWN DO-PYAZ

Ingredients	For 4	For 100
Prawns	500 gm	12.5 kg
Fat	50 gm	1.25 kg
Onions	225 gm	5.6 kg
Turmeric	½ tsp	50 gm
Red chilli powder	1 tsp	100 gm
Ginger	5 gm	115 gm

Ingredients	*For 4*	*For 100*
Garlic	6 cloves	50 gm
Green chillies	10 gm	250 gm
Lime	1	10-12
Coriander leaves	a few	1 bunch
Coconut	½	12
Salt	to taste	100 gm

Method

1. Shell prawns. Remove intestines. Wash thoroughly. 2. Slice half the onions finely. 3. Grind remaining onions with turmeric, chilli powder, garlic and ginger to a smooth paste. 4. Heat fat. Fry sliced onions till crisp and brown. Remove and drain. 5. In the same fat fry ground spices. 6. Add prawns and salt. Fry for a few minutes. 7. Add a little water. Cover and simmer for 20 minutes. 8. Grate coconut and extract thick milk. Add coconut milk and fried onions to prawn mixture. 9. When prawns are nearly cooked add green chillies slit lengthwise and juice of lime. 10. Serve hot garnished with coriander leaves.

55. PRAWN COCONUT CURRY (KONJU VEVICHATHU)

Ingredients	*For 4*	*For 100*
Large variety prawns or crayfish	500 gm	12.5 kg
Red chillies	15 to 20 gm	300 to 400 gm
Coriander	1 tsp	50 gm
Turmeric	a small piece or ¼ tsp powder	20 gm
Pepper	1 tsp	100 gm
Small red onions	4	50 gm
Garlic	4 flakes	50 gm
Ginger	1.25 cm. (½") piece	100 gm
Curry leaves	2 sprigs	1 bunch
Cocum	15-20 gm	300-340 gm
Coconut	½	12
Salt	to taste	100-120 gm
Coconut oil (fresh)	30 ml	500 ml

Method

1. Shell prawns. Remove intestines, wash thoroughly several times in cold water. 2. Roast or dry heat red chillies, coriander and turmeric. 3. Powder fine and grind to a smooth paste with onion, garlic and pepper. 4. Chop ginger into fine pieces. 5. Soak cocum in water. 6. Slice coconut

into thin quarter inch pieces. 7. In a stainless steel pan put in the curry leaves and half the cocum. 8. Mix together the ground paste, ginger, salt, remaining cocum, coconut and prawns. 9. Put into the stainless steel pan. Pour water to be in level with rest of ingredients. 10. Put on fire and bring to boil quickly. Reduce fire and simmer till prawns are cooked. 11. Test for salt. Pour fresh coconut oil on top and remove from fire. 12. Cool and cover. This can be kept for 2 days.

56. GOAN PRAWN (or fish) CURRY WITH MANGOES

Ingredients	*For 4*	*For 100*
Prawns	400 gm	10 kg
Red chillies	10 gm	250 gm
Coriander	10 gm	250 gm
Turmeric	¼ tsp	20 gm
Garlic	4 flakes	50 gm
Cumin	¼ tsp	20 gm
Grated coconut	½	12
Ginger	0.5 cm. (¼") piece	50 gm
Green chillies	2	50 gm
Raw mango slices	80 gm	1 kg
	(1 mango medium size)	(25 mangoes)
Onions	25 gm	725 gm
Coconut oil	30 ml	500 ml
Salt	to taste	100 gm

Method

1. Shell prawns. Remove intestines. Wash well. Apply salt and set aside. 2. Grind together red chillies, coriander, turmeric, garlic, cumin, ginger and coconut to a fine paste. 3. Slice onion. Heat oil and fry. 4. Add spices and fry. 5. Add water, slit green chillies and mango. Cook for five minutes and then add prawns. 6. Cook till prawns are done.

57. PRAWN CALDEEN (A)

Ingredients	*For 4*	*For 100*
Prawns	2 kg	10 kg
Ladies fingers	500 gm	2.5 kg
Coconuts	2	10
Ginger	2.5 cm. (1") piece	50 gm
Green chillies	30 gm	150 gm
Turmeric	½ tsp	10 gm
Garlic	10 flakes	25 gm
Onions	250 gm	1.25 kg

Ingredients	*For 4*	*For 100*
Tamarind	50 gm	250 gm
Lime	½	2-3
Coconut oil	150 ml	500 ml
Salt	to taste	100 gm

Method

1. Shell the prawns. Remove intestines. Wash well with salt and lime. 2. Slit green chillies. Slice ginger, garlic and onions. 3. Grate and grind coconut to a fine paste. 4. Heat oil. Add sliced onions and sauté without discolouration. 5. Add coconut, sliced garlic, ginger, green chillies and turmeric. 6. Add prawns and enough water to cook prawns. Cook on a slow fire. 7. Wipe ladies fingers with a damp cloth and cut into 5 cm. (2") pieces. 8. When prawns are half cooked, add tamarind juice and ladies fingers. Simmer till done.

N.B. If desired ladies fingers can be fried in a little oil before adding.

PRAWN CALDEEN (B)

Ingredients	*For 12*
Prawns	1 kg
Ladies finger (cut into 5 cm. (2") pieces) or	250 gm
Capsicums	4
Onions (sliced)	2 (200 gm)
Green chillies (slit)	2
Coconut oil	2 tbsp (25 ml)
Tamarind (size of a lime, soaked in a little water)	10 gm
Spices for grinding	
Coriander seeds	1 tbsp (8 gm)
Cumin	½ tsp (2 gm)
Peppercorns	12 (2 gm)
Garlic	2 flakes (1 gm)
Kashmiri red chilies	3 (3 gm)
Turmeric	½ tsp (2 gm)
Coconut (grated)	½

Method

1. Shell prawns. Remove intestines and wash well. 2. Heat oil. Add sliced onions and fry. 3. Add prawns and sauté till nearly dry. Grind spices with half the grated coconut. 4. Add finely ground spices and fry for a

few minutes longer. 5. Add about 500 ml of water and strained juice of tamarind. Bring to boil. 6. Add ladies fingers and cook till done, or cut capsicums into quarters. Remove seeds, wash well and add. Just before removing from the fire add slit green chillies and half a cup of thick coconut milk extracted from the remaining grated coconut. 7. Test for seasoning and remove.

58. PRAWN TEMPERADO

Ingredients	*For 10*
Large prawns	1 kg
Coconut	½ (extract milk twice)
Brinjal	200 gm
Pumpkin	200 gm
Garam masala	1 tsp
Salt	to taste
Oil	50 ml
Onions	2
Green chillies	12
Ginger	12.5 cm. (1") piece
Garlic	10 cloves
Coriander leaves	5 sprigs
Coriander seeds	2 tbsp
Turmeric	a pinch
Cumin	½ tsp

Slice onions, 6 green chillies, ginger and 4 cloves and garlic. Grind to a smooth paste with water, cumin, coriander seeds, turmeric, 6 cloves garlic, 6 green chillies, and coriander leaves.

Method

1. Shell, de-vein and wash prawns in several rinses of cold water. 2. Heat oil. Add sliced onions and sauté. Add remaining sliced spices. 3. Fry well. Add prawns and fry. When prawns change colour, add ground spices and the water used for grinding. Cook till oil floats on top. 4. Add cut brinjal and pumpkin. Add seoond extract. 5. Now add the first extract of coconut milk and garam masala powder. Bring to a boil and remove.

59. MASALA PRAWNS

Ingredients	*For 10*
Prawns	1 kg
Red chillies	8 to 10
Garlic	½ pod

Ingredients	*For 10*
Cumin	¼ tsp
Salt	to taste
Vinegar	2 tbsp
Onions	1 kg
Oil	50 ml

Method

1. Shell prawns, de-vein. 2. Wash well. 3. Grind to a fine paste, chillies, garlic, cumin and salt, using vinegar. 4. Apply well on prawns. Set aside for half an hour. 5. Heat oil. Lightly fry chopped onions. 6. Add prawns. Fry for 5 minutes. 7. Cover and cook over a slow fire in its own gravy till done. 8. Remove and serve hot.

60. PRAWN FRY

Ingredients	*For 4*	*For 100*
Prawns	500 gm	12.5 kg
Tomatoes	200 gm	5 kg
Chilli powder	1 tsp (2 gm)	50 gm
Turmeric	½ tsp	20 gm
Onions	100 gm	2.5 kg
Ginger	2.5 cm (1") piece	150 gm
Garlic	8 flakes	15 gm
Fennel	½ tsp	15 gm
Curry leaves	a few	1 bunch
Salt	to taste	100 gm
Fat	30 gm	750 gm

Method

1. Shell, de-vein and wash prawns and boil adding chilli powder, turmeric and salt in just enough water, to cook. 2. Blanch tomatoes, remove skin and slice. 3. Grind garlic and ginger into a smooth paste. 4. Chop onions. Powder fennel. 5. Heat fat, add fennel, onions, ground ginger and garlic and curry leaves. Fry till onions are slightly browned and a good aroma emanates. 6. Add the tomatoes and fry for a minute. 7. Add prawns and fry till quite dry.

61. LOBSTER CURRY (A)

Ingredients	*For 4*	*For 100*
Lobsters (average sized)	4 (225 gm)	100 (5.65 kg)
Onions	55 gm	1.35 kg

Ingredients	For 4	For 100
Fat	30 gm	500 gm
Garlic	a few flakes	50 gm
Ginger	1 piece	55 gm
Green chillies	6	85 gm
Spices for grinding		
Vinegar	30 ml	500 ml
Salt	to taste	80-100 gm
Masala		
Cumin	½ tsp	50 gm
Turmeric	¼ tsp	20 gm
Red chillies	3	85 gm
Cloves	3	10 gm
Peppercorns	4	10 gm
Cinnamon	a small piece	10 gm
Large cardamom	2	10 gm

Method

1. Boil live lobsters. 2. Remove the meat from tail, claws and body. 3. Chop onion, garlic, green chillies and ginger. 4. Grind remaining spices. 5. Heat fat. Fry chopped ingredients. 6. Add lobsters and ground spices. Continue frying for 2 or 3 minutes longer. 7. Add vinegar, water, salt, and let it simmer till cooked.

LOBSTER CURRY (B)

Ingredients	For 4	For 100
Lobsters	4 (225 gm)	100 (5.65 kg)
Oil	30 ml	500 ml
Onions	115 gm	2.8 kg
Coriander } roast	5 gm	115 gm
Cumin } roast	½ tsp	50 gm
Turmeric } roast	¼ tsp	20 gm
Cloves	4	10 gm
Chilli powder	1 tsp	100 gm
Ginger	2.5 cm. (1") piece	100 gm
Tomatoes	225 gm	2.8 kg
Tamarind	5 gm	115 gm
Salt	to taste	80–100 gm

Method

1. Boil live lobsters. Remove meat. 2. Chop onions. 3. Roast spices and grind with ginger. 4. Soak tamarind and extract juice. 5. Heat oil. Fry chopped onions. Add ground spices. 6. Add lobsters. Fry for a little longer. Add enough water to make the gravy and add salt. 7. Add blanched, chopped tomatoes and let it cook. 8. When about to remove, add tamarind juice. Test for seasoning and remove.

62. LOBSTER MASALA

Ingredients	*For 4–6*
Lobsters (large) or	2
Lobster meat	500 gm
Red chillies	10 gm
Garlic	10 gm
Ginger	10 gm
Cumin	1 tsp
Mustard seeds	1 tsp
Turmeric	a large pinch
Tomatoes	250 gm
Bay leaf (for flavour)	1
Cloves	2
Cardamom	2
Peppercorns	5
Onions	150 gm
Oil	50 ml
Salt	to taste

Method

1. Grind together red chillies, garlic, ginger, cumin, mustard seeds, turmeric, peppercorns cloves, cardamom and onions. 2. Heat the oil, add bay leaf and fry ground spices till oil floats on top. 3. Then put in lobster meat and chopped tomatoes. Add salt; cook slowly without water till done. If necessary, sprinkle a little water.

63. CRAB CURRY (A)

Ingredients	*For 4*	*For 100*
Crabs	455 gm (4)	11.3 kg (100)
Tomatoes	115 gm	2.8 kg
Coconut	115 gm	2.8 kg

Ingredients	*For 4*	*For 100*
Oil	30 ml	500 gm
Tamarind	10 gm	225 gm
Salt	to taste	100 gm
Kashmiri chillies	10 gm	225 gm
Coriander	10 gm	225 gm
Turmeric	a pinch	20 gm
Garlic	a few flakes	55 gm
Cumin	a pinch	20 gm
Ginger	5 gm	115 gm
Onions	225 gm	5.65 kg
Cinnamon	a small piece	15 gm
Spices for grinding		

Method

1. Wash crabs, pull the top shell from the body. 2. Discard the stomach bag attached to the shell below the eyes. 3. Discard greyish white "dead man's fingers" and wash well. 4. Cut each crab into 4 pieces. 5. Wash crab well. 6. Grind spices with coconut into a fine paste. 7. Heat oil and fry spices well. 8. Add crabs and fry. 9. Add chopped tomatoes and salt and cook on a slow fire. 10. When crab is cooked, add tamarind water (soak tamarind in a little water and squeeze pulp) and cook for 20 minutes.

CRAB CURRY (B)

Ingredients	*Quantity*
Crabs	500 gm
Onions	200 gm
Coconut	½
Garlic	1 pod
Green chillies	5-6
Coriander leaves	½ bunch
Ginger	10 gm
Curry leaves	1 sprig
Mustard seeds	a pinch
Oil	50 ml
Salt	to taste

Method

1. Wash crabs, pull the top shell from the body. 2. Discard the stomach bag attached to the shell below the eyes. 3. Discard greyish white "dead

man's fingers" and wash well. 4. Cut each crab into 4 pieces. Wash crabs well. 5. Grind together grated coconut, garlic, green chillies, coriander leaves and ginger. 6. Heat oil. Add mustard seeds, chopped onions and curry leaves. 7. When lightly fried, add ground spices. 8. Add salt. Mix well with the crab and set aside for half an hour. 9. Add the liquid from the grinding stone or very little water and cook over slow fire till crab is done and almost dry.

N.B. Chopped coriander leaves or a dash of lime juice may be added if desired when cooking crabs.

64. CRAB PULAO

Prepare curry as above using coconut milk from ½ grated coconut instead of water. Add sliced ginger and 2 or 3 slit green chillies. Boil rice till three-fourths done. Layer curry and rice in a pan. Sprinkle over with melted fat and a little milk. Bake, covered tightly, for 10 to 15 minutes and serve hot with sweet chutney.

65. OYSTER LONEVAS

Ingredients	*For 4*
Oysters	2 cups
Coconut	½
Curry powder	2 tbsp
Potatoes (boiled)	500 gm
Onions	200 gm
Tamarind pulp	¼ cup
Garam masala (cardamom, cloves, cinnamon)	1 tsp
Oil	

Method

1. Put the oysters into clean, fresh water. Remove beard and open shell. Drain the liquid inside the shell and set aside. 2. Grate coconut and make 2 extractions (½ cup thick and ½ cup thin milk). 3. Peel and quarter potatoes. Slice onions. Heat about 1½ tbsp oil. Fry onions till soft and light brown. Add curry powder. Fry for a few minutes. 4. Add a little of the oyster liquid and stir well. Add oysters and stir gently. Keep covered for 5 minutes. Add thin coconut milk and bring to a boil. Add the potatoes and the thick coconut milk, tamarind pulp and garam masala powder. 5. Simmer till the gravy is thick and oil floats on top.

MEAT

1. Mutton and Potato Curry
2. Mutton Indad
3. Mutton Vindaloo
4. Mutton Baffat
5. Malabar Mutton Curry
6. Mutton Khorma
7. Dum Pukhta (Kashmiri)
8. Mangsher Gota Maslar Curry
9. Nilgiri Khorma
10. Green Curry (meat, chicken or liver)
11. Shahi Khorma
12. Moghlai Khorma
13. Mutton Shahjahani
14. Dum ke Pasande
15. Mutton with Cauliflower
16. Mutton with Turnips
17. Mutton Papdi
18. Mutton Bhopla
19. Mutton Palak
20. Mutton with Mixed Bhaji
21. Chola-Ma-Gosht
22. Green Cow Peas with Mutton
23. Country Captain
24. Tomato Gosht
25. Hussainy Curry
26. Bamya Khuta
27. Chatani
28. Mulligatawny Curry
29. Mutton Curry
30. Mutton Curry (Mild)
31. Kolhapuri Mutton Curry
32. Rogan Josh
33. Mutton Do Pyaz
34. Mutton Do Pyaz with Lentils
35. Elaichi Mutton
36. Bhugal Gosht
37. Sel Gosht
38. Safed Mas
39. Mutton Chilli Fry
40. Meat Chilli Fry
41. Mutton and Potato Chips
42. Meat and Coconut Fry (Iraichi ulathiyathu)
43. Mutton Jhal Faraizi
44. Pal Porial (A)
    Pal Porial (B)
45. Masala Mutton Chops
46. Fried Meat
47. Musallum Raan
48. Lamb on the Bone
49. Mutton Kofta Curry
50. Ball Curry (Malabar)
51. Mince Balls
52. Nargisi Kofta Curry
53. Pork Kofta Curry
54. Hyderabadi Kheema
55. Kheema
56. Green Mince
57. Mutton and Carrot Kheema
58. Dal Kheema
59. Haleem
60. Rajmah Meat Curry
61. Mutton Cutlets
62. Seekh Kababs
63. Kabab Jeera
64. Kababs Broiled and Skewered
65. Steamed Kababs
66. Shami Kababs
67. Hussainy Kababs
68. Hamburger (Indian)
69. Liver Kababs
70. Boti Kababs
71. Reshmi Kababs
72. Shifta (Mutton, beef or fish)
73. Pork Curry
74. Pork Vindaloo
75. Sorpotel
76. Grilled Spare Ribs
77. Pork Kababs
78. Pork chops in Chilli Sauce

79. Goan Roast Suckling Pig
80. Alu Muckala (Chicken or mutton)
81. Murgh Do Pyaz
82. Murgh Musallam
83. Murgh Musallam (Stuffed)
84. Tomato Murgi
85. Rogini chicken
86. Chicken Curry (A)
    Chicken Curry (B)
    Chicken Curry (C)
87. Goan Chicken Curry
88. Chicken Moilee
89. Chicken Chacouti
90. Chicken Caldeen
91. Chicken Curry Malabar
92. Iraichi Mulugu
93. Chicken Khorma
94. Chicken Baffat
95. Chicken Mulligatawny Curry (Mild)
96. Chicken Chaat
97. Chicken Stew
98. Chicken Sauté—Indian style
99. Fried Chicken (A)
    Fried Chicken (B)
100. Devilled Chicken
101. Chicken Temperado
102. Chicken Pepper Fry
103. Methi Murg
104. Murg Adraki
105. Chicken Curry Mendes
106. Chicken Masala
107. Chicken Nawabi
108. Chicken Fry Coorg
109. Tandoori Chicken
110. Chicken Cafreal
111. Buttered Tandoori Chicken (Chicken makhanwalla)
112. Duck Buffado
113. Duck Mappas
114. Duck Fry
115. Duck Roast
116. Liver Curry
117. Liver and Potato Curry
118. Masala Trotters (Paya)

1. MUTTON AND POTATO CURRY

Ingredients	*For 4*	*For 100*
Mutton	500 gm	12.5 kg
Potatoes	225 gm	5.6 kg
Coriander powder	30 gm	680 gm
Garlic	4 flakes	50 gm
Green chillies	5 gm	115 gm
Onions	115 gm	2.8 kg
Turmeric	4 tsp	50 gm
Chilli powder	10 gm	225 gm
Ginger	1 piece	55 gm
Tamarind/vinegar	a little	225 gm
Fat	30 gm	500 gm
Salt	to taste	100 gm

Method

1. Wash and cut up the meat. 2. Wash, peel and cut the potatoes. 3. Slice onions, peel and slice half the garlic and ginger. 4. Soak tamarind. 5. Grind remaining half of garlic and ginger. 6. Heat fat. Fry onions,

sliced garlic, ginger and whole chillies. 7. Add turmeric, coriander powder and chilli powder. Fry well, sprinkling water from time to time. 8. When well fried add the ground ginger and garlic, meat and fry for 5 minutes. 9. Add potatoes and salt with warm water. 10. Cook gently till meat is tender. 11. Add tamarind water, bring to boil and remove from fire.

2. MUTTON INDAD

Ingredients	*For 4*	*For 100*
Mutton	500 gm	12.5 kg
Cloves	4	10 gm
Cinnamon	a small piece	10 gm
Cumin	a pinch	20 gm
Green chillies	5 gm	115 gm
Ginger	a small piece	5 gm
Vinegar	30 ml	400 ml
Red chillies (without seeds)	5 gm	115 gm
Turmeric	a pinch	20 gm
Garlic	3 flakes	30 gm
Potatoes	115 gm	2.8 kg
Fat	30 gm	500 gm
Salt	to taste	100 gm
Onions	115 gm	2.8 kg
Stock		
Sugar (optional)	to taste	100 gm

Method

1. Clean and cut meat. 2. Boil with cinnamon, cloves and salt till tender. 3. Grind together ginger, turmeric, red chillies, garlic and cumin, using vinegar. 4. Grind onions coarsely. 5. Heat fat. Sauté onions, spices and meat. Fry well. 6. When meat is well browned add stock, vinegar and salt to taste. 7. Add potatoes peeled and cut into quarters and slit green chillies. 8. Cook till potatoes are soft. Serve hot.

3. MUTTON VINDALOO

Ingredients	*For 4*	*For 100*
Mutton	500 gm	12.5 kg
Potatoes	225 gm	5.6 kg
Tomatoes	115 gm	2.8 kg
Cumin	a pinch	20 gm
Cinnamon	a small piece	50 gm
Red chillies	5 gm	115 gm
Mustard seeds	a pinch	50 gm
Garlic	a few flakes	50 gm

Ingredients	*For 4*	*For 100*
Ginger	a small piece	50 gm
Onion	30 gm	1.35 kg
Salt	to taste	100 gm
Vinegar	30 ml	600 ml
Fat	30 gm	500 gm

Method

1. Clean and cut meat. 2. Grind spices using vinegar. 3. Smear spices on meat and set aside for 2 to 3 hours. 4. Heat fat. Fry meat. 5. Add remaining vinegar and more water if required. 6. When three-fourths done, add potatoes peeled and cut into quarters and blanched chopped tomatoes. Add salt. 7. Remove when meat and vegetables are tender.

4. MUTTON BAFFAT

Ingredients	*For 4*	*For 100*
Mutton	500 gm	12.5 kg
Radish	150 gm	3.65 kg
Lime	¼	6
Split bengal gram	5 gm	115 gm
Ginger	a small piece	55 gm
Garlic	a few flakes	50 gm
Cloves	2	10 gm
Cinnamon	a small piece	10 gm
Pepper	a few	10 gm
Turmeric	a pinch	20 gm
Groundnuts	5 gm	115 gm
Poppy seeds	5 gm	115 gm
Green chillies	2	50 gm
Red chillies	5 gm	115 gm
Coconut	½	2.5 kg (10)
Onions	55 gm	1.35 kg
Fat	15 gm	250 gm
Salt	to taste	80-100 gm
Vinegar	15 ml	300 ml

Method

1. Clean and cut meat into 2.5 cm. (½″) pieces. 2. Boil radish in lime water till tender. 3. Grind together turmeric, red chillies, ginger, garlic, poppy seeds, gram, groundnut, cinnamon, cloves and pepper using a little vinegar. 4. Make 2 extractions of coconut-milk, the first one thick and the second medium. 5. Heat fat. Add sliced onion and brown. 6. Add green chillies (whole), spices and meat and second extract of coconut milk, vinegar and salt. 7. Cook till meat is tender. Add cooked radish

and first extract of coconut milk. 8. Temper with a few slices of onion fried in fat, and serve hot.

5. MALABAR MUTTON CURRY

Ingredients		*For 4*	*For 100*
Mutton		500 gm	12.5 kg
Potatoes		225 gm	5.6 kg
Green chillies		5 gm	115 gm
Ginger		a small piece	55 gm
Coconut		1	20
Coriander		15 gm	340 gm
Onion		55 gm	1.35 kg
Red chillies		10 gm	225 gm
Turmeric		a pinch	10 gm
Garlic		a few flakes	30 gm
Vinegar		15 ml	340 ml
Fat		15 gm	250 gm
Cinnamon	garam masala	a piece	50 gm
Cloves	garam masala	a few	50 gm
Cardamoms	garam masala	a few	50 gm
Curry leaves		1 sprig	1 bunch
Mustard seeds		1 tsp	10 gm
Salt		to taste	100 gm

Method

1. Clean and cut meat. Peel and cut potatoes. 2. Slice ginger and half the onion; slit green chillies. 3. Roast and grind coriander, red chillies, turmeric and garlic. 4. Grate coconut and make 3 extractions of coconut milk. The first extract must be thick, the second medium and third thin. 5. Heat some fat. Fry the ground spices lightly. 6. Add meat and the 3rd extract of coconut milk and simmer gently. 7. When half cooked, add 2nd extract of coconut milk, green chillies, ginger, sliced onion and potatoes; continue to simmer. 8. When meat is tender add vinegar, first extract of coconut milk and salt. Bring to boil. Remove and temper. 9. Heat a little fat and add a few pieces of chopped onions. When onions are browned, add mustard seeds, curry leaves and crushed garam masala. When seeds crackle pour into curry. Mix well and serve hot.

6. MUTTON KHORMA

Ingredients	*For 4*	*For 100*
Mutton	500 gm	12.5 kg
Dry coconut	30 gm	455 gm
Onions	115 gm	2.8 kg

Ingredients	*For 4*	*For 100*
Ginger	5 gm	115 gm
Garlic	a few flakes	50 gm
Red chillies	5 gm	115 gm
Curds	115 gm	2.8 kg
Coriander powder	15 gm	340 gm
Poppy seeds	10 gm	225 gm
Green chillies	2	30 gm
Cinnamon	2 gm	50 gm
Cloves	2 gm	50 gm
Peppercorns	2 gm	50 gm
Cardamoms	2 gm	50 gm
Fat	50 gm	1.25 kg
Salt	to taste	150 gm

Method

1. Wash and cut meat. 2. Soak in curds for half an hour. 3. Grind together poppy seeds, dry coconut, garlic, ginger, coriander powder, red chillies (seeds removed), green chillies and half the onions. 4. Heat fat, fry remaining sliced onions. 5. Add ground spices and meat. Fry for about 15 minutes. 6. Add remaining curds and tepid water and cook till meat is tender. 7. Add roasted and powdered cinnamon, cloves, peppercorns and cardamoms. 8. Cook for 5 to 10 minutes more and serve hot.

7. DUM PUKHTA (Kashmiri)

Ingredients	*For 4*	*For 100*
Mutton or chicken	500 gm	12.5 kg
Curds	115 gm	5.6 kg
Cloves	5	50 gm
Black cardamoms	7	50 gm
Peppercorns	15	100 gm
Butter	115 gm	2.8 kg
Saffron	a pinch	20 gm
Chilli powder	1 tsp	100 gm
Bay leaf	a few	3 to 5 gm
Raisins	10	50 gm
Almonds or cashewnuts	15	340 gm
Salt	to taste	100 gm
Flour	enough to seal the vessel	

Method

1. Blanch almonds. Slice. 2. Grind together cloves, cardamoms and peppercorns. 3. Clean and cut meat into even pieces or joint chicken.

4. Soak meat and ground spices in curds. 5. Melt butter. Add the marinaded meat and curds and remaining ingredients. 6. Seal the vessel with dough. (The dough should be quite hard.) 7. Cook until dough starts to crack. (About 45 minutes for small quantity and 1 to 1½ hours for large quantity.)

8. MANGSHER GOTA MASLAR CURRY

Ingredients	*For 4*	*For 100*
Mutton	500 gm	12.5 kg
Curds	60 gm	1.5 kg
Onions	225 gm	5.6 kg
Garlic	8 flakes	30 gm
Ginger	5 gm	115 gm
Coriander	5 gm	115 gm
Cardamoms	4	15 gm
Cumin	½ tsp	15 gm
Red chillies	3	85 gm
Salt	to taste	100 gm
Sugar	to taste	30 gm
Fat	30 gm	500 gm

Method

1. Clean and cut mutton into even pieces. 2. Peel and slice garlic, ginger and onions. 3. Crush garlic and steep in a little water for 15 minutes. 4. Pour this water over the mutton and let it stand for half an hour. 5. Heat fat. Add sliced onions, mutton soaked in garlic water and broken red chillies. 6. In a thin muslin bag tie the sliced ginger, coriander, cumin, and cardamoms. 7. Add the bouquet garni, salt and sugar and simmer till mutton is tender. 8. Remove the bouquet garni squeezing out as much as possible of the juice into the mutton. 9. Add beaten curds and fry the mutton till browned. Remove.

9. NILGIRI KHORMA

Ingredients	*For 4*	*For 100*
Mutton	500 gm	12.5 kg
Green chillies	5 gm	115 gm
Coriander leaves	a bunch	25 bunches
Ginger	a little	55 gm
Garlic	1 flake	20 gm
Poppy seeds	15 gm	340 gm
Curds	225 ml	4.25 litre
Coconut	30 gm	680 gm

Ingredients	*For 4*	*For 100*
Red chillies	5 gm	115 gm
Coriander	5 gm	115 gm
Garam masala	a little	30 gm
Onions	55 gm	1.35 kg
Fat	30 gm	500 gm
Salt	to taste	100 gm

Method

1. Wash, clean and cut (with bones) meat and soak in curds for half an hour. 2. Grind together half the onion, green chillies, coriander leaves, ginger, garlic, poppy seeds, coconut, red chillies and coriander. 3. Slice remaining onion. 4. Heat fat, fry onion slightly, add ground spices and fry for a few minutes. 5. Add meat, curds, salt and more water if required and cook till meat is tender. 6. When cooked add roasted and powdered garam masala and remove from fire.

10. GREEN CURRY (Meat, chicken or liver)

Ingredients	*Quantity*
Meat	680 gm
Coconut	¼
Coriander leaves	1 bunch
Onions	2
Salt	to taste
Lemon	½–1
Fat or oil	60 gm
Ginger	5 sq. cm. (2 sq.") piece
Garlic	8-10 cloves
Fennel	a little
Green chillies (large)	6
Potatoes (if required)	

Method

1. Grind coconut to thick paste. By adding water extract about half glass milk. 2. Grind 3 green chillies, fennel, turmeric, 7-8 garlic cloves, 2.5 sq. cm. (1 sq.") piece of ginger and some coriander leaves to a fine paste. 3. Cut up remaining 3 green chillies, 2.5 sq. cm. (1 sq.") ginger, and coriander leaves and keep aside. 4. Heat fat and add 2-3 bruised garlic cloves, 2 finely chopped onions, and cook till soft. 5. Add meat, salt and chopped chillies, ginger and coriander. 6. When water has evaporated, pour in coconut milk and a little water and cook till ready. Potatoes may be added. 7. Serve with a cut lemon.

11. SHAHI KHORMA

Ingredients	*For 4*	*For 100*
Mutton	500 gm	12.5 kg
Onions	200 gm	5 kg
Poppy seeds	10 gm	225 gm
Almonds	5 gm	115 gm
Coriander	15 gm	340 gm
Ginger	a small piece	85 gm
Kashmiri chillies	10 gm	225 gm
Cumin	a pinch	30 gm
Sultanas	5 gm	115 gm
Fat	50 gm	1.25 kg
Coconut	55 gm	1.35 kg (8)
Curds	115 gm	2.8 kg
Garlic	2 cloves	55 gm
Cloves	2 gm	50 gm
Cinnamon	2 gm	50 gm
Cardamoms	2 gm	50 gm
Dried milk	5 gm	125 gm
Salt	to taste	100 gm

Method

1. Wash and cut meat into 2.5 cm. (1") pieces. 2. Grind poppy seeds, cumin, coriander, ginger and garlic. 3. Remove seeds from red chillies. Soak in water and grind to a fine paste. 4. Grate coconut and extract milk. 5. Soak dry fruits and nuts in water. 6. Heat fat. Fry sliced onions, cloves, cinnamon and cardamoms, then the ground spices. 7. Add meat and fry. Add beaten curds, water and salt; cook till meat is tender. 8. Add coconut milk, dried milk, sultanas and almonds. Simmer for a few minutes. Remove. Serve hot.

12. MOGHLAI KHORMA

Ingredients	*For 8–10*
Mutton	1 kg
Fat	120 gm
Sugar and salt	to taste
For grinding	
Garlic	10 gm
Onions	50 gm
Ginger	10 gm
Red chillies	6-10
Cinnamon	2.5 cm. (1") piece

Ingredients	*For 8–10*
Cloves	5 gm
Small cardamoms	3 gm

Method

1. Cut mutton into big pieces. Wash and drain. Apply ground spices and set aside. 2. Heat 100 gm of fat. Add mutton, sugar and salt. Cover and cook over a slow fire till all the water that comes out of the meat is dried. 3. Add just sufficient water to cover meat. When meat is tender, add the remaining fat (melted) and remove from fire.

13. MUTTON SHAHJAHANI

Ingredients	*For 4*	*For 100*
Mutton	500 gm	12.5 kg
Onions	60 gm	1.5 kg
Garlic	6 flakes	75 gm
Ginger	10 gm	250 gm
Poppy seeds	5 gm	125 gm
Coriander leaves	1 bunch	25 bunches
Cinnamon	5 gm	125 gm
Cloves	5 gm	125 gm
Cardamoms	5 gm	125 gm
Asafoetida	a pinch	10 gm
Red chillies	a few	(to taste)
Fat	60 gm	1.5 kg
Salt	to taste	100 gm
Stock or water		
Garnish		
Almonds and silver paper		

Method

1. Clean and cut meat into 2.5 cm. (1") cubes. 2. Grind the spices to a smooth paste. 3. Slice onions and fry till brown. 4. Add ground spices and fry. 5. When fat starts oozing out, add mutton; fry for about 20 minutes. Add stock and salt. 6. Reduce temperature and simmer till meat is tender. 7. Remove onto a dish. 8. Garnish with slivers of almond and silver paper.

14. DUM KE PASANDE

Ingredients	*For 4*	*For 100*
Mutton	500 gm	12.5 kg
Potatoes	250 gm	6 kg
Tomatoes	500 gm	12.5 kg

Ingredients	For 4	For 100
Curds	150 ml	3.25 litre
Poppy seeds	50 gm	1 kg
Charoli nuts	50 gm	1 kg
Onions	250 gm	6 kg
Fat	100 gm	2.5 kg
Ginger and garlic	50 gm	1 kg
Chilli powder	15 gm	250 gm
Garam masala	10 gm	200 gm
Coriander leaves	¼ bunch	5-6 bunches
Salt	to taste	100 gm

Method

1. Fry sliced onions and grind them with the spices (except garam masala). 2. Mix all the spices with meat, add a little water and cook till half done. 3. Add beaten curds and cook till meat is fully tender. 4. Add sliced potatoes, tomatoes, salt and cook on a low fire. 5. When water has dried up, add garam masala powder. Remove from fire. Serve hot garnished with chopped coriander leaves.

15. MUTTON WITH CAULIFLOWER

Ingredients	For 4	For 100
Mutton	500 gm	12.5 kg
Onions	115 gm	2.8 kg
Turmeric	½ tsp	15 gm
Coriander powder	10 gm	225 gm
Ginger	1 piece	55 gm
Tomatoes	115 gm	2.8 kg
Curds	55 gm	1.35 kg
Cauliflower	225 gm	5.6 kg
Chilli powder	5 gm	115 gm
Fat	30 gm	500 gm
Salt	to taste	100 gm (approx.)

Method

1. Wash, clean and cut meat. 2. Wash and break cauliflower into flowerettes. 3. Peel and slice onions. Crush ginger. 4. Heat fat. Fry sliced onions. When brown add meat, turmeric, coriander powder and ginger. Fry well on a slow fire. 5. Add chopped tomatoes and beaten curds. 6. When tomatoes are cooked, add cauliflower, chilli powder and salt. Mix well and cook gently till mutton and cauliflower are well cooked. 7. Simmer till all liquid is reduced and serve hot.

16. MUTTON WITH TURNIPS

Ingredients	*For 4*	*For 100*
Mutton	500 gm	12.5 kg
Onions	115 gm	2.8 kg
Fat	55 gm	1.35 kg
Turmeric	½ tsp	15 gm
Whole red chillies	5 gm	115 gm
Small turnips	225 gm	5.6 kg
Garlic	2 cloves	50 gm
Ginger	a small piece	55 gm
Tomatoes	115 gm	2.8 kg
Cumin powder	¼ tsp	20 gm
Salt	to taste	100 gm (approx.)

Method

1. Clean and cut mutton into even sized pieces. 2. Peel and slice onions. 3. Heat fat; fry sliced onions; add mutton, turmeric, cumin and lightly bruised whole red chillies. 4. Fry the meat for 10-15 minutes, stirring all the time. Add turnips and stir. 5. Grind garlic and ginger and mix with blanched tomatoes. Add this to the meat. 6. Bring to boil, reduce flame, add salt and very small quantity of warm water. 7. Cover and cook on very gentle heat till meat is tender. Add more water if necessary.

17. MUTTON PAPDI

Ingredients	*For 4*	*For 100*
Mutton	250 gm	6.25 kg
Double beans (papdi or avra)	60 gm	1.5 kg
Potatoes	60 gm	1.5 kg
Onions	150 gm	3.75 kg
Ginger	5 gm	125 gm
Garlic	2-3 gm	50-75 gm
Coriander	5 gm	125 gm
Red chillies	2 gm	50 gm
Turmeric	½ gm	12
Cumin	½ gm	12 gm
Cloves	1	25 gm
Cinnamon	1¼ cm.	6 cm.
Fat	8 gm	200 gm
Oil	8 ml	200 ml
Salt	to taste	100 gm
Coriander leaves	⅛ bunch	3 bunches

Method

1. Clean and cut mutton into 2.5 cm. cubes. Peel and dice potatoes. Wash, but keep double beans whole. 2. Roast and powder coriander, red chillies, turmeric and cumin. 3. Peel and grind ginger and garlic to a smooth paste. 4. Chop onions. 5. Put the mutton into a vessel. Add curry powder, ground ingredients, all but 10 gm of onions and salt. Cover with water and simmer till mutton is tender. 6. Add potatoes and double beans. Simmer till vegetables are cooked and gravy is thick. 7. Remove from fire. Add washed and chopped coriander leaves. 8. Heat oil and fat in a fry pan. Add onions, cloves and cinnamon. When onions start browning, add curry. Stir well for 5 minutes. Remove.

18. MUTTON BHOPLA

Ingredients	*For 4*	*For 100*
Mutton	250 gm	6 kg
Red pumpkin (bhopla)	250 gm	6 kg
Green chillies	4 gm (2)	100 gm
Curds	150 gm	3.75 kg
Onions	150 gm	3.75 kg
Garam masala powder (cinnamon, cloves, pepper, cumin)	4 gm	100 gm
Chilli powder	4 gm	100 gm
Turmeric	4 gm	100 gm
Garlic	6 gm	150 gm
Ginger	10 gm	250 gm
Bay leaf	1	a few
Coriander leaves	⅛th bunch	3 bunches
Salt	to taste	100 gm
Fat	30 gm	750 gm

Method

1. Clean mutton, cut into 2.5 cm. (1") pieces., 2. Soak mutton in curds and salt for about 1 hour. 3. Grind together onions, ginger, garlic turmeric and chilli powder. 4. Heat fat. Fry ground ingredients till rich brown in colour and fat starts oozing out. Add garam masala. 5. Add bay leaf, green chillies (whole) and mutton soaked in curds. Fry till mutton becomes a rich brown colour. 6. Add water and simmer till mutton becomes tender. 7. Meanwhile peel, boil and mash pumpkin. Add to the mutton when it is tender and cook till the gravy is very thick. 8. Garnish with chopped coriander leaves and serve hot.

19. MUTTON PALAK

Ingredients	*For 4*	*For 100*
Mutton	500 gm	12.5 kg
Spinach	4 bunches	100 bunches
Fenugreek leaves	¼ bunch	5 bunches
Red chillies	5 gm	115 gm
Turmeric	a pinch	20 gm
Ginger	15 gm	340 gm
Cumin	a pinch	20 gm
Garlic	a few flakes	50 gm
Green chillies	5 gm	115 gm
Salt	10 gm	100 gm
Onions	115 gm	1.36 kg
Fat	30 gm	500 gm

Method

1. Wash and cut meat into even portions. 2. Grind red chillies, turmeric, cumin, ginger, green chillies and garlic. 3. Slice onions. 4. Heat fat. Fry sliced onions, add ground spices and fry well. 5. Add meat and a little water and let it cook till meat is nearly done. 6. Wash and chop spinach and fenugreek leaves. Add salt and cook without water. 7. Grind and add to the meat. 8. Cook till meat is tender. Serve hot.

N.B. Chicken Palak can be made in the same manner using chicken instead of mutton.

20. MUTTON WITH MIXED BHAJI

Ingredients	*For 8*
Mutton	500 gm
Amaranth	3 bunches (420 gm)
Spinach	2 bunches (200 gm)
Fenugreek leaves	1 bunch (135 gm)
Dil leaves	1 bunch (80 gm)
Chuka leaves	1 bunch (45 gm)
Red chilli powder	½ tsp (2 gm)
Fat	50 gm
Ginger	2.5 cm. (1") piece (10 gm)
Garlic	7-8 flakes (8 cm.)
Salt	to taste
Onions	200 gm
Turmeric	1 tsp (3 gm)
Coriander-cumin powder	1 tsp (3 gm)

Ingredients	*For 8*
Green chillies	6
Coriander leaves	1 bunch (100 gm)

Method

1. Wash and cut the mutton into pieces. Wash and chop the different types of leaves. 2. Slice onions; grind the ginger, garlic and green chillies. 3. Heat fat, fry three-fourths of the sliced onions to a golden brown. 4. Add mutton, ground spices, chopped leaves, sliced raw onions, salt and all the powdered spices. 5. Keep on stirring till the mixture dries up. Then add sufficient water to cook meat. When meat is well cooked, stir well and remove. 6. Serve hot with chapaties or bread.

21. CHOLA-MA-GOSHT

Ingredients	*For 8*
Mutton	500 gm
Cow peas (dry)	250 gm
Onions	150 gm
Ginger	2.5 cm. (1") piece
Garlic	6-8 flakes
Turmeric	½ tsp
Fat	1 tbsp
Pepper	½ tsp
Coriander-cumin powder	1 tsp
Salt	5-10 gm
Green chillies	3
Coriander leaves	½ bunch
Cherry tomatoes	100 gm
Chilli powder	5 gm
Vinegar	1 tbsp
Sugar (optional)	to taste

Method

1. Wash and cut mutton into pieces. Pick and wash the cow peas. 2. Chop half the onions and cut the rest into big pieces. 3. Boil mutton, peas and cut onions together. 4. Fry chopped onions till golden in colour; add ginger and garlic paste, turmeric, coriander and cumin powder, pepper and chilli powder. 5. Fry; remove and add to boiled mutton and cooked peas, add salt to taste. 6. Add chopped green chillies, coriander leaves and tomatoes; simmer on a slow fire. When mutton is cooked, add vinegar to taste. 7. Serve hot with bread or chapaties. Onion cuchumber could also be served with it.

22. GREEN COW PEAS WITH MUTTON

Ingredients	*For 8*
Mutton	500 gm
Cow peas (fresh)	500 gm
Ginger	2.5 cm. (1") piece
Garlic	6-8 flakes
Pepper powder	½ tsp
Fat	2 tbsp
Onions	250 gm
Salt	to taste
Turmeric	½ tsp
Chilli powder	1 tsp

Method

1. Wash and cut mutton. Grind ginger and garlic. 2. Wash, string and cut the cow peas into 1.25 cm. (½″) pieces. 3. Chop half the onions and fry to a golden colour, add mutton and fry. 4. Add ginger and garlic paste, dry spices and salt. Fry till completely dry. 5. Add the rest of the onions cut into pieces and water to cook. 6. When water boils, add prepared cow peas. 7. Cover and cook till done. Dry extra water if any. 8. Serve hot with bread or chapaties.

23. COUNTRY CAPTAIN

Ingredients	*For 4*	*For 100*
Mutton	500 gm	12.5 kg
Onions	115 gm	2.8 kg
Sugar	a pinch	55 gm
Vinegar	10 ml	250 ml
Kashmiri chillies (remove seeds)	5 gm	115 gm
Green chillies	5 gm	115 gm
Salt	to taste	100 gm
Ginger	5 gm	115 gm
Potatoes	225 gm	5.65 kg
Coriander	5 gm	115 gm
Cumin	a pinch	20 gm
Turmeric	a pinch	20 gm
Coriander leaves	¼ bunch	6 bunches
Fat	30 gm	500 gm

Method

1. Clean, wash and cut meat. 2. Chop onions and fry. 3. Add meat; fry lightly. 4. Add hot water and salt and cook. 5. Boil potatoes; slice and

fry till brown. 6. When meat is cooked, remove. Add ground coriander, Kashmiri chillies, cumin, turmeric, chopped ginger, green chillies and coriander leaves. 7. Add vinegar and sugar and cook till gravy is thick. 8. Add meat and potatoes. Cook for a few minutes longer and remove. Serve meat and gravy with potatoes on top.

24. TOMATO GOSHT

Ingredients	*For 8*
Beef (undercut)	1 kg
Tomatoes	1 kg
Onions	½ kg
Vinegar	30 ml
Salt	to taste
Fat	
For grinding	
Ginger	2.5 cm. (1") piece
Turmeric	½ tsp
Red chillies	30
Cumin	2 tsp
Pepper	1 tsp
Garlic	2 pods

Method

1. Cut meat into 5 cm. (2") diameter rounds of 0.25 to 0.50 cm. (⅛ to ¼") thickness. 2. Soften fibres using a steak hammer or a rolling pin. 3. Apply ground spices and vinegar. Set aside. 4. Slice tomatoes and chop onions. 5. In a strong-bottomed pan put a layer of meat. Cover with a layer of tomatoes. Sprinkle over with chopped onions. Continue till all the ingredients are used up. 6. Add the liquid from the plate in which the meat was marinaded. 7. Add salt and water to cook meat. 8. Cook over a slow fire till meat is tender and tomato well mashed up. 9. Heat fat and fry meat.

25. HUSSAINY CURRY

Ingredients	*For 4*	*For 100*
Mutton	500 gm	112.5 kg
Fat	30 gm	500 gm
Onions	225 gm	2 kg
Curds	15 ml	1.42 litre
Garlic	a few flakes	50 gm
Ginger	15 gm	340 gm
Green chillies	15 gm	225 gm
Tomatoes	225 gm	5.65 kg
Salt	to taste	100 gm

Ingredients	*For 4*	*For 100*
Potatoes for decoration	450 gm	11 kg
Milk	5 ml	100 ml
Tomatoes	55 gm	455 gm
Coriander leaves	5 gm	115 gm
For grinding		
Cumin powder	a pinch	20 gm
Coriander powder	5 gm	115 gm
Chilli powder	5 gm	115 gm
Turmeric	a pinch	15 gm

Method

1. Boil whole meat with salt and a few slices of ginger till tender. 2. Cut meat into even sized squares. 3. Cut ginger, garlic and green chillies into round slices and chop onions. 4. Crush part of the ginger and garlic and soak in water. 5. Thread ginger, garlic, onions, green chillies and meat on skewers. 6. Heat fat and brown remaining onions. 7. Add ground spices and fry well. 8. Sprinkle with garlic and ginger juice and add chopped tomatoes, well beaten curds and salt. 9. Arrange sticks neatly and allow to simmer 10-15 minutes. 10. Dish out on a flat dish and surround with mashed potato border decorated with tomato strips and green coriander leaves.

N.B. For border, boil potatoes and mash with milk.

26. BAMYA KHUTA

Ingredients	*For 4*	*For 100*
Mutton	500 gm	12.5 kg
Ladies fingers	450 gm	11 kg
Tomatoes	225 gm	5.6 kg
Onions	225 gm	5.6 kg
Fat or oil	50 gm	1.25 kg
Mint leaves	a few sprigs	2 bunches
Ginger	a small piece	55 gm
Garlic	3 flakes	50 gm
Turmeric	a pinch	20 gm
Garam masala (optional)	a pinch	20 gm
Lime or	1	20-25
Tamarind	10 gm	225 gm
Salt	to taste	100 gm

Method

1. Wash and prepare the ladies fingers and keep aside. 2. Wash and cut meat into even sized pieces. 3. Peel and slice onions and add to the meat.

4. Grind ginger and garlic. Add to meat with turmeric, salt, garam masala and oil. 5. Add a little water and keep pan on fire. Cook gently. 6. When water dries up, add chopped tomatoes. Stir constantly till tomatoes are well cooked. 7. Add ladies fingers. Brown for a little longer. 8. Add enough water to cover the meat and vegetables and cook gently until tender. 9. Add lime juice or tamarind and allow to boil well. Remove from fire and add finely chopped mint leaves. Serve hot.

N.B. This dish can be prepared in the same way by adding beetroot or red pumpkin or capsicum or white pumpkin instead of the ladies fingers. Chicken can be used instead of mutton.

27. CHATANI

Ingredients	*For 4*	*For 100*
Mutton or chicken	500 gm	12.5 kg
Tomatoes	450 gm	11 kg
Oil	50 ml	1.25 litre
Tamarind	10 gm	225 gm
Sugar	a little	50 gm
Onions	900 gm	22 kg
Ginger	a small piece	100 gm
Turmeric	a pinch	20 gm
Garlic	a few flakes	50 gm
Garam masala (optional)	a pinch	20 gm
Salt	to taste	100 gm

Method

1. Wash and cut up the meat. 2. Wash and slice tomatoes and keep them separate. 3. Peel and slice onions finely. 4. Grind ginger and garlic and powder garam masala if used. 5. In a pan heat oil. Fry onions till light brown. 6. Add mutton, ground garlic and ginger, turmeric and garam masala if used. Stir well for a few minutes. 7. Add chopped tomatoes and very little water. 8. Cook till all the water evaporates. Stir till meat browns and tomatoes and onions are well mashed. 9. Add more water and continue to cook till meat is tender and oil comes up. 10. Add tamarind, salt and sugar; simmer, let gravy thicken. Serve hot.

28. MULLIGATAWNY CURRY

Ingredients	*For 4*	*For 100*
Breast of mutton	500 gm	12.5 kg
Small onions	115 gm	2.8 kg
Garlic	5 gm	115 gm
Ginger	15 gm	340 gm

Ingredients	*For 4*	*For 100*
Cinnamon	2 gm	60 gm
Tomatoes	225 gm	5.65 kg
Water	1.8 litre	44.25 litre
Curry leaves	a few	1 bunch
Seasoning and thickening		
Red chillies (without seeds)	5 gm	115 gm
Coriander	15 gm	340 gm
Cumin	a pinch	20 gm
Fennel	5 gm	115 gm
Peppercorns	a few	20 gm
Split bengal gram	15 gm	340 gm
Coconut milk (thick)	300 ml	4.5 litre
Turmeric	a pinch	20 gm
Lime	1	20-25
Salt	to taste	100 gm
Tempering		
Fat	10 gm	250 gm
Red onions	5 gm	115 gm
Curry leaves	a few	½ bunch

Method

1. Cut mutton into neat pieces. Add all the first lot of ingredients and boil till meat is tender. 2. Roast and grind red chillies. Grind coriander, fennel, cumin and peppercorns. 3. Roast bengal gram and grind well. 4. Mix all the ingredients with the coconut milk and turmeric. 5. Add to mulligatawny with lime juice and salt. 6. Fry the onions and curry leaves in fat. Add to mulligatawny, stir well and remove from fire.

N.B. A mild Lamb Mulligatawny Curry can be made with Recipe No. 95, using 1 kg lamb instead of chicken.

29. MUTTON CURRY

Ingredients	*For 4*	*For 100*
Mutton (with bones)	500 gm	12.5 kg
Coriander	4 dsp. (20 gm)	500 gm
Peppercorns	1 tsp	50 gm
Turmeric	1 tsp (4 gm)	100 gm
Curry leaves	2 sprigs	1 bunch
Red onions	1 or 2 (2 gm)	50 gm
Mustard seeds	1 pinch	20 gm
Garlic	4 flakes	75 gm

Ingredients	For 4	For 100
Ginger	2.5 cm. (1") piece	250 gm
Green chillies	8	200 gm
Red onions	2 tbsp	750 gm
Oil	2 tbsp	750 ml
Salt	to taste	100 gm
Coconut	½	12
Potatoes	225 gm	5.6 kg
Vinegar	1 tbsp	375 ml
Tempering		
Cinnamon	1 piece	20 gm
Cloves	2	20 gm
Peppercorns	3	20 gm
Red onion	1	20 gm
Curry leaves	1 sprig	1 bunch
Oil or ghee (clarified butter)	1 tbsp	375 ml

Method

1. Cut mutton into 2.5 cm. (1") pieces with the bones. Clean. 2. Grind to a fine paste the coriander, peppercorns, turmeric, red onions (first lot) and garlic. 3. Slit green chillies, slice ginger and second lot of onions. 4. Heat oil. Add mustard seeds; when seeds crackle, add sliced onions (second lot) and curry leaves. When onions brown, add mutton and ground spices. Fry lightly. 5. Add ginger, green chillies, salt and enough water to almost cook mutton. 6. Meanwhile, grate coconut and prepare two extractions of coconut milk—the first thick, about 1 cup and the 2nd about 2 cups. (for 100, it will be 5 litres and 10 litres.) 7. Peel and cut potatoes into quarters. Add potatoes and 2nd extract of coconut milk to cooked meat with vinegar. 8. Test for salt. When potatoes are cooked, add 1st extract of coconut milk. Bring to boil. Remove. 9. Heat oil (or ghee). Add crushed cinnamon, cloves, peppercorns, sliced onion and curry leaves. 10. When onions brown, pour over curry and mix well.

Variations: Duck's eggs, hen's eggs, ladies fingers and sliced large fish can be prepared similarly. Boil eggs and shell. Prick and add. Fry ladies fingers separately before adding. Fish may also be fried. In all these cases, add potatoes at the start with ground spices.

30. MUTTON CURRY (Mild)

Ingredients	For 4	For 100
Mutton	500 gm	12.5 kg
Coriander powder	10 gm	250 gm
Poppy seeds	5 gm	75 gm

Ingredients	*For 4*	*For 100*
Turmeric	¼ tsp	25 gm
Ginger	2.5 cm. (1") piece	250 gm
Garlic	3 flakes	50 gm
Cashewnuts	15 gm	375 gm
Coconut	30 gm	750 gm
Garam masala	1 pinch	20 gm
Onions	1	2.5 kg
Vinegar	1 tsp	75 ml
Oil	25 ml	600 ml
Salt	to taste	100 gm (about)

Method

1. Clean and cut mutton into 2.5 cm. (1") pieces. 2. Grind together the spices, cashewnuts and coconut. 3. Slice onion. Heat oil. Fry onion till crisp brown. 4. Add spices and fry for 2 to 3 minutes longer. 5. Add mutton. Fry for a further 5 minutes. Add salt. 6. Cover pan. Cook over a very slow fire. Keep a little water over the lid of pan to stop meat from burning. 7. Add hot water as desired, a little at a time till meat is tender. 8. Add vinegar. Check for seasoning. Remove.

31. KOLHAPURI MUTTON CURRY

Ingredients	*For 8*
Mutton	1 kg
Coriander seeds	1 tbsp
Cumin	1 tsp
Ginger	3 gm
Garlic	12 gm (1 whole)
Onions	60 gm
Sesame seeds	1 tbsp
Poppy seeds	½ tbsp
Dry coconut	20 gm
Cloves	4
Peppercorns	4
Turmeric	½ tsp
Onions (finely sliced)	¼ kg
Chilli powder	to taste
Salt	to taste
Oil	100 ml

Method

1. Slightly fry all ingredients from coriander to peppercorns (each separately) except ginger and garlic. 2. Then grind all including the raw

garlic and ginger together to a paste. 3. Fry mutton in 50 ml of oil (slightly raw) and keep aside. 4. Then in 50 ml of oil, fry ¼ kg finely sliced onions to a golden brown colour. 5. Add ground masala and mix and fry together a little. 6. Add turmeric and the half cooked meat and mix well. 7. Add 4-5 cups (600 ml) water, chilli powder and salt to taste. 8. Allow to cook on a slow fire. 9. Keep curry thick or thin according to your taste.

32. ROGAN JOSH

Ingredients	*For 4*	*For 100*
Leg of mutton	50 gm	12.5 kg
Tomatoes	115 gm	2.72 kg
Coriander powder	10 gm	250 gm
Saltpetre	5 gm	100 gm
Fat	30 gm	500 gm
Kashmiri chillies (without seeds)	15 gm	225 gm
Ginger	10 gm	225 gm
Nutmeg	a pinch	15 gm
Saffron	a pinch	5 gm
Cumin	a pinch	45 gm
Mace	a pinch	15 gm
Garlic	a few flakes	85 gm
Onions	115 gm	2.72 kg
"Rattan jog"	a small piece	5 gm
Salt	to taste	100 gm
Stock		
Milk	enough to dissolve saffron	

Method

1. Clean and cut meat into 2.5 cm. (1") pieces with bones. 2. Chop onions, grind Kashmiri chillies, coriander, ginger, cumin and garlic. 3. Heat fat. Fry onion, add ground spices and fry well. Add tomatoes. 4. Add meat, half of the saffron and saltpetre. 5. Fry for about 5 minutes. Add stock, nutmeg, mace, salt and "rattan jog". 6. Cook gently till meat is tender. 7. When meat is cooked, add the red of the saffron dissolved in a little milk.

33. MUTTON DO PYAZ

Ingredients	*For 4*	*For 100*
Mutton (shoulder)	500 gm	12.5 kg
Fat	50 gm	1.25 kg

Ingredients	*For 4*	*For 100*
Onions (sliced)	115 gm	2.8 kg
Salt	10 gm	100 gm
Grind together		
Turmeric	a pinch	10 gm
Red chillies	5 gm	225 gm
Coriander	10 gm	225 gm
Ginger	10 gm	225 gm
Garlic	a few flakes	15 gm
Onions	115 gm	2.8 kg

Method

1. Clean and cut meat into even sized portions. 2. Heat fat and fry sliced onions till golden brown. Remove. 3. Add ground spices and fry well. 4. Add meat and continue frying. 5. Add onion, salt and hot water. 6. Cook till meat is tender and gravy is thickened.

34. MUTTON DO PYAZ WITH LENTILS

Ingredients	*For 4*	*For 100*
Mutton	500 gm	12.5 kg
Onions	225 gm	5.6 kg
Lentils	225 gm	5.6 kg
Garlic	2 flakes	55 gm
Cumin	¼ tsp	20 gm
Red chillies	5 gm	115 gm
Salt	to taste	100 gm
Curds	55 gm	1.36 kg
Fat	50 gm	1.25 kg
Peppercorns	6	50 gm
Turmeric	¼ tsp	20 gm

Method

1. Wash and cut up meat into 5 cm. (2") pieces. 2. Crush well half the onions, garlic and cumin. Grind red chillies fine. 3. Mix with salt and curds. 4. Rub curds mixture well into the meat and leave for half an hour. 5. Heat fat and fry remaining onions sliced. 6. Add meat. Cover the pan and shake well. 7. Add lentil and enough water to cover. 8. Cook over medium heat. 9. Put in crushed peppercorns and turmeric. Mix well. 10. Simmer till done and all the water is evaporated.

N.B. A proper do pyaz has no gravy save that of the fat and spices.

35. ELAICHI MUTTON

Ingredients	*For 4*	*For 100*
Mutton (with bones)	500 gm	12.5 kg
Cardamoms (small)	12	150 gm
Onions	1 small	1.25 kg
Oil	1 tbsp	375 ml
Salt	to taste	100 gm
Black pepper	½ tsp	50 gm
Coriander powder	1 tsp	125 gm

Method

1. Clean and cut mutton into 2.5 cm. (1") pieces. 2. Chop onion fine. Pound cardamom seeds. 3. Heat oil. Sauté chopped onion. 4. Add powdered cardamom seeds. Fry one minute. 5. Add prepared mutton, salt and coriander powder. Fry for a few minutes. 6. Add water. Cook over a slow fire till mutton is cooked and gravy is like a thin soup. Add pepper powder.

36. BHUGAL GOSHT

Ingredients	*For 4*	*For 100*
Mutton (with bones)	500 gm	12.5 kg
Onions	2 big (250 gm)	6.25 kg
Garlic	8-10 cloves (6 gm)	150 gm
Ginger	2.5 cm (1") piece (10 gm)	250 gm
Tomatoes	2 medium (160 gm)	
Coriander powder	2 tsp (10 gm)	250 gm
Chilli powder	½ tsp (2 gm)	
Garam masala (mixture of cinnamon, cloves, cardamom, carraway seeds and bay leaf)	1½ tsp (6 gm)	150 gm
Black pepper	¼ tsp	25 gm
Coriander leaves	⅛ bunch	6 bunches
Salt	to taste	100 gm
Fat	100 gm	2.5 kg

Method

1. Grind garlic and ginger. Fry chopped onions till nearly brown. 2. Add garlic and ginger and mutton. 3. Keep frying for 10-15 minutes, sprinkling a little water if desired. 4. Add coriander powder, red chilli powder, cumin powder and salt. 5. Fry for a further 10 minutes. 6. Add chopped tomatoes and fry for a further 10 minutes. 7. Add sufficient

water and coriander leaves and simmer over very slow fire. 8. When nearly done, add garam masala and pepper powder.

N.B. This mutton dish must be done on an extremely slow fire. Peeled quartered potatoes may be added half-way if desired.

37. SEL GOSHT

Ingredients	*For 4*	*For 100*
Mutton (with bones)	500 gm	12.5 kg
Onions (large)	2 (250 gm)	6.25 kg
Curds	100 gm	2.5 kg
Tomatoes (medium)	2 (160 gm)	4 kg
Green chillies	2	50 gm
Coriander leaves	⅛ bunch	6 bunches
Garlic	8-10 cloves (6 gm)	150 gm
Ginger	2.5 cm. (1") piece	250 gm
Coriander powder	2 tsp (10 gm)	250 gm
Chilli powder	½ tsp (2 gm)	50 gm
Cumin powder	1 tsp (4 gm)	100 gm
Turmeric	½ tsp (2 gm)	50 gm
Garam masala	1½ tsp (5 gm)	150 gm
Pepper	¼ tsp	25 gm
Salt	to taste	100 gm
Fat	100 gm	2.5 kg

Method

1. Into a strong bottomed pan, place fat, chopped onions, garlic, ginger, mutton mixed with curds, spices (except garam masala and pepper), salt and chopped tomatoes. 2. Cover and cook over very slow fire. 3. When mutton is cooked, add garam masala and pepper powder. 4. Mix well and serve hot.

38. SAFED MAS

Ingredients	*For 10*
Lamb	1 kg
Curds	1½ cup (225gm)
Fat	250 gm
Onions	150 gm
Garlic	6 cloves
Red chillies	7 gm
Black pepper	1 dsp (20 gm)
Cumin	3 gm
Poppy seeds	45 gm

Ingredients	For 10
Cashewnuts	25 gm
Salt	to taste
Water	½ litre

Method

1. Clean and cut lamb into 1" pieces with the bones. 2. Slice onions and garlic. 3. Grind together remaining spices. 4. Place all ingredients in a pressure cooker. 5. Cover and allow the steam to come up (about 10 minutes). 6. Place 10 lb. pressure on. Cook for a further 15 minutes. Cool pressure cooker slowly. 7. Open lid and take out the curry.

39. MUTTON CHILLI FRY

Ingredients	For 4	For 100
Mutton	500 gm	12.5 kg
Fat	30 gm	500 gm
Onions	55 gm	1.35 kg
Garlic	3 flakes	50 gm
Cloves	3 to 4	10 gm
Turmeric	a pinch	20 gm
Cumin	a pinch	20 gm
Ginger	a small piece	55 gm
Red chillies (without seeds)	10 gm	200 gm
Tamarind	10 gm	225 gm
Salt	to taste	100 gm

Method

1. Clean and cut meat. 2. Grind chillies, turmeric, ginger, cumin and half the onion. 3. Slice the other half of the onion and garlic. 4. Heat fat and fry onion and garlic lightly. Add powdered cloves and fry. 5. Add meat and the ground spices. Fry well; cover pan and cook on a slow fire without water for half an hour. 6. Add hot water and salt; simmer till meat is tender. 7. When meat is cooked, add tamarind pulp. Cook for a few minutes longer.

N.B. Chilli fry should have very little gravy.

40. MEAT CHILLI FRY

Ingredients	For 4	For 100
Mutton or beef	500 gm	12.5 kg
Onions	450 gm	11.00 kg
Green chillies	20 gm	500 gm
Ginger	10 gm	250 gm

Ingredients	*For 4*	*For 100*
Garlic	6 cloves	115 gm
Tomatoes	225 gm	5.6 kg
Coriander leaves (optional)	½ bunch	12 bunches
Salt	to taste	100 gm
Oil (coconut or sweet oil)	30 ml	500 ml

Method

1. Wash and cut meat into even pieces. Apply salt. 2. Boil in sufficient water to cook meat tender but dry. 3. Peel and slice onions, slit green chillies, slice the garlic and cut ginger into thin long pieces. Chop coriander leaves. 4. Add oil to meat. Add sliced ingredients and chopped tomatoes. Fry well. 5. Cook till fairly dry, stirring occasionally.

41. MUTTON AND POTATO CHIPS

Ingredients	*For 4*	*For 100*
Mutton	500 gm	12.5 kg
Potatoes	225 gm	5.6 kg
Onions	225 gm	5.6 kg
Garlic	10 gm	225 gm
Green chillies	5 gm	115 gm
Coriander leaves	½ bunch	12 bunches
Salt	to taste	100 gm
Fat	115 gm	2.8 kg

Method

1. Peel and cut potatoes in thin fingers. 2. Deep fry fingers till crisp. Remove and drain on paper; sprinkle salt and set aside. 3. Slice onions; grind together garlic, green chillies and coriander leaves. 4. Pour off extra fat and dry onions till brown. Add ground spices and meat. Fry well. 5. Add water and cook till meat is tender. 6. Serve hot garnished with fried potato fingers.

42. MEAT AND COCONUT FRY (IRAICHI ULATHIYATHU)

Ingredients	*For 4*	*For 100*
Beef or mutton	500 gm	12.5 kg
Coconut	115 gm (½)	2.8 kg (12)
Coriander	30 gm	450 gm
Red chillies	5 to 7 gm	150 gm
Turmeric	¼ tsp or a small piece	20 gm
Cinnamon	½ tsp	30 gm
Cloves	½ tsp	30 gm

Ingredients	*For 4*	*For 100*
Peppercorns	½ tsp	30 gm
Small onion	10 gm	250 gm
Garlic	6 flakes	50 gm
Ginger	1.25 cm (½") piece	50 gm
Curry leaves	2 sprigs	1 bunch
Salt	to taste	100-120 gm
Coconut oil	50 ml	1 litre

Method

1. Slice coconut into thin 1.25 cm. (½") pieces. Sprinkle a little turmeric powder. 2. Heat half the oil. Sauté coconut. Remove. 3. Clean and cut meat into 1.25 cm (½") pieces. 4. Roast and finely powder coriander, red chillies and turmeric. 5. Powder cinnamon, cloves and peppercorns. 6. Roast onion and garlic and grind to a fine paste. 7. Slice ginger. 8. Mix together meat, prepared spices, ground onions, and garlic, ginger, curry leaves, coconut, salt and enough water to cook meat dry. 9. Keep on fire. Bring to boil quickly. Reduce heat and cook over gentle heat till tender. Cover tightly so that no steam escapes. 10. When meat is tender and all water has evaporated stir well and remove. 11. Heat remaining oil. Add meat and fry well.

N.B. This meat can be kept for two to three days. Fry only as required.

43. MUTTON JHAL FARAIZI

Ingredients	*For 4*	*For 100*
Mutton (roast and cool)	500 gm	12.5 kg
Pepper	1 tsp	30 gm
Red chillies	10 gm	250 gm
Salt	15 gm	100 gm
Fat	50 gm	1.25 kg
Potatoes	450 gm	11 kg
Onions	450 gm	11 kg

Method

1. Boil potatoes. Peel, cool and dice. 2. Dice roast meat into even portions. 3. Chop onions. 4. Grind together chillies and pepper. 5. Heat fat, fry onions lightly. Add meat and potatoes and ground spices. 6. Fry on a slow fire till almost dry.

44. PAL PORIAL (A)

Ingredients	*For 4*	*For 100*
Meat	500 gm	12.5 kg
Chilli powder	1 dsp	200 gm

Ingredients	*For 4*	*For 100*
Onions	115 gm	2.8 kg
Oil	30 ml	500 ml
Fennel	5 gm	115 gm
Coconut	½	10
Salt	to taste	100 gm

Method

1. Clean and cut meat into even sized pieces. 2. Smear over with chilli powder and salt. 3. Slice onions. Roast and powder fennel. 4. Grate and extract coconut milk. 5. Heat oil. Sauté sliced onions. Add meat and fry. Add coconut milk. Cover and cook till meat is tender and dry. Sprinkle prepared fennel powder. 6. Remove from fire immediately.

N.B. If coconut milk is not available, fresh milk and water can be used instead.

PAL PORIAL (B)

Ingredients	*For 4*	*For 100*
Meat	500 gm	12.5 kg
Turmeric	1 tsp	20 gm
Salt	to taste	100 gm
Onions	115 gm	2.8 kg
Coconut	¼	6
Coriander	10 gm	250 gm
Red chillies	5 gm	115 gm
Turmeric	a small piece	20 gm
Cinnamon	a small piece	20 gm
Cloves	4	20 gm
Fennel	5 gm	115 gm
Lime	1	20-25

Method

1. Clean and cut meat into even sized pieces. 2. Apply turmeric and salt and set aside. 3. Grate and extract thick coconut milk. 4. Slice onions. Roast and powder all spices except fennel. 5. Roast fennel separately and powder. 6. Heat oil. Sauté onions. Add meat and fry. Cover and cook on a slow fire in its own juice. 7. When all the liquid has evaporated, add thick coconut milk and roasted and powdered spices. 8. Let it dry. Add fennel powder and lime juice. Remove from fire.

45. MASALA MUTTON CHOPS

Ingredients	*For 8*
Mutton	1 kg
Vinegar	3 tbsp

Ingredients	*For 8*
Garlic	6 cloves
Ginger	2.5 cm. piece
Chilli powder	½ tsp
Salt	to taste
Fat for frying	60 gm
Onions	2 (300 gm)

Method

1. Cut the mutton into about 1.25 cm. (½″) thick slices. Flatten with a steak hammer or a wooden roller. Soak in a mixture of vinegar, sliced garlic, finely chopped ginger and chilli powder. 2. Set aside for 10 to 12 hours (preferably in a refrigerator). Remove from the marinade. Add salt. 3. Heat fat. Fry the chops over a quick fire for a few minutes, on either side. Reduce heat. Sprinkle over with salt and pepper and cook for another 5 to 10 minutes. 4. Remove on to a hot plate. Fry roundels of onions in remaining fat and place over the chops. 5. Prepare a gravy by adding about half a cup of warm water to the dripping; add more seasoning and cook till gravy is brown and fairly thick.

46. FRIED MEAT

Ingredients	*For 4*	*For 100*
Mutton	500 gm	12.5 kg
Vinegar	30 ml	600 ml
Onions	225 gm	5.6 kg
Potatoes	115 gm	2.8 kg
Tomatoes	115 gm	2.8 kg
Carrots	115 gm	2.8 kg
Garlic	1 flake	30 gm
Red chillies (without seeds)	5 gm	115 gm
Ginger	a small piece	55 gm
Oil	100 gm	2.5 litre
Eggs	2	12
Breadcrumbs	30 gm	455 gm
Salt	to taste	100 gm

Method

1. Grind chillies, ginger and garlic to a fine paste. 2. Clean and cut meat, potatoes and carrots into even sized cubes. Chop onions. 3 Boil meat with vinegar, half the oil and salt. When half done add ground spices and cook till tender. 4. Fry potatoes and carrots in oil. 5. On fine sticks, 13 cm (5") long, thread onions, potatoes, meat, carrots and raw tomatoes

alternately. 6. Beat the eggs. Dip sticks in egg, sprinkle with breadcrumbs and deep fry.

47. MUSALLAM RAAN

Ingredients	*For 4*	*For 100*
Leg of mutton	500 gm	12.5 kg
Cashewnuts	55 gm	1.35 kg
Dry coconut	55 gm	1.35 kg
Raisins	55 gm	1.35 kg
Red chillies (without seeds)	5 gm	115 gm
Salt	to taste	100 gm
Garam masala	5 gm	115 gm
Garlic	3 flakes	55 gm
Coriander	10 gm	225 gm
Ginger	10 gm	225 gm
Curds	115 gm	2.80 kg
Fat	115 gm	2.80 kg
Lime	1	20-25
Raw papaya (peeled)	a small piece	225 gm

Method

1. Grind coriander, chillies and garam masala into a fine paste. 2. Grind coconut, cashewnuts, raisins, 3. Grind garlic, ginger and raw papaya. Mix with curds and salt. Add lime juice. 4. Wash the leg of mutton. With a pointed knife make several gashes all over. 5. Smear leg with curds mixture and keep aside for 15 to 30 minutes to allow mixture to seep in. 6. Smear ground chillies and garam masala paste over. 7. Finally smear the cashewnut paste. 8. Put the fat into a strong pan. Add the leg and turn till browned on all sides. Reduce fire to very slow. Cook covered till meat is cooked. Turn frequently. 9. Live coal may be put on the lid to help the cooking.

48. LAMB ON THE BONE

Ingredients	*For 15–20*
Leg of lamb	1 (about 2 kg)
Mint	1 bunch
Garlic	1 pod
Green chillies	5 to 6
Lime	1
Large-sized onion	1
Potatoes	250 gm
Brinjal	250 gm

Ingredients	*For 15–20*
Tomatoes	250 gm
Salt	to taste
Fat	50 gm

Method

1. Saw the leg of lamb into four or five pieces leaving the meat on the bone. 2. Grind together mint, green chillies and garlic. 3. Add lime juice and rub over meat. 4. Melt fat in a shallow pan. Brown meat lightly. 5. Reduce fire and cook covered over slow fire, sprinkling a little water every now and then, and turning the meat over. 6. When nearly done, add onion cut into rings, peeled and sliced potatoes, tomatoes and small brinjals, cut into halves, with the skin on. 7. Cook till vegetables and meat are tender. The meat must be very well cooked and almost falling off the bone. 8. Add salt. Mix well and remove.

49. MUTTON KOFTA CURRY

Ingredients	*For 4*	*For 100*
Mutton	500 gm	12.5 gm
Cloves	5	50 gm
Eggs	1	25
Cinnamon	a small piece	20 gm
Split bengal gram	55 gm	1.35 kg
Ginger	5 gm	115 gm
Green chillies	5 gm	115 gm
Salt	to taste	100 gm
Coriander leaves	¼ bunch	6 bunches
Ghee (absorption)	30 gm	340 gm
Curry		
Coriander powder	15 gm	340 gm
Red chillies	5 gm	115 gm
Turmeric	a pinch	20 gm
Dry coconut	30 gm	225 gm
Garlic	a few flakes	50 gm
Green chillies	a few	55 gm
Tomatoes	115 gm	2.8 kg
Lime	½	12
Salt	to taste	100 gm
Onions	55 gm	1.35 kg
Fat (to fry)	115 gm	1.00 kg

Method

1. Wash meat. Remove membranes and bones. 2. Mince meat. 3. Wash

and boil gram. 4. Grind together cooked gram, cinnamon, cloves, ginger, green chillies and meat. 5. Add salt, chopped coriander leaves and beaten egg. 6. Form into even sized balls with wet hands and fry lightly.

Curry

1. Slice onion. 2. Grind the spices. 3. Blanch tomatoes. 4. Heat some fat and fry onion. 5. Add spices and fry. 6. Add blanched tomatoes, and stock to cook the spices. 7. Add koftas and salt; simmer till meat is cooked. 8. Add lime juice before taking off the fire.

50. BALL CURRY (Malabar)

Ingredients	*For 4*	*For 100*
Meat (without bones)	250 gm	6.25 kg
Green chillies	2	50 gm
Onions	40 gm	1 kg
Ginger	2.5 cm. (½″) piece (5 gm)	125 gm
Salt	to taste	10 gm (approximate)
For curry		
Red chillies	4 gm	100 gm
Coriander	5 gm	125 gm
Ginger	1.25 cm. (½″) piece (2½ gm)	70 gm
Garlic	4 flakes (3 gm)	75 gm
Turmeric	⅛ tsp (½ gm)	12 gm
Cloves	3	50 gm
Cinnamon	1.25 cm. (¼″) piece	50 gm
Cardamoms	2	50 gm
Peppercorns	6	50 gm
Fennel	½ tsp	50 gm
Tomato	1	2.5 kg
Coconut	½	12
Water for grinding spices and preparation of coconut milk	2 cups	10.5 litre
For tempering		
Coconut oil	10 ml	250 ml
Ghee	10 gm	250 gm
Curry leaves	a few sprigs	1 bunch
Red onions (2 pods)	15 gm	375 gm
Mustard seeds	a pinch	25 gm

Method

1. Mince meat with the first lot of ingredients. Add salt and form into 8 (or 200) balls. 2. Roast red chillies and coriander. Grind together with remaining spices. 3. Grate coconut and extract milk, first thick, second after grinding, thinner. 4. Heat oil and ghee. Add mustard seeds. As seeds crackle, add curry leaves and sliced onions. When onions brown, add ground spices. 5. Fry for a further 5 to 10 minutes. 6. Add second extraction of coconut milk. Bring to boil. Add blanched tomato. 7. Add meat balls one by one to simmering liquid. 8. Cook over very slow fire for about 20 minutes. Test for seasoning and remove.

N.B. Instead of tomato, vinegar may be used.

51. MINCE BALLS

Ingredients	*For 4*	*For 100*
Minced meat	250 gm	6.25 kg
Small potatoes (new)	200 gm	5 kg
Green chillies	5 to 6	75
Onions	2 (200 gm)	5 kg
Ginger	2.5 cm. (1") piece (10 gm)	250 gm
Coriander	2 dsp.	250 gm
Turmeric	¼ tsp	25 gm
Garlic	2 flakes	30 gm
Salt	to taste	100 gm
Curry leaves	a few	1 bunch
Mustard seeds	½ tsp	10 gm
Fat	50 gm	1.25 kg

Method

1. Pass through the mincer, the minced meat, 2 green chillies, one onion and 1.25 (½") piece ginger. 2. Add salt and shape into balls. 3. Heat most of the fat in a strong bottomed pan. Put in mince balls. 4. Cover and let them cook in their own juice over a slow fire. 5. Meanwhile boil potatoes and peel. Roast and grind fine the coriander, red chillies, turmeric and garlic. 6. When meat is cooked, remove pan. 7. In a fry-pan, heat remaining fat. Add curry leaves and mustard. 8. As seeds start spluttering, add ground spices and remaining onion, green chillies and sliced ginger and salt to taste. 9. When the spices are cooked, add potatoes and minced meat balls and any liquid left in the pan. 10. Cook for a few minutes longer and remove.

52. NARGISI KOFTA CURRY

Ingredients	*For 4*	*For 100*
Meat (finely minced)	500 gm	12.5 kg
Eggs (hard-boiled)	4	100
Egg for binding	1	15
Cardamoms	a few	20 gm
Cloves	a small pinch	20 gm
Cinnamon	1 piece	20 gm
Onions	50 gm	1.35 kg
Green chillies	1	30 gm
Salt	to taste	80-100 gm
Fat to fry (absorption)	30 gm	500 gm
Seasoned flour to coat boiled eggs		
Curry		
Tomatoes	500 gm	12.5 kg
Turmeric	½ tsp	50 gm
Chilli powder	1 tsp	100 gm
Green chillies	1	30 gm
Garam masala	a small pinch	20 gm
Onions	115 gm	2.8 kg
Garlic	2 flakes	50 gm
Fat	15 gm	250 gm
Salt	to taste	50 gm
Garnish		
Coriander leaves	a few sprigs	1 bunch

Method

1. Mince meat finely. Add beaten egg. 2. Add finely chopped green chillies, onion, powdered cardamom, cloves and cinnamon and salt. 3. Dip eggs in seasoned flour. Coat with minced meat mixture. Deep fry. 4. Meanwhile heat fat for curry. Add sliced onions and sauté. Add finely chopped garlic, turmeric and red chilli powder. 5. Add puréed tomatoes and salt and let it simmer. Add garam masala. 6. Drop the koftas one by one into the gravy. Simmer for about 30 minutes. 7. Cut the koftas into two halves and let each piece float in the gravy with yolk side up. Garnish with coriander leaves.

53. PORK KOFTA CURRY (26 koftas)

Ingredients	*Quantity*
Shoulder of pork	1 kg
Onions	100 gm (1)

Ingredients	*Quantity*
Green chillies	4
Ginger	1½ inch piece
Split bengal gram	100 gm
Egg	1
Coriander leaves	to flavour
Salt	to taste
Fat	50 gm
Curry	
Chilli powder	1 tsp
Coriander powder	1 tsp
Turmeric	¼ tsp
Garlic	4 flakes
Onion	¼ (25 gm)
Coconut	½
Poppy seeds	50 gm
Onion	1 (sliced)
Tomatoes	150 gm (2 medium)
Oil	1 tbsp

Method

1. Boil pork and the gram separately. 2. Mince. Add finely chopped onion, ginger, green chillies, coriander leaves, salt and eggs. 3. Shape into small balls, size of a lime. Deep fry and set aside. 4. Grind to a fine paste all curry ingredients up to coconut. 5. Grind coconut and poppy seeds separately. 6. Heat 1 tbsp oil. Add fat left over in the pan in which pork was boiled. Heat till it stops spluttering. 7. Add sliced onion and fry till golden brown. Add ground spices: Fry well over slow fire. 8. Add chopped tomatoes. Cook for another 10 minutes adding more water as desired. 9. Add poppy seeds mixed in 1 cup water. Simmer for 5 minutes. 10. Add ground coconut mixed in another cup of water. Bring to boil. 11. Add salt. Check for seasoning. Add fried koftas. Boil for two minutes. 12. Add chopped coriander leaves and remove.

54. HYDERABADI KHEEMA

Ingredients	*For 4*	*For 100*
Mutton	500 gm	12.5 kg
Tomatoes	450 gm	11.00 kg
Ginger	2.5 cm. (1") piece	250 gm
Garlic	3 flakes	50 gm
Green chillies	5	100 gm

Ingredients	*For 4*	*For 100*
Garam masala	a pinch	20 gm
Potatoes	115 gm	2.80 kg
Onions	115 gm	2.80 kg
Curds	55 gm	1.36 kg
Fat	30 gm	500 gm
Salt	to taste	100 gm

Method

1. Clean and mince mutton. 2. Mince onions, garlic and ginger. Chop green chillies. 3. Heat fat. Fry gram, ground masala, onions, ginger, garlic and green chillies. 4. Add meat and fry for a few minutes. 5. Add cut tomatoes and cook covered on slow fire. 6. Sprinkle a little water occasionally. 7. When almost cooked, add diced potatoes, salt, and beaten curds. 8. Cook till potatoes are quite soft. Remove and serve hot.

55. KHEEMA

Ingredients	*Quantity*
Minced meat	500 gm
Fat	55 gm
Green chillies	6
Tomatoes	50 gm
Onions	60 gm
Cinnamon	2.5 cm. (1") piece
Cloves	3
Black cardamoms	2
Bay leaf	2
Chilli powder	2 tsp
Salt	to taste
Turmeric	1 tsp
Peppercorns	6
Coriander leaves	¼ bunch
Eggs (hard-boiled)	4
Green peas (shelled)	115 gm
Water	2 tbsp

Method

1. Chop onion and tomatoes and fry in hot fat. 2. Add all the ingredients except eggs, peas and coriander leaves. 3. Cook on a slow fire for 30 minutes or till the mince is tender. Add a little water if necessary. 4. When three-fourths done add peas. 5. Serve with hard boiled eggs cut into halves. Garnish with chopped coriander leaves.

N.B. Remove whole spices if desired.

56. GREEN MINCE

Ingredients	*For 4*	*For 100*
Mince	250 gm	6.25 kg
Onions (sliced)	1	2.5 kg
Tomatoes (chopped)	1	2.5 kg
Lime juice	of ½ lime	10 to 12 limes
Fat	2 tbsp (50 gm)	600 gm
Salt	to taste	100 gm
To be ground with water		
Coriander leaves	1 bunch	25 bunches
Mint leaves	½ bunch	12 bunches
Green chillies	6-8	200 gm
Ginger	a small piece	75 gm
Garlic	8 flakes	100 gm
Turmeric	1½ tsp	150 gm
Cumin	½ tsp	50 gm
Poppy seeds	1 tsp	75 gm
Peppercorns	¼ tsp	25 gm
Mustard seeds	¼ tsp	25 gm
Groundnuts	4	50 gm
Sultanas	4	30-50 gm

Method

1. Heat fat and sauté the onion till light brown. 2. Add the minced meat and cook till all the water is absorbed. 3. Put in the ground spices and fry well for 10 minutes, till you get a pleasant smell. 4. Add the tomato, salt to taste, and a cup of water and allow the mince to cook gradually. Add lime juice to taste. 5. Check for seasoning and remove. Green peas and potato fingers may be used to garnish this dish.

57. MUTTON AND CARROT KHEEMA

Ingredients	*For 4*	*For 100*
Mutton	500 gm	12.5 kg
Carrot	500 gm	12.5 kg
Green chillies	5 gm	125 gm
Garlic	5 gm	125 gm
Ginger	5 gm	125 gm
Onions	100 gm	2.5 kg
Turmeric	½ tsp	20 gm

Ingredients	*For 4*	*For 100*
Coriander leaves	a few sprigs	2 bunches
Salt & pepper	to taste	100 gm

Method

1. Mince the meat. Chop carrot into small pieces. 2. Chop garlic, ginger and onions. Keep green chillies whole. 3. Mix prepared ingredients, turmeric, salt, and pepper. Add sufficient water to cook minced meat fairly dry. 4. When meat is done and carrots well cooked, add chopped coriander leaves and remove. Serve hot.

58. DAL KHEEMA

Ingredients	*For 4*	*For 100*
Minced meat	250 gm	6.25 kg
Split bengal gram	50 gm	1.25 kg
Onions	100 gm	2.5 kg
Garlic	5 gm	125 gm
Ginger	5 gm	125 gm
Fresh coconut	30 gm	750 gm
Poppy seeds	1 tsp	125 gm
Clove	1	25 gm
Cinnamon	1 piece	25 gm
Coriander	5 gm	125 gm
Red chillies	1-2 gm	50 gm
Turmeric	a pinch	30 gm
Cumin	a pinch	30 gm
Coriander leaves	½ bunch	12 bunches
Oil	15 ml	375 ml
Tamarind	to taste	125 gm (about)
Salt	to taste	100 gm

Method

1. Pick and wash the gram and soak for one hour. 2. Roast and powder coriander, red chillies, turmeric and cumin. 3. Grind together ginger and garlic. Grind separately the coconut and poppy seeds. 4. Chop onions fine. Put minced meat into a vessel; add curry powder, ginger and garlic paste and all but 10 gm of the chopped onions. 5. Cook over moderate heat till minced meat is cooked. Add bengal gram along with the water in which it is soaked. 6. When gram is well boiled, add coconut and poppy seeds paste and salt, diluted in a cup of water. 7. Simmer for half an hour. Add tamarind juice. 8. Simmer for another 5 to 10 minutes. If gravy gets thick, add more water and bring to a boil. 9. Add washed and chopped coriander leaves. Remove from the fire. 10. Heat oil or fat. When

it starts to smoke, add the remaining finely chopped onions, clove and cinnamon stick. 11. When onions brown, pour a spoon of the gravy into the fry pan. 12. Mix well and add to the curry. Stir well.

59. HALEEM

Ingredients	*For 10*
Wheat	250 gm
Mutton (without bones)	300 gm
Green chillies	20 gm
Ginger	5 cm. (2") piece
Garlic	6 flakes
Limes	2
Salt	to taste
Fat	100 gm
Garam masala	2 tsp
Onions	100 gm
Coriander leaves	1 bunch
Turmeric	½ tsp

Method

1. Debran the wheat, wash, cook till very soft and mash well. 2. Clean and cook mutton with a little salt till tender. Mince and grind to a fine paste. 3. Grind ginger, garlic and green chillies to a fine paste. Heat fat, add finely sliced onions, fry till brown. Add the spices and ground mutton. Fry for some time. 4. Add mashed wheat and salt; cook on slow fire till it leaves the sides. Add lime juice. 5. Garnish with coriander leaves and finely sliced onions. Serve hot with fresh salad and nan roti.

60. RAJMAH MEAT CURRY

Ingredients	*For 4*	*For 100*
Kidney beans	50 gm	1.25 kg
Meat	250 gm	6.25 kg
Onions	50 gm	1.25 kg
Fat	10 gm	250 gm
Turmeric	½ tsp	50 gm
Chilli powder	1 tsp	125 gm
Coriander power	1 dsp.	250 gm
Coriander leaves	¼ bunch	6 bunches
Ginger	2.5 cm. (1") piece	250 gm
Garlic	2 to 3 flakes	50 gm
Salt	to taste	100 gm
Green chilli	1	25 gm

Ingredients	*For 4*	*For 100*
Garam masala powder (cinnamon, cloves, cardamom, cumin)	¼ tsp	25 gm

Method

1. Soak kidney beans overnight, or at least for 3 to 4 hours. Grind together onion, garlic, ginger and green chilli. 2. Heat fat. Fry ground ingredients with turmeric, chilli powder and coriander powder. When fat starts oozing out, add meat. Fry well. 4. Add water and simmer over slow fire till meat is half done. 5. Add soaked beans, salt, more water. Cook till meat and beans are tender and the gravy is thick. 6. Sprinkle garam masala over. Remove from fire. 7. Garnish with chopped coriander leaves and serve hot.

61. MUTTON CUTLETS

Ingredients	*For 4*	*For 100*
Leg of mutton	500 gm	12.5 kg
Potatoes	250 gm	6.25 kg
Pepper powder	to taste	50 gm
Salt	10 gm	100 gm
Onions	100 gm	2.5 kg
Egg	1	20
Breadcrumbs	55 gm	455 gm
Ginger	10 gm	250 gm
Green chillies	10 gm	250 gm
Curry leaves	¼ bunch	1 bunch
Fat to fry (absorption)	100 gm	2.5 kg

Method

1. Mince the mutton. 2. Boil and mash the potatoes. 3. Chop onions, green chillies and ginger fine. Heat a small quantity of fat. Sauté onions, green chillies, ginger and curry leaves. 4. Add potatoes, minced meat, pepper and salt. 5. Mix well, remove. The mixture should be moist but not wet. Test for seasoning. 6. Form into balls and flatten. 7. Coat with egg and breadcrumbs. 8. Deep fry and serve hot.

62. SEEKH KABABS

Ingredients	*For 4*	*For 100*
Mutton	500 gm	12.5 kg
Onions	55 gm	1.35 kg
Cardamoms	3	15 gm

Ingredients	*For 4*	*For 100*
Cloves	6	15 gm
Ginger	a small piece	55 gm
Mustard seeds	a pinch	20 gm
Cumin	a pinch	20 gm
Coriander	5 gm	115 gm
Garlic	3 flakes	55 gm
Salt	to taste	100 gm
Egg	1	20-25
Fat	30 gm	750 gm

Method

1. Wash and mince meat. 2. Grind together all the spices. Add meat, salt; grind well. Bind with beaten egg. 3. Divide mixture into even sized balls. 4. Grease skewers. Roll balls on to skewers. 5. Pour melted fat over and grill.

63. KABAB JEERA

Ingredients	*For 4*	*For 100*
Mutton	500 gm	12.5 kg
Cumin	10 gm	225 gm
Chilli powder	5 gm	115 gm
Onions	115 gm	2.8 kg
Coriander leaves	½ bunch	12 bunches
Salt	to taste	100 gm (approx.)
Fat		

Method

1. Clean and mince meat. 2. Chop onions fine. Roast and powder cumin, chop coriander leaves. 3. Mix first six ingredients. Shape like sausages and shallow fry.

64. KABABS BROILED AND SKEWERED

Ingredients	*For 4*	*For 100*
Lean meat	500 gm	12.5 kg
Curds	225 gm	5.6 kg
Red chillies	10 gm	250 gm
Coriander	1 tbsp	85 gm
Ginger	5 gm	115 gm
Lime (large)	1	20
Fat	30 gm	750 gm
Onions	115 gm	2.8 kg

Ingredients		For 4	For 100
Turmeric		1 pinch	20 gm
Peppercorns	garam masala	8	10 gm
Cloves		6	10 gm
Cinnamon		1 piece	10 gm

Method

1. Cut meat into neat 5 cm. (2") pieces. 2. Tie curds in a muslin bag and hang it to let water drip out of it. 3. Grind together red chillies, coriander and ginger using the juice of the lime. 4. Mix ground spices with half the quantity of curds. Add 1 tsp fat (melted). 5. Soak the meat pieces in the mixture for 10 to 20 minutes. 6. Place meat in a pan on fire. Add chopped onions and turmeric. 7. Grind garam masala and add. 8. Add remaining curds and cook meat on gentle heat. 9. When meat is half cooked take it out, cool and put on skewers. 10. Finish cooking over a slow coal fire turning the kababs constantly.

65. STEAMED KABABS

Ingredients	For 4	For 100
Mince meat	500 gm	12.5 kg
Cloves	5	30 gm
Red chillies	2-3	55 gm
Peppercorns	10	15 gm
Cardamom (large variety)	1	10 gm
Salt	to taste	100 gm
Fat	30 gm	500 gm

Method

1. Grind together meat, spices and salt. 2. Take small amounts of meat and roll them sausage fashion. 3. Lay these gently side by side in a wide shallow pan. 4. Put on a slow fire and cover pan with a lid for a few minutes. 5. Pour melted fat over the kababs carefully and fry until they are a nice brown. Serve hot.

66. SHAMI KABABS

Ingredients	For 4	For 100
Bengal gram	55 gm	2.8 kg
Mutton	500 gm	12.5 kg
Onion	55 gm	1.35 kg
Green chillies	10 gm	225 gm
Garlic	a few flakes	50 gm
Ginger	a small piece	105 gm
Pepper	to taste	20 gm

Ingredients	*For 4*	*For 100*
Coriander powder	10 gm	225 gm
Turmeric	a pinch	30 gm
Cumin powder	a pinch	15 gm
Cinnamon powder	a pinch	10 gm
Lime rind (grated)	a little	10 gm
Egg	1	10
Fat to fry	30 gm	500 gm
Salt	10 gm	100 gm
Coriander leaves	½ bunch	3 bunches
Onion rounds to decorate		

Method

1. Soak gram for 2 to 3 hours. 2. Clean and cut mutton. 3. Boil together meat and gram and mince. 4. Chop half of the onion, garlic, ginger, green chillies and coriander leaves. 5. Grind remainder. 6. Mix together gram, minced, meat, salt, all spices except chopped ones and lime rind; grind to a paste. 7. Bind with egg. Divide mixture into equal portions. 8. Place chopped spices and grated rind in the centre, form into balls. Flatten and shallow fry till brown. 9. Serve garnished with rounds of raw onion and chopped coriander leaves.

67. HUSSAINY KABABS

Ingredients	*For 4*	*For 100*
Mutton	500 gm	12.5 kg
Ginger	a small piece	115 gm
Garlic	6 cloves	50 gm
Red chillies	5	115 gm
Cumin	a pinch	20 gm
Salt	to taste	100 gm
Fat	225 gm	1.5 kg

Method

1. Cut mutton into small cubes. 2. Grind together ginger, garlic, red chillies, cumin and salt. 3. Mix mutton with ground paste and set aside for 1½ to 2 hours. 4. Thread 8 to 9 pieces meat on skewers about 15 cm. (6") long. 5. Heat fat and fry the skewered kababs slowly, turning them all the time until they become brown. Serve hot.

68. HAMBURGER (Indian)

Ingredients	*For 4*	*For 100*
Mutton	500 gm	12.5 kg
Ginger	5 gm	115 gm

Ingredients	*For 4*	*For 100*
Green chillies	5 gm	115 gm
Onions	115 gm	2.8 kg
Egg	1	15–20
Salt	to taste	80–100 gm
Fat to fry	30 gm	500 gm

Method

1. Clean and mince mutton. 2. Mince onion, chop finely green chillies and ginger. 3. Mix all ingredients. Divide into even sized portions. Flatten into cakes. 4. Shallow fry till cooked.

69. LIVER KABABS

Ingredients	*For 4*	*For 100*
Liver	500 gm	12.5 kg
Coriander powder	1 tsp	100 gm
Cinnamon	5 cm. (2") piece	30 gm
Cloves	6	10 gm
Garlic	½ pod	115 gm
Ginger	1.25 cm. (½") piece	50 gm
Pepper	1 tsp	50 gm
Curds	55 gm	1.36 kg
Salt	to taste	100 gm
Butter		

Method

1. Cut liver into 5 cm. (2") pieces. Wash and drain. 2. Grind to a fine paste, coriander, cinnamon, cloves, garlic and ginger. 3. Mix together curds, pepper, salt and ground spices. 4. Soak liver pieces in the mixture. 5. Put liver pieces on skewers and stand for 10 minutes. 6. Melt a little butter. Pour over liver and hold skewers over fire for about 10 minutes turning them occasionally.

70. BOTI KABABS

Ingredients	*Quantity*
Mutton (lamb)	250 gm
Cloves, cinnamon, cardamom, black cardamom	1 gm
Cumin	½ gm
Peppercorns	1 gm
Green chillies	2 gm
Ginger	2 gm

Ingredients	*Quantity*
Garlic	2 gm
Curds	50 ml
Lime	½
Green coriander	¼ bunch
Raw papaya	20 gm

Method

1. Cut mutton into even-sized pieces. Apply lime juice. 2. Roast and powder dry spices. 3. Grind green chillies, ginger, garlic and papaya. 4. Mix ground masala and powdered spices, curds and chopped coriander. 5. Add meat pieces and keep for 2 hours. 6. Thread on skewer and roast over a sigree. 7. When done, remove from skewer on to a hot paratha. 8. Roll paratha and fix with toothpicks or roll paratha in grease-proof paper. 9. Serve hot with onion rings.

71. RESHMI KABABS (4 portions)

Ingredients	*Quantity*
Chicken	2
Chopped chillies	10 gm
Garlic (chopped)	15 gm
Besan	100 gm
Butter	150 gm
Beaten curds	200 gm
Salt	to taste
Ginger-garlic paste	10 gm
Garam masala (aniseed, cardamom, cinnamon, mace)	2 gm

Method

1. Sauté garlic in butter, add besan and sauté till cooked without discolouring. 2. Cool mixture and add to the beaten curds with salt and ginger-garlic paste and garam masala. 3. Cut chicken into tikkas and marinade in the mixture. 4. Put the chicken tikkas on the seekhs (tandoori rods) and cook in the tandoor. 5. Garnish with lemon juice.

72. SHIFTA (Mutton, beef or fish)

Ingredients	*Quantity*
Minced beef or mutton or fish	500 gm
Onions (minced)	2
Mint	a little
Salt	to taste
Turmeric	a little

Ingredients	*Quantity*
Ginger	1.25 cm. (½″) piece
Eggs	2
Bread (soaked in water and well squeezed out)	1 slice

Method

1. Mince all ingredients and mix together with eggs and bread. Then divide into approximately a dozen portions. Ball each portion and pass a "seekh" through, moulding it in a long roll round the skewer. 3. Roast on open fire till it is stiff and slides off gently. 4. Before serving fry in oil and serve garnished with parsley.

73. PORK CURRY

Ingredients	*For 4*	*For 100*
Pork	500 gm	12.5 kg
Red chillies	5 gm	125 gm
Coriander seeds	10 gm	250 gm
Cumin	½ tsp	50 gm
Peppercorns	a few	30 gm
Turmeric	½ tsp	30 gm
Onions	250 gm	6.00 kg
Tamarind	5 gm	125 gm
Vinegar	30 ml	500 ml
Garlic	3-5 cloves	100 gm
Ginger	1.25 cm. (½") piece	125 gm
Green chillies	3	75 gm
Curry leaves	a few sprigs	1 bunch
Garam masala	¼ tsp	25 gm
Cinnamon and cloves	2 gm	50 gm
Potatoes	100 gm	2.5 kg
Fat	10 gm	250 gm
Salt	to taste	80-100 gm

Method

1. Clean and cut pork into 2.5 cm. (1") cubes. Roast coriander seeds and red chillies. 2. Grind to a fine paste with cumin, pepper, turmeric, half the onions and the tamarind. Slit green chillies slice ginger, garlic and remaining onions. 3. Boil pork with vinegar, curry leaves, cinnamon and cloves and just enough water to cook pork. 4. Add sliced ingredients and peeled and quartered potatoes. Cook over a slow fire. Meanwhile, in a large pan, fry the ground ingredients lightly. Add meat, potatoes and water, if required. Add salt. 5. Simmer for a few minutes till the fat floats

on top and meat and potatoes are cooked. Sprinkle with garam masala powder. Remove and serve hot.

74. PORK VINDALOO

Ingredients	*For 4*	*For 100*
Pork	500 gm	12.5 kg
Cumin	1 tsp	55 gm
Onions	225 gm	5-6 kg
Turmeric	¼ tsp	15 gm
Mustard	2 tsp	60 gm
Garlic	10 gm	250 gm
Ginger	10 gm	250 gm
Red chillies (remove seeds and soak in vinegar)	5 gm	115 gm
Cloves, Cinnamon, Peppercorns	5 gm	115 gm
Vinegar	100 ml	2.5 litre
Tomatoes	450 gm	11 kg
Curry leaves	a sprig	1 bunch
Salt	to taste	80-100 gm
Oil	30 ml	340 ml

Method

1. Clean and cut meat and wash in diluted vinegar. 2. Grind spices to a fine paste using vinegar. 3. Rub meat with ground spices and salt, and keep for a few hours. 4. Heat oil. Add curry leaves. When browned add meat and vinegar. 5. Add chopped tomatoes and simmer till meat is tender and tomatoes well mashed up.

75. SORPOTEL

Ingredients	*For 4*	*For 100*
Pork	340 gm	8.5 kg
Liver	115 gm	2.8 kg
Onions	30 gm	2.8 kg
Red chillies	5 gm	115 gm
Peppercorns	a few	15 gm
Cumin	a pinch	10 gm
Ginger	10 gm	250 gm
Garlic	4 cloves	30 gm
Garam masala	1 tsp	15 gm
Turmeric	½ tsp	10 gm
Tamarind	15 gm	240 gm
Sugar	½ tsp	10 gm

Ingredients	*For 4*	*For 100*
Vinegar	30 ml	680 ml
Salt	to taste	100 gm
Oil	15 ml	250 ml

Method

1. Boil pork and liver separately. Cut into cubes. 2. Mince the onion, chop ginger and garlic, grind red chillies, peppercorns, cumin, and turmeric to a fine paste. 3. Heat oil, fry onion. Add fresh spices and fry. 4. Add ground spices. Fry well. Add pork and liver. 5. Put in vinegar, tamarind juice, salt, sugar and garam masala and cook till meat is tender, adding a little water if necessary. Set aside for a couple of days before serving.

76. GRILLED SPARE RIBS

Ingredients	*Quantity*
Spare ribs (pork)	1.5 kg
Green chillies	20 gm
Ginger	10 gm
Garlic	10 gm
Papaya (green)	5 gm
Lime	½
Curds	390 ml
Chilli powder	5 gm
Kashmiri chilli powder	5 gm
Salad oil	15 ml
Orange colour	3 gm
Salt	to taste

Method

1. Grind together green chillies, ginger and garlic. Grind papaya separately. 2. Beat curds, add ground ingredients and the chilli powder. Beat well. 3. Add salad oil and colouring and pass through a fine sieve. Cut spare ribs into 10 cm. (4") pieces lengthwise along the bone. 4. Apply lime and salt and set aside for 10 minutes. Then marinade in prepared batter for about 2 to 3 hours. 5. Grill slowly over charcoal on a grid and turn occasionally to develop attractive colour and special flavour.

77. PORK KABABS

Ingredients	*Quantity*
Shoulder or loin of pork, cut in 4 cm. (1½") squares 2 cm. (1") thick.	

Ingredients	*Quantity*
For the marinade	
Salad oil	½ cup
Lime juice	1 tbsp
Onion (chop fine)	1
Garlic (chop fine)	6 cloves
Dry mustard	1 tsp
Pepper	½ tsp
Salt	to taste

Method

1. Mix together all the ingredients. Marinade meat for a several hours or overnight in the mixture. 2. Thread the meat on skewers. Put a grid over live coal in a charcoal stove and cook the kababs over this till done. 3. Brush meat with remaining marinade during cooking.

78. PORK CHOPS IN CHILLI SAUCE

Ingredients	*Quantity*
Pork chops	8
Garlic	8 cloves
Chilli powder	1 tsp
Vinegar	¼ cup
Ginger	a small piece
Salt	to taste

Method

1. Grind together garlic, chilli powder and ginger using vinegar. Apply on chops. Set aside in refrigerator overnight. 2. Add salt and bake in the marinade in a moderately hot oven, about 140°C (375°F), turning a couple of times until chops are done (about 45 minutes).

79. GOAN ROAST SUCKLING PIG

Buy a whole young pig, ask the butcher to clean it well and remove the entrails. Wash well three to four times.

Prepare the stuffing and stuff the belly. Stitch, using a trussing needle and strong thread. Apply salt all over. Place in a roasting tin and roast at 350°F basting frequently. When done, remove and immediately sprinkle over with chilli powder and turmeric (the heat of the roast pigling will cook the spices). Set aside. Into the roasting tin, add flour, chilli powder and turmeric and fry for a couple of minutes. Add water and vinegar and bring to boil. Simmer till gravy consistency is reached.

Ingredients	*Quantity*
The stuffing	
Kashmiri chillies	8
Mustard seeds	1 tsp
Cumin	1 tsp
Turmeric powder	½ tsp
Peppercorns	8
Ginger	5 cm. (2") piece
Garlic	½ pod
Garam masala (cinnamon, cloves, cardamom)	1 tsp
Vinegar and salt	to taste
Cooked potatoes	500 gm
Cooked peas	500 gm
Onions	250 gm
Breadcrumbs	250 gm
Liver	1
Heart	1
Kidney	1
Fat for frying	100 gm

Method

1. Grind dry spices using vinegar. Chop garlic and ginger. 2. Dice potatoes. Chop onions. Cut into fine pieces the liver, heart and kidney (these should be cleaned well by soaking in salt water to remove blood). 3. Heat fat. Fry onions, garlic and ginger. Add ground spices and fry for a few minutes longer. 4. Add vegetables, chopped organ meat and breadcrumbs and mix well.

80. ALU MUCKALA (Chicken or mutton)

Ingredients	*For 6 to 8*
Chicken (medium sized and tender)	1
Onions (medium)	1-2 (225 gm)
Ginger	2.5 cm. (1") piece
Garlic	4 cloves
Turmeric	½ tsp
Cinnamon	2 cm. (1") piece
Cloves	6
Cardamoms	6
Fat or oil	3 tbsp (approx.)

Method

1. Joint chicken into pieces after cleaning and washing. 2. Grind ginger,

garlic and onions into a paste and mix well with cut chicken adding turmeric, salt and oil. 3. Let it steep in this about an hour or more. 4. Settle the pieces well into a pan and pour over the oil and spices that you had steeped it in. 5. Cloves, cinnamon and cardamoms may be added at this stage. 6. Put just a little water—about ½ cup—and cook on a brisk fire until water dries and bottom of pan starts getting red. Keep turning the pieces until it gets evenly red all round. 7. Pour enough water to almost cover chicken. Bring to boil and simmer until water dries and oil comes up. 8. If chicken is still tough add a little more water and simmer on slow fire until ready.

N.B. Chicken should be served dry but moist and golden to reddish in colour.

81. MURGH DO PYAZ

Ingredients	*For 6 to 8*
Chicken (medium whole)	1
Onions	1.35 kg
Potatoes	500 gm
Tamarind	10 gm
Fat	115 gm
Spices for marinade	
Red chillies	2 to 3
Garlic	8 flakes
Cumin	1½ tsp
Mustard seeds	1½ tsp
Coriander	1½ tsp
Ginger	5 gm
Salt	to taste
Stuffing	
Coriander leaves	1 small bunch
Ginger	5 gm (a small piece)
Garlic	6 flakes
Cloves	6
Cardamoms	2
Green chillies	2
Turmeric	1 tsp
Coconut	½ (115 gm)
Salt	to taste

Method

1. Clean chicken but keep whole. 2. Grind the first lot of spices to a fine paste, mix with tamarind pulp extracted in half cup water. Marinade

chicken in this mixture for about 2 to 3 hours. 3. Grind together ingredients for stuffing to a fine paste and mix with fried chopped giblets. 4. Slice onions and halve peeled potatoes. 5. Stuff chicken with ground paste. 6. In a strong pan heat fat. 7. Spread a layer of onion and place chicken on top. Pour marinade mixture over. 8. Surround with halved potatoes. Dot with fat. 9. Cover tightly, and seal with dough. Cook in an oven about 350°F till chicken is tender.

82. MURGH MUSALLAM

Ingredients	*For 6 to 8*
Chicken	1
Turmeric	¼
Cumin	1 tsp
Cinnamon	5 cm. (2") piece
Cloves	4
Cardamoms	2
Ginger	2.5 cm. (1") piece (10 gm)
Garlic	a few flakes
Onions	115 gm
Red chillies	3 (remove seeds)
Salt	to taste
Tomatoes	900 gm
Fat	55 gm

Method

1. Clean and joint chicken into large pieces. 2. Grind spices with salt. Rub over the chicken pieces. 3. Blanch tomatoes and chop. 4. Heat fat, sauté chicken. Add any spice mixture left over in the pan. Cover tightly and cook till all liquid is evaporated. 5. Add blanched, chopped tomatoes, cook till chicken is tender and gravy thick.

83. MURGH MUSALLAM (Stuffed)

Ingredients	*For 6 to 8*
Chicken (large)	1
Eggs	4
Almonds	30 gm
Raisins	30 gm
Garlic	5 gm
Poppy seeds	5 gm
Pepper	5 gm
Cardamoms	2

Ingredients	*For 6 to 8*
Cloves	4
Onions	115 gm
Dry coconut	55 gm
Coriander	20 gm
Fat	225 gm
Curds	225 gm
Cumin	10 gm
Turmeric	½ tsp
Chilli powder	5 gm
Salt	to taste

Method

1. Clean and wash the chicken. 2. Wash insides with tepid water. 3. Mix together two raw eggs, two chopped hard boiled eggs, half the onions sliced, raisins, sliced almonds, a pinch of the pepper and a little salt. 4. Stuff the chicken with the mixture and stitch up. 5. Grind together remaining spices and dry coconut. Mix with 30 gm of curds. 6. Heat fat in a large strong pan. Fry spices. 7. Add remaining curds. Cook for 5 minutes longer. 8. Place stuffed chicken in the pan, cover tightly and cook on a gentle heat till done. 9. Turn the bird occasionally. 10. Remove when done. Take off the stitches. Pour gravy over and serve hot.

84. TOMATO MURGI

Ingredients	*For 6 to 8*
Chicken (fryer)	1
Onions	340 gm
Red chillies	5 to 6
Ginger	1.25 cm. (½") piece
Garlic	2 cloves
Cloves	3 to 4
Cinnamon	5 cm. (2") piece
Tomatoes	500 gm
Fat	45 gm (3 tbsp)
Vinegar	2 tbsp
Salt	to taste

Method

1. Clean and joint chicken. Boil together finely chopped tomatoes and a quarter of the onions (also chopped) with about 2 cups of water. When cooked, pass through a sieve. 2. Grind using the vinegar, the red chillies, ginger, garlic, cloves and cinnamon. 3. Slice the remaining onions. Heat

fat. Add onions and fry. Remove. 4. Add ground ingredients and fry lightly. Add chicken, fried onions, salt and remaining vinegar. Cook, covered, on a slow fire. When half done, add tomato and onion sauce. Cook gently till chicken is very tender. Serve hot.

85. ROGINI CHICKEN

Ingredients	*For 6 to 8*
Chicken	1
Curds	250 gm
Fat	100 gm
For grinding	
Red chillies	10 gm
Cashewnuts	30 gm
Poppy seeds	15 gm
Onion (sliced and browned)	100 gm (1)
Garlic	6-8 flakes
Ginger	2.5 cm. (1") piece (10 gm)
Salt	to taste.

Method

1. Joint chicken. Brown in fat. Do not overfry. Remove. 2. Add ground spices and fry over slow fire till the fat floats on top. Add chicken. 3. Stir well and cook gently sprinkling a little water if necessary. 4. When three-fourths done, beat curds into a smooth paste and pour over the chicken. 5. Cook again till chicken is tender. Do not stir. 6. Garnish with coriander leaves if desired.

N.B. Fat can be reduced by as much as 50 gm if you do not want the dish to be too rich.
A mix of green chillies and red chillies may be used. Add green chillies slit or whole along with the curds.

86. CHICKEN CURRY (A)

Ingredients	*For 6 to 8*
Chicken	1 (about 1.35 kg)
Onions	225 gm
Garlic	6 flakes
Salt	to taste
Lime	1
Fat	30 gm

Ingredients	*For 6 to 8*
For grinding	
Coriander powder	15 gm
Peppercorns	6
Ginger	10 gm
Red chillies	5
Poppy seeds	1 tsp
Cumin	½ tsp
Grated coconut	55 gm (¼)

Method

1. Clean, wash and joint chicken. 2. Slice onions and garlic. 3. Heat fat. Add onions and fry. Add the chicken pieces and brown well. 4. Add sliced garlic and ground spices. Fry for 2 to 3 minutes. 5. Add water and salt and simmer till chicken is tender and gravy is thick. 6. Add lime juice just before serving.

CHICKEN CURRY (B)

Ingredients	*For 6 to 8*
Chicken	1
Onions	150 gm
Tomatoes	150 gm
Salt	to taste
Peppercorns	10
Red chillies	4
Coriander	2 tbsp
Turmeric	1 tsp
Coconut	½
Fat	50 gm

Method

1. Grind coconut and coriander. 2. Grind onions, turmeric, red chillies and peppercorns. 3. In a pan, put in fat, ground ingredients and chicken; cover with a tight lid and cook on a slow fire for about 20 minutes. Add chopped tomatoes. 4. Sprinkle a little hot water and stir well for about 10 minutes. 5. Add more hot water and salt and cook on a slow fire till chicken is tender.

CHICKEN CURRY (C)

Ingredients	*For 8*
Chicken (large)	1
Coconut	½
Onions	2

Ingredients	*For 8*
Poppy seeds	1 tbsp
Turmeric	1 tsp
Garlic	8 cloves
Chilli powder	1 dsp.
Ginger	1.25 cm. (½" piece)
Coriander powder	1 tbsp
Cumin powder	2 tsp
Mustard seeds	1 tsp
Vinegar	2 tbsp (or to taste)
Cinnamon	2 small sticks
Cloves	3 to 4
Cardamoms	3 to 4
Raisins	½ cup (washed, cleaned and ground)
Cashewnuts	½ cup (half to be ground, other half to be left whole)
Onion (finely sliced)	1
Tomatoes (skinned)	2 (finely chopped)
Coriander leaves	1 small bunch (finely cut)
Fat	30 gm

Method

1. Clean, wash and joint the chicken. 2. Grind the coconut, two onions, poppy seeds, garlic, ginger and mustard seeds. Mix all the powdered spices to a paste with water. 3. Heat fat and add spices (cloves, cardamoms and cinnamon). Add the onion finely sliced and fry till light brown. 4. Now add the ground ingredients with the paste and fry for about 5 to 10 minutes till all raw smell disappears and the fat floats on top. 5. Add finely chopped skinned tomatoes and coriander leaves and fry for another 2 to 3 minutes. 6. Now add the chicken and fry for another few minutes till slightly browned. Add the vinegar with the ground raisins and cashewnuts, with 2 cups of water and salt to taste. 7. Cover tightly and cook on slow fire till chicken is cooked. Add whole cashewnuts and serve (if chicken is not well cooked, add a little more water and cook a little longer).

87. GOAN CHICKEN CURRY

Ingredients	*For 6 to 8*
Chicken	1

Ingredients	*For 6 to 8*
Coconut	1
Turmeric	2.5 cm (1") piece
Red chillies	8-10
Peppercorns	6
Cinnamon	5 cm. (2") piece
Cardamoms	4
Ginger	2.5 cm. (1") piece
Cumin	1 tsp
Garlic	1 small pod
Cloves	4
Tamarind	the size of a lime
Vinegar	2 tsp
Oil	2 tbsp
Onions	2
Salt	1 tsp
Sugar (optional)	1 tsp

Method

1. Clean and joint the chicken. Apply salt. 2. Grind turmeric, red chillies, ginger, peppercorns, cinnamon and cardamoms to a fine paste. Slice onions. 4. Heat oil, fry onions till golden brown. Add chicken pieces and fry well. Add a little water and let it cook, covered, till meat is tender. 5. Grate the coconut. Grind and extract milk. When chicken is cooked add spices, coconut milk, tamarind juice, vinegar, salt and sugar and simmer for a few minutes longer.

88. CHICKEN MOILEE

Ingredients	*For 6 to 8*
Chicken (fryer or broiler)	1
Coconut	1
Tomato	1
Onion	1
Fat	1 tbsp
Cumin	½ tsp
Turmeric	½ tsp
Ginger	2.5 cm. (1") piece
Garlic	3-4 flakes
Poppy seeds	1 tsp
Cinnamon	2.5 cm. (½") piece
Green chillies	4-5
Peppercorns	½ tsp
Salt	to taste

Method

1. Wash and joint chicken. 2. Grate coconut. Make three extractions of coconut milk. 3. Chop onion. Grind to a fine paste the cumin, turmeric, ginger, garlic and poppy seeds. 4. Heat fat and fry chopped onion. Add chicken, ground spices, whole cinnamon, pepper and green chillies, pulp of the tomato and second and third extractions of coconut milk. Add salt. 5. Simmer till chicken is tender and gravy is thick. Add first extraction of coconut milk (thick). 6. Bring to boil, test for seasoning and remove.

89. CHICKEN CHACOUTI

Ingredients	*For 6 to 8*
Chicken	1
Coconut	1
Coriander	30 gm
Cumin	1 tsp
Poppy seeds	1½ tbsp
Cardamoms	3
Cinnamon	2 gm
Cloves	2 gm
Ginger	3.5 cm. (1 ½") piece
Mustard seeds	5 gm
Peppercorns	2 gm
Garlic	5 flakes
Kashmiri chillies	12
Onions (large)	5
Turmeric	2.5 cm. (1") piece
Vinegar	½ cup
Tamarind	5 gm
Bayleaf	a few
Mace	a small piece
Dagadful (badyani)	a small piece
Oil	
Salt	to taste

Method

1. Clean and joint the chicken. Apply salt. 2. Chop one onion, apply it to the chicken with vinegar and keep aside. Slice ginger. 3. Fry all spices (except cumin, garlic and mustard seeds) in a little oil till coriander becomes golden brown, then add cumin, garlic and mustard seeds and remove. 4. Slice one onion and sauté till soft. Grate coconut and roast till light brown. 5. Grind spices with fried onion to a fine paste. Grind coconut coarsely, separately. 6. Fry remaining onions, add meat and fry,

then add spices, coconut, tamarind water and salt and a little water; allow to cook on slow fire till done.

90. CHICKEN CALDEEN

Ingredients	*For 6 to 8*
Chicken (tender)	1 (about 650 gm)
Ginger	2.5 cm. (½″) piece
Garlic	3 flakes
Onion	1
Coriander	1 tbsp
Red chillies	2 or to taste
Cumin	1 pinch
Turmeric	½ tsp
Cinnamon	1 small piece
Cloves	3
Peppercorns	5
Coconut	1
Vinegar	1 to 2 tbsp
Salt	to taste
Oil	50 ml

Method

1. Grind to a fine paste the coriander, red chillies, cumin, turmeric, cinnamon, cloves and pepper. 2. Sliçe onion, garlic and ginger. 3. Grate coconut and prepare three extractions. 4. Clean, wash and joint chicken. 5. Heat oil. Add sliced ingredients. Sauté. 6. Add ground paste and fry well. Add chicken and fry for a few minutes longer. 7. Add second and third extractions of coconut milk and simmer till chicken is tender. 8. When chicken is done, add salt, vinegar and first extraction of coconut milk and remove from fire.

91. CHICKEN CURRY MALABAR

Ingredients	*Quantity*
Chicken	1 (about 1.5 kg)
Coriander seeds	10 gm
Red chillies	3 to 4
Onions	225 gm
Coconut	1
Potatoes	500 gm
Curry leaves	2 sprigs
Peppercorns	6

Ingredients	*Quantity*
Turmeric	¼ tsp
Cinnamon	3 to 5 gm
Cloves	3 to 5 gm
Cardamoms	3 to 5 gm
Fennel	3 to 5 gm
Oil (coconut)	15 ml
Small onion	5 gm
Mustard seeds	a pinch
Salt	to taste
Ginger	5 gm
Tempering	
Fat	15 ml
Red onion	5 gm
Cinnamon	a small piece
Cloves (optional)	6

Method

1. Clean and joint chicken. 2. Roast coriander, red chillies, peppercorns, turmeric, cinnamon, cloves and cardamoms. 3. Powder fine and grind to a smooth paste with fennel. 4. Peel and slice onions. Peel and quarter potatoes. Peel and slice ginger. 5. Grate coconut and make three extractions. 6. Heat up oil. Fry small onion sliced and mustard seeds. 7. When seeds splutter add ground paste, chicken pieces sliced onions and curry leaves. 8. Sauté for 3 to 5 minutes. Add salt, cover and cook on slow fire till chicken is nearly done. 9. Add third extraction of coconut milk, potatoes and ginger. 10. When potatoes are cooked, add second extraction. Cook till gravy is fairly thick. 11. Add first extraction of coconut milk, bring to boil and remove. 12 Heat fat for tempering. Add sliced onion (small) and slightly crushed cinnamon and cloves; when onions brown, pour over curry. Mix well.

92. IRAICHI MULUGU

Ingredients	*For 6 to 8*
Chicken (medium)	1
Coconut (large)	1
Red chillies	10
Coriander	15 gm
Peppercorns	2-3
Cumin	a pinch
Red onions	40 gm
Turmeric	2 gm

Ingredients	*For 6 to 8*
Cinnamon	2.5 cm. (½″) piece
Cloves	2-3
Fennel	½ tsp
Ginger	2.5 cm. (1") piece
Coconut oil	1 tsp
Green chillies	2-3
Curry leaves	a few
Salt	to taste
Tamarind	a small ball
For tempering	
Ghee	15 gm
Oil	10 ml
Mustard seeds	one pinch
Red onion	1
Curry leaves	2 sprigs

Method

1. Heat frying pan. Add oil and fry red chillies. When lightly fried, add coriander, pepper, cumin, half of the red onions (sliced) and turmeric. Fry. Remove. 2. Add cinnamon, cloves and fennel in the frying pan while still hot and toss. 3. Grind the spices to a fine paste. Now clean and joint chicken. Smear with ground spices. Add half the coconut sliced, sliced ginger, green chillies, remaining onions (sliced), salt, curry leaves and water to cover and cook till three-fourths done. 4. Fry remaining coconut and grind to a fine paste. Soak tamarind in a cup of water and extract juice. Mix ground coconut in tamarind juice. Add to curry and cook till chicken is tender. There should be plenty of gravy. Remove from fire. Temper. 5. To temper, heat ghee and oil. Add sliced onion. When it browns, add mustard seeds and curry leaves. When seeds crackle, pour over curry and mix well.

93. CHICKEN KHORMA

Ingredients	*For 6 to 8*
Chicken	1 (about 2 kg)
Coconut	1
Poppy seeds	100 gm
Cashewnuts	100 gm
Red chillies	1-2 gm
Green Chilli	1
Coriander	10 gm
Onions	750 gm

Ingredients	*For 6 to 8*
Salt	to taste
Curds	500 gm
Fat	50 gm

Method

1. Clean and joint chicken. Grind together coconut, poppy seeds, cashewnuts, red chillies, green chilli, coriander and half the onions. 2. Heat fat and lightly sauté remaining onions (sliced). 3. Add ground ingredients and fry for a few minutes. 4. Add jointed chicken. Fry for a further 5 minutes. Add salt to taste and beaten curds. 5. Cook over low fire till done.

94. CHICKEN BAFFAT (Mild)

Ingredients	*For 6 to 8*
Chicken	1
Radish	150 gm
Lime	½
Turmeric	¼ tsp
Cinnamon	2.5 cm. (1") piece
Cloves	2
Garlic	3 flakes
Peppercorns	6-8
Poppy seeds	10 gm
Peanuts	5 gm
Split bengal gram	5 gm
Onion	½
Coconut	½
Vinegar	3 tbsp
Green chillies	2
Ginger	1.25 cm. (½") piece
Fat	30 gm
Butter	10 gm
Small onion	1
Curry leaves	1 sprig
Salt	to taste

Method

1. Clean and joint chicken. Roast lightly the gram and peanuts. 2. Grind to a smooth paste with turmeric, cinnamon, cloves, garlic, peppercorns and poppy seeds using vinegar. 3. Separately boil radish in water with the juice of ½ lime. 4. Heat fat in a pan. Sauté sliced ½ onion without discolouring. 5. Add ground spices and sauté for 2-3 minutes more.

6. Add chicken and sliced ginger and broken green chillies. Continue frying. Add salt and allow the water to come out. 7. Meanwhile make 3 extractions of coconut milk. Add the third extract to chicken and cook slowly till it is nearly done. 8. Add second extract and simmer till chicken is tender. Add boiled radish. 9. Now add the first extract and more vinegar and salt if desired. Remove. 10. Heat a little butter in a fry pan. Fry one small onion sliced and curry leaves if desired. Pour over curry and serve hot.

95. CHICKEN MULLIGATAWNY CURRY (Mild)

Ingredients	*Quantity*	
Chicken	1 kg	
Small onions (sliced)	115 gm	I
Garlic (sliced)	6 flakes	I
Ginger (sliced)	2.5 cm. (1") piece	I
Cinnamon	a small piece	I
Tomatoes	225 gm	I
Curry leaves		
Salt	2 tsp	
Kashmiri chillies	2	II
Coriander	10 gm	II
Cumin	a small pinch	II
Fennel	3 gm	II
Peppercorns	20	II
Split bengal gram	10 gm	II
Turmeric	¼ tsp	
Coconut	½ (1st and 2nd extract)	
Lime	1	
For tempering		
Clarified butter	10 gm	
Red onion	1	
Curry leaves	a few	

Method

1. Joint the chicken and simmer gently with the next seven ingredients for about 10 minutes. 2. Roast red chillies and bengal gram separately. Grind together second lot of ingredients to a smooth paste. 3. Add second extract of coconut milk and ground spices to chicken and cook till tender. 4. Add first extract of coconut milk and bring to boil. Remove. 5. Add lime juice and remove. Temper.

96. CHICKEN CHAAT

Ingredients	*For 8*
Chicken	1
Tomatoes	450 gm
Ghee	55 gm
Tamarind	10 gm
Sugar	a little
Onions	650 gm
Ginger	a small piece
Turmeric	a pinch
Garlic	a few flakes
Garam masala (optional)	a pinch
Salt	to taste

Method

1. Clean and joint chicken. 2. Wash and slice tomatoes and keep them separate. 3. Peel and slice onions finely. 4. Grind ginger and garlic and powder garam masala, if used. 5. In a degchi heat oil or ghee. Fry onions till light brown. 6. Add chicken, garlic, ginger, turmeric, salt and garam masala. 7. Stir well for a few minutes. 8. Add chopped tomatoes and very little water. 8. Cook till all the water evaporates. 10. Stir till chicken browns and tomatoes and onions are well dissolved. 11. Add more water and continue to cook till chicken is tender and oil comes up. 12. Add tamarind juice and sugar; simmer and let its gravy thicken. Serve hot.

97. CHICKEN STEW

Ingredients	*For 6 to 8*
Chicken (medium sized)	1
Ginger	10 gm
Onions	225 gm
Green chillies	20 gm
Curry leaves	2 to 3 sprigs
Salt	to taste
Coconut	1
Potatoes	450 gm
Refined flour	1 tsp
Vinegar	15 ml
Tempering	
Small red onion	1
Cinnamon	5 cm. (2") piece
Cloves	6
Clarified butter	15 ml

Method

1. Clean and joint chicken. 2. Peel and quarter onions and potatoes. Peel and slice ginger. Slit green chillies. 3. Make three extractions of coconut milk (thick, medium and thin). 4. In a pan put the chicken, onions, ginger, green chillies, curry leaves and salt. 5. Add a little water and cook till chicken is nearly done. 6. Add third extraction of coconut milk and potatoes. 7. When potatoes are cooked, add flour mixed in a little coconut milk, second extraction of coconut milk and vinegar. 8. Cook till gravy is thick. Add first extraction of coconut milk. Bring to boil and remove. 9. Heat clarified butter. Add sliced onion and slightly crushed cinnamon and cloves; when brown, pour over stew. Mix well.

98. CHICKEN SAUTÉ (Indian style)

Ingredients	*Quantity*
Chicken (broiler)	1
Red chillies	10
Peppercorns	a few
Cinnamon	
Cloves	3 gm
Fennel (saunf)	
Garlic	1 pod
Ginger	2.5 cm. (1") piece
Salt	to taste
Vinegar	1 tbsp
Onions	2 (200 gm)
Tomato	1 large

Method

1. Clean and joint chicken. 2. Grind together all the spices with salt, using vinegar. 3. Slice onions and chop tomato roughly. 4. Apply half the ground spices on chicken and set aside for about 10 minutes. 5. Heat oil. Fry lightly. 6. Fry remaining spices. 7. Add sliced onions, sauté. 8. Add chopped tomato and cook chicken gently till tender. 9. Check for seasoning. Remove.

99. FRIED CHICKEN

Ingredients	*Quantity*
Chicken (medium size)	1.3–1.5 kg
Kashmiri red chillies (remove seeds)	10-15
Sankeshwari chillies	8
Cloves	6
Pepper	5 gm

Ingredients	*Quantity*
Cinnamon	2" piece
Garlic	½ pod
Red onions	60 gm
Salt	to taste
Oil	to fry
Curry leaves	a few

Method

Clean, wash and joint the chicken. Grind together red chillies, pepper, cinnamon, garlic, red onions, and salt. Smear over chicken. Put the chicken in a pan. Add curry leaves and cook till chicken is tender without adding any water. Heat oil and fry the pieces of chicken. Serve hot or cold.

GRAVY (Optional)

Ingredients	*Quantity*
Potatoes	450 gm
Onions	10 gm
Ginger	5 gm
Coconut	115 gm
Vinegar	15 ml
Salt	to taste

Method

1. Peel and cut potatoes and onions into quarters. 2. Peel and slice ginger. 3. Extract coconut milk. 4. In the pan in which chicken was cooked put potatoes, onion and ginger. Add salt and a little water and cook till potatoes are tender. Add coconut milk and vinegar. 5. Bring to the boil and remove.

100. DEVILLED CHICKEN

Ingredients	*For 6 to 8*
Young chicken (broiler)	1
Red chillies	10
Peppercorns	5
Cloves	4
Turmeric	½ tsp
Cumin	1 tsp
Cinnamon	5 cm (2") piece
Cardamom	1
Garlic	1 to 2 cloves
Ginger	2.5 cm (1") piece
Onion	1 large

Ingredients	*For 6 to 8*
Vinegar	1 tsp
Tamarind	50 gm
Thick and thin milk of ½ coconut	
Butter or ghee	30 gm
Salt	to taste

Method

1. Clean and joint the chicken. Sprinkle over with a little salt and set aside. 2. Grind together to a fine paste red chillies, peppercorns, cloves, turmeric, cumin, cinnamon and cardamom. For less pungency, remove seeds from a few chillies. Fry chopped onion. Add sliced ginger and garlic and fry a little longer, then add ground ingredients and fry for another 2 to 3 minutes. 3. Add the chicken. Stir well. Cover and let it cook for about 15 to 20 minutes over a slow fire. Add the thin coconut milk and cook covered for a further 15 minutes. 4. Add tamarind juice and cook till chicken is tender (about half an hour). Add thick coconut milk and bring to boil. Add vinegar and let it simmer for 10 minutes. Remove and serve hot.

101. CHICKEN TEMPERADO

Ingredients	*For 6*
Chicken (small)	1
Red chillies	4
Tamarind	a very small ball
Vinegar	3 dsp.
Sugar	2 tsp
Onion	1 big
Oil	4-6 tsp
Cumin	1 tsp
Garlic	6 flakes
Cloves	4
Salt	to taste
For grinding	
Turmeric	2.5 cm. (1") piece
Ginger	2.5 cm. (1") piece
Peppercorns	12
Cinnamon	a small piece
Cardamom	1

Method

1. Clean and joint the chicken, apply salt and leave for about 20 minutes. 2. Slice onion, heat oil and fry till golden brown. Add chicken pieces and let it cook for about 10 minutes with the lid on. 3. Add tamarind juice

and continue cooking for another 15 minutes. 4. Crush cumin, garlic, cloves and add to the ground spices. 5. Add spices, mix well; add chillies and a little water. Cook for 15 minutes. 6. Add vinegar and sugar. Cook for five minutes and remove from fire.

102. CHICKEN PEPPER FRY

Ingredients		*For 6 to 8*
Chicken		1 small
Onions		2
Curry leaves		a few
Salt		to taste
Oil		3 tbsp
For grinding		
Turmeric	grind to a smooth paste	½ tsp (3 gm)
Chilli powder		1 tsp (5 gm)
Peppercorns		2 tsp (7 gm)
Cumin		1 tsp (5 gm)
Ginger		2.5 cm. (1") piece (12 gm)
Garlic		8 flakes

Method

1. Wash chicken pieces and cook in half a cup of water, adding salt and the ground spices, till tender. 2. Fry chopped onion and curry leaves in oil till golden brown. 3. Add the cooked chicken and fry for five minutes.

103. METHI MURG

A speciality of Hydrabad, Methi (fenugreek) Murg tastes best with fresh fenugreek leaves. The world's finest fenugreek comes from Qasur in Pakistan. *Kasoori methi* or dried fenugreek powder is an adequate replacement for the fresh vegetable.

Ingredients	*Quantity*
Chicken	1 kg
Curds	225 gm
Salt	to taste
Ghee	100 gm
Onions	300 gm
Garlic	30 gm
Ginger	50 gm
Green chillies	6
Turmeric	3 gm
Coriander powder	5 gm

Ingredients	*Quantity*
Red chilli powder	5 gm
Tomatoes	250 gm
Fenugreek (Kasoori methi or	2 tbsp
Fresh methi	2 bunches
Whole Garam Masala	
Green cardamoms	5
Black cardamom	1
Cloves	5
Cinnamon stick	1
Bay leaf	1
Mace	a pinch

Method

1. Clean and remove skin from chicken. Cut into 8 pieces. 2. Whisk the curds in a large bowl. Add salt and marinade chicken in this for at least half an hour. 3. Peel and chop onions and garlic. Chop 30 g of the ginger and cut the rest into juliennes for garnish. Slit, deseed and chop green chillies. Chop tomatoes and coriander. 4. Pre-heat oven to 350°F. 5. In a handi, heat ghee, add whole garam masala and saute till it crackles. Add onions and saute till brown. Add chopped ginger, garlic and green chillies dissolved in a quarter cup of water. Add tomatoes and fry until the fat separates. 6. Add the marinated chicken with the marinade and 3/4 cup of water. Bring to a boil. Cover and simmer until chicken is done and the fat separates. 7. Stir in the cream, sprinkle fenugreek, ginger juliennes and coriander. Cover with a lid. 8. To finish, seal the handi with atta dough and bake in the pre-heated oven for 15 minutes.

104. MURG ADRAKI

Ingredients	*Quantity*
Boneless chicken cubes	500 gm
Dry ginger powder	50 gm
Garlic-ginger paste	50 gm
Onions (chopped)	150 gm
Cinnamon powder	5 gm
Lemon	1
Coriander leaves	10 gm
Mint (chopped)	10 gm
Salt	to taste
Cooking oil	150 gm
Chilli powder	5 gm

Method

Heat oil, add onion and sauté till it turns golden brown. Add ginger-garlic paste and chicken cubes. Sauté for 10 minutes. Add lemon juice and cinnamon powder, mint leaves, salt to taste and garnish with fresh coriander leaves.

105. CHICKEN CURRY MENDES

Ingredients	*For 6 to 8*
Chicken	1 (medium)
Garlic	10 gm
Ginger	10 gm
Kashmiri chillies (remove seeds)	10 gm
Coriander	20 gm
Turmeric	5 gm
Onion (large)	1
Cloves	5
Cardamoms	2
Peppercorns	5
Bayleaf	1
Fat	100 gm
Tomatoes	250 gm
Salt	to taste
Coriander leaves	a few sprigs

Method

1. Clean and joint chicken. 2. Grind separately garlic, ginger and salt. 3. Apply on chicken and set aside. 4. Grind red chillies, coriander and turmeric to a fine paste. 5. Grind one onion separately. 6. Heat fat or oil. Fry one sliced onion till golden brown. 7. Add chicken and fry. Add ground spices and ground onion. 8. Fry over slow fire till flavour develops. 9. Add blanched and chopped tomatoes and about 1 cup of water. Cook till tender. 10. Roast and powder cloves, cardamoms, peppercorns and bayleaf. Sprinkle over chicken. 11. Test for seasoning and remove. Garnish with chopped leaves, and if desired, julienne potatoes.

106. CHICKEN MASALA

Ingredients	*For 6 to 8*
Chicken (fryer)	1
Cumin	1 tsp
Red chillies (remove seeds)	10
Ginger	2.5 cm. (1") piece
Coriander	2 tsp
Turmeric	½ tsp
Garlic	6 cloves
Vinegar	½ cup
Salt	to taste
Fat for frying	

Method

1. Grind the coriander, chillies, turmeric, garlic, ginger and cumin together with salt and vinegar. 2. Clean and joint the chicken. Mix well with the ground ingredients. Allow to stand for 1 hour. 3. Fry in 2 tbsp fat; sprinkle water and cook covered till chicken is tender and there is no gravy. Serve hot.

107. CHICKEN NAWABI

Ingredients	*Quantity*
Chicken	1 kg
Onions	350 gm
Tomatoes	350 gm
Broken cashewnuts	75 gm
Ginger	40 gm
Green chillies	30 gm
Garlic	25 gm
Jeera	5 gm
Cloves	
Cinnamon	3 gm
Cardamom	
Curds	150 ml
Red chilli powder	25 gm
Dhania powder (coriander powder)	20 gm
Coconut	½
Saunf (Fennel)	5 gm
Fat	100 gm
Ghee	20 gm
Kasuri methi	a large pinch
Salt	10 gm
Curry leaves	3 sprigs
Mustard	½ tsp
Coriander leaves	a few sprigs

Method

1. Clean and joint chicken. Wash well and drain. 2. Grind together 15 gms of red chilli powder, 10 gms of dhania powder, garlic and half of the ginger, saunf and jeera. Mix with curds and salt to prepare a marinade and soak chicken pieces in the marinade for half an hour. 3. Soak cashewnuts in hot water and grind to a fine paste. 4. Drain the chicken and cook on a skewer in a tandoor oven or over the sigree (if a tandoor or a sigree is not available brush oil and grill the chicken for at least 15 minutes). 5. Chop onions and tomatoes finely. Slice ginger into thin strips. Slit green chillies. Heat fat, sauté onions till they become pale brown, add tomatoes, ginger and green chillies, fry for a couple of

minutes. Then add cashewnut paste and the liquid in which the chicken was marinated plus the remaining chilli powder and dhania powder. Fry well. Add the chicken, continue frying till the masala is cooked. 6. Meanwhile make two extractions of coconut milk (thick and medium). 7. Add coconut milk — check for seasoning, add a few pieces of curry leaves and cook till the chicken is tender. Then add the roasted and powdered garam masala. Remove from fire. 8. Heat ghee. Add mustard seeds. When seeds crackle, add kasuri methi and curry leaves. Add to the chicken and mix well. 9. Serve hot garnished with chopped coriander leaves.

108. CHICKEN FRY COORG

Ingredients	*Quantity*
Chicken	800 gm (1)
Green chillies	12
Garlic	2 pods
Ginger	5 cm. (2") piece
Onion (large)	1
Cumin	1 tsp
Pepper	2 tsp
Salt	to taste
Fat	50 gm
Vinegar	1 tbsp

Method

1. Grind spices and salt with vinegar. 2. Apply over jointed chicken. Set aside for 1 hour. 3. Heat fat. Add chicken and fry over slow fire. 4. Cook covered till chicken is tender and fat floats on top.

109. TANDOORI CHICKEN

Ingredients	*For 6–8*	*For 100*
Chicken	1	10
Green chillies	20 gm	170 gm
Ginger	10 gm	115 gm
Garlic	10 gm	115 gm
Papaya (green)	5 gm	55 gm
Lime	½	4
Salt	to taste	80 gm
Batter		
Curds	390 ml	3.98 litre
Chilli powder	5 gm	55 gm
Kashmiri chilli powder	10 gm	115 gm
Salad oil	15 ml	250 ml

Ingredients	Quantity	Quantity
Orange colour (Erythrocyn)	3 gm	30 gm

Method

1. Prepare chicken (pluck, singe and skin). 2. Cut slits lengthwise over the breast portion and breadthwise over the leg portion carefully. 3. Apply salt all over. 4. Sprinkle lime juice and keep aside. 5. Grind together green chillies, ginger and garlic. 6. Beat curds thoroughly. Add ground spices. Grind papaya and add. Beat well again. 7. Add the chilli powders and beat well. 8. Add salad oil and colour and strain through a fine sieve. 9. Smear the batter all over the body of the chicken and well inside the slits. Let it soak in the batter for at least 12 hours. 10. Thread chicken on to a thin iron rod and place it well inside the tandoor. 11. Remove after 5-7 minutes. Smear with oil, and place again in the tandoor. 12. Remove when well done. Serve hot with onion rings and pieces of lime.

110. CHICKEN CAFREAL

Ingredients	For 6 to 8
Chicken	1
Ginger	1" piece
Garlic	½ pod
Coriander leaves	½ bunch
Cinnamon	1" (2 pcs.)
Cardamoms	5
Cloves	5
Green chillies	10
Black pepper	to taste
Salt	to taste
Oil	for frying (30 ml)
Butter	50 gm
Soya sauce	1 tsp
Lime	1
Vinegar	1 tbsp

Method

1. Clean and cut chicken into two from the backbone. Make gashes on the chicken. Wash, keep aside, apply salt, lime vinegar and soya sauce. 2. Grind dry ingredients along with coriander leaves. 3. Apply ground masala on chicken along with butter. 4. Heat oil in a frying pan and fry chicken. 5. Keep a small lid on the vessel and weight it down with a

heavy weight. Reduce heat and cook for ½ hour, if necessary keep basting with stock of chicken.

111. BUTTER TANDOORI CHICKEN (CHICKEN MAKHANWALA)

Ingredients	*Quantity*
Chicken	1
Butter for batter	125 gm (approx.)
Butter for basting	125 gm (approx.)
Tandoori masala	
Hot red chilli powder	5 gm
Kashmiri chilli powder	10 gm
Green chillies	20 gm
Ginger	10 gm
Garlic	10 gm

Method

1. Grind tandoori masala and mix with butter. 2. Make incisions or slits on the breasts and legs of the chicken. 3. Marinade chicken in the mixture for 10-12 hours. 4. Bake in the tandoor, basting frequently with butter, till chicken is cooked.

or

Remove when three-fourths done. Fry in butter, return again to the tandoor for 3-4 minutes. Keep basting till done.

Murgh Makhani

Prepare tandoori chicken. Melt butter. Sauté the leftover marinade in butter. Pour over the chicken.

112. DUCK BUFFADO

Ingredients	*For 6 to 8*
Duck	1
Potatoes	225 gm
Cabbage	115 gm
Green peas (unshelled)	225 gm
Vinegar	15 ml (1 tbsp)
Turmeric	¼ tsp
Green chillies	6
Cinnamon	2.5 cm (1") piece
Cloves	6
Onions	225 gm
Mint	a few sprigs

Ingredients	*For 6 to 8*
Fat	30 gm
Salt	to taste

Method

1. Clean and joint duck. 2. Peel and quarter potatoes. Cut cabbage into large pieces. Shell peas. 3. Peel and cut onions into quarters and slit green chillies. 4. In a strong pan, put in fat. Sauté onions without allowing them to brown. 5. Add duck and sauté. Add all the remaining ingredients except vinegar with just enough tepid water to barely cover the solids. 6. Simmer till duck is tender. Add vinegar and serve hot.

113. DUCK MAPPAS

Ingredients	*For 6 to 8*
Duck	1
Chilli powder	1 tbsp
Coriander powder	1 large pinch
Pepper	1 large pinch
Turmeric	1 tsp
Ghee or mixture of ghee and oil	½ cup
Onion	1 large
Vinegar	1 tbsp
Coconut	1
Salt	to taste
To temper	
Ghee	1 tbsp
Cinnamon	2.5 cm (1") piece
Cloves	3
Mustard seeds	1 tsp

Method

1. Clean and joint duck. Grind together chilli powder, coriander, pepper and turmeric, 2. Slice onion. Grate coconut and take out three extractions of coconut milk. Heat oil; add sliced onion and ground ingredients. Sauté. Add duck, fry for 5 minutes. Add salt and third extract of coconut milk and vinegar and bring to boil. Simmer. 3. When the duck is nearly done, add second extract of coconut milk. Simmer for 5-10 minutes. Add first extract. Bring to a boil. Remove from fire 4. Heat ghee. Add crushed cinnamon, cloves and mustard seeds. When the seeds crackle, pour over curry and mix well.

114. DUCK FRY

Ingredients	*For 6 to 8*
Duck	1
Chilli powder	1 tbsp
Coriander powder	2 tbsp
Pepper	½ tsp
Salt	to taste
Vinegar	1 tbsp
Oil	¼ cup
Small red onions	60 gm

Method

1. Clean duck and joint. 2. Grind together chilli powder and coriander, pepper and salt and apply on the duck. 3. Marinade in vinegar for half an hour. 4. Heat oil. Add onions. When they start to brown, add duck and brown well. 5. Add boiling water. 6. Cook on a slow fire till duck is done and no gravy remains.

115. DUCK ROAST

Ingredients	*For 6 to 8*
Plump duck	1 (about 1 kg)
Ginger	2.5 cm. (1") piece
Garlic	6 flakes
Vinegar	2 tbsp
Salt	to taste
Pepper	¼ tsp
Butter	15 gm
Oil	60 ml
Onions	115 gm
Tomatoes	225 gm
Kashmiri red chillies or red chillies with seeds removed	2
Sugar	¼ tsp

Method

1. Clean duck and keep it whole. 2. Grind ginger, garlic and pepper. 3. Apply on duck and prick with a fork to let the spices seep in. 4. Marinade in vinegar for half an hour. 5. Heat butter and oil in a large thick-bottom pan. 6. Add sliced onions, ground red chillies and chopped tomatoes. Add duck and brown. 7. Add two to three cups boiling water and salt. 8. Cook tightly covered till duck is tender. 9. Add sugar and remove from fire.

N.B. It can be served with roast or fried potatoes and boiled vegetables.

116. LIVER CURRY

Ingredients	*For 4*	*For 100*
Liver	225 gm	5.6 kg
Red chillies	5 gm	115 gm
Fennel	5 gm	115 gm
Curry leaves	1 sprig	½ bunch
Ginger	5 gm	115 gm
Turmeric	a pinch	15 gm
Red onions	30 gm	680 gm
Cardamoms	3	10 gm
Garlic	5 flakes	10 gm
Fenugreek powder	a pinch	5 gm
Vinegar	15 ml	340 ml
Coconut	½	12
Fat	30 gm	500 gm
Salt	to taste	80–100 gm

Method

1. Wash and boil the liver with salt. Cut into cubes. 2. Roast and grind red chillies. Grind fennel. Peel and slice ginger, garlic and onions. 3. Grate and extract thick coconut milk. 4. Put the liver into a pan with the coconut milk and all the ingredients except fat. 5. Boil till spices and onions are cooked. 6. Remove gravy. Add fat and fry the liver. 7. Pour back the gravy and cook for about 5 minutes.

117. LIVER AND POTATO CURRY

Ingredients	*For 4*	*For 100*
Liver	225 gm	5.6 kg
Potatoes	200 gm	4 kg
Red chillies	3	100 gm
Coriander	10 gm	250 gm
Cumin	a pinch	30 gm
Peppercorns	a few	30 gm
Onions	225 gm	5.6 kg
Green chillies	10 gm	250 gm
Garlic	a few flakes	30 gm
Ginger	5 gm	115 gm
Coconut	½	12
Fat	15 gm	250 gm
Vinegar	15 ml	340 ml
Curry leaves	a sprig	½ bunch
Salt	to taste	80–100 gm

Method

1. Clean, wash and cut liver into even cubes. 2. Roast and grind red chillies, coriander, cumin and peppercorns. Peel and slice onions, garlic and ginger. 3. Grate and make three extractions of coconut milk (thick, medium, thin) 4. Peel and cut potatoes into small cubes. 5. Cook together liver, third extract of coconut milk and salt for about one hour. 6. Add potatoes, second extract of coconut milk, vinegar, sliced onions, garlic and ginger and ground spices and whole green chillies. 7. When potatoes and liver are done, add thick coconut milk. Bring to boil. Taste for salt and remove. 8. Heat fat. Add curry leaves and a few pieces of onion. When they are brown, pour over curry. Mix well.

118. MASALA TROTTERS (Paya)

Ingredients	*For 6*
Trotters (cleaned)	1 doz.
Red chillies	10
Ginger	2.5 cm. (1") piece
Garlic	8 cloves
Salt	to taste
Turmeric	¾ tsp
Fat	2 tbsp
Chilli powder	½ tsp
Coconut	½
Cinnamon	2.5 cm (1") piece
Cloves	8
Cardamoms	8
Coriander leaves	a few sprigs
Onions	4
Coriander-cumin powder	1 tbsp
Rice flour (to wash trotters)	2 to 3 tbsp

Method

1. Wash trotters using rice flour to rub in. 2. Boil washed trotters in a cooker for 20 to 25 minutes with 5 cups of water. 3. Grind red chillies, coconut, ginger, garlic, cinnamon, coriader-cumin powder, cloves, cardamoms, turmeric powder, chilli powder and coriander leaves to be a fine paste. 4. Fry sliced onions in fat and remove. 5. In the same fat, fry spices to a golden brown colour. 6. Add fried onions, spices and salt to trotters and simmer till the gravy is thick. 7. Serve with onion cuchumber and chapaties.

INDIAN SWEETS

1. Balushai
2. Gaujas
3. Chiroti
4. Shakar Para
5. Semiya Payasam
6. Palpayasam
7. Payasa or Akki Paramanna
8. Sakarai Pongal
9. Pressed Rice with Jaggery and Coconut
10. Chana Dal Payasam
11. Falooda
12. Doodh Pak
13. Carrot Kheer
14. Badam Kheer
15. Sweet Potato Kheer
16. Phirnee
17. Mock Basundi
18. Doodh Kamal
19. Rabri
20. Carrot Hulwa
21. Beetroot Hulwa
22. Bottle Gourd Hulwa
23. Sooji Hulwa
24. Pumpkin Hulwa
25. Potato Hulwa
26. Wheat Hulwa White
27. Wheat Hulwa Black
28. Moong Dal Hulwa
29. Chakka Varattiathu
30. Peda
31. Vanilla Barfi
32. Coconut Barfi
33. Chocolate Barfi
34. Tricolour Barfi
35. Cashewnut Barfi
36. Besan Barfi
37. Semolina Ladoo
38. Boondi Ladoo
39. Til Ladoo
40. Besan Ladoo
41. Churma Ladoo
42. Magaj
43. French Toast
44. Shahi Tukra
45. Sewain
46. Coconut Chikki
47. Peanut Chikki
48. Til Chikki
49. Til and Gram Chikki
50. Coconut Sweet
51. Coconut Cubes
52. Chana Dal Toffee
53. Jallebi
54. Nut Balls
55. Jangri
56. Gulab Jamun (A)
    Gulab Jamun (B)
    Gulab Jamun (C)
57. Rasgullas
58. Shrikhand
59. Puran Poli
60. Sweet Potato Puran Poli
61. Obattu
62. Thali Sweet
63. Crullers
64. Kangan
65. Mohanthal
66. Karanjia
67. Nevri
68. Chandrakala
69. Malpuras (A)
    Malpuras (B)
70. Khoa Cakes
71. Mysore Pak (A)
    Mysore Pak (B)
    Mysore Pak (C)
72. Potato Pak
73. Amrit Pak
74. Stuffed Doodhi
75. Ijzer Koekjes
76. Achappam (Rose koekje)

77. Petha
78. Khaja
79. Sheera
80. Modaks
81. Kozhukutta
82. Bibique
83. Bhakra
84. Chapat (Sweet pancakes)
85. Rawo/Ravoo
86. Appam

I. BALUSHAI

Ingredients	*For 4*	*For 100*
Refined flour	115 gm	2.8 kg
Soda bicarbonate	a pinch	1 tsp
Fat	45 gm	900 gm
Curds	15 gm	680 gm
Cold water to mix		
Cardamoms	2	30 gm
Fat to fry (absorption)	30 gm	500 gm
Pistachio nuts	a few	115 gm
Syrup		
Sugar	115 gm	2.8 kg
Water	30 ml	900 ml
Lime juice	a few	drops

Method

1. Sieve flour with salt and soda bicarbonate. 2. Add crushed cardamoms. Rub in fat beaten curds. 3. Add cold water to make a soft dough. 4. Divide into equal sized balls. 5. Flatten each ball between the palms so as to have the centre thinner than the sides. 6. Put into deep hot fat on slow fire; leave them in without disturbance for 10 minutes. 7. Turn over and repeat process. 8. When cooked, remove from fat and drain. 9. When quite cold dip them in prepared sugar syrup and garnish with sliced pistachio nuts. 10. To prepare syrup boil water and sugar and stir till dissolved. Cook to one string consistency, sprinkle lime juice.

2. GAUJAS

Ingredients	*25 pieces*	*200 pieces*
Refined flour	115 gm	900 gm
Fat (hydrogenated)	15 gm	120 gm
Salt	a pinch	10 gm
Cardamoms	4	15 gm
Fat for frying (absorption)	15 gm	100 gm

Ingredients	*25 pieces*	*200 pieces*
Syrup		
Sugar	115 gm	0.90 kg
Water	30 ml	240 ml
Lime Juice	a few drops	1

Method

1. Mix flour, fat and salt and prepare a stiff dough using a little water (60 ml for 25 pieces). 2. Divide into even sized balls. Roll into thin poories about 7.5 cm. in (3") diameter. 3. Make slits in the centre taking care that the ends are not separated. 4. Roll from either side to the centre. Fold ends and twist. 5. Deep fry in hot fat 6. Remove and dip in prepared sugar syrup of 2 string consistency. 7. Sprinkle crushed cardamoms over.

N.B. Powdered sugar may be sprinkled over fried gaujas while they are still hot, instead of putting them in syrup.

3. CHIROTI

Ingredients	*25 pieces*	*100 pieces*
Refined flour	200 gm	1 kg
Rice flour	30 gm	120 gm
Fat	115 gm	460 gm
Sugar (powdered)	100 gm	400 gm
Salt	a pinch	1 level tsp
Fat for frying (absorption)	50 gm	150 gm
Rice flour for dusting	50 gm	150 gm

Method

1. Sieve flour with salt; rub in half the fat. Make dough as for puries using a little water (60 ml for 25 pieces). 2. Cream rice flour and remaining fat. Leave in cold water. 3. Divide dough into small balls and roll into thin chapaties. 4. Take one chapati, smear with the creamy mixture. Sprinkle with a little rice flour and place another chapati on top of it. Smear again with cream and dust over with rice flour. 5. Roll and cut into pieces; roll slightly and deep fry. Sprinkle powdered sugar over while it is still hot. 6. Repeat process.

4. SHAKAR PARA

Ingredients	*Quantity*
Refined flour	225 gm
Sugar	115 gm

Ingredients	*Quantity*
Fat	30 gm
Water	30 ml
Curds	1 tsp
Salt	a pinch
Cardamoms	2
Fat for frying	

Method

1. Sieve flour with salt. 2. Rub in fat. 3. Dissolve sugar in water. 4. Add to flour with curds and more water if necessary to make a stiff dough. 5. Roll out to 0.5 cm. (⅛″) thickness. 6. Cut into long strips and then cut into diamonds. 7. Fry in deep fat on slow fire till light brown. Sprinkle with crushed cardamoms.

5. SEMIYA PAYASAM

Ingredients	*For 4*	*For 100*
Vermicelli	55 gm	1.35 kg
Milk	250 ml	6.25 litre
Fat	30 gm	500 gm
Sugar	55 gm	1.35 kg
Saffron	a pinch	2 packages
Sultanas	30 gm	680 gm
Cashewnuts	30 gm	680 gm
Cardamoms	a few	15 gm

Method

1. Heat fat. Fry vermicelli. 2. Add milk and bring to boil quickly. 3. Add sugar and remove from fire. 4. Fry cashewnuts and sultanas and add to payasam with crushed cardamoms. Add saffron soaked in a little milk.

6. PALPAYASAM

Ingredients	*Quantity*
Milk	1 litre
Rice (small grain)	100 gm
Sugar	200 gm
Sultanas	15 gm
Cashewnuts	15 gm
Cardamoms	2 gm
Clarified butter	30 gm
Water	200 ml

Method

1. Wash and soak rice. 2. Cook rice in water with half the milk. Cook till soft. 3. Add remaining milk and sugar and cook till it becomes thick. Mix well. 4. Fry nuts and sultanas in clarified butter and add to payasam. 5. Powder cardamoms and sprinkle over.

7. PAYASA OR AKKI PARAMANNA

Ingredients	*Quantity*
Rice	1 kg
Jaggery or sugar	1½–2 kg
Coconut	1
Cardamoms	10 gm
Cashewnuts	50 gm
Nutmeg	a bit
Raisins	20-25 gm
Water as required (approx. 3–4 litres)	

Method

1. Boil in plenty of water till rice is soft, add jaggery, cashewnuts, raisins. 2. Boil till it is moderately thick, take off the fire, add coconut milk and powdered cardamoms and nutmeg.

N.B. In case sugar is used, coconut milk is not added; instead fresh milk is added.

8. SAKARAI PONGAL

Ingredients	*Quantity*
Split green gram	30 gm
Rice	90 gm
Jaggery	225 gm
Clarified butter (ghee)	50 gm
Banana (cooking)	1
Sultanas	15 gm
Cashewnuts	15 gm
Sugar candy	15 gm
Cardamoms	4

Method

1. Fry gram lightly. 2. Boil water, add gram and then rice. 3. Cook till soft and all water is evaporated. 4. Add jaggery and mix well and cook till dissolved. 5. Fry nuts in ghee and mix with rice. 6. Slice and add bananas. Add coarsely powdered sugar candy and cardamoms. 7. Mix well together.

9. PRESSED RICE WITH JAGGERY AND COCONUT

Ingredients	*Quantity*
Pressed rice	100 gm
Jaggery (grated)	100 gm
Coconut (grated)	75 gm

Method

1. Mix together and serve immediately.

10. CHANA DAL PAYASAM

Ingredients	*Quantity*
Split bengal gram	55 gm
Water	115 ml
Coconut	115 ml
Jaggery	115 ml
Cardamoms	15 gm
Clarified butter	30 gm

Method

1. Pick and wash gram. 2. Cook gram in water till soft. 3. Add jaggery to gram. Cook for 10 to 15 minutes. 4. Extract coconut milk. Add to gram. 5. Cook till it thickens. Add cardamom powder and clarified butter.

11. FALOODA

Ingredients	*Quantity*
Milk	1 litre
Cream	170 gm
Rose syrup	300 ml
Sugar	85 gm
"Tukmeri" or Sabja seeds	4 tbsp
Cornflour	60 gm

Method

1. Mix cornflower with a little cold milk to a smooth paste. 2. Boil half the milk. Add half the sugar. 3. Pour over cornflour paste stirring well. 4. Return to fire and cook till thick. 5. When thick, remove and pass through a colander on to ice cold water. 6. Meanwhile soak sabja seeds in cold water and allow them to swell. 7. Pour a small quantity of rose syrup in 6 glasses. 8. Put in soaked sabja seeds and the cornflour globules. 9. Mix remaining milk and sugar and pour into the glasses. 10. Top with cream and serve cold with crushed ice cubes.

12. DOODH PAK

Ingredients	*For 4*	*For 100*
Rice	30 gm	680 gm
Milk	590 ml	12.25 litre
Sugar	115 gm	2.8 kg
Charoli nuts	30 gm	680 gm
Cardamoms	a few	15 gm
Pistachio nuts	15 gm	340 gm
Almonds	15 gm	340 gm

Method

1. Heat milk in a thick-bottomed pan. 2. Stir till it boils. Add washed rice. 3. Simmer for half an hour stirring occasionally. 4. Add sugar and nuts. Cook on a very slow fire till thick. 5. Sprinkle powdered cardamoms. Serve hot or chilled as desired.

13. CARROT KHEER

Ingredients	*Quantity*
Carrots	250 gm
Milk	600 ml
Sugar	60 gm
Almonds or cashewnuts	30 gm
Cream	30 ml
Saffron	¼ tsp
Water	

Method

1. Wash, scrape and grate the carrots. 2. Place in a pan with enough water to half-cook carrots. 3. Cover pan and cook over slow heat till carrots are half-cooked. 4. Add milk, sugar and ground blanched almonds to carrots. 5. Cook gently stirring all the time. 6. Soak saffron in a dessertspoon of warm water. Mix to a paste. 7. When the carrots are cooked and mixture thick, add saffron. 8. Remove from fire and allow to cool (preferably over ice or in refrigerator). 9. When cold, stir in the cream. 10. Pour into a glass bowl. Garnish with silver paper and sliced almonds or cashewnuts.

14. BADAM KHEER

Ingredients	*For 4*
Almonds	50 gm
Milk	800 ml
Cardamoms	3
Sugar	50 gm
Saffron	a pinch

Method

1. Blanch and grind almonds into a smooth paste. 2. Boil the milk with sugar and almond paste. 3. Add powdered cardamoms and saffron. 4. Remove from heat. Chill and serve.

15. SWEET POTATO KHEER

Ingredients	*Quantity*
Milk	½ litre
Sweet potatoes	100 gm
Sugar	100 gm
Rose water to flavour	
Sultanas	30 gm
Cashewnuts	30 gm
Fat	20 gm
Cardamoms	2 to 4
Saffron or colour	

Method

1. Fry sultanas and cashewnuts and keep aside. 2. Boil or roast sweet potatoes in their jackets. Cool, peel and mash. 3. Boil milk. Add sugar and potatoes. 4. Add fried sultanas and nuts. 5. Finish off with rose water, powdered cardamom and saffron.

16. PHIRNEE

Ingredients	*For 4*	*For 100*
Rice flour	30 gm	680 gm
Sugar	60 gm	1.35 kg
Milk	300 ml	6 litre
Almonds or cashewnuts	15 gm	340 gm
Pistachio nuts	10 gm	250 gm
Cardamoms	a pinch	15 gm

Method

1. Mix rice flour with a little cold milk. 2. Boil remaining milk. Add to rice flour mixture. 3. Cook on slow fire till it becomes fairly thick. 4. Draw the pan to the side of the fire and sprinkle sugar. 5. When the sugar is dissolved and the contents are thick, remove from fire. Sprinkle with cardamom powder. 6. Pour into flat dishes (phirnee looks best if it is set in individual dishes). 7. Decorate with shredded nuts. Cool and serve.

N.B. Silver paper may be used to decorate.

17. MOCK BASUNDI

Ingredients	*For 15*
Milk	1 litre
Condensed milk	1 tin
Bread	400 gm
Nuts	25 gm
Silver foil	2
Almond or kewra or rose essence	a few drops

Method

1. Remove crust from the bread. Soak bread in milk for ½ hour. 2. Mix condensed milk into milk mixture. Pass the whole through a strainer. 3. Simmer for 15 to 20 minutes on a slow fire. Remove from fire, add nuts (chopped) and essence. 4. Chill thoroughly before serving. Serve garnished with silver foil.

18. DOODH KAMAL

Ingredients	*Quantity*
Milk	1 litre
Sugar	50 gm
Oranges	4
Rose water	a few drops

Method

1. Boil milk to a third. Add sugar and rose water. 2. Peel oranges. Remove skin and seeds from each segment, keeping each segment whole. 3. Pour milk into a glass bowl. Arrange segments of orange and chill. 4. Serve cold.

19. RABRI

Ingredients	*Quantity*
Milk	2.5 litre
Sugar	225 gm
Almonds	30 gm
Charoli nuts	30 gm
Cardamom	5 gm

Method

1. Boil milk until it gets thick. 2. Add sugar. Simmer for another 10 to 15 minutes. 3. Add blanched and sliced almonds, sliced charoli and coarsely powdered cardamom. 4. Cool and serve.

20. CARROT HULWA

Ingredients	*For 4*	*For 100*
Carrots	225 gm	5.65 kg
Sugar	115 gm	2.8 kg
Milk	500 ml	12.5 litre
Hydrogenated fat or clarified butter	55 gm	1.35 kg
Dried fruits and nuts	20 gm	450 gm
Cardamoms	a little	15 gm

Method

1. Wash carrots, scrape and grate. 2. Add carrot to milk and cook. 3. When milk dries up add fat and fry. 4. Add sugar, prepared fruits and crushed cardamoms.

21. BEETROOT HULWA

Ingredients	*For 4*	*For 100*
Beetroot	225 gm	5.65 kg
Sugar	115 gm	2.8 kg
Mawa	115 gm	2.8 kg
Clarified butter or hydrogenated fat	55 gm	1.35 kg
Cardamoms	a few	15 gm
Pistachio nuts	30 gm	680 gm
Silver paper		

Method

1. Peel and grate beetroot. 2. Heat fat. Fry grated beetroot. Add a little water and let it cook. 3. Add sugar and continue cooking. 4. When the mixture is almost dry, add mawa and powdered cardamoms. 5. Cook till it forms balls when tested with fingers. 6. Remove and spread on a greased plate. 7. Sprinkle with chopped nuts and garnish with silver paper.

22. BOTTLE GOURD HULWA

Ingredients	*For 4*	*For 100*
Bottle gourd	450 gm	11 kg
Milk	500 ml	12.5 litre
Sugar	340 gm	8.5 kg
Fat	115 gm	2.8 kg
Cardamoms	3	15 gm

Method

1. Peel and grate gourd. 2. Boil in milk; cook till all moisture is dried up. 3. Add sugar, fat and dry fruits and nuts if desired. 4. Fry for a few minutes. Sprinkle cardamom powder over.

23. SOOJI HULWA (4 portions)

Ingredients	*Quantity*
Semolina (sooji)	100 gm
Sugar	100 gm
Fat	40 gm
Cardamoms	4 to 5
Water	200 ml

Method

1. Melt fat and roast semolina till it is light brown. 2. Add hot water and mix well. Keep the degchi covered for 2 minutes. 3. Add sugar and mix well. Add cardamom powder. 4. Cook for five minutes till all the sugar melts. 5. Remove from fire and serve.

24. PUMPKIN HULWA

Ingredients	*For 4*	*For 100*
Pumpkin	225 gm	5.65 kg
Sugar	55 gm	1.35 kg
Milk	300 ml	7.5 litre
Clarified butter	30 gm	680 gm
Sultanas	10 gm	225 gm
Cashewnuts	10 gm	225 gm
Cardamoms	a few	30 gm

Method

1. Wash, peel and grate pumpkin. 2. Remove excess moisture by squeezing. 3. Add milk and sugar and boil till it is dry, stirring all the time. 4. Add ghee, sultanas and nuts, stir till quite dry. Add crushed cardamoms and remove.

25. POTATO HULWA

Ingredients	*Quantity*
Potatoes	400 gm
Sugar	300 gm
Cardamoms	4
Saffron	a pinch
Mawa	115 gm
Clarified butter	55 gm

Method

1. Boil potatoes. Peel and mash. 2. Put sugar and potatoes in a strong degchi and cook. 3. When half cooked add mawa, ghee, saffron and cardamoms. 4. When ready, spread on a greased plate and cut into pieces.

26. WHEAT HULWA WHITE

Ingredients	*Quantity*
Whole wheat or	1 kg
Wheat flour	450 gm
Sugar	1.8 kg
Milk	1.2 litre (2 bottles)
Water	4.75 litre (8 bottles)
Vegetable shortening	450 gm
Pure ghee	225 gm
Cashewnuts	225 gm
Cardamoms	10 gm

Method

1. Soak wheat in water for about 16 hours (change water twice during soaking period). 2. Grind in a round stone grinder. 3. Strain through a coarse jelly cloth. 4. If wheat flour is used, make a wet dough. Leave overnight. 5. Pass through a fine cloth. 6. Mix together wheat, milk, water and sugar. 7. Cook till thick, stirring all the time. When thick add fat and cashewnuts. 8. Continue cooking till a small portion rolled between thumb and forefinger forms a non-sticky ball. 9. Remove from fire. Add powdered cardamoms. 10. Spread in flat 2.5 cm. (1") deep metal trays. Leave to cool. Cut into 5 cm. (2") pieces. Tin and use as required.

27. WHEAT HULWA BLACK

Ingredients	*Quantity*
Wheat flour	450 gm
Molasses	1.35 kg
Water	4.75 litre
Coconut	2
Clarified butter	225 gm
Vegetable fat	225 gm
Cashewnuts	225 gm
Cardamoms	10 gm

Method

1. Prepare dough as for wheat hulwa (white). Leave overnight. 2. Pass through a fine cloth. 3. Dissolve molasses in the given water over gentle heat. 4. Grate coconut and extract coconut milk (about 1 litre). 5. Mix together wheat, molasses syrup and coconut milk and cook, stirring well till thick. 6. When quite thick add fat and cashewnuts. Cook till a small portion rolled between thumb and forefinger forms a non-sticky ball. 7. Remove from fire. Add powdered cardamoms. 8. Spread in flat 2.5 cm. (1") deep metal trays. 9. Leave to cool. Cut into 5 cm. (2") pieces. Tin and use as required.

28. MOONG DAL HULWA (Rajasthani)

Ingredients	*Quantity*
Split green gram	150 gm
Milk	150 ml
Sugar	100 gm
Fat	100 gm
For decorating	
Almonds	
Colour	
Cardamoms	
Cashewnuts	

Method

1. Soak the gram for 4-5 hours. Grind to a very fine paste. 2. Melt fat in a karai (fry-pan) and add ground gram. Fry to a slight brown colour over a very slow fire. 3. Boil milk separately with sugar. 4. When gram starts browning add milk. 5. Keep on stirring, (it should not stick to the sides of the pan) till all the milk gets dried up and fat starts oozing out from the halwa. 6. Remove and serve hot, garnished with the dry fruits.

29. CHAKKA VARATTIATHU

Ingredients	*Quantity*
Jackfruit pods with seeds removed	1 kg
Jaggery	500 gm
Fat (preferably clarified butter)	115 gm
Cardamom powder	a pinch

Method

1. Mince jackfruit. Prepare a thin syrup with jaggery and water and strain. 2. Place jackfruit in a deep and thick-bottomed pan. Cover with water and cook. 3. When nearly dry and cooked, add the jaggery syrup.

Stir continuously till all the moisture has evaporated. 4. Add the fat and continue stirring till the fat starts separating from the mixture. Sprinkle over with cardamom powder. 5. Mix well. Remove on to a greased plate and spread evenly. Cool, cut into squares and bottle.

30. PEDA

Ingredients	*16 pieces*	*100 pieces*
Mawa (dried whole milk)	225 gm	1.5 kg
Sugar	115 gm	750 gm
Cardamoms	a few	15 gm
Pistachio nuts	10 gm	250 gm
Silver paper	a few	15 gm

Method

1. Mix mawa with sugar. 2. Put into a karai or fry-pan and cook on a very slow fire stirring all the time. Add crushed cardamoms. 3. When mixture is ready (mixture forms balls when tested with fingers) pour into trays and leave to set. 4. Break up when set. Form into desired shapes and decorate with pistachios and silver paper.

31. VANILLA BARFI

Ingredients	*Quantity*
Mawa	2.75 kg
Sugar	1.35 kg
Vanilla	15 ml

Method

1. Mix sugar and mawa, put into a fry-pan and stir. Add vanilla essence. 2. When reddy (mixture forms balls when tested with fingers) put into a greased tray and allow to set and cool. 3. Cut into shapes and use.

32. COCONUT BARFI

Ingredients	*Quantity*
Mawa	2.75 kg
Sugar	1.35 kg
Coconut (grated fine and dried)	340 gm
Pink or green colour if desired	

Method

1. Mix sugar with mawa and put into a fry-pan over gentle heat and stir. 2. When mixture is ready (mixture forms balls which tested with fingers) remove from fire. Add coconut and stir well. 3. Spread on a greased tray

(keeping a little aside). 4. Mix colouring with the portion set aside (the colour should be light). 5. Put back on fire. Cook till it becomes creamy. 6. Spread on top of the first layer. Allow to cool, cut into cubes and use as desired.

33. CHOCOLATE BARFI

Ingredients	*Quantity*
Mawa	2.75 kg
Sugar	1.35 kg
Cocoa	255 gm

Method

1. Mix sugar with mawa; put into a fry-pan and stir. 2. When ready (mixture forms balls when tested with fingers), put half into a greased tray and allow to set. 3. Blend cocoa with the other half and heat till it becomes creamy. 4. Spread over the first layer and allow to cool. Cut into shapes and use.

34. TRICOLOUR BARFI

Ingredients	*Quantity*
Mawa	680 gm
Sugar	340 gm
Cocoa	30 gm
Almonds	55 gm
Pistachio nuts	55 gm
Glace cherries	55 gm
Pink colour, Silver paper	
Crushed cardamom	a little

Method

1. Rub mawa and sugar together and divide into 3 portions. 2. Cook one portion on a slow fire till sugar is dissolved. 3. Continue cooking slowly till mixture forms a ball when tested between finger and thumb. 4. Add finely shredded cherries and pink colour. 5. Turn out on to a greased tray and spread evenly. 6. Cook second portion same as the first; add crushed cardamom and sliced pistachio nuts. 7. Spread over first layer. 8. Cook third portion. Add cocoa and blanched chopped almonds. Spread over second layer. 9. Put silver paper over. Cut into diamonds.

35. CASHEWNUT BARFI

Ingredients	*Quantity*
Sugar	300 gm
Cashewnuts	100 gm

Ingredients	*Quantity*
Coconut	150 gm
Cardamom	2 gm
Fat	10 gm

Method

1. Soak cashewnuts in water for 1 hour. 2. Grind coconut and cashewnuts into a fine paste. 3. Add sugar and cook the mixture on a slow fire stirring constantly. 4. Add fat and keep stirring until the mixture leaves the sides of the pan. 5. Add cardamom powder, and remove the mixture, and put on a greased plate for cooling. 6. When cold, cut into cubes.

36. BESAN BARFI

Ingredients	*Quantity*
Bengal gram flour	500 gm
Fat or mixture of clarified butter	500 gm
Sugar	500 gm
Salt	a pinch
Cardamoms	5-10 gm
Nuts	30 gm

Method

1. Fry the gram flour in fat. Remove and set aside. 2. Prepare sugar syrup (use ½ the amount of water to sugar) of one-string consistency. 3. Add the fried flour and cook till it forms a lump in the centre of the pan. 4. Remove from fire, sprinkle crushed cardamom, add salt and chopped nuts. 5. Mix well and spread on to greased board 2.5 cm. (1") in thickness. 6. Cool and cut into diamond shapes.

37. SEMOLINA LADOO

Ingredients	*12 ladoos*	*120 ladoos*
Semolina	225 gm	2.25 kg
Sugar	225 gm	2.25 kg
Fat	100 gm	1 kg
Coconut	150 gm	1.5 kg
Milk	1 dsp	150 ml
Cardamoms	5 gm	115 gm

Method

1. Grate coconut and put it in the sun to dry. 2. Roast semolina in fat, sprinkle milk. 3. Stir well and remove from fire. 4. Mix semolina with grated coconut and powdered cardamom. 5. Add a little water to sugar and make a sticky syrup. When ready add mixture and prepare ladoos by shaping into balls.

38. BOONDI LADOO

Ingredients	*For 4*	*For 100*
Gram flour	115 gm	5.45 kg
Yellow colour	5 gm	15 gm
Soda bicarbonate	a small pinch	1 tsp
Sugar	115 gm	5.45 kg
Water	60 ml	2.95 litre
Cardamoms	a few	15 gm
Pistachios	5 gm	115 gm
Fat (absorption)	30 gm	370 gm

Method

1. Make a thick batter with gram flour and soda bicarbonate dissolved in water. 2. Heat fat in a deep fry-pan. 3. Drop batter through a perforated spoon. Fry for one to two minutes. 4. Prepare sugar syrup with sugar and water to two string consistency. 5. Put fried boondi into syrup. Add crushed cardamoms and pistachio nuts and form into balls. The colour can be added to the batter to make it yellower.

39. TIL LADOO

Ingredients	*Quantity*
Gingelly seeds	85 gm
Roasted peanuts	85 gm
Jaggery	115 gm
Fat	½ dsp

Method

1. Pick and roast (broil) gingelly seeds without discolouring. 2. Chop peanuts. 3. Cut jaggery into small pieces. Add 90 ml water and half a dessertspoon of fat to it. 4. Cook till syrup forms hard ball stage. 5. Add gingelly seeds and chopped nuts. Remove from fire and shape quickly into smooth balls, the size of a lime.

40. BESAN LADOO

Ingredients	*Quantity*
Bengal gram flour	500 gm
Fat	300 gm
Powdered sugar	500 gm
Cardamoms	10 gm

Method

1. Heat fat. Add gram flour and fry. 2. Remove pan from fire. Cool. Add powdered sugar. Mix well. 3. Add crushed cardamoms. Form into even shaped balls with the hands.

N.B. A sticky sugar syrup can be prepared and the fried gram flour added to it and then prepared into balls.

41. CHURMA LADOO (Rajasthani)

Ingredients	*Quantity*
Wheat flour	200 gm
Sugar (ground)	150 gm
Clarified butter (for frying and for the dough)	150 gm

Method

1. Make a dough as for chapaties by adding a little fat to the flour. 2. Divide into even round balls. 3. Flatten to about 5 cm. (2") in diameter and fry in fat on a slow fire till golden brown in colour. 4. Grind these balls to a fine powder. Sieve. 5. Heat about 2 tbsp of fat and add sieved powder and fry till light brown. 6. Remove from fire. Cool and when mixture is just warm, add ground sugar. 7. Mix well and form into ladoos.

42. MAGAJ

Ingredients	*Quantity*
Bengal gram flour	500 gm
Sugar	250 gm
Mawa	50 gm
Almonds	10 gm
Pistachio nuts	10 gm
Cardamoms	5 gm
Fat	250 gm

Method

1. Mix gram flour and half the fat and pass through a sieve. 2. Fry the mixture in the remaining fat till it browns. 3. Add mawa. Prepare sugar syrup (one-string consistency). 4. Add sugar syrup and powdered cardamoms to the mixture. 5. Mix it well. Pour onto a greased plate. 6. Decorate with almonds and pistachio nuts. 7. Mark into diagonals. Leave to cool. Cut into cubes.

43. FRENCH TOAST

Ingredients	*Quantity*
Bread	450 gm
Milk	500 ml
Eggs	2

Ingredients	Quantity
Sugar	30 gm
Vanilla	a few drops
Fat	115 gm

Method

1. Boil the milk and add half the sugar. 2. Beat eggs and mix with milk. 3. Add vanilla. 4. Soak slices of bread in the mixture for half an hour. 5. Shallow fry to golden brown. Turn over, fry the other side. Serve hot with sugar sprinkled on top.

44. SHAHI TUKRA

Ingredients	For 4	For 100
Bread slices	4	3 kg
Sugar	400 gm	10 kg
Milk	300 ml	7.5 litre
Cardamoms	2	10 gm
Saffron	a pinch	10 gm
Cashewnuts	a pinch	10 gm
Pistachio nuts	15 gm	340 gm
Fat to deep fry	15 gm	2 kg
Silver paper		

Method

1. Heat fat. Fry slices of bread. Remove. 2. Boil the milk. Simmer and reduce to half. 3. Add sugar and boil for another 10 minutes. 4. Heat saffron and soak in a little milk. Pour saffron on the fried bread. 5. Arrange fried bread in a tray without placing one on top of the other. Pour the prepared milk over the bread. 6. Garnish with crushed cardamoms, chopped nuts and silver paper. Serve hot.

45. SEWAIN

Ingredients	For 4	For 100
Vermicelli	225 gm	5.6 kg
Milk	300 ml	7.5 litre
Sugar	225 gm	5.6 kg
Saffron	a pinch	15 gm
Sultanas	30 gm	680 gm
Nuts	30 gm	680 gm

Method

1. Roast vermicelli in a hot pan. 2. Add boiling milk and sugar.

3. Simmer gently. When half done add sultanas, saffron and sliced nuts. 4. Cook till nearly dry. Serve hot or cold.

46. COCONUT CHIKKI

Ingredients	*Quantity*
Coconut	1 (225 gm)
Jaggery	340 gm
Fat	30 gm
Cardamom	½ tsp

Method

1. Grate coconut. Fry lightly in fat. 2. Melt jaggery in about 20 ml of water. Cook till it comes to the hard ball stage. 3. Add coconut, continue cooking stirring all the time till mixture is thick. 4. Add cardamom powder and pour onto a greased plate. Spread the mixture. Mark into squares. 5. When cold, cut into pieces.

47. PEANUT CHIKKI

Ingredients	*Quantity*
Jaggery	170 gm
Fat	1 tsp
Roasted peanuts	300 gm
Water	½ cup

Method

1. Remove skin of peanuts and crush them into big pieces. 2. Break jaggery. Add water and make a syrup. 3. When syrup reaches the hard ball stage, 120°C (250°F.), remove from fire. 4. Add nuts and mix well. 5. Pour onto a greased plate and spread evenly and cut into pieces.

48. TIL CHIKKI

Ingredients	*Quantity*
White gingelly seeds	115 gm
Chikki jaggery	55 gm
Oil	1 tsp

Method

1. Heat an iron fry-pan and roast the gingelly seeds till they puff up. 2. Heat fat in a pan. Add jaggery and cook on a slow fire till the bubbles become a pale brown in colour. 3. Put in the roasted gingelly seeds. Mix well. 4. Remove on to a greased board. Spread out evenly and cut into desired shapes immediately.

49. TIL AND GRAM CHIKKI

Ingredients	*Quantity*
Gingelly seeds (roasted)	85 gm
Split bengal gram	55 gm
Jaggery	115 gm
Water	

Method

1. Make a syrup with jaggery and water. 2. When syrup reaches the hard ball stage, 120°C (250°F), remove from fire and stir in gingelly seeds and gram. 3. Turn on to a greased plate. Spread evenly and cut into pieces before it hardens.

50. COCONUT SWEET

Ingredients	*Quantity*
Coconut	1
Sugar	680 gm
Cardamoms	5 gm
Pink colouring	

Method

1. Prepare a sugar syrup of one-string consistency. 2. Add finely grated coconut. Stir till thick. Add powdered cardamoms. 3. Remove from fire and spread half on a greased slab. 4. Add pink colouring to remaining portion and spread over the first layer. Roll out evenly. 5. Make into squares when still hot. 6. Cut when cold and tin.

51. COCONUT CUBES

Ingredients	*Quantity*
Coconut	225 gm
Almonds or cashewnuts	30 gm
Milk	600 ml
Butter	85 gm
Sugar	600 gm
Cochineal and vanilla	

Method

1. Grease a square tray with butter. 2. Blanch and mince almonds or chop cashewnuts. 3. Grate coconut (white part only). 4. In a strong pan put in the grated coconut, sugar and milk and keep on fire. 5. Cook at simmering point. When thick add nuts. 6. When mixture leaves sides of the pan, add butter. 7. Cook till dry. Add vanilla and cochineal (to get a pale pink colour). 8. Pour onto a greased tray. Spread evenly. 9. When cold cut into cubes.

52. CHANA DAL TOFFEE

Ingredients	*Quantity*
Split bengal gram	225 gm
Coconut	1 (225 gm)
Sugar	450 gm
Fat	1 tbsp
Almond	55 gm
Pistachio nuts	30 gm
Saffron	a pinch
Cardamom and nutmeg powder	1 tsp
Vanilla essence	1 tsp

Method

1. Blanch almonds. 2. Cut nuts into thin slices. 3. Grate coconut. 4. Wash and boil bengal gram. When boiled grind on a stone. 5. Mix together ground gram, grated coconut and sugar and cook on a slow fire. 6. When mixture leaves the sides of the pan and forms a lump, add flavouring (cardamom, nutmeg and vanilla) and powdered saffron. (Heat saffron to powder.) 7. Add prepared nuts. 8. Remove on to a greased thal or tray. Mark into squares. 9. When cold, cut into pieces.

53. JALLEBI

Ingredients	*20 Nos.*	*200 Nos.*
Refined flour	100 gm	1 kg
Bengal gram flour	20 gm	200 gm
Curds	20 gm	200 gm
Oil	20 gm	200 gm
Sugar	200 gm	2 kg
Rose essence	a few drops	10 ml
Fat	for frying	for frying

Method

1. Mix the above ingredients (except sugar and oil) together with water to form a thick batter. Set aside for 24 hours. 2. Make a sugar syrup of one-string consistency. 3. Heat oil in flat fry-pan "jallebi-kara". Pour batter through a coconut shell with one hole or through a cloth bag with a hole, to form patterns as shown below. 4. Fry till crisp (do not brown). 5. Put into prepared syrup (syrup must be cooled first). 6. Steep in sugar syrup. Remove and arrange in plates.

54. NUT BALLS

Ingredients	*Quantity*
Cashewnuts	50 gm
Walnuts	50 gm
Sultanas	50 gm
Honey	10 gm

Method

1. Mix together broken cashewnuts, walnuts, sultanas and just enough honey to form balls.

55. JANGRI

Ingredients	*Quantity*
Split black gram	250 gm
Rice	115 gm
Oil for frying	
Syrup	
Sugar	½ kg
Water	250 ml
Milk	a little

Method

1. Soak together the gram and rice for half an hour. 2. Grind to a smooth paste without adding any water. 3. Fill batter into a piping bag and pipe out in jallebi shapes into hot oil. 4. When it turns lightly brown and it starts floating on top of the oil remove and plunge into cold sugar syrup. 5. Prepare a syrup with ½ kg of sugar and 250 ml of water. Clarify with milk, bring to a 2 string consistency. Add yellow colour and remove from fire.

56. GULAB JAMUN (A)

Ingredients	*25 Pieces*	*100 Pieces*
Mawa	75 gm	1.8 kg
Sugar	75 gm	1.8 kg
Cardamoms (crushed)	a pinch	10 gm
Arrowroot	10 gm	225 gm
Water	35 ml	885 ml
Rose water	a few drops	5 ml
Soda bicarbonate	a small pinch	a pinch
Fat to fry		

Method

1. Prepare a syrup of one-string consistency with water and sugar. Add the rose water. 2. Pass the mawa through a sieve. Add crushed cardamoms, sieved arrowroot and a little cold water in which the soda bicarbonate has been dissolved. 3. Make a soft dough without kneading. 4. Divide into equal portions and shape into small balls. 5. Fry in deep fat till light brown. The frying should be done on a very slow fire and the fat should be stirred constantly. 6. Remove, cool for a short while and put into the cold syrup.

GULAB JAMUN WITH MILK POWDER (B)

Ingredients	*Quantity*
Glaxo (milk powder)	¼ cup
Flour	½ cup
Curds and butter for mixing	

Method

1. Mix together to form a stiff dough. 2. Make into balls and fry. 3. Put into prepared sugar syrup.

GULAB JAMUN WITH MILK POWDER (C)

Ingredients	*Quantity*
Amul (milk powder)	¾ cup
Cornflour	¼ cup
Ghee or butter to form a stiff dough	

Method

1. Mix together to form a stiff dough. 2. Make into balls and fry. 3. Put into prepared sugar syrup.

57. RASGULLAS

Ingredients	*Quantity (for 24)*
Pure cow's milk	1 litre
Whey water (2 days old)	½ litre
Sugar	½ kg
Water sufficient to make a syrup	
Rose water for flavouring	

Method

1. Boil the fresh cow's milk and curdle by adding the sour whey. 2. Strain through fine muslin and dip in cold water 4 for 5 times. 3. Hang to dry for ½ hr. to 45 minutes. 4. Cream the panir with palms of the

hand well till it is smooth and soft. 5. Divide into even-sized small balls. 6. Heat sugar with water to form a thin syrup and clarify. 7. When syrup starts to boil, add the rasgullas and allow to boil for 15 minutes on fast fire. 8. Sprinkle a little cold water on the boiling rasgullas at intervals of 5 minutes. 9. After half an hour, when the rasgullas become spongy and syrup froths over, remove from fire and immediately transfer into a dish containing ½ cup cold water. 10. Cool and flavour with rose water.

58. SHRIKAND

Ingredients	*Quantity*
Milk	approx. 2 ½ cups
Curds	1 tbsp
Powdered sugar	1 cup
Cardamoms	1-2
Pistachios	1 tbsp
Charoli	1 tbsp
Saffron	a pinch

Method

1. Boil the milk and leave to cool. When moderately hot, add beaten curds. Mix well by pouring from one pan to another and back. Keep aside, covered, for 10-12 hours. Pour into a clean muslin cloth and tie loosely. Hang the bag for two to three hours to let all the liquid drip through. Sprinkle crushed cardamoms and leave for one hour. Tie a strong cloth over a pan. Take small quantities of sugar and curds and mix well over the cloth. Put into a clean bowl. Continue till all the curds is mixed. Add saffron. Mix well, garnish with sliced pistachios and charoli. Cool and serve.

N.B. From 1 kg milk 250 gm of chakka can be obtained.

59. PURAN POLI

Ingredients	*Quantity*
Split bengal gram	450 gm
Sugar	450 gm
Whole wheat flour	100 gm
Refined flour	100 gm
Rice flour	100 gm
Oil	25 ml
Nutmeg	½

Method

1. Pick and wash gram. 2. Add just enough water to cook. 3. Cook till

water has evaporated and gram is tender. 4. Add sugar and cook until mixture becomes thick. 5. Pass mixture through a sieve while it is hot. Add grated nutmeg. 6. Make a very soft dough with rice flour, wheat flour, refined flour, water and oil. 7. Keep for one to two hours. 8. Make balls of the gram dal mixture (about the size of a small apple). 9. Take a small amount of dough (the size of a walnut) and spread over the gram dal balls. 10. Roll out and bake on a dosa stone or thick griddle till done. Turn over and bake the other side.

60. SWEET POTATO PURAN POLI

Ingredients	*Quantity*
Sweet potatoes	400 gm (4 medium size)
Sugar	200 gm
Cardamoms	8
Refined flour	50 gm (½ cup)
Fat	10 gm
Oil	a little

Method

1. Skin sweet potatoes; cook them in a little water. 2. Add sugar and cook till the mixture is dry. Mash well and add cardamom powder. 3. Make a very soft dough with flour, water and oil. Keep for one to two hours. 4. Make 8 balls of the sweet potato mixture and of the dough. 5. Spread the dough thinly over each sweet potato ball. Roll out and bake on a thick griddle till done. 6. Turn over and bake the other side. Apply fat or melted butter and serve hot.

61. OBATTU

Ingredients	*Quantity*
Fat	2 tsp
Fine semolina	100 gm
Flour	100 gm
Baking powder	
Salt	a pinch
Filling	
Split bengal gram	150 gm
Grated jaggery	75 gm
Cardamom powder	½ tsp

Method

1. Sift flour with baking powder and salt. Rub in 2 tsp fat. Add sufficient water to make a soft dough. 2. Cook gram until soft. Grind coarsely with jaggery. 3. Mix well and cook over a slow fire till thick and it gives out a pleasant aroma. 4. Add cardamom powder. Make into small balls. 5. Take a marble-size portion of dough. Roll thin. 6. Put the filling in the centre and press ends together. Flatten over a banana leaf smeared with fat or the back of a stainless steel pan. 7. Shallow fry on griddle (thick tawa). 8. Serve with pure ghee and milk.

62. THALI SWEET

Ingredients	*For 4*	*For 100*
Semolina	115 gm	2.8 kg
Almonds	30 gm	680 gm
Butter	115 gm	2.8 kg
Sugar	225 gm	5.6 kg
White of eggs	5	120
Rose water	½ wineglass	6 wineglasses (180 ml)

Method

1. Blanch and mince almonds. 2. Cream butter and sugar till fluffy and light. 3. Add semolina, mix well. Add minced almonds. 4. Beat egg whites stiffly and fold in gradually. 5. Add rose water, mix well and leave aside for half an hour. 6. Put the mixture into a greased tin. Decorate the top with thin strips of kneaded flour. 7. Bake in a moderate oven.

63. CRULLERS

Ingredients	*Quantity (57)*
Sugar	115 gm
Refined flour	340 gm
Eggs	3
Milk	1 tbsp
Cinnamon powder	½ tsp
Mace	½ tsp
Baking powder	1 tsp
Butter or	
Fat for frying	

Method

1. Cream together sugar and butter. 2. Add beaten eggs and beat mixture well. 3. Add cinnamon and mace powder. 4. Add 225 gm of refined flour

and milk and mix well. 5. Sift together remaining flour and baking powder. 6. Add to the mixture to form a dough. 7. Roll out 0.5 cm. (¼″) thick; cut like doughnuts. 8. Fry in deep fat till golden brown in colour.

64. KANGAN

Ingredients	*Quantity*
Sugar	75 gm
Fat	2 tbsp (30 gm)
Eggs	2
Milk	150 ml
Refined flour	250 gm
Baking powder	2 tsp
Salt	½ tsp
Almonds or any nuts	10 gm
Fat for frying	

Method

1. Cream sugar and fat till light and fluffy. 2. Add beaten eggs and milk. Mix well. 3. Sift together flour, baking powder and salt. 4. Add creamed mixture and finely chopped nuts and make a dough. 5. Roll out lightly. Cut out with doughnut cutter. 6. Fry in hot fat (deep frying) till light brown.

65. MOHANTHAL

Ingredients	*Quantity*
Bengal gram flour	115 gm
Pistachio nuts and almonds	30 gm
Milk	60 ml
Cardamoms	6
Fat	170 gm
Sugar	340 gm

Method

1. Mix gram flour, milk and 55 gm of fat. 2. Make a thick syrup of the sugar. 3. Blanch and slice almonds and pistachios. 4. Powder cardamoms. 5. Heat remaining fat. 6. Add gram flour mixture and fry. 7. Add sugar syrup. Mix well. Remove and pour onto greased plate and allow to set. 8. Sprinkle cardamom powder. Garnish with nuts. Cut into pieces.

66. KARANJIA

Ingredients	*Quantity*
Dough	
Refined flour	30 gm

Ingredients	*Quantity*
Semolina	85 gm
Fat	30 gm
Salt	a pinch
Milk and water as required	
Oil for frying	
Filling	
Mawa	30 gm
Fresh coconut	55 gm
Sugar	1 tbsp
Poppy seeds	1 tsp
Sultanas (optional)	10 gm

Method

1. Rub the fat into the flour and semolina. Add salt and liquid to make a fairly stiff dough. 2. Set aside for half an hour. 3. Break into pieces. Apply a little fat and knead each piece thoroughly till smooth. 4 Roll into rounds of 5-8 cm. (2-3") diameter. 5. Put filling in the centre. Fold over. Seal edges with a little water. 6. Deep fry till light brown. Drain and tin.

Filling

1. Pass mawa through a sieve. 2. Mix with grated coconut and sugar. 3. Add powdered poppy seeds and sultanas if used. Mix well and use as required.

67. NEVRI

Ingredients	*Quantity*
Refined flour	¼ kg
Coconut (tender)	1
Sugar	4–5 dsp
Gingelly seeds	100 gm
Fat	1 dsp
Salt	1 tsp (approx.)
Fat for frying	

Method

1. Sieve refined flour and salt. Rub in the fat to breadcrumbs consistency. Add sufficient water to make a dough. 2. Roll and cut into rounds. Fill with prepared filling. Fold them over to make half a circle and press the edges firmly. 3. Fry in hot fat or bake.

Filling

1. Mix sugar and grated coconut with half a cup of water and leave it till sugar is dissolved. 2. Mix well and cook. Add roasted gingelly seeds. Take it off the fire and let it cool.

68. CHANDRAKALA

Ingredients	*Quantity*
Refined flour	115 gm
Mawa (fresh whole milk)	115 gm
Sugar	115 gm
Sultanas	115 gm
Fat	30 gm
Pistachio nuts	55 gm
Coconut	15 gm
Cardamoms	5 gm
Almonds or cashewnuts	15 gm
Soda bicarbonate	a pinch
Salt	a pinch
Oil for frying	

Method

1. Rub fat into the flour. 2. Add soda, salt and enough water to make a stiff dough. 3. Let it stand for at least half an hour. 4. Knead well. Roll out and cut with a 7.5 cm. (3") diameter cutter. 5. Mix remaining ingredients. 6. Put a portion in each round. Turn over. 7. Seal edges with water. Decorate edges and deep fry in hot fat, till light brown.

69. MALPURAS (A)

Ingredients	*Quantity*
Semolina	340 gm
Refined flour	115 gm
Sugar	115 gm
Fat	30 gm
Lime juice	¼ tsp
Salt	a pinch
Soda bicarbonate	¼ tsp
Cardamom	10
Water	
Fat for frying	
Sugar syrup	
Sugar	340 gm

Ingredients	*Quantity*
Water	150 ml
Lime juice	1 tsp

Method

1. Sift flour and soda bicarbonate together, mix with semolina. 2. Add sugar, lime juice, fat, salt and cardamom powder and water to make a thin batter. Set aside for half an hour. 3. Prepare a sugar syrup with sugar and water. Clarify with lime juice; keep it lukewarm. 4. Heat a little fat in a fry-pan. 5. Pour a spoon of mixture. Spread it to a round of 10 cm. (4") diameter. 6. Pour a little hot fat around. 7. Turn over and fry. Remove excess fat and repeat process. 8. Put fried malpuras into prepared sugar syrup.

MALPURAS (B)

Ingredients	*Quantity*
Refined flour	450 gm
Sugar	115 gm
Fat	30 gm
Lime juice	¼ tsp
Soda bicarbonate	¼ tsp
Cardamoms	10
Salt	a pinch
Water	
Fat for frying	
Sugar syrup	
Same as for Malpura (A)	

Method

Same as for Malpura (A)

N.B. Semolina can be substituted for flour. Set aside batter for about an hour. Add more water to thin down batter if necessary.

70. KHOA CAKES

Ingredients	*Quantity*
Buffalo milk	2 litre
Citric acid or tartaric acid	¼ tsp
Powdered sugar	115 gm
Nuts to garnish	50 gm

Method

1. Grease a sandwich cake tin about 15 cm. (6") in diameter. 2. Heat the

milk. When it comes to the boil add a few grains of citric acid at a time and stir till it shows signs of curdsling (it should not curdsle completely). 3. Continue stirring till it thickens. 4. When it is quite thick and nearly dry add sugar. 5. When all liquid has dried up pour into the prepared tin. Spread and cover at once. 6. Leave overnight. Ease off from sides lightly with a knife. 7. Heat bottom gently and take on to a serving plate. Decorate with chopped or sliced nuts.

71. MYSORE PAK (A)

Ingredients	*25 pieces*	*360 pieces*
Bengal gram flour	125 gm	910 gm
Sugar	400 gm	3.63 kg
Fat	600 gm	4.3 kg
Cardamom	5 gm	115 gm
Water	100 ml	940 ml

Method

1. Heat fat to boiling point. Remove and set aside. 2. Add water to sugar and prepare a syrup of three-string consistency. 3. Take about 50 gm or 680 gm (for 360 pieces) of the fat and roast gram flour in it for about 2-3 minutes (do not allow to brown). 4. Sprinkle a little water on the gram flour to test whether it has been properly roasted in which case it will splutter. 5. Add sugar syrup to the roasted gram flour and stir well on fire. 6. Add gradually the remaining fat stirring continuously and vigorously till the fat starts floating on the top of the mixture. 7. Remove from the fire and pour the mixture on to a tray. 8. Allow the tray to cool in a slanting position so that the excess fat is drained off. 9. Sprinkle crushed cardamoms and cut into diamond shapes.

MYSORE PAK (B)

Ingredients	*Quantity*	
Bengal gram	1½ cups	(125 gm)
Sugar	2½ cups	(375 gm)
Fat	10 tsp	(200 gm)
Water	Sufficient for syrup	(120 ml)

Method

1. Put sugar into a deep pan. Add a little water and boil till the syrup gets to the soft ball stage. 2. Add flour by sprinkling over the syrup, little by little, and mix thoroughly to prevent lumping. 3. When well-mixed start adding hot fat slowly at intervals. 4. When the mass moves round and does not adhere to the vessel remove the vessel from the fire. 5. Transfer to a greased plate and cut into desired shapes while still hot.

MYSORE PAK (C)

Ingredients	*Quantity*
Bengal gram flour	1 cup
Sugar (grind coarsely, add water to prepare into a thick syrup)	1 cup
Oil	2 cups
Ghee	½ cup

Method

1. Fry gram flour in ghee. 2. Add sugar syrup and cook till it forms a ball. 3. Meanwhile, heat oil. Add flavouring. 4. Add oil to the flour mixture from a height. Stir for one minute and empty into a thali. Cut into desired shapes.

72. POTATO PAK

Ingredients	*Quantity*
Potatoes	200 gm
Flour	200 gm
Fat	100 gm
Cashewnuts	300 gm
Water	400 ml
Cloves	3
Rose essence	a few drops
Sugar	400 gm

Method

1. Boil, peel and mash potatoes. 2. Heat half the fat and mashed potatoes. Add flour to remaining fat and fry till light brown. 3. Mix potatoes and flour together. 4. Prepare a thick syrup with sugar and water, adding cloves while boiling. 5. Remove the cloves, add the potato mixture to the syrup and cook till the mixture sets. Remove from the fire. Add essence. 6. Pour the mixture on to a greased plate and decorate with chopped cashewnuts. 7. Cut into cubes and use as required.

73. AMRIT PAK

Ingredients	*Quantity*
Refined flour	225 gm
Salt	a pinch
Fat	60 gm
Sugar	225 gm
Mawa	225 gm
Almonds	60 gm

Ingredients	*Quantity*
Cardamoms	5 gm
Rose water	15 ml
Rose petals	
Cloves	
Silver leaves	
Fat to fry	

Method

1. Sieve flour with a pinch of salt. 2. Add 60 gm of hot fat and enough hot water to make a stiff dough. 3. Roll into small balls. Fry in hot fat till light brown. 4. Remove and drain. 5. Cool and pound in a mortar and pestle. 6. Sieve through a coarse sieve. 7. Mix sugar and mawa and cook on a very slow fire till sugar is dissolved. 8. Add rose water and cook till mixture forms a ball when tested between finger and thumb. 9. Add the sieved mixture, sliced almonds, and crushed cardamoms. Mix well. 10. Remove on to a greased plate. Spread evenly. Put silver leaf over and cut into even cubes. 11. Decorate with rose petals stuck on with fried cloves.

74. STUFFED DOODHI

Ingredients	*Quantity*
Bottle gourd (round)	1 (500 gm)
Mawa	225 gm
Almonds	60 gm
Pistachio nuts	60 gm
Rose essence	a few drops
Sugar	1 kg

Method

1. Peel gourd. Cut off the top part and scoop out seeds. 2. Mix together part of the sugar, mawa and sliced nuts. 3. Stuff gourd. Put back the lid and tie down to prevent stuffing from falling out. 4. Make a thin syrup with remaining sugar and water. 5. Cook the stuffed gourd in the sugar syrup till soft. Add rose essence. 6. When cold lift out the gourd and place on a silver plate. 7. Decorate gourd with silver paper. 8. Colour the rose syrup to a pale pink. 9. Pour over the gourd.

75. IJZER KOEKJES

Ingredients	*Quantity*
Refined flour	225 gm
Sugar	225 gm

Ingredients	*Quantity*
Egg yolks	2
Egg white	1
Thick coconut milk	300 ml
Cinnamon powder	1 tsp
Clove powder	1 tsp
Salt	a pinch

Method

1. Mix the flour and sugar together. 2. Add the egg yolks (well beaten) and then the coconut milk by degrees to obtain the consistency of a thick pancake batter. 3. Add cinnamon, cloves and salt. Mix well together. 4. Set aside for half an hour. 5. Beat the egg whites and mix in well with the butter. 6. Heat ijzer mould. Rub over with a little butter or ghee. Pour a dessertspoonful of the batter on to one side of the mould. Close and place over a hot fire. 7. When koekje is browned on one side, turn ijzer and cook second side. 8. As soon as koekje is taken out roll round a pencil. 9. As it cools it will slip off. Put into an air-light tin straight away.

76. ACHAPPAM (ROSE KOEKJE)

Ingredients	*Quantity*
Raw rice	910 gm
Eggs	4
Coconut	1
Sugar	450 gm
Salt	1 tsp
Coconut oil	1 litre
Coconut oil to fry (absorption)	about 50 gm

Method

1. Wash and soak rice for 2 to 3 hours. 2. Drain well (till nearly dry) and powder. Pass through a fine sieve. 3. Extract coconut milk from grated coconut. 4. Mix together rice flour, beaten egg, sugar, salt and coconut milk to prepare a medium batter (like pancake). 5. Heat oil. Heat mould in oil. 6. Dip mould in batter and straight away into hot fat. As koekjes form they will separate from mould. When golden brown drain on absorbent paper, cool and put into airtight tins.

77. PETHA

Ingredients	*Quantity*
Refined flour	200 gm

Ingredients	*Quantity*
Sugar	200 gm
Fat for frying	

Method

1. Sieve flour. Make a soft dough with a little fat (1 tablespoon) and water. 2. Roll out 0.5 cm (¼″) thick. With a sharp knife, cut into strips 1.25 cm. (½″) broad by 4 cm. (1 ½″) long. 3. Deep fry them till golden brown in colour on a very slow fire. 4. Prepare sugar syrup of one thread consistency with 3 tbsp of water and 200 gm sugar. 5. While it is hot, put prepared petha in it and shake the vessel well, so that the pieces get coated. 6. Sprinkle powdered cardamom over them.

78. KHAJJA

Ingredients	*Quantity*
Refined flour	500 gm
Sugar	200 gm
Yellow colour	a few drops
Fat (absorption)	150 gm
Water	

Method

1. Prepare a dough with flour and sugar syrup (like poori dough). 2. Mix yellow colour in it. 3. Divide into 40 small balls and roll thinly to the diameter of 13 cm. (5"). 4. Fry in hot fat.

N.B. Usually some designs or paintings are made with different colours on the thinly rolled pieces and then they are fried.

79. SHEERA

Ingredients	*Quantity*
Semolina	150 gm
Cashewnuts	8
Raisins or sultanas	20 gm
Cardamoms	4
Sugar	200 gm
Water	480 ml (approx.)
Rose water	a few drops
Salt	a pinch
Fat	30 gm

Method

1. Heat fat. Lightly brown semolina, add sugar, salt, water and sultanas or raisins. 2. Cook slowly till the grains swell and water is absorbed, stirring all the time. Remove when cooked. 3. Add cashewnuts, rose water and crushed cardamoms. Serve hot.

80. MODAKS

Ingredients	*Quantity*
Rice flour	400 gm
Salt	½ tsp
Water	600 ml
Oil	10 ml
Sugar	a pinch
Filling	
Coconuts	2
Sugar	200 gm
Cardamoms	10 gm
Mawa	100 gm
Poppy seeds	10 gm
Jaggery	200 gm

Method

1. To make rice flour, wash and soak rice. Drain and keep it for drying. When it is dry, grind to a smooth consistency. Sieve the flour with a fine mesh sieve. 2. Boil the water. Add salt, sugar and oil. 3. Add rice flour little by little without making any lumps. 4. Cook for 5 minutes. Remove from fire, knead the mixture when it is slightly hot, with an oily hand. 5. Divide it into 21 lime-sized portions. 6. Take one portion in the centre of the left palm and press with the right thumb at the centre, and sides with the fingers. 7. When it becomes like a katori or small bowl, put in some of the prepared filling. 8. With a wet hand, make about 7-8 pleats in the sides of the rice-flour 'bowl'. Now slowly try to close the left palm, and the pleats will come together. Press the pleats together with the right hand and shape the centre to a point. 9. Steam in a boiler for about 5–7 minutes. Serve hot.

Filling

1. Grate coconut. 2. Roast poppy seeds and powder the cardamoms. 3. Mix together coconut, sugar and jaggery. 4. Cook on a slow fire for about 10 minutes. 5. Add mawa and cardamom powder and poppy seeds; cook till mixture is slightly dry.

81. KOZHUKUTTA

Ingredients	*Quantity*
Rice flour (prepared)	1 cup
Hot water	¾ cup
Salt	a pinch

Filling

Sweet or savoury as desired. For sweet filling, use grated coconut and jaggery. For savoury, use a mixture of vegetables or minced meat.

Method

1. Mix together the rice flour, water and salt and knead well into a smooth dough. Divide into about 12 balls and divide filling into the same number of portions. 2. Fill centre of dough with filling by forming a depression with the thumb. Smooth over to cover. 3. Steam in a steam pan and serve hot.

To prepare the rice flour

1. Take raw and parboiled rice in the proportion of 1:3. Soak raw rice for about 2 to 3 hours and parboiled rice for about 20 minutes. Drain. 2. Dry slightly and pound. Sieve through a fine sieve. 3. Heat a thick-bottomed pan. Put in flour and roast for a few minutes till dry. 4. Sieve again and powder any hard lumps. Tin and use as required.

82. BIBIQUE

Ingredients	*Quantity*
Refined flour	380 gm
Sugar	2 kg
Coconuts	5
Fat	500 gm
Egg yolks	40
Grated nutmeg or	
a few drops of vanilla essence	

Method

1. Grate the coconut and grind to a fine paste. With 2 cups of water, extract milk. 2. Mix flour and sugar in a bowl. 3. Add beaten yolks and coconut milk and make into a thin batter (as for pancake). Add flavouring. 4. Melt ½ cup of fat in a thick- bottomed pan or pie dish and place it in an oven. 5. When hot, pour about 1–1½ cup of the batter. Close the oven and cook for about 20-30 minutes or until brown on top. 6. Put a spoon of fat on top and pour another layer of batter. Bake for

a further 20-30 minutes. 7. Repeat layer by layer till the batter is used up. When done, remove from fire, turn over and sprinkle icing sugar over.

83. BHAKRA

Ingredients	*Quantity (40)*
Whole wheat flour	400 gm
Semolina	140 gm
Egg	1
Salt	1 tsp
Fat	1½ tsp
Cashewnuts	50 gm
Powdered sugar	100 gm
Toddy	½ bottle
Fat to fry	150 gm (approx.)
Nutmeg powder	
Cardamom powder	

Method

1. Sieve flour and semolina and mix. Powder cashewnuts. 2. Mix in a bowl, flour, semolina, powdered cashewnuts, fat, salt, sugar, cardamom powder, nutmeg powder and egg. 3. Add toddy gradually and make it into a soft dough. Keep it covered near a warm place for 3 to 4 hours. Roll out into 1.25 cm (½″) thickness. 4. Cut into rounds with a cutter and deep fry on a slow fire. 5. Serve hot with tea or when cold, tin and use a required.

N.B. This will stay in tins for more than 15 days.

84. CHAPAT (SWEET PANCAKES)

Ingredients	*Quantity*
Eggs	4
Milk	½ litre (3 cups)
Sugar	4 tbsp
Refined flour	4 tbsp
Fat	100 gm
Vanilla essence	1 tsp
Cardamom and nutmeg powder	½ tsp
Charoli (crushed)	2 tsp

Method

1. Beat eggs and mix in sugar; add half a spoon of fat. 2. Add milk and flour slowly into the mixture mixing it with a wooden spoon to prevent

lumps. 3. Add charoli essence and cardamom and nutmeg powder. 4. Mix well and bring it to a dropping consistency. Keep batter for one hour. 5. Heat a frying pan, add one round spoon of batter and spread it thinly. 6. Cook on a slow fire, turn and cook the other side. 7. Repeat till all the batter is used up. 8. Fold into half or quarter and serve.

85. RAWO/RAVOO

Ingredients	*Quantity*
Semolina	115 gm
Fat	100 gm
Sugar	6 tbsp
Milk	1½ litre
Charoli nuts	50 gm
Sultanas	50 gm
Vanilla essence	1 tsp
Cardamom and nutmeg powder	1 tsp

Method

1. Clean, wash and dry sultanas. 2. Fry the sultanas and charoli lightly in a little fat and remove. 3. Divide milk into 2 parts; in one, add sugar. Heat both separately. 4. Heat fat, add semolina and fry very lightly on a slow fire. Do not discolour. 5. Add milk and stir well to prevent lumps. Go on stirring till it gets thick. Add sweet milk to this slowly, stirring all the time. 6. Add half of the charoli, sultanas, vanilla essence. cardamom and nutmeg powder. Remove from fire. 7. Pour into a serving dish. 8. Garnish with rest of charoli and sultanas.

N.B. Ravoo is served for breakfast on auspicious days, i.e. New Year or birthdays, with sweet curds, hardboiled eggs and bananas.

86. APPAM

Ingredients	*Quantity*
Rice	200 gm
Jaggery	150 gm
Coconut	½
Pepper	1 tsp
Fat to fry	

Method

1. Soak cleaned rice for one hour. Grind coarsely. Add jaggery and grind to a smooth paste. 2. Thin down to batter consistency with water. 3. Mix in pepper and grated coconut. 4. Heat fat in a deep frying pan. Pour a ladleful of this batter and deep fry till golden brown. 5. Drain on absorbent paper and serve hot.

SNACKS

1. Moong Dal Wada
2. Masala Wada
3. Potato Wada
4. Aloo Wada
5. Sabudana Wada
6. Sago Minced Meat Savoury Balls
7. Potato Bonda
8. Akki Vada (Rice vada)
9. Peanut Crispies
10. Pakoda
11. Assorted Pakoras
12. Panir Pakoras
13. Dahi Pakoda
14. Dahi Pakoda Chutney
15. Mysore Bonda
16. Potato Fritters
17. Potato Tikki (A)
    Potato Tikki (B)
18. Vegetable Patties
19. Samosas (Plain)
20. Butter Samosas
21. Cocktail Samosas
22. Cocktail Samosas with Liver Stuffing
23. Vegetable Samosas
24. Mutton Samosas
25. Bori Samosas (A)
    Bori Samosas (B)
    Bori Samosas (C)
26. Vegetable Puffs
27. Curry Puffs
28. Green Gram Bhajiya
29. Brinjal Bhajiya
30. Green Peas Gungra
31. Patrail (A)
    Patrail (B)
32. Kheema Patrail
33. Methi Balls
34. Uppuma
35. Semiya Uppuma
36. Bread Uppuma
37. Avil Uppuma
38. Sooji and Vegetable Uppma
39. Poha
40. Savoury Poha
41. Macaroni Uppuma
42. Pongal
43. Idli
44. Stuffed Idli
45. Rawa Idli
46. Vermicelli Nuts Idli
47. Sandnam
48. Dosa (Plain)
49. Dosa (Spiced)
50. Methi Dosa
51. Jaggery Dosa
52. Onion Dosa
53. Oothappam
54. Rawa Dosa
55. Moru Dosa
56. Masala Dosa
57. Coconut and Roasted Bengal Gram Chutney
58. Amaranth Adai
59. Pesarattu
60. Khaman Dhokla (A)
    Khaman Dhokla (B)
61. Khandvi
62. Pitla
63. Moongdal Kachories (A)
    Moongdal Kachories (B)
64. Potato Kachories
65. Potato Cakes
66. Corn and Green Pepper Fritters
67. Baked Corn
68. Macaroni and Tomato Fritters (Vegetarian)
69. Macaroni Cheese Fritters (Vegetarian)
70. Cheese Bouchees
71. Cheese Fritters
72. Cheese Jallebi
73. Cheese Toast
74. Potato Toast

75. Date Savoury
76. Savoury Cake
77. Chakli (A) (Murukku)
    Chakli (B)
78. Bhel Poori (A)
    Bhel Poori (B)
79. Pani Puri
80. Bhalle
81. Phafdas
82. Gantai (Plain)
83. Bhawnagari Gantia
84. Papri
85. Sev
86. Chiwda (A)
    Chiwda (B)
87. Nimki
88. Mathri
89. Mathia
90. Doodhi Muthia
91. Handwa
92. Vodde
93. Devilled Cashewnuts
94. Rose Poories
95. Kuzhalappam
96. Cheepappam
97. Achappam (Savoury)
98. Avilos
99. Paputtu
100. Fruit Chaat
101. Fried Vegetable Chaat
102. Dal Moth Chaat
103. Papdi chaat
104. Dahi Bhalle
105. Dahi Wada
106. Bati
107. Pappadam

1. MOONG DAL WADA

Ingredients	*Quantity*
Green gram with skin	225 gm
Ginger (chopped)	5 gm
Green chilli	1
Coriander (crushed)	5 gm
Cumin	a pinch
Grated coconut	30 gm
Salt	to taste
Gram flour	30 gm
Crushed peppercorns	2
Oil	2 tsp
Fat to fry	

Method

1. Clean, wash and soak the gram for 12 hours. 2. Remove husk as much as possible. 3. Grind coarsely. Add chopped chillies, ginger, coconut, coriander, cumin, pepper and salt. Mix well. 4. Rub oil in gram flour and add to mixture. 5. Fry this mixture in the shape of flat wadas in hot fat and serve hot.

2. MASALA WADA

Ingredients	*Quantity (10)*
Split red gram	115 gm

Ingredients	*Quantity (10)*
Onions	30 gm
Green chillies	2
Red chillies	2
Salt	to taste
Prawns (boiled and seasoned)	10

Method

1. Wash and soak gram for 2 hours. 2. Grind the gram coarsely (or pass through a mincer). 3. Mix finely chopped onions, green chillies, coarsely ground red chillies and salt. 4. Mix well together and shape into 10 small flat rounds about 0.8 cm (1/3") thick. 5. Place one prawn on the top of each wada. 6. Deep fry till crisp and cooked.

3. POTATO WADA

Ingredients	*Quantity*
Potatoes	225 gm
Onions	30 gm
Bengal gram flour	115 gm
Garam masala powder	½ tsp
Soda bicarbonate	a pinch
Salt	to taste
Green chillies	2
Coriander leaves	⅛ bunch
Garlic	2 flakes
Turmeric	⅛ tsp
Oil to fry	

Batter

Sift flour, soda bicarbonate and salt. Add enough water to make a thick batter.

Method

1. Boil and peel potatoes; chop. 2. Chop onions, ginger, green chillies, coriander leaves and garlic finely. 3. Heat one tbsp fat. Fry chopped ingredients. 4. Add potatoes, turmeric and salt. Mix well. 5. Remove from fire. Divide into equal sized balls. 6. Dip each ball in prepared batter and deep fry in fat till light brown. 7. Serve hot with chutney if desired.

4. ALOO WADA

Ingredients	*For 4*
Potatoes	115 gm
Pomegranate seeds	5 gm

Ingredients	*For 4*
Dry mango powder	5 gm
Mint leaves	1 sprig
Coriander leaves	1 sprig
Coriander (crushed)	2 gm
Cumin	2 gm
Chilli powder	2 gm
Salt	to taste
Gram flour	30 gm
Oil for frying	

Method

1. Boil, peel and mash potatoes. Chop coriander and mint leaves. 2. Mix all the ingredients (except gram flour) together and divide into 4 portions. 3. Prepare a batter of medium thickness with gram flour and water. 4. Whisk till light and frothy. Dip the potato balls in the batter and deep fry. Remove and press to make them flat. 5. Fry again till brown and crisp. Serve hot with mint or tamarind chutney.

5. SABUDANA WADA

Ingredients	*Quantity*
Potatoes	450 gm
Sago	225 gm
Peanut flour	225 gm
Green chillies	5 gm
Salt	to taste
Buttermilk	3 tbsp
Oil to fry	

Method

1. Soak sago in just enough water to cover it, leave for one to two hours. 2. Boil and mash potatoes; chop green chillies. 3. Mix all ingredients. 4. Flatten on banana leaves and deep fry.

6. SAGO MINCED MEAT SAVOURY BALLS

Ingredients	*For 4*
Sago	100 gm
Minced meat	180 gm
Onions	100 gm
Lime	½
Soda bicarbonate	a large pinch
Green chillies	3

Ingredients	*For 4*
Ginger	5 gm
Salt	to taste
Tomatoes	1 (115 gm)

Method

1. Wash, drain and keep aside sago for 30 minutes. 2. Boil the mincemeat in just enough water to cook it tender but dry. 3. Grind green chillies and ginger to a fine paste. 4. Mix together mincemeat, ground ingredients, finely chopped onions, gram flour, lime juice, chopped tomatoes, sago and 50 ml water to form a thick batter. Let it stand for 1 minute. Add soda bicarbonate. Mix well. 6. Form into balls and deep fry till golden brown. 7. Drain on absorbent paper and serve hot.

N.B. 250 gm of meat with bones when minced after removing the bones comes to 180 gm The above quantities make 40 savoury balls (the size of a lime).

7. POTATO BONDA

Ingredients	*Quantity (80)*
Potatoes	2 kg
Onions	500 gm
Ginger	50 gm
Green chillies	50 gm
Turmeric	1 tsp
Mustard seeds	1 tsp
Lime	1
Curry leaves	3 sprigs
Bengal gram flour	250 gm
Soda bicarbonate	¼ tsp
Salt	50-80 gm
Water	750 ml
Oil to fry	200 ml

Method

1. Boil and peel potatoes. Mash. 2. Chop onions, ginger and green chillies finely. 3. Heat 30 ml of oil. Add mustard seeds and curry leaves. 4. When mustard seeds crackle, add chopped spices potatoes, turmeric and salt. Add lime juice. Mix well. Remove. 5. Divide into 80 portions (the size of a large lime). 6. Dip in prepared batter and deep fry.

Batter

Sift together gram flour, soda bicarbonate, salt water to a smooth batter of medium thickness.

8. AKKI VADE (RICE VADA)

Ingredients	*Quantity*
Rice	1 kg
Split black gram	250 gm
Salt	50 gm
Cumin	20 gm
Green chillies	20 gm
Coriander	1 bunch
Oil for frying	

Method

1. Wash the rice, dry, then grind to powder. 2. Soak black gram in water for 1 hour, then grind it to make a thick paste. 3. Mix rice powder with this paste. Add salt and ground cumin, chillies and coriander. Press small portions of this paste on a banana leaf in the palm of the hand and fry in oil till they float on the surface.

9. PEANUT CRISPIES

Ingredients	*Quantity*
Peanuts shelled	250 gm
Bengal gram flour (besan)	1 cup
Rice flour	½ cup
Red chilli powder	½ tsp
Salt	a pinch
Water	½ cup (approx.)
Oil	3⅓ cup (approx.)

Method

Roast peanuts in the oven for 10-15 minutes. Prepare a batter of gram and rice flour, chilli powder, salt and water. Add roasted peanuts. Mix well. Heat oil. Drop peanuts into the hot oil, one at a time. Fry till crisp and drain on absorbent paper. Tin when cool.

10. PAKODA

Ingredients	*Quantity*
Bengal gram flour	115 gm
Rice flour	30 gm
Salt	to taste
Onions	50 gm
Green chillies	3 or 4
Cashewnuts	30 gm
Soda bicarbonate	a pinch

Ingredients	*Quantity*
Curry leaves	a few
Fat	1 tsp
Oil for frying	

Method

1. Chop onions, chillies and curry leaves. Add salt and soda bicarbonate and the mix well. 2. Mix together gram and rice flour. Add melted fat. 3. Add all the ingredients and mix to a thick batter adding enough water. 4. Heat the oil. Pour spoonfuls of the batter into the hot oil and deep fry till golden brown. 5. Drain on absorbent paper and serve hot.

11. ASSORTED PAKODAS

Ingredients	*Quantity*
Cauliflower	225 gm
Brinjal	225 gm
Ladies fingers	225 gm
Onions	225 gm
Potatoes	225 gm
Pumpkin	225 gm
Salt	to taste
Chilli powder	to taste
Bengal gram flour	125 gm
Soda bicarbonate	a pinch
Water to make batter	

Method

1. Prepare a batter with salt, chilli powder, gram flour and water to pouring consistency. 2. Peel and cut pumpkin and potatoes into thin slices. Break cauliflower into flowerettes. Cut onions into rings. Season with salt and chilli powder. Slit ladies finger from the sides and season lightly. 3. Dip in battter and fry in hot fat. 4. Serve hot with chutney.

N.B. Cauliflower and potatoes may be parboiled first or they must be fried slowly. Double frying, the first time in medium fat and then in hot fat may also be done.

12. PANIR PAKODAS

Ingredients	*Quantity*
Panir	
Milk	1 litre
Sour curds or	55 gm

Ingredients	*Quantity*
Alum or	1/4 tsp
Lime juice or	1/2 lime
Vinegar	1 dsp.
Peppercorns (crushed)	a few
Coriander leaves	a few sprigs
Batter	
Bengal gram flour	55 gm
Salt	to taste
Oil (to mix batter)	1 tsp
Chilli powder	1/4 tsp
Oil to fry	

Method

1. Prepare a smooth batter with salt, chilli powder, gram flour, oil and water (pouring consistency). 2. Dip panir cubes and fry in hot oil. Serve piping hot with chutney.

13. DAHI PAKODA

Ingredients	*Quantity (40) (5 portions)*
Moong dal	100 gm
Curds	250 gm
Coriander leaves	5 sprigs
Green chillies	5 gm
Chilli powder	a pinch
Jeera	
Peppercorns	4 gm
Coriander seeds	
Oil	70 ml

Method

1. Soak moong dal for 4 hours. Grind to a fine paste. Add chopped coriander leaves and green chillies. Add salt. 2. Heat oil. Make small balls with the moong dal paste. Fry on a slow fire. 3. When the pakodas are golden brown, take them out and dip them in cold water for 15 minutes. 4. Beat the curds. 5. Take out the pakodas from water and dip in curds. 6. Garnish with powdered, roasted coriander seeds, jeera and peppercorns and coriander leaves.

14. DAHI PAKODA CHUTNEY

Ingredients	*Quantity*
Tamarind	50 gm
Jaggery	30 gm

Ingredients	Quantity
Ginger powder	¼ pinch
Coriander or mint leaves	2-3 sprigs
Salt	to taste

Method

1. Soak tamarind and take out purée. 2. Grind coriander or mint leaves. 3. Add jaggery, ginger powder and coriander leaves to the purée. 4. Add salt.

15. MYSORE BONDA

Ingredients	Quantity
Split gram (urad dal)	115 gm
Green chillies	2 to 3
Coriander leaves	5 gm
Curry leaves	1 sprig
Coconut	10 gm
Ginger	5 gm
Peppercorns	2 to 3
Salt	to taste
Oil for frying	

Method

1. Soak gram for an hour. 2. Drain water completely and grind into a fine paste with salt and green chillies. 3. Chop coriander, ginger and curry leaves fine, crush peppercorns coarsely and cut coconut into small pieces. Add to the ground paste. 4. Meanwhile have oil ready for frying. 5. Make lime-sized balls of paste and deep fry till golden brown.

16. POTATO FRITTERS

Ingredients	Quantity
Potatoes	2 medium sized
Egg	1
Ginger	2.5 cm (½″) piece
Onions	½ (small)
Green chilli	1
Salt	to taste
Oil to fry	

Method

1. Peel and chop onion and ginger into very fine pieces. 2. Remove seeds from chilli and chop finely. Peel and grate potatoes. 3. Beat the egg well

and mix with grated potatoes and chopped ingredients. 4. Add salt to taste. Fry spoonfuls in hot oil. 5. Drain on absorbent paper and serve piping hot.

17. POTATO TIKKI (A)

Ingredients	*For 4*	*For 100*
Potatoes	450 gm	11.00 kg
Bread	55 gm	1.35 kg
Salt	to taste	80-100 gm
Green chillies	10 gm	250 gm
Coriander leaves	½ bunch	4 bunches
Breadcrumbs	30 gm	680 gm
Fat	to fry	to fry

Method

1. Wash and boil potatoes till tender. Peel and mash. 2. Soak bread in water. When soaked squeeze out water. 3. Mix potatoes, bread, salt, finely chopped coriander leaves and green chillies. 4. Make into balls. Flatten. Coat with breadcrumbs and shallow fry.

POTATO TIKKI (B)

Ingredients	*Quantity (60)*
Potatoes	2.5 kg
Bread	500 gm
Onions	50 gm
Green chili	1
Coriander leaves	few sprigs
Salt	to taste
Fat to fry	100 gm
Chutney	
Coriander leaves	1 bunch
Onions	150 gm
Green chillies	5
Lime	1
Salt	to taste

Method

1. Boil potatoes in their jackets till done. Peel and mash well. 2. Soak bread in a little water. Squeeze out moisture. 3. Chop green chillies, coriander leaves and onions finely. 4. Mix together prepared ingredients and salt. 5. Form into balls. Press. Put a small quantity of prepared chutney in the centre. 6. Seal edges. Shapes into rounds and shallow fry.

Chutney

1. Wash and drain coriander leaves. 2. Grind together onions, coriander leaves, green chillies and salt. Add lime juice to taste and mix well.

18. VEGETABLE PATTIES

Ingredients	*For 10*	*For 100*
Potatoes	800 gm	8 kg
Bread	80 gm	800 gm
Peas fresh or	180 gm	1.8 kg
Tinned	90 gm	900 gm
Green chillies	5 gm	50 gm
Ginger	a small piece	30 gm
Onions	100 gm	1 kg
Coriander leaves	5 gm	50 gm
Lime	a few drops	2
Garam masala	a pinch	2 tsp (6 to 10 gm)
Dry mango powder	½ tsp	2 tsp
Salt	to taste	100 gm
Fat to deep fry		

Method

1. Boil potatoes. Peel and mash when still hot. 2. Soak bread in water. Squeeze out moisture and mix with potatoes. Add salt and lime juice. 3. Shell the peas and crush them. 4. Grind green chillies and ginger. 5. Heat a little fat in a pan. Add chopped onions. When onions are light brown add ground green chillies and ginger. 6. Add peas and salt. Cook till peas are cooked. 7. When cooked add chopped coriander leaves, garam masala and dry mango powder. Mix well. 8. Divide potatoes and peas into equal portions (10 or 100). 9. Shape potatoes into cups and stuff with peas. Bind the edges together and shape into rounds. 10. Deep fry till crisp and brown.

N.B. A minced meat filling could be used instead of vegetables for mutton patties; mixed vegetables may be used instead of peas.

19. SAMOSAS (Plain)

Ingredients	*Quantity (80)*
Refined flour	500 gm
Fat	115 gm
Salt	50 gm
Green chillies	30 gm
Onions	500 gm
Mustard seeds	5 gm

Ingredients	*Quantity (80)*
Potatoes	1.5 kg
Lime	1
Turmeric	a small pinch
Oil to fry	

Method

1. Sift flour. Rub in fat. Add salt, cold water and make a fairly soft dough. 2. Set aside, covered, for at least half an hour. 3. Boil potatoes in their jackets. Peel and chop into small pieces. 4. Chop green chillies and onions finely. 5. Heat about 50 ml of oil. Add mustard seeds. As they crackle, add potatoes, turmeric, chopped onions, green chillies and salt. 6. Mix well over fire. Add lime juice and remove. 7. Knead dough well. Divide dough into small portions. Roll out each portion into a round about 7.5 cm (3") in diameter. 8. Cut down the centre. Make a cone of each portion. Put in prepared filling. 9. Seal edges with water. 10. Fry in deep fat till light brown. Serve hot.

20. BUTTER SAMOSAS

Ingredients	*Quantity (22)*
Refined flour	115 gm
Butter	50 gm
Salt	to taste
Fat	30 gm
Filling	
Green peas (fresh)	100 gm
Carrots	100 gm
Onions	100 gm
French beans	100 gm
Potatoes	100 gm
Salt	to taste
Green chillies	5 gm
Mustard seeds	1 gm
Lime	½
Turmeric	a pinch
Green coriander	2 sprigs
Curry leaves	a few leaves
Oil for frying	100 gm

Method

1. Make a smooth dough with flour, salt and butter. 2. Chop green chillies and onions. Chop the carrots, beans and potatoes into small pieces. 3. Heat the fat. Add mustard seeds. When they crackle, add the

vegetables, chopped onions, green chillies and turmeric. Sprinkle a little water and cook over slow fire till potatoes are cooked (about 15 minutes). 4. Add salt and mix well for about 5 minutes. Add lime juice and chopped leaves and remove. 5. Knead the dough again and make into small round balls. 6. Flatten and roll out on a floured board. Make these rounds the size of a saucer. Cut in half. 7. Make into a cone. Fill with the mixture. Wet the open edges with water and press together. 8. Heat oil to smoke point. Add samosas. Lower fire and fry till they are crisp and light brown.

21. COCKTAIL SAMOSAS

Ingredients	*Quantity*
Refined flour	115 gm
Fat (to rub in flour)	30 gm
Potatoes	115 gm
Carrots	55 gm
Peas	55 gm
Salt	to taste
Onions	50 gm
Chillies	2 gm
Garlic	a clove
Ginger	5 gm
Coriander leaves	¼ bunch
Pomegranate seeds	½ tsp
Garam masala	⅛ tsp
Oil to fry	

Method

1. Sift flour, add salt. Rub in fat. Add enough water to make a soft dough. Knead well and set aside, covered, for at least half an hour. 2. Dice potatoes and carrots. Shell peas and chop chillies. Chop onions, garlic, ginger and coriander leaves finely. 3. Heat about 30 ml oil. Put in chopped ingredients. Sauté without discolouring. Add diced vegetables and enough water to cook vegetables dry. Add salt. 4. When vegetables are cooked and moisture has evaporated, add pomegranate seeds and garam masala. Mix well and remove. 5. Knead dough. Divide into small portions. Roll out into rounds about 5 cm (2") in diameter and paper thin. Cut down the centre. Make a cone of each piece. Put in prepared filling. Seal the edges with water. Fry in deep fat till light brown. Serve hot.

N.B. For mutton samosas, the ingredients and method are the same as above except that 225 gm of minced mutton should be used instead of mixed vegetables. Lime may be used instead of pomegranate seeds.

22. COCKTAIL SAMOSAS WITH LIVER STUFFING

Ingredients	*Quantity*
Refined flour	115 gm
Butter	70 gm
Chicken liver	225 gm
Onions	100 gm
Bacon	50 gm
Worcestershire sauce	1 tsp
Salt	to taste
Fat to fry	

Method

1. Sift flour, add salt. Rub in fat. Add enough water to make a soft dough. 2. Knead well and set aside covered for at least half an hour. 3. Sauté chopped onions and bacon in melted butter. 4. Add chicken liver, cut into small pieces. 5. When cooked, add Worcestershire sauce and salt to taste. 6. Knead dough. Divide into small portions. 7. Roll out into rounds about 5 cm (2") in diameter and paper thin. Cut down the centre. 8. Make a cone of each piece. Put in prepared filling. 9. Seal the edges with water. 10. Fry in deep fat till light brown. 11. Serve hot.

23. VEGETABLE SAMOSAS

Ingredients	*Quantity (8 to 10)*	*Ingredients*	*Quantity (8 to 10)*
Refined flour	115 gm	**Green chillies**	2
Fat to rub in flour	30 gm	**Garlic**	1 flake
Potatoes	115 gm	**Ginger**	5 gm
Carrots	55 gm	**Coriander leaves**	¼ bunch
Peas	55 gm	**Pomegranate seeds**	1 tsp
Salt	to taste	**Garam masala powder**	⅛ tsp
Onions	50 gm	**Oil to fry**	

Method

1. Sift flour. Add salt. Rub in fat. 2. Add enough water to make a soft dough. Knead well and set aside covered for at least half an hour. 3. Dice potatoes and carrot. Shell peas. 4. Peel and chop fine, onions, garlic, ginger. Chop chillies and coriander. 5. Heat about 30 ml oil. Put in chopped ingredients. Sauté without discolouring. 6. Add diced vegetables and enough water to cook vegetables. Add salt. 7. When vegetables are cooked and moisture has evaporated, add pomegranate seeds and garam masala powder. Mix well and remove. 8. Knead dough. Divide into small

portions. Roll out into rounds about 7.5 cm (3") in diameter. 9. Cut down the centre. Make a cone of each piece. Put in prepared filling. Seal the edges with water. 10. Fry in deep fat till light brown. Serve hot.

24. MUTTON SAMOSAS

Ingredients and method same as above but use 225 gm of minced meat instead of mixed vegetables.

25. BORI SAMOSAS (A)

Ingredients same as for Vegetable Samosas. Rice flour to dust and roll out.

Method

1. Sift flour. Add salt and cold water and make a soft dough. 2. Divide into equal portions. Flatten the balls. Dip one side in melted fat and then in rice flour. 3. Press two balls together so that oiled and floured sides are joined and roll out into a thin chapati. 4. Keep a tawa upside down on fire. Cook chapati on tawa for a minute or two without browning. Turn over to cook the second side. 5. Separate two chapaties by beating lightly between the palms of the hands. 6. Wrap chapaties in a clean cloth. 7. Cut into strips 12 inches long and 4 cm (1½") wide 8. Make cones. Put in prepared filling of meat or vegetable. 9. Stick the edges with paste (flour and water). 10. Fry in deep fat till brown.

Paste

Ingredients	*Quantity*
Refined flour	30 gm
Water	170 ml

Method

1. Mix flour in 60 ml cold water. 2. Boil remaining water and add to mixture. 3. Return to fire and cook till thick.

BORI SAMOSAS (B)

Ingredients

Filling

Chopped hard boiled eggs
Chopped spring onions
Chopped green chillies
Powdered cumin
Lime juice
Boiled cubed carrots

BORI SAMOSAS (C)

Ingredients	*Quantity*
Filling	
Mawa	250 gm
Sugar	to taste
Raisins	30 gm
Poppy seeds	50 gm
Cardamoms	a few
Rose water	

26. VEGETABLE PUFFS

Ingredients	*Quantity*	*Ingredients*	*Quantity*
Refined flour	150 gm.	**Fat**	15 gm.
Fat	15 gm.	**Oil for frying**	
Salt	2 gm.	*Filling B*	
Creaming		**Potatoes**	115 gm.
Fat	50 gm.	**Cauliflower**	225 gm.
Rice flour	5 gm.	**Peas**	115 gm.
Filling A		**Onions**	115 gm.
Green peas	50 gm.	**Coriander leaves**	a few
Carrots	50 gm.	**Green chillies**	5 gm.
Onions	50 gm.	**Turmeric**	a pinch
Potatoes	100 gm.	**Chilli powder**	a pinch
French beans	50 gm.	**Cardamom**	a little
Salt	5 gm.	**Cloves**	a pinch
Green chillies	2 gm.	**Lime**	¼
Mustard seeds	1 gm.	**Salt**	to taste
Lime	½	**Fat to fry (absorption)**	30 gm.
Turmeric	a pinch		
Green coriander	2 sprigs		
Curry leaves	a few		

Method

1. Mix flour and salt. 2. Rub fat into flour. Add water to make a soft dough. Knead and set aside. 3. Divide the dough into even number of portions and roll each portion into thin rounds about 17.5 cm (7") in diameter. 4. Make a paste of rice flour and the fat. Leave in cold water. 5. Smear the rounds with the paste. Place 3 rounds one on top of the other. Roll firmly. 6. Cut into 2.5 cm (1") pieces. 7. Press each piece vertically. Roll into round shapes. 8. Fill with vegetable mixture and fold over forming a semicircle. Press edges well. 9. Deep fry till golden brown. Drain.

Filling A

1. Chop green chillies and onions. Chop the carrots, beans and potatoes into small pieces. 2. Heat the fat. Add mustard seeds. When they crackle, add the vegetables, chopped onion, green chillies and turmeric. Sprinkle a little water and cook over slow fire till potatoes are cooked (about 15 minutes). 3. Add salt and mix well for about 5 minutes. Add lime juice and chopped coriander leaves and remove.

Filling B

1. Boil potatoes and cauliflower and cut into small pieces. 2. Boil and mash the peas. Chop onions. 3. Heat fat. brown onion, and the spices, vegetables and salt, Sauté. 4. Cool and add lime juice.

27. CURRY PUFFS

Ingredients	*Quantity (12)*
Pastry	
Refined flour	115 gm
Egg yolk	1
Fat	15 gm
Thick coconut milk	40 ml
Salt	to taste
Fat or oil	to fry
Filling	
Prawns	500 gm
Billings or green tomatoes	225 gm
Small onions	30 gm
Red chillies	5 gm
Turmeric	a pinch
Curry leaves	a small sprig
Lemon grass	a small sprig
Powdered cloves and cinnamon	a pinch
Coconut milk (thick)	200 ml
Salt	to taste
Fat	15 gm

Method

1. Shell prawns. Remove intestines by slitting the back. Wash well in several lots of cold water. Drain and cut into small pieces. 2. Slice billings or green tomatoes and onions. 3. Grind red chillies. 4. Heat fat. Fry a quarter of the sliced onions, curry leaves and lemon grass. 5. Add minced prawns, the sliced billings or tomatoes, the remainder of the onions, the ground red chillies, turmeric, powdered cinnamon and cloves and salt.

6. Let it simmer for about 10 minutes. Then add the coconut milk and boil until gravy is absorbed. Test for seasoning. 7. Remove from fire. Take out the leaves and use as filling.

N.B. A vegetable or a meat filling can be used instead of the prawn filling.

28. GREEN GRAM BHAJIYA

Ingredients	*Quantity*
Green gram	225 gm
Coconut (grated)	30 gm
Garlic	4 flakes
Chilli powder	1 tsp
Onions	100 gm
Coriander leaves	½ bunch
Green chillies	5
Salt	1 tsp
Cumin	½ tsp
Soda bicarbonate	½ tsp
Turmeric	½ tsp
Vinegar	1 tbsp
Lime juice	1 lime
Oil to fry	

Method

1. Pick and wash gram. Soak in water for 5 to 6 hours. 2. Grind coconut, coriander, green chillies, cumin and garlic. 3. Mix with the gram. Add finely chopped onions, salt, soda bicarbonate, vinegar, turmeric, chilli powder, lime juice and a little oil. Mix well and keep aside for half an hour. 4. Heat oil (for deep frying). Put in teaspoons of mixture and fry till golden brown.

29. BRINJAL BHAJJIA

Ingredients	*For 4*	*For 100*
Brinjal	225 gm	5.65 kg
Bengal gram flour	30 gm	680 gm
Chilli powder	5 gm	115 gm
Turmeric	a pinch	15 gm
Salt	to taste	50-80 gm
Soda bicarbonate	a pinch	1 tsp
Oil to fry		

Method

1. Wash and slice brinjal into thin roundels. Apply turmeric and salt. 2. Make a batter with gram flour, soda flour, soda bicarbonate, chilli

powder and water. 3. Dip slices of brinjal in batter. Deep fry. Drain and serve immediately.

30. GREEN PEAS GUNGRA

Ingredients	*Quantity*
Filling	
Green peas	225 gm
Sweet potatoes	115 gm
Potatoes	115 gm
Green chillies	7 or 8
Onions	500 gm
Coriander leaves	a few
Salt	2 tsp
Sugar (optional)	1 tsp
Turmeric	¼ tsp
Chilli powder	½ tsp
Vinegar	1 tbsp
Oil	1 tbsp
Covering	
Refined flour	225 gm
Semolina	340 gm
Fat (creaming)	115 gm
Fat for dough	1 tbsp
Oil to fry	

Method

1. Shell the green peas. 2. Peel and cut potatoes and sweet potatoes into small cubes. 3. Chop coriander leaves and green chillies. In 1 tbsp oil, sauté green peas. Add potatoes, sweet potatoes, onions, green chillies, dry spices and coriander leaves. 4. Add sufficient water to cook it dry. Add salt. 5. When nearly done, add vinegar and sugar and cook till dry. Remove from fire. 6. Mix semolina and 1 tsp salt. Rub in fat (1 tbsp). 7. Add enough water to make a fairly stiff dough. 8. Cream together 115 gm of fat and the flour. 9. Keep on creaming till it forms a lump. 10. Keep the creamed mixture in water. 11. Roll out dough into thin chapaties. 12. Apply creamed mixture. Roll and cut into 2.5 cm slices. 13. Flatten the cut surface and roll out into rounds about 7.5 cm (3") in diameter. 14. Put in prepared filling. Turn over. Seal the edges with water and decorate. 15. Fry in deep fat till crisp and brown. Serve hot.

31. PATRAIL (A)

Ingredients	*Quantity*
Colocasia leaves (with black stems)	1 dozen

Ingredients	*Quantity*
Bengal gram flour	225 gm
Whole wheat flour	40 gm
Rice flour	20 gm
Onions	200 gm
Green chillies	50 gm
Coriander leaves	½ bunch
Ginger	2.5 cm (1") piece
Garlic	5 flakes
Cumin	½ tsp
Cooking banana	1
Fat	30 gm
Turmeric	½ tsp
Coriander-cumin powder	1 tsp
Fenugreek seeds	a few
Coconut	½ (115 gm)
Tamarind	30 gm
Vinegar	30 ml
Jaggery	50 gm
Salt	2 tsp
Sweet oil	2 tbsp
Oil to fry	

Method

1. Grate, grind and soak coconut (set aside a tablespoonful for grinding) in 75 ml of warm water, and extract milk. 2. Grind ginger, garlic, coriander, half the onions, green chillies, remaining coconut, fenugreek, cumin, salt. 3. Soak tamarind in half cup (about 75 ml) of water. Add vinegar. 4. Peel and chop banana. 5. Chop and fry remaining onions. Sieve and mix gram, rice, wheat flour, ground spices, fried onions with leftover fat, banana, turmeric, coriander-cumin powder, chilli powder and salt. 6. Mix tamarind pulp, jaggery and coconut milk and add to the mixture. 7. Add 2 tbsp sweet oil. 8. Apply mixture on a colocasia leaf on the wrong side. Put another leaf on top and apply mixture again. Repeat till 3 leaves are used up in each group. 9. Turn in the two ends and roll tightly. 10. Tie with thread and steam. Cut into slices. 11. Heat oil in a shallow fry pan and fry each piece. Serve hot.

PATRAIL (B)

Ingredients	*Quantity*
Colocasia leaves (with black stems)	6
Bengal gram flour	55 gm
Soda bicarbonate	a pinch

Ingredients	*Quantity*
Green chilli	1
Ginger	5 gm
Garlic	4 cloves
Jaggery	1 tsp
Gingelly seeds	1 tsp
Tamarind	15 gm
Garam masala powder	¼ tsp
Crushed coriander seeds	¼ tsp
Coconut (grated)	1 tsp
Coriander leaves (chopped)	a few
Oil	30 ml
Mustard seeds	a pinch
Salt	to taste

Method

1. Wash colocasia leaves. 2. Grind garlic, ginger and green chilli. 3. Sieve gram flour. 4. Make a pulp with tamarind and jaggery. 5. Make a thick batter with gram flour and tamarind pulp. Season. Add spices and soda bicarbonate. 6. Spread batter evenly on the wrong side of a leaf. Put another leaf on top and spread more batter. 7. Fold from both sides. Roll rightly. 8. Tie with a thread and steam for one hour. 9. Leave till quite cold. Slice. 10. Fry each slice and temper with mustard seeds. Serve hot, garnished with grated coconut and chopped coriander leaves.

32. KHEEMA PATRAIL

Ingredients	*Quantity*
Colocasia leaves (with black stems)	6 (medium-size)
Minced mutton	100 gm
Onions	50 gm
Salt	to taste
Ginger	5 gm
Turmeric	2 gm (a pinch)
Garlic	4 cloves
Chilli powder	2 gm (a pinch)
Green chilli	1
Coriander powder	4 gm (2 tsp)
Garam masala powder (cinnamon, cloves, cardamom, pepper and cumin)	3 gm
Lime	½
Salt	to taste
Bengal gram flour	50 gm

Method

1. Boil mutton with onions and salt. Grind together remaining spices and mix with gram flour and cooked minced meat. Add lime juice and mix well. 2. Spread on the back of one colocasia leaf. Put another leaf on top and apply more mixture. Repeat till all the leaves are used up. Turn in the two ends and roll rightly. 3. Tie with a thread and steam. Serve sliced or if preferred, fry each slice and serve hot.

33. METHI BALLS

Ingredients	*Quantity*
Fenugreek leaves	1 bunch
Potatoes	250 gm
Split bengal gram	250 gm
Spinach	1 bunch
Dill	1 bunch
Ridge gourd	250 gm
Green chillies	6-8
Garlic	4 cloves
Soda bicarbonate	a pinch
Dry mango powder	to taste
Garam masala (powdered cloves, cardamom, cinnamon)	to taste
Salt	to taste
Oil	15 ml
Oil for frying	

Method

1. Soak the gram for 3-4 hours. Boil, peel and mash the potatoes. 2. Wash and chop greens, green chillies and garlic. Peel and slice the ridge gourd. 3. Heat oil. Add garlic and garam masala. Fry for a minute. 4. Add drained gram, chopped greens, ridge gourd and green chillies. 5. Cook on a slow fire till all the ingredients are cooked and the liquid dries up. Grind to a fine paste. 6. Add mashed potatoes, soda bicarbonate, dry mango powder and salt and mix well. 7. Form into small balls and fry in hot fat till crisp. 8. Serve hot with coriander or mint chutney.

34. UPPUMA

Ingredients	*For 6*
Semolina	225 gm
Fat	30 gm
Onions	55 gm
Green chillies	5 gm

Ingredients	*For 6*
Ginger	5 gm
Coriander leaves	a few sprigs
Peanuts/Cashewnuts	15 gm
Bengal gram	15 gm
Split black gram	15 gm
Mustard seeds	3 gm
Curry leaves	2 sprigs
Water	
Lime	½
Salt	to taste

Method

1. Heat fat. Add mustard seeds, peanuts, split black gram and bengal gram and brown lightly. 2. Do not stir. Add chopped onions, ginger, green chillies and curry leaves. Sauté. 3. Add semolina. Roast till light brown. Add boiling water and salt. Allow to cook till dry. 4. Add a dash of lime juice and garnish with chopped coriander leaves. 5. Serve with or without chutney.

N.B. After step 2, water in the proportion of 1:2.3 can be added and brought to boil and semolina sprinkled over and allowed to cook over a slow fire without stirring, till dry, to obtain a slightly different flavour.

35. SEMIYA UPPUMA

Ingredients	*Quantity*
Vermicelli	200 gm
Fat (oil)	30 gm
Green chillies	5 gm
Ginger	5 gm
Coriander leaves	a few sprigs
Split bengal gram	10 gm
Split black gram	10 gm
Mustard seeds	2 gm
Curry leaves	2 sprigs
Salt	10-15 gm
Water	400-500 ml

Method

1. Heat half the fat. Fry vermicelli and remove. 2. Chop green chillies, ginger and coriander leaves finely. Heat remaining fat, add mustard seeds; when they crackle, fry chopped ingredients and the grams. 2. Add

curry leaves, water and salt. When the water starts boiling, add vermicelli. Stir and keep on a slow fire till cooked and dry.

36. BREAD UPPUMA

Ingredients	*Quantity*
Bread	200 gm
Onions	100 gm
Green chillies	10 gm
Lime	½
Mustard	¼ tsp (1 gm)
Turmeric	¼ tsp (1 gm)
Salt	5 to 7 gm
Sugar	2 gm
Fat	20 gm

Method

1. Cut the bread in very small cubes. Heat fat; add mustard, turmeric, chopped onions, and green chillies. Sauté. 2. Add bread cubes. Sprinkle water if required and cook covered for 10 to 12 minutes. 3. Add salt, a pinch of sugar and lime juice. Mix well, cook for 2 to 3 minutes more and remove.

37. AVIL UPPUMA

Ingredients	*Quantity*
Pressed rice	250 gm
Potatoes	225 gm
Ginger	5 gm
Onions	55 gm
Green chillies	5 gm
Split black gram	1 tsp
Coconut	55 gm
Fat	30 gm
Cinnamon	1 small piece
Red onion	1
Salt	to taste

Method

1. Peel and dice potatoes. 2. Peel and chop fine, ginger and onions. 3. Chop green chillies. 4. Grate coconut. 5. Heat fat. Add crushed cinnamon, red onion and black gram. 6. When gram browns, add potatoes, ginger, onions, green chillies, salt and just enough water to cook potatoes dry. 7. Keep pressed rice in a colander. Dip in cold water. Lift and drain. 8. When potatoes are nearly done, add pressed rice. Mix well.

Add grated coconut. 9. Cover and cook gently to allow steam to pass through coconut and cook it slightly. Remove.

38. SOOJI AND VEGETABLE UPPUMA

Ingredients	*Quantity*
Semolina	450 gm
Sprouted green gram	225 gm (60 gm before sprouting)
Carrots	115 gm
Green chillies	6 (20 gm)
Ginger	5 gm
Coriander leaves	1 bunch
Coconut	115 gm
Lime	1
Bengal gram	2 tsp
Split black gram	½ tsp
Mustard seeds	¼ tsp
Curry leaves	2 sprigs
Asafoetida	a pinch
Salt	to taste
Sugar	a pinch
Oil	150 ml

Method

1. Prepare vegetables. Heat 100 ml of oil. 2. Add bengal gram, black gram, mustard seeds, curry leaves and asafoetida. 3. Add chopped carrots and sprouted gram. Sauté. 4. Add chopped green spices and salt and stir well. Add water to vegetables and bring to boil. 5. Meanwhile heat remaining oil and lightly fry semolina. 6. Add semolina to vegetables. 7. Stir and keep on a slow fire till cooked and dry. 8. Add lime juice, sugar and grated coconut. Mix well. 9. Remove from fire and serve hot.

39. POHA

Ingredients	*Quantity*
Pressed rice	225 gm
Potatoes	225 gm
Onions	200 gm
Coriander leaves	⅛ bunch
Cumin	1 tsp
Mustard seeds	1 tsp
Asafoetida	a pinch
Turmeric	1 tsp

Ingredients	*Quantity*
Fat	45 gm
Salt	to taste
For garnish	
Coconut (grated)	30 gm
Coriander leaves (chopped)	

Method

1. Peel and dice potatoes. 2. Chop onions and coriander leaves finely. 3. Heat fat. Brown onions. Add remaining ingredients except rice. 4. Cook on a slow fire till potatoes are cooked (add a little water if necessary). 5. Put rice into a colander. Hold under a running tap or pour water over for about half a minute. Let it drain. 6. Add rice to potatoes. Cook for another 10 minutes. 7. Serve garnished with grated coconut and chopped coriander leaves.

40. SAVOURY POHA

Ingredients	*Quantity*
Pressed rice (poha)	100 gm
Green chillies	2 or 3
Spring onions	½ bunch
Coriander leaves	¼ bunch
Coconut milk	2 cups
Salt	to taste

Method

1. Mix together all ingredients and leave for 10 minutes before use.

41. MACARONI UPPUMA

Ingredients	*Quantity*
Tapioca macaroni (coarsely powdered)	115 gm
Salt	5 gm
Fat	15 gm
Bengal gram	5 gm
Black gram	5 gm
Mustard seeds	a few
Onions	15 gm
Green chillies	5 gm
Ginger	5 gm
Curry leaves	a few
Water	55 ml

Method

1. Chop green chillies, onions and ginger. 2. Heat half the fat. Lightly fry the powdered macaroni. 3. Heat remaining fat. Fry spices, grams and onions. 4. Add water and bring to boil. 5. Add salt and roasted macaroni. 6. Mix thoroughly. Cover and cook till water is absorbed.

42. PONGAL

Ingredients	*Quantity*
Rice (pressed)	115 gm
Split green gram	55 gm
Green chillies	5 gm
Peppercorns	5 gm
Ginger	10 gm
Fat	30 gm
Cashewnuts	15 gm

Method

1. Chop green chillies and ginger. 2. Heat fat and fry green chillies, ginger and peppercorns. 3. Fry the gram and pressed rice; add water and salt and allow it to cook. 4. Garnish with fried nuts and serve hot with chutney.

43. IDLI

Ingredients	*Quantity (20)*
Rice	225 gm
Split black gram	115 gm
Fenugreek	¼ tsp
Salt	to taste

Method

1. Wash and soak rice for about 30 minutes. Strain and dry. 2. Grind coarsely in the grinder. 3. Soak gram for one hour and grind with fenugreek till it is light and frothy. 4. Mix ground rice and ground gram and a little water and keep it overnight. 5. Add a pinch of salt and steam in idli steamer. Serve hot with coconut chutney.

N.B. If parboiled rice is used, the proportion of black gram to rice can be 1:3.

44. STUFFED IDLI

Ingredients	*Quantity*
Split black gram	50 gm
Parboiled rice or	150 gm

Ingredients	*Quantity*
Raw rice	100 gm
Fenugreek	a pinch
Salt	to taste
For the filling	
Mincemeat from leftover meat curry or green leafy vegetables.	

Method

1. Pour 1 ladle of batter into the idli mould. Sprinkle a layer of filling. 2. Cover with another ladle of batter and steam as usual. Serve hot.

45. RAWA IDLI

Ingredients	*Quantity*
Semolina (roasted and cooled)	2 cups (340 gm)
Split black gram	1 cup (175 gm)
Fenugreek seeds	a few
Salt	to taste

Method

1. Soak the gram and fenugreek seeds for 3-4 hours. 2. Grind till light and frothy. 3. Mix with roasted and cooled semolina. Add salt. Leave overnight. 4. Prepare as ordinary idlis.

46. VERMICELLI NUTS IDLI

Ingredients	*Quantity*
Vermicelli	675 gm
Semolina	225 gm
Curds	2 cups
Green chillies	12
Ginger	2.5 cm (1") piece
Mustard seeds	1 tsp
Split black gram	1½ tsp
Curry leaves	1 sprig
Chopped coriander leaves	1 tbsp
Asafoetida	a pinch
Fat	1 cup
Cashewnuts	1 cup
Salt	to taste

Method

1. Chop green chillies finely. Chop cashewnuts coarsely. 2. Heat fat in a

fry-pan; fry black gram and mustard seeds until seeds begin to splutter. 3. Add chopped ginger, coriander and curry leaves, chillies and cashewnuts. 4. Now add the vermicelli and fry to a light brown. 5. Add semolina and fry for a minute. Remove from the fire and cool. 6. Mix in the curds and enough water to make a thick batter. 7. Leave to ferment for two hours or more, covered with a piece of muslin. 8. Fill the idli katoris with this batter and steam in the idli steamer until done. 9. Serve hot with coconut chutney and sambar.

47. SANDNAM

Ingredients	*Quantity*
Rice	250 gm
Split black gram	100 gm
Salt	1 tsp (approx.)
Coconut	1
Toddy	

Method

1. Soak rice and gram separately and keep it overnight. 2. Drain and grind rice and gram to a paste, using toddy. Add salt. Leave it for some time to ferment. 3. Grate coconut fine and add to the mixture. Add a little water and mix it well to pouring consistency. Pour into moulds and steam. Eat with chicken curry.

N.B. Those who relish soft dosas would do well to have 3:1 proportion of parboiled rice to urad dal for the batter, with a small addition of one teaspoonful of methi to rice before soaking.

Crispy dosas, even to the special finish of the much-sought after 'paper thin' ones are easily obtained with a 4:1 proportion of raw rice to urad dal.

Uniform heating and longer retention of heat are best obtained by using a thick and heavy frying pan. To make dosas on a tawa add a little oil to the pan while hot, sprinkle a pinch of salt or mustard, allow it to crackle, wipe the frying surface clean and then start with dosa.

Covering the dosa for a minute or two immediately after spreading the dough into a circular shape, prevents it from getting torn while being turned over.

To facilitate spreading of the batter, clean the pan each time by sprinkling a little water and wiping with a small piece of brinjal or banana, using the stem as a handle.

When making paper thin dosas, uniform thickness is obtained by drawing the flat of the spatula (kurpi) over the dosa to even out the excess. The heat should be so regulated as to be uniform. The pan should be adequately heated.

48. DOSA (Plain)

Ingredients	*Quantity*
Rice	300 gm
Split black gram	100 gm
Salt	to taste
Gingelly oil	30 gm

Method

1. Soak rice and gram separately. 2. Grind rice coarsely and gram to a smooth and fluffy consistency. 3. Mix together. Leave to ferment overnight. 4. Add salt and lukewarm water to get pouring consistency. 5. Heat griddle. 6. Grease lightly with gingelly oil (a cut onion may be used to wipe surface of griddle if batter is inclined to stick). 7. Pour a spoonful of mixture. Spread to form a round about 13-15 cm (5- 6") in diameter. 8. Cook for 2 minutes. Turn over. Cook for another minute or two. 9. Serve hot with coconut chutney.

49. DOSA (Spiced)

Ingredients	*Quantity*
Rice	300 gm
Split black gram	100 gm
Salt	1 to 2 tsp
Soda bicarbonate	a pinch
Green chillies	3 to 4
Sugar	1 tsp
Whole wheat flour	10 gm
Fat for frying	30 gm (approx.)

Method

1. Soak gram and rice separately for about 8 hours. 2. Grind rice coarsely and gram to a smooth, light and frothy paste. 3. Grind green chillies to a smooth paste. 4. Mix together rice, split black gram, green chillies, sugar and salt. 5. Stir well and leave it covered overnight in a warm place. 6. Beat the mixture well and add wheat flour and soda bicarbonate. 7. Add more water if it is too thick and beat well to get pouring consistency (pancake batter consistency). 8. Heat griddle. Smear with fat. 9. Pour a spoonful of batter. Spread into a round (about 13 cm or 5" diameter). 10. In about 2 minutes, turn over. Cook for another minute. 11. Serve hot with coconut chutney.

50. METHI DOSA

Ingredients	*Quantity*
Split black gram	200 gm
Fenugreek	50 gm
Rice	1 kg

Method

1 Soak rice, gram, and fenugreek separately. Grind the gram and fenugreek to a smooth and fluffy consistency. 2. Grind rice coarsely. Mix together. Leave to ferment overnight. 3. Add salt and lukewarm water to obtain pouring consistency. Prepare like plain dosas.

51. JAGGERY DOSA

Ingredients	*Quantity*
Raw rice	250 gm
Whole wheat flour	500 gm
Jaggery	250 gm
Grated coconut (optional)	2 tbsp
Cardamom	
Clarified butter for frying	

Method

1. Soak and drain rice. Grind well. Add flour and broken pieces of jaggery with enough water to make a batter of pouring consistency. 2. Add grated coconut and mix well. Heat pan. Spread a tsp of ghee over. Pour batter and spread lightly. Turn carefully. Pour 1 tsp of ghee over. Remove.

N.B. Maize or jowar flour can be used instead of rice, if desired.

52. ONION DOSA

Ingredients	*Quantity*
Rice flour	60 gm (½ cup)
Whole wheat flour	45 gm (about ¼ cup)
Refined flour	30 gm (2 tbsp)
Bengal gram flour	2 tsp
Butter milk	½ cup
Onions (big)	1
Green chillies	3
Curry leaves	a few
Salt	to taste
Mustard seeds	½ tsp

Ingredients	*Quantity*
Water	½ cup
Soda bicarbonate	a pinch
Oil	1 tbsp

Method

1. Chop onion, chillies and curry leaves. 2. In a fry-pan, heat a tbsp of oil. Put in the mustard and as the seeds crackle, add chillies, curry leaves and fry till golden brown. 3. Mix all the flours together, add salt, buttermilk and soda and mix with enough water to form a thin batter of pouring consistency. 4. Add the fried ingredients and stir well. Pour a teaspoonful of oil on the griddle. Pour a ladle of batter over and spread thinly. 5. When one side is brown, turn over and brown the other side. 6. Remove. Serve hot with peanut chutney.

53. OOTHAPPAM

Ingredients	*Quantity*
Parboiled rice	125 gm
Split black gram	60 gm
Salt	to taste
Onions	2
Green chillies	a few
Ginger	a small piece
Coriander leaves	½ bunch
Fat to cook	

Method

1. Soak rice and gram separately overnight. 2. Grind them separately, then mix the two; allow to ferment for at least 24 hours. 3. Add onions, green chillies, ginger, coriander leaves, all chopped fine. Add salt and make batter into pouring consistency. 4. Cook as for pancakes or dosa.

54. RAWA DOSA

Ingredients	*For 4*	*For 100*
Semolina	300 gm	6 kg
Refined flour	30 gm	680 gm
Green chillies	5 gm	115 gm
Cumin	a pinch	10 gm
Buttermilk	120 ml	2.5 litre
Salt	to taste	100 gm
Fat	30 gm	50 gm

Method

1. Chop green chillies finely. 2. Mix together semolina, flour and butter milk. 3. Let the batter stand for at least half an hour. 4. Heat a little fat. Add green chillies and cumin. 5. When cumin crackles, add to batter. 6. Heat a griddle, smear surface with cut onion. 7. Pour a tsp of batter; spread round. Put a tsp of fat around it and turn over. 8. Remove when cooked. Serve hot with coconut chutney.

55. MORU DOSA

Ingredients	*Quantity*
Buttermilk	1 litre
Whole wheat flour	3 cups
Salt	to taste
Fat	60 gm
Green chillies	3 to 4
Ginger	2.5 cm (1") piece
Curry leaves	a small sprig.
Mustard seeds	a pinch
Soda bicarbonate	a large pinch
Fat for frying	

Method

1. Mix together buttermilk and flour and set aside for ½ to 1 hour. 2. Add salt and more water to form a pouring batter (dosa batter). 3. Heat 60 gm fat. Add chopped green chillies, ginger, curry leaves and mustard seeds. 4. When the seeds crackle, pour over batter and mix well. 5. Add soda bicarbonate dissolved in a little water and mix well. 6. Heat griddle. Grease and pour ladlefuls of batter and prepare dosas. 7. Serve hot with coconut chutney.

56. MASALA DOSA

Ingredients	*For 4*	*For 100*
Rice	500 gm	2 kg
Split black gram	175 gm	700 gm
Salt	to taste	50 gm approx.
Fat	30 gm	500 gm
Filling		
Potatoes	0.9 kg	3.64 kg
Onions	225 gm	900 gm
Curry leaves	2 sprigs	¼ bunch
Green chillies	30 gm	120 gm

Ingredients	*For 4*	*For 100*
Turmeric	5 gm	20 gm
Salt	to taste	30-50 gm
Mustard seeds	5 gm	20 gm
Oil or fat	15 gm	250 gm

Method

1. Soak black gram and rice separately. 2. Grind gram to a smooth, frothy paste. 3. Grind rice to a finely ground semolina consistency. Add salt and water to form a pouring consistency. Keep aside for 8 to 12 hours.

Filling

1. Boil potatoes. Peel and dice. 2. Slice onions, chop green chillies. 3. Heat three-fourths of the fat, sauté onions. Add turmeric and green chillies. 4. Add potatoes and salt and cook for a few minutes. 5. Remove from fire. Temper with mustard seeds and curry leaves.

Dosa

Heat a thick griddle. Smear with fat. Pour a ladle of batter and spread it to form an oval (paper thin). Pour teaspoons of fat from sides to cook dosa properly. The outside must be golden brown and crisp. Place filling in the centre and fold as for panroll. Serve with coconut chutney.

COCONUT CHUTNEY

Ingredients	*Quantity*
Coconut	1
Red chillies	5 gm
Ginger	10 gm
Onions	115 gm
Tamarind	10 gm

Method

1. Grate coconut and grind all ingredients together. If desired, this chutney may be tempered with mustard seeds and curry leaves and a little water may be added to moisten it.

57. COCONUT & ROASTED BENGAL GRAM CHUTNEY

Ingredients	*Quantity (15 portions)*
Coconut	½
Roasted chana dal (bhuna chana)	50 gm
Green chillies	10 gm
Ginger	5 gm
Salt	5 gm
Lime	1

Method

1. Grate coconut and grind to a coarse paste with roasted bengal gram, green chillies and ginger. 2. Mix with salt and lime juice.

58. AMARANTH ADAI

Ingredients	*Quantity*
Rice	250 gm
Split bengal gram	100 gm
Split red gram	100 gm
Split black gram	50 gm
Amaranth	1 bunch
Green chillies	1
Red chillies	2
Asafoetida	a large pinch
Curry leaves	a few
Fat (clarified butter) for frying	
Salt	to taste

Method

1. Soak rice (if parboiled rice is used, soak for 4 hours; if raw rice, soak for 2 hours). 2. Twenty minutes before grinding, clean and soak the grams. Grind together (rice and grams) coarsely with green chillies, red chillies and asafoetida. Set aside for 3 hours. 3. Add salt, chopped amaranth leaves and curry leaves. Heat pan and spread a tsp of fat. Pour a ladle of batter and spread to a round of 12.5 cm (5") diameter. When one side is done, turn over. Add another tsp of fat on top and fry till crisp. Serve hot with curds, honey or "mulaka-podi."

59. PESARATTU

Ingredients	*Quantity*
Green gram (whole)	115 gm
Green chillies	10 gm
Onions	30 gm
Ginger	20 gm
Salt	to taste
Fat to shallow fry	

Method

1. Soak gram in water for about 2 hours. 2. Grind coarsely with onions. Chop chillies fine and slice ginger. 3. Mix together ground gram, green chillies and salt. 4 Heat a fry-pan. Add a tsp of fat. 5. Spread half the mixture in pan to form a round about 12.5 cm in diameter. Top with thin

slices of ginger. Fry. 6. When one side is fried, turn over and fry other side. Add a little more fat if necessary.

60. KHAMAN DHOKLA (A)

Ingredients	*Quantity (24 pieces)*
Split bengal gram	2 tea cups
Soda bicarbonate	½ tsp
Oil	60 ml
Salt	to taste
Asafoetida	a pinch
Green chillies	3-4
Ginger	2.5 cm (½″) piece
Mustard seeds	1 pinch
Curry leaves	½ cup
Coriander leaves	2 sprigs

Method

1. Soak the gram overnight. Grind, but not too fine. 2. Beat with a circular motion to incorporate air. Leave to ferment till evening. 3. After it is fermented, add half the oil, salt, asafoetida, ground green chillies and ginger, and soda bicarbonate mixed with a little water. Beat again. 4. Grease a thali or a pyrex pie dish about 5 cm (2") deep with a little oil. Spread the mixture in it about 2.5 cm (1") thick. 5. Steam and remove. Allow to cool slightly. 6. Heat remaining oil. Add mustard seeds. As seeds crackle, add curry leaves and pour over 'Dhokla'. 7. Serve garnished with grated coconut and chopped coriander leaves.

N.B. 1 tbsp of buttermilk may be added along with spices and soda bicarbonate.

Dhokla may be served with coriander leaves chutney.

KHAMAN DHOKLA (B)

Ingredients	*Quantity (30 Pieces)*
Split bengal gram	200 gm
Black gram	75 gm
Ginger	10 gm
Green chillies	10 gm
Oil	100 gm
Asafoetida	5 gm
Sugar	10 gm (about 1 tsp)
Soda bicarbonate	½ tsp (3 gm)
Salt	10-15 gm

Ingredients	*Quantity (30 Pieces)*
Turmeric	¼ tsp (3 gm)
To temper	
Oil	50 gm
Mustard seeds	5 gm
Garnish	
Coconut	115 gm
Coriander leaves	30 gm

Method

1. Soak the grams together for 6 hours. 2. Grind finely in a round stone grinder, to allow it to froth up. 3. Add ground ginger, green chillies, salt, asafoetida, turmeric, soda bicarbonate and sugar. 4. Heat oil. Pour into the mixture. Mix well and keep for 12 hours. 5. When fermented, do not stir. Remove gently from side and put into a greased pan and steam (15–20 minutes). 6. Heat oil. Add mustard seeds. 7. Add pieces of dhokla. Fry for a few minutes. Serve garnished with grated coconut and chopped coriander leaves.

61. KHANDVI

Ingredients	*Quantity*
Buttermilk (thick)	150 ml (1 cup)
Bengal gram flour	115 gm
Water	150 ml
Green chillies	2
Ginger	2.5 cm (1") piece
Turmeric	½ tsp (3 gm)
Salt	10 gm
Tempering	
Red chilli	1
Asafoetida	a pinch
Mustard seeds	½ tsp (3 gm)
Vegetable fat	10 gm
For garnish	
Coconut	55 gm
Coriander leaves	30 gm

Method

1. Mix together buttermilk, gram flour and water. 2. Grind chillies and ginger to a paste. 3. Mix all ingredients (except those for tempering and

garnish) into a smooth solution and cook till water is almost absorbed and a soft dough consistency is obtained. 4. Grease plates with fat and spread mixture as thinly as possible while still hot. 5. Cut into 5 cm (2") strips. Grease finger and roll up each strip. 6. Heat fat. Add whole red chilli, mustard seeds and asafoetida. As seeds crackle, pour over prepared khandvi. 7. Garnish with grated coconut and chopped coriander leaves.

62. PITLA

Ingredients	*For 4*	*For 100*
Bengal gram flour	50 gm	1 kg
Onions	20 gm	500 gm
Green chillies	1	40 gm
Salt	to taste	30 gm
Turmeric	1 gm	10 gm
Red chilli powder	1 gm	10 gm
Mustard seeds	1 gm	4 gm
Cocum	10 gm	100 gm
Oil	15 ml	300 ml
Coconut	1 tbsp	1
Coriander leaves	a few sprigs	20 gm (1 bunch)

Method

1. Make a fairly thin batter with gram flour, turmeric, salt and water. 2. Heat oil, add mustard seeds. When they crackle, add chopped onions and green chillies and sauté. 3. Add the gram flour mixture, cocum and chilli powder. 4. Stir till mixture becomes dry (about 15 to 20 minutes). 5. Serve hot.

63. MOONG DAL KACHORIES (A)

Ingredients	*For 4*	*For 100*
Covering		
Refined flour	100 gm	2.5 kg
Soda bicarbonate	a pinch	10 gm
Sour curds	20 gm	500 gm
Fat	20 gm	400 gm
Salt	to taste	30 gm
Filling		
Split green dal	60 gm	1.5 kg
Garam masala	a pinch	10 gm
Coriander leaves	a few sprigs	1 bunch

Ingredients	*For 4*	*For 100*
Green chillies	3 gm	75 gm
Ginger	a small piece	30 gm
Fat	15 gm	250 gm

Method

1. Sieve flour with salt. 2. Rub in fat. 3. Beat the curds with a little water and add to flour. 4. Add soda bicarbonate dissolved in a little water. 5. Make a smooth dough and keep aside. 6. Soak gram overnight. 7. Chop green chillies, ginger and coriander leaves. 8. Heat fat. Sauté gram and chopped ingredients. Add garam masala. 9. Cover and cook gently till gram is cooked. Add salt. 10. Divide dough into equal portions. 11. Flatten dough between palms; fill with the gram filling. Seal edges on top. 12. Deep fry till golden brown; serve piping hot with chutney.

MOONG DAL KACHORIES (B)

Ingredients	*For 12*
Filling	
Split green gram	225 gm
Ginger	5 gm
Coriander leaves	50 gm
Asafoetida	a pinch
Turmeric	½ tsp
Sugar	1 tsp
Coriander and cumin powder	½ tsp
Fat	55 gm
Sultanas	50 gm
Coconut	30 gm
Chilli powder	5 gm
Lime	2
Salt	to taste
Covering	
Refined flour	115 gm
Semolina	55 gm
Fat	20 gm
Salt	1 tsp
Fat to fry	

Method

1. Wash and soak gram overnight and grind it coarsely. 2. Chop ginger and coriander leaves; grate coconut. 3. Heat fat, add the gram and cook. Add grated coconut, coriander and cumin powder, asafoetida, ginger,

coriander leaves, turmeric, chilli powder and salt. 4. Stir; add lime juice and sugar. Cook for a few minutes longer and remove. Add sultanas. 5. Sieve flour and semolina; add salt and rub in fat. 6. Make a dough and keep it covered for half an hour. Knead well. 7. Divide into equal portions; roll as for puries and put the gram mixture in the centre. Turn over and seal, using a little water. 8. Pinch the edges together. 9. Fry in deep fat. The fat should be quite hot.

64. POTATO KACHORIES

Ingredients	*For 4*	*For 100*
Covering		
Refined flour	100 gm	2.5 kg
Soda bicarbonate	a pinch	10 gm
Sour curds	20 gm	500 gm
Fat	20 gm	400 gm
Salt	to taste	30 gm
Filling		
Potatoes	160 gm	4 kg
Green peas	80 gm	2 kg
Green chillies	5 gm	115 gm
Ginger	a small piece	30 gm
Coriander leaves	a little	1 bunch
Turmeric	a small pinch	10 gm
Garam masala powder	a pinch	10 gm
Lime	¼	6
Mustard seeds	a few	5 gm
Salt	to taste	to taste
Oil for tempering	5 gm	60 gm
Oil for frying (absorption)	30 ml	500 ml
Imli chutney		
Tamarind	50 gm	1 kg
Jaggery	a little	60 gm
Green chillies	2	30 gm
Chilli powder	a pinch	30 gm

Method

1. Sieve flour with salt. 2. Rub fat into flour. 3. Beat the curds with a little water and add to flour. 4. Add soda bicarbonate dissolved in a little water. 5. Make a smooth dough and keep aside. 6. Boil potatoes in jackets. Peel and cut into cubes. 7. Boil peas and add to potatoes. 8. Remove seeds from green chillies and chop. Chop ginger and coriander leaves. 9. Add ginger, green chillies and coriander leaves and garam

masala to potato and peas-mixture. Mix well. 10. Heat oil. Add mustard seeds. As they crackle, add turmeric and mix with potatoes. 11. Add lime juice and mix thoroughly. 12. Divide dough into equal portions. 13. Divide potato mixture into same number of portions. 14. Flatten dough between palms; fill centre with prepared stuffing, seal edges on top. 15. Deep fry till golden brown and serve piping hot with tamarind chutney. 16. For chutney, soak tamarind and extract pulp. Mix all ingredients. Boil, strain and use.

65. POTATO CAKES

Ingredients	*Quantity*
Cooked potatoes	115 gm
Refined flour	30 gm
Butter	15 gm
Salt	to taste

Method

1. Mash potatoes. Add flour, butter and salt. 2. Roll out 0.25 cm (½″) thick. 3. Cut into rounds; cook on hot greased griddle. Brush with melted butter. Serve hot.

66. CORN AND GREEN PEPPER FRITTERS

Ingredients	*Quantity*
Capsicums	115 gm
Corn (tender) removed from cob	1 cob
Sugar	15 gm
Medium white sauce	120 ml
Baking powder	¼ tsp
Egg	1
Sifted flour	1 tbsp (about 15 gm)
Salt	to taste
Fat to fry	

Method

1. Cook the corn in the salted water. 2. Combine corn with sugar, salt, white sauce, egg and chopped capsicum. 3. Sift baking powder and flour and add it to the mixture. Mix well. 4. Fry in deep fat, like fritters.

67. BAKED CORN

Ingredients	*Quantity*
Refined flour	2 tbsp
Butter	1 tbsp

Ingredients	*Quantity*
Milk	1 cup
Corn (tender)	2 cobs
Capsicum	30 gm
Eggs	2
Salt	to taste

Method

1. Melt butter in a thick-bottomed pan. Add flour, and cook slowly without discolouring, stirring all the time. 2. Remove the pan from fire and add hot milk, a little at a time, to prevent lumps from forming. 3. When all the milk has been added and the batter is smooth, return to the fire and cook till the sauce is thick. Remove. 4. Add chopped capsicum, salt and beaten yolks of eggs. Remove corn from the cobs, and add to the sauce. 5. Beat the whites of the eggs till stiff and fold in. Pour into a greased pie dish and bake at 135°C. (300°F) for about 30 minutes.

68. MACARONI AND TOMATO FRITTERS (Vegetarian)

Ingredients	*For 4*	*For 100*
Macaroni	225 gm	5.6 kg
Tomatoes	450 gm	11.00 kg
Green chillies	5 gm	115 gm
Onions	115 gm	2.8 kg
Ginger	a small piece	55 gm
Bengal gram flour	55 gm	1.36 kg
Salt	to taste	80-100 gm
Oil to fry (absorption)	30 ml	500 ml

Method

1. Boil macaroni by the absorption method. 2. Cook tomatoes and pass through a sieve. 3. Make a thick batter with gram flour and water. Add tomato pulp, finely chopped onions, green chillies and ginger. Add cooked macaroni and salt. Mix well. 4. Heat oil. Drop teasponfulls of mixture into hot oil, when brown, remove. Drain and serve with chutney.

69. MACARONI CHEESE FRITTERS (Vegetarian)

Ingredients	*For 4*	*For 100*
Macaroni	225 gm	5.6 kg
Cheese	55 gm	1.36 kg
Onions	55 gm	1.36 kg
Green chillies	5 gm	115 gm
Coriander leaves	⅛ bunch	3 bunches

Ingredients	*For 4*	*For 100*
Bengal gram flour	55 gm	1.36 kg
Lime	½	6 to 8
Soda bicarbonate	a pinch	5 gm
Oil to fry (absorption)	30 ml	500 ml

Method

1. Boil macaroni by the absorption method. 2. Make a thick batter with gram flour and water. Add chopped onion, coriander, chillies; also soda, macaroni, cheese and lime juice. 3. Heat oil. Drop teaspoons of mixture into hot oil. When brown, remove. Drain and serve with chutney.

70. CHEESE BOUCHÉES

Ingredients	*For 4*
Cheese	225 gm
Refined flour	115 gm
Eggs	4
Salt and pepper	to taste
Oil for frying	

Method

1. Sieve flour, salt and pepper. 2. Add finely grated cheese. 3. Beat yolks of eggs and add to dry ingredients. Mix well. 4. Let the mixture stand for at least ½ hour. 5. Heat oil. 6. While oil is being heated beat egg whites stiff and fold into the mixture lightly but thoroughly. 7. Put teaspoonfuls of the mixture into the hot oil. Remove as it turns to a light golden-brown colour. 8. Drain on absorbent paper and serve hot in a hot dish over a folded napkin.

N.B. Do not allow bouchées to fry too long or else they become tough.

71. CHEESE FRITTERS

Ingredients	*Quantity*
Cheese	115 gm
Refined flour	225 gm
Salt and pepper	to taste
Oil for frying	
Water to mix	

Method

1. Sieve flour. Add salt and pepper. 2. Add water and prepare a medium batter. 3. Add grated cheese and leave the batter to stand for at least half an hour. 4. Heat oil and fry fritters till golden-brown.

72. CHEESE JALLEBI

Ingredients	*Quantity*
Grated cheese	55 gm
Refined flour	55 gm
Egg	½
Salt, pepper, mustard	a pinch each
Water to mix	
Oil to fry	

Method

1. Mix sieved flour, salt, pepper and mustard. 2. Add beaten egg and water to make a flowing batter. Let it stand for at least half an hour. 3. Add grated cheese. 4. Heat oil and fry like jallebis.

73. CHEESE TOAST

Ingredients	*Quantity*
Cheese (grated)	40 gm
(strong cheese)	
Worcester sauce	½ tsp
Mustard	1 tsp
Flour/Cornflour	1 tbsp
Egg(optional)	1
Baking powder	1 pinch
Cayenne pepper or chilli powder	to taste
Milk or water	1 dsp.
Bread slices	
Oil (to deep fry)	100 ml

Method

1. Cut bread slices into triangles or rectangles. 2. Mix all ingredients (except bread) together. 3. Spread on bread slices. 4. Deep fry in a deep karai and serve piping hot.

N.B. For variations, use ground garlic, ginger, chopped coriander leaves and green chillies or use tomato sauce instead of milk.

74. POTATO TOAST

Ingredients	*For 20*
Potatoes	2.5 kg
Bread	4 loaves or 80 slices (450 gm)
Eggs	6

Ingredients	For 20
Onions	250 gm
Green chillies	60 gm
Turmeric	1 level tsp
Coriander leaves	1 bunch
Lime juice	4
Salt	to taste
Fat	500 gm

Method

1. Peel and boil potatoes. Drain and dry on fire. Mash and cream. 2. Chop onions, green chillies and coriander leaves. 3. Heat a little fat. Sauté onions and green chillies. Add turmeric, creamed potatoes, chopped coriander leaves, lime juice and salt to taste. 4. Spread mixture about 1.25 cm thick on bread slices. Brush over with beaten egg seasoned with salt. 5. Fry in shallow fat. Brown both sides.

75. DATE SAVOURY

Ingredients	Quantity
Dates	200 gm
Cashewnuts or peanuts	55 gm
Cheese	75 gm
Egg yolk	1
Chilli powder	½ tsp
Butter	55 gm
Refined flour	200 gm
Salt	to taste
Fat for frying	

Method

1. Destone dates. 2. Mince nuts (if peanuts are used roast them first). 3. Fill dates with nuts. 4. Mix together grated cheese, butter, chilli powder, salt and egg yolk. 5. Add flour little at a time add make into a soft dough. 6. Roll and cut into small rounds. Into each round put one date and turn over to get a half moon shape. Seal the edges. 7. Bake or fry in deep fat.

76. SAVOURY CAKE

Ingredients	Quantity
Rice	115 gm
Split bengal gram	55 gm
Split black gram	55 gm

Ingredients	*Quantity*
Split green gram	55 gm
Shelled peas	115 gm
Curds	60 ml
Sultanas	55 gm
Peanuts	55 gm
Cashewnuts	55 gm
Green chilli	1
Ginger	5 gm
Garlic	5 gm
Coriander leaves	1 bunch
Salt	to taste
Mustard seeds	¼ tsp
Asafoetida	¼ tsp
Oil	120 ml
Soda bicarbonate	¼ tsp
Sugar	15 gm

Method

1. Wash and dry rice and grams. Powder coarsely (like semolina). 2. Heat half the oil and rub into the powdered ingredients. 3. Add beaten curds and warm water to make a thick batter. 4. Keep in warm place for 12 hours till fermented. Mix well. 5. Add finely chopped spices, nuts, sultanas, shelled peas, salt, soda bicarbonate and sugar. 6. Heat remaining oil. Add mustard seeds and asafoetida. 7. When mustard crackles, pour over mixture. 8. Pour into greased cake tin and bake at 135°C (300°F) for about 2 hours. 9. Serve in slices hot or cold with green chutney.

77. CHAKLI (A) (Murukku)

Ingredients	*Quantity*
Rice flour	340 gm
Split black gram	115 gm
Thick coconut milk	1
Pepper	10 gm
Garlic	10 gm
Cumin	2 tsp
Salt	to taste
Butter	100 gm
Oil to fry	

Method

1. Sift rice flour through a fine sieve. Roast slightly. 2. Roast gram and

powder. 3. Grind garlic, pepper and cumin. 4. Grate coconut and extract thick coconut milk. Add ground spices to it. 5. Mix flour and gram powder. 6. Add salt. Rub in butter. 7. Add coconut milk and make a stiff dough. 8. Knead well. Set aside for half an hour. 9. Knead again; press through mould and fry in hot fat.

CHAKLI (B)

Ingredients	*Quantity*
Raw rice	300 gm
Split bengal gram	200 gm
Split black gram	100 gm
Split green gram	50 gm
Coriander	10 gm
Cumin	5 gm
Oil	140 ml
Gingelly seeds	10 gm
Turmeric	6 gm
Chilli powder	15 gm
Salt	20 gm
Oil for frying	
Asafoetida	5 gm
Water	350 ml

Method

1. Roast rice, grams, coriander and cumin separately and powder. 2. Sieve the mixture and add gingelly seeds, asafoetida, chilli powder, turmeric and salt. 3. Heat 140 ml of oil and add to the mixture. 4. Make a dough using 350 ml of water. 5. Keep the dough for ½ hour. Divide into 7.5 cm (3") sized balls. 6. Put a ball into the chakli mould. Press on to paper to form a pattern as shown below. Slide gently into hot, deep fat. 7. Fry well on both sides. 8. Drain and cool and put into airtight tins.

N.B. When putting the mixture into the mould, knead the dough with a little water.

78. BHEL POORI (A)

Ingredients for sev	*Quantity*
Bengal gram flour	225 gm
Salt	15–20 gm

Ingredients for sev	*Quantity*
Asafoetida	a pinch
Chilli powder	1 level tsp
Baking soda	3 gm (3 pinches)
Oil for frying	140 ml
Cumin	5 gm
Gingelly seeds	10 gm
Ingredients for poories	
Semolina	55 gm
Refined flour	55 gm
Whole wheat flour	55 gm
Salt	to taste
Water to mix	
Oil	

Method

Sift gram flour with soda. Add asafoetida, chilli powder, salt, cumin, gingelly seeds, 2 tbsp of hot oil and some water to make a dough. Keep aside for half an hour. Heat oil for frying. Press the dough through the sev mould into the hot oil. Fry till light brown. Remove sev. Mix semolina, wheat flour, refined flour and salt. Add enough water to make a stiff dough. Let it stand for half an hour. Knead well. Divide into even portions, the size of a walnut. Roll out into thin rounds. Fry in hot oil till brown and crisp. Remove and drain. Allow poories to cool.

Hot chutney

Ingredients	*Quantity*
Coriander leaves	1 bunch
Green chillies	4
Ginger	5 gm
Garlic	2 flakes
Roasted gram	1 heaped tsp
Salt	to taste

Method

1. Wash and chop coriander leaves, green chillies, ginger and garlic. 2. Grind to a smooth paste with roasted gram and salt. 3. Mix with a little water if paste is too thick.

Sweet chutney

Ingredients	*Quantity*
Dates	100 gm
Tamarind	30 gm

Ingredients	*Quantity*
Sugar	1 tsp
Salt	to taste

Method

1. Destone dates. Soak tamarind in a little water for 15 minutes. Extract pulp. 2. Grind together dates and tamarind. Add sugar and salt.

Bhel

Method

Mix together 1 kg of puffed rice, sev, poories broken into pieces and the two chutneys. Add sliced, boiled potatoes, chopped onions and coriander leaves and add lime juice to taste.

N.B. Mixing can be done separately, as and when required.

BHEL POORI (B)

Ingredients	*For 25*
Poories	
Refined flour	225 gm.
Water to mix	
Salt	a pinch
Bhel	
Puffed rice	115 gm.
Fried split bengal gram	115 gm.
Fried sev	115 gm.
Fried split green gram	115 gm.
Onions (chopped)	455 gm.
Coriander leaves	½ bunch
Chutney no. 1	
Soak and grind together	
Dates	455 gm.
Tamarind	115 gm.
Chutney no. 2	
Grind all ingredients together	
Green chillies	5 gm.
Coriander leaves	¼ bunch
Mint leaves	a few
Cumin	1 tsp.
Lemon	½
Split bengal gram (roasted)	30 gm.
Salt	to taste
Turmeric	a pinch
Chutney no. 3	
Grind to a smooth paste using water	
Chilli powder	15 gm.
Coriander seeds	15 gm.
Garlic	30 gm.
Dry coconut	115 gm.
Peppercorns	8
Salt	to taste

Method

1. Make a stiff dough. Divide into small balls and roll into thin poories. Dry in the shade. Fry in deep fat till light brown.

Service

Mix crushed poories, puffed rice, split bengal gram, sev and fried green gram. Put about 30 gm of the mixture in a plate. Add chopped onions, chutney, chopped mango and coriander.

79. PANI POORI

Ingredients	*Quantity*
Refined flour	55 gm
Split black gram flour	115 gm
Semolina	115 gm
Cold water to mix	
Filling	
Sprouted green gram	55 gm
Pani	
Mint leaves	55 gm
Cold water	1.80 litre
Black pepper	15 gm
Black salt	15
Salt	15 gm
Cumin	2 tsp
Sweet cumin	15 gm
Cloves	4
Dry mango powder	115 gm
Ginger	2.5 cm (1") piece

Method

1. Sieve the refined flour and gram flour and semolina. Make a stiff dough. Knead well. Make small balls. Roll into fairly thick poories. Spread on a moist cloth and cover with another moist cloth. Fry in deep fat till light brown and crisp. Boil the sprouted gram in salted water.

Pani

1. Wash mint leaves. Grind cumin, sweet cumin, cloves and ginger. 2. Soak mango powder for an hour and sieve the pulp. 3. Powder salt and dissolve in cold water. 4. Mix the ground spices with pulp and salt water. 5. Strain and keep in an earthen pot.

Service

Make a hole in the poori and put in a few grains of sprouted gram. Dip the poori in the prepared liquid. Fill with pani and serve.

80. BHALLE

Ingredients	*Quantity*
Wada	
Split black gram	100 gm
Green chillies	10 gm
Ginger	5 gm
Salt	to taste
Cumin	5 gm

Method

1.Soak the gram overnight. Grind it coarsely and add chopped green chillies, ginger, cumin and salt. 2. Mix well. Shape into wadas 5 cm (2") in diameter and 0.5 cm (¼") thick. Fry in hot fat till golden brown. Drain the wadas and soak them in water for 5-10 minutes. Squeeze out the water and soak them in the tamarind chutney.

Chutney

Ingredients	*Quantity*
Tamarind	100 gm
Sugar	75 gm
Black salt	20 gm
Salt	to taste
Roasted chilli powder	1 tsp
Cumin	5 gm
Coriander	5 gm
Pepper	5 gm
Water	300 ml

Method

1. Soak the tamarind for 1 hour, take out the pulp and strain it. Roast and powder spices. 2. Add all the roasted and powdered spices, sugar and salt. Chill and serve.

81. PHAFDAS

Ingredients	*Quantity*
Bengal gram flour	115 gm
Split black gram flour	30 gm
Chilli powder	¼ tsp
Fat to rub in	1 tsp
Asafoetida	a pinch
Salt	⅛ tsp
Omum	to taste
Oil for deep frying	

Method

1. Sieve all flour. 2. Add spices, except chilli powder. Rub in fat. 3. Add salted water and make a stiff dough. 4. Divide into equal portions. 5. Roll out into very thin poories. 6. Deep fry. Remove and sprinkle over with chilli powder.

82. GANTIA (Plain)

Ingredients	*Quantity*
Bengal gram	
Flour	1 kg
Oil to mix	60 ml
Salt	1 tsp (full)
Water (approximately)	445 ml (3 cups)
Oil to fry	

Method

1. Sift gram flour. Rub in oil. 2. Add salt and water to make a stiff dough. 3. Press through sev moulds into hot fat. 4. When crisp and golden brown, remove and drain. 5. Tin and use as required.

N.B. 5 gm chilli powder and 5 gm turmeric could be mixed with the flour, if so desired.

83. BHAWNAGARI GANTIA

Ingredients	*Quantity*
Bengal gram flour	115 gm
Soda bicarbonate	½ tsp
Salt	to taste
Omum	¼ tsp
Asafoetida	a pinch
Crushed peppercorns	¼ tsp
Oil to rub in flour	30 gm
Oil for frying	

Method

1. Sift gram flour. Add crushed peppercorns, omum and asafoetida. 2. Add hot oil and rub in well. 3. Dissolve salt and soda bicarbonate in 60 ml of water. Bring to boiling point and cool. 4. Make a well in the centre of the flour and add prepared water, enough to make stiff dough. 5. Mix a tsp of oil to remaining water and sprinkle over the dough. 6. Knead the dough till quite smooth. 7. Press through sev mould into slightly hot, deep fat over slow fire. 8. Fry till crisp. Serve hot.

84. PAPRI

Same ingredients and method as for Gantia (plain) but rub through a Papri mould. Fry till crisp.

85. SEV

Ingredients	*Quantity*
Bengal gram flour	500 gm
Oil to mix	20 ml
Soda bicarbonate	2 pinches
Chilli powder	1 tsp
Water	590 ml
Salt	to taste
Asafoetida (optional)	5 gm
Oil to fry	125 ml

Method

1. Rub in oil into the flour. 2. Add all ingredients and make a stiff dough. 3. Press through a stiff mould into hot oil. 4. Fry till crisp. Stir lightly with end of a spoon as it hardens to prevent sev forming into lumps. 5. Remove. Drain and put into airtight tins or bottles.

86. CHIWDA (A)

Ingredients	*Quantity*
Pressed rice	115 gm
Peanuts	55 gm
Groundnuts/Cashewnuts	30 gm
Dry coconut (sliced)	15 gm
Green chillies	1
Sultanas	15 gm
Salt	to taste
Turmeric	½ tsp
Chilli powder	½ tsp
Chiwda masala powder	½ tsp
Curry leaves	1 tbsp
Garlic	2 flakes
White gingelly	1 tsp
Sugar (optional)	½ tsp
Fresh oil to fry	

Method

1. Heat oil. Fry pressed rice. Remove when it puffs up. Drain. 2. Mix turmeric with puffed rice. Set aside. 3. Fry cashewnuts till light brown.

4. Fry groundnuts, chilli, garlic, coconut, gingelly, sultanas, curry leaves separately. Remove after frying and drain. 5. Add fried ingredients to fried, pressed rice. Add chilli powder and chiwda masala powder. Mix well. 6. When the mixture is cold, add salt.

N.B. When frying pressed rice sprinkle small quantities of fat at a time or else it will not puff up properly.

Chiwda Masala

Ingredients	*Quantity*
Dry mango powder	1 tsp
Cumin	a pinch
Fenugreek	a pinch
Peppercorns	4
Cinnamon	0.5 cm (¼″) piece
Omum	a pinch
Red chilli	1

Method

1. Roast, powder and use as required.

CHIWDA (B)

Ingredients	*For 50*	*Ingredients*	*For 50*
Pressed rice	1 kg	**Turmeric**	15 gm
Peanuts	200 gm	**Curry leaves**	1 bunch
Bengal gram	200 gm	**Sugar (optional)**	225 gm
Dry coconut	200 gm		
Green chillies	55 gm	**Salt**	30–50 gm
Chilli powder	40 gm	**Oil to fry**	

Method

1. Soak gram overnight with a pinch of alum. 2. Slice dry coconut. Chop green chillies. 3. Heat oil. Fry pressed rice and remove as it puffs up. Drain. 4. Mix turmeric and chilli powder with fried rice. Set aside. 5. Fry gram, sliced coconut, green chillies, nuts, and curry leaves separately. Remove. 6. Mix fried ingredients with fried rice. 7. When cold, mix sugar and roasted and powdered salt.

87. NIMKI

Ingredients	*Quantity*
Refined flour	200 gm
Onions seeds	1 tsp

Ingredients	*Quantity*
Salt	to taste
Fat for rubbing in	15 gm
Water (absorption)	

Method

1. Sift flour. Add salt and onion seeds. 2. Rub in fat with sufficient water to form a soft, smooth dough. 3. Roll out about 0.1 cm (1⁄16″) thick. 4. Cut with a biscuit cutter. Prick. 5. Fry in deep fat till golden brown and crisp. 6. Drain on absorbent paper and tin.

88. MATHRI

Ingredients	*Quantity*
Refined flour	200 gm
Fat to rub in and for frying	
Salt	to taste
Omum seeds	

Method

1. Sieve flour. Add salt and omum seeds. Rub in 2 ½ tbsp of melted fat into flour. 2. Make a very hard dough adding a little water. Divide the dough into equal portions (about 10 to 12). 3. Flatten them slightly. Heat fat. Fry mathri to a golden brown colour on a very slow fire 4. Serve hot with any pickle.

89. MATHIA

Ingredients	*Quantity*
Refined flour	115 gm
Fat	30 gm
Crushed peppercorns	4
Sweet cumin	⅛ tsp
Curds	1 tbsp
Salt	to taste
Oil for frying	

Method

1. Sift flour. Add sweet cumin, salt and peppercorns. 2. Rub in fat. 3. Add curds and cold water to make a stiff dough. 4. Divide into equal portions. Roll into round poories. Double them. 5. Roll lightly. Fold again to form triangle. 6. Roll lightly again and fry in deep fat till light brown.

90. DOODHI MUTHIA

Ingredients	*Quantity*
Grated bottle ground	4 cups
Whole wheat flour	¾ cup
Bajra flour	¾ cup
Bengal gram flour	1 full cup
Salt	to taste
Sugar	2 tbsp
Cumin powder (roasted & powdered)	1½ tbsp
Turmeric	2 tsp
Green chillies (crushed)	10
Ginger (crushed)	5 cm (2") piece
Garlic (optional) (crushed)	½ pod
For frying	
Oil	6 tbsp (60 gm)
Gingelly seeds	1½ tsp
Asafoetida	a pinch
Garnish	
Grated coconut and chopped coriander leaves	

Method

1. Sqeeze out moisture from grated gourd. Add the flour and the remaining ingredients. Mix well and knead lightly. 2. Form into croquette shape. Steam for half an hour. Cool. Cut into 1.75 cm (¾″) pieces. 3. Heat oil. Add gingelly seeds and asafoetida. As seeds brown, add 'Muthia' and fry till pieces brown lightly on the outside. 4. Garnish with grated coconut and chopped coriander leaves.

N.B. Cabbage can be used instead of gourd. Fenugreek leaves may also be used instead, in which case do not squeeze. Two ripe bananas mashed up may also be used when preparing Muthia with fenugreek leaves.

91. HANDWA

Ingredients	*Quantity*
Rice flour (coarse)	1 kg
Bengal gram flour	500 gm
Black gram flour (coarse)	25 gm
Buttermilk	100 ml
Bottle gourd	500 gm
Oil	250 gm
Mustard seeds	5 gm

Ingredients	*Quantity*
Asafoetida	8 gm
Masala	
Green chillies	25 gm
Onions	50 gm
Cinnamon, cardamoms and cloves	8 gm
Turmeric	8 gm
Coriander	40 gm
Salt	to taste

Method

1. Grind masala to a fine paste. Mix the three types of flour with buttermilk, add more water to make a pouring consistency. 2. Add masala and peeled and grated bottle gourd to the mixture. 3. Heat oil in a thick pan. When hot, add mustard seeds and asafoetida. 4. When the mustard seeds crackle, pour the oil in the mixture. 5. Mix well and leave it for about 12 hours to ferment. 6. Pour into shallow ovenproof containers and bake the mixture for about 40 minutes. 7. Serve with green chutney.

92. VODDE

Ingredients	*Quantity*
Rice flour (raw rice flour)	½ kg
Parboiled rice flour	½ kg
Split black gram flour	¼ kg
Coconut	1
Salt	1 tsp approx.
Fat or oil for frying	

Method

1. Mix the rice flour, gram flour and salt, and make a dough using coconut milk or water. Leave it for about 12 hours. 2. Make small balls and roll like poories. Fry in hot oil.

N.B. A little powdered sugar may be mixed with the flour, if desired.

93. DEVILLED CASHEWNUTS

Ingredients	*For 4*	*For 100*
Cashewnuts	115 gm	2.8 kg
Cayenne pepper or chilli powder	a pinch	55 gm
Salt	to taste	100 gm
Fat	10 gm	200 gm

Method

1. Heat fat, fry cashewnuts. Drain 2. Mix together salt and cayenne pepper. Toss fried cashewnuts in the mixture.

94. ROSE POORIES

Ingredients	*Quantity*
Refined flour	225 gm
Fat	55 gm
Powdered sugar	55 gm
Rice flour	115 gm
Salt	2½ tsp
Oil for frying	

Method

1. Put the fat on a marble slab and beat with the palm of the hand. 2. When it gets smooth, add half the rice flour. 3. Cream well till it forms a lump. 4. Take out a tsp of mixture and put the rest in cold water. 5. Sift flour and salt. Add the tsp of the creamed mixture and water to make a fairly stiff dough. Divide into three portions. Colour one pink and one green. Make each portion into small balls. 6. Roll into thin chapaties. 7. Apply creamed mixture. Sprinkle a little rice flour over. Repeat process and put one of each colour to form 3 in one. 8. Roll. Cut into 2.5 cm (½″) slices. Press down rolled end. 9. Roll out into rounds of about 7.5 cm (3") diameter. 10. Deep fry in oil. Sprinkle over with powdered sugar.

95. KUZHALAPPAM

Ingredients	*Quantity*
Raw rice	910 gm
Coconut	1
Small onions	225 gm
Cumin	2 tsp
Garlic	50 gm
Salt	to taste
Refined coconut oil to fry (absorption)	1 kg (about 50 gm)

Method

1. Soak rice in water for 2 to 3 hours. 2. Drain well (till nearly dry) and powder. Sieve through a fine sieve. 3. Grind together onions, cumin, garlic and salt. 4. Extract coconut milk. Add ground ingredients. 5. Roast rice flour. When still hot, add coconut milk mixture to form a fairly stiff dough. 6. Divide into small balls. Roll out into 7.5 cm (3") diameter rounds. 7. Shape round a bamboo stick of 1.25–2 cm (½″–¾″) diameter

or around fingers to form tubes. 8. Fry in hot oil till crisp. 9. Drain well on absorbent paper. Cool and put into airtight tins.

N.B. This may be made sweet by putting into a thick sugar syrup (three string consistency) and mixing well. In this case less salt is added.

96. CHEEPAPPAM

Ingredients	*Quantity*
Raw rice	910 gm
Eggs	4
Coconut	2
Salt	to taste
Refined coconut oil (to fry) (absorption)	1 kg

Method

1. Soak rice in water for 2 to 3 hours. 2. Drain well (till dry) and powder. Sieve through a fine sieve. 3. Roast rice flour. Extract coconut milk. 4. Mix together rice flour, beaten eggs, coconut milk and salt to make a fairly stiff dough. 5. Make into small balls. Press between two barks of the banana tree, to form an impression or mark with a clean comb. 6. Heat oil and deep fry.

N.B. The fleshy bark of the banana tree is cut into a piece, 7.5 cm broad and 25 cm long. The thin inner membrane is removed before the bark is used to make the impression.

97. ACHAPPAM (SAVOURY)

Ingredients	*Quantity*
Refined flour	1 kg
Eggs	1 or 2
Sugar	1 tbsp
Salt	to taste
Cumin and gingelly seeds	

Method

1. Mix all ingredients together. 2. Prepare a batter adding sufficient water to form a pouring consistency. 3. Dip heated "koekjes mould" in batter and deep fry. 4. Drain well and tin.

98. AVILOS

Ingredients	*Quantity (88)*
Raw rice	910 gm
Coconut	2

Ingredients	*Quantity (88)*
Cumin	2 tsp
Gingelly seeds	2 tsp
Salt	to taste

Method

1. Soak rice in water for 2 to 3 hours. 2. Drain well (till nearly dry) and powder. 3. Sieve through a coarse sieve. 4. Mix grated coconut with flour thoroughly and set aside. 5. Heat a wide, shallow and thick-bottomed pan (jallebi karai or uruli). Put in the cumin and gingelly seeds. 6. When the seeds splutter add the rice mixture. Stir well. 7. As the rice flour starts browning, (pink-brown colour) remove and spread lightly on sheets of paper and cool. 8. If there are lumps, break and sieve. 9. Tin and use. Served with granulated sugar in powdered form or mixed with molasses or sugar syrup and made into balls.

N.B. If sugar is used, prepare sugar syrup of one-string consistency. Add lime juice, keep overnight. Reheat. Add avilos powder and shape into balls.

99. PAPPUTU (Coorg)

Ingredients	*For 4*
Broken rice (like large semolina)	100 gm (nearly 1 teacupful)
Milk	180 ml (1 teacupful)
Coconut (grated)	25 gm (½ teacup)

Method

1. Place rice in a shallow aluminium or enamel dish, about 0.5 cm (¼″) deep. Add a pinch of salt. 2. Pour milk over. Sprinkle over with grated coconut. Steam. 3. Serve hot with meat curry.

N.B. If desired, sugar to taste may be added by dissolving first in milk. Milk and water may also be added in the proportion of 1:1.

100. FRUIT CHAAT

Ingredients	*Quantity*
Bananas	2
Guava (ripe)	1
Red tomato (big)	1
Orange	1

Ingredients	*Quantity*
Potatoes (medium)	2
Limes	2
Salt and black pepper	to taste
Chaat masala	

Method

1. Boil potatoes, peel orange and bananas. Wash guava and tomato. 2. Cut up bananas, guava, tomato, orange and potatoes into even-sized pieces. 3. Place in a serving dish. Add chaat masala and lime juice as desired. Season. Mix well and serve.

101. FRIED VEGETABLE CHAAT

Ingredients	*Quantity*
Potatoes (big)	3
Sweet potatoes (big)	2
Limes (big)	2
Green peas	125 gm
Salt and pepper	to taste
Chaat masala	

Method

1. Boil potatoes and sweet potatoes. Boil peas separately. Peel potatoes and sweet potatoes. Cut into halves. 2. Heat a tawa or fry-pan, fry potatoes and sweet potatoes with a little fat to golden brown colour. 3. Fry peas lightly. Cut potatoes and sweet potatoes into cubes; mix with peas. 4. Add chaat masala, lime juice and salt to taste. Mix well. 5. Add chopped coriander and green chillies as desired and serve.

102. DAL MOTH CHAAT

Ingredients	*Quantity*
Sprouted green gram	100 gm
Sprouted bengal gram	100 gm
Green chillies	5 gm
Salt	to taste
Turmeric powder	a pinch
Limes	2
Cucumber	1

Method

1. Lightly cook the grams with a pinch of turmeric, salt and water till dry. 2. Cool. Serve garnished with slices of cucumber and green chillies. Pour lime juice over.

103. PAPDI CHAAT

Ingredients	*Quantity*
Refined flour	50 gm
Whole wheat flour	50 gm
Fat for frying	
Curds	150 gm
Chutney	
Tamarind	100 gm
Jaggery	75 gm
Salt, chilli powder and black salt	to taste
Potatoes (boiled)	2
Salt	to taste
Chilli powder	to taste
Cumin powder	to taste
Coriander leaves to garnish	

Method

1. Mix the two types of flour. Make a dough with a little water (not very hard, not very soft). Divide the dough into small balls, the size of grapes. Roll them thin. 2. Deep fry till golden brown in colour, cool. 3. Beat curds well with a little water. Boil potatoes. Peel and dice. 4. For the chutney, boil tamarind and jaggery for 5 minutes with ½ cup of water. Sieve this mixture thoroughly. Mix salt, chilli powder and black salt. 5. Put the papdis one by one on a plate. then spread potatoes over them. Add beaten curds and chutney over it. Sprinkle salt, chilli powder and cumin powder over it. 6. Garnish with coriander leaves just before serving.

104. DAHI BHALLE (Rajasthani)

Ingredients	*Quantity*
Split green gram	75 gm
Split black gram	105 gm
Oil for frying	
Green chillies	2
Garlic	2 flakes
Salt	to taste
Curds	200 gm
Cumin powder	½ tsp
Chilli powder	to taste
For Tamarind Chutney	
Tamarind	30 gm
Jaggery	15 gm

Ingredients	*Quantity*
Black salt	a pinch
Chilli powder	to taste
Salt	to taste
Cumin powder	a pinch

Method

1. Mix both the grams, soak for 4-5 hours. 2. Grind to a fine paste. 3. Add salt, chopped garlic, green chillies and 2 tsp oil. 4. Mix well. Then make round balls. 5. Flatten in the palm of a wet hand (this is to prevent dough sticking to palm) and fry in hot fat till golden brown. 6. Soak them in hot water, to which a little salt has been added, for 10-12 minutes. 7. For chutney, soak tamarind and jaggery for 2 hours. Then sieve it well through a thick sieve. Add black salt, chilli powder, cumin powder and salt.

Dahi Bhalle

1. Squeeze out the fried bhalle (wadas). 2. Arrange them in a plate. 3. Beat curds well. Add salt to taste. 4. Pour over the bhalle. 5. Pour tamarind chutney over and garnish with cumin powder, chopped green chillies, chilli powder and salt (a pinch) and serve.

105. DAHI WADA

Ingredients	*For 10*
Split black gram (urad dal)	200 gm
Green chillies	10 gm
Onions	50 gm
Soda bicarbonate (optional)	a pinch
Fresh curds (not sour)	1.5 litre
Chilli powder	2 gm
Cumin powder (roasted)	1 gm
Salt	to taste
Coriander leaves	50 gm

Method

1. Wash and soak gram in water for 8 to 10 hours. Drain water. 2. Grind to a fine paste (till light and frothy). 3. Add salt, finely chopped green chillies (seeds may be removed from chilli), onions and soda. Set aside for half an hour. 4. Beat well to enclose air. 5. Make mixture into round flat cakes (about 5 cm in diameter and 1.5 cm thick) in the palm of wet hands. 6. Make a hole in the centre and deep fry in hot oil till golden brown. 7. Soak fried wadas in salted hot water (for about 15 minutes) immediately after removing from the oil. 8. Squeeze out the water gently

by pressing vadas between the palms of both hands. 9. Put into beaten curds flavoured with chilli powder and cumin powder. 10. Garnish with finely chopped coriander leaves. Serve with or without tamarind chutney. Weight per portion : 20 gm

Tamarind Chutney

Ingredients	*For 10*
Tamarind	50 gm
Jaggery (gur)	10 gm
Green chillies (remove seeds)	1
Chilli powder	2 gm
Salt	to taste
Water	300 ml

Method

1. Soak tamarind in water. 2. Extract juice. 3. Mix all ingredients together. 4. Bring to boil. 5. Strain and use.

106. PAPPADAMS

Ingredients	*Quantity*
Black gram	115 gm
Pepper	⅛ tsp
Asafoetida	small pinch

Method

1. Soak black gram overnight. 2. Remove skin and dry in the sun. 3. Grind to powder. 4. Mix ingredients together and prepare a stiff dough with water. 5. Roll out dough into paper-thin rounds. 6. Dry in sun and store in airtight tins. 7. Fry in hot fat when desired.

N.B. Pappad khar is used to make pappads light and crisp. It consists of a mixture of potassium carbonate and sodium bicarbonate.

WESTERN COOKERY

Basic and Intermediate

SOUPS

1. Mixed Vegetable Soup
2. Vegetable Stock
3. Tomato Okra Soup
4. Scotch Broth
5. Scotch Vegetable Soup
6. Minestrone Soup
7. Cabbage Chowder
8. Chicken Chowder
9. Celery Chowder
10. Carrot Soup
11. Pumpkin Soup (Bresani potage)
12. Lentil Soup
13. Cream of Tomato Soup
14. Cream of Spinach Soup
15. Cream of Vegetable Soup
16. Cream of Cucumber Soup
17. Sundown Soup
18. Canadian Cheese Soup
19. Cream of Celery Soup
20. Cream of Potato Soup
21. Cream of Peas Soup
22. Cream of Leek Soup
23. Madras Soup
24. Mulligatawny Soup
25. Vegetable Mulligatawny Soup
26. Consommé Royale
27. Chilli Con Carne
28. Crab Soup

1. MIXED VEGETABLE SOUP

Ingredients	*For 4*	*For 100*
Potatoes	115 gm	2.8 kg
Carrots	115 gm	2.8 kg
Turnips	55 gm	1.35 kg
Onions	55 gm	1.35 kg
Peas	115 gm	2.8 kg
Tomatoes	55 gm	1.35 kg
French beans	55 gm	1.35 kg
Pepper	to taste	15 gm
Salt	10 gm	100 gm
Stock	1 litre	20 litre

Method

1. Prepare vegetables by cutting them into small pieces. Blanch tomatoes.
2. Cook in stock till tender. Serve hot.

N.B. Thickenings like sago or rice or macaroni can be added with the vegetables.

2. VEGETABLE STOCK

Ingredients	*Quantity*
Carrots	500 gm
Onions	500 gm
Turnip	250 gm
Parsely	2 sprigs

Ingredients	*Quantity*
Butter	30 gms
Peppercorns	3 to 4
Water	1 litre
Tomato puree	1 tspn
or	
Celery	a few pcs
Salt	

Method

1. Peel and dice or chop vegetables. 2. Saute in butter. 3. Add peppercorns and tomato puree or celery finely chopped and salt. 4. Bring to boil. 5. Cover pan and simmer for 2 hours or until the stock has developed a good flavour.

3. TOMATO OKRA SOUP

Ingredients	*For 4*	*For 100*
Rice	30 gm	680 gm
Butter	30 gm	340 gm
Celery	15 gm	340 gm
Tomatoes	340 gm	8.5 kg
Capsicum	55 gm	1.35 kg
Onions	30 gm	680 gm
Ladies fingers	55 gm	1.35 kg
Parsley	2 sprigs	3 bunches
Pepper	a pinch	15 gm
Salt	to taste	100 gm
Vegetable or meat stock	720 ml	18 litre

Method

1. Heat half the butter. Brown rice to golden brown. 2. Add stock. Bring to boil. 3. Chop celery, capsicum (with seeds removed and washed thoroughly) and onions. 4. Blanch and mash tomatoes. 5. Slice ladies fingers into roundels. 6. Heat remaining butter. Fry celery, capsicum and onions. Add tomatoes and bring to boil. 7. Pour into rice. Season; simmer covered till rice is tender. 8. Add ladies fingers and simmer for fifteen minutes more. Serve hot sprinkled with parsley.

4. SCOTCH BROTH

Ingredients	*For 4*	*For 100*
Scrag end of mutton	115 gm	2.8 kg
Pearl barley	30 gm	680 gm
Stock	885 ml	22 litre
Parsley	1 sprig	30 gm

Ingredients	*For 4*	*For 100*
Carrots	115 gm	2.8 kg
Turnip	55 gm	1.35 kg
Onions	55 gm	1.35 kg
Celery	55 gm	1.35 kg
Pepper	to taste	15 gm
Salt	10 gm	100 gm

Method

1. Wash barley. 2. Clean and cut meat. 3. Soak in cold stock for 15 minutes and cook for 1 hour. 4. Skim from broth and add diced vegetables, barley and seasoning and simmer for 2 hours. 5. Remove meat and dice. 6. Return to pan; add more seasoning if necessary. 7. Remove all fat and serve hot garnished with chopped parsley.

5. SCOTCH VEGETABLE SOUP

Ingredients	*For 4*	*For 100*
Carrots	115 gm	2.8 kg
Cabbage	30 gm	680 gm
Turnip	30 gm	680 gm
French beans	30 gm	680 gm
Ladies fingers	30 gm	680 gm
Onions	15 gm	340 gm
Potatoes	55 gm	1.35 kg
Tomatoes	115 gm	2.8 kg
Garlic	1 flake	10 gm
Fat	30 gm	340 gm
Marmite	1 tsp	55 gm
Parsley	a few sprigs	3 bunches
Salt	to taste	100 gm
Pepper	a pinch	15 gm
Quaker oats	30 gm	340 gm
Stock or water	890 ml	22 litre

Method

1. Wash, peel and dice carrots, turnip and potatoes. 2. Wash and dice cabbage, ladies fingers and french beans. 3. Chop onions, garlic and parsley. 4. Blanch and chop tomatoes. 5. Melt fat. Add prepared vegetables except potatoes and tomatoes, chopped onions and garlic. Cover and stew for a few minutes. 6. Add tomatoes, potato, stock, chopped onions, garlic and seasoning. 7. Cook gently for two hours. 8. Add oats. Mix well and simmer for 15 to 20 minutes. 9. Add marmite mixed in a little stock. 10. Remove and serve hot garnished with chopped parsley.

6. MINESTRONE SOUP

Ingredients	*For 4*	*For 100*
Cabbage	115 gm	2.8 kg
Tomatoes	115 gm	2.8 kg
Onions	115 gm	2.8 kg
Carrots	115 gm	2.8 kg
Turnip	30 gm	680 gm
Leeks	30 gm	680 gm
Celery	10 gm	250 gm
Parsley	1 sprig	a bunch
Macaroni	55 gm	1.35 kg
Cheese	30 gm	680 gm
Garlic	1 flake	10 gm
Salt	10 gm	100 gm
Pepper	to taste	15 gm
Stock	1 litre	25 litre
Oil	15 ml	55 ml

Method

1. Wash and dice into small pieces all the vegetables. Blanch tomatoes. 2. Mince onions and garlic. 3. Chop parsley. 4. Heat fat. Fry minced onions, garlic, parsley, carrots and turnip. 5. Add leeks, salt, pepper, blanched tomatoes, cabbage and celery. Add stock. 6. Bring to boiling point. Add macaroni cut into 1.25 cm (½″) pieces. 7. Simmer on slow fire till vegetables and macaroni are cooked. 8. Serve hot garnished with grated cheese.

7. CABBAGE CHOWDER

Ingredients	*For 4*	*For 100*
Cabbage	450 gm	11.00 kg
Onions	55 gm	1.35 kg
Tomatoes	225 gm	5.6 kg
Green pepper	55 gm	1.35 kg
Cold water	590 ml	14.75 litre
Butter	30 gm	680 gm
Refined flour	30 gm	680 gm
Milk	300 ml	7 litre
Cheese	30 gm	680 gm
Paprika	⅛ tsp	10 gm
Salt	to taste	80-100 gm
Pepper	a pinch	15 gm

Method

1. Wash and chop vegetables. All the seeds must be removed from the green pepper and it should be rinsed well before chopping. 2. Put

vegetables in a pan with water, salt and pepper. Bring to boil and simmer for about 15 minutes. 3. Prepare a white sauce with butter, flour and milk. 4. Add to the vegetable mixture. 5. Add cheese and paprika and stir until cheese is melted.

8. CHICKEN CHOWDER

Ingredients	*For 4*	*For 100*
Onions	40 gm	1 kg
Chicken fat	30 gm	680 gm
Refined flour	30 gm	680 gm
Chicken stock	300 ml	7 litre
Milk	450 ml	10 litre
Potatoes	115 gm	2.8 kg
Cooked chicken	115 gm	2.8 kg
Salt	to taste	80-100 gm
Pepper	a pinch	15 gm

Method

1. Peel and slice onions and potatoes. 2. Heat fat. Fry onions. Add flour and stir well. 3. Add chicken stock and potatoes. 4. Cook until soft. Add chicken and milk. Cook for 5 minutes longer. 5. Season and serve hot.

N.B. For Chicken Barley Chowder, add 30 gm or 680 gm of barley and cook till tender before adding the potatoes.

9. CELERY CHOWDER

Ingredients	*For 4*	*For 100*
Onions	40 gm	1 kg
Butter	30 gm	680 gm
Refined flour	30 gm	680 gm
Chicken stock	295 ml	7 litre
Milk	445 ml	10 litre
Potatoes	115 gm	2.8 kg
Celery	85 gm	2.12 kg
Salt	to taste	80-100 gm
Pepper	a pinch	15 gm

Method

1. Peel and slice onions and potatoes. Wash and chop celery into small pieces. 2. Heat fat. Fry onions. Add flour and stir well. 3. Add chicken stock, potatoes and celery. 4. Cook until soft. Add milk, season and serve.

10. CARROT SOUP

Ingredients	*For 4*	*For 100*
Carrots	455 gm	11.3 kg
Celery	115 gm	2.8 kg
Onions	55 gm	1.35 kg
Stock	885 ml	21 litre
Butter	30 gm	680 gm
Refined flour	15 gm	340 gm
Salt	to taste	80-100 gm
Pepper	a pinch	15 gm

Method

1. Wash, scrape and dice the carrots into even-sized pieces. Peel and chop onions, wash and chop celery. 2. Put the stock in a pan. Season with salt and pepper, add prepared vegetables and simmer till quite tender. 3. Mix the flour to a smooth paste with butter. Add to the soup and simmer for 10 minutes longer.

11. PUMPKIN SOUP (BRESANI POTAGE)

Ingredients	*For 4*	*For 100*
Pumpkin	455 gm	11.3 kg
Vegetable stock	590 ml	14.75 litre
Milk	300 ml	7.35 litre
Butter	15 gm	340 gm
Salt	to taste	80-100 gm
Pepper	a pinch	15 gm
Parsley	a few sprigs	2 bunches
Bread	115 gm	2.8 kg
Fat to fry bread	15 gm	250 gm

Method

1. Peel pumpkin. Remove seeds and the stringy part, cut into small cubes. 2. Add just enough water to cook. Boil till tender. 3. Press pumpkin through a sieve. 4. Return to pan with the butter, milk and stock. 5. Season. Bring to boil and serve hot, with fried croûtons and garnished with parsley.

12. LENTIL SOUP

Ingredients	*For 4*	*For 100*
Lentil	115 gm	2.8 kg
Carrots	55 gm	1.35 kg
Turnip	30 gm	680 gm
Onions	30 gm	680 gm
Celery	15 gm	340 gm

Ingredients	*For 4*	*For 100*
Stock	1 litre	22 litre
Milk	150 ml	3.75 litre
Butter	30 gm	680 gm
Refined flour	30 gm	680 gm
Pepper	a pinch	15-20 gm
Salt	to taste	80-100 gm
Croûtons		
Bread	30 gm	680 gm
Fat to fry	15 gm	250 gm

Method

1. Wash lentils and put into pan with stock. 2. Add sliced onions and celery and shredded carrots and turnip. 3. Add seasoning and boil gently until lentils and vegetables are tender (1 to 1½ hours). 4. Rub through a sieve. 5. Melt fat; add flour. Blend well. Add milk gradually to form a smooth sauce. 6. Add soup. Mix well. Bring to boiling point stirring all the time. Boil for about 3 minutes. 7. Serve hot with fried croûtons.

13. CREAM OF TOMATO SOUP

Ingredients	*For 4*	*For 100*
Tomatoes	350 gm	8.5 kg
Carrots	115 gm	2.8 kg
Turnip	30 gm	680 gm
Onions	30 gm	680 gm
Butter	30 gm	680 gm
Refined flour	30 gm	680 gm
Milk	300 ml	7.35 litre
Stock	750 ml	17.5 litre
Pepper	a pinch	15 gm
Salt	to taste	100 gm

Method

1. Clean and cut tomatoes. Chop onions, carrots and turnip. 2. Cover with stock or water. Add seasoning and cook till all vegetables are tender. 3. Put through a sieve to make a purée. 4. Prepare white sauce with milk, flour and butter. Cool. 5. Add purée gradually to the sauce. 6. Reheat, add more seasoning if required and serve hot with fried croûtons or chopped parsley.

N.B. To prepare a Cheemato Soup: for 4 portions, melt 115 gm of grated cheese in 50 ml milk. Reheat soup, add melted cheese. Remove. Garnish with parboiled matchstick-like strips of capsicum. Serve hot.

14. CREAM OF SPINACH SOUP

Ingredients	*For 4*	*For 100*
Meat stock	750 ml	17.5 litre
Spinach	250 gm	5.65 kg
Refined flour	30 gm	455 gm
Butter	30 gm	455 gm
Milk	300 ml	7.5 litre
Salt	to taste	80-100 gm

Method

1. Clean and wash spinach. 2. Cook in stock with salt. 3. Rub through sieve when cooked. 4. Prepare white sauce using flour, milk and butter. 5. Add spinach purée. Reheat and serve.

15. CREAM OF VEGETABLE SOUP

Ingredients	*For 4*	*For 100*
Vegetable stock	750 ml	18.75 litre
Celery	60 gm	1.5 kg
Onions	60 gm	1.5 kg
Potatoes	120 gm	3 kg
Carrots	60 gm	1.5 kg
Tomatoes	120 gm	3 kg
Turnip	60 gm	1.5 kg
Refined flour	30 gm	750 gm
Butter	30 gm	750 gm
Milk	300 ml	7.5 litre
Salt	to taste	80-100 gm

Method

1. Chop all cleaned vegetables. 2. Cook in cold stock or water till tender. 3. Pass through a sieve and make a purée. 4. Prepare white sauce with flour, butter and milk. 5. Add to purée, season to taste. Reheat and serve hot.

16. CREAM OF CUCUMBER SOUP

Ingredients	*For 10*
Cucumber (large)	1
Onions (medium)	1
Chicken stock	1 litre
(this can be made from stock cubes)	
Butter	30 gm
Refined flour	30 gm
Cream	4 tbsp
Egg yolk	1

Ingredients	*For 10*
Green colouring	a few drops
Salt & pepper (if you are not using a stock cube)	

Method

1. Skin the cucumber with a potato peeler and keep a little of the skin for the garnish. 2. Slice the cucumber and add it to stock with the chopped onions. 3. Simmer the vegetables gently for about 20 mins. until they are tender. 4. Sieve the soup or liquidise it. 5. Rinse the pan, put in the butter and melt it over gentle heat, then take it off the heat and stir in the flour. 6. Whisk in the sieved liquid and stir gently until the soup is smooth. 7. Simmer the soup for a few minutes then take it off the heat. 8. Beat the egg yolk and cream together and add two tablespoonsful of the hot soup. 9. Add the mixture to the soup, stirring it in gradually. 10. Stir the soup over gentle heat for a few minutes to enrich and thicken it, but be careful not to let it boil. 11. Season the soup if necessary, colour it a delicate green, cool and chill it. 12. Just before serving, cut a little of the cucumber skin into fine shreds and add them to the soup.

N.B. This soup is also good served hot.

17. SUNDOWN SOUP

Ingredients	*For 6*
Fresh curd	150 ml
Milk	150 ml (1 cup)
Cucumber (large)	½
Salt and pepper	
Tomato juice	150 ml (1 cup)
Cold chicken stock	150 ml (1 cup)
Cream	1 tbsp
Prawns (boiled)	30 gm
Hard-boiled egg (chopped)	½
Chopped mint	1 level tbsp
Garlic	½ clove

Method

1. Mix the curd and milk and keep them aside. 2. Peel and dice the cucumber into 0.5 cm (¼″) cubes and sprinkle with salt. 3. Mix tomato juice, chicken stock and cream and add the curd and milk mixture along with the diced cucumber. 4. Season the soup with salt and pepper, stir in the chopped hard-boiled egg, the prawns and the chopped mint. 5. Crush garlic and rub round the inside of a large bowl and pour the soup into it; chill before serving.

18. CANADIAN CHEESE SOUP

Ingredients	*For 4*
Chicken stock	1 litre
Flour	30 gm
Milk	300 ml
Cheese	100 gm
Shredded carrot	45 gm (½ cup)
Thinly sliced celery	30 gm (½ cup)
Onions (chopped)	20 gm (½ cup)

Method

1. Add vegetables to stock. Cover and cook for 10- 12 mins. or till tender. 2. Blend the flour in 1 cup milk. Add to vegetable mixture. 3. Add another cup of milk and cook till thickened. 4. Add grated cheese and stir until melted.

19. CREAM OF CELERY SOUP

Ingredients	*For 4*	*For 100*
Potatoes	120 gm	3 kg
Celery	250 gm	6.25 kg
Stock	750 ml	18.75 litre
Onions	60 gm	1.5 kg
Parsley	5 gm	75 gm
Butter	30 gm	750 gm
Refined flour	30 gm	750 gm
Milk	300 ml	7.5 litre
Pepper	to taste	15 gm
Salt	10 gm	100 gm

Method

1. Prepare vegetables and boil in stock till tender. 2. Rub through a sieve and make a purée. 3. Prepare a white sauce with flour, butter and milk. 4. Add sauce to purée. Add seasoning. 5. Bring to boil and serve hot, garnished with finely chopped celery hearts.

20. CREAM OF POTATO SOUP

Ingredients	*For 4*	*For 100*
Potatoes	250 gm	6.25 kg
Onions	30 gm	680 gm
Celery	30 gm	680 gm
Salt	10 gm	100 gm
Parsley	1 sprig	3 bunches
Milk	300 ml	7.5 litre

Ingredients	For 4	For 100
Refined flour	15 gm	340 gm
Butter	15 gm	340 gm
Stock	900 ml	18.75 litre

Method

1. Peel and quarter potatoes. 2. Chop onions and celery. 3. Put vegetables in stock; add salt; cook till potatoes are soft. 4. Form a purée by passing through a sieve. 5. Prepare a thin white sauce with flour, butter and milk. 6. Add potato purée to sauce; bring to boil slowly. 7. Serve hot garnished with chopped parsley.

21. CREAM OF PEAS SOUP

Ingredients	For 4	For 100
Peas	350 gm	8.5 kg
Carrots	120 gm	3 kg
Onions	30 gm	750 gm
Turnip	60 gm	1.5 kg
Stock	750 ml	18.75 litre
Milk	300 ml	7.5 litre
Refined flour	30 gm	750 gm
Butter	30 gm	750 gm
Pepper	to taste	15 gm
Salt	10 gm	100 gm
Mint	1 sprig	1 bunch

Method

1. Shell peas, grate carrots, turnip and onions. 2. Cook vegetables in cold stock. Add mint. 3. Prepare a white sauce with flour, butter and milk. 4. When vegetables are tender, sieve to make a vegetable purée. 5. Mix sauce with vegetable purée. Add seasoning. 6. Reheat. Bring to boil and serve garnished with chopped mint.

22. CREAM OF LEEK SOUP

Ingredients	For 4	For 100
Leeks	455 gm	11.3 kg
White stock	750 ml	18.75 litre
Milk	300 ml	7.5 litre
Butter	30 gm	750 gm
Refined flour	30 gm	750 gm
Pepper	to taste	15 gm
Salt	10 gm	100 gm

Method

1. Wash and trim the leeks, slice thinly. 2. Cook leeks in stock till tender.

3. Press through a sieve to form a purée and return to fire. 4. Thicken with the butter and flour, well creamed together. 5. Season to taste. 6. Add hot milk. Bring to boil and remove from fire.

23. MADRAS SOUP

Ingredients	*For 4*	*For 100*
Tomatoes	500 gm	12.5 kg
Carrots	55 gm	1.35 kg
Onions	55 gm	1.35 kg
Coconut	½	12
Milk	300 ml	7.5 litre
Refined flour	30 gm	680 gm
Butter	30 gm	680 gm
Stock or water	600 ml	14.75 litre
Peppercorns	a few	15 gm
Salt	to taste	100 gm
Parsley	a sprig	a bunch

Method

1. Wash and slice tomatoes. 2. Peel and slice onions. 3. Peel and grate carrots. Grate coconut. 4. Place tomatoes, onions and carrots in a heavy pan. 5. Add hot stock or boiling water. Add pepper and salt. 6. Cook till vegetables are almost done. 7. Add grated coconut and cook till vegetables are well cooked. 8. Rub through a soup sieve. 9. Prepare a white sauce with flour, butter and milk. 10. Add vegetable purée gradually (the sauce and purée should be of the same temperature). 11. Reheat and serve garnished with chopped parsley.

24. MULLIGATAWNY SOUP

Ingredients	*For 4*	*For 100*
Mutton	200 gm	5 kg
Stock	885 ml	22 litre
Coconut	1	10
Lime	1	10
Curry leaves	1 sprig	1 bunch
Oil	15 ml	115 ml
Tomatoes	200 gm	5 kg
Garlic	a few flakes	15 gm
Onions	15 gm	340 gm
Ginger	5 gm	55 gm
Cinnamon	a small piece	15 gm
Coriander	10 gm	225 gm
Cumin	10 gm	225 gm
Fennel	10 gm	225 gm
Turmeric	a pinch	15 gm

Ingredients	For 4	For 100
Fenugreek	a pinch	5 gm
Boiled rice	55 gm	1.35 kg
Salt	to taste	100 gm

Method

1. Clean and cut the mutton into small pieces. 2. Add stock and let it simmer till meat is tender. 3. Roast and powder coriander, fennel, and cumin and add along with turmeric, fenugreek, half the onions, garlic, ginger, cinnamon, curry leaves, tomatoes and salt. Simmer till tomatoes are well cooked. 4. Strain stock, return best pieces of mutton to stock. 5. Extract thick coconut milk from coconut. Add to stock. 6. Heat fat in a pan. Add remaining sliced onions and fry till crisp. 7. Add soup, lime juice and more salt if necessary. Bring to boil, remove and serve hot garnished with boiled rice.

25. VEGETABLE MULLIGATAWNY SOUP

Ingredients	For 4	For 100
Potatoes	115 gm	2.8 kg
Carrots	55 gm	1.35 kg
Turnip	55 gm	1.35 kg
Tomatoes	225 gm	5.6 kg
Veg. stock	590 ml	15 litre
Coconut	1	10
Lime	1	10
Curry leaves	1 sprig	1 bunch
Oil	15 ml	250 ml
Garlic	2 cloves	30 gm
Onions	15 gm	240 gm
Ginger	a small piece	45 gm
Cinnamon	a small piece	10 gm
Coriander	10 gm	225 gm
Cumin	10 gm	225 gm
Fennel	10 gm	225 gm
Turmeric	a pinch	15 gm
Fenugreek	a pinch	5 gm
Boiled rice	30 gm	680 gm
Salt	to taste	100 gm

Method

1. Clean and cut vegetables into small pieces. Roast and powder coriander, cumin and fennel. 2. Add vegetables, stock, coriander, fennel and cumin powders, turmeric, fenugreek, half the onions, garlic, cinnamon, curry leaves, tomatoes and salt. Simmer till vegetables are tender. 3. Strain and pass vegetables through a sieve, saving a few pieces

for the garnish. 4. Extract thick coconut milk from the coconut and add to the soup. 5. Heat fat in a pan. Add remaining sliced onions and fry till crisp. 6. Add soup lime juice and more salt if necessary. Remove and serve hot garnished with boiled rice and pieces of vegetables.

26. CONSOMMÉ ROYALE

Ingredients	*For 4*	*For 100*
Good mutton stock	885 ml	17.7 litre
For clarification		
Minced mutton (lean)	115 gm	910 gm
Egg white	1	6
Egg yolk	1	3
Carrots	55 gm	455 gm
Celery	30 gm	225 gm
Peppercorns	a few	15 gm
Onions	10 gm	55 gm
Cloves	2 gm	10 gm
Salt	10 gm	100 gm
Vinegar	10 ml	30 ml
Royale garnish		
Egg yolk	1	4
Milk or stock	15 ml	115 ml
Seasoning		

Method

1. Cool stock well and strain. 2. Chop the vegetables and mix with minced meat and eggs. 3. Add mixture to stock and whisk thoroughly. 4. Add vinegar, spices and onions to the stock. 5. Keep on a slow fire and bring to boil whisking all the time. 6. When it starts boiling stop whisking and allow to simmer for one hour. 7. Strain through a muslin twice if necessary. 8. Reheat and garnish with cubes of royale. 9. For garnish, beat yolk, add stock and seasoning and steam in small greased moulds.

27. CHILI CON CARNE

Ingredients	*For 4*	*For 100*
Minced meat (beef or mutton)	500 gm	12.5 kg
Onions	115 gm	2.8 kg
Garlic	2 cloves	15 gm
Fat	15 gm	340 gm
Capsicum	60 gm	1.36 kg
Haricot beans	225 gm	5.6 kg
Tomatoes	225 gm	5.6 kg
Chilli powder	1 level tsp	60 gm
Salt	to taste	80–100 gm

Method

1. Wash and soak beans overnight in cold water. 2. Cook with a little soda until tender. 3. Brown meat in hot fat. Add chopped onions, garlic and green pepper. 4. Add blanched tomatoes and seasoning. 5. Cover and simmer for one hour, adding a little water if needed. 6. Add cooked beans. Reheat and serve hot.

28. CRAB SOUP

Ingredients	*Quantity*
Crabs	6
Tomatoes (large)	3
Onions	1
Capsicum	1
Bay leaf	1
Ladies fingers	6 to 7
Butter	2 tbsp
Salt	to taste
Pepper	to taste
Boiled rice for garnish	

Method

1. Prepare crabs. Blanch tomatoes and chop. Chop onions. Cut ladies fingers into roundels. Remove seeds, wash well. Chop capsicum. 2. Heat fat. Fry the crabs lightly. Add chopped onions and capsicum. Sauté. Add ladies fingers and fry for a couple of minutes more. 3. Add tomatoes, bay leaf, salt and pepper to taste and about 1–1½ liters of water. Cover and simmer for an hour. Serve hot, garnished with boiled rice.

EGGS

1. Hard Boiled Eggs
2. Soft Boiled Eggs
3. Poached Eggs
4. Scrambled Eggs
5. Scrambled Eggs on Toast
6. Scrambled Eggs with Tomato
7. Scrambled Eggs with Ham
8. Fried Eggs
9. Fried Eggs and Bacon
10. Omelette
11. French Omelette
12. Puffy Omelette
13. Cheese Omelette
14. Tomato Omelette
15. Stuffed Eggs
16. Eggs au Gratin
17. Egg Croquettes
18. Egg Nests
19. Devilled Eggs
20. Curried Eggs

1. HARD BOILED EGGS

Place eggs in cold water (water level at least 2.5 cm (1") above eggs). Do not cover. Bring to boil. Reduce heat and allow to simmer for 7 to 10 minutes depending on size of eggs. Crack shell lightly and plunge eggs into cold water (this is to prevent the formation of the blue rim round the yolk). Cool and shell.

N.B. Duck's eggs must be boiled for about 15 minutes.

2. SOFT BOILED EGGS

Place the eggs in cold water; bring to boil. Reduce heat. Simmer for 2 to 3 minutes. Remove from water and serve at once in an egg cup.

3. POACHED EGGS

Fill oiled shallow pan with water to depth sufficient to cover eggs completely. Add salt and vinegar (1½ teaspoon salt and 1 tablespoon vinegar to 1 litre of water). Heat water to boiling. Break eggs one at a time into a shallow and wet cup. Slide gently into the water. Reduce heat to simmering point and cook until white is jelly like and a film forms over yolk. Remove eggs individually with a perforated skimmer. Slip on to slice of hot buttered toast. Season with salt and pepper.

N.B. The whites of eggs may be trimmed or they may be cooked in oiled rings or in special egg poachers to make them look attractive.

4. SCRAMBLED EGGS

Ingredients	*Quantity*
Eggs	8
Butter	60 gm
Milk	30 ml
Salt	to taste
Pepper	a pinch

Method

1. Break the eggs into a bowl. Add pepper and salt and beat lightly. Add milk. 2. Melt half the butter in a thick-bottomed pan. Add the eggs and cook over gentle heat till eggs are lightly cooked, stirring lightly as eggs set. 3. Remove from heat. Check for seasoning and mix in remaining butter.

5. SCRAMBLED EGGS ON TOAST

Prepare as above serving each portion on a slice of freshly buttered toast with the crust removed.

6. SCRAMBLED EGGS WITH TOMATO

Ingredients	*Quantity*
Eggs	8
Butter	60 gm
Milk	30 ml
Salt	to taste
Pepper	¼ tsp
Tomatoes	450 gm
Onions (chopped)	30 gm
Fat	30 gm
Parsley	a few sprigs

Method

1. Prepare scrambled eggs as per basic recipe. 2. Blanch tomatoes. Cut into halves. Remove seeds. 3. Chop roughly. 4. Heat fat. Sauté onions without discoloring. 5. Add the tomatoes and season. 6. Simmer over gentle heat till moisture is evaporated. 7. Serve eggs in individual dishes. Place a spoonful of tomato in the centre of each dish of egg and a little chopped parsley on top of the tomato.

7. SCRAMBLED EGGS WITH HAM

Ingredients	*Quantity*	*Ingredients*	*Quantity*
Eggs	8	**Salt**	to taste
Butter	60 gm	**Pepper**	a pinch
Milk	30 gm	**Ham**	115 gm

Method

1. Prepare eggs as for the basic recipe. 2. Trim off all fat from the ham. Cut into 1.25 cm (½″) pieces. 3. Add to the eggs along with the butter.

N.B. Shrimps, cheese, asparagus tips, kidney etc. can be served with scrambled eggs.

8. FRIED EGGS

Ingredients	*Quantity*
Eggs	1 or 2 per portion
Pepper and salt	to taste

Method

1. Melt a little fat in the pan. 2. Add the eggs. Season lightly. 3. Cook gently until lightly set. Lift out gently. 4. Serve on a plate or a flat dish.

9. FRIED EGGS AND BACON

Ingredients	*Quantity*
Eggs	1 or 2 per portion
Bacon	3 rashers per portion (about 60 gm)

Method

1. Fry eggs as in the above recipe. 2. Remove the rind off the bacon. 3. Fry in a little fat or grill on a flat tray. 4. Dress neatly around the eggs.

N.B. Fried eggs may also be served with grilled or fried tomatoes, mushrooms, sautéd potatoes, etc.

10. OMELETTE

Ingredients	*Quantity*
Eggs	2 per portion
Pepper	to taste
Salt	to taste
Fat	15 gm

Method

1. Break the eggs into a bowl. Season with pepper and salt. 2. Beat well with a fork or a whisk until yolks and whites are thoroughly combined and no streaks of white can be seen. 3. Heat the omelette pan. Wipe thoroughly with a clean cloth. 4. Add the fat. 5. When fat melts add egg mixture, moving the mixture continuously with a fork until lightly set. 6. Remove from heat. 7. Half-fold the mixture over at right angles to the handle. 8. Gently lift out and serve in the centre of a flat silver dish. 9. Neaten shape if necessary and serve immediately.

11. FRENCH OMELETTE

Ingredients	*Quantity*
Egg	1
Liquid (milk, tomato juice or cream)	1 tbsp
Salt	a pinch
Pepper	
Fat	10 gm

Method

1. Beat egg just enough to mix. 2. Add liquid and seasoning. 3. Melt fat in an omellete pan. 4. Pour in egg mixture. 5. Cook slowly keeping heat low. 6. As under-surface becomes set, start lifting it slightly with a

spatula to let uncooked portion flow underneath and cook. 7. When whole mixture is creamy, brown the bottom lightly. 8. Fold and remove on to a plate. Serve immediately.

12. PUFFY OMELETTE

Ingredients	*Quantity*
Egg	1
Milk	1 tbsp
Salt	to taste
Pepper	a pinch
Fat	10 gm

Method

1. Separate egg white and yolk. 2. Beat yolk slightly. Add milk and seasoning. 3. Beat until thick and lemon coloured. 4. Fold in stiffly beaten egg white. 5. Heat omelette pan. Wipe with a clean cloth. 6. Add fat. When fat melts add egg mixture. 7. Spread evenly and cook slowly 2 to 5 minutes until delicately brown underneath and top is dry and firm. 8. Loosen with a spatula. Fold and serve immediately on a hot plate.

13. CHEESE OMELETTE

Ingredients	*Quantity*
Eggs	2
Pepper and salt	to taste
Fat	15 gm
Cheese	30 gm

Method

1. Prepare omelette as for basic recipe. 2. Before folding, add grated cheese. 3. Fold and serve hot.

14. TOMATO OMELETTE

Ingredients	*Quantity*
Eggs	2
Salt and pepper	to taste
Fat	30 gm
Tomatoes	225 gm
Onions	30 gm
Chopped parsley	a few sprigs

Method

1. Blanch tomatoes. Cut into halves, remove seeds and chop roughly. 2. Chop onions. 3. Heat 15 gm fat. Sauté onions without discolouring.

4. Add tomatoes. Simmer gently till all moisture is evaporated. 5. Prepare omellete as for basic recipe. 6. Fill with prepared tomato. 7. Fold. Place on a hot plate, sprinkle chopped parsley on top and serve at once with tomato sauce (served separately).

N.B. A variety of fillings such as mushrooms, chicken liver, kidney, shrimp, ham, bacon, etc. can be used.

15. STUFFED EGGS

Ingredients	*For 4*	*For 100*
Eggs	4	100
Margarine	60 gm	1.35 kg
Tomato ketchup, anchovy essence or mayonnaise	1 tbsp	340 ml

Method

1. Hard-boil the eggs. Cool and shell. Cut in halves and remove the yolk. 2. Cream the margarine. Add the yolk and sauce and beat until smooth. 3. Pipe the filling into the egg whites. 4. Serve with salad.

16. EGGS AU GRATIN

Ingredients	*For 4*	*For 100*
Eggs	4	100
Yolk of egg	½	12
Pepper	a pinch	15 gm
Salt	to taste	100 gm
Breadcrumbs	30 gm	680 gm
Cheese	55 gm	1.36 kg
Mustard	½ tsp	55 gm
White sauce		
Margarine	30 gm	680 gm
Refined flour	30 gm	680 gm
Milk	295 ml	7 litre

Method

1. Hard-boil eggs and put into cold water. 2. Grate cheese. 3. Prepare sauce. 4. Add cheese, mustard and seasoning to the sauce. 5. Stir in the yolk of egg. Keep warm. 6. Shell eggs, slice the eggs and keep a few for decoration. 7. Put sliced eggs in a hot dish. Pour cheese sauce over. 8. Sprinkle breadcrumbs over. Keep under a grill for a few minutes. 9. Serve hot garnished with parsley and slices of eggs cut into half.

17. EGG CROQUETTES

Ingredients	*For 4*	*For 100*
Eggs	4	100
Raw egg	½	12
Milk	150 ml	3.65 litre
Margarine	30 gm	680 gm
Refined flour	45 gm	1.05 kg
Pepper	a pinch	15 gm
Salt	to taste	100 gm
Cream	15 ml	355 ml
Breadcrumbs	30 gm	680 gm
Fat to fry (absorption)	30 gm	500 gm

Method

1. Hard-boil eggs. Put in cold water. 2. Shell and chop. 3. Prepare sauce with margarine, flour and milk. Add seasoning. 4. Add chopped hard-boiled eggs and cream and mix well. 5. Turn out on to a plate and allow to get cold. 6. Divide into even portions, form into cork shapes. 7. Coat with raw egg and breadcrumbs and deep fry. 8. Drain and serve on hot dish over absorbent paper; garnish with parsley.

18. EGG NESTS

Ingredients	*For 4*	*For 100*
Eggs	4	100
Potatoes	910 gm	25 kg
Margarine	20 gm	450 gm
Milk	30-50 ml	680 ml to 1 litre
Salt and pepper	to taste	to taste

Method

1. Prepare, cook and mash the potatoes. 2. Melt the margarine and beat half of it and the milk into the potatoes. 3. Place the potatoes in 7.5 cm deep baking tins. Smooth over the top. 4. Use egg shell to make nests; break an egg into each. 5. Sprinkle the rest of the margarine over the top and place in a hot oven until the eggs are cooked and the potato is brown. 6. Serve hot.

19. DEVILLED EGGS

Ingredients	*For 4*	*For 100*
Eggs	4	100

Ingredients	*For 4*	*For 100*
Chilli powder or		
Cayenne pepper	a pinch	55 gm
Salt	to taste	100 gm
Margarine	15 gm	340 gm

Method

1. Hard-boil eggs, put in cold water, shell and cut into halves. 2. Heat fat. Add chilli powder and salt. Remove from fire and toss eggs in the pan.

20. CURRIED EGGS

Ingredients	*Quantity*
Hard-boiled eggs	4
Curry sauce	300 ml
Rice	60 gm

Method

1. Boil the rice and keep hot. 2. Shell the eggs. Cut into halves. 3. Arrange neatly in a dish. Border with boiled rice. 4. Pour hot curry sauce over the eggs and serve hot.

FISH

1. COURT BOUILLON FOR BOILING FISH

Ingredients	*Quantity*
Carrots	225 gm
Onions	225 gm
Parsley	a few sprigs
Thyme	1 sprig
Salt	a
Peppercorns	10
Vinegar	300 ml
Water	1 litre

Method

1. Prepare vegetables. Mix all ingredients together. 2. Simmer for 3 hours. Strain before using.

2. FISH CAKES

Ingredients	*For 4*	*For 100*
Pomfret, ghol or salmon	500 gm	12.5 kg
Potatoes	450 gm	11.00 kg
Egg	1	12
Chopped parsley	1 sprig	2 bunches
Pepper	to taste	15 gm
Salt	10 gm	100 gm
Breadcrumbs	30 gm	340 gm
Fat to fry (absorption)	30 gm	500 gm
Court bouillon		

Method

1. Clean, cut and boil fish in court bouillon. 2. Flake and skin fish and remove bones. 3. Boil and mash potatoes. 4. Mix fish, potatoes and seasoning. 5. Divide into equal portions, shape and coat with egg and toss in breadcrumbs. 6. Reshape and fry in hot fat. Drain and serve hot garnished with parsley.

3. FISH CROQUETTES

Ingredients	*For 4*	*For 100*
Fish	500 gm	12.5 kg
Shrimps (cleaned) or	115 gm	2.8 kg
Anchovy essence		
Cayenne pepper or	a pinch	15 gm
Chilli powder	a pinch	10 gm
Lime juice	½ lime	6 limes

Ingredients	*For 4*	*For 100*
Salt	to taste	100 gm
Refined flour	30 gm	340 gm
Butter	30 gm	340 gm
Milk	150 ml	3.75 litre
Eggs	1	12
Breadcrumbs	30 gm	340 gm
Fat to fry (absorption)	30 gm	500 gm

Method

1. Boil and flake fish. 2. Clean, boil and chop shrimps. 3. Make a panada with flour, butter and milk. 4. To the panada add fish, shrimp and seasoning. Turn out on to a plate and cool. Add lime juice. 5. Divide into even portions. Form into croquette shapes on floured board. 6. Coat with egg and toss in breadcrumbs. 7. Deep fry in hot fat. Drain on absorbent paper. Serve hot.

4. FISH KEDGEREE

Ingredients	*For 4*	*For 100*
Fish	500 gm	12.5 kg
Rice	200 gm	5 kg
Eggs	4	100
Margarine	55 gm	1.36 kg
Milk	30 ml	680 ml
Parsley	½ bunch	3 bunches
Salt	to taste	100 gm
Pepper	to taste	15 gm

Method

1. Boil rice, drain well. 2. Hard-boil the eggs. Sieve yolk of hard-boiled eggs and chop whites. 3. Clean and cut fish. Boil in a court bouillon. 4. Skin and flake fish. Remove the bones. 5. Add rice and seasoning to fish. 6. Add about half the cooked eggs, margarine and milk. 7. Reheat. 8. Turn out on to a hot dish and pile up. Garnish with hard-boiled eggs and chopped parsley.

5. FISH AND MUSHROOM RING

Ingredients	*For 4*	*For 100*
Pomfret or any other white fish	500 gm	12.5 kg
Rice	225 gm	5.6 kg
Capsicum	55 gm	1.35 kg

Ingredients	For 4	For 100
Tomatoes	115 gm	2.8 kg
Mushrooms	115 gm	2.8 kg
Peas (shelled)	55 gm	1.35 kg
Onions	55 gm	1.35 kg
Curry sauce	300 ml	7.5 litre
Salt and pepper	to taste	to taste
Butter	30 gm	450 gm

Method

1. Boil rice. Wash and boil the fish with seasonings. 2. Slice a few thin pieces of capsicum and chop the rest. Chop tomatoes and onions. Cook peas and mushrooms. 3. Melt fat. Sauté finely chopped onions and tomatoes. Remove from fire. Add rice, peas and mushrooms, mix well. Add seasoning. 4. Pack an oiled ring mould with rice mixture and keep mould in hot water. 5. Skin, flake and bone fish and stir into the curry sauce. 6. Turn out rice on to a hot dish. Fill centre with fish mixture. Garnish with sliced capsicum and a few mushrooms.

6. FISH AND POTATO PIE

Ingredients	For 4	For 100
Fish	500 gm	12.5 kg
Potatoes	450 gm	11 kg
Tomatoes	225 gm	5.6 kg
Pepper	a pinch	15 gm
Salt	to taste	100 gm
Onions	55 gm	1.35 kg
Butter	30 gm	680 gm
Milk	30 ml	590 ml
Egg	½	2

Method

1. Boil fish. Remove skin and bones and flake. 2. Boil and mash potatoes. Add the milk and half the butter. 3. Slice tomatoes and mince onions. 4. Grease a pie dish, put in a layer of fish, then a layer of sliced tomatoes. Sprinkle with onions, pepper and salt. Continue till dish is three-fourths full. 5. Pour melted butter over. 6. Pile mashed potatoes on top of fish. 7. Roughen the surface with a fork and brush over with beaten egg. 8. Bake in a moderate oven for 30-40 minutes. Serve hot.

N.B. Grated cheese can be added to the potatoes or chopped hard-boiled egg to fish. A medium white sauce can be mixed with the fish.

7. FISH PUDDING

Ingredients	*Quantity*
Boiled fish (without bones)	450 gm
Butter	30 gm
Potatoes	450 gm
Top of milk	2 tbsp
Cream of tomato soup	100 ml
Salt, pepper	to taste
Refined flour	30 gm

Method

1. Boil and mash potatoes. Add top of milk and butter. Beat well. 2. Flake fish. Add seasoning, and cook with flour. 3. Grease well, a pie dish or casserole. 4. Line the casserole with a third of the potato. 5. Add a layer of fish and a third of the soup. 6. Continue with a layer of potato, then fish. 7. Mix the remainder of the tomato soup with the remaining potatoes. When evenly coloured, spread over the fish. 8. Roughen the surface with a fork bringing it up to a point in the centre. 9. Bake until heated through and nicely browned.

8. FRYING BATTER FOR FISH (A)

Ingredients	*For 10*
Refined flour	225 gm
Yeast, fresh or	15 gm
Dry yeast	8 gm
Milk or water	300 ml
Salt	to taste

Method

1. Sift the flour and salt into a basin. 2. Dissolve the yeast in a little of the water. 3. Make a well in the flour. 4. Add the yeast and the liquid. 5. Mix the flour gradually and beat to a smooth mixture. 6. Allow to rest for at least one hour before using.

FRYING BATTER FOR FISH (B)

Ingredients	*For 10*
Refined flour	225 gm
Egg	1
Water or milk	300 ml
Oil	30 ml
Salt	to taste

Method

1. Sift the flour and salt into a basin. 2. Make a well. 3. Add the egg and the liquid. 4. Mix flour gradually and beat to a smooth mixture. 5. Mix in the oil. 6. Allow to rest before using.

FRYING BATTER FOR FISH (C)

Ingredients	*Quantity*
Refined flour	225 gm
Oil	30 ml
Egg whites	2
Water or milk	300 ml
Salt	to taste

Method

1. Sift the flour and salt into a basin. 2. Make a well. 3. Add the liquid and mix in the flour gradually. Beat to smooth mixture. 4. Mix in the oil. 5. Allow to rest. 6. Just before using fold in stiffly beaten egg whites.

FRYING BATTER FOR FISH (D)

Ingredients	*Quantity*
Refined flour	225 gm
Milk or water	300 ml
Baking Powder	1 tsp
Salt	to taste

Method

1. Sift the flour, salt and baking powder into a basin. 2. Make a well in the centre. Add the liquid and mix in the flour gradually. Beat to a smooth mixture.

9. FRIED FILLETS OF FISH

Ingredients	*For 4*	*For 100*
Pomfret	500 gm (one fish)	12.5 kg (25 fish)
Salt	10 gm	100 gm
Pepper	to taste	15 gm
Eggs	1	8
Breadcrumbs	55 gm	900 gm
Fat to fry (absorption)	55 gm	340 gm
Lime	1	6

Method

1. Clean and wash fish thoroughly. 2. Fillet each fish into 4 even fillets. Skin. 3. Season with pepper and salt. 4. Dip in beaten eggs. Coat with pepper and salt. Coat with breadcrumbs. 5. Deep fry till golden brown. Garnish with lime slices.

10. FILLET OF POMFRET OR SOLE ORLY

Ingredients	*For 4*	*For 100*
Pomfret or sole	500 gm (one fish)	12.5 kg (25 fish)
Marinade		
Salad oil	10 gm	250 gm
Vinegar	10 gm	250 gm
Onions chopped	15 gm	340 gm
Salt	to taste	30-50 gm
Parsley	¼ bunch	6 bunches
Batter		
Refined flour	15 gm	340 gm
Eggs	½ to 1	12
Soda bicarbonate or baking powder	a pinch	
Olive or salad oil	10 gm	250 gm
Tepid water	a little	200 gm (about)
Salt	to taste	30-50 gm
Fat to fry (absorption)	30 gm	340 gm

Method

1. Sift flour, baking powder and salt into a basin. Add yolk of egg, oil and water and mix to a smooth batter. Leave aside for half an hour. 2. Clean, fillet, and skin fish. Wash thoroughly in cold water. 3. Prepare a marinade with the given ingredients. 4. Soak fish in the marinade for at least 10 minutes. 5. Add stiffly beaten egg white to batter. 6. Dip fish in batter; deep fry. Drain and serve hot, garnished with fried parsley. Serve tomato sauce separately.

11. POMFRET COLBERT

Ingredients	*For 4*	*For 100*
Pomfret	500 gm	12.5 kg
Milk	10 ml	250 ml
Seasoned flour	15 gm	225 gm
Breadcrumbs	30 gm	455 gm
Fat to fry (absorption)	55 gm	340 gm
Eggs	1	10

Ingredients	*For 4*	*For 100*
Maître d'hotel butter		
Butter	30 gm	500 gm
Parsley	1 sprig	1 bunch
Lime	½	6

Method

1. Clean and fillet pomfret. 2. Dip in milk. Roll in flour. 3. Coat with beaten egg and breadcrumbs and deep fry. 4. Serve garnished with Maitre d' hotel butter. 5. To make Maître d'hotel butter, cream butter, add chopped parsley and lime juice. Mix well, set in a cool place and use as required.

12. FISH MEUNIÈRE

Ingredients	*For 4*	*For 100*
Pomfret or sole	500 gm	12.5 kg
Clarified butter	50 gm	1 kg
Refined flour	10 gm	225 gm
Lime	4	12
Parsley	3 sprigs	60 gm
Pepper	a pinch	15 gm
Salt	to taste	80-100 gm

Method

1. Clean, fillet and skin fish; wash and dry. 2. Sprinkle over with seasoned flour (this can be done by putting seasoned flour and fillet in a brown paper bag and shaking well). 3. Heat half the clarified butter to smoking point. Put in the fish. 4. When fish is sufficiently coloured on one side, turn over and brown the other side. 5. Remove to a hot dish. Sprinkle over with lime juice. Garnish with chopped parsley. 6. Brown remaining butter. Pour over fish and serve immediately. (The froth produced by butter and parsley must be seen as it is served.)

13. GRILLED FISH

Ingredients	*For 4*	*For 100*
Pomfret or any other small fish like herring	500 gm	12.5 kg
Butter	15 gm	340 gm
Lime	1	12
Pepper	a pinch	15 gm
Salt	to taste	10 gm

Method

1. Wash and clean the fish keeping it whole. Wash again. 2. Make gashes on the fish. Season and smear with lime juice. Keep aside for some time. 3. Heat the grill. Grill on both sides basting with melted butter. 4. When browned on both sides, reduce heat and let the fish cook for 5 to 15 minutes. Serve hot.

14. BAKED FILLETS IN TOMATO SAUCE

Ingredients	*For 4*	*For 100*
Pomfret, sole, etc.	500 gm	12.5 kg
Fat	50 gm	1 kg
Onions	115 gm	2.8 kg
Celery	115 gm	2.8 kg
Capsicum	115 gm	2.8 kg
Refined flour	30 gm	680 gm
Tomatoes	225 gm	5.6 kg
Pepper	a pinch	15 gm
Bayleaves	1	5 gm
Cloves	1	5 gm
Cayenne pepper	a pinch	10 gm

Method

1. Clean, wash, fillet and skin fish. 2. Place in a well-greased baking dish. 3. Chop onions, capsicum (remove seeds) and celery. 4. Blanch tomatoes and make a purée. 5. Melt fat. Add onions, celery and capsicum. Cook until tender but not brown. 6. Blend in the flour. 7. Add tomato purée and seasonings and cook, stirring constantly until thickened. Remove bayleaves and cloves. 8. Pour sauce over fish. 9. Bake, retain heat at 175ºC (350ºF) for about 30 minutes or until tender.

15. STUFFED BAKED POMFRET

Ingredients	*For 4*	*For 100*
Pomfret	500 gm	12.5 kg
Lime	½	6
Forcemeat stuffing	55 gm	1.35 kg
Butter or fat	30 gm	680 gm
Pepper	a pinch	15 gm
Salt	to taste	100 gm

Method

1. Scale and wash fish. 2. Fillet from one side but do not detach. 3. Remove entrails and centre bone. 4. Wash thoroughly. 5. Stuff with forcemeat stuffing. Tie. Sprinkle with lime juice and seasoning. 6. Melt

fat in a baking tray. When hot, put in the fish. Cook at moderate heat till tender. 7. Baste frequently.

16. STUFFED HERRINGS

Ingredients		*Quantity*
Herrings		4
Oatmeal stuffing		
Oatmeal	mix all the ingredients together	115 gm
Parsley		2 sprigs
Onions (grated)		15 gm
Margarine or butter		60 gm
Egg		1
Salt and Pepper		a little

Method

1. Clean and split herrings. Remove the bones by inserting the thumb under the tail end of each herring and lifting carefully. 2. Mix all the stuffing ingredients and place a portion of the mixture carefully in each herring and roll up. 3. Lay side by side on a greased baking dish. Sprinkle with salt, pepper and oatmeal. 4. Cover with greased paper and bake for 30 minutes in a moderately hot oven. 5. Serve with slices of lemon or mustard sauce.

17. BAKED FISH A LA COLLEGE

Ingredients	*For 4*	*For 100*
Pomfret, sole, salmon or mackerel	500 gm	12.5 kg
Anchovy sauce	15 ml	340 ml
Tomato ketchup	30 ml	680 ml
Salad oil	30 ml	680 ml
Lime (juice)	1	25
Salt	to taste	80-100 gm

Method

1. Clean fish, wash well and make gashes at 2.5 cm intervals. 2. Mix together remaining ingredients. 3. Marinade fish in the mixture for about half an hour. 4. Bake in a moderate oven till done. Serve hot.

18. FISH BIRDS

Ingredients	*For 4*	*For 100*
Pomfret or sole	500 gm	12.5 kg

Ingredients	*For 4*	*For 100*
Salt	to taste	80-100 gm
Pepper	a pinch	15 gm
Bacon sliced	30 gm	680 gm
Bread stuffing		
Onions	55 gm	1.35 kg
Celery	55 gm	1.35 kg
Butter or margarine	30 gm	680 gm
Bread crumbs (soft)	150 gm	3.75 kg
Lime	1	10
Salt	to taste	50 to 80 gm
Parsley	a few sprigs	5 bunches

Method

1. Prepare stuffing. Fry chopped onions and celery till tender but not brown. 2. Combine all ingredients and mix well. If too dry, add a little milk or stock. 3. Clean, fillet and skin fish. 4. Place a small roll of stuffing on each piece of fish. 5. Roll fish around stuffing and fasten with toothpicks. 6. Place rolls on well-greased baking pans and lay a slice of bacon on top of each. 7. Bake in moderate oven 175°C (350°F) for about 30 minutes. 8. Take out fastenings. Garnish and serve immediately with an egg sauce.

19. SALMON LOAF

Ingredients	*For 4*	*For 100*
Salmon	500 gm	12.5 kg
Celery	115 gm	2.8 kg
Onions	115 gm	2.8 kg
Butter or margarine	30 gm	250 gm
Milk and salmon liquor	100 ml	2.5 litre
Breadcrumbs	200 gm	5 kg
Salt	to taste	80-100 gm
Pepper	a pinch	15 gm
Lime	1	10
Egg	1	25
Court bouillon		

Method

1. Clean and boil salmon in court bouillon. 2. Drain but reserve liquor. Remove bones, skin and flake. 3. Melt fat and fry finely chopped onions and celery till tender but not brown. 4. Combine all ingredients and mix well. 5. Pack into a well-greased loaf tin. 6. Bake in moderate oven 175°C

(350°F) for about 1 hour or until slightly brown. 7. Serve with Spanish sauce.

SPANISH SAUCE

Ingredients	*For 4*	*For 100*
Onions	30 gm	680 gm
Celery	115 gm	2.8 kg
Capsicum	50 gm	1 kg
Fat	15 gm	340 gm
Tomatoes	450 gm	11.00 kg
Salt	to taste	80-100 gm
Cayenne	a pinch	10 gm
Refined flour	15 gm	340 gm

Method

1. Melt the fat. Add finely chopped onions, celery and capsicum. Fry till browned. 2. Blanch tomatoes and make a purée. 3. Add tomato purée to the fried vegetables. Add seasoning and simmer slowly until vegetables are tender. 4. Add a small amount of water to the flour. Stir into a smooth paste. 5. Add flour mixture to sauce and cook until slightly thick. 6. Serve hot.

20. FISH MORNAY

Ingredients	*For 4*	*For 100*
Pomfret or sole	500 gm	12.5 kg
Lime juice	1 tsp	12
Milk	1 tbsp	340 ml
Shallots (chopped)	1 tsp	115 gm
Mornay sauce	300 ml	7.5 litre
Grated cheese	30 gm	680 gm
Parsley	1 sprig	2 bunches
Salt	to taste	80-100 gm
Pepper	to taste	15 gm
Mornay sauce		
Butter	30 gm	680 gm
Refined flour	30 gm	680 gm
Milk and stock	300 ml	7.5 litre
Cheese	30 gm	680 gm
Seasoning		

Method

1. Clean fish. Fillet and skin. 2. Arrange in a baking dish. 3. Season and sprinkle with lemon juice and milk. Sprinkle with chopped shallots.

4. Cook in moderately hot oven. 5. Prepare a Mornay sauce using milk and fish stock, herbs and seasoning. Cook for 10 minutes. 6. Remove shallots and put fish into a pyrex pie dish. 7. Coat with sauce and sprinkle with cheese. 8. Brown under a grill. Garnish with parsley.

21. TOMATO FISH

Ingredients	*Quantity*
Pomfret or other white fish	150 gm
Tomato (large)	1
Capsicum	½
Lime	½
Onions (small)	1
Salt	to taste

Method

1. Clean, wash and boil fish. Blanch tomato and extract juice. 2. Mix with finely chopped capsicum, onions and lime juice. Add salt to taste. 3. Add boiled fish and mix well. Add more seasoning if necessary.

22. FILLET DE POMFRET CRÉME

Ingredients	*For 4*	*For 100*
Pomfret or sole	500 gm	12.5 kg
Margarine	20 gm	500 gm
Refined flour	20 gm	500 gm
Milk	300 ml	7.5 litre
Bayleaf	1	5 gm
Mace	1 blade	2-3 gm
Salt	to taste	80-100 gm
Pepper	a pinch	15 gm
Cayenne pepper	a pinch	15 gm
Cream (optional)	20 gm	500 gm

Method

1. Clean, fillet and skin fish. 2. Season fillets and roll up with the skinned side inside. 3. Cook in greased baking tins covered with greased paper for about 15 minutes. 4. Infuse the milk with the bones, white skin, bayleaf and mace. 5. Strain the milk and prepare a sauce using margarine, flour and infused milk. 6. Dish the fillets. Coat with sauce and garnish with chopped parsley and cayenne pepper.

23. POMFRET FLORENTINE

Ingredients	*For 4*	*For 100*
Pomfret	500 gm	12.5 kg
Spinach	455 gm	11.3 kg
Butter	30 gm	680 gm
Lime	a few drops	115 ml
Salt	10 gm	100 gm
Cayenne pepper	a pinch	10 gm
Mornay sauce		
Refined flour	15 gm	340 gm
Butter	15 gm	340 gm
Cheese	30 gm	680 gm
Fish stock	295 ml	7.5 litre
Milk	145 ml	3.5 litre

Method

1. Wash, trim and fillet fish. 2. Place in a buttered dish, sprinkle with lemon juice and seasoning. Steam. 3. When cooked, place fish in fire proof dish; coat with Mornay sauce. Sprinkle with grated cheese. 4. Brown under a grill or in a very hot oven. 5. Garnish with cooked spinach.

N.B. Cooked spinach can be spread in a pyrex pie dish, the fillets placed over, covered with the mornay sauce and grilled or baked.

24. POMFRET À LA PORTUGAISE

Ingredients	*For 4*	*For 100*
Pomfret	500 gm	12.5 kg
Tomatoes	225 gm	5.6 kg
Mushrooms	55 gm	1.4 kg
Fresh breadcrumbs	30 gm	455 gm
Butter	30 gm	455 gm
Shallots or onions	115 gm	2.8 kg
Cheese	15 gm	340 gm
Lime	1	6
Salt	10 gm	100 gm
Pepper	to taste	15 gm

Method

1. Fillet the fish and skin, wash in several rinses of cold water. 2. Skin the tomatoes and slice them. 3. Sauté shallots or onions and mushrooms in butter. 4. Grease pyrex dishes and line the bottom with thinly sliced

tomatoes. 5. Place one layer of fillet of fish on top, sprinkle with salt, pepper and lemon. 6. Spread mushrooms and onions. 7. Repeat in layers till dish is full and the top layer is tomatoes. 8. Sprinkle breadcrumbs and grated cheese. 9. Dot with butter and bake in moderate oven for 30 minutes. 10. If not sufficiently brown finish under a grill.

25. BAKED FISH SOUFFLE

Ingredients	*For 4*	*For 100*
Fish	500 gm	12.5 kg
Butter	30 gm	680 gm
Refined flour	30 gm	680 gm
Milk	300 ml	7.5 litre
Eggs	2	50
Pepper	to taste	80-100 gm
Salt	to taste	15 gm

Method

1. Melt butter in a pan, add flour evenly and cook. 2. Add warm milk gradually to form a smooth consistency. Cook to form a sauce of medium consistency. 3. Remove from fire and cool. 4. Clean and boil fish. 5. Flake fish and remove skin and bones. 6. Rub fish through a wire sieve; add seasoning. Add the sauce. 7. Beat yolks and add to fish and sauce stirring all the time. 8. Whisk white of eggs to a stiff froth and fold in lightly. 9. Pour into greased dishes and bake until brown. Serve immediately with shrimp sauce or anchovy sauce.

26. POMFRET MAYONNAISE

Ingredients	*For 4*	*For 100*
Pomfret	500 gm	12.5 kg
Mayonnaise sauce	150 ml	3.75 litre
Lettuce	1 bunch	25 bunches
Tomatoes	225 gm	5.6 kg
Cucumber	225 gm	5.6 kg
Lime	1	10
Court bouillon		

Method

1. Clean fish. Remove fins. Wash well. 2. Fillet fish from one side only and remove centre bones. Wash again. 3. Poach fish in a court bouillon. 4. Drain and place in a serving dish. 5. Coat with mayonnaise sauce. 6. Garnish with lettuce, slices of cucumber, tomatoes and lime.

COURT BOUILLON

To every litre of water add

Salt	15 gm	**Vinegar**	75 ml
Carrot (sliced)	60 gm	**Peppercorns**	6
Bayleaf	1	**Onion (sliced)**	60 gm
Parsley stalks	2 to 3	**Thyme**	a sprig

Method

Simmer for 3 hours. Strain before using.

27. PRAWNS FRIED IN BATTER

Ingredients	*For 4*	*For 100*
Prawns (medium-sized)	500 gm	12.5 kg
Refined flour	50 gm	1.25 kg
Eggs	½	12
Salt	to taste	80-100 gm
Milk	100 ml	2.5 litre
Cayenne pepper	a pinch	10 gm
Salad oil	15 ml	340 ml
Fat to fry (absorption)	30 gm	500 gm

Method

1. Prepare a batter with flour, yolk of egg, milk, seasoning and salad oil. Mix well and set aside. 2. Shell prawns. Remove intestines. Wash thoroughly. Drain on cloth to dry. 3. Beat white of egg stiffly and fold into the batter. 4. Heat enough fat to deep fry prawns. 5. Dip prawns in batter and deep fry. 6. Drain on absorbent paper and serve hot.

28. PRAWN AND NOODLE CASSEROLE

Ingredients	*For 4*	*For 100*
Prawns	500 gm	12.5 kg
Noodles	115 gm	2.8 kg
Milk	300 ml	7.5 litre
Refined flour	30 gm	680 gm
Butter or margarine	30 gm	680 gm
Capsicum	55 gm	1.36 kg
Onions	55 gm	1.36 kg
Cheese	55 gm	1.36 kg
Salt	to taste	80-100 gm
Pepper	a pinch	15 gm

Method

1. Shell and wash prawns. Remove intestines. Wash again. Boil in court

bouillon. Cool and drain. 2. Cook noodles in boiling salted water. Boil for 10 to 15 minutes or until tender and drain. 3. Make a white sauce with flour, butter and milk. 4. Cook chopped capsicum and onions in salted water till tender. Drain and add to white sauce. 5. Arrange noodles and prawns in layers in a well greased pyrex dish. 6. Cover with white sauce and sprinkle with grated cheese. 7. Bake in moderate oven at 190°C (375°F) for about 10-15 minutes.

MEAT

A General Guide to Roasting and Boiling Meat

1. Irish Stew
2. Brown Stew
3. Summer Stew
4. Exeter Stew
5. Ragoût of Mutton
6. Mutton Fricassée
7. Hungarian Goulash with Caraway Dumplings
8. Haricot Mutton
9. Navarin Printanier
10. Casserole of Mutton
11. Spaghetti Mutton and Tomato Casserole
12. Tomato Mutton Chop Casserole
13. Ham Noodle Casserole
14. Mutton Hot Pot
15. Lancashire Hot Pot
16. Meat and Potato Cutlet
17. Durham Cutlets
18. Hamburgers (A)
    Hamburgers (B)
    Hamburgers (C)
19. Meat Balls
20. Scotch Eggs
21. Pan Rolls
22. Cornish Pasties
23. Shepherd's Pie
24. Meat and Potato Pie
25. Meat Loaf
26. Mince Mould
27. Pot Roast
28. Roast Lamb or Mutton
29. Miroton of Mutton
30. Tournedos of Mutton
31. Mutton Andalouse
32. Mutton Olives
33. Olivetti Romane
34. Stuffed Mutton
35. Mutton Chops with Potato Covering
36. Momo (A)
    Momo (B)
37. Toad in the Hole
38. Roast Heart
39. Braised Liver
40. Stuffed Baked Liver
41. Brain Cutlets
42. Spaghetti Bolognese
43. Mixed Grill
44. Kidney Sauté
45. Roast Chicken with Dressing
46. Rancher's Fried Chicken
47. Masala Roast Chicken
48. Baked Chicken and Noodle Casserole
49. Chicken Tetrazini
50. Devilled Chicken
51. Homemade Bacon
52. Boiled Ham (A)
    Boiled Ham (B)
53. Baked Ham
54. Homemade Ham

A GENERAL GUIDE TO ROASTING AND BOILING MEAT

	Roasting	*Roasting*	*Boiling*
Meat	*Method 1* Put at 230°C (450°F) for 15 to 20 minutes. Reduce to 190°C (375°F) till done *Method 2* Roast at constant temperature of 163°C to 190° (375°F.)	*Method 3* Slow roasting at a constant temperature of 163°C (325°F)	
Beef and mutton	*Thick cut* 25 minutes per 500 gm and 25 minutes over *Thin Cut* 20 minutes per 500 gm and 20 minutes over	*Thick cut* 35 minutes per 500 gm and 35 minutes over *Thin cut* 25 minutes per 500 gm and 25 minutes over	*Fresh* 25 minutes per 500 gm and 25 minutes over *Pickled or salted* 30 minutes per 500 gm and 30 minutes over
Lamb	20 minutes per 500 gm and 20 minutes over	30 minutes per 500 gm and 30 minutes over	
Pork	*Thick cut* 35 minutes per 500 gm and 35 minutes over *Thin cut* 30 minutes per 500 gm and 30 minutes over	*Thick cut* 45 minutes per 500 gm and 45 minutes over *Thin cut* 35 minutes per 500 gm and 30 minutes over	*Fresh* 25 minutes per 500 gm and 30 minutes over *Salt (bacon and ham)* 30 minutes per 500 gm and 30 minutes over
Veal	30 minutes per 500 gm and 30 minutes over	40 minutes per 500 gm and 40 minutes over	

	Roasting	*Roasting*	*Boiling*
Chicken and goose	Approximately one hour for 1.35 kg 2 or 3 hours according to size (may be parboiled and then roasted if tough)		1-2 hours according to size
Turkey	*Drawn weight* 3 to 4.5 kg, 2 hours. 4.5–5.4 kg, 3 hours 9 kg, 3½ hours.		
Venison	25 to 35 minutes per 500 gm		
Heart (sheep)			1½ to 2 hours
Tongue (sheep)			1½ hours

WHY DID IT GO WRONG?

Tough Roast Meat

There are three main causes of meat being tough after roasting:

1. The meat itself. When choosing a joint for roasting, it is important to select one that is well "marbled" with fat, i.e. fat evenly distributed throughout the joint.
2. Failure to thaw a chilled joint. It is important that the joint be completely thawed out before cooking is commenced.
3. Cooking in too hot an oven for a long period. The oven should be kept at 220°C (425°F) until the outside of the meat is lightly browned. This coagulates the protein and seals the joint, thus preventing the juices from running out. The oven should then be reduced to 212°C (400°F) for the remainder of the cooking time. If the temperature of the oven is not reduced, the meat may become tough and there will be considerable shrinkage. When roasting by

the low temperature method, there is little danger of the meat hardening and becoming tough, but because of the low temperature there may be a certain loss of flavour.

1. IRISH STEW

Ingredients	*For 4*	*For 100*
Mutton (middle or scrag end of neck or breast)	500 gm	12.5 kg
Potatoes	1 kg	25 kg
Onions	225 gm	2.8 kg
Pepper	a pinch	30 gm
Salt	10 gm	100 gm
Stock or water	590 ml	14.75 litre

Method

1. Wash and cut meat into neat pieces. 2. Peel and slice onions. 3. Peel and cut potatoes into large pieces. 4. Put meat, onions, seasoning and a quarter of the potatoes thinly sliced into a pan and add water or stock. 5. Cook till meat is three- fourths done. 6. Place the remaining potatoes on top of the meat and onions and cook till meat and potatoes are cooked. 7. Serve hot with the meat in the centre and the potatoes and gravy around.

2. BROWN STEW

Ingredients	*For 4*	*For 100*
Shoulder of mutton	500 gm	12.5 kg
Onions	115 gm	2.8 kg
Carrots	225 gm	5.6 kg
Turnips	115 gm	2.8 kg
Stock	590 ml	14.75 litre
Refined flour	30 gm	340 gm
Salt	10 gm	100 gm
Pepper	to taste	15 gm
Fat	30 gm	340 gm

Method

1. Trim, wash and cut meat. 2. Heat fat and fry meat till brown. Remove. 3. Fry sliced onions. Pour away surplus fat. 4. Add stock and seasoning and when hot, replace meat and simmer till almost done. 5. Add prepared vegetables and cook till tender. 6. When meat and vegetables are cooked, add blended flour and cook for 15 minutes stirring occasionally. 7. To

dish out, place meat in the centre of a hot dish with the vegetables round it and strain the gravy over.

3. SUMMER STEW

Ingredients	*For 4*	*For 100*
Middle neck of lamb	500 gm	12.5 kg
Turnips (young)	115 gm	2.8 kg
Carrots (young)	225 gm	5.65 kg
New potatoes	450 gm	11.00 kg
Green peas	450 gm	11.00 kg
Onions	115 gm	2.8 kg
Salt	to taste	100 gm
Pepper	to taste	15 gm
Mint	½ bunch	3 bunches

Method

1. Wash lamb and cut into pieces 2. Peel and slice onions. 3. Scrape and cut turnips and carrots. 4. Peel potatoes, shell peas and chop mint. 5. Put the meat, onions and seasoning in a pan. Add sufficient water to cover the meat. Simmer for one hour. 6. Add vegetables, potatoes and mint and cook till vegetables and meat are tender. 7. Remove from fire and serve hot.

4. EXETER STEW

Ingredients	*For 4*	*For 100*
Shoulder of mutton	500 gm	12.5 kg
Onions	115 gm	2.75 kg
Carrots	225 gm	5.6 kg
Turnips	115 gm	2.75 kg
Stock	590 ml	14.75 litre
Refined flour	30 gm	340 gm
Salt	to taste	100 gm
Pepper	to taste	15 gm
Fat	30 gm	340 gm
Dumplings		
Refined flour	55 gm	910 gm
Fat	30 gm	455 gm
Baking powder	½ tsp	45 gm
Salt	a pinch	100 gm

Ingredients	*For 4*	*For 100*
Onions	15 gm	225 gm
Parsley	1 sprig	2 bunches

Method

Stew

1. Prepare a brown stew. 2. Put the dumplings in the stew 40 minutes before removing from fire. 3. Place the stew in a hot dish surrounded by the dumplings.

Dumplings

1. Mix the dry ingredients. 2. Rub in fat. Add chopped onions and parsley. 3. Add sufficient water to make a light dough. 4. Divide into even-sized balls. 5. Cook in stew for 40 minutes.

5. RAGOÛT OF MUTTON

Ingredients	*For 4*	*For 100*
Breast of mutton	55 gm	12.5 kg
Refined flour	30 gm	680 gm
Onions	115 gm	2.8 kg
Carrots	225 gm	5.65 kg
Celery	30 gm	680 gm
Turnips	55 gm	1.35 kg
Fat	55 gm	1.35 kg
Tomato paste	225 gm	5.65 kg
Salt	to taste	100 gm
Pepper	to taste	15 gm
Stock	590 ml	14.75 litre

Method

1. Cut mutton into 2.5 cm (1") cubes and dip in seasoned flour. 2. Sauté carrots, turnips, chopped onions and celery in hot fat. 3. Add mutton and fry till all the surfaces are sealed and brown. 4. Remove excess fat. Add tomato paste and simmer gently. 5. Add stock, season, stir well and cook gently till meat is tender. 6. Now thicken gravy by adding remaining flour blended in water.

6. MUTTON FRICASSÉE

Ingredients	*For 4*	*For 100*
Breast of lamb or mutton	500 gm	12.5 kg
Onions	115 gm	2.8 kg

Ingredients	*For 4*	*For 100*
Bayleaf	1	10 gm
Parsley	a sprig	3 bunches
Mace	a pinch	5 gm
Stock	590 ml	14.75 litre
Refined flour	30 gm	680 gm
Carrots	450 gm	11.00 kg
Fat	15 gm	340 gm
Salt	to taste	100 gm
Pepper	to taste	15 gm

Method

1. Trim the meat and cut into neat pieces. 2. Melt fat and sauté sliced onions. 3. Add bayleaf, mace and parsley. 4. Add meat and cook slowly for 10 minutes stirring frequently. 5. Add stock and simmer on a gentle fire, till meat is tender. 6. Blend the flour with a little stock and add to fricassée. Bring to boiling point and season. 7. Boil carrots separately. 8. Dish the meat in a pile and strain the gravy over. Surround with cooked carrots. 9. Garnish with chopped parsley.

7. HUNGARIAN GOULASH WITH CARAWAY DUMPLINGS

Ingredients	*For 4*	*For 100*
Veal beef or mutton	500 gm	12.5 kg
Refined flour	10 gm	225 gm
Onions	115 gm	2.8 kg
Pepper	to taste	15 gm
Salt	10 gm	100 gm
Capsicum	55 gm	1.35 kg
Fat	30 gm	225 gm
Tomatoes	115 gm	2.8 kg
Nutmeg	a pinch	10 gm
Stock	590 ml	14.75 litre
Bayleaf	1 leaf	5 gm
Paprika	1 pinch	15 gm
Parsley	1 sprig	30 gm

Method

1. Clean and cut meat into even-sized cubes and dip in seasoned flour. 2. Remove seeds from capsicum; wash well, drain and chop. Chop onions. Sauté onions and capsicum in heated fat. 3. Add meat and fry lightly on all sides. 4. Stir in blanched tomatoes, seasoning and remaining flour.

Add stock and bouquet garni. 5. Simmer gently till meat is tender. 6. Serve with caraway dumplings.

CARAWAY DUMPLINGS

Ingredients	*For 4*	*For 100*
Caraway seeds	½ tsp	30 gm
Pepper	a pinch	5 gm
Fat	30 gm	455 gm
Refined flour	55 gm	1.35 kg
Baking powder	½ tsp	45 gm
Salt	a pinch	30 gm

Method

1. Mix dry ingredients. 2. Rub in fat. 3. Add cold water and prepare a light dough. 4. Divide into walnut-sized portions and form into balls. 5. Cook in boiling water or stock for 25 minutes.

8. HARICOT MUTTON

Ingredients	*For 4*	*For 100*
Mid neck mutton or loin chops	500 gm	12.5 kg
Fat	30 gm	455 gm
Carrots	115 gm	2.8 kg
Turnips	115 gm	2.8 kg
Haricot beans	30 gm	680 gm
Onions	55 gm	1.35 kg
Refined flour	15 gm	340 gm
Pepper	a pinch	15 gm
Salt	10 gm	100 gm
Stock or water	590 ml	14.75 litre

Method

1. Soak haricot beans overnight. 2. Cut meat into even-sized pieces with bone. 3. Heat fat and fry meat. 4. Remove meat and add sliced onions and fry. 5. Pour off fat. 6. Add stock and seasoning. When hot, add meat. 7. Simmer till meat is nearly done. 8. Blend flour with water. Add to meat and cook for a few minutes, stirring all the time. 9. Cut carrots and turnips into cubes and cook with previously soaked haricot beans. 10. Put meat in centre of a hot dish with beans and garnish with vegetables.

9. NAVARIN PRINTANIER

Ingredients	*For 4*	*For 100*
Breast, neck and shoulder of mutton	500 gm	12.5 kg
Fat	30 gm	680 gm
Sugar	a pinch	55 gm
Salt	10 gm	100 gm
Pepper	to taste	15 gm
Refined flour	15 gm	340 gm
Stock	590 ml	14.75 litre
Small onions	55 gm	1.35 kg
Carrots (young)	115 gm	2.72 kg
Turnip (young)	55 gm	1.35 kg
New potatoes	115 gm	2.72 kg
Beans	55 gm	1.35 kg
Bouquet garni		
Tomatoes	225 gm	5.6 kg
Garlic	1 clove	10 gm
Bayleaf	1	5 gm
Cloves	2	5 gm
Onions	a small piece	30 gm
Peppercorns	a few	5 gm
Celery	30 gm	680 gm
Parsley	a sprig	15 gm

Method

1. Clean and cut the mutton with the bones. 2. Heat fat, add mutton and brown lightly. 3. Add seasoning and sugar and fry over a brisk fire. The sugar settles at the bottom of the pan where it turns to caramel. It is then dissolved by moistening which gives the required colour. 4. When meat is well fried, remove all the fat. 5. Sprinkle the flour and cook for a few minutes stirring all the time. 6. Add the liquid and bring to boil stirring all the time. 7. Add blanched tomatoes and bouquet garni and simmer till meat is tender. 8. Add prepared vegetables and continue cooking till the vegetables are cooked.

10. CASSEROLE OF MUTTON

Ingredients	*For 4*	*For 100*
Mutton chops or breast	500 gm	12.5 kg
Onions	115 gm	2.8 kg
Carrots	115 gm	2.8 kg

Ingredients	For 4	For 100
Turnips	115 gm	2.8 kg
Fat	30 gm	340 gm
Refined flour	30 gm	340 gm
Pepper	to taste	15 gm
Salt	10 gm	100 gm

Method

1. Clean and cut meat with bones. 2. Prepare the vegetables and cut into 3 cm (1") cubes. 3. Melt the fat, then add the meat and vegetables and cook with lid on over gentle heat for about 15 minutes stirring once or twice. 4. Remove from heat and warm stock. 5. Transfer into a casserole dish and cook in the oven at 160°C (320°F.) or gas mark 3 with lid on till meat is tender. 6. Blend the flour with a little stock. Add with seasoning to stock. 7. Return to oven and cook for 10 minutes.

N.B. If meat is tough, cook on top of range as for stews till half done and then transfer to casserole dish.

11. SPAGHETTI MUTTON AND TOMATO CASSEROLE

Ingredients	For 4	For 100
Mutton	500 gm	12.5 kg
Eggs	1	12
Breadcrumbs	30 gm	680 gm
Fat	55 gm	1.35 kg
Spaghetti	225 gm	5 kg
Tomatoes	500 gm	12.5 kg
Refined flour	15 gm	340 gm
Butter	15 gm	340 gm
Onions	55 gm	1.35 kg
Carrots	55 gm	1.35 kg
Salt	to taste	100 gm
Pepper	to taste	20 gm

Method

1. Clean and mince mutton. 2. Add seasoning and shape into balls. Dip in egg and breadcrumbs and fry lightly. 3. Boil spaghetti in salted water till done. 4. Prepare a tomato sauce using remaining ingredients. 5. In a casserole dish place a good layer of spaghetti. 6. Cover with tomato sauce. 7. Top with meat balls. 8. Cover and bake in a moderate oven at 175°C (350°F) for 25 minutes.

12. TOMATO MUTTON CHOP CASSEROLE

Ingredients	*For 4*	*For 100*
Mutton chops	500 gm (4)	12.5 kg (100)
Carrots	115 gm	2.8 kg
Peas	115 gm	2.8 kg
Onions	115 gm	2.8 kg
Celery	55 gm	1.35 kg
Potatoes	225 gm	5 kg
Tomatoes	115 gm	2.8 kg
Stock	600 ml	14.75 litre
Pepper	to taste	15 gm
Salt	to taste	80-100 gm

Method

1. Blanch and pierce the tomatoes. 2. Clean and slice carrots and onions and dice potatoes and celery. 3. Mix all ingredients together. 4. Put into a casserole dish. Cover and cook in a moderate oven till meat is tender (about 2–2½ hours).

13. HAM NOODLE CASSEROLE

Ingredients	*Quantity*
Small shell noodles	115 gm
Leeks	2
Milk	400 ml
Lean cooked ham	115 gm
Grated cheese	60 gm
Salt and pepper	

Method

1. Wash leeks very thoroughly, removing any discoloured outside leaves. 2. Chop into rings. 3. Dice ham. 4. Grease casserole. Layer leeks, ham and noodles (seasoning each layer) and a little grated cheese. 5. Pour milk over and sprinkle grated cheese. Bake at 175°C (350°F) or gas mark 4 for about half an hour. The casserole is ready when all the milk is absorbed.

N.B. This is also made very tasty with tinned celery hearts instead of leeks. It only needs half a tin, i.e. 2 hearts.

14. MUTTON HOT POT

Ingredients	*For 4*	*For 100*
Mutton	500 gm	12.5 kg
Potatoes	680 gm	15 kg

Ingredients	For 4	For 100
Onions	115 gm	2.8 kg
Peppercorns	a few	30 gm
Salt	to taste	100 gm
Butter	30 gm	340 gm

Method

1. Wash and trim meat, cut into pieces. 2. Peel and slice onions. 3. Peel and cut potatoes into thin slices. 4. Put the onions, meat, seasoning and potatoes in a casserole in layers, ending with a thick layer of potatoes. 5. Add stock and cover with greased paper. 6. Cook in a moderate oven for at least 2 to 2½ hours. 7. Remove paper half an hour before removing from the oven. Dot with butter and let the potatoes brown. 8. Serve hot in the dish in which it is cooked with a table napkin pinned round.

15. LANCASHIRE HOT POT

Ingredients	For 4	For 100
Mutton	340 gm	8.5 kg
Kidneys	4	100
Potatoes	450 gm	11.00 kg
Onions	115 gm	2.8 kg
Carrots	115 gm	2.8 kg
Turnip	55 gm	1.35 kg
Pepper	a pinch	15 gm
Salt	to taste	80-100 gm
Stock (Strong)	590 ml	14.75 litre
Fat	30 gm	340 gm

Method

1. Clean and prepare meat and kidneys. 2. Parboil potatoes. Peel and cut into roundels. 3. Cut half of the onions into quarters and the other half into slices. 4. Dice carrots and turnip. 5. Heat fat. Brown meat and sliced onions. Add remaining ingredients except potatoes and cook till meat is fairly tender. 6. Arrange in a casserole dish with layers of vegetables, meat and potatoes with a thick layer of potatoes on top. 7. Pour stock over and cover with a lid or paper. Cook at moderate heat for about 2 hours. 8. About 15 minutes before serving, remove the lid or paper to allow potatoes to brown.

16. MEAT AND POTATO CUTLET

Ingredients	For 4	For 100
Leg of mutton	500 gm	12.5 kg

Ingredients	*For 4*	*For 100*
Potatoes	225 gm	5.6 kg
Onions	115 gm	2.75 kg
Milk	15 ml	225 ml
Parsley	¼ bunch	2 bunches
Pepper	to taste	15 gm
Salt	10 gm	100 gm
Egg	1	12
Breadcrumbs	55 gm	455 gm
Fat to fry (absorption)	30 gm	340 gm

Method

1. Boil and mince meat. 2. Peel, boil and mash potatoes with a little milk. 3. Mince onions, sauté in a little fat. Mix with mutton. Add seasoning and chopped parsley. 4. Make a roll of the mutton mixture and cover with mashed potatoes. 5. Coat with egg and breadcrumbs and deep fry. 6. Serve hot with tomato sauce.

17. DURHAM CUTLETS

Ingredients	*For 4*	*For 100*
Mutton	500 gm	12.5 kg
Parsley	a few sprigs	30 gm
Eggs	1	12
Breadcrumbs	55 gm	900 gm
Worcester sauce	5 ml	115 ml
Pepper	a pinch	15 gm
Salt	to taste	100 gm
Fat to fry (absorption)	30 gm	380 gm
Macaroni	30 gm	115 gm
Refined flour	30 gm	380 gm
Butter	30 gm	380 gm
Milk	145 ml	1.75 litre

Method

1. Prepare panada (thick white sauce). 2. Boil and mince meat. Add seasoning and Worcester sauce. 3. Add to panada. 4. Spread mixture on to a plate. 5. When cool divide into even portions. 6. Form into cutlets. Coat with egg and crumbs inserting a piece of macaroni at one end. 7. Fry in deep fat until golden. Drain and serve hot. Serve garnished with parsley.

18. HAMBURGERS (A)

Ingredients	*For 4*	*For 100*
Mutton	500 gm	12.5 kg
Salt	to taste	80-100 gm
Pepper	to taste	15 gm
Fat to fry	30-45 gm	340-400 gm

Method

1. Clean and mince meat. 2. Mix with pepper and salt. Form into hamburgers. 3. Shallow fry till meat is cooked. Serve hot between hamburger buns. Size of portion, 50 gm For (4) 8 small or 4 large for (100) 200 small or 100 large.

HAMBURGERS (B)

Ingredients	*For 4*	*For 100*
Mutton	500 gm	12.5 kg
Onions	115 gm	2.8 kg
Eggs	1	12
Fat to fry	30-40 gm	340-400 gm
Salt	to taste	80-100 gm
Pepper	a pinch	15 gm

Method

1. Clean and mince meat. Add pepper and salt. 2. Peel and mince onions. Add to meat. 3. Bind with egg. Form into even-sized flat cakes and shallow fry till cooked. Serve hot between hamburger buns.

HAMBURGERS (C)

Ingredients	*For 4*	*For 100*
Mutton	500 gm	12.5 kg
Bread (fresh)	50 gm	1.25 kg
Pepper	a pinch	15 gm
Salt	to taste	80-100 gm
Onions	115 gm	2.8 kg
Fat to fry	30-45 gm	340-400 gm

Method

1. Clean and mince meat. Mix with fresh breadcrumbs, salt, pepper and minced onions. 2. Form into even-sized cakes. 3. Shallow fry till cooked and serve hot with barbecue sauce.

BARBECUE SAUCE

Ingredients	*For 4*	*For 100*
Tomatoes	115 gm	2.8 kg
Onions	20 gm	500 gm
Chillies (ripe)	2	10 gm
Sugar	30 gm	800 gm
Vinegar	35 ml	900 ml
Salt	to taste	80-100 gm

Method

1. Place in a thick-bottomed pan, the tomatoes peeled and quartered, diced onions, sugar, salt and vinegar. 2. Cook for 1½ hours or until mixture ceases to look watery. 3. Add finely chopped chillies (without seeds) and cook for half an hour. 4. Place in sterilized jars and process by immersing in hot water for 15 minutes. 5. Use for hamburgers or cold meats.

19. MEAT BALLS

Ingredients	*For 4*	*For 100*
Mutton	500 gm	12.5 kg
Onions	115 gm	2.75 kg
Pepper	to taste	15 gm
Salt	to taste	100 gm
Fat for frying (absorption)	30 gm	340 gm

Method

1. Mince mutton. 2. Chop onions fine, add to minced mutton with pepper, beaten eggs and salt. 3. Form into balls and deep fry.

20. SCOTCH EGGS

Ingredients	*For 4*	*For 100*
Hard-boiled eggs	4	100
Raw egg	1	10
Mutton	500 gm	12.5 kg
Onions	55 gm	1.35 kg
Potatoes	225 gm	5.65 kg
Parsley	1 sprig	55 gm
Refined flour	15 gm	115 gm
Breadcrumbs	115 gm	1.8 kg
Pepper	to taste	15 gm

Ingredients	For 4	For 100
Salt	10 gm	100 gm
Fat to fry (absorption)	30 gm	340 gm

Method

1. Shell hard-boiled eggs. Roll in seasoned flour. 2. Boil and mash potatoes. Clean, boil and mince the mutton. Mix minced onions, mashed potatoes and mutton with the seasoning. 3. Coat egg with the minced meat mixture. 4. Brush with beaten egg. Roll in breadcrumbs. 5. Deep fry in hot fat. 6. Cut into halves and serve cold, set in lettuce leaves or hot with tomato sauce.

N.B. Sausage meat can be used instead of mutton in which case the potatoes are not necessary.

21. PAN ROLLS

Ingredients	For 4	For 100
Refined flour	115 gm	2.8 kg
Eggs	1	25
Milk	145 ml	3.6 litre
Salt	5 gm	30 gm

Method

1. Sieve flour and salt into a bowl. 2. Make a well in the centre, add the beaten yolk of egg and milk. 3. Beat well to form a smooth batter and let it stand for an hour. 4. Beat egg white stiff. Fold it into the batter and prepare pancakes. 5. Fill with prepared filling. Fold envelope fashion. 6. Dip in egg, coat with breadcrumbs and deep fry. 7. Serve hot.

Filling

Ingredients	For 4	For 100
Mutton	500 gm	12.5 kg
Potatoes	225 gm	5.6 kg
Onions	55 gm	1.36 kg
Salt	to taste	80-100 gm
Pepper	a pinch	15 gm
Ginger	3-5 gm	100 gm
Fat	10 gm	225 gm
Coating		
Eggs	1	12
Breadcrumbs	115 gm	1.8 kg
Fat to fry		

Filling

1. Boil mutton in just enough water till tender. 2. Mince mutton. Chop onions fine. Peel and grate ginger. 3. Boil and mash potatoes or dice into small pieces. 4. Heat fat in a large pan. Sauté onions and ginger. 5. Add meat, potatoes, salt and pepper and mix thoroughly. Remove from fire and use as required.

22. CORNISH PASTIES

Ingredients	*For 4*	*For 100*
Refined flour	170 gm	4.25 kg
Butter or margarine	85 gm	2.1 kg
Salt	a pinch	30 gm
Baking powder	¼ tsp	25 gm
Cold water to mix		

Method

1. Sieve flour with baking powder and salt. 2. Rub in the butter or margarine to breadcrumb consistency. 3. Add sufficient water to make a dough that is neither too dry nor wet. 4. Roll out and cut into rounds about 10 cm (4") in diameter. Fill with prepared filling. 5. Fold them over to make half a circle and press the edges firmly and flute them. 6. Brush them over with a little milk. Bake at 220ºC (425ºF) for about 15 minutes.

Filling

Ingredients	*For 4*	*For 100*
Meat	455 gm	11.3 kg
Potatoes	225 gm	5.65 kg
Onions	55 gm	1.35 kg
Tomato ketchup	15 ml	375 ml
Stock	30 ml	750 ml
Fat	15 gm	250 gm
Salt	to taste	50-80 gm

Filling

1. Boil or roast meat and dice into even-sized small pieces. 2. Boil and dice potatoes. Chop onions. 3. Heat fat. Sauté onions. Add meat and potatoes. 4. Remove from fire. Add ketchup, stock and salt. Mix well and use as required.

23. SHEPHERD'S PIE

Ingredients	*For 4*	*For 100*
Beef or mutton	500 gm	12.5 kg
Potatoes	450 gm	11.00 kg
Butter	30 gm	680 gm
Onions	115 gm	2.8 kg
Refined flour	10 gm	250 gm
Stock	150 ml	3.75 litre
Salt	to taste	80-100 gm
Pepper	a pinch	15 gm
Milk	75 ml	1.8 litre
Tomatoes	115 gm	2.8 kg

Method

1. Boil or roast meat, cool and mince. 2. Chop onions. 3. Melt half the fat in a pan and fry onions till pale brown. 4. Stir in flour, add stock gradually, stir until thick. 5. Blanch tomatoes, chop and add to stock. 6. Add seasoning and meat. 7. Put into greased pie dish. 8. Boil and mash potatoes with milk. 9. Spread over the meat, make a rough surface with a fork. 10. Dot with butter. 11. Bake at 190ºC (375ºF) for about 20-25 minutes.

24. MEAT AND POTATO PIE

Ingredients	*For 4*	*For 100*
Mutton	500 gm	12.5 kg
Potatoes	1 kg	22 kg
Onions	225 gm	2.8 kg
Pepper	to taste	15 gm
Salt	to taste	100 gm
Stock or water	590 ml	14.75 litre
Shortcrust pastry		
Refined flour	115 gm	1.35 kg
Butter	60 gm	680 gm
Baking powder	¼ tsp	30 gm
Salt	a pinch	10 gm
Cold water to mix		

Method

1. Wash and cut meat. 2. Peel and cut potatoes. 3. Peel and slice onions. 4. Put meat, onions and seasoning in a pan, cover with stock and cook for 20 to 30 minutes. 5. Add potatoes and cook till meat is tender. Cool.

6. Transfer into pie dish, cover with shortcrust pastry, decorating top with leaves. 7. Bake at 205°C (400°F) for 15 minutes.

Shortcrust pastry

Make as in Method 1 to 3 of Cornish Pasties (Recipe no. 22 above)

25. MEAT LOAF

Ingredients	*For 4*	*For 100*
Meat	500 gm	12.5 kg
Breadcrumbs	55 gm	2.75 kg
Eggs	1	15
Hard-boiled egg	1	15
Onions	20 gm	500 gm
Bacon	55 gm	1.35 kg
Parsley	a sprig	2 bunches
Stock	15 ml	250-340 ml
Pepper	a pinch	15 gm
Salt	10 gm	100 gm
Fat	10 gm	30 gm

Method

1. Clean and mince meat. 2. Heat fat. Fry chopped onions and chopped bacon. 3. Add minced meat, breadcrumbs, beaten egg and seasoning and a little stock to moisten. 4. Grease a bread loaf tin. Dredge with breadcrumbs. 5. Arrange sliced hard-boiled egg. Press in prepared meat. 6. Cover with grease-proof paper and bake in a moderate oven at 175°C (350°F) for 1 hour. 7. Serve hot or cold with tomato sauce or brown gravy.

26. MINCE MOULD

Ingredients	*Quantity*
Cooked minced meat	500 gm
Potatoes	500 gm
Bread slices	2
Butter	15 gm
Salt and pepper	to taste
Green peas	
Hard boiled egg	1
Mint leaves	
Grated cheese	
Meat gravy	

Method

1. The minced meat can be freshly prepared or left-over roast chicken or mutton, ham, pork etc. can be used. Mince well. 2. Soak bread in hot water. Squeeze off moisture and add to the minced meat. Add a little meat gravy to keep the meat moist. 3. Peel, boil in salted water, drain dry and mash potatoes adding a little butter, salt and pepper. 4. Line a buttered mould evenly with mashed potato. Fill with minced meat. Cover the top with grease-proof paper or banana leaves. 5. Steam for half an hour. Cool and turn out. Sprinkle grated cheese over. 6. Decorate with slices of hard-boiled egg, strips of carrot, peas and mint leaves. Serve set in lettuce leaves.

27. POT ROAST

Ingredients	*For 4*	*For 100*
Breast of mutton or leg of mutton	500 gm	12.5 kg
Fat	55 gm	455 gm
Gravy		
Refined flour	15 gm	340 gm
Stock	145 ml	3.6 litre
Salt	to taste	100 gm
Pepper	to taste	15 gm

Method

1. Wipe the meat. 2. If breast of mutton is being used, bone and stuff it with forcemeat. 3. Sprinkle fat in a heavy iron pan and fry the meat lightly on all sides until evenly browned. 4. Sprinkle a little water. Put the lid on and cook on slow fire. 5. Turn frequently. Sprinkle water if necessary. 6. When meat is tender, remove, pour off excess fat and prepare gravy in the same pan. (See method for gravy in next recipe.)

28. ROAST LAMB OR MUTTON

Allow approximately 170 gm of meat on the bone (legs, shoulder, saddle or loin and breast).

1. Season the joints with salt and pepper. 2. Place on a trivet in a roasting tray. 3. Place a little fat on top and cook at 205°C (400°F) for 100 minutes. 4. Reduce heat to 190°C (375°F). Baste frequently and reduce the heat gradually to 175°C (375°F). (Roasting time approximately 20 minutes per 450 gm and 20 minutes over.)

Test to see if cooked. The joints should be cooked through. Allow to stand for approximately half an hour before carving. (If this is not done, the meat will shrink and curl.)

Roast gravy

Place the roasting tray on the stove over gentle heat, to allow the sediment to settle. Carefully strain the fat, leaving the sediment in the tray. Return to the stove. Add a little cornflour. Brown carefully, swill with brown stock. Allow to simmer for a few minutes. Correct seasoning, strain and skim.

29. MIROTON OF MUTTON

Ingredients	*For 4*	*For 100*
Mutton leg	500 gm	12.5 kg
Tomato sauce	470 ml	11.75 litre
Refined flour	15 gm	340 gm
Butter	15 gm	340 gm
Onions	15 gm	340 gm
Potatoes	450 gm	11.00 kg
Parsley	¼ bunch	2 bunches
Mint	a sprig	2 bunches
Pepper	to taste	15 gm
Salt	10 gm	100 gm
Stock	590 ml	14.75 litre

Method

1. Clean and roast leg of mutton, cool and carve into thin slices. 2. Boil potatoes and mash. 3. Prepare a brown sauce with flour, butter, onions and stock. 4. Chop mint and parsley fine. 5. Dredge meat with pepper, salt and chopped parsley and mint. 6. Arrange slices of meat overlapping in a greased pyrex dish. 7. Pipe a border of mashed potatoes all around. 8. Pour the sauces mixed together over the meat. Sauce should be enough to cover the meat. 9. Bake in a fairly quick oven and dust the top of the sauce with finely chopped mint before serving.

30. TOURNEDOS OF MUTTON

Ingredients		*For 4*	*For 100*
Mutton leg		500 gm	12.5 kg
Bread		115 gm	2.8 kg
Salt		to taste	100 gm
Pepper	for mashed potatoes	a pinch	15 gm
Milk	for mashed potatoes	20 ml	295 ml
Butter	for mashed potatoes	10 gm	225 gm
Potatoes		450 gm	11 kg
Parsley		½ bunch	2 bunches
Fat to fry		50 gm	1 kg

Method

1. Clean and cut the meat into neat round pieces about 1.75 cm (¾″) thick and 7.5 cm (3") in diameter. 2. Beat with a steak hammer. Season with pepper and salt and keep aside for a while. 3. Heat fat. Put in meat quickly, sear the outside of the meat. Lower flame and let meat cook till it is tender. 4. Boil and mash potatoes. 5. Fry slices of bread in fat. 6. Pipe a double line of mashed potato down the centre of a hot dish, in which the meat is to be served. 7. Place croutons of fried bread around and pipe roses of potato mixture between each. Decorate with small sprigs of parsley. 8. Place a piece of meat on each crouton and pour hot brown sauce over, allowing some of it to soak into the fried bread. Serve very hot.

BROWN SAUCE

Ingredients	*For 4*	*For 100*
Refined flour	20 gm	455 gm
Onions	115 gm	2.8 kg
Fat	20 gm	455 gm
Tomatoes	50 gm	1 kg
Carrots	20 gm	455 gm
Stock	590 ml	14.75 litre
Pepper	to taste	15 gm
Salt	to taste	100 gm

Method

1. Heat fat. Fry onions till brown and crisp. 2. Add flour and brown. 3. Add stock, chopped tomatoes, carrots. Season. Cook till vegetables are tender, stirring occasionally. 4. Press through a sieve.

31. MUTTON ANDALOUSE

Ingredients	*Quantity*
Leg of mutton	500 gm
Bacon	50 gm
Meat glaze	1 cup
Capsicums (medium sized)	225 gm
Vegetable pulao	1 cup
Brinjal	1
Tomato	1
Sausages (small variety)	3 or 4
Oil	30 ml

Method

1. Clean and trim leg of mutton. 2. Tie over with strips of bacon and roast. 3. Remove seeds from capsicum halves and fill with rice. 4. Fry roundels of brinjal in oil. Chop tomatoes roughly and toss in oil. 5. Cut meat into 5 cm (2") rounds, 0.25-0.5 cm (⅛–¼") thick. 6. Arrange neatly in an oval dish. Brush over with meat glaze. 7. Surround with capsicums, fried brinjal, and small heaps of tomatoes. 8. Place a fried or grilled sausage between each. Serve hot with gravy prepared from pan drippings left after meat is roasted.

32. MUTTON OLIVES

Ingredients	*For 4*	*For 100*
Forcemeat		
Fresh breadcrumbs	30 gm	680 gm
Butter or margarine	15 gm	340 gm
Grated lime rind	a pinch	10 gm
Parsley	a little	55 gm
Mixed herbs	1 pinch	30 gm
Egg for binding or	½	3
Milk	10 ml	115 ml
Olives		
Leg of mutton	455 gm	11.3 kg
Fat	30 gm	455 gm
Stock	590 ml	14.75 litre
Pepper	to taste	15 gm
Salt	to taste	100 gm
Refined flour	15 gm	340 gm
Garnish		
Small tomatoes	55 gm	2.35 kg
Peas	30 gm	680 gm
Turnip	15 gm	340 gm
Beans	15 gm	340 gm
Potatoes	15 gm	340 gm
Carrots	15 gm	340 gm

Method

1. Prepare forcemeat by mixing all ingredients together. 2. Wash, wipe and cut meat into thin strips 7–10 cm (3"–4"). 3. Spread stuffing on each, roll and tie up with cotton thread so that they look like "olives". 4. Melt

fat. Fry olives and pour off surplus fat. 5. Add stock and seasoning and simmer till olives are tender (2 hours). 6. Prepare vegetables. Halve tomatoes, shell peas, dice other vegetables. Boil peas and diced vegetables. 7. Add trimmings of vegetables in the stew. 8. Lift out the olives, remove thread and arrange on a hot dish. 9. Blend flour with water. Add to stew and cook for 5 minutes. 10. Strain over the meat and garnish with prepared vegetables.

33. OLIVETTI ROMANE

Ingredients	*For 4*	*For 100*
Mutton	500 gm	12.5 kg
Carrots	30 gm	680 gm
Onions	60 gm	1.55 kg
Garlic	1 flake	15 gm
Tomato purée	60 ml	1 litre
Chopped parsley	a few sprigs	3 bunches
Stock	250 ml	5.75 litre
Eggs	1	25
Butter	30 gm	680 gm
Salt and pepper	to taste	100 gm
Bay leaf	½	5 gm
Lime	a few	drops

Method

1. Clean and mince mutton. 2. Peel and mince carrots, onions and garlic. 3. Mix together minced mutton, salt, pepper, half the onions. 4. Shape into olives. 5. Heat butter. Add garlic, remaining onions and carrots. 6. Cover and cook till tender but not brown. 7. Add the tomato purée and the remaining seasoning. 8. Add stock. Put in the olives. Simmer for 15 minutes. 9. Serve hot with a dash of lime juice and chopped parsley.

34. STUFFED MUTTON

Ingredients	*For 4*	*For 100*
Leg, shoulder or breast of mutton	500 gm	12.5 kg
Dripping or fat	30 gm	225 gm
Refined flour	10 gm	250 gm
Stock	590 ml	14.75 litre
Pepper	a pinch	15 gm
Salt	10 gm	100 gm
Forcemeat stuffing		
Fresh breadcrumbs	30 gm	900 gm

Ingredients	For 4	For 100
Butter or margarine	15 gm	455 gm
Grated lime rind	a pinch	15 gm
Parsley	1 tsp	55 gm
Mixed herbs	a pinch	30 gm
Pepper	to taste	10 gm
Salt	to taste	50 gm
Egg for binding or	½	3
Milk	10 ml	115 ml

Method

1. Wash and wipe the meat. 2. With a sharp pointed knife remove the bones. 3. Prepare the stuffing. 4. Spread out the meat and season and then place the stuffing. 5. Roll up being careful to tuck in any stuffing. 6. Tie securely with a string. 7. Weigh and allow 30 minutes to each 450 gm and 30 minutes over. 8. Place the joint in a baking tin. Baste with dripping and cook in an oven at 190°C (375°F) or gas mark 5. 9. After 10 minutes reduce the temperature to 165°C (330°F) or gas mark 3 and cook till done, basting occasionally. 10. Dish the meat and remove the string. 11. Remove extra fat from baking tray. 12. Add flour and brown. 13. Add stock and seasoning, keep on fire, stir well till it starts boiling. 14. Strain and serve with the meat.

35. MUTTON CHOPS WITH POTATO COVERING

Ingredients	For 4	For 100
Mutton chops	500 gm	12.5 kg
Potatoes	450 gm	11.00 kg
Eggs	1	12
Breadcrumbs	50 gm	1 kg
Pepper	a pinch	15 gm
Salt	to taste	80-100 gm
Onions	30 gm	340 gm
Butter	30 gm	340 gm
Milk	a little	295 ml
Fat to fry (absorption)	30 gm	500 gm

Method

1. Wash and clean chops. 2. Beat with blunt side of knife. Season with salt and pepper. 3. Heat a little fat. Fry sliced onions. Add chops and a little water and boil till chops are tender and no moisture is left. 4. Make mashed potatoes. Cover chops Coat with egg and breadcrumbs and deep fry.

36. MOMO (A)

Ingredients	*Quantity*
Flour	1.25 kg
Salt	
Yeast (optional)	1 tsp
Soda bicarbonate (optional)	¼,
Filling	
(Mix together)	
Minced pork or beef	1 kg
Chopped onions	250 gm
Oil (Dalda melted)	1 cup
Ajinomoto	½ tsp
Soya sauce	3 tbsp
Salt	to taste
Water	1 cup
Egg (optional)	1

Method

1. Sieve together maida and salt. 2. Add warm water to flour and make a soft dough. 3. Knead well and set aside for 2-3 hours. 4. If yeast is used, dissolve it in lukewarm water. Add to flour sifted with salt and soda bicarbonate. This dough must be left to rise for 5-6 hours or overnight. 5. Roll into sausage shape, cut into 2.5 cm (1") pieces. 6. Roll out like luchis (edges thinner than the centre). Put a tsp of prepared filling. 7. Pleat the edges together firmly, sealing as you proceed. 8. Steam for 30 minutes if pork filling is used and for 20 minutes if beef filling is used.

MOMO (B)

Ingredients	*Quantity (50 Momos)*
Dough	
Refined flour	½ kg
Egg	1
Salt	5 gm
Filling	
Mincemeat (fatty)	½ kg
Onions	250 gm
Green chillies	10 gm
Ginger	5 gm
Salt	10 gm
Soya sauce (optional)	1 tsp
Ajinomoto (optional)	¼ tsp
Oil (optional)	1 tbsp

Method

For dough

1. Mix flour, salt and egg. 2. Add tepid water and make a soft dough, kneading vigorously for about 20 minutes. 3. Set the dough aside for approximately 1 hour.

For filling

1. Chop onions, green chillies and ginger. 2. Mix them with the mincemeat. 3. Add salt, soya sauce and ajinomoto and mix well (only salt, if soya sauce and ajinomoto are not used).

To shape momos

1. Divide the dough evenly into small balls weighing approximately 10 gm each. 2. Roll to about 6 cm in diameter. 3. Put 1 tsp of mincemeat filling in the centre.

To steam momos

1. Boil water in the bottom compartment of momo steamer, idli steamer or pressure cooker with idli steamer. 2. Grease the perforated compartments and place momos keeping at least ½" space round each momo. 3. Steam momos for 25-30 minutes. (If pressure cooker is used, do not put the weight.) 4. Serve steaming hot with tomato-garlic chutney.

TOMATO-GARLIC CHUTNEY

Ingredients	*Quantity*
Tomatoes (ripe)	250 gm
Garlic	5 gm
Red chillied (dried)	5 gm
Methi seeds	2 gm
Oil	20 ml
Salt	10 gm

Method

1. Blanch/roast tomatoes and remove the skin. 2. Heat oil. Add methi seeds. When seeds splutter, add garlic pods and fry them to golden brown. 3. Add dry red chillies and fry till they are crisp and brown. 4. Remove from fire and drain them out of the oil. 5. Grind together the above fried ingredients, along with blanched tomatoes, to a very smooth paste. 6. Return the ground paste to the frying pan with remaining oil. Add salt and fry till the raw smell of tomatoes goes. 7. Remove from fire. Cool and serve with momos.

37. TOAD IN THE HOLE

Ingredients	*For 4*	*For 100*
Batter		
Refined flour	115 gm	2.8 kg
Milk	395 ml	5.6 litre
Eggs	1	25
Salt	to taste	100 gm
Meat or loin chops or sausage	500 gm	12.5 kg

Method

1. Cut meat into neat pieces or skin sausages. Place in a greased pie dish. 2. Mix flour and salt in a bowl. Make a well in the centre. 3. Add the egg. Stir from the centre, working in the flour gradually adding the milk till it looks like cream. 4. Beat well and mix thoroughly. 5. Stir in the remaining milk and leave to stand for at least half and hour. 6. Pour batter over meat or sausage. 7. Bake in a hot oven for 45 minutes–1 hour. Reduce heat slightly after 15 minutes. 8. Serve hot.

N.B. If meat is inclined to be tough, boil first.

38. ROAST HEART

Ingredients	*For 4*	*For 100*
Sheep's heart	4	100
Dripping	55 gm	225 gm
Forcemeat stuffing		
Fresh breadcrumbs	30 gm	680 gm
Butter or margarine	15 gm	340 gm
Grated lime rind	a pinch	10 gm
Parsley	few sprigs	55 gm
Mixed herbs	a pinch	30 gm
Pepper	to taste	10 gm
Salt	to taste	50 gm
Egg for binding or	½	6
Milk	10 ml	115 ml

Method

1. Clean hearts well. Remove tubes. 2. Make forcemeat stuffing. 3. Fill up the hearts and sew or skewer openings. 4. Bake at 190°C (375°F) covered with greased paper, basting frequently. 5. Serve with thickened gravy.

39. BRAISED LIVER

Ingredients	*For 4*	*For 100*
Liver	340 gm	8.4 kg

Ingredients	*For 4*	*For 100*
Salt	to taste	80-100 gm
Pepper	a pinch	30 gm
Onions	115 gm	2.8 kg
Parsley	a few sprigs	3 bunches
Refined flour	10 gm	225 gm
Fat	30 gm	500 gm

Method

1. Season liver with salt and pepper. 2. Heat fat, brown onions. Add liver and sauté. 3. Remove surplus fat. Add hot water. 4. Cover and cook till tender. 5. Add flour mixed with water to form a smooth paste. 6. Bring to boil, add chopped parsley and keep in a moderate oven for 10-20 minutes.

40. STUFFED BAKED LIVER

Ingredients	*For 4*	*For 100*
Liver	500 gm	12.5 kg
Breadcrumbs	85 gm	2.1 kg
Onions	30 gm	680 gm
Parsley	1 sprig	3 bunches
Salt	to taste	100 gm
Pepper	to taste	15 gm
Eggs	½	6
Stock	145 ml	2.95 litre
Tomato ketchup	15 ml	350 ml
Refined flour	5 gm	115 gm
Bacon (fat)	115 gm	2.85 kg

Method

1. Prepare forcemeat stuffing with breadcrumbs, onions, parsley, seasoning and egg. 2. Wash and dry the liver, cut into thin slices 2.5 cm (½″) thick and put them in a greased baking tin. 3. Cover each piece of liver with stuffing. 4. Remove rind from bacon and place pieces on top of the stuffing. 5. Pour the stock round the meat and bake slowly for about an hour. 6. Dish neatly, add the ketchup to the liquid in the tin. 7. Thicken with the blended flour and pour round the liver.

41. BRAIN CUTLETS

Ingredients	*For 4*	*For 100*
Brains	2	50
Breadcrumbs	30 gm	680 gm
Eggs	1	12

Ingredients	For 4	For 100
Salt	to taste	50 gm
Pepper	a pinch	15 gm
Fat to fry (absorption)	15 gm	250 gm

Method

1. Soak brain in brine solution. 2. Remove and wash roughly and slice. 3. Sprinkle salt and pepper. 4. Coat with egg and breadcrumbs and deep fry.

42. SPAGHETTI BOLOGNESE

Ingredients	For 4	For 100
Spaghetti	225 gm	5.65 kg
Meat (minced)	115 gm	2.8 kg
Salad oil	30 ml	500 ml
Onions	115 gm	1.35 kg
Celery	30 gm	680 gm
Carrots	55 gm	1.35 kg
Tomatoes	115 gm	2.8 kg
Mushrooms	55 gm	1.35 kg
Salt	to taste	100 gm
Garlic	1 flake	4 flakes
Bayleaf	1 gm	5 gm
Cheese	30 gm	680 gm

Method

1. Chop onions and garlic finely and fry in oil. 2. Add meat, fry for a few minutes and add mushrooms. 3. Add blanched tomatoes, chopped carrots, celery, bay leaf and salt. 4. Simmer gently until meat is cooked. 5. Cook spaghetti in plenty of boiling salted water till tender. 6. Drain, put in a hot dish, add the meat sauce; mix well and serve garnished with grated cheese.

43. MIXED GRILL

Ingredients	For 4	For 100
Sausages	4 (225 gm)	100 (5.6 kg)
Kidneys	4 (115 gm)	100 (2.8 kg)
Mushrooms	4 (30 gm)	100 (680 gm)
Cutlets	4 (225 gm)	100 (5.6 kg)
Tomatoes	4 (450 gm)	100 (11 kg)
Streaky bacon rashers	4 (60 gm)	100 (1.5 kg)
Garnish		
Straw potatoes	115 gm	2.8 kg
Parsley butter		

Method

1. Grill in the order given (prick sausages before grilling). 2. Dress neatly in silver flats. Garnish with straw potatoes and place a slice of parsley butter on each kidney.

44. KIDNEY SAUTÉ

Ingredients	*For 4*	*For 100*
Sheep's kidneys	8	200
Sauce demiglace	300 ml	7.5 litre
Butter or fat	55 gm	680 gm

Method

1. Skin and halve kidneys. Remove the sinews and cut each half into three to five pieces. Season. 2. Fry quickly in a frying pan for about 4 to 5 minutes. 3. Place in a colander to drain. Add to the finished sauce. Do not reboil. Serve hot.

45. ROAST CHICKEN WITH DRESSING

Ingredients	*Quantity (6 servings)*
Moist bread dressing	
Roasting chicken	1
Salad oil	
Paprika	¼ tsp
Pepper	⅛ tsp
Salt	
Small onions, quartered	1
Water	
All-purpose flour	3 tbsp
Parsley sprigs for garnish	

Method

1. Prepare moist bread dressing. 2. Remove giblets and neck from chicken; reserve for gravy. Rinse chicken with running cold water and drain well. Spoon some of the dressing lightly into neck cavity (do not pack dressing; it expands during cooking). Fold neck skin over dressing; fasten neck skin to back with skewer. With chicken breast-side up, lift wings up towards the neck, then fold under back of chicken so they stay in place. 3. Spoon remaining dressing lightly into body cavity.* Close by folding skin lightly over opening; skewer closed if necessary. With string,

*Bake any leftover dressing in covered, greased, small casserole dish during last 30 minutes of roasting chicken.

tie legs and tail together. 4. Place chicken, breast-side up, on rack in open roasting pan; brush with salad oil; sprinkle with paprika, pepper and ½ tsp salt. Roast at 350°F for about 2½ hours. Start checking if done towards last 30 minutes. (If you like, use a meat thermometer. Before placing chicken in oven insert meat thermometer into thickest part of meat in the oven between breast and thigh, being careful that pointed end of thermometer does not touch bone.) 5. When chicken turns golden, cover loosely with a "tent" of folded foil. Remove foil towards end of roasting time and, with pastry-brush, brush chicken generously with pan drippings. Chicken is done when thickest part of leg feels soft when pinched with fingers protected by paper towels. (If using meat thermometer, chicken is done when temperature reaches 175° to 180°F.) 6. While chicken is roasting, prepare giblets and neck for use in gravy: In a 1-quart saucepan over high heat, heat giblets, neck, onions, 1 cup water, and ¼ teaspoon salt to boiling. Reduce heat to low; cover and simmer 30 minutes or until giblets are tender. Drain, reserving broth; discard onions. Pull meat from neck; discard bones; coarsely chop neck meat and giblets; refrigerate. 7. When chicken is done, place on warm platter; keep warm. Prepare gravy. Remove rack from roasting pan; pour pan drippings into a 2 cup measure or small bowl (set pan aside); let stand a few seconds until fat separates from meat juice. Skim 3 tablespoons fat from drippings into a 1-quart saucepan; skim off and discard any remaining fat. Add reserved giblet broth to roasting pan; stir until brown bits are loosened; add to meat juice in cup to make 1½ cups (add water if necessary). Into the fat in saucepan over medium heat, stir in flour and ¼ teaspoon salt until blended; gradually stir in meat juice mixture; cook, stirring constantly until mixture is thickened. Add reserved giblets and meat; cook until heated through. Pour gravy into gravy boat. 8. To serve, arrange parsley sprigs around chicken. Serve with gravy. Makes 6 servings.

Moist bread dressing

In a 4-quart saucepan over medium heat, melt ½ cup butter or margarine; add 1 medium celery stalk diced and 1 medium onions, diced; cook until vegetables are tender (about 10 minutes) stirring frequently. Remove saucepan from heat. Stir in 2 tablespoons minced parsley, ¾ teaspoon salt, ½ teaspoon poultry seasoning and ¼ teaspoon pepper. Add 9 cups white-bread cubes, ¼ cup water, and 1 egg, slightly beaten; mix well.

46. RANCHER'S FRIED CHICKEN

Ingredients	*Quantity (4 Servings)*
Chicken	4 legs, 4 breasts

Ingredients	*Quantity (4 Servings)*
Eggs	3
Breadcrumbs	250 gm
Worcestershire sauce	
Salt as required	
Pepper as required	
Oil to fry	
Flour	100 gm
Oriental Sauce (see recipe below)	150 ml
French fries	400 gm

Method

1. Season the flour with salt and pepper. 2. Marinade the chicken in Worcestershire sauce, salt, pepper, mustard. 3. Roll the chicken in flour until evenly coated. 4. Break eggs and beat lightly. 5. Dip in egg and then coat with breadcrumbs. 6. Deep fry. 7. Serve with French Fries and Oriental Sauce.

ORIENTAL SAUCE

Ingredients	*Quantity*
Tomatoes (medium)	6
Green chillies	12 gm
Coriander leaves	5 gm
Salt	to taste
Oil to cook	
Peppercorns	2
Bayleaf	1
Onions	1
Garlic	15 gm
Ginger	2 gm
Tabasco	a pinch

Method

1. Clean the tomatoes, slit and keep aside. 2. Chop garlic, ginger, green chillies and coriander leaves. 3. Keep water for boiling. 4. Blanch the tomatoes and remove the skin. Remove the pulp and seed. Keep it aside. 5. Heat the oil. 6. Add peppercorns, bayleaf and sauté. 7. Add garlic and sauté. 8. Add chopped onions and sauté till transparent. Add ginger, green chilli and sauté till you get an aroma. 9. Add the blanched tomato pulp. 10. Cook for 20 minutes. 11. On cooking check for seasoning (salt). 12. Strain the sauce. Finish off with tabasco and stir to taste. 13. Garnish it with juliennes of ginger and chopped coriander. 14. Serve hot with any fried vegetarian and non-vegetarian items.

47. MASALA ROAST CHICKEN

Ingredients	*Quantity*
Chicken (medium-sized)	1
Butter	30gm (2 tbsp)
Good stock	1 cup
Grind to a fine paste	
Red chillies (without seeds)	5
Cloves	6
Cinnamon	½″ piece
Peppercorns	a few
Salt	
Garlic	6 cloves

Method

1. Clean chicken. 2. Apply ground spices inside and out. 3. Put back giblets into the chicken. 4. Smear the breast with butter. 5. Place in a roasting tin. 6. Pour stock around. 7. Roast the chicken in a fairly hot oven, Gas mark 6 or 400ºF for about 1 hour 15 minutes, or till done. 8. Dish out. 9. Surround with straw potatoes. 10. Serve gravy in a sauce boat. 11. Serve vegetable pulao, mint raita, pickle and pappad separately.

48. BAKED CHICKEN AND NOODLE CASSEROLE

Ingredients	*For 4*	*For 100*
Stewing chicken	500 gm	12.5 kg
Butter	40 gm	1 kg
Refined flour	25 gm	680 gm
Chicken broth	200 ml	5 litre
Milk	100-150 ml	2.5-3.75 litre
Salt	to taste	100 gm
White pepper	a pinch	1 tsp
Nutmeg	a pinch	½ tsp
Mushrooms (cooked)	30 gm	680 gm
Noodles	40 gm	1 kg
Bread	40 gm	1 kg
Butter (melted)	10 gm	225 gm

Method

1. Wash chicken, place in large kettle and cover with cold water. 2. Simmer chicken until tender. Cool, remove chicken, and reserve broth. 3. Cut chicken into 1.25 - 1.75 cm (½″ to ¾″) pieces. 4. Melt butter, add flour and blend well. 5. Gradually add milk and chicken broth, stirring constantly with a wire whip. 6. Add salt, pepper and nutmeg. 7. Cook until sauce is of medium thickness, and flour is thoroughly cooked.

8. Add chicken and mushrooms to sauce, and bring mixture to a simmering point. 9. In the meantime, cook noodles in boiling salted water until almost tender. Drain. 10. Stir cooked noodles into chicken mixture. 11. Toss bread cubes in melted butter. 12. Place approximately 160 gm (5 oz.) chicken noodle mixture in each individual greased casserole. 13. Top with buttered bread cubes. 14. Bake in a 175°C (350°F) oven until sauce is bubbly and bread cubes are golden brown (about 25 minutes).

49. CHICKEN TETRAZINI

Ingredients	*Quantity*
Cooked noodles	115 gm
Leeks or	2
Onions	1
Milk	400 ml
Cooked chicken	60 gm
Cooked ham	60 gm
Grated cheese	30 gm
Pepper, Salt	to taste
Shredded capsicum	

Method

1. Wash leeks, chop into rings. Dice ham; sliver chicken. Grease casserole. 2. Layer leeks, ham, chicken and noodles and chopped capsicum with salt, pepper and grated cheese. 3. Pour milk over. Bake at 193°C (380°F) for about half an hour. When ready, milk should be absorbed.

50. DEVILLED CHICKEN

Ingredients	*Quantity*
Chicken (broiler)	1
Onions	250 gm
Red chillies	5 gm
Mustard seeds	30 gm
Worcester sauce	
Vinegar	1 tbsp
Sugar	1 tsp
Salt	to taste
Lemon grass	½
Butter or fat	30 gm

Method

1. Grind mustard seeds and red chillies to a smooth paste using the

vinegar. 2. Mix together with Worcester sauce, sugar, salt and chopped lemon grass. Smear over chicken and set aside for an hour. 3. Melt butter or fat in a strong pan. Lightly fry chicken on both sides. Add quartered onions and sauté. Keep over slow fire and cook gently. The pan must be covered tightly. 4. Turn frequently and sprinkle with coconut milk or water to allow the chicken to roast evenly.

51. HOMEMADE BACON

Ingredients	*Quantity*
Pork	500 gm
Saltpetre	¾ tsp
Brown sugar	1 tsp
Salt	1 tbsp

Method

1. Select a piece of pork without bones. Do not wash but wipe it dry. 2. Mix saltpetre, sugar and salt and rub into pork. Put into a dish and keep in the refrigerator. 3. Turn daily for a fortnight. It is then ready for use.

52. BOILED HAM (A)

Ham
Raspings (browned breadcrumbs)
Brown sugar

Method

1. Soak ham for 12 hours. (24 hours if very salty). 2. Clean and trim. 3. Put into a pan with sufficient cold water to cover and simmer gently until tender—a little over an hour per kg 4. Remove from fire and let ham remain steeped in the water till cold (keep lid on). 5. Remove and strip off the skin. Leave in refrigerator to set. Sprinkle with browned breadcrumbs and sugar.

N.B. To ensure that the ham is sweet insert a sharp knife close to the bone. When withdrawn there should be no unpleasant smell.

BOILED HAM (B)

Ingredients	*Quantity*
Ham	1 kg
Vinegar	1 tsp
Onions	1
Raspings (browned breadcrumbs)	
Celery	1 head
Turnip	1
Savoury herbs	

Method

1. Soak ham in cold water for 12 hours. 2. Remove and soak in vinegar and water (1 tsp to 600 ml of water) for a few hours. 3. Remove, put into a pan and cover with cold water. Add sliced vegetables and herbs. Simmer gently till tender (allow a little over an hour per kg) 4. Cool in the same liquid. 5. Remove and strip off the skin, cover with raspings and put a paper frill round the knuckle.

53. BAKED HAM

Ingredients

Ham
Refined flour
Brown sugar
Cloves

Method

1. Soak ham in cold water for 12 hours. 2. Wipe well and trim. 3. Coat with a flour and water paste crust which must be sufficiently thick to keep the juices in. 4. Place the ham in an oven at 205ºC (400ºF)or Gas mark 6 for 15 minutes. 5. Reduce heat to 155 ºC (310ºF) or Gas mark 2 and cook till done (30 minutes per 450 gm and 30 minutes over). 6. Remove the crust and skin. Score squares in the fat and place a clove in each square sprinkling brown sugar over the fat. Decorate the knuckle with paper frill.

54. HOMEMADE HAM

Ingredients	*Quantity*
Pork (leg)	2.7 kg
Salt	250 gm
Lime juice	¼ cup.
Saltpetre	60 gm

Method

1. Wipe pork well. Prick with a fork all over and apply salt and lime juice. 2. Put the saltpetre into a strong empty tin. Burn a few coconut shells and put into the tin taking care to see that your face is not too close to the tin as the flame leaps up immediately. 3. When burnt, add one cup of cold water. Strain the liquid through a clean cloth. Pour over the pork and mix well. 4. Put the pork into a clean bowl and set aside for six days. After the 6th day, strain the liquid. Cover with fresh water. Add a pint of beer and boil for use.

VEGETABLES

1. Boiled Potatoes
2. Rice Potatoes
3. Roast Potatoes
4. Scalloped Potatoes
5. Macaire Potatoes
6. Parsley Potatoes
7. Creamed Potatoes
8. Potato Chips
9. Duchess Potatoes
10. Savoury Potatoes
11. Pommes de Terre Lyonnaise
12. Potato Salad
13. Potato Hongroise
14. Bubble and Squeak
15. Sweet Potato
16. Creamed Carrots
17. Glazed Carrots
18. Sautéd Carrots
19. French Beans
20. Boiled Peas
21. Boiled Cauliflower
22. Scalloped Cauliflower
23. Boiled Cabbage
24. Scalloped Marrow
25. Sautéd Tinda
26. Cauliflower Fried in Batter
27. Creamed Spinach
28. Spinach au Beurre
29. Purée of Spinach
30. Fried Aubergine (Egg plant)
31. Aubergine à la Turque
32. Grilled Tomatoes
33. Stuffed Tomatoes
34. Creamed Ladies Fingers
35. Sanfaina Verduras
36. Baked Beans
37. Mixed Vegetable Salad
38. Lettuce Salad
39. Green Salad
40. Tossed Salad
41. Cabbage Salad
42. Cole Slaw (A)
    Cole Slaw (B)
43. Capsicum Salad
44. Carrot and Celery Salad
45. Spring Onion Surprise
46. Boiled Beetroot
47. Waldorf Salad
48. Clock Salad

1. BOILED POTATOES

Ingredients	*For 4*	*For 100*
Potatoes	450 gm	11 kg
Salt	to taste	100-150 gm

Method

1. Wash, peel and rewash potatoes. 2. Cut into even-sized pieces. 4. Cook carefully in salted water till well cooked. 4. Drain well and serve hot.

2. RICE POTATOES

Ingredients	*For 4*	*For 100*
Potatoes	450 gm	11 kg
Salt	to taste	100-150 gm

Method

1. Wash, peel and rewash potatoes. 2. Cook in salted water till done. 3. Drain off the water. Place a lid on the saucepan and return to a low heat so as to dry out the potatoes. 4. Pass through a medium sieve or a special potato-masher directly into the serving dish. 5. Serve without further handling.

3. ROAST POTATOES

Ingredients	*For 4*	*For 100*
Potatoes	450 gm	11 kg
Salt	to taste	80-100 gm
Fat	250 gm	3 kg

Method

1. Wash, peel and rewash potatoes. 2. Cut into even-sized portions. 3. Parboil in salted water. Drain well. 4. Heat fat in a roasting tray. 5. Add the potatoes and lightly brown on all sides. 6. Cook in a hot oven turning the potatoes once or twice. 7. Cook to a golden brown. Drain. 8. Serve hot with roast meat.

N.B. Approximate cooking time: 1 hour.

4. SCALLOPED POTATOES

Ingredients	*For 4*	*For 100*
Potatoes	450 gm	11 kg
Refined flour	15 gm	340 gm
Butter	15 gm	340 gm
Milk	295 ml	7.37 litre
Onions	115 gm	1.36 kg
Parsley	1 sprig	45 gm

Method

1. Boil and peel potatoes and cut into thin round slices. 2. Prepare white sauce, add chopped parsley and grated onions. 3. Arrange sliced potatoes in a greased pie dish. 4. Pour sauce over it. Dot with butter and bake in a hot oven till top is browned.

N.B. Sauce should cover the potatoes.

5. MACAIRE POTATOES

Ingredients	*For 4*	*For 100*
Potatoes	455 gm	11.3 kg

Ingredients	For 4	For 100
Butter	20 gm	450 gm
Fat to fry	30 gm	500 gm
Salt	to taste	100 gm
Pepper	to taste	15 gm

Method

1. Parboil potatoes in their jackets. 2. Bake potatoes till well-cooked. 3. Cut into half and scoop out the flesh. 4. Mash well with butter and seasoning. 5. Spread and press down the preparation on a greased fry pan. 6. Brown both sides and serve hot.

6. PARSLEY POTATOES

Ingredients	For 4	For 100
Potatoes (medium, even-sized)	450 gm	11 kg
Butter	15 gm	250 gm
Parsley	a few sprigs	55 gm
Salt	to taste	80-100 gm

Method

1. Boil potatoes in their jackets till well-cooked. 2. Drain. Dry off moisture. Cool and peel. 3. Melt butter in a sufficiently large pan. Add salt. 4. Put in the peeled potatoes. Toss well. Serve hot garnished with chopped parsley.

7. CREAMED POTATOES

Ingredients	For 4	For 100
Potatoes	450 gm	11 kg
Milk	30 ml	640 ml
Butter	30 gm	680 gm
Salt	10 gm	100 gm

Method

1. Peel and boil potatoes with salt. 2. When well-cooked drain off water. Dry on fire and mash well. 3. Add milk and butter and beat well to a fluffy consistency.

8. POTATO CHIPS

Ingredients	For 4	For 100
Potatoes	450 gm	11 kg
Salt	10 gm	100 gm
Fat to fry (absorption)	30 gm	500 gm

Method

1. Peel potatoes. Wash and cut into fingers. 2. Deep fry till crisp. Add salt.

N.B. An alternative is to parboil potatoes and then peel and cut into fingers and deep fry.

9. DUCHESS POTATOES

Ingredients	*For 4*	*For 100*
Potatoes	225 gm	5.65 kg
Eggs	1	8
Hot milk	30 ml	475 ml
Butter	15 gm	340 gm
Salt	10 gm	100 gm
White pepper	a pinch	15 gm

Method

1. Peel and boil potatoes till tender. 2. Strain and mash or sieve. 3. Stir the fat into the hot sieved potatoes. 4. Mix well; add beaten egg and milk. 5. Add seasoning. 6. Fill forcing bag and squeeze mixture out on to a greased baking sheet in the shape of roses or pyramids. 7. Brush with beaten egg or melted butter. 8. Bake in a quick oven till brown, at 205ºC (400ºF) or Gas mark 6 for 10 minutes.

10. SAVOURY POTATOES

Ingredients	*For 4*	*For 100*
Potatoes (even-sized)	500 gm	12.5 kg
Cheese	30 gm	680 gm
Butter	30 gm	680 gm
Milk	60 ml	1.5 litre
Breadcrumbs	30 gm	455 gm
Salt	to taste	100 gm
White pepper	to taste	15 gm

Method

1. Bake potatoes in a hot oven in their jackets. 2. Cut in two lengthwise, scoop out the inside. 3. Mash scooped potatoes and season, add butter, milk and grated cheese. 4. Mix thoroughly and put mixture back into jackets. 5. Top with breadcrumbs and bake in a moderate oven till brown. Serve hot.

N.B. Potatoes may be parboiled in their jackets before baking to hasten cooking process.

11. POMMES DE TERRE LYONNAISE

Ingredients	*For 4*	*For 100*
Potatoes	450 gm	11 kg
Onions	115 gm	2.8 kg
Parsley	a few sprigs	4 bunches
Pepper	a pinch	15 gm
Salt	to taste	80-100 gm
Fat	30 gm	680 gm

Method

1. Boil potatoes, peel and cut into rounds. 2. Slice onions and fry till golden brown. Remove. 3. Toss potatoes in fat. Add onions. Mix well. Remove and serve hot garnished with chopped parsley.

12. POTATO SALAD

Cold cooked potatoes sliced neatly make a popular salad. Sprinkle the slices well with dressing and top with a little chopped parsley.

Chopped onions may be sprinkled over if required.

Potato and beetroot combine well but remember not to arrange them together until required or the beetroot will discolour the potato. Sliced or chopped nuts can be mixed with the dressing and added.

13. POTATO HONGROISE

Ingredients	*For 4*	*For 100*
Potatoes	450 gm	11 kg
Tomatoes	115 gm	2.8 kg
Onions	115 gm	2.8 kg
Salt	10 gm	100 gm
Paprika	5 gm	115 gm
Stock		
Parsley	¼ bunch	2 bunches
Fat	15 gm	225 gm

Method

1. Boil potatoes in the skin. Peel. 2. Cut into roundels. 3. Slice onions and fry. 4. Add paprika and blanched tomatoes. 5. Add potato roundels and salt. 6. Put the whole thing into a pyrex dish (as for scalloped potato). Add a little stock if necessary. 7. Cook in a slow oven till potatoes are tender and moisture reduced. Sprinkle with chopped parsley and serve hot.

14. BUBBLE AND SQUEAK

Ingredients	*For 4*	*For 100*
Potatoes	225 gm	5.45 kg
Cabbage	225 gm	5.45 kg
Onions	30 gm	680 gm
Pepper	to taste	15 gm
Salt	10 gm	100 gm
Capsicum (optional)	30 gm	455 gm
Fat	30 gm	500 gm

Method

1. Wash and boil potatoes and cabbage and mash. 2. Mince onions and capsicum (remove seeds first). 3. Mix all the ingredients with seasoning. 4. Heat a frying pan, smear with fat. 5. Press down the mixture to fill the pan. 6. When brown on one side, turn over and brown the other. 7. Cut in portions and serve hot.

15. SWEET POTATO

Ingredients	*For 4*	*For 100*
Sweet potato	450 gm	11 kg

Method

1. Wash sweet potatoes; parboil. 2. Grease a baking dish. Place potatoes in a tray and bake in a slow oven till quite tender.

16. CREAMED CARROTS

Ingredients	*For 4*	*For 100*
Carrots	225 gm	5.65 kg
Butter	15 gm	340 gm
Salt	to taste	80 gm

Method

1. Wash and peel carrots. 2. Cut into thin roundels. 3. Barely cover with water. Add salt. 4. Simmer gently until tender. 5. Drain well. 6. Mash with a fork or pass through a sieve. 7. Return to the pan, reheat, and mix in the butter, and correct the seasoning. 8. Serve dome-shaped in a hot vegetable dish. Decorate with a palette knife.

17. GLAZED CARROTS

Ingredients	*For 4*	*For 100*
Carrots	225 gm	5.6 kg

Ingredients	For 4	For 100
Sugar	10 gm	225 gm
Butter	15 gm	340 gm
Salt	10 gm	100 gm
Parsley	1 sprig	2 bunches

Method

1. Wash, scrape and dice carrots or cut in roundels. 2. Cook together carrots, sugar, butter and salt with enough water to cook carrots. 3. When all the liquid has evaporated and carrots are tender, remove from fire. 4. Dish out, garnish with chopped parsley. Serve hot.

18. SAUTEED CARROTS

Ingredients	For 4	For 100
Carrots	450 gm	11 kg
Butter	30 gm	680 gm
Salt	to taste	80-100 gm

Method

1. Scrape or peel carrots. Dice or cut into rounds. 2. Boil in salted water. Drain and sauté in butter. Serve hot.

19. FRENCH BEANS

Ingredients	For 4	For 100
French beans	450 gm	11 kg
Butter	30 gm	680 gm
Salt	to taste	80-100 gm

Method

1. Boil just enough water to cover beans. 2. Wash, string and slice beans diagonally. 3. Add beans to boiling water. Cook till tender. Add salt. 4. Drain and save liquid for soup or stock. 5. Melt butter and toss beans in the butter.

20. BOILED PEAS

Ingredients	For 4	For 100
Peas (whole)	1 kg	25 kg
Salt	to taste	80-100 gm
Mint	1 sprig	1 bunch
Butter	30 gm	500 gm
Sugar	½ tsp	60 gm

Method

1. Shell and wash peas. 2. Cook in boiling salted water, with the mint, until tender. 3. Drain in a colander. 4. Add butter and powdered sugar and toss gently. 5. Serve in a vegetable dish with mint leaves.

21. BOILED CAULIFLOWER

Ingredients	*For 4*	*For 100*
Cauliflower	450 gm (1)	11 kg (25)
Salt	to taste	80-100 gm

Method

1. Trim the stem and remove outer leaves. 2. Hollow out the stem with a peeler. 3. Wash well. 4. Cook in boiling salted water till done. 5. Drain well and serve whole on a serviette, placed on a flat dish or with each cauliflower cut into 4 even portions in a vegetable dish.

N.B. One medium-sized cauliflower takes about 20 minutes to cook.

22. SCALLOPED CAULIFLOWER

Ingredients	*For 4*	*For 100*
Cauliflower	450 gm	11 kg
Milk	225 ml	5.9 litre
Refined flour	15 gm	340 gm
Butter	15 gm	340 gm
Onions	55 gm	1.35 kg
Parsley	1 sprig	2 bunches
Butter for dotting	10 gm	200 gm

Method

1. Boil cauliflower in salted water. 2. Prepare white sauce using flour, butter, milk and cauliflower liquor. 3. Add grated onions and chopped parsley. 4. Arrange cauliflower in pyrex dish. 5. Pour sauce over. Sauce should cover the cauliflower completely. 6. Dot with butter and bake in quick oven or under a griller to brown top.

23. BOILED CABBAGE

Ingredients	*For 4*	*For 100*
Cabbage	450 gm	11 kg
Butter	30 gm	680 gm
Salt	to taste	100 gm

Method

1. Wash cabbage. Cut into quarters. 2. Boil in salted water till tender. 3. Drain. Pour melted butter over and serve chopped into smaller pieces or cut into half.

24. SCALLOPED MARROW

Ingredients	*For 4*	*For 100*
Vegetable marrow	450 gm	11 kg
Milk	150 ml	3.75 litre
Vegetable stock	295 ml	7.5 litre
Butter	15 gm	340 gm
Refined flour	15 gm	340 gm
Salt	5-10 gm	100 gm
Pepper	a pinch	15 gm
Onions	115 gm	1.35 kg
Parsley	½ bunch	3 bunches

Method

1. Peel and parboil vegetable marrow. 2. Prepare a white sauce (medium) with flour, butter, milk and stock. Add seasoning, minced onions and chopped parsley. 3. Put marrow in a greased casserole dish; cover with sauce and brown in an oven.

25. SAUTÉD TINDA

Ingredients	*For 4*	*For 100*
Round Gourds (Tinda)	450 gm	11 kg
Onions	115 gm	1.35 kg
Fat	30 gm	680 gm
Salt	to taste	80-100 gm

Method

1. Wash and peel gourds. 2. Cut into quarters. 3. Barely cover with water, add salt. 4. Simmer till tender. 5. Drain. 6. Slice onions. 7. Heat fat, sauté onions. Add boiled tinda and sauté. Remove and serve hot.

26. CAULIFLOWER FRIED IN BATTER

Ingredients	*For 4*	*For 100*
Cauliflower	450 gm	11 kg
Refined flour	30 gm	680 gm
Eggs	1	12
Milk	150 ml	3.75 litre
Pepper	a pinch	15 gm

Ingredients	*For 4*	*For 100*
Salt	to taste	80-100 gm
Fat to fry (absorption)	30 gm	500 gm

Method

1. Parboil cauliflower in salted boiling water. 2. Drain and keep liquor. 3. Prepare a batter with egg, milk and flour using cauliflower liquor if more liquid is necessary. 4. Break cauliflower into flowerettes. Dip in batter and deep fry. 5. Drain on absorbent paper. Serve hot.

27. CREAMED SPINACH

Ingredients	*For 4*	*For 100*
Spinach	4 bunches	100 bunches
Butter	30 gm	680 gm
Salt	to taste	80-100 gm
Pepper	a pinch	15 gm

Method

1. Wash the spinach thoroughly in cold water after removing any coarse leaves. 2. Place in a saucepan with only the water adhering to the leaves after washing. 3. Cook till tender. Drain. 4. Chop and rub through a sieve. Add butter and seasoning.

N.B. Cream may be added instead of butter or a little flour may be mixed with the butter and added to the spinach.

28. SPINACH AU BEURRE

Ingredients	*For 4*	*For 100*
Spinach	450 gm	11 kg
Butter	30 gm	680 gm
Salt	to taste	80-100 gm

Method

1. Wash spinach very well. 2. Put into a pan with salt. Bring to boil quickly. Reduce heat and let it cook. 3. Add a little water if necessary. 4. When cooked remove, chop fine. Add melted butter. Mix and serve hot.

29. PURÉE OF SPINACH

Ingredients	*For 4*	*For 100*
Spinach	450 gm	11 kg
Onions	55 gm	1.35 kg
Butter	55 gm	1.35 kg
Salt	to taste	100 gm

Method

1. Wash spinach several times. 2. Add salt and onions and bring to boil quickly. 3. Cook on a slow fire till spinach is cooked and water is evaporated. 4. Mash—reheat and add butter.

30. FRIED AUBERGINE (Egg plant)

Ingredients	*For 4*	*For 100*
Aubergine	450 gm	11 kg
Oil to fry	30 ml	500 ml
Salt	to taste	30-50 ml
Pepper	a pinch	15 gm

Method

1. Cut the aubergine into thin roundels. 2. Season and dredge them. 3. Fry in smoking oil. 4. Dish them on a napkin and serve immediately.

31. AUBERGINES À LA TURQUE

Ingredients	*For 4*	*For 100*
Aubergine	450 gm	11 kg
Pepper	a pinch	15 gm
Salt	to taste	30-50 gm
Egg yolks	1	12
Cheese	30 gm	640 gm
Oil to fry		
Batter		
Refined flour	15 gm	455 gm
Egg white	1	12
Water		
Salt	to taste	30-50 gm

Method

1. Cut aubergine lengthwise into thin slices. 2. Season and fry these slices in oil. 3. Pair them off and join them together by means of a very firm preparation of raw egg yolk and grated cheese. 4. When ready to serve, dip them in batter and deep fry in smoking oil. 5. Serve hot.

32. GRILLED TOMATOES

Ingredients	*For 4*	*For 100*
Tomatoes	225 gm	5.65 kg
Salt	to taste	80-100 gm
Pepper	to taste	15 gm
Butter	15 gm	115 gm

Method

1. Wash and cut tomatoes in halves. 2. Season and dot them with butter; grill till cooked.

33. STUFFED TOMATOES

Ingredients	*For 4*	*For 100*
Tomatoes (even-sized)	500 gm (4)	12.5 kg (100)
Potatoes	115 gm	2.8 kg
Turnip	55 gm	1.35 kg
Carrots	115 gm	2.8 kg
Peas	115 gm	2.8 kg
Onions	55 gm	1.36 kg
Mayonnaise sauce	150 ml	2.95 litre
Lettuce leaves	55 gm	1.35 kg
Salt	to taste	80-100 gm

Method

1. Select good round tomatoes. Slice top, scoop out inside, sprinkle salt and leave to drain upside down. 2. Dice and boil vegetables, mix with mayonnaise, and stuff tomatoes. Chill. 3. Serve on a bed of lettuce leaves.

34. CREAMED LADIES FINGERS

Ingredients	*For 4*	*For 100*
Ladies fingers	225 gm	5.6 kg
Refined flour	15 gm	340 gm
Butter	15 gm	340 gm
Milk	295 ml	7.35 litre
Salt	10 gm	100 gm
Pepper	a pinch	15 gm
Fat	30 gm	225 gm

Method

1. Prepare ladies fingers and parboil in salted water. 2. Prepare a thick white sauce with flour, butter and milk. 3. Heat fat and toss ladies fingers in fat. 4. Cohere with the sauce and serve hot.

N.B. 115 ml of cream can be added to every 590 ml of milk used.

35. SAFAINA VERDURAS

Ingredients	*For 4*	*For 100*
Potatoes	450 gm	11 kg
Aubergine	115 gm	2.8 kg

Ingredients	For 4	For 100
Tomatoes	450 gm	11 kg
Onions	225 gm	5.6 kg
Capsicum	55 gm	1.36 kg
Oil	30-50 ml	680 ml–1 litre
Salt	to taste	80–100 gm
Tomato sauce or vegetable stock		

Method

1. Parboil potatoes. 2. Peel and cut into thin roundels. 3. Wash and cut aubergine into roundels. 4. Slice tomatoes and onions. 5. Remove seeds from capsicum and slice. 6. Heat oil. Fry each vegetable separately. 7. Arrange in layers in a pie dish. Pour some tomato sauce or vegetable stock over. 8. Bake in a moderate oven for 10-15 minutes.

36. BAKED BEANS

Ingredients	For 4	For 100
Haricot beans	30 gm	680 gm
Tomatoes	450 gm	11 kg
Molasses	10 gm	250 gm
Bacon	15 gm	340 gm
Vinegar	15 ml	340 ml
Salt	to taste	100 gm
Pepper	to taste	15 gm

Method

1. Wash and soak beans overnight. 2. Boil till tender in the same liquid. 3. Drain (use liquor for stock). 4. Blanch tomatoes and make a purée. Add vinegar. 6. Pour into pyrex or aluminium pie dishes and bake covered in a moderate oven for 15–20 minutes.

37. MIXED VEGETABLE SALAD

Ingredients	For 4	For 100
Carrots	225 gm	5.6 kg
Cucumber	115 gm	2.8 kg
Tomatoes	115 gm	2.8 kg
Red radish	30 gm	340 gm
Lettuce leaves	1 bunch	25 bunches

Method

1. Wash and grate carrots. 2. Peel and slice cucumber. 3. Slice tomatoes

and radish. 4. Wash and drain lettuce without squeezing. 5. Arrange as desired. Serve with a salad dressing.

N.B. Hard-boiled eggs and strips of ham may be included to make the salad more substantial.

38. LETTUCE SALAD

When lettuce is served alone as a salad it is generally called a French salad. The lettuce is washed and drained (not squeezed) and just before serving, a French dressing is mixed with the lettuce. If the dressing is added any length of time before serving, the vinegar in the dressing will break down the fibres of the lettuce and it will become soft and unappetising.

FRENCH DRESSING FOR LETTUCE SALAD

Ingredients (mix well together)	*Quantity*
Vinegar	1 tbsp
Oil	3 tbsp
Sugar	1 salt spoon
Salt	1 salt spoon
Black pepper	1 salt spoon

39. GREEN SALAD

Ingredients	*For 4*	*For 100*
Cabbage	225 gm	5.66 kg
Capsicum	55 gm	1.35 kg
Onions	30 gm	680 gm
Salad oil	30 ml	700 ml
Vinegar	10 ml	250 ml
Salt	10 gm	100 gm
Garlic	1 small piece	1 clove

Method

1. Shred cabbage fine. 2. Remove seeds from capsicum. Chop fine. Chop onions and garlic fine. 3. Mix all ingredients together one hour before serving.

40. TOSSED SALAD

Ingredients	*For 4*	*For 100*
Lettuce	1 bunch	25 bunches
Tomatoes	225 gm	5.65 kg
Carrots	115 gm	2.8 kg

Ingredients	For 4	For 100
Red radish	115 gm	2.8 kg
French dressing	100 ml	2.5 litre

Method

1. Wash and prepare vegetables. Break lettuce and cut radish into flowers. Chill. 2. Cut tomatoes into wedges, slice carrots. 3. Combine together prepared vegetables in bowl. 4. Pour French dressing over vegetables just before serving and gently mix.

41. CABBAGE SALAD

Ingredients	For 4	For 100
Cabbage (fresh)	225 gm	5.65 kg
Onions	55 gm	1.35 kg
Capsicum	55 gm	1.35 kg
Salad oil	30 ml	680 ml
Lime juice	1	12
Salt	to taste	80-100 gm

Method

1. Shred cabbage fine. Remove seeds from capsicum and chop fine. Chop onions finely. 2. Mix all ingredients together.

N.B. Finely diced carrots can be used to garnish.

42. COLE SLAW (A)

Ingredients	For 4	For 100
Cabbage	225 gm	5.65 kg
Cream dressing		
Sugar	15 gm	340 gm
Salt	a pinch	50 gm
Pepper	a pinch	15 gm
Cayenne pepper	a small	pinch
Onions	30 gm	680 gm
Green pepper (without seeds)	15 gm	340 gm
Cream	30 ml	680 ml
Vinegar (mild)	10 ml	250 ml

Method

1. Shred cabbage finely. 2. Mix dry ingredients of the sauce, minced onions and finely chopped green pepper. 3. Add cream and vinegar. Beat until thickened. 4. Mix with shredded cabbage.

COLE SLAW (B)

Ingredients	*For 4*	*For 100*
Cabbage	225 gm	5.6 kg
Vinegar	60 ml	1.4 litre
Sugar	45 gm	1.2 kg
Salt	a pinch	80-100 gm

Method

1. Shred cabbage fine. Mix all ingredients.

43. CAPSICUM SALAD

Ingredients	*For 4*	*For 100*
Capsicums	225 gm	5.65 kg
Lime	1	12
Sugar	a pinch	30 gm
Salt	to taste	80-100 gm

Method

1. Slit capsicums into two. Remove seeds and wash well. 2. Cut into fine slices. Add sugar, salt and lime juice. Mix well.

44. CARROT AND CELERY SALAD

Ingredients	*For 4*	*For 100*
Carrots	225 gm	5.6 kg
Celery	1 head	1.36 kg
Nuts	55 gm	1.25 kg
Mustard	1 tsp	15 gm
Pickled onions	4	25 gm
Mayonnaise	30 ml	680 ml
Cabbage lettuce	¼ bunch	25 bunches

Method

1. Clean and grate carrots. 2. Take out the white part of celery and chop fine. 3. Chop nuts. 4. Wash lettuce and arrange in a circle around the salad dish. 5. Mix finely chopped pickled onions and mustard with mayonnaise. Mix carrots, celery and nuts. 6. Place in the centre.

45. SPRING ONION SURPRISE

Method

Wash carefully and shred, the heart of a lettuce and mix with a few finely chopped spring onions and olive oil. Add two chopped olives, some chopped chives and a little parsley. Garnish with sliced, hard-boiled egg and serve with cold sliced potatoes sprinkled with salad cream and parsley.

46. BOILED BEETROOT

Method

Wash and cook in the steamer or in gently simmering water till tender (test by skinning). Cool and peel. Dice or cut into slices. Serve plain with vinegar or sprinkled with vinaigrette.

47. WALDORF SALAD

Ingredients	*Quantity*
Apples (diced)	10 cups
Celery (diced)	5 cups
Broken walnuts	2½ cups
Mayonnaise or cooked salad dressing	1 cup
Heavy cream	¼ cup

Method

1. Combine apples and celery; marinade with French dressing or sprinkle with lemon juice to prevent discolouring. 2. Just before serving, add nuts and mix with mayonnaise or cooked salad dressing thinned with cream. 3. Serve on crisp lettuce. Garnish with cherries, if desired.

N.B. For colour, do not peel apples.

48. CLOCK SALAD

Ingredients	*Quantity*
Hard-boiled eggs	6
Potatoes	¾ kg
Cucumber (large)	1
Tomatoes	½ kg
Chopped parsley	1 tbsp
Mayonnaise	½ cup
Onions (minced)	1 tsp
Salt, pepper	to taste
Pink colouring	125 gm

Method

1. Peel potatoes thinly, cook in the usual way until just tender. 2. Drain and dice. 3. When quite cold mix with mayonnaise, parsley, onions, salt and pepper to taste. 4. Spread over base of a large platter rising slightly towards centre. 5. Smooth surface with a knife-blade. 6. Cut strip of skin from cucumber and fashion hands of clock. 7. Score rest of unpeeled cucumber, cut into thin slices and arrange around edge of platter. 8. Shell eggs, cut into halves lengthwise and arrange around platter in

same position as numbers on a clock. 9. Place tomato wedges between egg halves, giving scalloped edge to platter. 10. Soften cream cheese with a little milk, beat with wooden spoon until soft and smooth. Colour pink. 11. Pipe cream cheese onto eggs in the form of figures. Arrange cucumber hands in position. 12. Chill before serving. Extra salad ingredients such as lettuce, cress, radish, pineapple wedges etc. may be served in a separate bowl.

MAYONNAISE

Ingredients	*Quantity*
Egg yolk	1
Mustard	1 tsp
Sugar	1 pinch
Salt	to taste
White pepper	a pinch
Vinegar	1 tbsp
Salad oil	130 ml
Lime	½

Method

1. Put yolk of egg into a bowl with sugar, salt, mustard and pepper. 2. Cream well. 3. Add salad oil drop by drop. Keep beating vigorously with a wooden spoon all the time. 4. As sauce gets thicker moisten slightly with vinegar. 5. Keep adding salad oil and beating. 6. Taste for seasoning and add lime juice. Mix well.

COLD SWEETS

1. Fruit Salad
2. Fairy Pudding
3. Banana Custard
4. Banana Whip
5. Stewed Guavas
6. Blancmange
7. Marshmallow Pudding
8. Neapolitan Mousse
9. Coffee Mousse
10. Honeycomb Mould
11. Butterscotch Sponge
12. Amber Cream
13. Spanish Cream or Crème d'Espagne
14. Lemon Sponge
15. Pineapple Sponge
16. Mango Fluff
17. Caramel Custard
18. Fruit Trifle
19. Sago Cream
20. Prune Mould
21. Summer Pudding
22. Moss Jelly
23. Diplomat Pudding
24. Mawa and Almond Pudding
25. Refrigerator Cake
26. Ice-cream in a Refrigerator
    Basic Recipe (A)
    Basic Recipe (B)
27. Ice-cream with Evaporated Milk

28. Ice-cream with Condensed and Evaporated Milk
29. Condensed Milk Ice-cream
30. Tutti Frutti
31. Almond Ice-cream
32. Pineapple Ice-cream
33. Vanilla Ice-cream
34. Coffee Ice-cream
35. Banana Ice-cream
36. Custard for Ice-cream

1. FRUIT SALAD

Ingredients	*For 4*	*For 100*
Oranges	1	25
Pineapple	225 gm	5.5 kg
Bananas	2	50
Cherries (fresh or tinned)	110	2.8 kg
Apples	55 gm	1.35 kg
Cinnamon	a small piece	10 gm
Cloves	2	10 gm
Cream	55 gm	1.35 kg
Sugar	115 gm	2.8 kg

Method

1. Boil water and sugar. Add cinnamon and cloves. 2. When syrup is quite thick, remove and cool. Strain and mix with prepared fruit. 3. Serve with cream or custard sauce.

2. FAIRY PUDDING

Ingredients	*For 4*	*For 100*
Water	300 ml	7.5 litre
Sugar	60 gm	1.5 kg
Lime or	½	12
Lemon	1	25
Egg white	1	25
Cornflour	15 gm	340 gm

Method

1. Boil the water with grated lemon rind and sugar. 2. Blend the cornflour with the lemon juice. 3. Strain sugar solution on to blended cornflour. 4. Return to pan and boil for 6 to 8 minutes. 5. Whip the white of egg stiffly and fold into the mixture when it has cooled slightly. 6. Pour into wet moulds and turn out when set. 7. Serve with custard sauce.

CUSTARD SAUCE

Ingredients	*For 4*	*For 100*
Egg yolk	1	25

Ingredients	*For 4*	*For 100*
Milk	150 ml	3.5 litre
Sugar	10 gm	250 gm
Salt	a pinch	5 gm

Method

1. Beat egg. Add sugar and salt. 2. Pour hot milk over. Stir well. 3. Pour into a double boiler and cook till thick.

3. BANANA CUSTARD

Ingredients	*For 4*	*For 100*
Bananas	4	100
Custard powder	15 gm	340 gm
Milk	150 ml	3.75 litre
Sugar	30 gm	680 gm
Vanilla essence	a few drops	10 gm
Lime	a few drops	1

Method

1. Blend custard powder, sugar and a little cold milk to form a smooth paste. 2. Boil remaining milk. Pour over paste. Blend well and return to fire. 3. Cook till custard coats the back of a wooden spoon. Add vanilla to flavour. 4. Cool and add sliced bananas.

N.B. A few drops of lime juice must be sprinkled over the sliced bananas to prevent discoloration.

4. BANANA WHIP

Ingredients	*Quantity*
Bananas (green)	3
Egg whites	2
Sugar	10 gm
Cashewnuts (chopped)	a few
Vanilla essence	
Lime juice	a few drops

Method

1. Mash bananas. 2. Add lime juice, egg whites and sugar. Whisk with a rotary beater. 3. Add vanilla. chill for 5 minutes. 4. Garnish with chopped cashewnuts or walnuts and serve.

5. STEWED GUAVAS

Ingredients	For 4	For 100
Guavas	450 gm	11 kg
Sugar	30 gm	680 gm
Cloves	a few	10 gm
Lime	½	6

Method

1. Clean, wash and peel guavas and cut into quarters. 2. Add enough water to stew. When half done take off fire, and remove seeds. 3. Put back on fire and when water boils add sugar and cloves. 4. When guavas are tender and syrup thickens add lime juice and take off the fire. Cool. Remove the cloves and serve with custard sauce.

6. BLANCMANGE

Ingredients	For 4	For 100
Cornflour	30 gm	680 gm
Milk	590 ml	14.75 litre
Sugar	55 gm	1.35 kg
Cocoa (optional)	5 gm	115 gm

Method

1. Mix together cornflour, sugar and enough cold milk to form a smooth paste. 2. Boil remaining milk. Add to the paste, stirring well. 3. Put back on fire. Cook till thick. 4. Add colouring and flavouring and set in wet moulds in layers.

N.B. To add cocoa, mix with a little cold milk and add to one portion, cook for a few minutes longer and set over the previous layers.

7. MARSHMALLOW PUDDING

Ingredients	For 4	For 100
Eggs	2	50
Gelatine	10 gm	300 gm
Hot water	20 ml	500 ml (about)
Sugar	30 gm	680 gm
Vanilla essence	a few drops	20 ml
Pink and green colouring		

Method

1. Separate whites and yolks of eggs carefully. Keep yolks aside for sauce. 2. Whisk whites very stiffly. 3. Add sugar gradually. 4. Dissolve gelatine in warm water and add drop by drop to the sugar and egg mixture. 5. Add vanilla essence. 6. Separate into 3 bowls. Colour one pink, one

green, and keep one white. Pour in layers into wet moulds and chill. Serve with chocolate sauce.

CHOCOLATE SAUCE

Ingredients	*For 4*	*For 100*
Egg yolks	1	25
Milk	150 ml	3.75 litre
Cocoa	10 gm	250 gm
Sugar	10 gm	250 gm

Method

1. Beat the yolks, add milk and sugar and heat over low flame. 2. Add cocoa to a little cold milk. Make into a smooth paste. Add to the sauce. Cook for a few minutes longer. Serve hot with cold marshmallows.

8. NEAPOLITAN MOUSSE

Ingredients	*For 4*	*For 100*
Milk	500 ml	8.85 litre
Eggs	2	30
Gelatine	15 gm	215 gm
Cream	15 gm	340 gm
Cherries	10 gm	225 gm
Sugar	55 gm	1.35 kg
Coffee, almond and raspberry essence and pink and green colouring		

Method

1. Soak gelatine in a little water for 5 minutes. 2. Separate yolks and whites of eggs. 3. Beat yolks and sugar thoroughly. Add soaked gelatine. 4. Warm milk and pour over the mixture. 5. Put into a double saucepan over flame and cook until gelatine dissolves and mixture thickens like custard. Do not boil. 6. Remove from heat and divide evenly into 3 bowls. 7. Flavour one with coffee essence, one with almond essence and one with raspberry essence. Tint with green and pink (colours should be pale). 8. Divide stiffly beaten egg whites into 3 and fold in one part into each bowl. 9. When mixture is cold, set in layers in refrigerator. 10. Decorate with whipped cream and cherries.

9. COFFEE MOUSSE

Ingredients	*For 4*	*For 100*
Milk	500 ml	8.85 litre
Eggs	2	30

Ingredients	For 4	For 100
Gelatine	15 gm	215 gm
Cream	15 gm	340 gm
Cherries	10 gm	225 gm
Sugar	55 gm	795 gm
Coffee essence		

Method

1. Soak gelatine in a little warm water for 5 minutes. 2. Separate yolks and whites of eggs. 3. Beat yolks and sugar thoroughly. 4. Warm milk and pour over the mixture. 5. Put in double saucepan over low flame and cook till custard thickens. 6. Remove from fire and add dissolved gelatine and essence. 7. Cool and fold in stiffly beaten egg whites. 8. Set in refrigerator. 9. Turn out and decorate with whipped cream and glacé cherries.

10. HONEYCOMB MOULD

Ingredients	For 4	For 100
Eggs	2	50
Gelatine	15 gm	225 gm
Milk	590 ml	9.45 litre
Sugar	30 gm	680 gm
Vanilla essence	a few drops	15 ml
Water	80 ml	1.18 litre

Method

1. Prepare a custard with the yolk of eggs, sugar and milk. 2. Add gelatine dissolved in warm water. 3. Allow to cool and add the flavouring. 4. Beat egg whites very stiffly and fold into the custard. 5. Keep bowl over ice or in cold water and stir occasionally. 6. When on the point of setting, pour into a wet mould and leave to set in the refrigerator.

11. BUTTERSCOTCH SPONGE

Ingredients	For 4	For 100
Eggs	2	36
Brown sugar	30 gm	680 gm
Butter	30 gm	680 gm
Gelatine	10 gm	200 gm
Milk	295 ml	4 litre
Salt	a small pinch	a pinch
Vanilla essence	to flavour	2¼ tsp

Method

1. Caramelize butter and sugar over a slow fire. 2. Pour boiling milk over the caramel. When sugar is dissolved, pour over beaten egg yolks, stirring vigorously. 3. Return to fire and cook till thick. 4. Leave aside and add dissolved gelatine when custard is just warm. 5. Leave on ice. 6. When it starts setting, fold in stiffly beaten egg whites. 7. Pour into moulds and set in refrigerator.

12. AMBER CREAM

Ingredients	*For 4*	*For 100*
Gelatine	3 tsp (½ pkt.)	150 gm
Hot water	150 ml	3.75 litre
Golden syrup	2 tbsp (40 gm)	1 kg
Eggs	1	25
Salt	a pinch	10 gm
Milk	150 ml	3.75 litre
Vanilla essence	to taste	3 tsp

Method

1. Heat milk. Add to beaten egg yolk. 2. Return to fire. 3. Cook till mixture thickens. Remove and cool. 4. Dissolve gelatine in hot water. 5. Add golden syrup. Stir into custard. 6. Beat together egg whites and salt till stiff. 7. Fold into the mixture. Add vanilla to flavour. 8. Place in a mould and leave to set in refrigerator.

13. SPANISH CREAM OR CREME D'ESPAGNE

Ingredients	*For 4*	*For 100*
Gelatine (if Davis, 1 pkt.)	12-15 gm	240 gm
Sugar	75 gm	1.5 kg
Salt	a pinch	10 gm
Eggs	2	40
Milk	500 ml	10 litre
Vanilla	1 tsp	2 tbsp (30 ml)

Method

1. Mix together gelatine, 2 tablespoons sugar and a pinch of salt. Heat in a double boiler till melted. 2. Beat egg yolks. Add milk. 3. Add to gelatine mixture. Cook over boiling water stirring constantly until gelatine is thoroughly dissolved (about 10 minutes). 4. Remove from heat. Add vanilla. Chill to unbeaten egg consistency. 5. Beat egg whites with remaining sugar until stiff. 6. Fold into gelatine mixture. 7. Chill until firm.

14. LEMON SPONGE

Ingredients	*For 4*	*For 100*
Gelatine	20 gm	500 gm
Egg whites	2	50
Sugar	60 gm	1.5 kg
Lime or	½	12
Lemon	1	25
Water	150 ml (approx.)	3.5 litre

Method

1. Put the rind and juice of lime, sugar, gelatine and water into a saucepan. Cover and bring to boil. 2. Infuse for half an hour. 3. Strain and cool. Whisk egg whites stiffly in a large bowl. Add the cool lime mixture slowly, whisking well. 4. Whisk till it starts to set. 5. Pour into a wet mould and turn out when set. Serve with custard sauce.

CUSTARD SAUCE

Ingredients	*For 4*	*For 100*
Egg yolks	1	25
Milk	150 ml	3.5 litre
Sugar	10 gm	250 gm
Salt	a pinch	5 gm

Method

1. Beat egg yolks. Add sugar and salt. 2. Pour hot milk over. Stir well. 3. Pour into a double boiler and cook till thick.

15. PINEAPPLE SPONGE

Ingredients	*For 4*	*For 100*
Gelatine	15-20 gm	340-400 gm
Lime	½	12
Egg whites	2	50
Pineapple (tinned)	225 gm	5.6 kg
Sugar	45 gm	1.1 kg
Water and pineapple juice	300 ml	7.5 litre

Method

1. Dissolve gelatine in the liquid. Add sugar and lime juice and allow to cool. 2. Dice pineapple. 3. Whisk egg whites till stiff in a large bowl and add the liquid gradually and continue whisking till mixture starts to set. 4. Add two-thirds of the pineapple and whisk well together. 5. Pile at

once into a glass dish and decorate with remaining pineapple. 6. Serve with custard sauce (see recipe 14).

16. MANGO FLUFF

Ingredients	*For 4*	*For 100*
Mango (ripe)	1	25
Egg whites	1	25
Gelatine	10 gm	250 gm
Cream	30 gm	680 gm
Sugar	30 gm	680 gm

Method

1. Prepare a mango purée. Add half the gelatine dissolved previously in a little warm water. 2. Prepare marshmallow as for marshmallow pudding. 3. Set a layer of marshmallow in a wet mould. 4. Pour mango purée over. Cover with another layer of marshmallow. Leave to set in the refrigerator. 5. Turn out and decorate with whipped and flavoured cream.

17. CARAMEL CUSTARD

Ingredients	*For 4*	*For 100*
Milk	300 ml	7.5 litre
Eggs	2	50
Sugar	30 gm	680 gm
Nutmeg	a pinch	1
Caramel		
Loaf sugar	15 gm	450 gm
Water	1½ tsp	230 ml

Method

1. Dissolve sugar for caramel in water in a strong pan. 2. Bring to boil till it becomes golden brown. 3. Pour at once into warm dry pudding moulds and mask evenly all over. 4. Bring the milk almost to boiling point. 5. Pour over beaten eggs and sugar. 6. Strain into prepared moulds. Sprinkle over with grated nutmeg. 7. Cover moulds with greased paper and steam gently for 1 to 1½ hours or bake in the oven in a water bath. 8. Remove, cool for a few minutes and turn on to a dish. Serve either hot or cold.

N.B. Do not allow the water to boil while the custard is steaming or baking.

18. FRUIT TRIFLE

Ingredients	*Quantity (10 portions)*
For fatless sponge	
Flour	90 gm
Grain sugar	90 gm
Eggs	3
Filling	
Oranges	2
Chickoos	2
Apples	2
Bananas	2
Dried apricots (soak in water for 1 hour, remove seeds and cut into bits)	100 gm
Preparation	
Fresh cream	200 gm
Grain sugar for syrup	100 gm
Jam	30 gm
Brandy	50 ml
Cherries	a few
Castor sugar	1 tsp

Method

1. Make a fatless sponge by whipping grain sugar, eggs and flour. 2. Cut the sponge cake into half, sandwich with the jam and cut into cubes. 3. Peel the fruits and dice. 4. Arrange the sponge cake cubes in an oval dish and soak in the thin sugar syrup and brandy. 5. Arrange all the fruits in layers over the cake. 6. Whip cream and sugar. Add flavouring and pile on top. 7. Decorate with cherries on top.

N.B. Stewed dried apricot can be added to the fruits. Also a few pieces of chopped nuts. Egg whites stiffly beaten with sugar can be used to decorate instead of whipped cream. A layer of fruit jelly may be poured over custard for variation.

19. SAGO CREAM

Ingredients	*For 4*	*For 100*
Sago	45 gm	1.12 kg
Milk	590 ml	14.75 litre
Sugar	30 gm	680 gm
Cream	150 ml	3 litre

Ingredients	*For 4*	*For 100*
Sherry	1 tbsp	340 ml
Vanilla essence	½ tsp	30 ml
Ratafia biscuits	30 gm	680 gm
Pistachio nuts	10 gm	250 gm

Method

1. Simmer the sago in milk until cooked. 2. Add sugar and cool, stirring occasionally. 3. When cold add the sherry, vanilla and slightly whipped cream. 4. Pour into a glass dish, and decorate with Ratafia biscuits and chopped nuts.

20. PRUNE MOULD

Ingredients	*For 4*	*For 100*
Prunes	225 gm	5.6 kg
Sugar	60 gm	1.5 kg
Water	590 ml	14.75 litre
Cinnamon	1 small stick	15 gm
Lime	¼	6
Gelatine	15 gm	340 gm
Jam	1 tbsp	500 gm

Method

1. Wash and soak prunes overnight in water. 2. Stew with lime rind until soft. 3. Add sugar and cinnamon and cook for 5 minutes. 4. Take out cinnamon and lime rind. 5. Remove stones from prunes and cut up roughly. 6. Measure prunes and juice and make up to the original amount of water. 7. Add gelatine, jam and lime juice. Heat till gelatine is dissolved. 8. Cool and mould when on the point of setting. 9. When set, turn out and serve with cream.

21. SUMMER PUDDING

Ingredients	*Quantity*
Stale bread	
Dried apricot	
or prunes	450 gm
Sugar	15 gm

Method

1. Soak fruit overnight. Stew with sugar. 2. Stone fruits. 3. Line a pint pudding basin with bread, leaving no space. 4. Fill with hot fruit, reserve juice, cover with bread, put a saucer with a weight on top. 5. Leave

overnight or for several hours. 6. Turn out and pour fruit juice over. Serve with custard.

22. MOSS JELLY

Ingredients	*For 4*	*For 100*
China grass	5 gm	125 gm
Water	450 ml	11.25 litre
Sugar	115 gm	2.8 kg
Lime juice	to taste	12 limes

Method

1. Wash and soak china grass in cold water, in which it is to be cooked, for at least 3 hours. 2. Dissolve on slow fire. Add sugar. 3. Remove from fire, strain. Add lime juice and colouring. Leave to set. 4. When set, serve with custard sauce.

N.B. Fruit juice may be added and the amount of water reduced or jelly could be served with fruit salad and custard sauce.

23. DIPLOMAT PUDDING

Ingredients	*For 4*	*For 100*
Milk	250 ml	5.75 litre
Gelatine	10 gm	250 gm
Eggs	2	50
Sugar	60 gm	1.35 kg
Sultanas	20 gm	500 gm
Currants	20 gm	500 gm
Angelica	20 gm	500 gm
Wafer biscuits	20 gm	500 gm
Glucose biscuits	20 gm	500 gm
Cherries	20 gm	500 gm

Method

1. Cream together egg yolks and sugar till light and fluffy. 2. Pour boiling milk over. Return to heat and cook to a custard consistency. 3. Remove from heat. Add gelatine dissolved in a little warm water. Mix well. 4. Cool and fold in stiffly beaten egg whites. 5. Decorate bottom of greased jelly moulds with some angelica and cherries. Fill half. 6. Put a layer of glucose biscuits dipped in fruit juice. 7. Put some currants over. Fill with remaining mixture. Set in refrigerator. 8. Turn out when cold and decorate with wafer biscuits, and remaining fruits.

24. MAWA AND ALMOND PUDDING (Cold)

Ingredients	*Quantity*
Hariali mawa	100 gm (½ cup)
Milk	100 ml (½ cup)
Eggs	2
Grated almonds or cashewnuts	40 gm (½ cup)
Almond essence	a few drops
Sugar	75 gm (½ cup)
Gelatine	8 gm (1 level tbsp)

Method

1. Separate egg yolks and whites. 2. Blend the mawa, milk, egg yolks, sugar and nuts in the blender for 5 minutes. 3. Add essence. Add dissolved gelatine to the well blended mixture and whip over ice. 4. When the mixture is semi-solid, lightly fold in stiffly beaten egg whites and pour into a greased jelly mould. 5. When set, turn out and garnish with glacé cherries and slivered almonds.

25. REFRIGERATOR CAKE

Ingredients	*Quantity*
Vanilla ice-cream wafers	
Sweetened condensed milk	1 large tin
Strong black coffee	150 ml
Sugar to sweeten	if necessary

Method

1. Mix the condensed milk in a basin with strong black coffee. Add castor sugar to sweeten, if necessary. 2. Stir the mixture in the basin over a pan of boiling water for five minutes. 3. Line a cake tin with waxed paper. Pour a layer of coffee mixture into bottom of tin and cover with layer of wafers. 4. Repeat till coffee mixture is used up. Finish with a layer of wafers. Place in refrigerator and chill for 12 hours. 5. Turn out on a dish, remove the wax paper and decorate with whipped cream. 6. Serve straight from the refrigerator.

26. ICE-CREAM IN A REFRIGERATOR

Points to remember

1. Use a good recipe, i.e. one with sufficient fat content. This is obtained by using canned or fresh cream, full cream condensed milk or evaporated milk. 2. Freeze quickly. To do this turn indicator to coldest position before starting to freeze the mixture. 3. Beat at least once to give a light texture. 4. When ice-cream has frozen, return indicator to normal position.

BASIC RECIPE (A)

Ingredients	*Quantity*
Full cream milk	600 ml
Eggs	2
Gelatine	½ tsp
Sugar	115 gm
Flavour and colour as desired	
Cream	50 ml

Method

1. Cream egg yolks and sugar. Pour boiling milk over. 2. Place on fire and cook till custard is quite thick (it should coat the back of a wooden spoon). 3. Remove from heat. Add gelatine dissolved in a dessertspoon of warm water. Mix well. 4. Cool. Add well-beaten egg whites, flavouring and colouring. Mix well. 5. Pour into trays and freeze (set refrigerator at coldest). 6. Remove from freezer when it starts to set. Beat with a rotary beater till double its volume, adding cream gradually. 7. Return to freezer. Set at coldest position. When ice-cream is frozen, return indicator to normal.

BASIC RECIPE (B)

Ingredients	*Quantity*
Full cream milk	600 ml
Egg yolks	4
Sugar	120 gm
Pure cream	50 ml

Method

1. Prepare a custard with egg yolks, milk and sugar. Cool. 2. Add the cream. Freeze as for Basic Recipe (A).

27. ICE-CREAM WITH EVAPORATED MILK

Ingredients	*Quantity*
Evaporated milk	600 ml
Castor sugar	115 gm
Gelatine	1 tsp
Boiling water	1 tbsp
Vanila essence	1 tsp

Method

1. Dissolve gelatine in boiling water. 2. Mix together milk, sugar and gelatine. Pour into the freezer tray. 3. Chill until mixture starts to freeze

round the edges. 4. Pour into a cold bowl. Add vanilla and whisk well until thick and creamy. Return to freezing tray until firm.

28. ICE-CREAM WITH CONDENSED & EVAPORATED MILK

Ingredients	*Quantity*
Full cream condensed milk	1 tin
Evaporated milk	150 ml
Water	150 ml
Flavouring	

Method

1. Chill the condensed milk mixed with the water. 2. Whip the evaporated milk until thick. 3. Fold into the condensed milk. Add flavouring. 4. Freeze until thick. 5. Turn into a cold bowl and beat until very smooth. 6. Replace in the trays and freeze again.

ICE-CREAM FLAVOURINGS

1. Add 1½ dessertspoons of soluble coffee dissolved in about 60 ml of water to 600 ml of ice-cream. 2. Melt 115 gm of chocolate in 150 ml of water and add to the ice-cream. 3. Stir 300 ml of thick fruit purée into the ice- cream. 4. Use less sugar and add 115 gm of jam to the ice-cream.

29. CONDENSED MILK ICE-CREAM

Ingredients	*Quantity*
Condensed milk	1 tin (Nestlé)
Water	1 cup
Whipping cream	2 cups
Nescafé and cocoa	mix together 1 tbsp

Method

1. Mix together condensed milk, water, coffee and cocoa and chill. 2. Chill cream separately. 3. Whip and fold into condensed milk mixture. 4. Pour into freezer trays and freeze. 5. As it starts to set, remove and whip well. 6. Return to freezer and serve garnished with chopped nuts.

30. TUTTI FRUTTI

Ingredients	*Quantity*
Milk	600 ml
Castor sugar	115 gm
Egg yolks	4

Ingredients	Quantity
Cream	120 ml
Mixed candied peel	115 gm
Mixed chopped nuts	55 gm
Orange juice	1 tbsp
Lemon juice	1 tsp

Method

1. Cream egg yolks and sugar. 2. Add boiling milk and cook till custard is quite thick (cook in a double boiler). 3. Pass through a sieve and set in the freezer (keep refrigerator at coldest). 4. As it starts to set take out. Pour into a chilled mould and beat till stiff gradually adding cream, fruit juice and chopped nuts and peel.

31. ALMOND ICE-CREAM

Ingredients	Quantity
Milk	2.5 litre
Almonds (125 gm shredded and 125 gm ground finely)	250 gm
Sugar	to taste
Rose water	
Kesar (saffron)	2 packets (about ½ gm)

Method

1. Boil the milk down to two-thirds of the original quantity. 2. Add sugar and ground almonds. 3. Add rose water, shredded almonds and kesar. 4. Keep half in an ice tray and half in a bowl. 5. Scrape and mix when serving.

N.B. Half cashewnuts and half almonds could be used instead of just almonds in which case, add a few drops of almond essence.

32. PINEAPPLE ICE-CREAM

Ingredients	Quantity
Pineapple	450 gm
Castor sugar	180 gm
Lemon juice	½
Cream	600 ml

Method

1. Cut up the pineapple. Pound it in a mortar and rub through a hair sieve. 2. Add the pulp, sugar and lemon juice to the cream and freeze.

33. VANILLA ICE-CREAM

Ingredients	*Quantity*
Egg (whole)	1
Egg yolks	5
Milk	600 ml
Castor sugar	4 tbsp
Vanilla essence	a few drops
Thick cream	300 ml

Method

1. Make the eggs and milk into a custard, add sugar and vanilla. 2. Beat the cream stiffly. 3. When cold, partly freeze the custard and then mix in cream and continue to freeze until the right consistency is reached.

34. COFFEE ICE-CREAM

Ingredients	*Quantity*
Egg yolks	8
Cream	600 ml
Coffee beans (roasted but not ground)	¼ lb. (170 gm)
Castor sugar	4 tbsp

Method

1. Make the egg yalks and cream into a custard. 2. Add to it the coffee beans and let it stand until they have flavoured the mixture well. 3. Then strain it, add the sugar, and when the custard is quite cold, freeze.

35. BANANA ICE-CREAM

Ingredients	*Quantity*
Bananas (large, ripe)	4
Lemon juice	1
Custard	600 ml

Method

1. Peel bananas, pound to a pulp and pass through sieve. 2. Add strained lemon juice and mix with custard. 3. Freeze in the usual way. 4. If desired, add 50 ml of cream.

36. CUSTARD FOR ICE-CREAM

Ingredients	*Quantity*
Milk	600 ml

Ingredients	*Quantity*
Sugar	115 gm
Egg yolks	4
Egg whites	2
Vanilla	a few drops

Method

1. Beat the egg yolks and mix in the sugar. 2. Bring the milk to nearly boiling point; take it off the fire and add to the egg mixture stirring all the time. 3. Return the saucepan to the fire and stir carefully until the mixture thickens but do not let it boil or the egg will curdle. 4. When cold, flavour to taste and just before freezing stir in egg whites, beaten to a stiff froth. 5. This custard forms the basis of many ice-creams. 6. You can make this plainer or richer by using fewer or more eggs. 7. The ice-cream can be named after the flavouring used.

HOT SWEETS

1. Bread Pudding
2. Cabinet Pudding
3. Queen of Puddings
4. Canary Pudding (A)
   Canary Pudding (B)
5. College Pudding
6. Mawa and Almond Pudding
7. Albert Pudding
8. Ginger Pudding
9. Marmalade Pudding
10. Chocolate Pudding
11. Baked Coconut Pudding
12. Baked Chocolate
13. Eplakaka
14. Plum Pudding
15. Christmas Pudding (A)
    Vanilla Sauce
    Hard Sauce
    Christmas Pudding (B)
16. Jamaican Sweet Potato Pudding
17. Caribbean Banana
18. Apricot Charlotte
19. Rice Pudding (A)
    Rice Pudding (B)
20. Semolina Pudding
21. Vattilappa
22. Almond Soufflé
23. Pineapple Soufflé
24. Pancakes
25. Pancake with Coconut Filling
26. Banana Fritters
27. Liberian Cassava Cake

1. BREAD PUDDING

Ingredients	*For 4*	*For 100*
Bread	115 gm	2.85 kg
Butter	30 gm	680 gm
Milk	250 ml	4.72 litre
Sugar	60 gm	1.5 kg

Ingredients	For 4	For 100
Eggs	2	50
Sultanas	30 gm	680 gm
Nutmeg	a pinch	½
Cashewnuts	30 gm	680 gm
Lime rind	a pinch	1 lime

Method

1. Butter bread and break into small pieces. 2. Boil milk and pour over bread and set aside for half an hour. 3. Beat eggs well. Add sugar, lime rind and nutmeg. 4. Pour over bread. Add sultanas and cashewnuts. Mix well. 5. Pour into greased mould. Cover with greaseproof paper and steam till set. 6. Serve hot with lemon juice.

2. CABINET PUDDING

Ingredients	For 4	For 100
Bread	225 gm	5.9 kg
Eggs	2	50
Butter	30 gm	680 gm
Milk	295 ml	9 litre
Sugar	115 gm	2.8 kg
Sultanas	55 gm	1.35 kg
Cashewnuts	30 gm	680 gm
Vanilla essence or lime rind		

Method

1. Butter the pudding mould and decorate bottom and sides with nuts and sultanas. 2. Butter slices of bread, cut off the crust and cut the bread into cubes. 3. Arrange a layer of bread in the prepared mould and sprinkle with sultanas and sugar. 4. Continue in layers till mould is half full. 5. Beat eggs in a bowl. Boil milk and pour over beaten eggs stirring well. Add flavouring and a little sugar. 6. Pour over bread and let it stand for ½ hour to soak bread thoroughly. 7. Cover mould with butter paper and steam for one hour. 8. Turn out and serve hot with jam or custard sauce.

3. QUEEN OF PUDDINGS

Ingredients	For 4	For 100
Milk	250 ml	4.75 litre
Butter or margarine	30 gm	680 gm
Fresh bread	115 gm	2.9 kg
Jam	30 gm	455 gm

Ingredients	*For 4*	*For 100*
Lime rind	a little	2 lemons
Eggs	2	50
Sugar	55 gm	1.35 kg

Method

1. Heat milk and butter together and pour over bread. 2. Add half the sugar, egg yolks and grated lime rind. Mix well and allow to stand for half an hour. 3. Pour into a greased pie dish and bake till quite firm. 4. Heat jam and spread over the pudding. 5. Beat egg whites stiffly. Fold in sugar and pile on pudding. 6. Bake in a slow oven for about 15 minutes till meringue is set and pale brown in colour.

4. CANARY PUDDING (A)

Ingredients	*For 4*	*For 100*
Eggs	2 (90 gm)	50 (2.25 kg)
Refined flour	90 gm	2.25 kg
Butter	90 gm	2.25 kg
Sugar	90 gm	2.25 kg
Baking powder	a pinch	30 gm
Vanilla essence	to taste	to taste

Method

1. Cream butter and sugar. 2. Add beaten egg yolks and then the flour sieved with baking powder. 3. Fold in well-beaten egg whites. Add essence. 4. Pour into greased moulds and steam; serve with jam sauce.

CANARY PUDDING (B)

Ingredients	*For 4*	*For 100*
Eggs	1	25
Refined flour	85 gm	2.125 kg
Fat	55 gm	1.35 kg
Sugar	55 gm	1.35 kg
Milk	55 gm	1.35 kg
Baking powder	to mix	to mix
Vanilla essence	¼ tsp	45 gm

Method

1. Cream butter and sugar. 2. Add beaten egg yolk and flour sieved with baking powder. 3. Fold in well-beaten egg white. Add milk and essence. 4. Pour into greased mould and steam (1–1½ hours). 5. Serve with jam sauce.

5. COLLEGE PUDDING

Ingredients	*For 4*	*For 100*
Refined flour	55 gm	1.35 kg
Fresh breadcrumbs	55 gm	1.35 kg
Fat	45 gm	1.12 kg
Baking powder	½ tsp	45 gm
Eggs	1	25
Milk (if necessary)	to mix (2 tbsp)	500 ml (about)
Sultanas	45 gm	1.10 kg
Candied peel	15 gm	340 gm
Golden syrup	2 tbsp	500 gm
Mixed spice	a pinch	10 gm

Method

1. Mix dry ingredients together. 2. Add beaten egg, golden syrup and milk if necessary, to make a soft paste. 3. Put into a greased mould and steam for 2 to 2½ hours.

6. MAWA AND ALMOND PUDDING (Hot)

Ingredients	*Quantity*
Hariali mawa	100 gm (½ cup)
Milk	100 ml (½ cup)
Eggs	2
Grated almonds or cashewnuts	40 gm (½ cup)
Almond essence	a few drops
Sugar	75 gm (½ cup)

Method

1. Blend the mawa, milk, eggs, sugar and nuts in the blender for 5 minutes. Add essence. 2. Lightly caramelize a jelly mould and pour in the mixture. 3. Seal the mould with greaseproof paper or aluminium foil. Place in water bath and bake in the oven for 45 minutes. 4. Garnish with slivered almonds.

7. ALBERT PUDDING

Ingredients	*For 4*	*For 100*
Refined flour	170 gm	3.4 kg
Baking powder	½ tsp	30 gm
Eggs	2	40
Sugar	115 gm	2.3 kg
Margarine	115 gm	2.8 kg
Glacé cherries	15 gm	300 gm
Milk (if necessary)	1 tbsp	300 ml

Method

1. Cream margarine and sugar. 2. Beat eggs and add gradually, beating mixture well with each addition of egg. 9. Sift flour and baking powder together. Fold in gradually. 4. Grease a pudding mould. Decorate with cherries. Pour in the mixture to fill three-fourths of the basin. 4. Cover with greaseproof paper and steam for 1½ to 2 hours. 6. Serve hot with jam sauce.

8. GINGER PUDDING

Ingredients	*For 4*	*For 100*
Refined flour	155 gm	2.8 kg
Eggs	1	25
Butter	55 gm	1.35 kg
Sugar	55 gm	1.35 kg
Dry ginger powder	1 tsp	55 gm
Baking powder	½ tsp	30 gm
Milk	to mix	to mix

Method

1. Cream butter and sugar well. 2. Add egg yolk and beat. 3. Sieve flour and baking powder. 4. Beat egg white stiffly and add flour and white alternately. 5. Fold in ginger powder. 6. Grease pudding mould, pour in mixture and cover with greaseproof paper. 7. Steam for 1½ hours. 8. Serve hot with custard sauce or jam sauce.

9. MARMALADE PUDDING

Ingredients	*For 4*	*For 100*
Refined flour	55 gm	1.1 kg
Breadcrumbs	55 gm	1.1 kg
Salt	a pinch	10 gm
Baking powder	½ tsp	30 gm
Sugar	30 gm	680 gm
Shredded suet or vegetable shortening	45 gm	900 gm
Marmalade	115 gm	2.3 kg
Eggs	1	25

Method

1. Mix dry ingredients together. 2. Add beaten egg and marmalade. 3. Put into well-greased mould and steam for 1½ to 2 hours. Serve with marmalade sauce.

10. CHOCOLATE PUDDING

Ingredients	*Quantity*
Sugar	100 gm
Butter	75 gm
Milk	75 ml
Flour	150 gm
Baking powder	10 gm
Salt	2 gm
Cocoa	25 gm
Walnut	70 gm
Sugar	70 gm
Brown sugar	70 gm
Cocoa powder (to sprinkle)	25 gm

Method

1. Cream together 100 gm sugar and butter and stir in milk. 2. Sift the flour, baking powder, salt and cocoa powder and add to the creamed mixture. Add chopped pieces of walnut. 3. Mix 75 gm white sugar, 70 gm brown sugar and 25 gm cocoa powder together and sprinkle over the batter (placed in a baking dish) and pour 150 ml boiling water over it. 4. Bake immediately at 350°C for 35-40 minutes. Serve with ice-cream.

11. BAKED COCONUT PUDDING

Ingredients	*For 4*	*For 100*
Fresh breadcrumbs	55 gm	1.35 kg
Coconut	55 gm	1.35 kg
Milk	295 ml	7.375 litre
Granulated sugar	30 gm	680 gm
Castor sugar	30 gm	680 gm
Grated lemon rind	a little	2 limes
Margarine	30 gm	680 gm
Eggs	2	50

Method

1. Heat the milk and margarine together. 2. Pour over the breadcrumbs. 3. Add coconut, lemon rind and granulated sugar. 4. Beat egg yolks and add to mixture. 5. Allow to stand for half an hour or longer. 6. Put into a greased pie dish and bake till quite firm at 175°C (350°F). 7. Whisk the egg whites firmly. Fold in castor sugar and pile on top of pudding. 8. Put into a cool oven at 93°C (200°F) for 15 minutes or until the meringue mixture is crisp and pale brown in colour.

12. BAKED CHOCOLATE PUDDING

Ingredients	*For 4*	*For 100*
Breadcrumbs (fresh)	85 gm	2 kg
Milk	300 ml	7.5 litre
Sugar	70 gm	1.75 kg
Butter	20 gm	500 gm
Cocoa	10 gm	250 gm
Eggs	2	50
Salt	a pinch	2 tsp

Method

1. Boil milk, cocoa and butter and pour over breadcrumbs and sugar. 2. Cover and keep aside for 10 minutes. 3. Add beaten egg yolks and pour into a greased pie dish and bake in a moderate oven till set (20-30 minutes). 4. Whip egg whites stiffly and add 2 tsp sugar. Spread on top of the pudding and brown in a slow oven.

13. EPLAKAKA

Ingredients	*Quantity*
Breadcrumbs (soft)	2 cups
Sugar	¾ cup
Butter	½ cup
Apple sauce	2 cups
Jam	½ cup
Thick cream (whipped)	½ cup
Apple sauce	
Cooking apples	4
Lemon peel	
Sugar	½ cup
Raisins (soaked in warm water)	¼ cup
Egg yolk (slightly beaten)	1

Method

1. Prepare the sauce. Cut apples into eighths and cover with cold water. 2. Add lemon peel and cook for 20-30 minutes or until apples are soft. Put the cooked apples through a strainer to remove peel and core. Add sugar and raisins. 3. Whip egg yolk into the mixture to make it fluffy. Combine breadcurmbs and sugar. Sauté in butter slowly until browned. 4. Place alternate layers of breadcrumbs and apple sauce in a glass dish. Put thin layers of jam between layers. Serve chilled with whipped cream.

14. PLUM PUDDING

Ingredients	*Quantity*
Flour	85 gm
Breadcrumbs	55 gm
Finely chopped suet or margarine	115 gm
Brown sugar	115 gm
Eggs	3
Nutmeg	a pinch
Mixed spice	½ tsp
Salt	a pinch
Sultanas	55 gm
Currants or black raisins	115 gm
Mixed peel	55 gm
Almonds or cashewnuts	30 gm
Lemon (rind and juice)	½
Valencia raisins	115 gm
Brandy (optional)	15 ml

Method

1. Put flour and breadcrumbs into a basin. 2. Add all the dry ingredients and well-beaten eggs and beat the mixture to a stiff consistency. 3. Put into a well-greased pudding mould. 4. Press down and steam for 4-6 hours. 5. Steam again for 2 hours before serving. 6. Serve with custard sauce or rum butter.

15. CHRISTMAS PUDDING (A)

Ingredients	*For 4*	*For 100*
Carrots (grated)	60 gm	1.2 kg
Potatoes (grated)	85 gm	1.7 kg
Raisins	60 gm	1.2 kg
Dates	60 gm	1.2 kg
Butter	45 gm	900 gm
Sugar	85 gm	1.7 kg
Nuts (chopped)	30 gm	600 gm
Soda bicarbonate	¼ tsp	3 tbsp
Cinnamon (powder)	¼ tsp	2 tbsp
Cloves (powder)	¼ tsp	2 tbsp
Nutmeg	¼ tsp	2 tbsp
Salt	a pinch	½ tsp
Refined flour	45 gm	900 gm

Method

1. Mix together grated carrots, potatoes, chopped raisins, dates, nuts and

sugar and butter. 2. Mix together soda, cinnamon, cloves, nutmeg, salt and flour. 3. Add to first mixture. 4. Put into a greased bun tin. 5. Steam for about 2 hours. 6. Serve with vanilla sauce or hard sauce.

VANILLA SAUCE

Ingredients	*Quantity*
Sugar	450 gm
Cornflour	85 gm
Salt	½ tsp
Boiling water	1.8 litre
Vanilla	2 tbsp
Butter	30 gm

Method

1. Mix together, sugar, cornflour and salt. Add boiling water. Cook until clear. Add vanilla and butter. Serve hot.

HARD SAUCE

Ingredients	*Quantity*
Butter	340 gm
Brown sugar	540 gm
Whipped cream	¾ cup (180 ml)
Vanilla	2 tsp

Method

1. Cream butter. Add sugar gradually. Cream well. Fold in whipped cream and vanilla.

CHRISTMAS PUDDING (B)

Ingredients	*Quantity*
Almonds or cashewnuts	15 gm
Sultanas and currants	225 gm
Large raisins	225 gm (after stoning)
Candied peel	115 gm
Brown sugar	225 gm
Breadcrumbs (fresh)	225 gm
Lime (juice and finely grated rind)	1
Suet or margarine	115 gm
Refined flour	225 gm
Salt	¼ tsp
Ground cinnamon	1 tsp

Ingredients	*Quantity*
Ground nutmeg	1 tsp
Ground cloves	½ tsp
Eggs	3
Cider, stout, or brandy	1 glass.

Method

1. Christmas pudding should be made well in advance. On the first day, prepare ingredients and on the second day prepare the basins and steam puddings. Set aside, and on Christmas day, reheat the pudding by steaming for another 2 hours.

1. Blanch almonds and chop, or chop cashewnuts fine. 2. Mix prepared sultanas, currants, chopped raisins and candied peel together in a large basin. 3. Stir in chopped nuts, sugar, breadcrumbs, lemon rind and fat. 4. Sift flour, salt and spices together. 5. Beat eggs (yolk and white) and add lime juice and cider (if brandy is used, add enough fruit juice to a wineglass of brandy to make one full glass). Mix with flour. 6. Add flour and egg mixture to the other ingredients and mix well. Set aside. 7. On the second day, brush basin with melted fat and fill with pudding mixture. 8. Cover the basin with greaseproof paper and tie with a string. 9. Steam large puddings for 8 hours and smaller ones for 6 hours. 10. When the pudding is cold, cover with fresh greaseproof paper and store in a cool dry place till Christmas. 11. Steam again and sprinkle icing sugar over. 12. Serve with grape sauce or brandy butter.

16. JAMAICAN SWEET POTATO PUDDING

Ingredients	*Quantity*
Sweet potatoes	500 gm
Butter	50 gm
Sugar	75 gm
Refined flour	25 gm
Nutmeg	2
Ginger powder	a pinch
Coconut (grated)	100 gm
Vanilla essence	a few drops
Raisins	10 gm
Salt	a pinch

Method

1. Wash, peel and grate sweet potatoes. Cream butter and sugar. Add grated sweet potatoes. 2. Sift flour with nutmeg, ginger and salt. Add to the sweet potato mixture. 3. Extract thick coconut milk from freshly grated coconut and add a little to the mixture. Add vanilla and raisins.

4. Pour the mixture into a greased mould and bake at 190°C (375°F) for 1½ hours. Serve hot or cold with remaining coconut milk.

17. CARIBBEAN BANANA

Ingredients	*Quantity*
Bananas	4
Orange juice	1 orange
Butter	60 gm
Lemon juice	¼ lemon
Rum	1 wine glass
Castor sugar	2 tsp
Brandy	1 wine glass

Method

1. Over steady flame, melt the butter and place the peeled bananas. 2. While gently shaking the pan, turn the bananas, add the sugar, continuing to heat until caramelization starts. 3. Add the fruit juice, continuing to heat so that the liquid is well-reduced as the bananas cook. 4. Add the brandy, turning and basting the bananas thoroughly. 5. With the flame high, add the rum, and lower flame. Serve immediately.

N.B. Caribbean banana may be served with praline ice-cream if desired. Slivered almonds or sliced cashewnuts may also be added.

18. APRICOT CHARLOTTE

Ingredients	*For 4*	*For 100*
Apricots (dried)	225 gm	5.6 kg
Sugar	30 gm	680 gm
Butter	55 gm	1.36 kg
Lemon	¼	4½

Method

1. Grease jelly mould. 2. Cut bread into thin fingers. Dip in melted butter and line the jelly mould with the buttered side touching the dish. 3. Put in the prepared filling. Cover the top with bread slices. 4. Bake in a hot oven for 30 to 45 minutes. The bread should be brown and crisp. 5. Allow to stand for a few minutes, then turn on to a hot dish. 6. Sprinkle over with powdered sugar.

Filling

1. Soak apricots overnight. 2. Stone. Remove nuts from stone and mix with fruit. 3. Add lime juice, rind and sugar. Cook till mixture thickens.

19. RICE PUDDING (A)

Ingredients	*For 4*	*For 100*
Milk	600 ml	14.75 litre
Sugar	60 gm	1.5 kg
Vanilla essence	a few drops	2 tsp
Rice	45 gm	1 kg
Butter	15 gm	340 gm
Grated nutmeg	a pinch	½

Method

1. Wash the rice; place in a pie dish. 2. Add sugar and milk. Mix well. 3. Add butter, essence and nutmeg. 4. Place on a baking sheet; clean the rim of the pie dish. 5. Bake in a moderate oven until the milk starts simmering. 6. Reduce heat and allow the pudding to cook slowly for about 1½ to 2 hours.

RICE PUDDING (B)

Ingredients	*For 4*	*For 100*
Milk	600 ml	14.75 litre
Sugar	60 gm	1.5 kg
Vanilla essence	a few drops	2 tsp
Rice	45 gm	1 kg
Butter	15 gm	340 gm
Grated nutmeg	a pinch	½

Method

1. Boil the milk in a thick-bottomed pan. 2. Add washed rice. Stir to a boil. 3. Simmer gently, stirring frequently until the rice is cooked. 4. Mix in the sugar, flavouring and butter (one egg yolk per 590 ml of milk may also be added). 5. Pour into a pie dish. Put under the grill and brown slightly. Serve hot.

20. SEMOLINA PUDDING

Ingredients	*For 4*	*For 100*
Milk	600 ml	14.75 litre
Sugar	60 gm	1.5 kg
Butter	15 gm	340 gm
Semolina	45 gm	1 kg
Lime juice	a few drops	3 limes
Egg yolk (optional)	1	25

Method

1. Boil the milk in a thick-bottomed pan. 2. Sprinkle the semolina and stir to boil. 3. Simmer for 15 to 20 minutes. 4. Add sugar, butter, flavouring and egg yolk if included. 5. Pour into a pie dish. 6. Brown under a grill. 7. Serve hot.

21. VATTILAPPA

Ingredients	*For 4*	*For 100*
Eggs	2	50
Thick coconut milk	150 ml (1 cup)	3.75 litre
Palm jaggery	30 gm	680 gm
Grated nutmeg	a pinch	2 nutmegs
Lime rind	½ lime	10 limes

Method

1. Extract thick coconut milk. 2. Add grated jaggery and mix till dissolved. 3. Add beaten eggs, grated nutmeg and lime rind. 4. Pour into a greased mould and steam gently till set.

22. ALMOND SOUFFLÉ

Ingredients	*For 4*	*For 100*
Egg whites	4	100
Lime	a dash	1 tsp
Salt	a pinch	1 tsp
Almonds	30 gm	680 gm
Castor sugar	45 gm	1.125 kg
Sugar for caramel	15 gm	340 gm

Method

1. Beat egg whites with lime till stiff. 2. Add sugar gradually and beat in; add salt. 3. Fold in finely sliced almonds. 4. Caramelize sugar in a jelly mould. 5. Pour meringue mixture into the mould, filling two-thirds of the mould. 6. Cover with greaseproof paper and steam over simmering water for about 10 to 15 minutes. 7. Cool and turn out and serve with cream or custard.

23. PINEAPPLE SOUFFLÉ

Ingredients	*Quantity*
Butter	60 gm
Eggs	3
Breadcrumbs (fresh)	85 gm
Castor sugar	100 gm
Pineapple (small tin)	1 (about 400 gm)

Method

1. Cream butter and sugar and beat in egg yolks, breadcrumbs and pineapple pieces. 2. Beat egg whites till stiff and fold half into the mixture. 3. Pour into a greased pyrex dish. Pile remaining egg whites on top. 4. Bake at 175°C (350°F) for 45 minutes in a hot water bath.

24. PANCAKES

Ingredients	*For 4*	*For 100*
Refined flour	115 gm	2.8 kg
Salt	½ tsp	30 to 50 gm
Eggs	1	25
Milk	300 ml	75. litre
Sugar	30 gm	680 gm
Lime	½	10
Fat for frying	30 gm	680 gm

Method

1. Mix flour and salt in a bowl. 2. Make a well in the centre. Break egg and drop into the centre. 3. Stir in from the centre working in the flour, gradually adding milk until one-third to half is used and the flour is the consistency of thick cream. 4. Beat well and mix thoroughly. 5. Stir in the remainder of the milk and leave to stand for at least half an hour. 6. Take a pan and heat a little fat in it. 7. Pour in sufficient batter to cover the bottom of the pan thinly. 8. Fry quickly until golden brown. 9. When the batter is nearly set, loosen by shaking the pan gently and easing the edge of the batter with a knife. 10. Toss or turn with a knife and fry until golden brown on the second side. 11. Turn on to sugared paper. 12. Sprinkle with sugar and lemon juice. 13. Roll up and keep hot until all the pancakes are fried and serve immediately.

25. PANCAKE WITH COCONUT FILLING

Ingredients	*For 4*	*For 100*
Refined flour	115 gm	2.8 kg
Eggs	1	25
Milk	295 ml	7.5 litre
Sugar	30 gm	680 gm
Salt	a small pinch	10 gm
Filling		
Coconut	55 gm	1.36 kg
Sugar	30 gm	680 gm
Cardamoms	a few	10 gm

Method

1. Sieve together flour and salt into a bowl. 2. Make a well in the centre. Add beaten egg yolk and milk. Add sugar. 3. Beat well to form a smooth batter and let in stand for an hour. 4. Whisk egg white stiffly. Fold into batter and prepare pancakes, cooking only on one side. Put in the filling and roll.

Filling

Scrape coconut. Add sugar and crushed cardamoms.

26. BANANA FRITTERS

Ingredients	*For 4*	*For 100*
Bananas	2	50
Milk	50 ml	1.18 litre
Refined flour	30 gm	680 gm
Eggs	½	12
Castor sugar	30 gm	455 gm
Fat to fry		

Method

1. Peel bananas and cut into long pieces. 2. Prepare a batter with flour, eggs and milk. 3. Dip slices of bananas in batter. Deep fry. 4. Drain and toss in castor sugar. 5. Serve on a dish lined with a paper napkin.

27. LIBERIAN CASSAVA CAKE

Ingredients	*Quantity*
Tapioca (raw, grated)	1½
Milk	½ cup
Egg (beaten)	1
Butter	6 tbsp
Sugar	1 cup
Grated coconut	¾ cup
Refined flour	½ cup
Baking powder	2½ tsp
Salt	a pinch
Vanilla	1 tsp

Method

1. Wash, peel and grate the tapioca and soak in milk for 5 minutes. 2. Cream butter and sugar; add beaten egg, grated coconut and tapioca mixture. 3. Sift flour with baking powder and add to the batter. Add a few drops of vanilla essence. Pour the mixture into a greased and floured cake tin. Bake at 200°C (about 400°F) for 40 minutes.

VEGETARIAN DISHES

1. Vegetable Stew
2. Vegetable Stew with Haricot Beans
3. Egg and Vegetable Stew
4. Vegetable Ragoût
5. Aubergine and Cauliflower Ragoût
6. Egg and Vegetable Ragoût
7. Vegetable Goulash with Caraway Dumplings
8. Casserole of Vegetable
9. Swedish Onion Casserole
10. Baked Spanish Onions
11. Vegetable Hot Pot
12. Sweet Potato Hot Pot
13. Ratatouille
14. Vegetable Kedgeree
15. Risotto a l'Italienne
16. Rice and Lentil Savory
17. Vegetable Cutlets
18. Vegetable Cakes
19. Vegetable Balls
20. Carrot Rissoles
21. Lentil Rissoles
22. Vegetable Rissoles
23. Bird's Nest
24. Rice Croquettes
25. Vegetable Hamburger
26. Vegetarian Sausages
27. Savoury Sausages
28. Mock Salmon Steak
29. Mock Beef Rissoles
30. Mock Fillets of Sole
31. Nut Cutlets
32. Vegetable Panrolls
33. Egg and Pea Panrolls
34. Macaroni and Tomato Fritters
35. Corn and Green Pepper Fritters
36. Cauliflower au Gratin
37. Vegetable and Egg au Gratin
38. Vegetable Exotica
39. Egg and Vegetable Savoury
40. Cauliflower and Egg Savoury
41. Macaroni Cheese
42. Baked Savoury Macaroni
43. Spaghetti with Mushroom and Cheese Sauce
44. Spaghetti with Barbecue Sauce
45. Vegetable Pie
46. Vegetable Pie with Cheese Sauce
47. Egg, Potato and Rice Pie
48. Cheese, Egg and Potato Pie
49. Golden Cheese Bake
50. Cheese Soufflé
51. Cheese and Corn Soufflé
52. Cheese Soufflé Dubois
53. Cheese and Cauliflower Soufflé
54. Spinach Soufflé (A)
    Spinach Soufflé (B)
55. Savoury Mould a l'Italienne
56. Savoury Vegetable Ring
57. Japonaise Tomatoes
58. Potato Basket
59. Aubergines Stuffed and Baked
60. Stuffed Sweet Pepper
61. Stuffed Vegetable Marrow (Vellari)
62. Eggs in Tomatoes
63. Egg and Potato Fry
64. Lentil Roast
65. Nut Roast
66. Vegetable Loaf
67. Cheese and Lentil Pie
68. Cheese and Onion Flan
69. Baked Brinjal with Sage and Onion Stuffing
70. Mushroom Flan
71. Golden Onion Quiche
72. Tomato Cheese Pizza
73. Tomato Cheesecake
74. Baked Vegetable Pie

1. VEGETABLE STEW

Ingredients	*For 4*	*For 100*
Potatoes	115 gm	2.8 kg
Carrots	115 gm	2.8 kg
Cabbage	225 gm	5.6 kg
Peas	115 gm	2.8 kg
Celery	55 gm	1.35 kg
Onions	55 gm	1.35 kg
Vegetable stock or water	590 ml	14.75 litre
Milk	150 ml	3 litre
Refined flour	15 gm	240 gm
Peppercorns	a few	20 gm
Bayleaf	1	5 gm
Salt	to taste	80-100 gm

Method

1. Prepare vegetables. 2. Put all vegetables, seasoning and vegetable stock into a pan and cook till vegetables are tender. 3. Add flour mixed into a smooth paste with milk. Bring to boil stirring all the time.

N.B. There must be a fair amount (about 150 ml) of liquid per person in the stew after cooking. If desired, tomatoes can be used instead of celery but double the quantity.

2. VEGETABLE STEW WITH HARICOT BEANS

Ingredients	*For 4*	*For 100*
Potatoes	225 gm	5.65 kg
Carrots	225 gm	5.65 kg
Turnip	115 gm	2.8 kg
Haricot beans	115 gm	2.8 kg
Onions	115 gm	2.8 kg
Milk	150 ml	2.36 litre
Refined flour	10 gm	225 gm
Butter to fry	15 gm	340 gm
Pepper	to taste	15 gm
Salt	to taste	80-100 gm

Method

1. Soak beans overnight in hot water. 2. Prepare vegetables. 3. Boil beans till tender in the water in which they were soaked. 4. Heat fat. Brown onions. Add prepared vegetables and just enough tepid water to cook vegetables. 5. When vegetables are tender add Haricot beans. 6. Add seasoning, flour and milk. 7. Simmer for 10 minutes stirring all the time.

N.B. Stew should have a fair amount of liquid.

3. EGG AND VEGETABLE STEW

Ingredients	*For 4*	*For 100*
Eggs	4	100
Potatoes	225 gm	5.65 kg
Peas	115 gm	2.8 kg
Carrots	115 gm	2.8 kg
Tomatoes	115 gm	2.8 kg
Capsicum	55 gm	1.36 kg
Onions	55 gm	1.36 kg
Butter	15 gm	340 gm
Salt	to taste	80–100 gm
Peppercorns	a few	15 gm
Bayleaves	1 bunch	5 gm

Method

1. Prepare vegetables. 2. Slice onions and sauté in melted fat. 3. Add all the vegetables and a quarter of the potatoes thinly sliced. 4. Add seasoning and water and let it cook. 5. When half-cooked add remaining potatoes and halved hard-boiled eggs. 6. Cook till potatoes are tender and serve hot.

4. VEGETABLE RAGOÛT

Ingredients	*For 4*	*For 100*
Haricot beans	115 gm	2.8 kg
Carrots	225 gm	5.6 kg
Turnip	115 gm	2.8 kg
Tomatoes	225 gm	5.6 kg
Onions	55 gm	1.35 kg
Butter	40 gm	900 gm
Refined flour	15 gm	340 gm
Salt	to taste	80-100 gm
Pepper	a pinch	15 gm

Method

1. Wash and soak beans overnight. 2. Boil with a few pieces of onion and part of the butter till tender. 3. Drain liquor but keep it. 4. Dice carrots, turnip and fry lightly. 5. Add to beans, add blanched tomatoes and cook till vegetables are tender. 6. Fry sliced onion; add flour and brown. Add bean liquor and season; simmer for 10 to 15 minutes stirring all the time. 7. Add vegetables. Bring to boil and remove. Serve hot.

5. AUBERGINE AND CAULIFLOWER RAGOÛT

Ingredients	*For 4*	*For 100*
Cauliflower	225 gm	5.6 kg
Aubergine (brinjal)	225 gm	5.6 kg
Onions	115 gm	2.8 kg
Tomatoes	225 gm	5.6 kg
Fat	30 gm	680 gm
Peppercorns	a few	15 gm
Salt	to taste	80-100
Bayleaves	2	5 gm
Boiling water	590 ml	14.75 litre

Method

1. Wash and boil cauliflower in hot water. 2. Strain but keep liquor. 3. Cut brinjal into long pieces. Chop onions. 4. Heat fat. Fry brinjal and onions. Add sliced tomatoes. Cook for a few minutes. 5. Put the onions, brinjal and tomato mixture in a casserole dish. Add cauliflower. Pour liquor over with more hot water if necessary. Add seasoning. 6. Cook gently in an oven for 30-45 minutes.

6. EGG AND VEGETABLE RAGOÛT

Ingredients	*For 4*	*For 100*
Hard-boiled eggs	4	100
Haricot beans	225 gm	5.65 kg
Carrots	225 gm	5.65 kg
Turnip	115 gm	2.8 kg
Onions	115 gm	2.8 kg
Butter	30 gm	680 gm
Refined flour	15 gm	340 gm
Tomatoes	225 gm	5.65 kg

Method

1. Wash and soak beans overnight. 2. Boil beans in the same water with a few pieces of onion and part of the butter, till tender. 3. Drain but keep the liquor. 4. Slice carrots and turnip. 5. Heat half the remaining butter and fry carrots and turnip lightly. Add beans and blanched tomatoes and cook till vegetables are tender. 6. Heat butter and fry sliced onions. Add flour and brown. Add bean liquor and simmer for 10 minutes. 7. Add gravy and halved hard-boiled eggs to vegetables. Bring to a boil stirring all the time.

7. VEGETABLE GOULASH WITH CARAWAY DUMPLINGS

Ingredients	*For 4*	*For 100*
Cauliflower	225 gm	5.6 kg
Potatoes	225 gm	5.6 kg
Peas	225 gm	5.6 kg
Carrots	225 gm	5.6 kg
Refined flour	10 gm	225 gm
Onions	115 gm	2.8 kg
Capsicum	55 gm	1.36 kg
Tomatoes	115 gm	2.8 kg
Salt	10 gm	100 gm
Pepper	to taste	15 gm
Nutmeg	a pinch	10 gm
Parsley	a sprig	1 bunch
Bayleaf	1 leaf	5 gm
Paprika	a pinch	15 gm
Fat	15 gm	250 gm

Method

1. Prepare cauliflower, potatoes, peas and carrots and dip in seasoned flour. 2. Chop onions and green pepper and sauté in heated fat. 3. Add prepared vegetables and fry lightly on all sides. 4 Stir in blanched tomatoes, seasoning and remaining flour. Add stock and seasoning. 5. Simmer gently till vegetables are cooked. 6. Serve with caraway dumplings.

N.B. For caraway dumplings see Meat Section (recipe no. 7).

8. CASSEROLE OF VEGETABLE

Ingredients	*For 4*	*For 100*
Carrots	115 gm	2.8 kg
Peas	115 gm	2.8 kg
Beans	115 gm	2.8 kg
Potatoes	225 gm	5.6 kg
Turnip	55 gm	1.8 kg
Onions	115 gm	2.8 kg
Pepper	to taste	15 gm
Salt	10 gm	100 gm
Refined flour	30 gm	340 gm
Fat	30 gm	340 gm

Method

1. Prepare vegetables. 2. Heat fat, add vegetables and cook with lid on,

for about 15 minutes. 3. Remove, add warm vegetable stock and transfer to casserole dish. 4. Cook in oven at 160°C (320°F) or Gas mark 3 with lid on, till vegetables are tender. 5. Blend flour in a little stock. Add to casserole with seasoning. 6. Return to oven and cook 10 minutes longer.

N.B. For an egg and vegetable casserole, one boiled egg per person can be included. Hard-boil eggs. Shell and cut and into half and add to casserole 10 minutes before removing.

9. SWEDISH ONION CASSEROLE

Ingredients	*For 4*
Onions	225 gm
Eggs (hard-boiled)	4
Cheese sauce	
Butter	45 gm
Refined flour	3 level tbsp
Milk	400 ml
Grated cheese	115 gm
Salt and pepper	to taste
Mustard	¼ tsp

Method

1. Peel, slice and fry onions in melted butter until tender and pale golden brown. 2. Place in a casserole or ovenproof dish. Arrange sliced hard-boiled eggs over top. 3. Cover with prepared cheese sauce and cook in a hot oven at 205°C (400°F) or Gas mark 6 for 15 to 20 minutes until heated through and golden brown.

Cheese sauce

1. Melt butter, cook flour over gentle heat stirring continuously for one minute. 2. Remove pan from heat, gradually blend in milk to form a smooth sauce. Return to heat. Bring to a boil and simmer gently for 3 minutes stirring throughout. 3. Stir in grated cheese and season to taste with salt, pepper and mustard.

10. BAKED SPANISH ONIONS

Ingredients	*Quantity*
Medium-sized onions	3
Garlic	½ clove
Butter	30 gm
Parsley (finely chopped)	1 tsp
Lime juice	a few drops
Fresh white breadcrumbs	2 tbsp

Ingredients	Quantity
Salt and pepper	to taste

Method

1. Peel and cook onions in boiling salted water for 15 minutes. 2. Drain well. Cut into two crosswise. 3. Arrange on buttered baking dish, cut sides up. 4. Chop garlic fine. Blend garlic with butter, parsley, salt and pepper. Gradually beat in lime juice. 5. Spread mixture evenly over the six half-onions. 6. Cover and bake in moderate oven at 175ºC (350ºF) or Gas mark 4 for about 45 minutes basting from time to time. 7. Sprinkle with the breadcrumbs, return to oven and bake for another 10 to 15 minutes.

11. VEGETABLE HOT POT

Ingredients	For 4	For 100
Potatoes	225 gm	5.6 kg
Onions	115 gm	2.8 kg
Carrots	225 gm	5.6 kg
Turnip	115 gm	2.8 kg
Tomatoes	115 gm	2.8 kg
Capsicum	55 gm	1.35 kg
Celery	55 gm	1.35 kg
Beans	115 gm	2.8 kg
Salt	to taste	80-100 gm
Butter	10 gm	225 gm
Pepper	a pinch	15 gm

Method

1. Wash and prepare vegetables. 2. Cut potatoes into roundels, slice onions, dice carrots and turnip. Chop capsicum and celery, cut tomatoes into quarters, cut beans. 3. Arrange in layers in a casserole dish with a thick layer of potatoes on top. 4. Mix seasoning in vegetable stock; pour over the prepared vegetables. 5. Cover with greaseproof paper and cook till vegetables are cooked (about 1½ hours in a moderate hot oven). 6. Remove paper. Brush potatoes with melted butter and brown.

12. SWEET POTATO HOT POT

Ingredients	For 4	For 100
Sweet potatoes	450 gm	11 kg
Carrots	225 gm	5.6 kg
Onions	225 gm	5.6 kg
Peas	225 gm	5.6 kg

Ingredients	*For 4*	*For 100*
Turnip	115 gm	2.8 kg
Salt	to taste	80-100 gm
Stock	300 ml	7.5 litre
Parsley	a sprig	5 bunches
Butter	30 gm	630 gm

Method

1. Parboil sweet potatoes in jackets. 2. Peel and cut into roundels. 3. Peel and dice carrots, onions and turnip; shell peas. 4. Arrange vegetables in layers in a hot pot dish or casserole, keeping a layer of sweet potato on top. 5. Dot with butter. Add stock mixed with seasoning. 6. Cover with greasepaper or lid. 7. Cook in a moderate oven until vegetables are tender. 8. Remove paper and brush potato with a little melted butter. 9. Brown the top in a hot oven. Garnish with chopped parsley. 10. Serve with a folded napkin pinned round the dish in which it was cooked.

13. RATATOUILLE

Ingredients	*For 4*	*For 100*
Green pepper	225 gm	5.6 kg
Tomatoes	225 gm	5.6 kg
Young marrow	115 gm	2.8 kg
Aubergine (brinjal)	225 gm	5.6 kg
Onions	55 gm	5.6 kg
Olive oil	30 ml	450 ml
Garlic	1 flake	30 gm
Salt	10 gm	100 gm
Pepper	to taste	15 gm
Bread	115 gm	2.8 kg

Method

1. Split the green pepper in half, scoop out and discard the seeds, shred the flesh fairly fine. 2. Skin the tomatoes (put them into boiling water for a minute and the skin will come away easily) and slice. 3. Peel marrow and aubergine thinly and dice. 4. Skin onions and slice finely. 5. Heat oil till very hot. Add the onions and the green pepper. Sauté lightly until they are tender, add the diced marrow and aubergine and continue cooking; season with salt and pepper. 6. Stir in tomatoes and crushed garlic. Cover pan. 7. Simmer slowly for about 30 minutes, stirring occasionally. 8. Serve piping hot, surrounded with triangles of toast.

14. VEGETABLE KEDGEREE

Ingredients	*For 4*	*For 100*
Rice	225 gm	5.6 kg
Split green gram	115 gm	2.8 kg
Peas	225 gm	5.6 kg
Carrots	115 kg	2.8 kg
Eggs	4	100
Milk	30 ml	680 ml
Parsley	1 sprig	2 bunches
Salt	to taste	100 gm
Pepper	to taste	15 gm
Margarine	55 gm	1.35 kg

Method

1. Boil and drain rice. 2. Boil gram till tender and dry. 3. Dice carrots and shell peas, Boil. 4. Hard-boil eggs, sieve yolks and chop whites. 5. Mix rice, gram, vegetables, half the eggs, milk, margarine, seasoning and parsley. 6. Reheat, serve piled up in a dish garnished with remaining eggs.

15. RISOTTO A l'ITALIENNE

Ingredients	*For 4*	*For 100*
Pulao rice	450 gm	11 kg
Butter	55 gm	1.35 kg
Onions	115 gm	2.8 kg
Cheese	30 gm	680 gm
Nutmeg	a pinch	10 gm
Saffron	a pinch	5 gm
Tomato sauce	120 ml	2.95 litre
Vegetable stock	790 ml	20 litre
Pepper and salt		

Method

1. Wash rice and drain well. 2. Peel and mince onions. 3. Melt the butter. When hot add the onions and fry lightly. 4. Add rice, pepper, salt, nutmeg and saffron. 5. Add part of the stock and as rice starts swelling, add remainder of the stock. 6. As the stock is used up, add the sauce gradually. 7. When the rice is tender, add grated cheese; mould and turn over and serve.

N.B. In preparing this dish remember that the rice should be neither too dry nor too moist.

16. RICE AND LENTIL SAVOURY

Ingredients	*For 4*	*For 100*
Rice	115 gm	2.8 kg
Lentils	60 gm	1.35 kg
Eggs	1	25
Onions	115 gm	2.8 kg
Cheese	60 gm	1.35 kg
Garlic	1 clove	15 gm
Parsley	3-4 sprigs	4 bunches
Salt	to taste	100 gm
Cayenne pepper	a pinch	15 gm
Fat	15 gm	250 gm
Oil to fry	30 ml	500 ml

Method

1. Heat fat. Fry washed rice lightly. 2. Add double the quantity of water and cook till tender and dry (the rice grains should be separate). 3. Add half the beaten egg. 4. Cook lentils till tender. 5. Slice onions and fry well in the oil. 6. Mix together lentils, fried onions and remaining beaten egg. Add flaked cheese, chopped parsley and seasoning. 7. Put half the rice mixture in a well-greased pie dish. Add the lentil mixture. 8. Cover with remaining rice. 9. Cook at 190°C (375°F) or Gas mark 5 for half an hour. 10. Serve hot with cooked greens.

17. VEGETABLE CUTLETS

Ingredients	*For 4*	*For 100*
Potatoes	450 gm	11 kg
Carrots	115 gm	2.8 kg
Peas	115 gm	2.8 kg
Onions	55 gm	1.35 kg
Celery	1 stick	30 gm
Capsicum	15 gm	225 gm
Lime	1	6
Pepper	to taste	15 gm
Eggs	1	12
Breadcrumbs	55 gm	455 gm
Fat (absorption)	30 gm	500 gm
Refined flour	1 tsp	30 gm
Salt	to taste	100 gm

Method

1. Boil and mash potatoes. 2. Boil and chop carrots and peas. 3. Mince onions and celery; chop capsicum finely. 4. Mix chopped vegetables,

onions, celery and capsicum with mashed potatoes. Add lime juice, pepper and salt. 5. Shape into cutlets, dip first in flour then in egg and breadcrumbs and deep fry. 6. Serve hot with tomato sauce.

18. VEGETABLE CAKES

Ingredients	*For 4*	*For 100*
Potatoes	225 gm	5.6 kg
Peas	225 gm	5.6 kg
Carrots	115 gm	2.8 kg
Cauliflower	115 gm	2.8 kg
Onions	55 gm	1.35 kg
Lime	½	12
Ginger	a little	30 gm
Marmite	5 gm	115 gm
Salt	to taste	80-100 gm
Fat to fry (absorption)	30 gm	500 gm
Eggs	1	12
Breadcrumbs	30 gm	680 gm

Method

1. Clean and cut vegetables. 2 Boil and mash. 3. Add finely chopped onions, lime juice, marmite, ginger and salt. 4. Form into rounds, 7.5 cm. (3") in diameter. 5. Coat with egg and breadcrumbs and deep fry. Drain and serve hot.

19. VEGETABLE BALLS

Ingredients	*For 4*	*For 100*
Carrots	115 gm	2.8 kg
Peas	115 gm	2.8 kg
Cauliflower	115 gm	2.8 kg
Capsicum (without seeds)	55 gm	1.35 kg
Potatoes	225 gm	5.6 kg
Onions	115 gm	2.8 kg
Fresh bread	30 gm	680 gm
Eggs	1	20
Pepper	to taste	15 gm
Salt	to taste	100 gm
Fat to fry (absorption)	30 gm	500 gm

Method

1. Boil, peel and mash potatoes. 2. Prepare peas, carrots and cauliflower. Boil and crush. 3. Chop fine or mince capsicum and onions. 4. Soak bread in water, squeeze out moisture. 5. Mix together potatoes, vegetables,

capsicum, onions, bread, seasoning and beaten egg. 6. Shape into small balls (the size of a small lime) 7. Heat fat and deep fry vegetable balls. 8. Drain on absorbent paper and serve hot, plain or as garnish for pulaos, spaghetti etc.

20. CARROT RISSOLES

Ingredients	*For 4*	*For 100*
Carrots	450 gm	11 kg
Salt	to taste	80-100 gm
Nutmeg	a pinch	30 gm
Eggs	1	12
Butter	30 gm	680 gm
Breadcrumbs	30 gm	680 gm
Fat to fry (absorption)	30 gm	500 gm
Parsley	a few sprigs	3 bunches

Method

1. Wash and boil carrots in very little water till tender. 2. Mash or press carrots through a sieve. 3. Add salt, nutmeg and butter and mix thoroughly. 4. Form into shapes resembling carrots. 5. Coat with egg and roll in breadcrumbs and fry till brown. Drain. 6. Stick a sprig of parsley on top and serve at once.

21. LENTIL RISSOLES

Ingredients	*For 4*	*For 100*
Lentils	450 gm	11 kg
Powdered herbs	a pinch	30 gm
Parsley	1 sprig	3 bunches
Cheese	55 gm	1.35 kg
Fresh breadcrumbs	15 gm	340 gm
Margarine	15 gm	900 gm
Dry breadcrumbs	30 gm	340 gm
Egg yolks	1	20
Egg to coat	1	8
Fat to fry	30 gm	500 gm
Salt	a pinch	100 gm

Method

1. Wash and soak lentils for half an hour. 2. Cook till tender, beat until smooth and dry over fire. 3. Remove from fire. Add margarine, cheese, parsley, herbs, seasoning and fresh breadcrumbs. Mix well with beaten egg yolk. 4. Shape into rolls, dip in egg and breadcrumbs and deep fry. 5. Drain well and serve hot with tomato sauce.

22. VEGETABLE RISSOLES

Ingredients	*For 4*	*For 100*
Potatoes	225 gm	5.6 kg
Peas	225 gm	5.6 kg
Carrots	225 gm	5.6 kg
Cauliflower	225 gm	5.6 kg
Celery	55 gm	1.35 kg
Onions	55 gm	1.35 kg
Salt	to taste	80-100 gm
Pepper	to taste	15 gm
Powdered herbs	1 tsp	55 gm
Chopped parsley	a little	30 gm
Grated cheese	15 gm	340 gm
Margarine	30 gm	680 gm
Eggs	1	12
Breadcrumbs	30 gm	680 gm
Fat to fry (absorption)	30 gm	680 gm

Method

1. Prepare and cook vegetables till tender. 2. Mash vegetables and dry over a fire. 3. Add margarine, cheese, parsley, herbs and seasoning. Form into rissoles. 4. Dip in egg, roll in breadcrumbs and deep fry till golden brown. Drain well and serve with tomato sauce.

23. BIRD'S NEST

Ingredients	*For 4*	*For 100*
Potatoes	455 gm	11.3 kg
Peas	225 gm	5.6 kg
Vermicelli	55 gm	1.35 kg
Green pepper	15 gm	340 gm
Salt	10 gm	80-100 gm
Onions	115 gm	2.8 kg
Eggs	1	12
Parsley	2 sprigs	15 gm
Lime juice	to taste	8
Fat (absorption)	30 gm	500 gm
Lettuce	1 bunch	a few bunches

Method

1. Boil potatoes and peas separately. 2. Mash potatoes well. 3. Chop green pepper, onions and parsley. 4. Heat a little fat, add chopped ingredients and sauté. 5. Add potatoes and salt to taste. 6. Shape like eggs, stuff with boiled salted peas. 7. Coat with egg and vermicelli and

deep fry in hot fat. 8. Cut into halves lengthwise and set in lettuce leaves to resemble a bird's nest.

24. RICE CROQUETTES

Ingredients	*For 4*	*For 100*
Rice	225 gm	5.6 kg
Grated cheese	30 gm	680 gm
Parsley	3 sprigs	4 bunches
Onions	60 gm	1.35 kg
Salt	to taste	80-100 gm
Cayenne pepper	a pinch	10 gm
Eggs (beaten)	1	12
Eggs (hard-boiled)	2	50
Oil to fry (absorption)	30 ml	500 ml

Method

1. Boil rice, cool. 2. Mix with well-beaten egg. 3. Peel and mince onions. 4. Heat a little oil. Sauté minced onions without discolouring. 5. Remove from fire. Add chopped hard-boiled eggs, grated cheese, chopped parsley, salt and cayenne pepper. 6. With hands previously rinsed in cold water take a handful of rice. 7. Make a hollow in the middle, fill with prepared mixture. 8. Mould into a ball. Dip in browned breadcrumbs and fry in a deep pan of boiling oil till brown. 9. Drain well on absorbent paper. Serve hot with tomato sauce.

25. VEGETABLE HAMBURGERS

Ingredients	*For 4*	*For 100*
Potatoes	225 gm	5.6 kg
Carrots	225 gm	5.6 kg
Onions	55 gm	1.35 kg
Peas	115 gm	2.8 kg
Capsicum	55 gm	1.35 kg
Cayenne pepper	a pinch	10 gm
Bread	30 gm	680 gm
Eggs	1	25
Salt	to taste	80-100 gm
Oil	10 ml	200 ml

Method

1. Boil and mash potatoes. 2. Boil and mash carrots and peas. 3. Chop onions and capsicum fine. 4. Soak bread. 5. Heat oil. Sauté onions and capsicum. 6. Add mashed vegetables and bread with moisture squeezed

out. 7. Add cayenne pepper, salt and beaten egg. Mix well. 8. Shape into hamburgers 5 cm. (2") in diameter. 9. Shallow fry.

26. VEGETARIAN SAUSAGES

Ingredients	*For 4*	*For 100*
Lentils	115 gm	2.8 kg
Bread	55 gm	1.35 kg
Rice	55 gm	1.35 kg
Eggs	1	12
Marmite	¼ tsp	30 gm
Capsicum	30 gm	680 gm
Butter	15 gm	220 gm
Salt	to taste	80 gm
Breadcrumbs	20 gm	455 gm
Fat to fry	30 gm	500 gm

Method

1. Boil lentils and rice separately. 2. Put them into a pan, add fresh breadcrumbs and marmite, salt and pepper. 3. Parboil capsicum, chop fine and add to above mixture. 4. Add melted butter. Mix well. 5. Keep on fire and cook lightly. 6. Turn out and leave till cold. When cold, flour the hands and form into small sausages; coat with egg and breadcrumbs and deep fry.

27. SAVOURY SAUSAGES

Ingredients	*For 4*	*For 100*
Rice	115 gm	2.8 kg
Lentils	60 gm	1.36 kg
Eggs (hard-boiled)	2	50
Eggs (beaten)	1	12
Curry powder	a large pinch	30 gm
Pepper	a pinch	15 gm
Salt	to taste	100 gm
Ginger	a small piece	100 gm
Tomato purée	1 tbsp	500 gm
Breadcrumbs	30 gm	500 gm
Oil to fry (absorption)	30 ml	500 ml

Method

1. Boil rice and lentils separately. Cool. 2. Chop hard-boiled eggs finely. 3. Mix with cold cooked rice, lentils, pepper, curry powder, salt, tomato purée and finely chopped ginger. 4. Shape into sausages. Coat in egg and breadcrumbs. Fry in deep fat till brown. Drain on absorbent paper. Serve hot with fried or mashed potatoes.

28. MOCK SALMON STEAK

Ingredients	*For 4*	*For 100*
Potatoes	450 gm	11 kg
Rice	115 gm	2.8 kg
Butter	50 gm	1.25 kg
Onions	30 gm	680 gm
Fresh bread	115 gm	2.8 kg
Tomatoes	450 gm	11 kg
Eggs	2	50
Milk	30 ml	680 ml
Breadcrumbs	15 gm	340 gm
Fat	50 gm	1.25 kg
Salt	to taste	80-100 gm
Pepper	to taste	15-30 gm

Method

1. Heat butter in pan. Add chopped onions and fry. 2. When onions brown, add milk and bring to a boil. 3. Add boiled rice and mashed potatoes. 4. Add breadcrumbs and tomato purée, seasoning and eggs. Mix well. 5. Form into the shape of small steaks. 6. Coat with egg and breadcrumbs and fry.

29. MOCK BEEF RISSOLES

Ingredients	*For 4*	*For 100*
Rice	115 gm	2.8 kg
Radish	115 gm	2.8 kg
Mustard	½ tsp	75 gm
Onions	30 gm	680 gm
Capsicum	30 gm	680 gm
Milk	295 ml	7.37 litre
Lime	1	12
Eggs	1	12
Breadcrumbs	30 gm	680 gm
Oil to fry (absorption)	15 ml	250 ml
Salt and pepper		

Method

1. Cook the rice in milk till tender. 2. Add grated radish, onions and chopped capsicum. 3. Add mustard, pepper, salt and lime juice. 4. Fold in whipped egg white. 5. Roll in breadcrumbs. Deep fry. Drain and serve hot with tomato sauce.

30. MOCK FILLETS OF SOLE

Ingredients	*For 4*	*For 100*
Potatoes	450 gm	11 kg
Rice	115 gm	2.8 kg
Butter	55 gm	1.35 kg
Bread	55 gm	1.36 kg
Milk	295 ml	7 litre
Onions	10 gm	250 gm
Mace	a pinch	10 gm
Eggs	2	24
Lime	½	8
Salt	to taste	80-100 gm
Pepper	to taste	15-30 gm

Method

1. Slice onions and fry in butter without browning. 2. Add the milk and when it boils, add rice and mace. 3. Boil and mash potatoes. 4. When rice is cooked, add mashed potatoes and fresh breadcrumbs. 5. Beat eggs well and add half to above mixture. 6. Add pepper and salt and set to cool. 7. Shape into small fillets. Coat with egg and breadcrumbs and deep fry. 8. Serve hot garnished with slices of lime.

31. NUT CUTLETS

Ingredients	*For 4*	*For 100*
Mixed nuts	115 gm	2.8 kg
Mace	a pinch	10 gm
Chopped parsley	½ tsp	2 bunches
Onions	30 gm	680 gm
Milk	150 ml	3.65 litre
Butter	15 gm	340 gm
Refined flour	30 gm	680 gm
Salt	to taste	100 gm
Pepper	a pinch	15 gm
Eggs	½–1	12
Breadcrumbs	30 gm	680 gm
Fat to fry (absorption)	30 gm	500 gm

Method

1. Make a thick sauce with flour, butter and milk. Add seasoning and flavouring. 2. Peel and grind nuts. 3. Mince onions. 4. Mix together sauce, nuts and onions and leave to cool. 5. Divide into even portions and shape on a floured board. 6. Brush with egg and toss in breadcrumbs. 7. Fry quickly in hot fat, drain and serve hot.

32. VEGETABLE PANROLLS

Ingredients	*For 4*	*For 100*
Batter		
Refined flour	115 gm	2.8 kg
Egg	1	25
Milk	145 ml	3.625 litre
Salt	to taste	50 gm
Filling		
Carrots	225 gm	5.65 kg
Peas	115 gm	2.8 kg
Potatoes	450 gm	11.00 kg
Onions	115 gm	2.8 kg
Salt	to taste	80-100 gm
Pepper	a pinch	15 gm
Ginger	5 gm	100 gm
Lime	¼	6
Coating		
Egg	1	12
Breadcrumbs	55 gm	455 gm
Fat to fry	30 gm	500 gm

Method

Pancakes

1. Sieve flour and salt into a bowl. 2. Make a well in the centre, add the beaten yolk of egg and milk. 3. Beat well to form a smooth batter and let it stand for an hour. 4. Beat white stiff. Fold into the batter and prepare pancakes. 5. Fill with prepared filling. Fold envelope fashion. 6. Dip in egg, coat with breadcrumbs and deep fry.

Filling

1. Peel and dice potatoes and carrots to very small pieces. 2. Shell peas and chop onions; grate ginger. 3. Heat fat, sauté onions; add rest of vegetables, salt, pepper, ginger and just enough water to cover the vegetables. 4. Cook till vegetables are tender and moisture has evaporated. 5. Add lime juice. Remove from fire and use as required.

33. EGG AND PEA PANROLLS

Ingredients	*For 4 (2 per portion)*	*For 100 (2 per portion)*
Pancake Batter		
Refined flour	115 gm	2.8 kg
Salt	½ tsp	50 gm

Ingredients	*For 4 (2 per portion)*	*For 100 (2 per portion)*
Eggs	1	25
Milk	300 ml	7.5 litre
Filling		
Hard-boiled eggs	2	50
Peas	450 gm	11 kg
Milk	115 ml	2.8 litre
Refined flour	30 gm	680 gm
Butter	30 gm	680 gm
Cheese	30 gm	680 gm
Onions	30 gm	680 gm
Cayenne pepper	a pinch	15 gm
Oil	60 ml	1.5 litre
Salt	to taste	50 gm

Method

1. Shell and boil peas. 2. Prepare a white sauce with flour, butter and milk. Add grated onions, cook for 5 minutes. Remove from fire. Cool. 3. Add chopped hard-boiled eggs, peas, grated cheese, cayenne pepper and salt. 4. Mix flour and salt for pancake in a bowl. 5. Make a well in the centre. Break the egg and drop into it. 6. Stir from the centre working in the flour, gradually adding milk until a third to half of it is used up and the whole is the consistency of thick cream. 7. Beat well and mix thoroughly. 8. Stir in the remainder of the milk and let it stand for at least half an hour. 9. Prepare pancakes (see pancake recipe) but do not turn. 10. Put a spoonful of filling in the centre. 11. Fold to form a parcel. Add a teaspoon of oil more into the pan and brown on both sides. Serve hot.

34. MACARONI AND TOMATO FRITTERS

Ingredients	*For 4*	*For 100*
Macaroni	225 gm	5.6 kg
Tomatoes	225 gm	5.6 kg
Carrots	55 gm	1.35 kg
Pepper	to taste	15 gm
Onions	10 gm	250 gm
Cornflour	15 gm	340 gm
Butter	10 gm	250 gm
Eggs	1	12
Breadcrumbs	30 gm	680 gm
Fat to fry (absorption)	30 gm	500 gm

Method

1. Boil macaroni in salted water using the absorption method. 2. Chop up fine. 3. Prepare a thick tomato sauce using cornflour to thicken. Mix with macaroni and leave it to cool. 4. When cold, form into fritters. Coat with egg and breadcrumbs and deep fry.

35. CORN AND GREEN PEPPER FRITTERS

Ingredients	*For 4*	*For 100*
Capsicum	225 gm	5.6 kg
Corn	450 gm	11 kg
Sugar	a pinch	30 gm
Eggs	1	12
Refined flour (sifted)	15 gm	340 gm
Baking powder	a pinch	1½ tsp
Salt	to taste	80-100 gm
Fat to fry (absorption)	30 gm	500 gm
White sauce		
Butter	15 gm	340 gm
Refined flour	15 gm	340 gm
Milk or milk and cornliquor	150 ml	3.75 litre
Salt	to taste	15 gm

Method

1. Cook the corn in salted water till tender. 2. Combine corn, sugar, salt, chopped capsicum, eggs and white sauce. 3. Mix baking powder with flour and sift over the corn mixture. Mix well. 4. Heat oil. Fry dessertspoonfuls in hot oil. Drain and serve hot.

36. CAULIFLOWER AU GRATIN

Ingredients	*For 4*	*For 100*
Cauliflower	225 gm	5.6 kg
Cheese	55 gm	1.35 kg
Milk and Cauliflower liquor	295 ml	7.3 litre
Refined flour	30 gm	680 gm
Butter	30 gm	680 gm
Pepper	a pinch	15 gm
Salt	to taste	100 gm

Method

1. Wash and boil the cauliflower in salted water. 2. Make a sauce with

flour, butter and liquid. 3. Add seasoning and three-fourths of the cheese. 4. Put the cauliflower into a greased pan. 5. Pour sauce over the cauliflower, sprinkle cheese and brown under the grill or high up in the oven.

37. VEGETABLE AND EGG AU GRATIN

Ingredients	*For 4*	*For 100*
Small onions	450 gm	11 kg
Peas	450 gm	11 kg
Potatoes	450 gm	11 kg
Milk	15 ml	200 ml
Butter	10 gm	250 gm
Eggs	4	100
Béchamel sauce	295 ml	7.4 litre
Breadcrumbs	15 gm	340 gm
Cheese	15 gm	340 gm
Béchamel sauce		
Onions	10 gm	250 gm
Carrots	15 gm	340 gm
Mushrooms	10 gm	250 gm
Bouquet garni	10 gm	100 gm
Butter	30 gm	680 gm
Milk	845 ml	18.6 litre
Refined flour	15 gm	340 gm
Salt	to taste	80-100 gm
Pepper	a pinch	15 gm
Nutmeg	a small pinch	10 gm

Method

1. Prepare a white sauce with half the butter, flour and three-fourths of the milk. 2. Stew vegetables in remaining butter. Add remaining milk and bouquet garni. 3. Simmer till vegetables are well cooked. 4. Strain essence into the Béchamel sauce, then season and cook 5 minutes longer. 5. Cook small onion in a casserole in the oven. 6. Boil peas. Boil and mash potatoes. 7. Hard-boil the eggs. 8. Line a buttered pie dish with the mashed potatoes. 9. Put in the cooked onion and peas. 10. Put the hard-boiled eggs on top, pour in the sauce. 11. Sprinkle with fine breadcrumbs, then with grated cheese. Brown lightly under the grill.

38. VEGETABLE EXOTICA

Ingredients	*Quantity*
Brussels sprouts	100 gm

Ingredients	*Quantity*
Baby corn	50 gm
Fresh peas	50 gm
Mushrooms	50 gm
Carrots	100 gm
Spring onion bulbs	50 gm
Salt	
Pepper	to taste
Mustard	
Parmesan cheese	50 gm
Pesto Sauce	
Basil	1 bunch
Garlic	a few flakes
Pine nuts (chilkosas)	50 gm
Olive oil	50 ml

Method

1. Wash, scrape if necessary, and prepare vegetables. 2. Break broccoli into flowerettes, cut Brussels sprouts into quarters. Leave mushrooms, baby corn and onion bulbs whole. The peas should be shelled and carrots turned. 4. Parboil in slightly seasoned boiling water. Drain. 5. Prepare sauce. Pound together in a mortar the basil (about 50 gm after stalks are removed). 6. Grind garlic flakes and pine nuts fine. Add half the cheese grated. When it forms a thick smooth paste, add olive oil gradually to blend well with the other ingredients. Add pepper, salt and a pinch of mustard. Mix with prepared vegetables and place in an oven-proof dish. 7. Top with the remaining shredded cheese. Bake in a quick oven to form a crust. Serve hot.

39. EGG AND VEGETABLE SAVOURY

Ingredients	*For 4*	*For 100*
Onions	250 gm	5.6 kg
Potatoes	450 gm	11 kg
Carrots	115 gm	2.8 kg
Peas	250 gm	5.6 kg
Tomatoes	115 gm	2.8 kg
Eggs	2	50
Butter	30 gm	680 gm
Cheese sauce	300 ml	7.5 litre
Pepper	a pinch	15 gm
Cayenne pepper	a pinch	15 gm

Method

1. Cook potatoes, carrots, onions and peas separately. 2. Dice cooked potatoes, carrots, onions and fresh tomatoes. Stir in the peas and butter. 3. Beat the eggs with the seasoning. Stir into the cheese sauce. 4. Add prepared vegetables to sauce. 5. Turn into a greased casserole dish. Bake for half an hour in a moderate oven.

40. CAULIFLOWER AND EGG SAVOURY

Ingredients	*For 4*	*For 100*
Cauliflower	225 gm	5.65 kg
Tomatoes	115 gm	2.8 kg
Onions	115 gm	2.8 kg
Capsicum	115 gm	2.8 kg
Hard-boiled eggs	1	25
Cheese	30 gm	680 gm
White sauce	292 ml	7.35 litre
Butter	15 gm	340 gm
Chopped herbs	¼ tsp	15 gm
Pepper	a pinch	15 gm
Salt	to taste	80-100 gm

Method

1. Parboil cauliflower. Drain and keep liquor for preparing the sauce. 2. Stew sliced tomatoes, onions and capsicums with the butter. 3. Put in a baking dish alternately with the cauliflower. 4. Put a layer of sliced hard-boiled egg. Cover with white sauce. Sprinkle with grated cheese. Dot with butter. 5. Brown lightly in a quick oven. Serve hot with roast potatoes and cheese sauce.

41. MACARONI CHEESE

Ingredients	*For 4*	*For 100*
Macaroni	115 gm	2.8 kg
Cheese	55 gm	1.35 kg
Butter	15 gm	340 gm
Refined flour	15 gm	340 gm
Milk	295 ml	7.35 litre
Pepper	to taste	15 gm
Salt	10 gm	100 gm
Breadcrumbs	30 gm	455 gm
Tomatoes	115 gm	2.8 kg

Method

1. Grate cheese. 2. Boil macaroni in salted water till cooked. 3. Drain and put into a colander, hold under a running tap. 4. Prepare white sauce and add half the grated cheese. 5. Grease a mould, put in the boiled macaroni and tomato slices. Pour hot sauce over. 6. Sprinkle with grated cheese and breadcrumbs. Dot with butter and bake for 25 minutes at 205°C (400°F).

42. BAKED SAVOURY MACARONI

Ingredients	*For 4*	*For 100*
Macaroni	225 gm	5.6 kg
Milk	295 ml	7.35 litre
Cheese	55 gm	1.36 kg
Onions	115 gm	2.8 kg
Eggs	2	50
Garlic	1 flake	10 gm
Parsley	1 sprig	1 bunch
Pepper	a pinch	15 gm
Salt	to taste	80-100 gm
Nutmeg	a small pinch	10 gm

Method

1. Boil the macaroni till tender. Drain well. 2. Add hot milk, grated cheese, minced onions, beaten eggs, minced garlic, chopped parsley, pepper, salt and nutmeg. 3. Mix well and put into a buttered pie dish, keeping the mixture not more than 2.5 cm. (1") deep. 4. Bake in a moderate oven for about 45 minutes. 5. Serve hot with grilled tomatoes and peas or greens.

43. SPAGHETTI WITH MUSHROOM AND CHEESE SAUCE

Ingredients	*For 4*	*For 100*
Fresh mushrooms or	225 gm	5.6 kg
Dried mushrooms	115 gm	2.8 kg
Onions	60 gm	1.36 kg
Butter	10 gm	250 gm
Milk	150 ml	3.75 litre
Salt	to taste	50-80 gm
Pepper	a pinch	15 gm
Refined flour	15 gm	340 gm
Tomato sauce	30 ml	680 ml
Cheese	60 gm	1.36 kg
Spaghetti	340 gm	8.5 kg
Butter (for spaghetti)	30 gm	340 gm

Method

1. Wash and soak mushrooms overnight if dry or wipe mushrooms if fresh. Cut into large pieces. 2. Melt butter. Sauté finely chopped onions without discolouring. 3. Add mushrooms, milk and seasoning. Cover pan and simmer for 10 minutes. 4. Make the flour into a smooth paste with a little milk and tomato sauce. 5. Stir into mushroom mixture. Bring to boil stirring all the time. 6. Boil for one or two minutes. Remove from the fire and stir in the cheese until melted. 7. Meanwhile cook the spaghetti (hold spaghetti in a bundle and lower the ends into boiling salted water, then gradually wind the rest round the inside of the pan as it becomes supple enough to bend). Boil for 10 to 12 minutes until just tender. Drain; return to the pan and toss in melted butter. 8. Turn cooked spaghetti on to a hot dish. 9. Pour the mushroom sauce over and garnish with half slices of tomato and sprigs of parsley.

44. SPAGHETTI WITH BARBECUE SAUCE

Ingredients	*For 4*	*For 100*
Spaghetti	340 gm	8.5 kg
Oil	30 ml	680 ml
Onions	55 gm	1.36 kg
Cornflour	15 gm	340 gm
Tomatoes	500 gm	12.5 kg
Water	590 ml	14.75 litre
Brown sugar	30 gm	680 gm
Paprika	½ level tsp	15 gm
Worcester sauce	15 ml	340 ml
Vinegar	10 ml	250 ml
Tabasco sauce	a few drops	30 ml
Stuffed olives	15 gm	340 gm
Cheese	60 gm	1.35 kg
Butter	10 gm	250 gm
Salt	to taste	50-80 gm

Method

1. Cook spaghetti in salted boiling water till done. 2. Drain and hold under a running tap to prevent sticking. 3. Heat oil. Add chopped onions and cook for a few minutes without browning. 4. Stir in the cornflour and mix well. 5. Add peeled and sliced tomatoes and water and simmer for 10 to 15 minutes. 6. Add sugar, paprika, Worcester sauce, vinegar and tabasco sauce and cook for a few minutes more. 7. Check for seasoning. 8. Stir in sliced olives. 9. Melt butter and toss spaghetti in the butter to warm it. 10. Put the spaghetti into a serving dish. Pour the hot sauce over. 11. Sprinkle over with grated cheese and serve hot.

45. VEGETABLE PIE

Ingredients	*For 4*	*For 100*
Potatoes	680 gm	17 kg
Beans	225 gm	5.6 kg
Carrots	225 gm	5.6 kg
Peas	225 gm	5.6 kg
Capsicum	55 gm	1.35 kg
Celery	30 gm	680 gm
Onions	30 gm	680 gm
Refined flour	15 gm	340 gm
Salt	to taste	100 gm
Pepper	a pinch	15 gm
Milk	150 ml	3 litre
Butter	15 gm	340 gm

Method

1. Make a thick white stew with half the potatoes and all the other vegetables. 2. Boil and mash remaining potatoes. 3. Grease a pie dish. Put in the vegetable stew. 4. Cover with mashed potatoes. Top with butter and bake.

46. VEGETABLE PIE WITH CHEESE SAUCE

Ingredients	*For 4*	*For 100*
Potatoes	450 gm	11 kg
Peas	225 gm	5.65 kg
Carrots	225 gm	5.65 kg
Tomatoes	225 gm	5.65 kg
Celery	115 gm	2.8 kg
Onions	115 gm	2.8 kg
Salt	to taste	50-100 gm
Pepper	a pinch	15 gm
Butter	15 gm	340 gm
Sauce		
Milk	295 ml	7.35 litre
Refined flour	15 gm	340 gm
Butter	15 gm	340 gm
Cheese	55 gm	1.35 kg

Method

1. Prepare a white stew with half the potatoes and all the other vegetables. 2. Make a cheese sauce with flour, butter, milk and cheese. 3. Boil and mash remaining potatoes. 4. Mix cheese sauce with

vegetables; put into a pie dish. 5. Cover with creamed potatoes; fork it as for shepherd's pie. 6. Dot with butter and grill till brown or brown in an oven.

47. EGG, TOMATO AND RICE PIE

Ingredients	*For 4*	*For 100*
Hard-boiled eggs	2	50
Rice	340 gm	8.6 kg
Onions	115 gm	8.6 kg
Garlic	2 flakes	15 gm
Cheese	55 gm	1.36 kg
Tomatoes	225 gm	5.6 kg
Green pepper	115 gm	2.8 kg
Parsley sauce	295 gm	7.35 gm
Salt	to taste	100 gm
Butter	10 gm	225 gm
Parsley Sauce		
Milk	295 ml	7.3 litre
Refined flour	15 gm	340 gm
Butter	15 gm	340 gm
Parsley	½ bunch	8 bunches

Method

1. Boil rice. 2. Chop garlic and onions fine. Fry in melted fat. 3. Mix rice with parsley sauce, pepper, salt, fried onions and garlic. 4. Lay in pyrex dish with sliced eggs, sliced tomatoes and chopped green pepper. 5. Sprinkle with grated cheese. 6. Bake at 175°C (350°F) for 15 minutes.

Parsley sauce

1. Prepare white sauce. Add finely chopped parsley.

48. CHEESE, EGG AND POTATO PIE

Ingredients	*For 4*	*For 100*
Potatoes	450 gm	11 kg
Eggs	2	50
Cheese	60 gm	1.5 kg
White sauce	590 ml	14.75 litre
Celery	50 gm	1 kg
Pepper	a pinch	15 gm
Salt	to taste	80-100 gm
Butter	15 gm	340 gm

Method

1. Boil potatoes. Peel and slice. 2. Hard-boil eggs. Shell and chop. 3. Chop celery. Grate cheese. 4. Mix eggs and potatoes. 5. Put into a buttered dish. Sprinkle over with chopped celery, pepper and salt. 6. Mix half the cheese into the white sauce. 7. Pour sauce into the dish. Sprinkle with remaining cheese. Dot with butter and bake in a hot oven at 218ºC (425ºF) or Gas mark 7 for half an hour.

49. GOLDEN CHEESE BAKE

Ingredients	*Quantity*
Cooked rice	220 gm
Shredded carrots	170 gm
Grated cheese	115 gm
Milk	50 ml
Beaten eggs	2
Minced onion	30 gm
Salt	1½ tsp
Pepper	¼ tsp

Method

1. Combine rice, carrots, 100 gm cheese, milk, eggs, onion and seasoning. 2. Pour into greased baking dish. 3. Sprinkle with remaining 15 gm cheese. 4. Bake at 175ºC (350ºF) for one hour.

50. CHEESE SOUFFLÉ

Ingredients	*For 4*	*For 100*
Butter	15 gm	340 gm
Refined flour.	15 gm	340 gm
Milk	150 ml	3.7 litre
Cheese	55 gm	2.8 kg
Eggs	2	50
Salt	to taste	50-80 gm
Pepper	a pinch	15 gm

Method

1. Melt butter in a pan. Add flour and cook for a few minutes. Do not allow it to brown. 2. Add hot milk and cook till sauce thickens, stirring all the time. Remove and cool. 3. Add grated cheese and seasoning and beaten egg yolks. 4. Whip egg whites very stiffly and fold into the mixture. 5. Pour into a greased soufflé mould and bake in a hot oven at 205ºC (400ºF) for 15 to 20 minutes. Serve immediately.

51. CHEESE AND CORN SOUFFLÉ

Ingredients	*Quantity*
Butter	¼ cup (180 gm)
Refined flour	¼ cup (about 60 gm)
Salt	to taste
Milk	1 cup
Cheese	100 gm
Dry mustard	1 tsp
Corn (boil till tender, corn on the cob in salted water; drain and scrape)	1 cup
Soft breadcrumbs	½ cup
Eggs	3
Cream of tartar	¼ tsp

Method

1. Prepare a white sauce with flour, butter and milk. Add salt to taste and mustard. Add grated cheese, breadcrumbs and corn. 2. Cook stirring until cheese is melted. Cool for a few minutes. Add beaten egg yolks and blend well. 3. Beat egg whites and cream of tartar, until stiff. Fold into the mixture. Pour into ungreased pan, set in a large pan of hot water. Bake at 163°C (325°F) till set. Serve immediately.

52. CHEESE SOUFFLÉ DUBOIS

Ingredients	*For 4*	*For 100*
Milk	295 ml	7.3 litre
Fresh breadcrumbs	115 gm	2.8 kg
Cheese	85 gm	2.125 kg
Eggs	2	50
Salt	to taste	50 gm
Mustard	a pinch	15 gm
Pepper	a pinch	15 gm
Sugar	a pinch	15 gm

Method

1. Bring the milk to a boil, remove from fire and drop the breadcrumbs gradually stirring vigorously with a wooden spoon. 2. Beat well. Add seasoning and leave to cool, stirring occasionally. 3. Add the cheese and well-beaten egg yolks. 4. Lastly fold in stiffly beaten egg whites. 5. Pour into deep fire-proof dishes and bake in a moderate oven till set.

53. CHEESE AND CAULIFLOWER SOUFFLÉ

Ingredients	*For 4*	*For 100*
Cauliflower	340 gm	11 kg

Ingredients	*For 4*	*For 100*
Refined flour	15 gm	340 gm
Butter	15 gm	340 gm
Milk	150 ml	3.75 litre
Stock	150 ml	3.75 litre
Cheese	55 gm	1.35 kg
Eggs	2	50
Salt	a pinch	80-100 gm
Pepper	a pinch	15 gm

Method

1. Parboil cauliflower in salted water. 2. Drain and break cauliflower into flowerettes. 3. Prepare a medium-consistency white sauce with flour, butter, milk and cauliflower stock. Cool. 4. Add well-beaten egg yolks and grated cheese. 5. Beat egg whites stiff and fold into mixture. 6. Put cauliflower into greased pie dish and pour sauce over. 7. Bake in a moderate oven. 8. Serve immediately.

54. SPINACH SOUFFLÉ (A)

Ingredients	*For 4*	*For 100*
Spinach	225 gm	5.65 kg
Cheese	70 gm	1.75 kg
Eggs	2	50
Refined flour	30 gm	680 gm
Milk	150 ml	3.75 litre
Pepper	to taste	15 gm
Salt	to taste	100 gm
Butter	30 gm	680 gm

Method

1. Wash and boil spinach till tender and all moisture has evaporated. 2. Make into a purée. 3. Prepare mornay sauce with flour, butter, milk and most of the cheese. 4. Add sauce to spinach purée. Add beaten egg yolks. Mix well. 5. Beat egg whites to a stiff froth and fold into the mixture. 6. Put mixture into a soufflé mould and bake at 175°C (350°F) for 25-30 minutes.

SPINACH SOUFFLÉ (B)

Ingredients	*For 4*	*For 100*
Spinach	225 gm	5.65 kg
Eggs	3	75
Cheese	70 gm	1.75 kg
Pepper	to taste	15 gm
Salt	to taste	100 gm

Method

1. Wash and boil spinach till tender and all moisture has evaporated. 2. Make into a purée. 3. Add egg yolks and grated cheese, reserving a little for sprinkling on top. 4. Beat egg whites stiff, fold into the mixture. 5. Put into a soufflé mould, sprinkle with remaining cheese and bake at 175°C (350°F) for 25-30 minutes.

55. SAVOURY MOULD a l'ITALIENNE

Ingredients	*For 4*	*For 100*
Spaghetti	225 gm	5.6 kg
Bread	225 gm	5.6 kg
Tomatoes	225 gm	5.6 kg
Cheese	55 gm	1.35 kg
Milk	50 ml	1.25 litre
Browned breadcrumbs	30 gm	340 gm
Salt	10 gm	100 gm
Pepper	to taste	15 gm
Paprika	5 gm	115 gm
Parsley	½ bunch	2 bunches
Butter	30 gm	680 gm

Method

1. Boil the spaghetti in salted boiling water. 2. Cool and strain. 3. Cut fresh bread (without crust) into small cubes, cover with warm milk. 4. Blanch and mash tomatoes; grate cheese. 5. Butter a pyrex mould, sprinkle the inside thickly with browned breadcrumbs. 6. Fill the mould alternately with layers of spaghetti, tomatoes, bread and cheese keeping spaghetti as the top layer. 7. Season each layer with salt, pepper and paprika. 8. Pour remaining melted butter over the spaghetti. 9. Bake in a moderately hot oven for about 35 minutes.

56. SAVOURY VEGETABLE RING

Ingredients	*For 4*	*For 100*
Potatoes	565 gm	15 kg
Butter	15 gm	340 gm
Eggs	1	25
Onions	100 gm	2.5 kg
Cheese	30 gm	680 gm
Mushrooms	30 gm	680 gm
Carrots	225 gm	5.6 kg
Peas	115 gm	2.8 kg
Breadcrumbs	10 gm	250 gm

Ingredients	*For 4*	*For 100*
Tomato ketchup	30 ml	680 ml
Brown gravy or vegetable stock	150 ml	3.75 litre
Pepper	a pinch	15 gm
Salt	to taste	80-100 gm

Method

1. Peel and slice carrots, mushrooms and a quarter of the potatoes. Shell peas. 2. Boil remaining potatoes. Peel and mash. 3. Add beaten egg, half the onions grated, and grated cheese. 4. Put into a ring mould previously greased and sprinkle with breadcrumbs. 5. Bake at 175°C (350°F) for 30 to 40 minutes. 6. Meanwhile stew prepared vegetables and remaining onions in the brown gravy. 7. Add tomato ketchup and seasoning. 8. Turn cooked mould on to a large serving dish. Fill hole in centre with vegetable mixture. 9. Garnish with a few whole mushrooms and serve hot.

57. JAPONAISE TOMATOES

Ingredients	*For 4*	*For 100*
Medium-sized tomatoes	500 gm	12.5 kg
Butter	30 gm	680 gm
Rice	115 gm	2.75 kg
Cheese	55 gm	1.36 kg
Breadcrumbs	15 gm	340 gm
Parsley	1 bunch	4 bunches
Salt	10 gm	100 gm
Pepper	to taste	15 gm

Method

1. Wash tomatoes, cut a slice off the top, scoop out pulp and drain shells. 2. In a pan put in the tomato pulp and butter and put over a fire. 3. When hot, add fully boiled rice. Add pepper and salt. 4. Add grated cheese. 5. Remove from fire and fill prepared tomatoes with the filling. 6. Sprinkle breadcrumbs over top of each tomato. Dot with butter and bake in a fairly hot oven for 15 minutes. 7. Serve garnished with crisply fried parsley.

58. POTATO BASKET

Ingredients	*For 4*	*For 100*
Potatoes	500 gm	12.5 kg
Oil	to fry	to fry
Salt	to taste	to taste
Mixed vegetable filling		
Peas (unshelled)	115 gm	2.8 kg

Ingredients	*For 4*	*For 100*
Carrots	60 gm	1.36 kg
Beans	60 gm	1.36 kg
Turnip	30 gm	680 gm
Salt and pepper to taste		

Method

1. Peel and cut potatoes into very thin, long strips. 2. Put into salted water and leave for 10 minutes. 3. Drain and spread on a clean cloth. 4. Arrange the strips in a small sieve (with handle) so as to form a design like a basket. 5. Put a few more strips so as to bind the strips together. 6. Place another sieve over and press tightly. 7. Hold the handles together and immerse in hot oil and fry till light brown. 8. Drain and fill with a macédoine of prepared vegetables. 9. Put a handle of either lettuce stem or spring onion. Serve on a salad bed.

59. AUBERGINES STUFFED AND BAKED

Ingredients	*For 4*	*For 100*
Aubergines	4 (450 gm)	100 (11 kg)
Onions	225 gm	5.6 kg
Tomatoes	225 gm	5.6 kg
Rice	115 gm	2.8 kg
Garlic	1 clove	15 gm
Cheese	30 gm	680 gm
Fat	30 gm	500 gm

Method

1. Boil unpeeled aubergines for 5 minutes. 2. Cool. Halve lengthwise and remove a little of the pulp to leave thick shells. 3. Boil rice and cool. 4. Brown chopped onions in fat. 5. Add the diced, peeled tomatoes, grated garlic and the chopped brinjal pulp. 6. Cook gently together for 4 or 5 minutes more. 7. Mix with the rice and grated cheese. Pile the mixture into the shells. 8. Bake on a greased dish in a moderate oven for 35 minutes.

60. STUFFED SWEET PEPPER

Ingredients	*For 4*	*For 100*
Capsicums (large)	4 (450 gm)	100 (11 kg)
Tomatoes	225 gm	5.65 kg

Ingredients	*For 4*	*For 100*
Stuffing 'A'		
Rice	115 gm	2.8 kg
Mushrooms	30 gm	680 kg
Onions	50 gm	1.36 kg
Butter	15 gm	340 gm
Cayenne pepper	a pinch	15 gm
Salt	to taste	80-100 gm
Stuffing 'B'		
Rice	115 gm	2.8 kg
Cheese	50 gm	1.36 kg
Eggs	1	25
Fresh breadcrumbs	15 gm	340 gm
Salt	to taste	to taste

Method

1. Simmer whole capsicums in enough water to cover, for 12 minutes. 2. Halve and remove seeds. 3. Fill with prepared stuffing. Place in a buttered baking dish. 4. Place tomato halves in between. Bake for 45 minutes in a moderate oven. Add a little gravy to the baking dish after the first 2 minutes.

1. Chop the onions fine. Brown in butter. 2. Add minced mushrooms and cook for about 3 minutes. 3. Mix in boiled rice and seasoning.

Stuffing 'B'

1. Boil rice and cool. 2. Add beaten egg, flaked cheese and breadcrumbs. Add salt.

61. STUFFED VEGETABLE MARROW (Vellari)

Ingredients	*Quantity*
Vegetable marrow (medium-sized)	1
Butter	2 tbsp
Nuts (chopped finely)	½ cup
Potato	1
Onions (small)	1
Milk (small cup)	1
Egg	1
Marmite or vegetable extract	½ tsp
Grated cheese	1 heaped tbsp
Parsley	½ bunch
Salt and pepper	to taste

Method

1. Wash and scrub marrow but do not peel. 2. Cut in half lengthwise. Scoop out seeds and pith. 3. Boil potato. Dice 4. Mix together chopped nuts, diced potato, milk, seasoning, egg and chopped parsley. 5. Melt butter. Fry chopped onion and the seeds of marrow if tender, in half the butter. 6. Add chopped nuts etc., and marmite and fry for a couple of minutes longer. 7. Parboil vegetable marrow (it should still be hard). 8. Fill with fried mixture. Place in a buttered pie dish. 9. Top with butter and grated cheese. 10. Bake for about half an hour in a medium oven at 175ºC (350ºF). 11. Serve with tomato sauce.

62. EGGS IN TOMATOES

Ingredients	*For 4*	*For 100*
Tomatoes (medium, even-sized)	4 (450 gm)	100 (11 kg)
Eggs	4	100
Cheese	60 gm	1.35 kg
Breadcrumbs	30 gm	680 gm
Fat	10 gm	250 gm
Salt	to taste	to taste

Method

1. Cut a thin slice from the top (not the stem end) of each tomato. 2. Carefully remove pulp. Place tomatoes in a greased baking dish. 3. Break egg and drop one into each tomato. 4. Mix tomato pulp, grated cheese and breadcrumbs. Season to taste. 5. Roll into marbles. 6. Place around the tomatoes. 7. Bake until eggs are set.

63. EGG AND POTATO FRY

Ingredients	*For 4*	*For 100*
Potatoes	450 gm	11 kg
Onions	225 gm	5.6 kg
Eggs	3	75
Fat	30 gm	500 gm
Pepper	a pinch	15 gm
Salt	to taste	80-100 gm

Method

1. Slice onions thick. Brown lightly in fat. 2. Add thickly sliced, boiled potatoes. 3. Cook for 5 minutes stirring well. 4. Beat eggs with seasoning. Increase heat. Pour in beaten eggs. 5. Lift edges to let egg fluid flow under. 6. Cook till eggs set. Serve unfolded and hot.

64. LENTIL ROAST

Ingredients	*For 4*	*For 100*
Lentils	225 gm	5.6 kg
Cheese	115 gm	2.8 kg
Eggs	1	25
Breadcrumbs	60 gm	1.35 kg
Onions	170 gm	3 kg
Garlic	1 flake	10 gm
Parsley	1 bunch	10 bunches
Dried thyme	a pinch	10 gm
Pepper	a pinch	15 gm
Vegetable stock	150 ml	3 litre
Salt	to taste	80-100 gm
Fat to fry	15 gm	250 gm

Method

1. Simmer washed lentils till cooked dry. 2. Chop onions and garlic fine. 3. Fry both till well-browned. 4. Flake the cheese. 5. Beat the egg. Mix all the ingredients together using vegetable stock to moisten. 6. Bake in a moderately hot oven, at Gas mark 5 or 190°C (375°F) for 35 to 40 minutes. Serve hot with gravy.

65. NUT ROAST

Ingredients	*For 4*	*For 100*
Mixed nuts	115 gm	2.8 k.g
Egg	1	12
Butter	15 gm	340 gm
Breadcrumbs	30 gm	680 gm
Pepper	a pinch	15 gm
Salt	to taste	100 gm
Tomatoes	255 gm	5.6 kg
Onions	30 gm	680 gm
Lime rind	a little	3–4 limes
Mixed herbs	½ tsp	15 gm

Method

1 Grind nuts. 2. Chop onions and tomatoes. 3. Heat butter, cook tomatoes and onions. 4. Mix all ingredients. 5. Bind with beaten egg. 6. Bake for 40–50 minutes in a moderate oven, serve with tomato sauce.

66. VEGETABLE LOAF

Ingredients	*For 4*	*For 100*
Peas	55 gm	1.35 kg

Ingredients	*For 4*	*For 100*
Carrots	55 gm	1.35 kg
Beans	55 gm	1.35 kg
Cauliflower	55 gm	1.35 kg
Potatoes	455 gm	11.3 kg
Eggs	1	25
Onions	30 gm	680 gm
Marmite	a little	15 gm
Breadcrumbs	30 gm	455 gm
Fat	15 gm	250 gm

Method

1. Boil and mash potatoes and line a bread tin. 2. Heat fat. Fry chopped onion, minced vegetables and seasoning; cook on a slow fire. 3. Add beaten egg and breadcrumbs. 4. Put the prepared filling into the tin; moisten if required. Bake for 35-40 minutes in a moderately hot oven at Gas mark 5 or 190°C (375°F).

67. CHEESE AND LENTIL PIE

Ingredients	*Quantity*
Short crust pastry	
Flour	500 gm
Fat	250 gm
Salt	to taste
Cold water	to mix
Filling	
Egg	1
Cheese	170 gm
Lentils	170 gm
Carrots (cooked)	170 gm
Milk	625 ml
Salt and pepper	

Method

1. Sieve the flour and salt. Rub fat into the flour. 2. Add just sufficient cold water to form a stiff dough. 3. Roll out and use as desired. Cook lentils till soft and drain. 4. Mince cooked carrots. Grate cheese. Line a pie dish with pastry (keeping one half for covering). 5. Add beaten egg, lentils, cheese and carrots to milk. Season well. 6. Pour filling into the pastry-lined tin and cover with remaining pastry. 7. Bake in a hot oven until the pastry is cooked. 8. Serve hot.

68. CHEESE AND ONION FLAN

Ingredients	*For 4*	*For 100*
Pastry:		
Refined flour	140 gm	2.38 kg
Butter	85 gm	1.3 kg
Baking powder	¼ tsp	15 gm
Salt	a pinch	1 tsp
Cold water	to mix	to mix
Filling		
Milk	180 ml	3 litre
Refined flour	15 gm	255 gm
Butter	15 gm	255 gm
Eggs	1	17
Cheese	55 gm	935 gm
Onions	55 gm	935 gm
Tomatoes	100 gm	1.7 kg
Mustard	½ tsp	30 gm
Salt	to taste	50-80 gm
Pepper	a pinch	15 gm

Method

1. Make pastry as in Recipe no. 67. (shortcrust pastry). 2. Roll out and line a flan tin. Decorate edges by using trimmings and bake for 9 minutes at 190°C (375°F). 3. Make a white sauce with flour, half the butter and milk. Beat till cool. 4. Sauté chopped onions without discolouring. 5. Add grated cheese, mustard and beaten egg. Add pepper and salt. 6. Pile into flan and bake at 190°C (375°F) for 10 minutes. 7. Blanch and slice tomatoes. Decorate flan by placing slices over. 8. Bake for 5 minutes more at 190°C (375°F). 9. Serve hot or cold.

N.B. A little cheese may be reserved from the sauce and sprinkled over tomatoes for added flavour.

69. BAKED BRINJAL WITH SAGE AND ONION STUFFING

Ingredients	*Quantity*
Brinjal (medium-sized—black variety)	4
Oil as desired	
Salt	to taste
Sage and onion stuffing	
Cheese (preferably mozzarella)	50 gm
Pepper	
Salt	to season

Method

1. Wash, wipe and cut brinjal into halves. 2. Salt and set aside for about half an hour. 3. Remove moisture from top and chisel out the pulp keeping skin intact. 4. Coat skin generously with oil. Heat about a tbsp of oil (15 ml) in a fry pan. 5. Add the brinjal pulp and sauté. Add sage and onion stuffing, adding more seasoning if desired. 6. Sauté till cooked. 7. Blend with grated cheese (setting aside some for topping). 8. Stuff brinjal halves. 9. Top with cheese and bake at 300°F for about 15 minutes or grill.

SAGE AND ONION STUFFING

Ingredients	*Quantity*
Onions	225 gm
Bread crumbs	50-60 gm
Sage (fresh or dried) chopped	½–1 tsp
Butter	30 gm
Salt	
Pepper	as desired
Green chillies	2
(remove seeds if pungent)	
Ginger (finely chopped)	½″ piece
(can be added to the seasoning if desired)	

Method

1. Parboil onions. Drain off water. 2. Chop finely and blend all ingredients together.

70. MUSHROOM FLAN

Ingredients	*Quantity*
Pastry	
Refined flour	140 gm
Butter	85 gm
Baking powder	¼ tsp
Salt	a pinch
Cold water	to
Filling	
Mushrooms	170 gm
Butter	60
Milk	360 ml
Bayleaf	1
Thyme	1 sprig
Flour	30 gm

Ingredients	*Quantity*
Salt and pepper	to taste
Egg	1
Cream	3 tbsp

Method

1. Prepare pastry as in cheese and onion flan and line a flan tin reserving scraps of pastry for decoration. 2. Wash mushrooms in cold water. Slice thinly, reserving a few for decoration. 3. Melt the butter and fry mushrooms gently until they are tender. Remove whole ones and keep aside. 4. Infuse thyme and bayleaf into the milk and bring to the boil slowly. Strain. 5. Stir in the flour with the mushrooms. Add the milk which should be hot and whisk well into the sauce. 6. Stir with salt and pepper. 7. Break the egg into a bowl, beat well and add the cream. Take out 2 tsp for glazing the pastry. 8. Add a little mushroom sauce to the egg and cream and then pour this mixture gradually into the sauce. Allow the filling to get quite cold and pour into the lined flan ring. 9. Roll out the scraps of pastry. Cut into strips 0.5 cm. (¼") wide. Twist them and lay them crisscross in a trellis pattern over the flan. Brush the pastry with the remaining egg and cream mixture. 10. Bake the flan at 205°C (400°F) or Gas mark 6 for 25 minutes. Reduce heat to 197°C (380°F) or Gas mark 5 and bake for a further 5 to 10 minutes. Heat the mushrooms reserved for garnish and place in the trellis spaces.

71. GOLDEN ONION QUICHE

Ingredients	*Quantity*
Shortcrust pastry:	
Refined flour	170 gm
Butter	85 gm
Baking powder	¼ tsp
Iced water to mix	
Filling	
Onions	225 gm
Milk	300 ml
Cheddar cheese (finely grated)	85 gm
Egg	1
Salt and pepper	to taste

Method

1. Prepare shortcrust pastry. Roll out and line a 20 cm. (8") sandwich tin or flan ring. Trim edges neatly. 2. Peel and slice onions thinly and cook in boiling salted water until soft. 3. Blend milk with two-thirds of the cheese, beaten egg, well-drained cooked onions and salt and pepper to

taste. 5. Pour into prepared pastry case and sprinkle with remaining cheese. 5. Bake on the shelf above centre in hot oven at 205°C (400°F) or Gas mark 6 for 10 minutes. Then reduce temperature of oven to moderate 149°C (300°F) or Gas mark 4 and cook for another 25 to 30 minutes or until the filling is golden brown and set and pastry cooked through.

72. TOMATO & CHEESE PIZZA

Ingredients	*For 6*
Flour	250 gm
Fresh yeast or	15 gm
Dry yeast	10 gm
Milk	50 ml
Salt	½ tsp
Egg	1
Fat	20 gm
Butter for brushing	15 gm
Tomatoes	500 gm
Onions	200 gm
Mushrooms	4 (15 gm)
Cheese	100 gm
Olives	10 gm (2)
Capsicums	100 gm
Red chilli powder	½ tsp
Pepper powder (optional)	½ tsp

Method

For the filling

1. Chop onions and half the capsicums into fine pieces and slice the remaining capsicums into roundels. 2. Blanch tomatoes and chop into fine pieces. 3. Sauté the onions and chopped capsicums in the fat and add chopped tomatoes. 4. Add 50 gm of grated cheese and salt, red chilli powder and pepper powder. Mix well and set aside.

For the dough

1. Make a soft dough with flour, yeast, egg, milk and salt and keep covered for half an hour for fermentation. 2. Divide into 6 portions and roll into 10 cm. (4") diameter rounds. 3. Keep them on a lightly greased baking sheet. 4. Keep them for proving for 20 minutes. 5. When proved enough, prick them nicely with a fork. 6. Bake at 205°C (400°F) for about 10 minutes. 7. Remove and brush with melted butter. 8. Spread the tomato filling over and decorate with mushrooms, olives and sliced capsicums. 9. Sprinkle the remaining cheese over and bake again for another 5 minutes at 205°C (400°F) and serve hot.

73. TOMATO CHEESECAKE

Ingredients	*For 6*
For the crust	
Plain flour	115 gm
Salt, pepper, dry mustard	a pinch
Butter	60 gm
Grated cheese	30 gm
For the filling	
Firm ripe tomatoes	340 gm
Butter or margarine	85 gm
Eggs	2
Cottage or cream cheese	340 gm
Thin cream or top of milk	2 tbsp
Seasoning	

Method

1. Sieve the flour and seasoning, rub in the butter or margarine, add the cheese and water to bind. 2. Roll out and line a 17.5 cm. (7") flan ring. 3. Skin half the tomatoes and slice thinly; put at the bottom of the pastry case. 4. Cream butter with seasoning until soft, gradually beat in eggs, cheese and finally cream. 5. Put into the pastry-lined case and set in the middle of a hot oven at 218°C (425°F) for 10 minutes, then lower the heat to 163°C (325°F) for a further 35-40 minutes until firm to the touch. 6. Cool, then top with skinned sliced tomatoes.

74. BAKED VEGETABLE PIE

Ingredients	*Quantity*
Cabbage (medium)	1
Mushrooms	100 gm
Spring onions	50 gm
Eggs	3
Fat	30 gm
Milk	50 ml
Grated cheese	30 gm
Breadcrumbs	30 gm
Salt and pepper	to taste
Butter	15 gm

Method

1. Separate leaves from cabbage and boil in salted water for a short time. Remove when half done. Drain. 2. Set aside the large leaves and chop the remaining cabbage. 3. Chop mushrooms and spring onions with tender leaves. 4. Prepare scrambled eggs with eggs and milk, seasoning

to taste. In a little of the fat, sauté onions and mushrooms. 5. In a greased baking dish, spread a layer of cabbage leaves. Over this, put a layer of scrambled eggs. Cover with a layer of mushrooms and onions. 6. Continue till all the vegetables are used up. Cover with grated cheese and breadcrumbs. Dot with butter. 7. Bake at 175ºC (350ºF) for about 30 minutes, or until the top is golden brown. 8. Serve with gravy.

GRAVY

Ingredients	*Quantity*
Butter	30 gm
Milk	1 cup
Refined flour	60 gm
Vegetable stock	½ cup
Onions	1
Marmite or other yeast extract	2 tsp
Bayleaf	1
Salt	to taste

Method

1. Melt the fat. Add chopped onion and fry until golden brown. 2. Add the flour and blend well till it becomes brown (about 5 to 7 minutes) stirring all the time. 3. Remove pan from fire. Cool and add stock and milk stirring well to form a smooth mixture. 4. Mix in marmite dissolved in a little stock. Add salt. 5. Return to fire and simmer till gravy is of the required consistency (thinner than a sauce) and well-cooked.

SAUCES

73. Tartare Sauce (Campus)
74. Celery Dressing
75. Chantilly Dressing
76. Club Dressing
77. Egg Dressing
78. Egg and Green Pepper Dressing
79. Savoury
80. Green Sauce
81. Thousand Island Dressing with Mayonnaise Sauce
82. Roquefort Dressing
83. French Dressing (A)
    French Dressing (B)
84. Dieters Dressing
85. Zero Salad Dressing
86. Chef's Dressing
87. Cottage Dip
88. Crab Cheese Dip
89. Cucumber Dip
90. Egg Dip
91. Garlic Mayonnaise
92. Indian Dressing
93. Thousand Island French Dressing
94. Salad Cream
95. Sour Cream Dressing
96. Yoghurt Dressing
97. Salad Dressing (A)
    Salad Dressing (B)
    Salad Dressing (C)
98. Boiled Salad Dressing
99. Cole Slaw Dressing
100. Cream Dressing for Cole Slaw
101. Ravigotte Sauce (A)
    Ravigotte Sauce (B)
102. Jam Sauce (A)
    Jam Sauce (B)
103. Apricot Sauce
104. Marmalade Sauce
105. Orange Sauce
106. Lemon Sauce
107. Custard Sauce (A)
    Custard Sauce (B)
108. Sherry Sauce
109. Sabayon Sauce
110. Chocolate Sauce (A)
    Chocolate Sauce (B)
111. Coffee Sauce
112. Syrup Sauce
113. Melba Sauce
114. Almond Sauce
115. Rum Butter (A)
    Rum Butter (B)
116. Rum Butter
117. Rum Butter Sauce
118. Rum Sauce
119. Brandy Butter or Hard Sauce
120. Brandy Butter
121. Sauce for Sweet Pudding
122. Grape Sauce
123. Veal Forcemeat
124. Sage and Onion Stuffing
125. Coral Butter
126. Maitre D'Hotel Butter
127. Mint Butter
128. Chutney Butter
129. Mustard Butter
130. Paprika Butter
131. Curry Butter
132. Vinaigrette

STOCKS

Stocks are the foundation of many important kitchen preparations; therefore the greatest possible care should be taken in their production.

1. Stale meat or bones and decaying vegetables will give stock an unpleasant flavour and cause it to deteriorate quickly.

2. Scum should be removed, otherwise it will boil into the stock and spoil the colour and flavour.
3. Fat should be skimmed, otherwise it will taste greasy.
4. Stock should always simmer gently, for if it is allowed to boil quickly, it will evaporate and go cloudy.
5. It should not be allowed to go off the boil, otherwise, in hot weather, there is a danger of it going sour.
6. Salt should not be added to stock.
7. When making chicken stock, if raw bones are not available, then a boiling fowl can be used.

GENERAL PROPORTIONS OF INGREDIENTS FOR ALL STOCKS EXCEPT FISH STOCK

Ingredients	*Quantity*	*Ingredients*	*Quantity*
Water	4.75 litre	**Bouquet garni**	
Raw bones	1.8 kg	**(thyme, bayleaf,**	
Vegetables	450 gm	**parsley stalks)**	
(onions, carrots,		**Peppercorns**	12
celery, leeks)			

General method for all white stocks (except fish stock)

1. Chop up the bones, remove any fat or marrow. 2. Place in a stock pot; add cold water and bring to a boil. 3. If the scum is dirty then blanch and wash off the bones, re-cover with cold water and reboil. 4. Skim, wipe round sides of the pot and simmer gently. 5. Add the washed, peeled, whole vegetables, bouquet garni and peppercorns. Simmer for 6-8 hours. Skim and strain.

During the cooking, a certain amount of evaporation will take place; therefore add 1 pt. cold water just before boiling point is reached. This will also help to throw the scum to the surface and make it easier to skim.

General method for all brown stocks

1. Chop the bones and brown well on all sides either by: (a) Placing in a roasting tin, or an oven, or (b) Carefully browning in a little fat in a frying pan. 2. Drain off any fat and place the bones in a stock pot. 3. Brown any sediment that may be in the bottom of the tray, deglacé (swill out) with a pint of boiling water, simmer for a few minutes and add to the bones. 4. Add the cold water, bring to the boil and skim. 5. Wash, peel and roughly cut the vegetables, fry in a little fat till brown, strain and add to the bones. 6. Add the bouquet garni and peppercorns. 7. Simmer for 6-8 hours. 8. Skim and strain.

FISH STOCK (4.5 litre)

Ingredients	*Quantity*	*Ingredients*	*Quantity*
Water	4.75 litre	**Bayleaf**	1
Fish bones (pomfret, sole)	1.80 kg	**Lime (juice)**	½
		Parsley stalks	a few
Onions	225 gm	**Peppercorns**	6
Margarine	55 gm		

Method

1. Melt the margarine in a thick-bottomed pan. 2. Add sliced onions, well-washed fish bones and the remaining ingredients. 3. Cover with greaseproof paper and lid and sweat for 5 minutes. Remove greaseproof paper. 4. Add the water, bring to the boil, skim and simmer for 20 minutes, then strain.

1. WHITE SAUCE (300 ml)

Ingredients	*Pouring Consistency*	*Coating*	*Panada*
Refined flour	15 gm	30 gm	55 gm
Fat (butter or margarine)	15 gm	30 gm	55 gm
Liquid (milk and stock)	300 ml	300 ml	300 ml
Pepper	to taste	to taste	to taste
Salt	to taste	to taste	to taste

Method

1. Heat milk and stock. Remove and keep hot. 2. Melt the fat in a pan. 3. Add flour. Mix smoothly and cook over gentle heat (2-3 minutes) without discolouring. 4. Remove from heat. Add the liquid, a little at a time to the roux until mixture is light and creamy. Stir all the time (if the liquid is not added gradually lumps are formed). 5. Add remaining liquid and mix thoroughly. 6. Return to heat and bring to boil stirring well all the time. 7. Continue boiling and stirring for 4 to 5 minutes, to cook flour thoroughly. If the boiling is not continued the sauce will be raw in flavour and dull instead of glossy. 8. Season carefully.

N.B. The liquid depends on the kind of food with which the sauce is to be served.

For meat: half milk and half stock or pot liquor.

For fish: half milk and half fish stock.

For vegetables: half milk and half vegetable stock.

For sweets: milk or milk and water.

2. BROWN SAUCE (300 ml)

Ingredients	*Quantity*	*Ingredients*	*Quantity*
Refined flour	15 gm	**Stock**	300 ml
Fat (butter or margarine)	15 gm	**Carrot**	30 gm
		Onions	115 gm

Method

1. Heat liquid. Remove and keep warm. 2. Prepare vegetables and slice them. 3. Melt the fat and fry the vegetables until brown. 4. Add the flour. Cook slowly together until roux becomes a good brown colour. 5. Remove from heat and add the liquid, a little at a time, mixing smoothly with the roux. 6. Allow to simmer for about 30 minutes. 7. Skim, strain and reheat.

3. ROAST GRAVY (300 ml) (10 portions)

Ingredients	*Quantity*	*Ingredients*	*Quantity*
Raw bones	225 gm	**Carrot**	55 gm
Onions	55 gm	**Stock or water**	590 ml
Celery	30 gm		

Method

1. Chop bones and brown in oven or brown in a little fat on top of the stove in a fry-pan. 2. When half-browned add finely minced celery, carrot, and onion. 3. Drain off all fat. 4. Place in a saucepan with stock or water. 5. Bring to boil. Skim and allow to simmer. 6. Simmer for 1½ to 2 hours. 7. Remove the joint from the roasting tin when cooked. 8. Return tray to low heat to allow sediment to settle. 9. Carefully strain off the fat leaving the sediment in the tin. 10. Return to the stove and brown carefully. Swill with the brown stock. 11. Allow to simmer for a few minutes. 12. Check for seasoning. 13. Strain and skim.

4. BROWN GRAVY

Ingredients	*For 4*	*For 100*
Carrots	30 gm	455 gm
Onions	30 gm	455 gm
Refined flour	20 gm	225 gm
Fat	20 gm	225 gm
Salt	5 gm	100 gm
Pepper	a pinch	15 gm
Stock	300 ml	7.37 litre

Method

1. Slice onions, scrape and chop carrots. 2. Heat fat. Brown onions and carrots. Add flour and brown. 3. Add stock and cook till vegetables are tender and gravy is thick. 4. Season, remove and strain. Serve hot.

5. JUS LIE (300 ml) (10 portions)

Ingredients	*Quantity*	*Ingredients*	*Quantity*
Chicken bones	115 gm	**Thyme**	1 small sprig
Chicken giblets		**Tomato purée**	5 ml
Celery	15 gm	**Arrowroot or cornflour**	10 gm
Onions	30 gm	**Stock**	500 ml
Carrot	30 gm	**Mushroom trimmings**	a few
Bayleaf	¼		

Method

1. Chop the bones and brown in a little fat. 2. Add chopped giblets, mushroom trimmings, finely chopped carrot, onion, celery, bayleaf and thyme. Brown well. 3. Mix in the tomato purée and stock. 4. Simmer for 2 hours. 5. Dilute the arrowroot or cornflour in a little cold water. 6. Pour into the boiling stock, stirring continuously till it re-boils. 7. Simmer for 10 to 15 minutes. 8. Correct the seasoning. 9. Pass through a fine strainer.

6. ANCHOVY SAUCE (300 ml) (10 portions)

Serve with fish

Ingredients	*Quantity*
White sauce	300 ml
Anchovy essence	1 dsp.

7. CAPER SAUCE (300 ml) (10 portions)

Serve with boiled mutton or poached fish

Ingredients	*Quantity*
White sauce	300 ml
Capers (chop slightly)	1 tbsp

8. CHEESE SAUCE (300 ml) (10 portions)

Serve with fish & vegetables

Ingredients	*Quantity*
White sauce	300 ml
Grated cheese	55 gm
Prepared mustard	½ tsp

9. EGG SAUCE (300 ml) (10 portions)

Serve with boiled or steamed fish

Ingredients	*Quantity*
White sauce	300 ml
Hard-boiled egg (chop into pieces)	1

10. MUSTARD SAUCE (300 ml) (10 portions)

Serve with grilled herrings, mackerel etc.

Ingredients	*Quantity*
White sauce	300 ml
Prepared mustard	1 tsp
Vinegar	1 tsp

11. ONION SAUCE (330 ml) (10 portions)

Serve with boiled mutton, roast leg of mutton and tripe

Ingredients	*Quantity*
White sauce	300 ml
Cooked onion (finely chopped)	1

12. PARSLEY SAUCE (300 ml) (10 portions)

Serve with veal, fish, boiled fowl & vegetables

Ingredients	*Quantity*
White sauce	300 ml
Parsley (finely chopped)	1 tsp (½ bunch)

13. SHRIMP SAUCE (300 ml) (10 portions)

Serve with fish soufflé, vegetable soufflé etc.

Ingredients	*Quantity*
White sauce	300 ml
Shrimps* (cooked)	70 gm

N.B. This sauce could be made using Béchamel as the base.

14. DUTCH SAUCE (300 ml) (10 portions)

Ingredients	*Quantity*
Margarine or butter	20 gm
Refined flour	20 gm

---

*Shell shrimps. Remove intestines, wash thoroughly in cold water. Boil in salted water or court bouillon.

Ingredients	*Quantity*
Milk	300 ml
Lime (juice)	¼–½
Egg yolk	1
Cream	1 tbsp
Pepper	to taste
Salt	to taste

Method

1. Heat milk. Set aside but keep hot. 2. Melt fat. Stir in flour. 2. Add seasoning. 3. Stir over heat without discolouring for a few minutes. 4. Remove from heat and stir in milk gradually. 5. Cook carefully, stirring all the time till it thickens. Boil for 2 minutes. 6. Cool slightly and add egg yolk and lemon juice. 7. Reheat but do not boil.

15. TOMATO SAUCE (A)

Serve with Fish Orly, fried fish, meat, fish, or vegetable cutlets, pastas, etc.

Ingredients	*For 4*	*For 100*
Tomatoes	225 gm	5.66 kg
Bacon	5 gm	115 gm
Butter	15 gm	340 gm
Carrot	20 gm	455 gm
Turnip	20 gm	455 gm
Onions	20 gm	455 gm
Refined flour	15 gm	340 gm
White pepper	to taste	15 gm
Salt	to taste	100 gm
Stock or tomato liquid	300 ml	7 litre
Sugar	1 tsp	100 gm

Method

1. Slice onion and tomatoes finely. 2. Shred carrot and turnip. 3. Put all of them into a pan with stock, bacon, butter and seasoning. 4. Cook until tender. 5. Rub through a sieve and blend in flour. 6. Return to pan and stir until it boils. 7. Boil for 4-5 minutes and remove.

N.B. Depending on the quality of the tomatoes, it may be necessary to increase the quantity of tomatoes used.

TOMATO SAUCE (B)

Ingredients	*Quality*
Butter	30 gm
Flour	30 gm
Water	300 ml

Ingredients	*Quality*
Tomatoes	500 gm
Salt / **Pepper**	to taste
Bouquet garni (parsley, thyme, bayleaf crushed and tied in a bag)	

Method

1. Melt the butter. Stir in the flour. Take pan off the heat and blend in the water without forming lumps. Return to heat and stir till in boils. 2. Blanch tomatoes (dip in boiling water). Skin, pulp and remove seeds. Add tomato to the sauce and add seasoning, bouquet garni and sugar. Cook for 20 to 30 minutes. 3. Remove bouquet garni and strain pressing through a sieve. Return to the rinsed out pan. 4. Check for seasoning and simmer for 5 minutes or until you get a smooth, flowing consistency.

16. BREAD SAUCE (300 ml) (10 portions)

Serve with roast poultry, partridge, pheasant etc.

Ingredients	*Quantity*	*Ingredients*	*Quantity*
Milk	300 ml	**Cloves**	2
Onion	30 gm	**Mace**	1 blade
Margarine	30 gm	**Lemon rind**	1 lemon
Fresh bread-crumbs	45 gm	**Salt**	to taste
		Pepper	a pinch

Method

1. Simmer onion stuck with clove and mace in milk for half an hour. 2. Put breadcrumbs, margarine and seasoning into a bowl. 3. Strain flavoured milk over the breadcrumb mixture. 4. Stand in a warm place to thicken. 5. Reheat and beat well. One tbsp of cream may be added if desired.

17. HORSERADISH SAUCE (150 ml) (5 portions)

Serve with roast beef, grilled chicken, smoked trout etc.

Ingredients	*Quantity*	*Ingredients*	*Quantity*
Grated horse-radish	4 tbsp (120 gm raw wt. approx.)	**Salt**	¼ tsp
		Vinegar	1½ tbsp (22 ml)
Sugar	⅛ tsp	**Milk**	75 ml
Dry mustard	½ tsp	**Cream**	75 ml

Method

1. Scrub, peel and grate radish. 2. Mix mustard, sugar and salt. 3. Add

slightly whipped cream. 4. Add the vinegar gradually, stirring gently. 5. Add horseradish gradually.

18. APPLE SAUCE (300 ml) (10 portions)

Serve with roast duck, pork and goose

Ingredients	*Quantity*	*Ingredients*	*Quantity*
Cooking apples	450 gm	**Margarine**	30 gm
		Sugar	60 gm

Method

1. Peel, core and wash the apples. 2. Place with the sugar, margarine and a little water in a saucepan with a tightly-fitting lid. 3. Cook to a purée. 4. Pass through a sieve. 5. Serve with roast pork, duck and goose.

19. CURRY SAUCE

Ingredients	*For 4*	*For 100*
Flour	45 gm	1 kg
Butter	45 gm	1 kg
Onions	50 gm	1.36 kg
Curry powder	1 tbsp	250 gm
Good stock	600 ml	15 litre
Tomatoes	115 gm	2.8 kg
Bayleaf	1	3 gm
Salt	to taste	80-100 gm

Method

1. Melt the butter. Add the finely chopped onion. 2. When it turns light brown, stir in the flour and curry powder. 3. Blend well and cook for 5 minutes. 4. Pour in the stock gradually. Blend well. 5. Add chopped tomatoes and bayleaf. 6. Bring to boil stirring all the time; cook for 20 minutes. 7. Strain and serve.

N.B. Red wine or sherry may be added to flavour the curry sauce.

20. MINT SAUCE (60 ml) (4 portions)

Serve with roast lamb

Ingredients	*Quantity*	*Ingredients*	*Quantity*
Vinegar	60 ml	**Water**	1 tbsp (optional)
Chopped Mint	2 tbsp (1 bunch raw mint)	**Salt**	to taste (about 10 gm)
Sugar	1 tbsp		

Method

1. Wash mint. Sprinkle a little sugar over it and chop finely. 2. Mix all ingredients together. Serve with roast lamb. If required it can be served with cold ham or bacon.

N.B. A bouquet garni of 6 peppercorns, 1 clove, 1 blade mace, 6 allspice, ½ bayleaf, 1 sprig parsley and a pinch of mixed herbs could be used.

21. ESPAGNOLE SAUCE (600 ml)

A basic sauce

Ingredients	*Quantity*	*Ingredients*	*Quantity*
Butter	55 gm	**Flour**	55 gm
Lean bacon	55 gm	**Stock**	600 ml
Carrot	55 gm	**Bouquet garni**	
Mushrooms	30 gm	**(parsley, thyme,**	
Tomato pulp	150 ml	**marjoram, basil,**	
Onions	115 gm	**bayleaf, lime rind)**	
	(1 medium)	**Sherry (optional)**	75 ml
		Salt	to taste (15-20 gm)

Method

1. Cut bacon and vegetables into small pieces. 2. Fry lightly in butter. Add flour and cook very slowly till golden brown. 4. Add stock, tomato pulp and bouquet garni. Simmer for 30 minutes. 5. Strain through a tammy. Reheat and add sherry, if desired.

22. REFORME SAUCE (300 ml) (10 portions)

Serve with lamb cutlets

Ingredients	*Quantity*	*Ingredients*	*Quantity*
Espagnole sauce	300 ml	**Redcurrant jelly**	1 tsp
Wine vinegar	150 ml	**Wine**	75 ml (optional)
Peppercorns	12 (crushed)	**Salt**	to taste

Method

1. Add peppercorns to vinegar. Reduce vinegar to about 15 ml 2. Add espagnole sauce, jelly and wine. 3. Boil. Strain and use as required.

N.B. Roselle jelly could be used as a substitute for red currant jelly, if the latter is not available.

23. SAUCE AMBASSADRICE (300 ml) (10 portions)

Serve with roast, mutton cutlets, etc.

Ingredients	*Quantity*	*Ingredients*	*Quantity*
Espagnole sauce	300 ml	**Sugar**	1 pinch
Redcurrant jelly or roselle jelly	1 tsp	**Salt**	each
		Cayenne	
		Raisins	55 gm
		Lime juice	½ tbsp

Method

Boil all ingredients except raisins together. Add raisins and serve.

24. SAUCE RAIFORT (Horseradish) (300 ml) (10 portions)

Serve with roast beef and Chicken Maryland

Ingredients	*Quantity*
Grated Horseradish	150 gm
Béchamel sauce	300 ml
White stock	150 ml
Cream	300 ml
Egg yolks	2
Mustard	1 tsp
Vinegar	8 ml (1 tbsp)
Breadcrumbs	15 gm
Butter	10 gm

Method

1. Peel and clean the horseradish and place in a pan. 2. Add stock and boil gently for 20 minutes. 3. Add Béchamel sauce and breadcrumbs and pass through a tammy cloth. 4. Add a liaison of cream and egg yolks and mustard dissolved in vinegar. 5. Finish with a knob of butter.

25. SAUCE HACHÉE (300 ml) (10 portions)

For meat dishes

Ingredients	*Quantity*
Demi glacé	600 ml
Tomato sauce	300 ml
Shallots (chopped)	30 gm
Onions (chopped)	60 gm
Butter	10 gm
Parsley (chopped)	1 tsp
Ham (diced)	60 gm

Ingredients	*Quantity*
Capers (chopped)	30 gm
Vinegar	75 ml
Duxelle	60 gm
Seasoning	

Method

1. Melt butter. 2. Add onions and shallots. Sauté. 3. Add the vinegar lightly and reduce until almost dry. 4. Add the remaining ingredients. Bring to a boil; and simmer for 5 minutes skimming well.

26. SAUCE HACHÉE (300 ml) (10 portions)

For fish dishes

Ingredients	*Quantity*
Fish veloute	1 litre
Shallots (chopped)	30 gm
Onions (chopped)	60 gm
Capers (chopped)	30 gm
Anchovies (chopped)	60 gm
Vinegar	75 ml
Parsley (chopped)	1 tsp
Duxelle	60 gm

Method

1. Heat a pan. Add chopped onions and shallots. 2. Cover, to allow them to sweat. 3. Add the vinegar and reduce until almost dry. 4. Add veloute and other ingredients. 5. Bring to a boil. Skim. 6. Correct seasoning and consistency.

27. SAUCE CERVELLE (250 ml) (8 portions)

Serve with sheep's and calves' heads

Ingredients	*Quantity*	*Ingredients*	*Quantity*
Sheep's or		**Parsley (chopped)**	1 tsp
calves' brains	4	**Court bouillon**	1 litre
White roux	115 gm	**Seasoning**	
Brain liquor	1 litre		

Method

1. Wash and soak the brains in cold water. 2. Remove the small membranes round the brains using warm water so that they can be removed easily. 3. Place the brains in court bouillon, bring slowly to a boil and simmer for about 20 minutes. 4. Prepare a sauce with the white roux and the liquor in which the brains were cooked. 5. Slice the brains

finely and add to the sauce with parsley. 6. Check for seasoning and finish with a tbsp of fresh cream, if desired.

28. SAUCE AURORE (300 ml) (10 portions)

Serve with fish, eggs and boiled chicken

Ingredients	*Quantity*
Chicken veloute or fish veloute	1 litre
Red tomatoes (concassed)	200 gm
Tomato purée	30 ml
Butter	115 gm
Cream	60 gm

Method

1. Cook the veloute sauce and concassed tomatoes and purée together. 2. Pass through a strainer. 3. Finish off with cream and butter added gradually.

29. BORDELAISE SAUCE (300 ml) (10 portions)

Serve with fried or grilled steaks, grilled meat & sautés

Ingredients	*Quantity*	*Ingredients*	*Quantity*
Espagnole sauce	300 ml	**Parsley (chopped)**	1 tsp
Shallot or		**Meat glaze**	1 tsp
small red onion	1	**Claret (optional)**	75 ml
(chopped)		**Salt**	to taste

Method

1. Cook shallot in claret or in a little stock. 2. Add espagnole and meat glaze. 3. Boil for 5 minutes. 4. Strain through tammy cloth. Add parsley, salt and reheat.

30. MEAT GLAZE (A) (1 litre)

Ingredients	*Quantity*
Strong brown stock	2.35 litre

Method

1. Reduce the stock by boiling until dark in colour and thick; use as required.

MEAT GLAZE (B) (150 ml)

Ingredients	*Quantity*	*Ingredients*	*Quantity*
Strong brown stock	150 ml	**Pepper**	a pinch
Meat extract	¼ tsp	**Salt**	to taste
Gelatine	7-10 gm		

Method

1. Put the stock in a small pan. Add meat extract, gelatine and seasoning. 2. Heat until gelatine has dissolved and use as substitute for Meat Glaze (A).

31. SAUCE DEMIGLACÉ (300 ml) (10 portions)

Ingredients	*Quantity*	*Ingredients*	*Quantity*
Liquid glaze	150 ml	**Sherry (optional)**	75 ml
Espagnole sauce	150 ml	**Seasoning**	

Method

Boil all ingredients together. Season and strain.

32. BIGRADE SAUCE (1 litre) (20 portions)

Serve with roast duck, goose, pork, ham and venison

Ingredients	*Quantity*
Demiglacé	1.5 litre
Stock (prepared from duck bones)	400 ml
Seasoning	
Port wine or red wine	150 ml
Rind and juice of 3 oranges	
Juice of 1 lemon or ½ lime.	

Method

1. Peel the rind of the oranges very thinly, taking care that no white pith is used. 2. Cut into juliennes. Cover with cold water. 3. Bring to a boil. Strain, and dry well. 4. Mix the demiglacé, stock and orange juice and boil until reduced to half. 5. Strain, and return to saucepan. 6. Add the prepared orange rind, lemon juice, port wine and the cooking juices from the duck. 7. Bring to a boil and correct the seasoning.

33. POIVRADE SAUCE (1 litre) (20 portions)

Serve with venison

Ingredients	*Quantity*
Demiglacé	1 litre
Mirepoix (carrots, onions, bacon scraps cut into small cubes, fried and used to flavour stocks, sauces and braised meats)	400 gm
Butter	120 gm
Vinegar	150 ml
Seasoning	
White wine	300 ml

Ingredients	*Quantity*
Bayleaves	2
Thyme	1 sprig
Peppercorns	20

Method

1. Melt half the butter. Fry the mirepiox golden brown. 2. Remove excess fat. Add wine, vinegar, bayleaves and thyme. Reduce by half. 3. Add the demiglacé and allow to simmer for 20-30 minutes. 4. Add peppercorns and simmer for a further 5 minutes. 5. Correct seasoning and strain the sauce. 6. Blend in remaining butter in small knobs.

34. SAUCE SMETANE (600 ml) (10-15 portions)

Serve with beef entrées, game and poultry

Ingredients	*Quantity*
Demiglacé	600 ml
Game liquor	600 ml
Juice of 2 lemons	
Sour cream	300 ml
Butter	60 gm
Seasoning	

Method

1. Reduce the game liquor to a glaze. 2. Add the demiglacé and sour cream and bring to a boil. 3. Add lemon juice and strain through muslin. 4. Blend in butter gradually. Check for seasoning.

35. SAUCE ZINGARA (1 litre) (20 portions)

Serve with small cuts of meat and poultry

Ingredients		*Quantity*
Demiglacé		600 ml
Tomato sauce		300 ml
Madeira wine or red wine		60 ml
Truffle	cut into	60 gm
Mushrooms	julienne	60 gm
Ox tongue	strips	60 gm
Ham		60 gm
Butter		15 gm
Seasoning		

Method

1. Melt butter. Add juliennes. Cover and cook for about 5 minutes. 2. Add the demiglacé and tomato sauce and bring to a boil. 3. Correct seasoning. Skim well and finish with the wine.

36. SAUCE ITALIENNE (300 ml) (10 portions)

Ingredients	*Quantity*	*Ingredients*	*Quantity*
Shallots	2	**Bayleaf**	a small piece
Mushrooms	3	**Sherry**	75 ml
Butter	30 gm	**Salt**	to taste
Refined flour	45 gm	**Pepper**	a pinch
Stock	450 ml		

Method

1. Chop shallots and fry in butter. 2. Add flour and brown very slowly. 3. Wash, peel and chop mushrooms, using stalks as well. 4. Add to flour along with bayleaf. 5. Cook for a few minutes longer. Add sherry if used. Reduce a little. 6. Add the stock. Boil for 10 minutes. 7. Add seasoning. Strain through tammy and use.

37. VELOUTE SAUCE (600 ml)

A basic sauce

Ingredients	*Quantity*	*Ingredients*	*Quantity*
Refined flour	30 gm	**White stock**	600 ml
Butter	60 gm	**Mushroom liquor**	30 ml

38. VICTORIA SAUCE

Serve with fish and shellfish.

To Veloute Sauce, add a little cooked tomato purée. Chopped lobster can also be added.

39. SAUCE SUPREME (1.5 litre) (25 portions)

Serve with chicken, veal and white entrées.

Ingredients	*Quantity*
Veloute sauce	1.5 litre
Cream	150 ml
Lemon juice	a little
Butter	60 gm
Seasoning	

Method

1. Bring the sauce to a boil. 2. Finish with butter added in small knobs and lemon juice. Remove from fire. 3. Blend in cream. Season to taste.

40. WHITE WINE SAUCE (1.5 litre) (25 portions)

Serve with dressed fish

Ingredients	*Quantity*
Veloute sauce	1.5 litre
White wine	30 ml
Egg yolks	3
Butter	120 gm
Lemon juice	
Seasoning	

Method

1. Reduce the white wine to half. Allow to cool. 2. Add egg yolks and whisk in a double boiler, as for Hollandaise sauce. 3. Bring the veloute to boil and gradually add the whisked mixture. 4. Add a little lemon juice and pass through a tammy. 5. Add butter in small knobs and blend well. Season.

41. GREEN HERB SAUCE (Vert-pre sauce) (300 ml) (10 portions)

Serve with cold salmon

Ingredients	*Quantity*	*Ingredients*	*Quantity*
Shallots	2	**Spinach**	30 gm
Butter	85 gm	**Parsley**	6 sprigs
White vinegar	30 ml	**Chives**	2-3 sprigs
	(2 tbsp)	**Salt**	to taste
Veloute sauce	300 ml	**Pepper**	to taste

Method

1. Peel and chop the shallots finely. 2. Put shallots, vinegar and 30 gms. of butter into a stew pan and place on fire. 3. Cook with lid on and allow to reduce to about half of its original quantity. 4. Add Veloute sauce and simmer for a few minutes. 5. Wash, pick and parboil spinach and herbs. 6. Drain and cool. Press out all water and pound in a mortar with about 30 gms. butter. 7. Rub through a sieve and mix with sauce. 8. Whisk in remaining butter. Season to taste and serve.

42. BÉCHAMEL (600 ml)

A basic sauce

Ingredients	*Quantity*	*Ingredients*	*Quantity*
Butter	45 gm	**Bayleaf**	½
Refined flour	30 gm	**Carrot**	30 gm
Milk	600 ml	**Celery**	5 cm
Onions	100 gm		(2") piece
	(1 small)	**Salt**	a pinch

Ingredients	Quantity	Ingredients	Quantity
Clove	1	**Nutmeg (grated)**	a pinch
Peppercorns (white)	10	**Lime juice**	½ tsp

Method

1. Melt 30 gm of butter. Add flour and cook without discolouring, stirring well all the time. Remove from heat. 2. Stir in boiling milk gradually, to prevent formation of lumps. 3. Return to heat. Add onion stuck with clove, sliced carrot, celery, peppercorns, salt and grated nutmeg. 4. Stir until it boils and allow to simmer for 15 minutes. 5. Pass through a tammy cloth. Return to pan and finish with remaining butter and lime juice.

43. SWEET BUTTER SAUCE (1 litre) (20-30 portions)

Serve with steamed puddings

Ingredients	Quantity
Béchamel sauce	1 litre
Sugar	120 gm
Vanilla essence	

Method

1. Mix sugar with Béchamel sauce. 2. Flavour as desired.

44. ALLEMANDE (600 ml)

A basic sauce

Ingredients	Quantity	Ingredients	Quantity
Butter	45 gm	**Nutmeg**	a pinch
Refined flour	30 gm	**Pepper**	a pinch
Chicken stock	600 ml	**Salt**	to taste
Cream	1 tbsp	**Lime (juice)**	1 tsp
Egg yolks	2		

Method

1. Melt 30 gm of butter. Add flour and cook without discolouring. 2. Remove pan from fire. Add stock gradually, stirring well to prevent formation of lumps. 3. Season with pepper, salt and nutmeg. 4. Simmer for half an hour. 5. Beat egg yolks. Add cream. 6. Add a little of the hot stock gradually and mix well. Whisk in butter. 7. Add to sauce. Heat without boiling. 8. Add lime juice. Remove and pass through a tammy cloth.

45. SHRIMP SAUCE (Rich) (Sauce aux écrevisses) (300 ml) (10 portions)

Serve with fish, soufflé, steamed fish, boiled lobster etc.

Ingredients	*Quantity*	*Ingredients*	*Quantity*
Shrimps	250 gm	**Seasoning**	
Béchamel sauce	150 ml	**Coral butter (see below)**	
Cream	4 tbsp		

Method

1. Shell shrimps. Remove intestines. Wash well and boil in court bouillon or salted water. 2. Pound fine. Add to sauce. Pass through a sieve. 3. Reheat with coral butter; add cream and seasoning.

CORAL BUTTER

Ingredients	*Quantity*	*Ingredients*	*Quantity*
Lobster coral	30 gm	**Seasoning**	
Butter	15 gm		

Method

Wash and dry the coral and pound with butter. Season and rub through a hair sieve.

46. CREAM SAUCE (300 ml) (10 portions)

Serve with sole, sweetbreads, chicken and vegetables.

Ingredients	*Quantity*
Béchamel sauce	300 ml
Cream or fullcream evaporated milk	150 ml

Method

1. To the Béchamel, while still hot, add cream and mix well.

N.B. When this sauce is made for fish, prepare the Béchamel with half milk and half strong fish liquor.

47. CUCUMBER SAUCE (Sauce aux concombres) (150 ml) (5 portions)

Serve with boiled or poached fish and white entrées

Ingredients	*Quantity*	*Ingredients*	*Quantity*
Cucumber	55 gm	**Butter**	30 gm
Spinach (cooked)	1 tbsp	**White sauce**	150 ml
	(30 gm raw)	**Cream**	75 ml
Seasoning			

Method

1. Peel cucumber and cut into 2.5 cm. (1") slices. Soak in cold water. 2. Drain and sauté in 15 gm of butter with the lid on. 3. Pound well with spinach. Pass through a hair sieve. 4. Reheat along with the sauce. Add cream and seasoning.

48. SAUCE CARDINAL (300 ml) (10 portions)

Serve with fish and shellfish

Ingredients	*Quantity*	*Ingredients*	*Quantity*
Fish roe	15 gm	**Cayenne**	a pinch
Butter	20 gm	**Salt**	to taste
Refined flour	20 gm	**Lime juice**	to taste
Fish stock	300 ml	**Cream**	75 ml

Method

1. Wash roe. Pound with butter and pass through a hair sieve. 2. Make sauce with this butter, flour and stock. 3. Boil well and add lemon juice, Cayenne and salt to taste. 4. Strain through tammy cloth. Reheat and add cream.

49. SAUCE MORNAY (300 ml) (10 portions)

Serve with boiled leg of mutton, roast leg of mutton and tripe

Ingredients	*Quantity*	*Ingredients*	*Quantity*
Butter	30 gm	**Cheese**	30 gm
Refined flour	30 gm	**Milk**	300 ml
Seasoning			

Method

1. Proceed as for Cheese Sauce, adding cheese after cooking.

50. SAUCE SOUBISE

Ingredients	*Quantity*	*Ingredients*	*Quantity*
Butter	30 gm	**Pepper**	a pinch
Refined flour	30 gm	**Salt**	to taste
Milk	400 ml	**Cream**	2 tbsp
Onions	150 gm		

Method

1. Chop onions finely and cook slowly in milk for 10 minutes. 2. Melt fat. Add flour and cook slightly without browning. 3. Add milk and onions and stir till it boils. Cook slowly for 10 minutes. 4. Strain through tammy cloth. 5. Add cream and seasoning.

51. BROWN ONION SAUCE (Sauce Lyonnaise) (300 ml) (10 portions)

Serve with steaks, sausages, bittocks

Ingredients	*Quantity*	*Ingredients*	*Quantity*
Onions (sliced)	115 gm	**Demiglacé**	300 ml
Margarine	30 gm	**Vinegar**	2 tbsp (30 ml)

Method

1. Melt the margarine in a pan. 2. Add onions and cover with a lid. 3. Cook gently till tender. 4. Remove the lid and allow to brown slightly. 5. Add vinegar and reduce completely. 6. Add demiglacé. Simmer for 5 to 10 minutes. 7. Skim and add seasoning.

52. ASPIC JELLY (1 litre)

Ingredients	*Quantity*	*Ingredients*	*Quantity*
Stock	885 ml	**Turnip**	1 (115 gm)
Sherry	150 ml	**Onion**	1 (100 gm)
Mixed vinegar (tarragon, malt, chilli)	75 ml	**Celery**	1 stick
		Salt	½ tsp
		Parsley stalk	
Lime (rind and juice)	½	**Peppercorns (white)**	10
		Gelatine	70 gm
Carrot	1 (55 gm)	**Eggs (white and shell)**	2

Method

1. Remove fat from stock. 2. Put all ingredients together into a strong pan. 3. Keep on fire and whisk till nearly boiling. 4. Allow to simmer for 30 minutes. 5. Strain through a scalded jelly cloth.

53. BARBECUE SAUCE (A)

Serve with hamburgers, grilled poultry, cold meat, etc.

Ingredients	*For 4*	*For 100*
Tomatoes	115 gm	2.8 kg
Onions	20 gm	500 gm
Chillies (ripe)	2	115 gm
Sugar	30 gm	800 gm
Vinegar	35 ml	900 ml
Salt	to taste	80-100 gm

Method

1. Place in a thick-bottomed pan, the tomatoes peeled and quartered, diced onion, sugar, salt and vinegar. 2. Cook for 1½ hours or until mixture ceases to look watery. 3. Add finely chopped chillies (without seeds) and cook for half an hour. 4. Place in sterlized jars and process in a hot water bath for 15 minutes. 5. Use for hamburgers or cold meats.

BARBECUE SAUCE (B)

Serve with hamburgers, grilled poultry, cold meat, etc.

Ingredients	*For 4*	*For 100*
Onions	30 gm	680 gm
Oil	1 tbsp	225 ml
Tomato ketchup	30 ml	680 ml
Worcester sauce	10 ml	250 ml
Water	30 ml	680 ml
Sugar	15 gm	340 gm
Lime	½	6
Mustard	a pinch	3 tsp
Pepper	a pinch	15 gm
Salt	to taste	80-100 gm

Method

1. Heat oil. Sauté chopped onion. 2. Add remaining ingredients. Simmer for 15 minutes. Strain and use as required.

BARBECUE SAUCE (C)

Serve with hamburgers, grilled poultry, cold meat, etc.

Ingredients	*For 4*	*For 100*
Meat stock	20 ml	500 ml
Chilli sauce	10 ml	250 ml
Ketchup	20 ml	500 ml
Worcester sauce	1 tsp	15 ml
Vinegar	10 ml	250 ml
Brown sugar	10 gm	250 ml
Salt	to taste	80-100 gm
Pepper	a pinch	15 gm
Onions (finely minced)	10 gm	250 gm

Method

Mix all the ingredients together.

BARBECUE SAUCE (D)

Serve with hamburgers, grilled poultry, cold meat, etc.

Ingredients	*For 4*	*For 100*
Vinegar	100 ml	2.5 litre
Sugar	30 gm	680 gm
Ketchup	150 ml	3.75 litre
Salt	to taste	80–100 gm
Onions (finely minced)	10 gm	250 gm

Method

Mix all the ingredients together.

54. SPICY BARBECUE SAUCE (1–2 litre) (20–25 portions)

Serve with hamburgers, grilled poultry, cold meat, etc.

Ingredients	*Quantity*
Vinegar	½ cup
Tomato juice	3 cups
Brown sugar	¼ cup
Prepared mustard	¼ cup
Garlic salt	2 tsp
Salt	2 tsp
Pepper	½ tsp
Small onions (sliced)	2
Ketchup	½ cup
Worcester sauce	3 tbsp

Method

1. In a saucepan, combine vinegar, tomato juice, brown sugar, mustard, salt, pepper, onions. 2. Simmer uncovered for 20 minutes. 3. Then stir in ketchup and Worcester sauce. 4. Bring to a boil. 5. Leftover sauce may be refrigerated or frozen for later use.

55. HOLLANDAISE SAUCE (200 ml) (5-8 portions)

Serve with hot poached fish, asparagus, cauliflower, etc.

Ingredients	*Quantity*	*Ingredients*	*Quantity*
Butter	225 gm	**Egg yolks**	2
Salt	to taste	**Peppercorns (crushed)**	6
Cayenne pepper	a small pinch	**Vinegar**	1 tbsp (15 ml)

Method

1. Place the peppercorns and vinegar in a small pan and reduce completely. 2. Add 1 tbsp cold water and allow to cool. 3. Mix in egg yolks with a whisk. 4. Return to gentle heat and whisking continuously cook to a sabayon (this is the cooking of egg yolks to a thickened consistency like cream, sufficient to show the mark of the whisk). 5. Remove from heat and cool slightly. 6. Whisk in melted butter until thoroughly combined. 7. Check for seasoning. 8. Pass through a muslin or tammy cloth. 9. Keep at a slightly warm temperature until thick. 10. Serve in a slightly warm sauce-boat.

N.B. Should the sauce curdle, put a tsp of boiling water in a small pan and gradually whisk in the curdled sauce.

56. MOUSELINE SAUCE

Serve with fish and chicken

Method

Proceed as for Hollandaise sauce. For 500 ml of sauce, beat in 250 ml of whipped cream at the last moment.

MOCK HOLLANDAISE SAUCE (300 ml) (10 Portions)

Ingredients	*Quantity*	*Ingredients*	*Quantity*
Béchamel sauce	300 ml	**Lime juice**	1 tsp
Egg yolks	2	**Seasoning**	to taste
Butter	30 gm	**Cream**	1 tbsp

Method

1. Whisk sauce till boiling. 2. Add beaten egg yolks and butter in small quantities. 3. Whisk over gentle heat without boiling. 4. Season to taste and stir in lime juice. Season. Add cream. 5. Pass through a tammy cloth if necessary.

57. BEARNAISE SAUCE (A) (280 ml) (5-8 portions)

Serve with grilled meat and fish

Ingredients	*Quantity*	*Ingredients*	*Quantity*
Butter	225 gm	**Egg yolks**	3
Shallots (chopped)	15 gm	**Peppercorns (crushed)**	6
Tarragon	1 tbsp	**Vinegar**	15 ml

Method

1. Mix together shallots, peppercorns, and vinegar. 2. Reduce completely. 3. Add 1 tbsp cold water. Allow to cool. 4. Mix in egg yolks with a whisk. 5. Return to gentle heat and whisking continuously, cook till it becomes like cream. 6. Remove from heat and cool slightly. 7. Whisk in the melted warm butter until thoroughly combined. 8. Add seasoning to taste. 9. Pass through a tammy cloth. 10. Serve warm with grilled meat and fish.

BEARNAISE SAUCE (B) (150 ml) (5-8 portions)

Ingredients	*Quantity*	*Ingredients*	*Quantity*
Béchamel sauce	150 ml	**Egg yolks**	2
Shallot	1	**Butter**	15 gm
Tarragon		**Peppercorns (crushed)**	6
Vinegar	75 ml		

Method

1. Chop the shallot and put into a pan with vinegar and pepper corns. 2. Boil till reduced to 1 tbsp 3. Add béchamel sauce and whisk well. 4. Add egg yolks and continue whisking taking care that sauce does not boil. 5. Remove from heat and gradually whisk in the butter. 6. Pass through a tammy and reheat. 7. Use as required.

58. SAUCE CHORON

Serve with grilled poultry and meat

Method

Make a thick Bearnaise sauce combined with a reduction of tomato purée and tomato concassee to colour slightly.

When serving the sauce—usually on top of a grilled steak—decorate with a thin spiral of meat glaze.

59. BERCY SAUCE (300 ml) (10 portions)

Serve with poached, fried or grilled fish

Ingredients	*Quantity*	*Ingredients*	*Quantity*
Onions	55 gm	**Salt and pepper**	to taste
White wine or		**Parsley (chopped)**	1 tsp
Fish liquor	300 ml	**Lime juice**	1 tsp
Butter (melted)	55 gm		

Method

1. Simmer finely minced onion in wine or fish liquor. 2. Add butter and mix thoroughly, season to taste. 3. Stir in parsley and lime juice.

N.B. When used for meat as in Rognon Sauté, add meat glaze instead of fish liquor when wine is not available.

60. SAUCE NORMANDE (1 litre)

Serve with fish dishes

Ingredients	*Quantity*
Bercy sauce	1 litre
Egg yolks	4
Cream	150 ml
Butter	60 gm

Method

1. Strain Bercy sauce through a tammy cloth. 2. Blend together egg yolks, cream and butter and add to sauce.

61. CHASSEUR SAUCE (Sauce Chasseur) (300 ml) (10 portions)

Serve with steaks, cutlets, sauté of chicken

Ingredients	*Quantity*	*Ingredients*	*Quantity*
Button mushrooms (sliced)	55 gm	**Shallots (chopped)**	15 gm
Butter	30 gm	**Demiglacé**	300 ml
Parsley and tarragon (chopped)	1 tsp	**Tomatoes (concassed)**	115 gm
		White wine (dry)	75 ml

Method

1. Melt the butter in a small pan. 2. Add chopped shallots and cook gently for 2 to 3 minutes without discolouring. 3. Add mushrooms. Cover with a lid and cook gently for 2 to 3 minutes. 4. Strain off the fat. 5. Add wine and reduce to half. 6. Add tomatoes. 7. Add demiglacé. Simmer for 5 to 10 minutes. 8. Check for seasoning and add tarragon and parsley. 9. Serve with fried steaks, chops, chicken, etc., e.g. Noisette d'Agneau Chasseur.

62. CHÂTEAUBRIAND SAUCE (A) (300 ml) (10 portions)

Serve with grilled fillets of beef

Ingredients	*Quantity*	*Ingredients*	*Quantity*
Shallots	30 gm	**Meat gravy**	300 ml
Thyme	1 sprig.	**Butter**	115 gm
Bayleaf	1	**Lime juice**	½ lime
Mushrooms (parings)	30 gm	**Parsley**	¼ bunch

Method

1. Prepare parsley butter with butter, parsley and lime. 2. Put all the remaining ingredients into a stew pan and cook to reduce to half the quantity. 3. Strain through muslin, add the prepared parsley butter. Serve hot with Chateâubriand or grilled fillet of beef.

CHÂTEAUBRIAND SAUCE (B) (200 ml) (8 portions)

Serve with fried or grilled steaks, fillets of beef

Ingredients	*Quantity*
Jus lie (made out of veal stock)	600 ml
Maitre d'hôtel butter	225 gm
Thyme	1 sprig
Bayleaf	1
Shallots (chopped)	60 gm
Mushroom trimmings	60 gm
White wine	300 ml

Method

1. Put shallots, thyme, mushroom trimmings, bayleaf and wine into a pan and reduce to one-third. 2. Add the jus lie (veal gravy) and reduce to half again. 3. Strain through a muslin cloth. 4. Finish away from heat, with maitre d'hôtel butter.

63. PIQUANT SAUCE (300 ml) (10 portions)

Serve with pork, duck, brown entrées, Durham cutlet, etc.

Ingredients	*Quantity*	*Ingredients*	*Quantity*
Shallots (chopped)	55 gm	**Vinegar**	75 ml
Demiglacé	300 ml	**Capers (chopped)**	15 gm
Gherkins (chopped)	30 gm	**Parsley (chopped)**	1 tsp

Method

1. Put vinegar and shallots in a small pan and reduce by half. 2. Add demiglacé. Simmer for 15 to 20 minutes. 3. Add the rest of the ingredients. 4. Skim and correct seasoning.

64. ROBERT SAUCE (Sauce robert) (300 ml) (10 portions)

Ingredients	*Quantity*	*Ingredients*	*Quantity*
Onions	55 gm	**Demiglacé**	300 ml
Margarine	15 gm	**Mustard**	1 tsp
Vinegar	75 ml	**Castor sugar**	¼ tsp

Method

1. Melt the margarine in a small pan. 2. Add finely chopped onion. 3. Cook gently without discolouring. 4. Add vinegar and reduce completely. 5. Add the demiglacé. Simmer for 5 to 10 minutes. 6. Remove from heat and add mustard mixed with a little water and sugar. 7. Skim and check for seasoning.

65. CHARCUTIÈRE SAUCE (300 ml) (10 portions)

Serve with pork chops or cutlets, mutton cutlets.

Proceed as for Robert Sauce and finally add 30 gm of sliced gherkins. This sauce can also be served with pork.

66. WHITE CHAUDFROID (300 ml)

Used for masking poultry and meat

Ingredients	*Quantity*	*Ingredients*	*Quantity*
Béchamel sauce	300 ml	**Gelatine**	7-10 gm
Cream	75 ml	**Aspic jelly**	150 ml

Method

1. Warm the sauce. 2. Dissolve gelatine in aspic jelly and add to sauce. 3. Mix well. Add cream. Strain through tammy cloth and use as required.

67. TOMATO CHAUDFROID SAUCE (300 ml)

Used for masking fish and vegetables

Ingredients	*Quantity*	*Ingredients*	*Quantity*
Tomato purée	300 ml	**Aspic jelly**	150 ml
Gelatine	7-10 gm		

Method

1. Dissolve gelatine in jelly. Add to purée. 2. Boil up together and strain.

68. BROWN CHAUDFROID SAUCE (300 ml) (10 portions)

Used for masking poultry and meats.

Ingredients	*Quantity*	*Ingredients*	*Quantity*
Espagnole sauce	300 ml	**Aspic jelly**	150 ml
Gelatine	10 gm		

Method

1. Dissolve gelatine in aspic jelly. 2. Add to Espagnole sauce. 3. Boil up together and strain.

69. GREEN CHAUDFROID SAUCE

Method

Add spinach purée to white Chaudfroid mixture till desired colour is obtained.

USE OF CHAUDFROID SAUCES

White: Joints of chicken or rabbit, cutlets, white fish, eggs, galantine of chicken.

Brown: Cutlets, joints of game, galantines of game, fillets of beef.

Tomato: Cutlets, game, eggs, fish.

Green: Cutlets, fish, eggs.

70. DEVILLED SAUCE (Sauce diable) (300 ml) (10 portions)

Serve with grilled or fried fish and meats

Ingredients	*Quantity*	*Ingredients*	*Quantity*
Shallots or onion (chopped)	55 gm	**Vinegar (white)**	40 ml
Mignonette pepper	10 gm	**Cayenne pepper**	a large pinch
White wine	30 ml	**Demiglacé**	300 ml

Method

1. Mix together the chopped onion, Mignonette pepper, wine and vinegar. 2. Reduce by half. 3. Add the demiglacé. 4. Simmer 5 to 10 minutes. 5. Season liberally with Cayenne pepper. 6. Pass through a fine muslin. 7. Serve with grilled or fried fish or meats.

71. MAYONNAISE SAUCE (A) (150 ml) (5-8 portions)

A basic sauce with many uses. Served with cold fish, poultry, eggs and vegetables.

Ingredients	*Quantity*
Egg yolk	1
Mustard	1 tsp
Sugar	1 pinch
Salt	to taste
White pèpper	a pinch
Vinegar	1 tbsp
Salad oil	130 ml
Lime	½

Method

Mix egg yolk with sugar, mustard and pepper. 2. Cream well. 3. Add salad oil drop by drop. Keep beating vigorously with a wooden spoon all the time. 4. As sauce gets thicker moisten slightly with vinegar. 5. Keep adding salad oil and keep beating. 6. Taste for seasoning and add lime juice. Mix well.

N.B. Remedy for curdled mixture is to whisk a fresh egg yolk slowly into the mixture.

MAYONNAISE SAUCE (B) (5 litre) (200-250 portions)

Ingredients	*Quantity*	*Ingredients*	*Quantity*
Egg yolks	30	**Mustard**	2 tbsp
Salt	60 gm	**Vinegar**	120 ml

Ingredients	*Quantity*	*Ingredients*	*Quantity*
Paprika	1 tbsp	**Salad oil**	5 litre
Cayenne pepper	a pinch		

Method

1. Mix well egg yolks, salt, paprika, Cayenne pepper and mustard. 2. Add half (60 ml) of the vinegar. 3. Add slowly half the salad oil. The oil must be added very slowly, beating steadily until an emulsion is formed. After emulsion forms, oil can be added in amounts of half-cup and later one cup at a time, beating well. 4. Add remaining vinegar. Beat well. 5. Add remaining salad oil, continue beating until all oil is emulsified.

72. TARTARE SAUCE (A) (60 ml) (2-3 portions)

Serve with fried and grilled fish, some meats and salads

Method

Take four tbsp of mayonnaise and add 2 tsp of chopped capers and 1 level tsp of chopped parsley. Generally served with hot, fried fish.

TARTARE SAUCE (B) (300 ml) (10 portions)

Ingredients	*Quantity*	*Ingredients*	*Quantity*
Mayonnaise	300 ml	**Gherkins (pickled)**	55 gm
Capers	30 gm	**Parsley**	

Method

1. Chop capers, gherkins and parsley. Combine with mayonnaise.

TARTARE SAUCE (C)

To mayonnaise add ½ cup pickled gherkins and cucumber, 30 gm green pepper, 2 tbsp chopped parsley, ½ cup olives, 60 ml of vinegar, 2 tsp minced onion, a few drops of Worcester sauce and a few drops of tabasco.

73. TARTARE SAUCE (Campus) (2 litre) (15-20 portions)

Ingredients	*Quantity*	*Ingredients*	*Quantity*
Mayonnaise	2.36 litre	**Parsley**	1 bunch
Mixed vinegar	450 gm	**Tomato (chopped)**	450 gm
Pickle			

Method

Blanch tomato, remove seeds and cut into small cubes. Chop pickles and parsley. Combine all ingredients with mayonnaise.

74. CELERY DRESSING (300 ml) (10 portions)

Serve with chicken, fish and vegetable salads.

Ingredients	*Quantity*	*Ingredients*	*Quantity*
Mayonnaise	2 cups	**Green pepper (chopped)**	55 gm
Parsley (chopped)	2 tbsp	**Celery (diced)**	85 gm

Method

Mix well together.

75. CHANTILLY DRESSING (400 ml) (12-15 portions)

Serve with poached fish and fish, chicken and vegetable salads.

To 2 cups of mayonnaise add 120 ml of whipped cream.

76. CLUB DRESSING (4.75 litre) (30-35 portions)

Serve with fish, chicken and vegetable salads.

To 4.75 litres of mayonnaise, add 30 gm currants, 30 gm chopped raisins and 30 gm chopped nuts.

77. EGG DRESSING (300 ml) (10 portions)

Serve with salads

To 2 cups of mayonnaise add 2 eggs hard-boiled and chopped.

78. EGG AND GREEN PEPPER DRESSING (2 litre) (15-20 portions)

Serve with fish, chicken and vegetable salads

Ingredients	*Quantity*	*Ingredients*	*Quantity*
Mayonnaise	5½ cups (2 litre)	**Green pepper (chopped finely)**	55 gm
Eggs (hard-boiled and chopped)	6	**Onion (chopped)**	15 gm
		Cayenne pepper	a pinch

Method

Mix carefully.

79. SAVOURY (300 ml) (10 portions)

Serve with grilled meats, fried or grilled fish

To 2 cups mayonnaise add 85 gm celery diced, 55 gm green pepper chopped and 2 tablespoons onion chopped.

80. GREEN SAUCE (300 ml) (10 portions)

Serve with cold fish

Ingredients	*Quantity*
Spinach or chives	60 gm
Mayonnaise	300 ml

Method

1. Pick, wash and blanch the spinach leaves or chives. 2. Squeeze dry. 3. Pass through a fine sieve. 4. Mix with mayonnaise. 5. Serve with cold salmon.

81. THOUSAND ISLAND DRESSING WITH MAYONNAISE SAUCE (2.7 litre) (25 portions)

Ingredients	*Quantity*	*Ingredients*	*Quantity*
Mayonnaise sauce	2.7 kg (9 cups)	**Chilli sauce**	340 ml
Onions (minced fine)	115 gm	**Eggs (hard-boiled and chopped)**	10
Pimento (chopped)	85 gm	**Olives (chopped)**	115 gm
		Cayenne	¼ tsp

Method

Mix all the ingredients together and blend well.

82. ROQUEFORT DRESSING (100 ml) (4 portions)

Ingredients	*Quantity*	*Ingredients*	*Quantity*
French dressing	5 tbsp (75 ml)	**Roquefort cheese**	30 gm
Mayonnaise sauce	2 tbsp	**Worcester sauce**	½ tsp

Method

Mix together mayonnaise and roquefort cheese broken into small pieces. Blend in French dressing very slowly and add Worcester sauce. Serve with green salads.

83. FRENCH DRESSING (A)

For salads

Mix together 3 parts of salad oil to one part of vinegar. Season to taste with salt, pepper and mustard. Add chopped herbs to taste. Toss the salad in the dressing only just before serving. For a variation lime juice can be used instead of vinegar.

FRENCH DRESSING (B) (4 litre) (30-35 portions)

Ingredients	*Quantity*	*Ingredients*	*Quantity*
Salt	55 gm	**Salad oil**	2.36 litre
Mustard	2 tbsp	**Vinegar**	1.18 litre
Paprika	2 tbsp	**Onion juice**	4 tbsp
Pepper	1 tbsp		

Method

Mix together dry ingredients. Add oil, vinegar and onion juice. Put into a jar and shake well or beat well with an electric beater.

N.B. ½ cup of poppy seeds can be added to above recipe for **POPPY SEED DRESSING**.

84. DIETERS DRESSING (250 ml) (8-10 portions)

For salads

Mix together 8 tbsp each of orange juice and grapefruit juice. Add a tablespoonful of lemon juice, ½ tsp salt, ¼ tsp paprika and ¼ tsp Worcestershire sauce. Shake until the ingredients are thoroughly blended. Chill. Shake well before serving.

85. ZERO SALAD DRESSING (100 ml) (4-6 portions)

Ingredients	*Quantity*
Tomato juice	½ cup
Lemon juice or vinegar	2 tbsp
Onions (finely chopped)	1 tbsp
Salt & pepper	to taste
Chopped parsley or green pepper	to taste
Horseradish or mustard may be added if desired.	

Method

Combine ingredients in a jar with a tightly-fitted lid. Shake well before using.

86. CHEF'S DRESSING (250 ml) (8-10 portions)

Ingredients	*Quantity*
Tomato sauce	½ cup
Salad oil	½ cup
Vinegar	¼ cup
Salt	to taste

Ingredients	*Quantity*
Pepper	a pinch
Mustard	½ tsp
Soya sauce (optional)	¼ tsp
Onions (chopped)	1 tbsp

Method

Combine all the ingredients and shake well.

87. COTTAGE DIP (250 ml) (8-10 portions)

Ingredients	*Quantity*
Chef's dressing	1 cup
Uncreamed cottage cheese	1 cup

Method

Purée the above ingredients in a blender or by rubbing them together through a fine sieve. Add a pinch of Cayenne pepper.

88. CRAB CHEESE DIP (100 ml) (4-6 portions)

Ingredients	*Quantity*
Cheese	115 gm
Milk	about 60 ml
Lime juice	2 tsp
Worcester sauce	1 tsp
Garlic	1 flake
Salt and pepper	to taste
Crab meat cooked	115 gm

Method

1. Grate cheese. Put into a bowl. Add milk, a little at a time and cream well to get the consistency of cream cheese. 2. Add lime juice, Worcester sauce, finely chopped garlic, salt, pepper and finely chopped crab meat. 3. Chill and serve with wafers, salt biscuits, cream crackers or pieces of freshly baked bread.

89. CUCUMBER DIP (250 ml) (8-10 portions)

Ingredients	*Quantity*
Fresh curd	200 gm
Cucumber	1
Green chillies	2
Onions	1
Chives	a few sprigs
Salt	to taste

Method

1. Put the fresh curd into a muslin bag to remove the water. Beat well to a smooth consistency. 2. Add finely chopped cucumber, green chillies (seeds removed), onion, chives and salt to taste.

90. EGG DIP (100 ml) (4 portions)

Ingredients	*Quantity*
Eggs (hard-boiled)	6
Mayonnaise sauce	⅓ cup
Prepared mustard	2 tsp
Lime juice	1–1½ tsp
Worcester sauce	1–1½ tsp
Chilli sauce	a few drops
Crisp slices of fried bacon	4

Method

1. Sieve hard-boiled eggs. Mix other ingredients except bacon and beat to a smooth consistency. 2. Just before serving, fold in crumbled bacon. Serve with waters or salt biscuits.

91. GARLIC MAYONNAISE

Ingredients	*Quantity*
Lump of soft white bread (size of a walnut)	
Milk	2 tsp
Garlic	4 cloves
Salt and pepper	to taste
Lemon juice	1 tsp
Egg yolk	1
Olive oil	⅓ pint

Method

1. Soak the bread in milk and squeeze it out. 2. Peel and chop the garlic. Mash the two together in a basin, with a wooden spoon, into a smooth paste. 3. Add salt and pepper, lemon juice and egg yolk, and beat in about a tsp of oil. 4. Pour the rest of the oil into a jug, and then trickle it drop by drop into the mixture, beating with the spoon as you do so. 5. It is important when making any kind of mayonnaise to add the oil gradually, a few drops at a time, and then to beat those in. If it curdles, another egg yolk may correct matters.

GARLIC SAUCE

One type of garlic sauce served in Italy with fresh water fish and other types of heavy fish is very similar to the Aioli sauce made with breadcrumbs. Another is a bit stronger and should be tackled only by those with tough and resilient digestions. It is especially designed for serving with pasta. Cooking time 8 minutes. Serves 6-8.

Ingredients	*Quantity*
Olive oil	¼ cup (3 tbsp)
Butter	¼ cup (10 gm)
Garlic	4 cloves
Parsley	4 tsp
Dried basil	1 tsp
Salt	¼–½ tsp
Pepper	to taste

Method

1. Heat the oil and butter in a small saucepan. Add chopped garlic and fry very gently for 5 minutes. 2. Add all the remaining ingredients and cook over low heat for a further 5 minutes. 3. Toss with freshly cooked hot pasta and serve immediately.

92. INDIAN DRESSING (150 ml) (5-8 portions)

Serve with hard-boiled eggs and salads.

Ingredients	*Quantity*	*Ingredients*	*Quantity*
Salad oil	6 tbsp	**Sugar**	½ tsp
	(100 ml)	**Eggs (hard-boiled)**	3
Vinegar	4 tbsp	**Green pepper**	60 gm
	(60 ml)	**Pickled beetroot**	15 gm
Pepper	½ tsp	**Parsley**	a few sprigs
Mustard	1 tsp		(1 tsp chopped)
Paprika	a pinch		

Method

1. Mix together dry spices and sugar. 2. Add vinegar and salad oil and blend well by shaking in a bottle. 3. Blend in sieved yolks of hard-boiled eggs. 4. Add finely chopped green pepper, chopped pickled beetroot and chopped parsley. 5. Mix well and chill before serving. Excellent with hard-boiled eggs.

93. THOUSAND ISLAND FRENCH DRESSING (150 ml) (5-8 portions)

Ingredients	*Quantity*	*Ingredients*	*Quantity*
Olive oil	150 ml	**Stuffed olives**	8
Orange (juice)	½	**(sliced fine)**	
Lemon (juice) or	½	**Worcester sauce**	1 tsp
Lime (juice)	¼	**Dry mustard**	¼ tsp

Ingredients	*Quantity*	*Ingredients*	*Quantity*
Salt	1 tsp	**Onion**	10 gm
Paprika	¼ tsp	**(finely minced)**	
Parsley	1 bunch		
	(1 tbsp chopped)		

Method

1. Mix all the ingredients together thoroughly. 2. Chill. 3. Shake well before using.

94. SALAD CREAM (Cooked) (200 ml) (5-8 portions)

For salads, cole slaw etc.

Ingredients	*Quantity*	*Ingredients*	*Quantity*
Butter	30 gm	**Egg yolks**	2
Refined flour	15 gm	**Vinegar**	30-45 ml
Salt	½ tsp		(2-3 tbsp)
Pepper	a pinch	**Cream or**	10 ml
Mustard (dry)	1 tsp	**Cottage cheese or**	10 gm
Sugar	1 tsp	**Salad oil**	10 ml
Milk	150 ml		

Method

1. Melt butter. Stir in flour. 2. Add salt, pepper, mustard and sugar. 3. Stir in the milk and bring to a boil stirring carefully. 4. Cool slightly. 5. Beat egg yolks. Add sauce gradually, stirring well. 6. Return to fire and cook slowly till sauce thickens. 7. Remove and gradually add vinegar. Leave to cool. 8. To get extra creaming, add cream or sieved cottage cheese or salad oil before serving.

95. SOUR CREAM DRESSING (150 ml) (5-8 portions)

For salads

Ingredients	*Quantity*	*Ingredients*	*Quantity*
Sour cream	150 ml	**Sugar**	¼ tsp
Onions	15 gm	**Horseradish**	15 gm
(finely chopped)		**(grated)**	
Salt	¼ tsp	**Tabasco sauce**	¼ tsp

Method

1. Blend all ingredients together. Fresh cream can be made sour by adding a tbsp of lemon juice to 15 ml of fresh cream.

96. YOGHURT DRESSING (300 ml) (10 portions)

For salads or as accompaniment to pilaffs

Ingredients	*Quantity*	*Ingredients*	*Quantity*
Yoghurt (curd)	300 ml	**Chives (finely minced)**	½ tsp
Lemon juice	1 tsp		
Paprika	½ tsp	**Salt**	½ tsp
Mustard	½ tsp		

Method

1. Mix all the ingredients well. Chill before serving.

97. SALAD DRESSING (A) (150 ml) (5-8 portions)

For salads

Ingredients	*Quantity*	*Ingredients*	*Quantity*
Eggs (hard-boiled)	2	**Vinegar (white)**	3 tbsp (45 ml)
Castor sugar	1 tsp		
Mustard	¼ tsp	**Cream or evaporated milk**	150 ml
Salt	¼ tsp		

Method

1. Rub egg yolks through a sieve. 2. Add seasoning and mix well together. 3. Moisten with vinegar and work till smooth. 4. Add gradually and carefully, cream or milk.

SALAD DRESSING (B) (150 ml) (5-8 portions)

Ingredients	*Quantity*
Evaporated milk	150 ml
Vinegar	3 tbsp (45 ml)
Sugar	2 tsp
Mustard	¼ tsp

Method

1. Mix dry ingredients with vinegar. 2. Stir in the milk gradually. If too thick, add a little water or milk.

SALAD DRESSING (C) (300 ml) (10 portions)

Ingredients	*Quantity*	*Ingredients*	*Quantity*
Salad oil or	1 tbsp	**Mustard**	½ tsp
Margarine	20 gm	**Sugar**	1 tsp
Flour	20 gm	**Salt and pepper**	to taste
Egg	1	**Vinegar**	1-2 tbsp (30 ml)
Milk and water	300 ml		
Cream (optional)	75 ml		

Method

1. Make a sauce with salad oil or margarine, flour, milk and water. 2. Add seasoning. Cool slightly and add beaten egg. 3. Reboil. Add vinegar to taste and cream. 4. Allow to get cold stirring occasionally.

98. BOILED SALAD DRESSING (150 ml) (5-8 portions)

For salads

Ingredients	*Quantity*	*Ingredients*	*Quantity*
Eggs	2	**Milk**	150 ml
Oil	1 tbsp	**Cream**	1 tbsp
Mustard	½ tsp	**Vinegar**	1 tbsp
Sugar	1 tsp		(15 ml)
Salt	1½ tsp		

Method

1. Mix oil, mustard, sugar, salt and vinegar. 2. Beat eggs and add milk and cream. 3. Strain into the bowl with oil etc. 4. Place in a pan of hot water and whisk till mixture begins to thicken. 5. Pour into a cold basin.

99. COLE SLAW DRESSING (100 ml) (4 portions)

Ingredients	*Quantity*
Vinegar	2 tbsp
Salt	a pinch
Pepper	a pinch
Dry mustard	¼ tsp
Sugar	1 tsp
Butter	1 tsp
Egg (beaten)	1
Cream	100 ml

Method

1. Heat seasoning and butter to boiling point. Slowly stir into beaten egg. 2. Cook until mixture thickens. Remove from heat. Stir in cream. 3. While hot, pour over shredded cabbage. 4. Chill and serve cold.

100. CREAM DRESSING FOR COLE SLAW (100 ml) (4-7 portions)

Ingredients	*Quantity*	*Ingredients*	*Quantity*
Cream	100 gm	**Lime**	1
Capsicum	25 gm	**Sugar**	½ tsp (2 gm)
Onions	25 gm	**Salt and pepper**	to taste

Method

1. Remove seeds from capsicum. 2. Chop fine and soak in water. 3. Chop the onion fine. 4. Beat cream, add all ingredients. 5. Mix well.

101. RAVIGOTTE SAUCE (A) (600 ml) (20 portions)

Serve with fried fish and boiled poultry

Ingredients	*Quantity*	*Ingredients*	*Quantity*
White wine	150 ml	**Shallots**	30 gm
Vinegar (white)	75 ml	**Tarragon**	
Veloute sauce	600 ml	**Chervil (chopped)**	1 tsp
Butter	30 gm	**Chives**	1 tsp

Method

1. Mince shallots. Pound with butter. 2. Reduce by half the vinegar and wine. 3. Add Veloute sauce. Boil gently for 5 minutes. Add shallots, butter and chopped chervil, tarragon and chives.

RAVIGOTTE SAUCE (B) OR VINAIGRETTE (600 ml) (20 portions)

Serve with salads, vegetables, calf's head

Ingredients	*Quantity*	*Ingredients*	*Quantity*
Salad oil	590 ml	**Parsley**	1 tbsp
Vinegar	200 ml	**Tarragon**	
Salt and pepper	to taste	**Chervil (chopped)**	½ tbsp
Onions (finely chopped)	1 tbsp	**Chives**	

Method

1. Put all the ingredients into a bowl. Mix thoroughly. 2. Serve with calf's head, foot or sheep's trotters etc. 3. Add 2 to 3 tbsp of the liquor in which the solids have been cooked, before serving.

102. JAM SAUCE (A)

Serve with sweet puddings

Ingredients	*For 4*	*For 100*
Jam	40 gm	1 kg
Cold water	500 gm	7 litre
Lemon juice	½	6
Sugar	40 gm	1 kg

Method

1. Put all ingredients into a strong pan. Boil until reduced to two-thirds. Strain and colour if necessary.

JAM SAUCE (B) (300 ml) (10 portions)

Ingredients	*Quantity*	*Ingredients*	*Quantity*
Jam	225 gm	**Water**	120 ml
Cornflour	10-15 gm		

Method

1. Boil jam and water together. 2. Adjust consistency with a little cornflour. 3. Re-boil until clear and pass through a sieve.

103. APRICOT SAUCE (Sauce apricot) (100 ml) (3-10 portions)

Ingredients	*Quantity*	*Ingredients*	*Quantity*
Apricot jam	225 gm	**Water**	120 ml
Cornflour			

Method

Proceed as for Jam Sauce (B).

104. MARMALADE SAUCE (200 ml) (5-8 portions)

Serve with steamed hot puddings

Ingredients	*Quantity*	*Ingredients*	*Quantity*
Marmalade	2 tbsp	**Lime juice**	¼ tsp
Cold water	300 ml	**Sugar**	2 tbsp

Method

1. Put all ingredients into a small pan. 2. Boil until reduced to two-thirds.

105. ORANGE SAUCE (300 ml) (10 portions)

Serve with steamed puddings and ice-creams

Ingredients	*Quantity*	*Ingredients*	*Quantity*
Orange	1	**Sugar**	55 gm
Water	300 ml	**Cornflour**	15 gm

Method

1. Boil the sugar and water. 2. Add cornflour diluted with water, stirring continuously. 3. Re-boil till clear. Strain. 4. Add blanched julienne of orange peel and orange juice.

106. LEMON SAUCE

Method

Proceed as for Orange Sauce using a lemon instead of an orange.

107. CUSTARD SAUCE (A) (With fresh eggs) (300 ml) (10 portions)

Serve with fruit, steamed or baked puddings.

Ingredients	*Quantity*
Milk	300 ml
Castor sugar	30 gm
Egg yolks	2
Vanilla essence	2-3 drops

Method

1. Mix egg yolks, sugar and essence in a basin. 2. Whisk in boiled milk. 3. Return to a thick-bottomed pan. 4. Place on low heat and stir with a wooden spoon till it coats the back of the spoon. Do not boil. 5. Pass through a fine strainer.

CUSTARD SAUCE (B) (300 ml) (10 portions)

Ingredients	*Quantity*
Milk	300 ml
Castor sugar	30 gm
Custard powder	15 gm

Method

1. Dilute the custard powder with a little cold milk. 2. Boil remaining milk. 3. Pour the boiled milk gradually over custard powder. 4. Return to the saucepan. 5. Stir till it boils. Mix in the sugar.

108. SHERRY SAUCE (70 ml) (4 portions)

Serve with trifle, steamed puddings and cold puddings

Ingredients	*Quantity*
Egg yolks	2
Sherry	75 ml
Castor sugar	1 tsp
Cream	1 tbsp

Method

1. Whisk egg yolks, sugar and sherry well together over gentle heat till the mixture becomes thick and frothy, taking care not to allow it to curdle. 2. Add cream and serve.

N.B. Fruit juice can be used instead of sherry.

109. SABAYON SAUCE (75 ml) (4 portions)

Serve with soufflés, puddings, sweets

Ingredients	*Quantity*	*Ingredients*	*Quantity*
Egg yolk	1	**Fruit juice**	75 ml
Sugar	$1\frac{1}{2}$ tsp		

Method

1. Whisk over gentle heat till thick and frothy. Use immediately. If too thick, thin down with a little cream.

110. CHOCOLATE SAUCE (A) (300 ml) (10 portions)

Serve with ice-creams, soufflés, puddings

Ingredients	*Quantity*	*Ingredients*	*Quantity*
Milk	300 ml	**Chocolate (block) or**	30 gm
Sugar	45 gm	**Cocoa**	15 gm
Butter	10 gm	**Cornflour**	15 gm

Method

With cocoa

1. Dilute cornflour and cocoa with a little cold milk. 2. Boil remaining milk. Pour gradually over cornflour mixture. 4. Return to the pan. 5. Stir till it starts to boil. 6. Mix in the sugar and butter.

With chocolate

Shred the chocolate. Add to the milk and proceed as above, omitting cocoa.

CHOCOLATE SAUCE (B) (200 ml) (5-8 portions)

Ingredients	*Quantity*	*Ingredients*	*Quantity*
Chocolate	45 gm	**Salt**	a pinch
Water	200 ml	**Sugar**	30 gm
Cornflour	2 tsp	**Vanilla**	
Butter	15 gm		

Method

1. Break up the chocolate. Add half the water and dissolve over gentle heat. 2. Mix the cornflour and salt to a smooth cream with a little of the remaining cold water. 3. Heat the rest; when it starts boiling, pour over the blended cornflour, stirring well. 4. Add the dissolved chocolate, butter and sugar and cook for 4 to 5 minutes stirring and beating well. Add a few drops of vanilla essence.

111. COFFEE SAUCE (300 ml) (10 portions)

Serve with ice-creams and cold puddings

Ingredients	*Quantity*	*Ingredients*	*Quantity*
Butter	30 gm	**Sugar**	30 gm
Flour	15 gm	**Vanilla**	a few drops
Black coffee	300 ml	**Egg yolk**	1

Method

1. Melt the butter in a small saucepan and mix in the flour. 2. Add coffee gradually and stir until boiling. 3. Simmer slowly for 5 minutes. Add sugar and flavouring. 4. Just before serving, stir in egg yolk. Do not allow the sauce to boil again.

112. SYRUP SAUCE (300 ml) (10 portions)

Serve with ice-creams, soufflés or puddings

Ingredients	*Quantity*	*Ingredients*	*Quantity*
Golden syrup	230 ml	**Water**	150 ml
Lime (juice)	½	**Cornflour**	15 gm

Method

1. Bring the syrup, water and lime juice to a boil. 2. Thicken with diluted cornflour. 3. Boil for a few minutes.

113. MELBA SAUCE (500 ml) (15 portions)

Serve with vanilla ice-cream

Ingredients	*Quantity*	*Ingredients*	*Quantity*
Raspberry jam	450 gm	**Water**	150 ml

Method

1. Boil together and pass through a strainer.

114. ALMOND SAUCE (300 ml) (10 portions)

Serve with steamed puddings

Ingredients	*Quantity*	*Ingredients*	*Quantity*
Milk	300 ml	**Almond essence**	a few drops
Castor sugar	30 gm	**Almonds**	15 gm
Cornflour	15 gm		

Method

1. Dilute the cornflour with a little cold milk. 2. Boil remaining milk. 3. Whisk into the cornflour. 4. Return to pan and stir till it starts boiling.

5. Simmer for 3 to 4 minutes. 6. Mix in sugar and essence. 7. Pass through a strainer. 8. Add slices of almonds and serve.

115. RUM BUTTER (A) (150 gm) (5-8 portions)

Ingredients	*Quantity*	*Ingredients*	*Quantity*
Butter	55 gm	**Castor or**	
Rum	1 dsp	**icing sugar**	115 gm

Method

1. Cream butter and sugar. Flavour with rum and set aside to cool. Serve with Christmas pudding or other steamed puddings.

RUM BUTTER (B) (200 ml) (5-8 portions)

Ingredients	*Quantity*
Butter	115 gm
Icing sugar (sifted)	115 gm
Rum	to taste

Method

1. Beat the butter to a very soft cream (an electric mixer is excellent for this) and gradually beat in the sifted icing sugar. 2. Add the rum from a spoon; it is easier to control than from a bottle.

N.B. The rum butter can be frozen but it keeps well in a refrigerator and is then just the right temperature for serving. Spoon it into a glass dish and serve it chilled with Christmas pudding or other steamed puddings.

116. RUM BUTTER (With brown sugar) (300 ml) (10 portions)

Serve with Christmas pudding

Ingredients	*Quantity*
Butter	170 gm
Light coloured, soft brown sugar	170 gm
Rum (depending on taste)	1-2 tbsp

Method

1. Beat the butter to a soft cream, add the light brown sugar and beat again very thoroughly. 2. Beat in the rum gradually, then either pipe or heap it into a dish for serving. Serve straight from the refrigerator.

N.B. Pipe the rum butter into the dish from which it is to be served, let it harden, then wrap it loosely with polythene. As it is served cold, use it straight from the refrigerator.

117. RUM BUTTER SAUCE (150 ml) (5-8 portions)

Ingredients	*Quantity*
Cornstarch	1 tbsp
Sugar	1/3 cup
Salt	1/8 tsp
Water	2 tbsp
Egg yolk (beaten)	1
Butter or margarine	1½ tsp
Lemon juice	1½ tsp
Grated lemon rind	½ tsp
Rum	2 tsp
Egg white (stiffly beaten)	1

Method

1. Combine cornstarch, sugar, and water on top of double boiler. Cook over hot water until thick, stirring constantly. 2. Gradually add cornstarch mixture to beaten egg yolk. Return to pan and cook for 5 more minutes, stirring constantly. 3. Remove from heat; add butter and cool. Add lemon juice, lemon rind and rum. 4. Fold stiffly beaten egg white into sauce. Serve either hot or cold. 5. Make 1½ cup sauce for apple or mince pie.

118. RUM SAUCE (300 ml) (10 portions)

Ingredients	*Quantity*
Cornflour	15 gm
Water	300 ml
Sugar	2 tbsp
A pinch of powdered cinnamon	
Rum	2 tbsp
Butter	30 gm

Method

1. Mix the cornflour with a little cold water. 2. Boil the remaining water and pour on to the cornflour, mixing well. 3. Pour into a saucepan and stir till it boils. 4. Add sugar, powdered cinnamon, rum and last, the butter broken in small pieces.

119. BRANDY BUTTER OR HARD SAUCE (200 ml) (5-8 portions)

Serve with Christmas pudding or ice cream

Ingredients	*Quantity*
Butter	60 gm
Icing sugar	115 gm
Brandy	1 tbsp

Method

1. Beat the butter and sugar to a white fluffy cream. 2. Gradually beat in brandy. 3. Leave in a cool place until required. Serve piled up in a fancy dish.

120. BRANDY BUTTER (200 ml) (5-8 portions)

Serve with Christmas pudding

Ingredients	*Quantity*
Butter	100 gm
Icing sugar	100 gm
Brandy	½ cup

Method

1. Cream butter till fluffy. Add icing sugar. 2. Continue beating. Add brandy slowly, blending well.

121. SAUCE FOR SWEET PUDDING (150 ml) (5-8 portions)

Ingredients	*Quantity*
Butter	60 gm
Castor sugar	60 gm
Rum or brandy	1 full wine glass
Hot milk or water	1 tbsp

Method

1. Beat the butter to a cream. 2. Add sugar. Cream well. 3. Add brandy or rum little by little and beat in till blended and serve.

N.B. This sauce can be served round the pudding or in a sauce boat.

122. GRAPE SAUCE (150 ml) (5-8 portions)

Serve with steamed puddings or ice-creams

Ingredients	*Quantity*
Arrowroot	1 level tsp
Concentrated black grape juice	4 tbsp
Water	1 glass
Lime juice	1 tsp
Sugar as desired	

Method

1. Blend arrowroot with a little cold water. 2. Add grape juice, water, lime juice, and sugar. 3. Bring to a boil slowly, stirring all the time. 4. Serve hot or cold.

123. VEAL FORCEMEAT

Ingredients	*Quantity*	*Ingredients*	*Quantity*
Suet, margarine or dripping	30 gm	**Parsley (finely chopped)**	1 tsp
Breadcrumbs (fresh)	55 gm	**Grated lime rind**	a pinch
Mixed herbs	a pinch	**Egg or milk**	to bind

Method

Mix all the dry ingredients. Bind with egg or milk.

124. SAGE AND ONION STUFFING

Ingredients	*Quantity*	*Ingredients*	*Quantity*
Onions	225 gm	**Sage fresh (chopped)**	1 tsp
Breadcrumbs (fresh)	55 gm	**or**	
Dripping or margarine	30 gm	**Dried sage**	½ tsp

Method

1. Parboil onions. Drain off water. Chop finely. 2. Mix all the ingredients together.

125. CORAL BUTTER (3-4 portions)

Ingredients	*Quantity*
Lobster coral	30 gm
Butter	15 gm
Seasoning	

Method

1. Wash and dry the lobster coral and pound with the butter. 2. Season and rub through a hair sieve.

126. MAITRE D'HÔTEL BUTTER (15 gm)

Serve with Fish Colbert or grilled fish

Ingredients	*Quantity*	*Ingredients*	*Quantity*
Butter	15 gm	**Parsley (chopped)**	1 tsp
Lime juice	a few drops		
Seasoning	to taste		

Method

1. Cream the butter and add the other ingredients. Mix well. 2. Leave in a cool place till firm and use as required.

127. MINT BUTTER (30 mg.) (3-4 portions)

Serve with grilled lamb chops

Ingredients	*Quantity*	*Ingredients*	*Quantity*
Butter (unsalted)	30 gm	**Mint (finely chopped)**	2 tsp
Lime juice	a few drops		

Method

1. Mix all the ingredients together and blend well.

128. CHUTNEY BUTTER (300 gm) (10 portions)

Serve with grilled meat and poultry

Ingredients	*Quantity*	*Ingredients*	*Quantity*
Mango chutney	115 gm	**Fresh butter**	225 gm
Mustard	2 tsp	**Lime juice**	½ tsp

Method

1. Pound the chutney in a mortar, add mustard and work in the butter; season to taste and add a few drops of lime juice. Rub through a hair sieve. 2. Place on ice and use as required.

129. MUSTARD BUTTER (4-6 portions)

Serve with grilled fish or meat

Ingredients	*Quantity*
Butter	115 gm
French mustard	1 tsp
Lime juice for flavour	

Method

1. Cream butter. Work the mustard into it and add the lime juice.

130. PAPRIKA BUTTER (4-6 portions)

Use as garnish for canapes for hors d'oeuvres

Ingredients	*Quantity*
Butter	115 gm
Paprika	1 tsp

Method

Cream butter lightly and blend in paprika.

131. CURRY BUTTER (4-6 portions)

Serve with grilled meat or fish

Ingredients	*Quantity*
Butter	115 gm
Curry powder	30 gm

Method

Soften the butter. Blend in curry powder.

132. VINAIGRETTE (50 ml) (4 portions)

For salads

Ingredients	*Quantity*	*Ingredients*	*Quantity*
Salad oil	3 tbsp (45 ml)	**Vinegar**	1 tbsp (15 ml)
Mustard	1 tbsp	**Salt and pepper**	to taste

Method

Combine all the ingredients together.

Variations

(a) Add chopped chives or parsley.
(b) Add chopped hard-boiled egg.
(c) Use lemon juice instead of vinegar.

INDEX

INDEX